Hiraeth: Beyond My Father's House

A Woman's Journey Home

Gwendolyn Evans Caldwell

ISBN 10: 1492731110
ISBN 13: 9781492731115

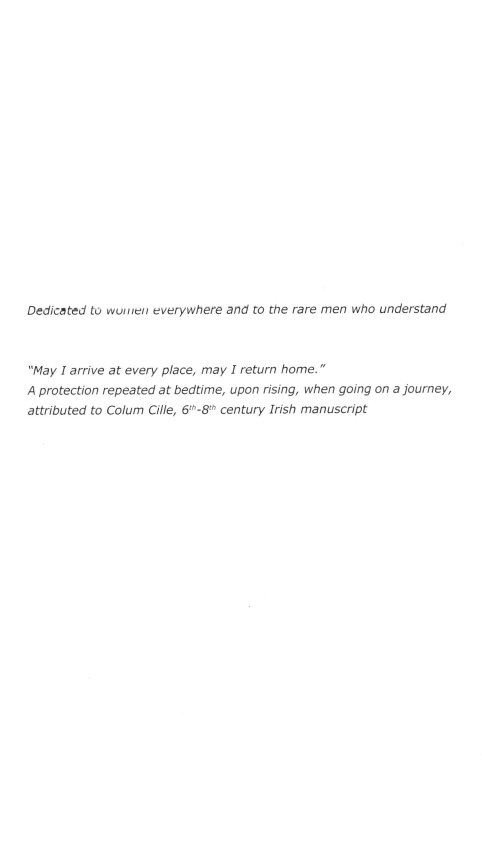

Dedicated to women everywhere and to the rare men who understand

"May I arrive at every place, may I return home."
A protection repeated at bedtime, upon rising, when going on a journey, attributed to Colum Cille, 6th-8th century Irish manuscript

Contents

Preface

Virginia Woolf once commented: "very few women yet have written truthful autobiographies." It is my desire to be one of the few.

My purpose in telling my life story is to leave an accurate record for my family, close friends, and women seeking inspiration for their own journeys. This more-than-memoir has been a labor of love, requiring immense dedication (and sometimes frustration) for three decades. Honesty has driven this writing, but since telling truth may not always please those about whom one tells it, I have changed several names, for I intend no harm, simply truth.

I am among those many artists who are not "numbers persons;" nevertheless, I have painstakingly endeavored to get dates, facts, and statistics correct. I've provided footnotes for most references and quotations, but in the few instances I could not relocate a source, I included the quotation anyway. My forty journals and reams of letters were invaluable references as were my *friends*: the books that have inspired and influenced my life. The letters, addresses, talks by and conversations with my dad are given verbatim per his files, my notes, journals, tape recordings, letters, and research. Flashbacks—and sometimes flash forwards—serve my *kairos*, not *chronos*, sense of time, as do changing tenses.

This is perhaps my greatest work—aside from creating three wonderful children and a number of acceptable paintings and I hope it conveys a *universal* as well as deeply personal story, touching lives beyond my own.

one

Quest

On a high hill beyond the moor, stone stairs, overgrown with nettles and ivy, lead to layers of hidden rooms. It could be 17 AD or 1070. Clodius, King of the West Franks or Henry, Prince of Scotland, or Malcolm, Earl of Angus, or perhaps a wandering Welsh bard, stands between crumbling parapets and signals me—or is it just a tattered cloth caught on a briar? I wave back and call out a greeting. I think it is returned—or is it the valley echo? I seek to know this place—my roots, my story, myself—and climb the craggy terrain toward home.

If my father hadn't been born dead, my life might have turned out differently. But he was. Born dead. Laid on the floor. Covered with a cloth. The attending physician and specialist could do no more, nor could more be expected at a home-birth in a humble section of Indianapolis, Indiana, in 1915. The doctors had told Robert, my grandfather, they could either save his wife, Norma, or the infant; not both. Robert paced nervously, staring at the lifeless lump that was to have been his second son while Norma, exhausted, closed her eyes in sleep. In the parlor, Lewis, their first-born, fidgeted with the hole in his pocket as he stared out the window at two boys trying to make a bike from old tires, wondering if their invention would sustain a ride to the end of the street, wondering if he could join them and get out of this house where death had taken hold.

The windows of the small gray-brown home never let in much light, but this May 19th seemed especially quiescent and dark—until Aunt Meda's knock. Seconds after the infant's arrival, Meda entered, eagerly asking, "How's my sister? Has she delivered yet?"

Her sparkling blue eyes found answer in Robert's sad brown ones.

Pressing past him to her sister's side, she saw the lifeless newborn and instantly refuted the tragic scene: "*No*! That child is *not* dead! *God* is his life! God is his *life!*"

Suddenly, to everyone's surprise, except Aunt Meda's, the infant let out a primal yowl—an exuberant wail as if shouted from a craggy sea cliff, befitting his ancient Welsh and Scottish roots. His hue became rosy; his life certain. God-launched, fighting the odds, small yet fearless, attracting everyone's attention, my father, Glenn Arthur Evans—the most remarkable man I've ever known—entered the world with indisputable originality that continued all his days.

What magic had Meda worked? Had she special powers? No medical explanation was given. However, for Norma and Meda there was only one reason for this extraordinary birth. Both women had recently encountered Christian Science. Barely neophytes of this unusual Christian religion— which holds no orthodox sense of liturgy, baptism, symbolism, Eucharist, or acceptance of Jesus as God—they had, in studying its textbook, *Science and Health with Key to the Scriptures* by Mary Baker Eddy, come to believe that life is spiritual and healing natural. Founded in New England in 1866 by Mary Baker Eddy, Christian Science teaches that God is Supreme Good, omniscient, omnipresent, omnipotent, defined by seven synonyms: Spirit, Life, Truth, Love, Principle, Mind, Soul. Scientists, as adherents call themselves, hold to the spiritual fact that all was created in the image and likeness of God, Spirit, and that evidence to the contrary is mortal belief or suggestion—not the truth of being. Through deeply prayerful practice of the teachings of Christ Jesus, as well as others in Old and New Testaments, Scientists demonstrate that healing can happen today as it did in biblical times, because the Christ principle is ever-present. One awakens out of sin, sickness, or death to harmony through a deeper understanding of God and by *sticking* to the truth that God's creation is spiritually intact. Such was Meda's basis for declaring my father alive. Denying what was unlike God, she didn't see a dead child. As startling as it may seem to some, Christian Scientists learn to *unsee* much of what appears.

Though I would depart from it decades later, I was born into this extraordinary belief system, the foundation of my grandmother's spirituality—profoundly proven to her by my father's birth, the cornerstone of our family's faith. No matter how many times I was told this story of Dad's arrival, tiny hairs on the back of my neck would rise and I'd feel my father's life had unique divine purpose. No ordinary birth, his seemed to have behind it the same life-force that controls tides, generates glaciers, and explodes super novas.

So perhaps it is not so surprising it was *his* car that saved my own life in 2004.

I'd taken the road to Springtown before. From my Pocono village home, down 611 South to 212 West, into beautiful Bucks County, Pennsylvania where I hoped to find a new home.

Searching for home has been my lifetime occupation—equally important to my being an artist. I've needed to create beauty and light in my living space, just as I've delineated space with brush on canvas or paper. Home— like art-making—is a *process* more than a product and each of my thirty-four moves has added to the composition.

Hiraeth, an ancient Welsh word, captures my meaning. I once read that each of us has a particular word at our very core that defines, compels, and guides us. Once discovered, we spend our life living into that word. *Hiraeth* is mine. *Hiraeth* is the deep inner yearning for home that rises within one's soul, the longing for a place where we aren't but where we'd like to be, where we feel connected and know we belong. It is a *quest for place*—love for where we ache to return, or, a place we hope to discover, a place often unknown, unnamed. More than nostalgia for the past or hope for the future (but inclusive of both), *hiraeth* has a poetry and music about it and sometimes an agony. It's inner promptings carry me like a seed on the wind from one location to another. Like Celtic *peregrini* following an exodus beyond their control, I seek, as 5ᵗʰ century Welsh St. Brynach says: "to find a home, to be at home, in all the many levels that that word can carry" (*The Celtic Way of Prayer*, Esther De Waal, p.8).

But this particular overcast August morning, driving to meet a realtor in Springtown, I am not thinking of these things. Alone, listening to an NPR interview about the upcoming 2004 election, settled in my father's big Oldsmobile Regency 98, with it's cushy gray leather seats and computerized bells and whistles, that I'd inherited when Dad died in January, 2002, and early for my appointment, the straight country road in front of me, I never expect a car to miss its stop sign, slam into the Olds with horrific force, sending me head-on into a ditch and telephone pole.

The mind is amazing at a time like this. A plethora of thoughts come in a second. Peripherally I see—or is it feel?—the thundering car crashing into me (I learn later that the cross street from which this car came is, ominously, Gallows Hill Road, just as I will learn the accident occurred 13 hours before Friday the 13th). Certainly it's stopping … but it's not! …*this is an automobile accident!*… I'm having an *automobile accident!*… I *can't* have an automobile accident! I'm not speeding…I'm on the main road… doing everything right! Then the impact, airbags deploy, gray soot in my face, and an unbelievable calm as I surprise myself by declaring, "I will not lose the presence of God nor the lucidity of my thought."

I watch the windshield shatter in front of my face and notice the telephone pole, oddly, seems only inches away. Through the windshield —now an aqua-colored mosaic of quarter-inch pieces—I see thick black smoke rising from where the engine had been. Though my glasses are gone from my face, I see through the cracked driver's side window the young blonde driver of the other car walk towards my vehicle—she is unharmed. Good. Then she runs back as if she needs to get something from her car…or is she leaving me here?...does she know I'm alive?

I hear my voice cry out as if detached from me: "Please help! I can't get out! Please don't leave me here!"

I bang on the window with my left hand, but it won't break. I try to open my driver's door, but it won't budge. Before I began this trip, per habit, I'd automatically locked all the doors and windows when I put on my seat belt. Now, securely held in by these safety measures, I can't move. My ribs won't let me reach to the passenger door. My legs, almost immediately discolored and immobile, begin to bulge as if they contain rumpled grapefruit. I look at my right arm—my painting arm—now shaped like an isosceles triangle between wrist and elbow, and realize no anatomy I'd studied in art school resembles this!

Black smoke ascends from the crumpled hood. Cars on television catch on fire after an accident, but my husband Bill once told me this never happens in real life. Nevertheless, I feel the need to get out–*now*. Nothing moves well. I see specks of blood on the gray leather. Why? I don't think I'm bleeding.

A woman in a black and red Mickey Mouse t-shirt is yelling at the back window: "Get out! You have to get out NOW!" Unable to open either front door due to the ditch, she encourages me to climb into the back where she has managed to open the back door several inches. I cannot fit in the tiny space between the seats and tell myself, "I'll go on a diet when this is over;" apparently, my sense of humor is intact. Cradling my right arm—which looks like a miniature Mt. Hood, the Oregon mountain I'd climbed with my sons a few years ago—I somehow manage to undo my seat belt and try once more to reach across my body with my left hand to the passenger door but it still won't open. Again comes that woman's encouraging voice. And again I try. This time, with much pain and difficulty, I manage to miraculously open the front passenger door. My continuing lucid thought directs me to find my purse and broken glasses on the floor before I attempt to step out.

Having been a Christian Scientist for the first three-quarters of my life, I know instinctively to stand, walk, and not give in to whatever awful evidence the material picture presents. I keep checking that the presence of God is with me. It is.

The woman who called at the window tells me her name is Eileen and that she's a nurse at St. Luke's Hospital in Bethlehem. Imagine that! What are the chances that the first car to stop would contain a nurse?! She helps me walk slowly to a safe hill across the street where the young driver who hit me has her head in her hands, crying. All I can say is "My arm…I am an artist and *this* is the arm I paint with! My *arm*!" I know there are other injuries but it is my right arm—my means to create and be who I am—now in grotesquely inaccurate anatomy cradled in my left arm that matters most.

I look back at the crumpled metal that had once been my father's car. *How did I survive this crash?!*

The State police and EMS people arrive. The policeman asks my name.

"Gwendolyn Caldwell...I don't live here...I live in Shawnee-on-Delaware in the Poconos." I answer his questions about the accident; he takes a brief statement and promises to call me later. He and the EMS people ask what hospital I want to go to.

"I don't go to hospitals," I answer, "I don't use medicine; I used to be a Christian Scientist." A man from another car says with fear in his eyes "You'll go to the hospital *this* time! You need immediate attention!"

"I was on my way to my realtor," I respond, "he will wonder where I am...I've got to phone him...we have a 10:30 meeting...he's not more than a mile or two down this road...my husband is in Washington, DC ... my daughter works in the Poconos. Please, someone call the realtor or my daughter—take my planner, it's in my purse." My planner-wallet is passed around. The policeman copies down my license information but no one is able to get a cell phone signal in this rural area to call the realtor or my daughter. An EMS worker repeats "What hospital do you want to go to?"

I look at the nurse in the Mickey Mouse T-shirt and ask, "Is Saint Luke's a good place?"

"Yes, they'll take good care of you there."

The officer says, "Go, just go in the ambulance!"

Everyone is urging me to go.

"But I haven't gotten my things out of the car...I haven't gotten the name of the other driver or her insurance company..." Instinctively, I want to do the right thing—I'd paid attention in driver's ed. decades ago.

"Go! Your things will be secured." The officer assures me. "Call the Dublin Bucks County station—they will give you all that information later. Just, go with the EMS!"

The EMS workers put me on a stretcher and into the back of the ambulance. They check my ribs, neck, head, stomach, legs, arm, pulse, blood pressure, tell me I am lucky to have survived and that it is a good thing I don't wear a girdle, easier to check for injuries.

"It's a *miracle* you walked away from that crash site! *That big Olds saved your life!* Any smaller car and you'd be *dead!*"

Even after his death my father is powerfully in my life. Had I not inherited his tank of a car—which my daughter's fiancée affectionately referred to as "The Steamship Gwendolyn"—I would have been driving my less crashworthy 12-year old Mitsubishi Eclipse. Even though I inherited the Olds, I never called it mine. Every time I got in it, it seemed my father had just stepped out of it —his old Cape Cod map book in the back seat pocket, his Boston Prudential Parking sticker on the side window, his nap pillow for road trips still on the back window ledge. I'd left all his things just as they were. I never thought about it before, but maybe, subconsciously, it was to keep him close.

An hour later I find myself in St. Luke's emergency room in Bethlehem, Pennsylvania, waiting another hour for X-rays. A nurse with multi-colored curly hair whose lapel pin tells me she's Gretchen offers me painkillers, which I decline (my Christian Science background kicks in again).

The laugh of the day comes when I am wheeled through double doors into the X-ray room.

"Are you pregnant?" the nurse asks routinely. I laugh in spite of my painful ribs. "I'm 60, not likely!", I say, "though I'd enjoy it if I were."

"You can't be 60! You don't look over 40!" I'd heard that comment before. Must be the long brown hair.

"Plain living," I answer, "No smoking, drinking, drugs, not even aspirin."

She smiles, takes the X-rays, and returns me to my room.

My daughter, Charissa, arrives—the EMS worker who rode in the ambulance with me called her on her cell phone. Charissa left work immediately and drove the hour and twenty minutes to St. Luke's from the Poconos.

"Your mother was a real trouper!" the nurse says to her.

The doctor on duty finally enters and explains I fractured a left rib, have some major hematomas (I had to ask what these are), bruises, concussion, and broke one of the two bones in my forearm, which he puts in a splint. After several days, time for the swelling to go up and down, I should call an orthopedic he says.

As Charissa drives me home from the hospital, I read the hospital's four pages of computerized instructions, which begin: *You have broken your wrist.* I am confused. Clearly what I saw was a broken *arm*. Clearly the on-call doctor said I'd broken one of two bones in my *arm* – not my wrist. Can't anything medical ever be clear? No wonder medical care is the third leading cause of death in the U.S.—a recent statistic I'd heard on PBS. The only other time I sought medical attention was eight years prior for a fall on wet pavement which resulted in my right arm being put in a cast for too long, apparently a misdiagnosis, the result being something called Reflex Sympathetic Dystrophy, or so I was told. After therapy and much effort on my part, I was able to paint again. I never dreamed my painting arm would sustain a second injury.

I decide not to wait the several days to see an orthopedic surgeon. My daughter finds me the best in our area, who fits me into his busy schedule the next morning. He tells me surgery is necessary *immediately* (good I'd not waited the several days per hospital instructions!); I believe him, for along with showing me the x-ray, knowing I am an artist, he draws a picture of my arm, locating and labeling the bones, and I see the broken radius bone in two pieces, each end frayed.

"If you want to use this arm again you'll need a permanent plate and screws to hold the bone together," the surgeon tells me. "I cannot promise you will have the fine motor skill to be able to do art as before. But if you don't have this surgery, you will *never* have use of your arm."

As if a balloon pierced by a pin, I'm deflated. But a strong clarity within tells me he is right. In two days, I will have surgery and seven screws will permanently secure a steel plate inside my painting arm.

For one brought up in Christian Science to be told she must have surgery is ejection from reality.

Christian Science, the very premise of our family's existence, had kept us free of drugs, medicine, and surgery for four generations—from my grandparents down through the raising of my own three children. Facing an operation, I was now in very foreign territory!

This was a distressing position to be in, for I'd experienced healing myself as well as witnessed the power of prayer in my Dad's dynamic example. Devoted to practicing the religion that had given him life, his quest to understand God and apply this understanding to daily living was no less holy than King Arthur's quest for the Holy Grail. Devoted to divine quests, King Arthur and Glenn Arthur—both with roots in mystical Wales—were known for their high standards, courageous leadership, fearlessness, and the ability to fight evil. Embellished legends followed them. King Arthur's grail may yet be proven tangible, some golden chalice or platter hidden for centuries, per-haps raised at the Last Supper, but, object or no, at least the symbol of great transforming power. Glenn Arthur's quest was to help mankind by following the healing path he'd found in Christian Science. Nothing mattered more to him. Not even his family.

As his first-born child and only daughter, I understood this intellectually better than I did as his daughter. My brother seemed to accept better than I this hierarchy that relegates family to second place in a father's devotion. Being male, possibly he more easily understood the detachment that enables a Cause to supersede the intimate. Carol Gilligan's *In A Different Voice* sug-gests the male species seeks *separation,* the female, *attachment.* I had the curse many a daughter experiences of never quite attaining the longed for relation-ship with her father, never feeling fully worthy not being a son, and, thus, eternally in search of a father's love and approval.

I am a "father's daughter." Father's daughters seek to be like their fathers, to make their fathers proud, and to imitate their father's values. Maureen Murdock explains the term in her book on the subject: "A father's daughter is a woman who over-identifies with or hero worships her father" (Murdock, *Father's Daughters*, pg.XIII). A father's daughter attempts to emulate her father's successes and beliefs. Often a firstborn child, she dutifully follows her father's rules and guidelines with such intensity that growing up she may not acknowledge her own identity.

Elizabeth Cady Stanton, definitely a father's daughter, was so influenced by her father that when his beloved son died, she attempted to replace her brother. She became an avid reader, superior student, Greek scholar, horse-woman, an outspoken public speaker, and an articulate writer at a time when these accomplishments eluded most women. In the process of measuring up to sonship she became one of the most significant thinkers of 19th century America, as well as one of the most important advocates for women's rights. All this and the mother of seven!

Jane Addams of Hull House fame (and so much more) is another father's daughter. She identified with her father to such a degree that it was difficult for her to separate herself from him. Even her health was affected. A friend wrote to her at the time of her father's death, "By a word you spoke at one time I know your father's life transfused itself through yours" (source lost).

My life is tangled, too, in my father's story. Like two gold chain necklaces left in a box to twist together over time, they've become so entwined that only painstaking care over more time can untie the troubled knots. Now and then I leave my routine and responsibilities to untangle the two. Two decades ago I began serious de-knotting. The place I chose for this work is a mere spec in the Midwest, a quaint tranquil town of barely one thousand people along the banks of the Wabash River: New Harmony, Indiana.

Indiana is where my paternal great-grandfather William Richard Evans settled (following a brief time in Cincinnati) after leaving the Evans homestead in Wales in 1867. His six children were born in Indiana, among them Robert Benjamin, my grandfather, and later Robert's three sons, among them Glenn, my father. I learned recently that my Grandmother Norma, her sister Meda and their siblings Veda, Verly, Buley, Lula, and twins, Lawrence and Clarence, were also born and raised in Indiana—in Huntingburg, coincidentally, just 50 miles from New Harmony. On one of my last trips to New Harmony, I made a point of driving to the Huntingburg courthouse where I touched the graceful ink signatures of Norma's parents, my paternal great grandfather, Norman Comstock Kelso, and his wife, Elizabeth Alexander (Elizabeth's dates: 1854-1933). According to the tax register, #1 H, Norma Ethel, their eighth child (my grandmother) was born September 18, 1890 and her father, Norman, was a 'car builder' (I presumed a street car builder, given the place and period). Norman Kelso's family came from Tyrell County, North Carolina, to Indiana in the mid 1700's; before that from Kelso, Scotland. Like my father's maternal lineage, so, too, my mother's lineage can be traced to Scots (and Irish and English), among them Henry, Prince of Scotland and Malcolm, Earl of Angus, and as far back as the 7th century.

But Indiana did not intrigue me because of family history. I had but the vaguest memory of one childhood visit to Indianapolis to see my Dad's great aunts and great uncle in their lace-doillied Victorian home and of another family trip, years later, to see my mother's brother, George Hunt, named after his father, my maternal grandfather. On my bedroom wall hangs a photo of George Hunt, my maternal grandfather, standing beside "The Hunt Special", a 1931 racing car he developed, for he was a pioneer in the auto industry and Indianapolis 500 speedway races. I recall no other ties to Indiana prior to finding New Harmony on my own while looking for a respite from a hot summer in St. Louis, where we lived, for my two toddler sons, my husband John, and myself in 1974.

From the first I read of New Harmony I felt *called* to the place—the way an artist is called to paint a particular scene. After my enchanting first visit there with my young sons—who delightedly rode their tricycles up and down safe streets and chased each other through garden mazes—I returned to New Harmony almost annually for nearly 25 years. It remains in my mind a mystical place of *home* coming.

In New Harmony, the past seems as real as the present. Founded in 1814 by God-fearing Harmonists, sometimes called Rappites, a German separatist religious group, New Harmony was purchased eight years later by Utopia-seeking Owenites, followers of forward thinking Robert Owen who sought to create a better society through education and progressive ideas. Though neither group exists today, their ideas, architecture, and contributions permeate the town. Historic buildings, the roofless church, gardens, woods, quiet paths, sanctuaries, chapels, a Shaker-style inn, art galleries, antique shops, and an old-fashioned sense of time feed the soul of every visitor.

Much of the preservation and artistic beauty of the place is due to the vision, philanthropy, intellect, spiritual intuition, and attention to detail of one woman: Jane Owen, wife of Robert Owen, descendant of the Owenites' founder. I first met Jane Owen in her garden in 1993, nearly two decades after my first visit to New Harmony. Many months earlier, I'd applied to live in The Poet's House, one of Jane Owen's historical homes, which she bestows upon an artist or writer for a week or more for creative pursuits. I was granted the privilege of having this 1814 former Harmonist home all to myself for two weeks mid-summer 1993 for the purpose of painting and writing.

That summer, when I checked in at the New Harmony Inn, a blue-trimmed formal white card in Jane Owen's own handwriting invited me to drop by and meet her. Having been captivated by her village for years prior to our meeting, I was already an admirer of this woman. I knew her by the grace and beauty she'd created in the place I'd come to love. She was clipping roses when I timidly opened the garden gate in front of one of her several homes. An iconic, vibrant, ageless woman, the same age as my father, she wore a long skirt, practical shoes, a large straw hat tied under her chin and pruning gloves. Removing a glove to shake my hand, she greeted me with interest and a wide Carol Channing smile. For the next dozen years, she and I would know each other; several of my paintings and one of my framed poems hang in her homes. Though our contact became merely the exchange of Christmas cards after 2000 and ended with her death in 2010, I continue to esteem her spiritual depth, her patronage of the arts, her humanitarian work and her ability to get things done. She remains part of what I love about New Harmony.

Whenever I arrive in New Harmony, the tension of duties, responsibilities, career and motherhood melt away. Here blooming things invigorate. Nothing stifles. It is as if I am cleansed in a kind of invisible shower the minute I step out of my car, as if I am wrapped in loving arms for the duration of my stay. I always find inspiration and renewal. I watch waterfowl on the pond, walk a secret pine needle path lined with inspiring thoughts carved out of metal, admire flower and herb gardens, sit on a low log pew tracing shadows with my eyes that become a cross on old plaster walls in the *Chapel of the Little Portion*, where an ancient mill wheel serves as alter, its circle pattern winding inward to its center, a design repeated on the stationery in my Inn room, symbol of what happens here.

New Harmony enables my centering and trimming of self. Here, I stop life's hectic pace and find balance, symmetry, renewed purpose. I trim away accumulation, get down to my essential being. Focused in stillness, I am free to be fully me. I create paintings and poems, painting late into the day and writing late into the night. Centered like a potter at her wheel, I don't *do* – I *dwell*.

New Harmony is like a potter throwing pots. Though a two-dimensional artist, not a potter, I admire the potter's art—especially since taking a course at Penland School of Crafts where I discovered that throwing pots is a metaphor for life. The potter does not center clay with her hands, but with her *whole being*. Only stillness directs the clay. No pot emerges if the potter is not focused mind and body. Closing my eyes, I could feel the form better. The less I struggled, the stiller I became and the more perfect my pot. When I tried too hard, the torque ripped off the lip, the mass wobbled, the hollow developed unevenly. Only when *centered*—a calm euphoria—could I lift the clay into cylinder or bowl. Then, when the spinning stopped and the pot dried leather hard, I trimmed away the excess, leaving the desired form. New Harmony enables me to find my form, to trim away life's excess and seek answers uninterrupted. Like my father, I, too, was born for spiritual quest.

In early June, 1993, my father phoned me at my home in Memphis from his home in Boston suggesting we get together. Our relationship, that had once been deeply close, had in recent years become awkward, strained. We'd put off facing each other, even when we were face to face. I had asked months earlier if we might get together, but he wasn't ready then; too many bridges to cross. Now he was ready.

His call caught me on a ladder with a dripping paintbrush in my hand. My husband Bill, daughter Charissa, and I had just moved into a 30-year old story-and-a-half house three days before. I was painting old beige grass-cloth walls red. On the previous day I'd painted the kitchen white, planning on a blue and white print wallpaper later. This new home –brick, conservative, and uninteresting, had two advantages: 1) it was in easy walking distance to our daughter's high school where Bill taught history and I, art, and 2) we could afford it. Plus, I knew I could transform it into something special, as I had previous homes.

Surrounded by stacks of unopened boxes, I fought my way to the kitchen phone before the last ring.

"Dad!" I was surprised to hear his voice. Since my mother's death in 1991 he rarely phoned. "Hello! Sure, I can talk now; no I'm just painting the living room." A crimson glob of latex fell on the kitchen floor, as I climbed over large cartons to put the wet brush in the sink. "Yes, we moved in a couple days ago. Boxes everywhere, you know what it's like."

"Can we get together in two weeks?," he asked. "I'll have some time then, just for the weekend."

"Sure," I heard myself say, as I shoved piles off my desk to locate a calendar, determined to wedge in any date he wanted. I'd been eager to meet for a year. As busy as he'd been as a corporation's CEO, my father's last 30 years as a Christian Science teacher, practitioner, and lecturer were even more demanding. Some days he answered as many as 40 phone calls while keeping appointments with patients and students.

"In two weeks? That'll be fine, Dad." I figured I could unpack the rest of the cartons after I returned. The weekend he chose was prior to the

Monday I was to move into New Harmony's Poet's House for my special two-week painting/writing retreat. If we could meet in New Harmony, that would help.

"Dad, what would you think about meeting in Indiana, your native state? I know a restful place: The New Harmony Inn. I think you'd really like it. You could fly into Evansville. Yes, I'll make all the arrangements. I can pick you up at the airport if you like.... Sure, if you prefer, you can take a taxi. Okay… looking forward to it."

Phone calls from Dad were always to the point, brief, and abrupt in ending. Though we had not spoken in six months, chitchat was never on his agenda. I did not mention to him that Nathan, my middle child, a college junior, would be driving back from working in a fishing cannery in Alaska with a friend that Friday, nor that my husband would be leaving the week after to hike part of the Appalachian Trail. I didn't tell him that Jason, my oldest son, following years attending local colleges and working in Memphis, would soon be leaving Memphis for Savannah College of Art and Design. Nor did I mention that my 14-year old daughter would be sponsoring a summer camp for kindergarteners the same week. No. I did not mention my life. Painting rooms, unpacking boxes, fixing meals, doing laundry, taking pets to vets, maintaining children's lives, preparing to teach a new school year, even writing and painting at the Poet's House just wouldn't seem important compared to his healing work. I'd learned long ago not to mention that to which he couldn't relate. I would squeeze in this weekend visit when it suited *him*, for my father is a busy man.

Our weekend arrives. I pack my suitcase, easel, art materials, writing notebooks and journals, into my compact Eclipse and drive the six hours from Memphis, Tennessee to New Harmony, Indiana. Arriving early, I stroll through gardens while waiting for the taxi that will bring Dad from the airport. I worry about his leaving patients, appointments, and an active Boston schedule to come see me. What if he views our visit as a waste of his time? Will we be able to talk deeply, metaphysically explore ideas, the way we used to before my divorce from John? Before my mother's death? Before I left the Church? Before I married Bill? Will it be a reunion or a familial Armageddon? Some unfamiliar flower scent distracts me for a moment. It is so lovely here in New Harmony, I cannot worry for long. I call the airport and check; his plane will be an hour late. Down paths of perennials I've time to reflect on our tarnished relationship.

I have been the devoted daughter all my life. I have been Dad's little girl, his student, supporter, defender, listener, ardent fan, obedient servant, and confidante. I have baked his favorite pies and cookies, created overwhelming Thanksgiving dinners and Christmases, mailed him thousands of letters and dozens of original poems, shared my deepest thoughts, listened devotedly to his teachings and ideas, fought for the same causes he cares about, stood the same ground, and given him grandchildren of which he could be proud. Throughout my life he has been my teacher, my hero, my role model, my provider, and my inspiration. I have craved his attention and aimed to measure up to the glory-place reserved for the perfect son I wasn't and that my younger brother genuinely was. I have striven to live up to my father's standards, adopted his values and views. Perfection was his goal, and, for too long it was also mine. For his many loving and noble deeds, his grand accomplishments, and shining ability to heal, I joined others in keeping him on a pedestal. Now, for me, that pedestal has toppled.

Like my father, I was a devoted Christian Scientist. For forty-six years his beloved religion was mine, too. Faith in God governed our family. Aunts, uncles, cousins, all found their way to this extraordinary religion that Meda and Norma introduced to the family. It more than influenced our lives; it *was* our life. Christian Science directed our every thought and action and our perception of the world. We did not smoke, drink alcohol, visit doctors—nor was there ever so much as an aspirin in our home. Our family was a model of the religion's teachings.

Like my father, I joined The Mother Church at age twelve and branch churches wherever I happened to live, serving on committees and in many leadership capacities. Like my father, I was a First Reader, a church board chairman, Sunday School superintendent and Sunday School teacher for more than twenty years. Like my father, I became a Christian Science practitioner in the public healing practice, though briefly, unlisted, and never to his degree. I gave speeches at regional meetings and wrote for the Church's international periodicals. Like my father, I raised my children to be practicing

Christian Scientists (though today none are). Like my father, I believed in the unreality of evil, the sinless nature of true man, and the power of God to heal anything.

Like my father, I relied on God as the supreme, omniscient and loving Father-Mother of all, guiding even the minutia of my life. God's omnipresent goodness and omnipotence are the bases of Christian Science practice; and healing as Christ Jesus healed is expected of the faithful. Healing, as it was for our entire family, was my norm. The theological premise for healing is that God, Spirit, being perfect, His creation can only be perfect and spiritual; therefore, any material evidence of imperfection—sin, sickness, or death—is illusion. Sickness is a lie, a dream from which one can awake by knowing, *clinging* to the truth that the perfection of God and his spiritual creation is intact. A Christian Scientist learns to deny anything unlike God (Life, Truth, Love, Principle, Mind, Soul, Spirit)—and steadfastly affirms God's Allness wherever material evidence suggests the opposite. Like most sincere Scientists, I worked at this daily. A Christian Scientist's health and well-being depends upon consciousness staying in the spiritual, seeing beyond the five senses, beyond brain, blood, bones to the man and woman made in God's image and likeness—*spiritual*—not material. For the genuine Christian Scientist who knows God, Mind, to be "*the only I*" (Eddy, *Science and Health*, p.591:16), body is not real, neither pained nor pleasured—nor one's identity.

At times I have, with a smile, described myself to "non-Science" friends as a member of the "Hasidic Branch" of Christian Science—my term, derived from reading Hiam Potok's *My Name is Asher Lev*. I recognized parallels between my own religious upbringing and those of Hasidic Jews. Asher Lev and I share the impact of deeply religious parents and powerful belief systems to influence one's life and art. For both of us, a strong religious family is both cause for, and in conflict with, artistic endeavor. Asher learns that "*every great artist is a man who has freed himself from his family, his nation, his race. Every man who has shown the world the way to beauty, to true culture, has been a rebel, a 'universal' without patriotism, without home, who found his people everywhere*" (Potok, *My Name is Asher Lev*, p. 195). And Asher Lev learns, as I did when I left the Christian Science Church in 1992, the devastation and isolation that departure from sacred family beliefs can cause as well as the exhilarating launching into a larger universe.

At all costs, an artist is responsible to truth, to her vision, and must follow where that vision leads. Lev, Van Gogh, and others have said that art *is* religion and painting is prayer. It is difficult, if not impossible, to belong to two religions at the same time—especially two such opposing ones. As a Christian Scientist, I was at odds with the material world, but as an artist I use my senses to create material objects that reveal my vision. At times the very material I work with—the *impasto* of paint, for example—can seem divine.

Making art and reading widely, along with spiritual and intellectual curiosity, life experiences, the passage of time, and much reflection in solitude carried me away from my father's world.

Yet, I find myself also grounded by my early faith. Medical concepts are still foreign to me.

The day prior to driving to New Harmony for the reunion with Dad—three months before my fiftieth birthday—I underwent my *first* medical exam ever, a process which most humans take for granted, but which I'd compare to blasting into outer space. No longer a Christian Scientist, thus, no longer legally exempt from my employer's medical requirements, I enrolled in the labyrinth called healthcare insurance and made an appointment with a female primary care physician. Sitting in her waiting room staring at anatomical charts for an hour had seemed not only a huge waste of time but, also, a bizarre experience. I'd been exempt from most high school biology classes and escaped all college sciences other than astronomy and geology. I found the posters, diagrams, tools and apparatus of a doctor's office quite overwhelming. To be asked the simplest of questions about childhood illnesses defied my very upbringing and all that I had known to be true up to this point in my life; the nurse might as well have asked me about plant life on Mars. To be ushered behind one door after another by programmed uniformed people thrusting paperwork at me, squeezing my arm, stabbing a vein, pushing my breasts, collecting my fluids, weighing, measuring, and evaluating my body— a body which for 50 years I declared did not really exist—in numerical lingo that might as well have been advanced calculus for all I knew, was a shocking and alien experience; about as strange as practicing Christian Science would seem to any doctor-visiting, medicine-imbibing ordinary person. The exam found me in perfect health with one exception. My mammogram indicated some uncertainty.

"Nothing's certain," the doctor said, "but you should see a surgeon in the next few weeks when you return from your trip." That would be the week school starts, when art supplies have to be inventoried, when my sons head off to college and my daughter starts high school. Not to mention the postponed unpacking since our recent move.

Nothing's certain. Is *anything* ever certain? Throughout the six-hour drive from Memphis to New Harmony, these words played in my mind along with re-runs of my life: leaving a twenty-one year marriage, divorce, marriage to Bill, my mother's death, art career, new house, children's lives and needs, religion, painting ideas, half-baked poems longing to be complete, and the restlessness that comes from doing too much and accomplishing too little while turning fifty—and the apprehension of this weekend with my father.

But all concerns fade in New Harmony's light. They can't play here. New Harmony's colors, textures, and sounds overtake mental re-runs. A bird sings overhead and a sweet breeze blows my hair. Waiting for my father on a rustic bench with summer surrounding me, I revise my opinion: "Nothing is certain—*except* New Harmony." Though I've never lived here, each visit assures me I've come *home*.

A fleck of distant yellow grows closer until it becomes a cab at the curb, the back door swings open and out steps my father.

two

The Poet's House

I am in this house again. A spacious country home with vistas, vast fields of green and distant forests. Two sides of the house are separated from the main section by corridors of doors and stairs: the cupola room in a far wing, up several flights; and, in a completely different direction, down four wide steps, a lower room as huge as a hotel lobby. I struggle to make my way to each. Both are unused, closed off from the main house. I have been living here for years without using them; it's as if I forget they exist. Then I remember them and am eager to use them. But some unknown dread hovers over my getting to these rooms. Someone—I think a husband—says he will go with me; but he gets preoccupied; so I take my flashlight and go alone. When I reach the lower room I notice its stone floor, massive beams, and huge fireplace like the jowls of some giant beast. Though furnished in warm tones, brown leather, olive paisley prints, textured fabrics, and the yellow glow of lamps, this room includes mysterious dark corners. I desperately want to redeem this space. The cupola room, up a complex set of stairs and doors, is not more than 12' by 12' but has very high ceilings that angle and meet, gothic-like, in the center. Everything is painted white. There are no furnishings, only secret panels, cupboards, and closets on all four sides, and, high up, windows all around. Even on a cloudy day—which it often is when I am in this house—there's light here.

This room would make a perfect retreat. I love its whiteness, simplicity, austerity. It is my favorite, but it, too, has a foreboding about it—something to do with the secret cupboards and closets. I believe if I put it to use, the ominous feeling will vanish. But tonight I worry about the main house. My furniture is gone, moved out, and why was I not told? I feel homeless. Someone says, "Don't you remember the movers came and got it all? We are moving again." I insist we cannot move until I make full use of the two remote rooms. Adamant, alone, I return to the rooms and stare down the fear that permeates them with thoughts of how to use both. And just as I begin to make plans for change—as each time I've had this dream—I wake.

A dwelling expresses the thoughts of its past and present residents. The beliefs, convictions, fears, loves, and character of those who have lived in a house give pattern, form, color and texture to that house as surely as fabric or furnishing. More than a physical place or roof over one's head, home is a power beyond occupied space. It is an atmosphere, presence, mood, intangible substance, a kind of poem reflecting one's thought and identity. Home is the location-less place where consciousness dwells. It is where one cultivates who she is. A home reflects the love that created it and any cruelty it has known. Home is where we put who we are, and a bit of who we are remains in every house we leave.

In every one of my thirty-four homes, I left some bit of me behind. And, in each dwelling I have felt something remaining from those who lived there before me. In my 1700s Pennsylvania house, I felt the presence of Charlotte, one of its former owners, and others unnamed before her. This is not a ghostly matter. It is about *presence* and *continuity*. We have a relationship with those with whom we have shared *home*. Something drew each of us to the same place, though at different times, and that something unites us.

Time seems suspended when we are truly home. Artists and poets understand this timelessness for they create in it. Madeliene L'Engle writes that "artists often have a more profound sense of what time is all about"

(L'Engle, *Walking on Water*, p.96). It has nothing to do with *chronos* time, "wrist watch and alarm clock time," but, rather, with unmeasured *kairos* time, "God's time, real time" (L'Engle, p. 93). I pray, paint, and write in *kairos* time, especially in New Harmony.

In 1993, following the weekend at New Harmony Inn with my father, Monday morning I move into the Poet's House for my two-week painting/ writing retreat as planned. This 1814 ivy-covered Harmonist house is more perfect than I'd imagined. Like a Rothko painting. Books, antiques and art furnish the house in a quiet austerity and relaxed simplicity. Pared down. Essence. In its sparseness, a feast for the artist's eye.

There are two floors, two rooms each. A 25 by 35-foot sitting room with wide hearth, nudged floor to ceiling by bookshelves, offers several grand antique farm-style tables, each big enough to serve dinner for eight. I set out my brushes and paints in orderly fashion on one table and create a writing center on another. Under the south window table, I mark my claim with legal pads, a pot of pencils and pens, a file box, and writing folders—my things tell me that I belong here and work will be done. I place my books, journals, candles, and a pot of dried grasses on the old brick mantel facing the rosy-peach sofa where I fall asleep reading during my first afternoon in this house. Behind the sofa stands a dry-sink on which rests a hand-blown glass lamp—the size of a giant pumpkin— providing home to a creative spider in its woven, muted-green shade. The graceful, straight-back, rush-seat rocker is not quite comfortable enough to spend the day in, but the Arts and Crafts movement style chaise of wood and cane is. The plank floor is bare but for one thick white rug in front of the sofa—a handsome contrast. French doors open to the grape arbor patio, another perfect place for writing.

The other room on the first floor is a kitchen, with olive-colored eating area, aquamarine linoleum, slate countertop, and warm wood cabinetry the hue of browned butter. Above the cabinets into which I unload my week's groceries, perch handsome earth-toned pottery pieces, envied by this would-be potter. Hand-thrown pottery and hand-blown plates of fragile turquoise glass fill the cabinets. I'll enjoy doing dishes here in the unusual color harmony, craftsmanship, and artful clutter of tools, hand-made crocks, hanging baskets, herbs, and fresh linens. A wedge of light streaks across the floor from the half-open door. Along with the carpet of sunshine, enter sounds and smells from summer gardens.

A corner stair closed off by a latched door—so quaint I will draw it one afternoon—connects the two floors. At the top of the stairway is a long built-in writing desk made of beautiful old wood; a window centered above it looks out to lawn and garden, an inspiration for any writer seated beneath it. On the opposite wall more bookshelves lure me. Off the hall, a spacious bathroom—something the Harmonists did not have—invites me to consider the luxury of a bath in the huge soaking tub every night of my stay. Also off the hall is the generous bedroom furnished entirely in mellow wood antiques with white walls and plain white bed linens. A high double bed, a twin bed, an armoire, a long cupboard, a side table, a bed stool and several unusually low chairs provide more than I need, yet, there is beautiful simplicity here. One exposed section of my bedroom ceiling reveals the mud and straw "biscuit" construction used by 19th century Harmonists to insulate their homes. I feel as if I am in a museum; a certain reverence for the past is in order.

Have I gone back in time? Possibly it *is* 1814 again. I think I hear voices—German perhaps? Yet, I understand their pleasant chatter as they work. I am included in their industrious sorting of fresh-picked vegetables for dinner. Some are praying, for they are a devout group, but these Harmonists do not seem to object that I am in their home to write and paint. Somehow they understand my twentieth-century need. They have accommodated many guests for nearly two centuries; I am only one more intruder seeking their peace. We work side by side.

I hear the rustle of Frances Wright's long dark skirts—the early feminist who wrote for Owen's newspaper and admired this community as much as I. Will her hand lift the stair-door latch, and will she walk into the room discussing her passion for women's rights? How many questions I will have for her! Perhaps it is Robert Frost on the stair, for he, too, was once a resident here. Maybe he will recite his latest poem for me from the rocking chair while a Rappite carries an iron pot to the hearth. Maybe I can sit at the feet of Thomas Merton and Paul Tillich, both once Poet House visitors, and ask theological questions tonight after dinner. From the shelf old friends call—Shakespeare, Emily Dickinson, Sylvia Plath, Adrienne Rich—and writers new to me. I am not alone in my solitude.

A dwelling of mystery and tranquility, this old Harmonist home has a life of its own. I watch the sun mold the house in different shapes, changing the symmetry and patterns of light and dark throughout the day. I move through the house as the hours unfold and am in significant new places, created by new shadows, new light. Like stations. Stations of the cross? It is as if *within* the house is a journey. Home is the "still point" for journey but can it also be the journey itself? For two weeks, this house will be both journey and home to me. I will thrive here. For more than a place of history, aesthetics, comfort, the Poet's House is a spiritual place. It is, as true home always is, *incarnational.* Function, form, and beauty are inseparable from the spirit that creates them. The thoughts of hundreds of writers who have visited here or whose works line the shelves are now part of me.

I cannot tell where New Harmony's identity and mine separate. Whenever I visit, New Harmony seems to be my essence, the blood in my veins, the breath in my lungs. It is as if every historic log, brick, and stone breathes for me, as if the gardens are my laughter. Light and shadow on New Harmony's textured paths play out my moods. The peaceful parks are my place of worship. The simplicity of this safe place hushes any self-doubt, fills me with joy and balance. I am affirmed by all I hear and see. The New Harmony in me and the *me* I pour into New Harmony stir into one fine blend.

This visit in 1993 had a unique preface: two days with my father.

Dad arrived at the Inn late Friday afternoon for our weekend together. Not having seen each other in over a year, nor deeply connected for half a dozen years, I had anticipated our meeting with some trepidation. But New Harmony's peace took over and by the time Dad's taxi pulled up to the curb I was eager to greet him, hopeful for the renewal our visit might bring.

"Hi, Dad! Welcome to New Harmony!" I attempt to open the taxi door for him but his strong hands beat me to it.

My father always arrives with flourish. Vitality, love, and dynamism— these characteristics bound out of the taxi all at once. His deep-set brown eyes never fail to twinkle. He habitually sports a generous smile from years of practice with colleagues and students. In the 1980s, this innate warmth attracted many when he and my mother traveled to several hundred cities on a lecture circuit throughout the U.S., Europe, and Asia. At 78 he looks like a man in his early sixties. His 5' 9" trim frame in navy sports coat, crisp white shirt and striped tie, shows the vigor of a man who loves to walk along Boston's Charles River and once played tennis daily but does not reveal his fondness for Mom's or my homemade chocolate chip cookies.

"So good to be here." His hearty hug makes me feel he really means this. Perhaps things really will go well this weekend. But he is good with words.

We check him into his Shaker-style room and then stroll over to The Red Geranium Restaurant. A delicious dinner is accompanied by unusually stiff talk on safe subjects. This is not normal for either of us. We are both being particularly cautious.

Unlike this night, dinnertime growing up in our home was lively and instructional, with a free exchange of ideas. When my father was not away on business, we ate in the dining room—china, candles, cloth napkins and plenty of conversation. Sometimes the topic would be my Dad's day, dealing with corporation or ethical issues. He would ask my brother and me how we would handle a union difficulty, a production problem, or an issue that challenged one's integrity. He took our answers seriously. I enjoyed this; perhaps it nurtured my love of problem-solving; certainly it influenced my brother's future business career. Often Dad would include an explanation of moral decision-making. He would tell of his experiences in making "right" choices, how to base one's decisions on "what God would have me do," on the Christly method of solving a problem he'd gleaned from study of the Bible and Christian Science textbook. Dad saw mealtime as an opportunity to feed us life lessons.

Whether we were at the table or in his office, Dad told my brother and me Bible stories of Christ Jesus, Paul, Moses, Abraham, Daniel, Ruth, and all the rest. He made them real. Their examples of integrity set the pattern we were to follow, offering lessons for daily life. Daniel in the lion's den illustrated how I might overcome fear of standing up in front of my 6th grade class to recite a poem. If someone were rude, that was merely an opportunity for me to love the same way Old Testament Joseph loved his treacherous brothers after they sold him into slavery. Our struggle with any sickness was like Jacob's wrestling with the angel. Our guide for behavior was the Sermon on the Mount. Jesus' healings stood with us through colds, flu, mumps, falls and injuries, enabling us to work at being victors over pain.

Frequently Dad's teachings focused on God's "names" as given in the Christian Science textbook: Principle, Mind, Soul, Spirit, Life, Truth, Love. He pointed out many times that if I understood God to be the only Mind, then I could rely on Him going into exams and be unafraid. In like manner, God as Principle, taught me to be principled in my standards, habits, and actions. Such practice of one's understanding of God is called *demonstration* in Christian Science and is *proof* of Christian Science's validity. A healing is not about cure, but about growing in spiritual understanding; physical improvement is the by-product.

Lessons discerned from the weekly Bible lesson or a healing we experienced molded the substance of our days. Success in sports or academics, our health and well-being, depended upon our faithfulness to Supreme Good. It was our job to be good because Goodness was the standard set in our home and our reason for being.

I remember when I first learned that the world is not entirely good. I was about nine, in the fifties, watching "I Remember Mama" on our new black and white TV. Someone planned to poison Mama's husband. I can still feel the shock I felt then that maliciousness existed. Certainly I had heard the word "evil" before (it was mentioned in the Lord's Prayer) but this time evil itself was in front of me, happening to a good man. How could anyone want to harm another child of God?! Is *BAD* out there?! Can it touch me? Though my sheltered concept of the world as totally good was suddenly shattered, I didn't lose my belief in the power of goodness

I accepted my mother's good expectations for my brother and me and never tired of hearing my father tell about the good Bible characters whose lives I was supposed to emulate. Ours was a harmonious home, without heated argument or a swear word. Raised on a steady diet of goodness, I remained drawn to all things good, beautiful, and true and was confused by anything less. I naively believed the standards in our home were in *every* home. As kids often do, I assumed all families lived the way we did. I did not realize then that our standards were untypical, that my father's children needed to be perfect in order to be *his* children.

If I felt sad it was not Truth I was feeling. If I fell down, or made a mistake, or got a low grade, these things could have been prevented if I were only better, more like my father, more reflective of God's qualities. I was convinced of everyone's goodness—except my own.

Deep down I *knew* I wasn't perfect; all I had to do was look in the mirror. In 5th grade, slightly chunkier than most, with an ugly perm or, later, an equally unattractive Dutch-boy cut (both selected by my mother), I saw the evidence for myself. If that weren't enough, I was shy and unsure of myself on into high school; I would rather have disappeared than talk—not a bit like my articulate brother and father. Math gave me problems and I was among the last to be chosen for kickball teams. My mother was always insisting I be more social, go to and give parties. Her message was that I didn't measure up to her expectations for *her* daughter. I felt different, *not* perfect.

Taught that God is the only I or Ego, (Eddy, *Science and Health*, p. 588:21), I had a difficult time finding myself. In order to survive (though I didn't realize it at the time) I retreated into my imagination: a wonderful world of my own making—of story, dolls, paper dolls, books, drawing and writing. I invented a place for myself where it was safe to create and question.

As I grew older I went into my father's office with deep metaphysical questions. His fascinating and illuminating answers always shot down doubt. His wisdom, seasoned generously with testimonies of healing and real-life experiences, many of which I had witnessed, fascinated me. In his strong voice of certitude, he would tell me how he, or people he knew and helped as a Christian Science practitioner, had overcome difficulties. Whether in childhood or as an adult I loved being called into his office to hear his inspiring stories and to have private time with this amazing man with whom everyone wanted time. Even at nearly fifty years of age in New Harmony I looked forward to time alone with my father.

But by our 1993 New Harmony meeting, with all that had transpired in recent years in our lives, I felt some apprehension. A fragility hung about our meeting. Only five years prior, contemplating divorce and leaving the church, I had been the recipient of Dad's rarely seen rage and we had not had a sit-down, intimate interchange of ideas since. Our last "talk" was on the eve of my divorce in July, 1990, as he tried to persuade me not to go through with it. He and Mom did not approve of divorce and did everything in their power to stop it. Two days before I was to fly to Memphis to appear in court to finalize the divorce, he drove from Boston to Providence, Rhode Island, where I was in the last busy days of completing my Master's Degree at Rhode Island School of Design (RISD). Dad spent four hours trying to convince me that divorce was wrong. "Divorce is against Jesus' biblical command!" he bellowed at one point. For the first hour and a half (I timed it) he lectured nonstop, questioning me without room for my answers, relentlessly trying to persuade me to see the error of my action.

What would he ask me this weekend in New Harmony? Would he blame me for my mother's death as some had? Would he criticize my new marriage to a liberal intellectual younger than I? And what would he say about my leaving the Christian Science Church? This last issue would be the rub. I had found my voice in adulthood, stood up to him that night in Providence, but could I endure two intense days of personal scrutiny? Would I lose myself? Would I once more become his agreeable little girl under his powerful influence? The same way I lost my *self* whenever I entered my mother's kitchen as an adult, once more following her orders as if I were a third grader instead of a grown mother of three and an accomplished cook in my own right?

The divorce process made me stronger. In September 1989 I separated from my husband, after several attempts, under pressure, to return and try once more. But on July 4,1990—Independence Day—the divorce became final. Six months later, Christmas, 1990, I experienced my first family event as a divorcee: my parents' 50th anniversary, celebrated by aunts, uncles, and cousins in Bermuda. Merely polite, neither Dad nor I took off our safety masks on that occasion. My children's activities buffered the iciness of some relatives, and the courage I'd gained in going through a divorce enabled me to enjoy bits of the island vacation despite being the black sheep.

My mother's unexpected death the following May was another issue Dad was sure to bring up. In the eyes of several aunts, an uncle, and some Christian Scientists, I robbed my father of his wife by breaking my mother's heart, thereby causing her death.

Another topic was certain to be my pursuing a Master's Degree at RISD for three summers (1988-1990), leaving my then husband at home and my kids at camp and summer jobs. "How can you leave your family duties?!," I still hear Dad's booming words. Yet, he had left his family for the same amount of time to serve NATO in Europe as well as for countless business trips. Wasn't nine weeks away from home for a Master's Degree in my field of employment as important as his business trips? My sons were not young children but college and high school age, working each summer; my daughter was in summer camp. But my parents regarded my absence from my family as unforgivable.

Until her death, Mom grew critical and phoned frequently to question how I could "desert" my family for "all that liberal thinking at an art school!" My parents had never shared nor understood my love of art, though Mom framed my more realistic paintings, decorating her Boston penthouse with them.

My marriage to Bill would be another issue. This non-Christian Scientist, a humorous, witty, intellectual, guitar-playing, bearded historian eight years my junior was definitely a blow to Dad. Following a year of dating, Bill and I married October 19, 1991, six months after Mom's death.

But of all the things I'd done, in Dad's view, none was more intolerable than my leaving the Church in 1992. He fought hard to keep me on board. This promised to be the most difficult theme of the weekend, and of our lives.

My father was an integral part of the Church I left, involved in its hierarchy, its headquarters, its deepest core. He lived, worked, wrote, spoke, taught its teachings, and healed with its principles. It was his daily life and greatest love. And I left it. I left all that mattered to him. Indeed, my leaving caused many to cast me out. This took its toll on my relationship with my father. What had once been a deeply metaphysical relationship, grounded in close sharing of ideas and the search for truth, became fragile—like the fine hand-blown glass plates in the Poet's House cupboard which one clumsy movement could shatter.

Our first evening of our 1993 "reunion" weekend, after dinner at The Red Geranium, we stroll through the town of New Harmony—all two or three blocks. We amble through Carol's Garden, the Roofless Church, and then wander to the town band shell where John Phillip Sousa tunes fill the warm summer air. I half expect *The Music Man*'s Forrest Tucker to come around the Methodist Church, parading down Main Street, a boys' band following in turn-of-the-century uniforms. The curiously old-fashioned evening eases our being together. We might have walked pleasant streets all evening, but a history of deep discussion informs my father and me; we know our unspoken agenda is Truth—the one thing each of us most values and the concept each of us now views differently.

My father and I share an affinity for honesty to the point of boldness. Honesty is freeing. It cancels fear, enables one to look over any precipice with courage and leap when called. I grew up knowing that healing demands honesty. "Honesty is spiritual power; dishonesty is human weakness which forfeits divine help" the Christian Science textbook taught me (Eddy, *Science and Health*, p 453:16). I still believe this. I've never understood dishonesty nor am I comfortable around anyone who functions deceptively. Honesty frames my friendships, work, and problem-solving. It is the basis for my thinking and action, what causes I take up, and what environs I live in or leave. I'm sure I got this concept initially from my father and Christian Science, but life has made it mine.

By sunset, Dad and I sit on a bench under an old oak immersed in conversation. We tell amusing family anecdotes, re-live Christmases, family vacations, catch up on grandchildren and healings. A cool breeze eventually moves us inside to two Shaker rockers in Dad's room.

I am in his "office" again. Only this time I have a voice and our rockers face each other. It is not easy to stand up to an immensely powerful patriarch—especially one dearly loved by so many. The force that enables my father to support the sick and dying also empowers his strength of opinion and influence. Habitually leaned upon and looked up to by colleagues, patients, friends, and family, he is accustomed to being in charge and to taking charge when no one else will. To me, when I was younger, his power seemed directly linked to God. He appeared to always have the right answer, the unswerving might, an infallible ability to solve any crisis. Never to be denied, he spoke the final word on any issue. I was not afraid of him, but I knew I never wanted to go against him; though in recent years I had done just that.

Our conversation develops carefully, neither one wanting to make a battle of our New Harmony time. Both seem ready to find a common ground. Actually, we search for more: a foundation on which to build a new relationship as valuable as the old one had been. Four years ago, words of betrayal left both pairs of lips. Misunderstandings replaced a life-long treasured closeness and love's thread sometimes seemed invisible.

Like metronomes to our words, our rockers keep mismatched beats until late into the night.

My father expects people to agree with him. Tonight is no different. When my truth does not agree with his, I am unheard. His inquisition and sermons, designed to drive me to his perspective, lengthen. He talks firmly to convince me of his certitude.

When I was a child we conversed safely because I did two things exceedingly well: I was obedient and I listened. Listening was easy; it was talking that was difficult. During my high school years when Dad brought Japanese and Mid-Eastern businessmen home to dinner, I didn't open my mouth except to eat. After dinner, while they talked, I sat quietly on the floor, observing and absorbing everything, while drawing their portraits in my sketchbook.

Now thirty years later, I sit across from my father and dare to speak my mind when he asks about my divorce.

"Divorce is a dry, hard desert place, Dad. I wouldn't wish its agony on an enemy. But it made me strong and it was necessary. For twenty-one years I had given my all to my marriage. But I was so *alone* in that marriage! John was in an ivory tower, avoiding life and love, incapable of intimate—or any real—communication . To survive I had to leave. So I found the courage to do just that. I was led the whole way—each step was clear. I left everything I'd had or known—except the kids."

"I know John wasn't a good provider—I tried to talk to him about that." Dad interjected.

"It wasn't about his losing jobs or the struggle to make ends meet." I tried to correct Dad; I wanted him to understand why I left. "It was about *us*, our relationship. He seemed distant from me and the kids. While teaching and exhibiting my art and being PTA president and Sunday School Superintendent, and raising our kids, I also paid the bills, cleaned, cooked, gardened, ironed his shirts, planned the vacations, made the decisions. He gave little. I left because I was losing myself and I needed to be me."

"What do you mean: 'I needed to be me'? A marriage is not a selfish undertaking! I've seen all sorts of marriages put back together! It just has to be worked on in Science! I can tell you healing after healing I've helped with in marriages that were struggling! Today they are harmonious, happy couples! I *know* it is possible!"

"Dad, I tried for *twenty-one* years. I was devoted to making my marriage work, making a good home, being a good wife and mother. Nothing was more important to me!"

"You have three wonderful children that prove what you did in the home department; I'm not questioning that. I've enjoyed many Thanksgiving and Christmas dinners in your home; you're a good cook like your mother. A good homemaker. You've raised good kids. That's why it is so hard to understand what went wrong! John never beat you, he wasn't an alcoholic—he was a good man, a sincere Christian Scientist."

"Yes, but he didn't communicate, talk, touch, hold, share, read or venture into life. He didn't see the value of expressing love humanly, deeply, fully. He existed in his own silence, never caring to know the woman he had married, never questioning what life was all about, never seeking beyond his own certitude. So I threw myself into children, church work, art, and community causes. Until I just couldn't do it anymore. Couldn't live without love, intellect, connection. Couldn't go through the paces. Couldn't play the perfect homemaker and problem-solver for everyone anymore. I prayed about all of this, you know. One day it came to me—I am *not* my father's daughter, I am *not* my husband's wife, I am *not* my children's mother. First and foremost, I am *me—God's child. A person with an individuality of her own*. It was time to be who I was created to become."

"What do you mean you are *not* my daughter, *not* your children's mother?"

"Of course, I'm your daughter—gratefully so! And my children's mother—I love every part of that! I just mean, that above all, I must be *faithful to who I am*."

"You are a mother, a daughter, a wife—what more is there to know?! There is no higher occupation than motherhood! Look at your own mother—no one exemplified what motherhood means better than Ruth did! No one kept a better, cleaner home, was a finer cook than your mother! She was a good woman with high standards!" His brown eyes pierced my own brown eyes as he added sternly, "It broke her heart to see your marriage break up, you know."

"Yes, Dad, I know. She called and told me—often." I could tell by his surprised expression what I suspected: he was unaware of her many calls to me. "I know she died of a broken heart and I know that some in the family blame me."

"I never said you caused her death!" My father defends himself unnecessarily.

I take the opportunity to ask about my mother's death. At 75 she died somewhat mysteriously. He tells me only the little I already know. How she had been ill and he had prepared her meals and taken care of her—something he was not used to doing—especially on top of all the work he had to do for his practice and class. And how when she passed in her sleep he had tried to bring her back through prayer and then failing to do so, called 911, but she was already gone. How he knelt in prayer, asking God why and what he was to do, and the answer he received was to go right on doing his healing and teaching work.

"Your mother exemplified purity. She expressed all the mother qualities of God. We reflect both the male and female qualities of God, you know. It's all right here in the textbook." He fumbles through his briefcase for a *Science and Health* as if I'd never seen one before. "Here, take this and read what Mrs. Eddy has to say." As if I'd never read it before.

He hands me his well-worn leather copy. I read the two paragraphs he instructs me to read aloud, familiar passages that I have read countless times throughout my life. Then I listen to him lecture on the topic of marriage for twenty minutes. Familiar words I have heard many times. Finally, his question: "So, do you mean to tell me that self is more important than God?"

"I didn't say that, Dad. God is essential to me. I divorced because I couldn't live a lie anymore. Hidden tears had become a way of life for me. My divorce was not about being selfish; it was about *survival!*"

He starts to speak but holds himself back. I can see this is not easy for him. His huge knuckles—from working on an auto-assembly line as a young man—flex on the chair arms. He has more to say than he dares. He desperately wants to persuade me to his point of view. He is trying even harder not to alienate me. What he doesn't know is that we cannot be alienated, that neither of us wants that and won't let it happen.

"So why did you feel the need to leave the church?" At last the primal question.

"Prayer led me away." I have no problem being blunt. That was precisely how it happened.

His brow furrows and he starts to speak but sits back in his chair, as if controlling himself once again.

I continue, slowly, "It was more about following Love's impulse than making a decision. I keep discovering…"

Dad interrupts: "You can be very impulsive! One has to watch that!" He could not wait for my full answer. "We must act out of thoughtful deliberation, not impulse!"

"No, that's not what I mean, Dad. Please let me finish. What I was about to say is that Love is bigger than a denomination. It is *universal.* I keep running into God in all sorts of unexpected places. God isn't just in Christian Science anymore, for me. I find God in literature, philosophy, an inner-city Methodist church, the outreach of a downtown Episcopal congregation, Buddhism, Hinduism, my art, in my classroom, and in ordinary daily life itself! I don't know that I can explain this so you'll understand." I pause, knowing he needs to have a turn.

"The one thing I do understand is that if it weren't for this religion," Dad holds the textbook up reverently as he continues, "I wouldn't be here right now! I owe my health, my success in business, everything I have, to this healing truth founded by that dear woman, Mary Baker Eddy! I don't know what I would do without Christian Science! Every difficulty, every adversity in my life has been healed by this truth! Mrs. Eddy left us a powerful tool. I have seen it heal every disease or problem you can name. I owe my life to it—and so do you!" His voice reaches a crescendo and then softens some as he follows with healings I have heard many times. He includes some of my own.

He talks for another hour without stopping, which I have known him to do on many occasions when speaking of Christian Science. I listen to his impressive true stories just as I did as a child on into adulthood. I hear how he was healed of a football injury in high school and of an automobile accident when a young man and how a patient of his was healed of cancer and another one of drug addiction. I hear the lessons he and his patients learned. I still enjoy hearing them. Only now these healings make me wonder what *universal* truth is at their core, for healing must be as universal as love; it must be available to all—regardless of denomination. It isn't just about one woman's discovery. But I am not allowed to speak a word.

When he finishes, he looks at his watch. "It's nearly midnight. I think we should call it a night and continue where we left off in the morning." He rises. The decision as to when to end a conversation is always his. I remember more than once hearing him say to guests in our home as the hour grew late, "You may stay as long as you like, but I'm going to bed." And off he'd go.

We hug. I feel his protruding bony shoulder—some unhealed tennis injury? We say goodnight.

Saturday morning we rise early, meet for breakfast, then sit on the bank of the creek that flows behind the inn. I had decided before this weekend that I wanted to interview my father—to know fully this amazing man who is clearly the most intriguing individual I have ever known. I tell him I would like to interview him. He likes my idea; eager, really. I take out my legal tablet and ask him questions about every aspect of his life—part of my untangling the interlocking gold chains. I take copious notes. Writing, like drawing and painting, has always been my way of understanding things, and I do want to deeply understand my father.

Dad enjoys reflecting on his childhood, his careers in three major industries, and his healing work. By noon I have ten pages of notes, both sides. Perhaps this seems strange, to interview one's father, but it is not the first time I have transcribed his words. This time it is not religious wisdom I seek from him but my father himself. What was he like as a child? What did he do in high school besides play football? How exactly did he meet my mother? What was their relationship like? What was it like during WWII to help in the production of the *Enola Gay*? How did Christian Science direct his business decisions? What matters most to him? I ask these questions and many more. Old familiar stories gain new meaning and a few new ones pop up. We laugh together at some and soberly share our insights on others. Before we know it, it is noon and my brother arrives.

My father had invited my brother, Rich, to join us for part of the weekend. The three of us have not been alone together for years, aside from a few days following Mom's death. When we meet in New Harmony, my brother is a handsome, dark-haired, dark-eyed forty-something businessman with a law degree and a poet's heart who leaves behind on seven sublime New Jersey acres, an historic home, a vibrant wife who is my friend and four exceptionally talented children, plus assorted dogs and cats. A decade after our New Harmony gathering, Rich would surprise some by divorcing, remarrying, living in Arizona with his new wife and her six children, a couple of horses, more dogs and cats. Thoughtful, sensitive, a take-charge provider and soccer-coaching father, a music lover, devoted Christian Scientist, and successful lawyer-businessman, my busy brother and I see each other less than once a year. However, we are close in thoughts and viewpoint and know we can count on each other when there's a need; I have always been very proud of him.

In New Harmony, Rich and I sit in Dad's room late Saturday afternoon, sharing with our father the realities of our lives. Along with the good stuff—a child's lead in a play, another's football wins, one's academic honors—we include the occasional experience of a child smoking cigarettes, trying alcohol, or experimenting with drugs. These facts appear to surprise Dad, for he holds his grandchildren to the same perfection he held his own children.

My father uses his family's accomplishments as illustrations in his speeches. We become examples of the power of God at work in individual lives. I never felt comfortable with this. What if I messed up? Some of my better experiences were out there in Dad's lectures and I couldn't fail in the face of them, but I knew I was *not* infallible; in fact, I could be a real disappointment. What kind of an example could I possibly be for anyone? Nevertheless, my father's narratives about real people's healings sometimes included my brother and me.

Rich finishes a story about one of his sons, which launches Dad's speech about what it takes to raise good children in today's world. When Dad finishes, I add my point of view:

"I don't think love for our children is based on how good they are. We simply love them! They are amazing individuals! But like us, they make mistakes. It's *not* about being perfect—being human means not being perfect. Nor is it about living up to some imposed standard as much as it is about learning and growing. None of us is perfect. We have to be tolerant in understanding other points of view and must not judge anyone. We listen to know who each individual is, to become aware of each one's particular story. There will always be light and dark in life—like light and shadow in a drawing—*both* are necessary. Try to imagine a drawing without one or the other—impossible!" I'm not sure Dad follows my analogy. He is not really listening to me, but seems busy formulating his own thoughts. I restate my view more concisely: "I believe, for what they teach, challenges and mistakes are as important as achievements. We need the lessons of adversity in order to grow."

"I agree that adversity is a great teacher..." Dad adds. In fact, this is one of my father's lifetime themes. He picks out of my remarks what he can respond to safely; then re-directs the conversation in the only direction any conversation with the man can go: toward Christian Science. Dad continues, "...but, at the same time, we must hold to certain *standards*. Standards are essential! That's what's wrong today—not high enough standards! If everyone governed himself with the standards set out in the Bible and the Christian Science textbook, why, we'd end all our problems as a society! We must never give in to anything less than perfection! We are capable of that! We must behold the perfect man! That's the only man there is! We climb that mountain to perfect being every time we demonstrate the truth taught in Christian Science in our daily lives. The world needs our example! The world needs better standards! And Christian Science has them all laid out in the textbook that dear woman, Mary Baker Eddy, gave us!"

The expectation of integrity, morality, industry, order and cleanliness in our home grew directly from my father and mother's standards, which in turn were based on their understanding of God and Christian Science. I realize my father's standard of perfection is still an influence on Rich and me—and on most who knew him. I never thought about this as a child; it was just the way things were. Now as an adult I see that Dad's need for certitude was connected to his need for perfection. He inspected everyone and everything for moral fiber, unselfish compassion, and integrity—individuals, businesses, governments. He looked for God's likeness in every man, woman, and child. How a waitress takes an order, the way a family crosses the street, a taxi driver's humor, an employee's work ethic or lack thereof—to my father every action indicated quality or the need for quality. He weighed and measured perfection in everything from a gesture to an annual report. His inspection for perfection was daily, hourly, minute-by-minute.

"One's path is not necessarily straight up the mountain, Dad," I offer. "Life is more complex than that. Meandering left or right—often two steps backward for one forward—can be useful. No one's path is perfectly straight and no one travels another's path. So, no one can dictate what another's direction or standards should be. No one has all the answers, nor has anyone the right to judge another."

"I judge no one!" Visibly angry, Dad has taken my words personally rather than philosophically.

"I didn't say you did. I was just expressing what I believe." I answer calmly, hoping to cool the tension.

Timely enough, my brother asks if we can take a walk so he can see some of New Harmony, which we do. As always, the peace of New Harmony takes over. How glad I am we came here. Truthful dialogue is not always easy but it is cleansing, edifying, freeing.

A pleasant dinner follows with all three of us sharing memories. We recall the special treat, when we were little, of being gotten out of bed for ice cream on a hot Baltimore night. We recall blizzard-winters along Lake Michigan, our vacation on a working ranch in Wyoming, years at Christian Science summer camp where Rich was both camper and counselor, church experiences from the many different branch churches we'd belonged to wherever we moved. Rich and I remind Dad of how we loved the bedtime stories he invented for us, each one a different episode in the saga he made up of Jochko and Pinto a little Indian Christian Science boy living in the Southwest and his spotted pony—who had many exciting adventures and healings. Tonight Rich and I hear Dad tell of true and extraordinary healings he's helped people experience recently. The evening grows warm and tender as we remember and appreciate family experiences with both depth and laughter—a good conclusion before Dad leaves in the morning.

As I walk back to my room, I realize that no matter what else, above all, I see in my father a *loving soul*. This is a man who has relied on God continually for every step taken, who devotes his time to healing and teaching others because of his love for his God. He is there for his students in a most remarkable way, never failing to put the patient's need ahead of his own. I have known him to sacrifice what many would consider entitlements in order to help one suffering individual. How many nights he missed sleep! How many missed family dinners or vacations! For what? To answer that phone or go to that distressed home in the middle of the night because he is needed. Committed to his holy task, he would reach all mankind with the Truth (as he perceives it) if he could—in fact, like Don Quixote, he believes it to be possible and chases that dream. I have, and do sometimes still, share his dream: for Truth to reach and uplift humanity, though as to precisely what that truth is, our dreams may differ. I realize that though our journeys may have veered one from the other, neither of us has left the same highway.

I also realize that Dad's religion deals with the divinely perfect, dismissing the merely human. It claims absolute answers, not accepting mystery. Dad knows only one religious truth, ignoring thousands of years of wise teaching and religious diversity. Confident in his certitude, he doesn't see a reality outside of his own nor does he tolerate opposing viewpoints. For him, the material world holds little pleasure or importance. Spirit alone matters. Though he would deny it, he labels, classifies, and judges, placing some individuals on pedestals and dismissing others.

In contrast, life has taught me to accept ambiguity, to embrace change, and to learn from the journey itself rather than from set answers; to be open to mystery and centuries of wisdom and diverse thought; to find the glow of truth in the most surprising places; to cherish goodness, truth, and beauty without perfection as the goal; and never to place persons on pedestals. What we place on a pedestal is bound to fall off and shatter like glass.

There's a good bit of evidence that the world is not perfect. Where is the need for *mercy* or a Messiah in a perfect world? Perfection is a dead-end state, intolerant of diversity, not allowing a thing or person to change or be "in process." To me, the selectivity and exclusivity of perfectionism and idealism do not allow for the inclusive, connecting nature of compassion which creates relationship.

The honest eye notices the inter-relatedness of all things, identifies us as works in progress—growing, changing, being transformed by experience. If there is any certainty at all, it seems to me, it pertains to *love*, a word with many meanings and even more demands. I tried to express some of these views to my father, hoping we might share as truth-seekers.

Several times during the weekend when Dad handed me the Christian Science textbook and had me read aloud pages he considered pertinent to our conversation, it was clear he needed me to be reading from the textbook of the Church I had left. I realized he would never be able to accept my having resigned from his Church, his truth. I also realized that my desire for total honesty between us—something we always had before—might be difficult from now on. Some subjects would be painful for him and I could not bear to cause him hurt. We both realized this weekend that our relationship can never be what it once was.

Change is the only constant. We do not have the same bodies we had at two or ten, nor even all the cells that composed us last week. From the relatively calm changes of the seasons which bring us pleasurable variety, to the violent volcanic eruptions of the Pacific rim, change is part of earth's pattern. Even our thought processes and ideas change. The opposite of certitude, change terrifies some people. But an artist embraces change. It is what an artwork does—from concept to the first pencil scratches to completed piece. New ideas come and an artist goes with them, unsure of where they will lead. Change is at the core of creation. An artist knows this from experience and accepts constant flux—even chaos sometimes—in order to create. He is unafraid of change because it is part of his daily work. In fact, an artist must seek change, and its accompanying risk. I embrace this messy process.

Just as I think I am beginning to understand the design of who I am, some startling fuchsia bolts across my life composition. I discover that the pattern I knew so well has changed, and with it the meaning. What I previously understood is gone. In its place is something new. It's as if a small black mark grows into a huge ugly shape ruining the established order of my life design, or so it seems, until an array of unexpected hues splash across the black, subduing it with dazzling color. Then I am suddenly in awe of the surprising beauty and orderly placement of all the elements—even the black, once perceived to be so ugly, now precisely the right backdrop for the profusion of color. What happened? My perception was *transformed*.

In the same way I make art, I reach out for a newly designed relationship with my father, as if I were fine-tuning a drawing, learning from the line that appears what marks to make next. Dad and I are not erasing our relationship just re-defining it. This will be a strong work, for we both have the desire to craft it over time.

I am glad I never let go of the possibility of reuniting with my father. Most of us are given only one pair of parents. It seems to me, we must never give them up no matter how hurtful the relationship becomes. We honor our parents not merely because a commandment says so (though there is merit in that) but because it is the way of blessing for all concerned, because the parent-child relationship is the one most like our relationship to God. What would either my father or I have gained if we had forsaken each other? What good could come of separation? With a little risk-taking of meeting for one intense weekend, came an improved union. What a simple thing to do for the rebirth of a relationship! Through sharing our stories we discovered our indelible *inter-relatedness*. We found a closeness—not as years ago when we were close because we saw things the same way and took pride in our agreement; but rather, close because we *chose* closeness *in spite of* our differences.

Before leaving for Boston, forty-eight hours after his arrival, Dad said to me "I'm so glad we had this time together. It's been an important weekend for me. Let's keep in touch."

"Maybe you can come for Thanksgiving?" I asked, adding a whispered, "I love you, Dad."

Our words are as genuine as our differences. But as we part, we are held together as if wrapped in one warm quilt made from fragments of our past *and present* in an inter-related pattern of light and shadow, stitched with love's strong thread.

The inter-relatedness of all things surrounds me as I sit writing on the arbor-covered patio of the Poet's House. Clusters of cherries smile down from the tree overhead where a friendly chorus of birds serenade. A finch flies closer, cocks his head as if curiously interested in what I am doing; he seems to say our worlds are not so different. A butterfly lands on my table for a second and I appreciate the beauty of her pattern, dare to imagine she appreciates mine, too. The blooming profusion around me is no mere backdrop to human activity, but central to it: rhubarb, corn, cabbages, herbs, bachelor's buttons, white and lavender lilies *talk* to me with their colorful shapes. I love flowers less for their perfect beauty and more for their audacity to bounce, vulnerable and delicate, into an often mean and ugly world, transforming it.

The splendor before me suggests I might very well be basking in the French countryside. Monet might drop by and invite me to paint with him late this afternoon when the light will be just right. He would appreciate the complimentary hues of the moss-covered alizarin brick paths that lead to this ivy-covered cottage, its paint a fine match to the moss. He would enjoy my placement of a ripe peach on a turquoise glass plate, set atop a cadmium yellow mat on the glass-topped table that reflects the bobbing purple and green grapes above. He would marvel at the composition, the relationship of seemingly unrelated things. Always the abundant message in New Harmony is *inter-relatedness*.

My first night alone in the Poet's House I chose serendipitously from the shelves a copy of Thomas Merton's *Asian Journals* for evening reading in which Merton refers to Murti's ideas, writing that it is not escape into ideal-ism we really want, but, rather, the "*transformation of consciousness by a detached and compassionate acceptance of the empirical world in its* **inter-relatedness**. *To be part of this* **inter-relatedness**." Yes! Perhaps here lies the secret beneath the mystery of New Harmony: where spirit, beauty, nature, art, creatures and creation—past and present—dwell together, are loved and honored, har-mony exists.

Today, I am poignantly aware of my inter-relatedness with all things, sit-ting in the garden of the Poet's House, pondering this past weekend with my father, while slicing a peach on a fragile turquoise plate of hand-blown glass.

three

Ancestral Home

One stormy, thunderous night in the Llynfi Valley of Wales, a farmer, walking home by the ancient oak grove, came upon a downed limb. Dark as it was, he could not see the peculiarly small man who called out to him for help. "Please sir, if it not be too much trouble for ye, would ye move the limb from off our home?" The farmer had heard of these woodland creatures all of his life, but by St. David, he'd never laid eyes on one until now!—not that he could actually see him clearly. He guessed the little fellow to be no taller than his dog. With a heave the farmer removed the limb and accepted the sprite's kind thanks. "We Bwbachod pay our debts!," called the little man after the farmer as he went on his way.

The next morning the farmer awoke to the gleeful shouts of his wife. "What's that you're carrying on about, Wife?" the old Welshman asked as he reached for his boots.

The wife answered, "The Bwbachod came last night! When everyone was sleepin', they set our house in order—just as they'd promised you! The little folk swept the floors, washed the dishes, stacked the fire-wood, milked the cows, baked the bread and set the table! My chores are all done! And I never heard a word nor caught a sight of 'em!" "And see, here, my girl! What's this in my boot?" The farmer found his own reason for merriment. "Why, its one...two... three gold coins!"

In the New Harmony museum one can read about Welsh-born Robert Owen, the textile industrialist and social reformer who purchased New Harmony in the 1800s from the Harmonists. He and his son, Robert Dale Owen, and their followers sailed from Scotland to establish a community in America that valued human rights, scientific studies, agricultural experimentation, and the improvement of society. Owen's Welsh birth may explain in part why he and his son could take on the challenge of starting an innovative cultural community in the austere frontier that was Indiana in the early 1800s, and why his son, who took over the leadership of the community, supported women's rights and the abolition of slavery when few did. Those inventive Welsh, always ready for a worthy fight and creative to the core!

Most say Welsh history begins in 383 AD; others claim its prehistory cannot be separated from its story. But I think Gwyn A. Williams in his *When Was Wales?* captures what one need know about Wales and her people:

> *"This is the first point to grasp about the history of this people. Wales is impossible. A country called Wales exists only because the Welsh invented it. The Welsh exist only because they invented themselves. They had no choice. A tiny handful of people occupying two western peninsulas of Britain had, in the Bronze Age, lived for perhaps a thousand years (maybe even longer) as an integral element in some kind of human society which made Stonehenge a focus. For perhaps six or seven hundred years they had lived in a fragmented and warlike Celtic-speaking society as four or five tribes within a British complex of tribes. For a further four hundred years they lived under Rome; for half that time, their freemen as Roman citizens of Britannia, in at least three city-state Romano-British commonwealths. With the breaking of Britannia, they emerged in a welter of little British kingdoms, gradually shaking out as four major polities, one of them controlled by immigrants from Ireland, another probably by an intruder dynasty from elsewhere in Britain. By the eighth century they found that Britain had been removed. They were stuck in their peninsulas behind a great dyke and rampart raised by an alien people who called them foreigners—in that alien language 'weallas'—Welsh. By that time they themselves were*

beginning to call what was left of the Britons Cymry *or fellow-countrymen. Pretty soon there was nobody left to call* Cymry *except themselves. Their stronger kings started to hammer the whole bunch together and to make a country called* Cymru: *Wales.*
…the Welsh have made themselves…against the odds. There were not enough of them…to keep out much more numerous and much more powerful peoples. From birth, they lived with the threat of extinction.

They survived by making and re-making themselves and their Wales over and over again. So far, they have survived for over a millennium and a half: one of the minor miracles of history…one of the oldest peoples in this land even if they are now unrecognizable. Their patron saint is St. David…But their patron spirit they captured in their lavish wealth of imaginative stories (the quickest way over the mountains), some of which survive in the Mabinogion. *The presiding spirit of Welsh history has been the shape-shifter, Gwydion the Magician, who always changed his shape and always stayed the same."*
(Williams, *When Was Wales?*, pp. 2-6)

Impossible existence. Re-inventing themselves. Fighters. Survivors. Adapters. And story-tellers. My ancestors. I've other Celtic blood, too—mostly Scottish and Irish; some English, some French, a touch of German, and probably a smattering of everything else as well. But I *feel* especially Welsh. I feel that alien nature that's at the root of Welshness.

I like to think that my Welsh background accounts for my ability to re-invent myself from time to time. I know what it is to fight against the odds, to live an impossible existence. Like the Welsh I, too, am a survivor. At times a shape-shifter, like Gwydion. I like the thought of coming from a country of changes and contrasts: hills and valleys, woods and seaside, mines and minds. I like coming from a country of bards and poets, saints and Druids, where storytelling is not merely entertainment but a way of life.

I once read somewhere that the old Welsh word for "story", *cyfarwyddyd*, means instructive guidance, and its root means "to see". A Welsh story-teller is a *seer*—a teacher who *"guides the souls of his listeners through the world of mystery"*(source lost). If I could be anything, I would be such a storyteller.

For the ancient Welsh, *everything* had meaning. I am especially Welsh in this regard, having experienced wonder in ordinary things—from twigs to mountaintops. The spirituality of Celtic Christians reflected *hud*, a Welsh word signifying "a sense of wonder and awe at the divine residing in everything" (Edward C. Sellner, *Wisdom of the Celtic Saints*, Revised and Expanded, p. 30). The first Christians in Wales, rooted in the spirituality of the desert fathers and mothers—those earliest Christians who journeyed into the desert for silence, solitude, and prayer—believed that the supernatural pervaded every aspect of life and that spirits existed everywhere in oak grove, mountaintop, rock, river, spring, well, and stream.

Maintaining a deep respect for the Druid culture that preceded them, the early Christians in Wales and Ireland built their monasteries in places where Druid and Druidesses once taught. Like the Druids, they, too, honored nature and loved animals, frequently retreating to cave or mountaintop. As they had previously in the desert, they entered the "cave of the heart" to encounter God and deepest self. The influence of these desert hermits is evidenced today in 500 place names that reference *desert* throughout Wales and Ireland (De Waal, *The Celtic Way of Prayer*, p.95).

The first Christians to come to the British Isles cherished home, yet they left all and wandered to explore the unknown, journeying to spread the truth of Christ. Enduring many hardships, they experienced what for them was the worst suffering to bear: the absence of home and family, what they called "the *white martyrdom* of living years far from home and hearth for the sake of the gospels" (Sellner, p. 32). The Celts' word, *hiraeth*, captured their "extreme yearning for home" (Sellner, p. 32). I have come to see many Celtic concepts as part of me, but none more than *hiraeth*.

The Celts saw no clear distinction between past, present, and future. They believed "the present contains within itself both past events, which continue to live on, as well as the seeds of future events waiting to be born." (Sellner, earlier edition, p. 25). For them there is "only a very thin divide between past, present, and future"…there are "places where a person is somehow able, possibly only for a moment, to encounter a more ancient reality within present time; as places where perhaps only in a glance we are somehow transported into the future." (Sellner, earlier edition, p. 16).

I have experienced these thin places, where past, present, and future come together. Though I did not study Celtic Christianity until the late 1990s, long after my visit to Wales, I know now how very Celtic I am—not just because of my ancestry, but in my ways of functioning, in how I think and perceive, in what I honor and value. I cannot work or live outside of nature and beauty—I need gardens, flowers, and blue sky the way a starving person needs food. Big segments of alone quiet time are essential to my wellbeing. Cats, numerous Newfoundlands, one Samoyed and several Bernese Mountain dogs have helped to make my life complete. I have long disregarded *chronos* time in favor of God's time. Healing, though not associated with a spring, has always been part of my life, as it was for the Celts. Like the Celts, too, myth (which is also truth) is more real than factual history to me. Intuition rules over the rational. That voice within guides my every step, not convention, prudence or procedure. Like Native American Shamans, the Celts found the spiritual in the ordinary, relied on dreams and vision to show them their path. I hike the same trail. I could have been part of the wandering Celtic band who "valued poetic imagination and artistic creativity, kinship relations and the warmth of the hearth, the wonder of stories and the guidance of dreams. It was a spirituality profoundly affected by the beauty of the landscape, the powerful presence of the sea, and the swift passage at night of the full moon across open skies." (Sellner, p. 24)

Before I knew any of this, I visited Wales for the first time at age twenty while traveling on a college abroad trip. I was the first of our branch of the American Evanses to meet our Welsh relatives residing in the Evans' 12th century ancestral home, *Gelli Lenor*. I traveled by train from London to Bridgend where I was met by relatives I'd never seen before, and driven, in the car they rented for the occasion, to Maesteg in Glamorganshire.

According to what my family has told me, my great-great-great-great grandmother married William Evans (1730-1792) and bore him twin sons: Thomas Evan and Evan William. I am descended from the Evan William twin (1760-1836). His son, Morgan Evans married Lettice (his second wife) by whom he had William Richard Evans (1847-1925), father of Robert Benjamin, my paternal grandfather (1890-1967). Uncle Thomas, whose guest I was in Wales, himself a twin, was descended from Thomas Evan, the twin brother of Evan William.

On the train to Bridgend, my eyes were fastened to the window. Eager to meet my Welsh relatives, I was also captivated by the rugged landscape, mountainous jewel-green hills dotted with sheep, cattle, and mud-colored houses topped with smoking chimneys. It was as if the 20th century had disappeared and the past was tangible. The rhythm of the locomotive wheels suggested a Celtic tune. The textures and changing sky lured me to a distant time of *Mabinogi* tales and Authurian legends. Watching the scenery closely, I thought I glimpsed her come round a cairn: a filmy vision with flowing auburn hair whose intense dark eyes looked through me before she vanished in an oak grove as quickly as she'd appeared. Had the other passengers seen her, too? A glance told me they had not, for their heads were nodding in sleep or buried in books. Perhaps there were others from the past roaming out there. I searched, but only lush green valleys and blue-gray sky were in view now. Perhaps she had not been there at all. I switched focus to my reflection in the window, straightening my hair. This compelling and strangely familiar country, comfortable yet eerie, was not like any place I'd ever been! This *Cymru*, this Wales, called me out of myself—or, to myself—I wasn't sure which.

When I got off the train, I was greeted at the station by Uncle Thomas—typically short like most Welshmen (and all the men in my family), ruddy-faced, sporting a bowler hat, black umbrella, a hearty handshake and sparkling smile from under a carefully groomed white moustache. His daughter, Mair, (about my parents' age), and her husband, Peter, kindly led me to the car they had rented for this occasion and Peter drove us while Uncle Thomas described, in his Welsh brogue, every historic landmark en route home.

Home was *Gelli Lenor*, a thick-walled feudal farmhouse located in the Llynfi Valley, in the Parish of Llangynwyd in Tir Iarll, where my great-grandfather was born and his ancestors before him for over ten centuries. Since 1100 *Gelli Lenor* has been inhabited by Evanses. Uncle Thomas himself is quoted in a history of the area vouching in the 1970s that *Gelli Lenor* farm was at least 800 years old, saying he could trace his ancestors on his mother's side for 300 years and his paternal ancestors for 500 years (*History of the Llynfi Valley* by Brinley Richards, South Glamorgan, 1982, p.52). Surrounded by mountains, between the iron and coal mining town of Maesteg and the farming village of Llangynwyd, near River Llynfi, not far from Castell Coch (also known as Llangynwyd Castle), Gelli Lenor lies in an area proposed by some to be the general location of King Arthur's fall. It is an area of coal mines, stone quarries, thick woods, agricultural land producing corn, oats, and barley, a few scattered sheep farms, and bleak moorlands. *Gelli Lenor*, meaning "on a high hill", can be found on maps of the 1300s and may have been originally known as *Gelli Eleanor*. Ancient remnants, including seven healing springs, castle ruins, the Bodvoc Stone (which details generations of a royal Celtic dynasty and dates to about 550 AD) and the Sychbant Stone (possibly a portion of an 11th century Celtic cross once in front of Llangynwd Church, now being used as a flower container by it's innovative owner) were found on farms near *Gelli Lenor* (Richards, pp. 29-30). *Gelli Lenor*'s own bit of history which Uncle Thomas shared, concerns a stone on the property that marks the stump of a tree where legend has it, Edward II climbed in 1337 to escape capture by his enemies (who eventually murdered him). The tree itself might still be there if my great-great-grandfather had not inadvertently cut it down.

When we arrived, Mair served tea in the main sitting room where a wide hearth was flanked by sofas facing each other. A lovely Welsh dresser, filled with blue and white china and metal mugs, covered one entire wall. The dresser, they said, was made centuries earlier by one of our ancestors, an early Evans carpenter. I had known my grandfather was a carpenter and his father and brothers, but now I learned that I come, apparently, from a long line of carpenters. This may explain my penchant for making things— like paintings and art and a table out of an old antique window I found in my garage. Perhaps my heritage has influenced my building and remodeling homes over the years. Perhaps I may be a skilled Evans carpenter in my next life.

Mair draped a large sturdy round table with embroidered linen and carried out delights fit for a coronation: sponge cake filled with raspberries and whipped cream; chocolate nut cake; delicate crustless salmon sandwiches; thin buttered bread with home-made jam, shortbread cookies; and, of course, tea with milk. I enjoy beautifully prepared food and this lovely presentation was truly unexpected. I couldn't think of a thing I had done to deserve this production but I was thrilled.

Kathryn and Susan, Mair and Peter's daughters, arrived home from school soon after tea had begun, wearing uniforms of striped black ties, knee socks, black sweaters and skirts. Charles, the demanding three year-old, went to bed early, leaving the rest of us to conversation followed by a dinner so sumptuous that it seemed we'd never had tea only a few hours before. The feast resembled an American Thanksgiving: turkey, stuffing, potatoes, Brussel sprouts, sausage, gravy, and fresh fruit for dessert. Mair, a teacher by profession, was also quite the cook.

While Uncle Thomas was sharing Welsh history and family stories at the table, he reminded me of my grandfather, Robert Evans. They both had pride in their pasts, respected people for their character, loved telling stories, and held strong religious beliefs—though vastly different ones. Uncle Thomas was active in the Welsh Presbyterian Church. My grandfather was a Christian Science practitioner. Uncle Thomas told me about a famous clergyman in the family: his brother Gwyn Evans, Minister of the Welsh Presbyterian Church, Charing Cross Road, London, who had been moderator for the 1957 Bristol Congress. It struck me that spiritual concerns seem hereditary in the Evans clan.

The first to leave *Gelli Lenor*, my great-grandfather, William Richard Evans came alone to America in 1867, bringing little more than his exceptional carpentering skill. He met and married his wife and settled in Indianapolis, Indiana, raising two daughters, Margaret and Sara, and four sons: William, Morgan, Arthur, and Robert Benjamin—the last being the youngest, my grandfather. When Robert was only two, his mother died, so William's sister, Sally, came over from Wales to care for her brother's six children, leaving behind her own prospects for marriage. She never married but kept house for her brother and his children until she died. I remember my father and his brothers speaking often of their Great Aunt Sally's kind heart and praising her famous pies they consumed enthusiastically as small boys on infrequent visits to their grandfather's home. Those visits also revealed the strong patriarchal household William demanded. My father told me no one ever dared sit down before their grandfather, nor could one leave the table until he stood, nor sit in his armchair in the living room. Beyond that, my father had little to share about his grandfather's home at 2845 Capital Avenue, Indianapolis, which William had built after his staircase carpentry business had become successful. In those days carpentry was an art and the stairway was the outstanding interior art form in private homes and public buildings.

Evans' stairs were known throughout the Midwest for their beauty and sturdy construction. From a Masonic Lodge write-up (Evanses were Masons for three generations, stopping short of my father) I learned that at least two examples of Evans construction were in public buildings: the stair railings in the Indianapolis' Federal building and in the Typographical Building on North Meridian Street. Recently, I saw a photo online of the exterior of the Federal Building—a very impressive piece of architecture. I am eager to make another trip to Indiana—this time to Indianapolis—to see the Federal Building, to walk inside and climb the stairway my great-grandfather William built a century ago. William continued his carpentry business until he retired in 1920 when his plant was destroyed by fire. He died five years later at age seventy-eight.

By the time I visited his home as a child with my father in the 1950s, only Robert's brother, Arthur, and his two sisters, Sara (Dowelle by marriage) and Marge (Margaret), lived there. "The Aunts," as they were known within the family, looked remarkably like Carey Grants charming aunts in the 1944 film *Arsenic and Old Lace*. They served my brother and me grape ice cream sodas on their big Victorian front porch and one of them entertained us with playing, by ear, the baby grand piano in the parlor. My only other memories are of a dark olive-green mustiness, smells of old things, and Uncle Art ensconced in an over-stuffed armchair, his cane always close by. I don't recall the stairway. Now with my adult eyes, I want to see this home again. When I take my trip to Indianapolis, I want to find this house, go inside, hold the railing and walk up the stairway my great-grandfather built for his family. I want to *touch* my past.

William's son Robert (later I would hear him called by his sons "Pop," or "Ben" after his middle name, Benjamin) worked with his brothers in his father's carpentry shop into adulthood. Perhaps my grandfather learned generosity by seeing the opposite in his father, for William never paid salaries to his sons. Sons were simply part of the family work force, just as daughters, Margaret and Sara, took care of the family household. Their needs were met by their father William, as he saw fit. Even as a married adult, Robert had to ask his father for money anytime he needed anything. Forced dependence on his father, and lack of schooling beyond seventh grade, restricted Robert's freedom.

It is not surprising that in 1909 he struck out on his own, using his carpentry skills in designing and constructing the first wood and linen structures for the new aircraft industry. Later Robert and his wife, Norma Kelso Evans, moved with their young sons to Fairfield Air Depot (eventually Wright Patterson Air Force Base) in Fairborn, Ohio where his skill was very much needed.

I never saw my grandfather make anything out of wood. By the time I came along he had been in the public practice of Christian Science for some time and had given up all carpentry work. On our rare visits—usually a holiday or my parents' Christian Science Association day—he was always soft-spoken and kind to us, his grandchildren. He loved being with kids and entertained us by playing music on spoons in his mouth and performing magical tricks, such as making his finger disappear. A true Welshman, he loved to sing and dance and was especially fond of show tunes. When he came to visit us, our neighborhood friends knocked on our door to ask "Can your grandpa come out and play?" He bought me books of paper dolls (usually movie stars) every time I saw him, and slipped my brother and me dollar bills when Grandma wasn't looking.

Norma was the more stalwart of the two. She controlled the purse strings and ran the household. By the time I was in school she was the major bread-winner, earning her living as a Christian Science practitioner. She was devoted to her work. Whenever I think of her, I picture her on the phone taking another patient's call for help. I do not recall eating one meal in her home, though I must have. She was not domestic—neither cook nor homemaker—nor was she particularly maternal, according to my father, nor from what I observed. In the days I knew her, she was committed to one thing: Christian Science. A popular healer in Dayton, she took phone calls for help day and night. I recall lying awake in bed on any visit listening to the ringing of the phone and her firm comforting words to the caller. My only other memory of her, was hearing her stern voice chastising Robert for not measuring up to some task. He would mumble to himself, waddling his nearly 300 pounds back and forth, rubbing his hands, as he went off alone to remedy his failure or to listen to a favorite piece of music. The caring one of the pair always seemed to me to be my grandfather.

Uncle Thomas seemed to share his cousin's kind and generous nature. In my brief stay with him I received a silver charm bracelet with Welsh symbols, a nicely illustrated book about Wales, a British pound note and his attention.

Uncle Thomas was different from my grandfather, too. Ideas and social causes mattered more to him than physical comforts and food. My rotund grandfather, however, could hardly wait to sit down to a meal and would have adored teatime at Gelli Lenor. Also unlike my grandfather, Uncle Thomas read widely and often. He was exceptionally alert to news and current events, culling opinions about everything. He spoke about agriculture in Wales and how it had changed over the years. He was against the mechanization of farming and industrial growth, which he saw destroying farms and the quality of life. He did not think much of twentieth century progress and feared the loss of the human spirit. What would he think of twenty-first century America if he were alive today? Our commercial, materialistic, media-saturated, crowded, hi-tech and violent society would have been a great disappointment, no doubt. I would like to talk to him about that—and more. I would love to ask him questions about what I have learned about the Celts and Welsh since my visit. We never seem to grab and hold the present moment fully enough, and by the time we've grown to know its value, its gone. Certainly in 1964 I was too naive to fully appreciate the opportunity I had in meeting him; he died about 10 years later.

I wish I'd not been so shy. I wanted to be more talkative, expressive, but at twenty that was not possible for me. I had not yet learned to be myself; whatever little bit I knew of me, I kept inside. But I did draw portraits of Mair's girls, which pleased everyone.

Susan's room was mine for the night. The freshly ironed embroidered cases on the plump pillows, the extra comforter at the foot of the bed, the neatness of the room, the care of details, made me feel special. These people I had never met before welcomed me like a princess. I absorbed all I could, as they were a link to my past.

I lay in the thick-walled bedroom under comforting feathers wondering who had slept here centuries ago. What was it to be Welsh? To live in this village, not just visit it? To daily walk the rocky paths through pasture and hillside? To come home to this farmhouse, night after night, and crawl into bed? For ten centuries Evanses had walked here, resting after a long day's work, gathering around a dinner table—just as I had today. Perhaps they had stared out the same window into the dark night, listening to the same woodland sounds I was hearing—could it be the *Bwbachod* dancing in the moonlight? Certainly my ancestors had touched the same door, rested a hand on the same stone wall, climbed up the same winding stair, I had tonight. I let my hand linger on the cool plaster surface as if I could touch my past, as if by touching my past I might know my present and future and discover who I am. I lay awake for hours contemplating the intertwining of past, present, and future.

I know now that the Welsh bard of long ago is alive in the poet-writer-artist-me today. The Celtic fire has been burning in my soul, even beneath the shyness. My hunger to create, to build home in harmony with nature, to honor earth, is as ancient as the Celts themselves. I pick vegetables and flowers for my table from soil I've cultivated with my own hands, stand in my backyard waterfall to watch a blue heron fly overhead, my animals beside me, and softly hum a tune like any ancient Celt. And like any ancient Celt, I trust my intuition to tell me truth, to heal, to invent (or re-invent) myself, to change yet always stay the same, to follow my *hiraeth* sense in finding my home.

On that first visit to Wales, I did not know how deeply my roots molded me. I would discover that over time. All I could do at twenty was question who I was, who I would become, and wonder from under a warm quilt how to thank these relatives who had given me much more than a comfortable bed and delicious meals. They had shown me my Welsh home and given me the priceless gift of *story*—the story of my people and my beginning. They had given me a piece of me that I had not known. That night I wrote in my journal before turning off the light: "My source is in these hills and in this solid dwelling rooted to this rugged land. My coming here is providential." Then I fell asleep, snug and secure, more aware of how necessary finding my roots was to finding my self.

four

In My Father's House

I saw Arthur in a prism, briefly, at the waterfall. He was alone at his Round Table. Merlin, gaudy in purple and silver garb, had just left him in the mist, having warned the king once more about those who would block His Majesty's efforts to find the Grail. Now in solitude, Arthur dropped to his knees and prayed, "I will find the lost treasure and bring it to light for all the world. It alone holds the power to sustain, renew! By it, the world will be healed! No risk is too great in seeking this treasure! No battle too great. No foe too fearsome to prevent my quest! For it is not by my power alone that I seek the Grail but by the very power of the Holy Grail itself!" Then Arthur arose, took his sword and mounted his steed to lead his men into battle, their cheers following him up the mountain path.

My first morning at The Poet's House, I take my easel and watercolors outdoors and set up in front of one of the Harmonists' early log cabins. Small, efficient dwellings, they confined a family in close space. As I paint broad washes across my paper house, I wonder what it must have been like to live here in the early 1800s. Did winter wind whirl through those gapping cracks? I think I see in the space between two carefully hewn logs on the lowest tier a moving boot. Black leather. Coated lightly with brown dirt. A child laughs and another pair of feet, smaller, in dark stockings, prance past the crevice into shadow. A soft voice calls in German from somewhere inside and boots and stockings hustle behind tight logs that hide my view. The sun is very hot today. I feel the perspiration on the back of my neck and wipe it with my bandana. A fly flits across my paper. The voices and traces of the past vanish as a tour guide leads a group between my view and me. I wait.

My father's childhood home was no more pretentious than this Harmonist cabin. Their plain two-bedroom home in civilian barracks, heated by a pot-bellied stove, and as Dad described it, "with never a picture on the wall," was at Fairfield Ohio's Air Depot, (now Wright Patterson Air Force Base). Robert had left his father's carpentry business in Indianapolis in order to begin a career in Ohio crafting airplanes from wood and cloth for the new aviation industry. Three year-old Glenn, seven year-old Lewis, and Bill not yet a year, shared one bedroom, while their parents, Robert and Norma, shared the other.

Robert was eager for this new job that would pay him regularly and allow him to provide a modest home for his growing family. But Dad told me pay-day always meant an argument between his parents. Dad remembers shaking under his covers in the next room listening to his father demand fiercely, "Norma, what did you do with that money I gave you?!" It wasn't that Norma was a spendthrift; there simply was not enough money for a family of five. Norma's deep-set brown eyes registered calmly but firmly her defense. She came from a long line of Scotsmen, after all, and was neither frivolous nor ignorant of the value of a day's hard-earned wages. Bold and innately curious, her expectations exceeded her eighth grade education. Norma did not intend to remain poor—and she wasn't years later, after becoming a Christian Science practitioner, earning her own income.

Typical of many in the Depression Era, Dad and his brothers shared a bed. Children of the Depression lived very different lives from today's kids with their celebrity athletic shoes, computer games, iPods, and organized sports. Children of the '20s and '30s owned few clothes, and what they did have usually was passed down from older brothers or neighbors. To own anything of one's own was rare. Nor was focus on children's desires but on how to survive. Fun was a bunch of guys gathering in a field to play ball— often without even a ball, using some makeshift substitute. My father told us he couldn't remember ever having a store-bought toy of his own. A pair of socks, a cap or an orange might be his whole Christmas and family vacations were practically nonexistent.

Dad remembered few family gatherings in his childhood. In a visit with Dad in 1999, he told me that his father never accepted his mother's people, "a cultural difference existed between the two, creating a jealousy." Had I not had a list of more pressing questions to ask my father at the time, I might have pursued the nature of this cultural difference. In retrospect, this bit of information intrigues me because throughout my own childhood, Dad rarely took us to see Mom's relatives, just as his own father didn't connect to his wife's family. Though in later years, Dad developed relationships with several of Mom's relatives.

Dad recalled one trip when he was a boy. His parents took him, his younger brother, Bill, and Aunt Meda to New England to see the homes of Mary Baker Eddy, the founder of Christian Science. Dad recalled a chicken salad picnic beside Mrs. Eddy's pond at Pleasant View, her estate in Concord, Massachusetts, that no longer exists. Her article "Pond and Purpose" refers to this pond and was always an important teaching for Dad on practical Christian Science, on how to find one's purpose by being "spiritually baptized in the infinite ocean of love," which he included in a 1988 speech (Glenn Evans Speach, October 8,1988, Concord, N.H.).

One time when Dad was about twelve he took his savings from caddying on the base golf course to buy himself a second-hand bike. Later he traded it for a goat (he never said why). His mother was angry about the goat in the yard and so his father took it, sold it for three chickens which the family ate for several Sunday dinners. Depression days were tough on kids and pets.

But through a young boy's eyes, the 20s and early 30s were also adventurous years, especially if you had the good fortune to live on an airbase during the romantic days of early flight. Dad loved wandering the military salvage yard. Shy, independent and inventive, he created aviator's silk scarves out of old parachutes, found discarded parts from which he built "planes" and dressed up in pieces of old uniforms, imagining himself flying. He often lived in his thoughts and daydreams, much like my imaginative childhood of paper dolls and drawings—another link we shared.

Fascinated by flight, Dad hung out with the military men on the base, becoming their mascot. They often took him and Snubs, the stray mutt Dad adopted (who lasted a bit longer than the goat), on their maneuvers and outings. Snubs, named after a cartoon strip character, went everywhere with Dad. Dad loved Snubs more than anything. When Snubs bit the mailman, the field manager said that the dog would have to go. Snubs had never done anything like this before and Dad was very upset. The thought of losing his beloved dog was overwhelming. It was the one thing that was his. The mess sergeant, who was being transferred, agreed to take the dog with him. Dad cried for days after giving up Snubs.

Dad told me his prized possession was a flyer's leather cap, complete with flaps, that a pilot had given him. He wore it every day to school. Walking to school he loved to imagine himself flying in a plane. Sometimes even the school bell couldn't bring him back to reality, for he would tell his teacher, "You know, Miss Deck, I was flying in a plane this morning high over Fairborn and when I looked down I saw the school yard and you were as tiny as an *ant!*" Fortunately this was the sweet teacher on whom Dad had a crush, and *not* one he had earlier in his elementary years who lined up her students and spanked them *all*, first thing, routinely, every morning—before they even had a chance to do anything right or wrong! No wonder Glenn flew away in his imagination.

Once when Lindbergh landed at Wright Patterson, Dad got to sit in the *Spirit of St. Louis*. At the time, Dad was caddying for the officer of the day, Captain (or Colonel?) Bartron, whose duty it was to greet any arriving officers or planes. Bartron saw Lindbergh's plane circle and taxi. Quickly he got in his car, taking Glenn with him, and hurried to the airfield which was next to the base golf course.

Lindbergh had just left his reception in New York and was on his way to the reception to be held for him in St. Louis. He landed at the Fairfield base to re-fuel and see General Fellois. When Lindy got out of the plane, Bartron, a couple of mechanics, and my father greeted him. Dad had met many flying heroes, but none "so high a hero for me as Lindy!" While receiving Captain Bartron's greeting, Lindbergh did not ignore the little wide-eyed, open-mouthed caddy. "Would you like to sit in the Spirit?" Lindy asked Dad. Sitting in the Spirit of St. Louis was one of the highlights of Dad's childhood. Figuratively, he sat in Spirit throughout his life.

Spirit was everything to Norma and she raised her three sons to follow her strong faith. Her conversion began at a street car stop. Thinking about money and family problems, Norma must have looked disturbed, for a stranger handed her a Christian Science Journal. Norma read it and liked its positive statements. Not long afterward, Norma's oldest son, Robert Lewis, called "Lewie" by his brothers and later known to me as "Unkie," was invited by a neighbor to visit the Christian Science Sunday School. Norma was frightened to let Lewis go because he had been sickly from birth, requiring diet restrictions and daily medicine, and his behavior was very difficult. Norma was afraid he would not be able to sit still or be obedient and was certain he would get into trouble. The neighbor assured her he'd be fine. When Lewis returned calm and happy Norma asked what they did in that Sunday School and let him attend regularly and she began to attend church and read the literature—against her husband's protests. Like her sister, Meda, she earnestly studied this new religion, having purchased the Christian Science textbook, *Science and Health*, with pennies saved from grocery money and hiding it under their bed because her temperamental husband disapproved of the religion (though his opinion would change over time).

A year or so after finding Christian Science, Norma became staunchly grounded in Christian Science through my Dad's birth. By the time her third child, William (Bill), was born, Norma had been practicing Christian Science for several years. At age two Bill experienced a series of convulsions that left him unconscious. Norma did not hesitate to rely on Christian Science. While she rocked her son, declaring spiritual truths, her frightened husband left the house to drink, not wanting to witness the death of his son, which he felt was imminent. Norma asked Lewis, to read from the textbook and Glenn, who was too young to read, to pray the Lord's Prayer aloud. Norma continued to rock Bill in her arms while singing hymns. About 3 AM, when Robert came home, all was well. He could not believe his eyes. A complete healing had taken place. The baby was breathing normally, peacefully asleep. Moved by what he had witnessed, Robert walked directly into the bathroom, flung open the cabinet, and threw out all medicines. From that time on, he, too, studied Christian Science and attended church with his family. Eventually he gave up smoking and drinking and was healed of his fiery temper. By the time I came along it was difficult to imagine my grandfather as ever having been anything other than gentle and kind. Both he and my grandmother were *Journal*-listed Christian Science practitioners for more than thirty years, and healing work was their primary activity.

Dad often told the story of one Sunday morning's drive to church when he was a boy. He and his brothers were in the back of the family's Model T Ford, their parents in the front. Lewis, who probably thought anything would be more fun than the very long drive to church and back, continuously muttered from the backseat, "I don't want to go to Sunday School!" Robert pulled the Model T to the side of the road, turned off the engine, leaned over the seat, looked straight into Lewis' eyes, and pointing a firm finger in his face said in no uncertain terms, "YOU *WILL* GO TO SUNDAY SCHOOL! AND YOU WON'T COMPLAIN ABOUT IT!" That was the end of that. Never again did any of the three ever doubt that Sunday School was their right place on a Sunday morning! I saw upon occasions a similar firmness in my own father.

Dad's resolve began early. His first healing by himself was of a seriously sprained ankle from playing football. Dad loved football and was captain of his team all four years of high school. After one game his injury necessitated keeping off his foot. The ankle looked so bad that the coach had wanted to rush him to the hospital but Dad had some of his teammates take him home instead. They carried him to a chair where his badly swollen foot was elevated on a footstool. It was a Wednesday night and his parents were gone to church, a several hour trip from their home. Alone and in pain, Glenn could not move and picked up the *Christian Science Journal* lying on the table beside him. All evening he read inspiring articles and testimonies of healing. By the time his parents arrived home, he was able to walk to the door, free of any pain. The next day he walked his usual three miles to school and played in every minute of Friday night's big game—and, as my father often reminded me, "those were the days when you played *both* offense and defense." This was an important experience, Dad told me, because "I proved I could heal on my own".

His parents were consistent in instilling standards in their three sons and never let the boys get away with a thing. Dad remembered spankings. But he also recalled life lessons that stayed with him throughout adulthood.

One such lesson centered on a friend's BB gun and warehouse windows. I probably heard this story more than a hundred times in my life. On one visit with Dad, about a year before his death, I heard it four times in one weekend. He used it with patients and students, in speeches and addresses. Obviously it was a profound learning experience for him and he never forgot it.

His friend, Eddie, got a BB gun for Christmas—an especially handsome rifle. The warehouse was full of small-paned windows, dozens of them. It was just too tempting to the 10-year old boys. "It just seemed like fun to see if we could shoot out each of the windows without missing any—we never thought about the consequences," Dad recounted. So the two friends took turns aiming carefully and shooting until not a window was left. That night at the dinner table, Robert was telling his wife about the conversation he had had with the warehouse superintendent, how someone had broken every window in his warehouse and that he had no idea how it had been done or who had done it. Robert questioned how anyone could do such a senseless thing, expressing much concern for his acquaintance's predicament. After all, this was the Depression and one did not simply run out and buy new glass windowpanes; glass was not cheap. The warehouse contents were now exposed and the economic loss could potentially ruin the owner. Glenn said nothing but left the dinner table, his dinner unfinished, and went to his room where he cried long and hard. Then he mustered his courage and went to the living room where his father sat reading the paper.

"Pop, I'm the one who broke all the windows in the warehouse," Dad said directly.

Shocked, his father looked up from the paper. "You don't even have a gun, Glenn."

"But Eddie does," Glenn replied, "We each shot out half the windows, taking turns. We didn't know it was wrong. I'm really sorry."

Robert replied, "Somebody's got to tell the superintendent."

"Will *you?*" Glenn asked sheepishly.

"No, *you* will," his father answered firmly. "But I'll pay for the windows because you don't have that kind of money. And you'll earn and pay me back every penny of it!"

"So," Dad said, "I was sent off to the superintendent's house immediately. The superintendent was not as mad as he might have been because he was so pleased that I had come forward and told him I'd done it. When I got back home Pop put his arms around me and told me how glad he was that I had told the truth. This lesson in telling the truth was one of the most important of my life. Pop would have whipped me or at least shown a terrible temper if this had occurred prior to his transformation in Christian Science. I will never forget that he wasn't angry with me, just eager to have me see what I had done was wrong and what needed to be corrected. I worked many jobs to pay back every penny that my dad paid for the windows."

Moral lessons abounded in my father's youth, and the playing field was no exception. Sports were always important to Dad, especially football. He played center his first two years and quarterback his senior year. He got his varsity letter in 1932, his junior year.

His football coach made a big impression on Dad. A highly moral man, the coach required of his players strong moral behavior on and off the field. If a player swore once, he was out of the game for its duration. If he were caught smoking or drinking, he was kicked off the team. The game was coached from a perspective of teamwork. Getting along with others was part of the game. Winning was not everything with this coach, though his team was tough and did extremely well. Lessons learned on the playing field stayed with my father, so much so that when he went back in the 1980's as one of only six honorary recipients to receive a plaque in his high school's hall of fame, he chose to speak about his coach and the moral character he instilled in his players.

During high school, Dad was president of his class his sophomore, junior, and senior years, and also student body president. He liked people and they liked him. This trait was true throughout his life. What a change from the little boy who once stood in a garden so he would grow and who told his second grade teacher that he was an orphan!

Aside from school, most of Dad's youth was spent working. In fact, he spent virtually all of his life working. Work was foundational to the man, an essential to be revered. He told me once he could never remember not working. In fact, he said, "I didn't know you couldn't get a job during the Depression because I always had one." He usually had *more* than one. When he was ten he began caddying on the base golf curse, washing cars for the big wigs, and setting pins in a bowling alley. By age twelve, and for many years, he worked at Marie Groth's grocery store.

Dad stocked, packaged, and weighed groceries and also drove the delivery truck every day after school (before age sixteen) until time for his football practice. After football he went back to work in the store until 10:00 PM. Marie Groth expected precision of her employees. Dad described Marie Groth as "a German immigrant, honest, exacting, disciplined". He continued, "Her integrity was a model for me over the years. She kept an immaculate store and I was expected to keep it that way. If I did not do something precisely right, I had to do it over until I got it right. She expected every item to be weighed with utmost accuracy. Once when a customer was mistakenly over-charged, she sent me to deliver the change to the home with apologies. I remember grumbling at the time, as it was a long hot walk. But I never forgot the lesson."

In 1974 in Chicago, Dad spoke of Marie Groth in an address to the Association of Home Appliance Manufacturers: *"When you weighed meat you were to see that it was a couple ounces in favor of the customer. When sacking peaches you never put one with a bad spot in the bag…Marie…demanded everyone work almost as hard as she did, and I can't remember her having an idle moment. But she was always fair, always just, in her dealings. And I developed a great respect and appreciation for her. One day a customer was short-changed twenty-three cents, and Marie didn't realize it until the lady had returned home. She asked me to walk the mile and a half to the home of the customer and return the twenty-three cents. At the time I thought she surely could have waited a few days until the purchaser returned. But Marie didn't want her customer believing even for a few days that she might have been cheated."* Glenn's next line in his speech suggests Marie's influence: *"I'm grateful I can say that for more than 30 years in 3 major industries I was never asked nor pressured to do anything unethical or dishonest."* And a few paragraphs down: *"My conclusion is that high ethical standards can be maintained from a corner grocery store to a giant enterprise if the top management set a good example."* (Glenn Evans Speech, 1974 to Home Appliance Manufactueres, *The Image of Business—Whom Can You Trust?*)

While working several jobs throughout his youth, Glenn's conscientious nature kept his grades from suffering, though Glenn was, by his own admission, "no scholar." School work was always his responsibility. "My parents never knew enough to help us with homework," Dad told me. "Neither of them had a high school education. They never really cared about grades, so long as we weren't failing or in trouble."

There was a time in Dad's eighth grade when his marks hit bottom. It was another significant turning point in his life and a story he frequently told. Every morning his mother would rise and work with him—not on English or math nor other school subjects—but reading and discussing the weekly Bible Lesson in the Christian Science Quarterly. Norma read this lesson aloud with her son daily as they discussed it and she explained its relevance to her son's academic difficulty. She taught him to apply the lessons of the Bible to his school problems. They studied the meaning of the Beatitudes and connected them to Glenn's needs. His grades improved rapidly and it became another experience of trusting God Glenn never forgot.

At our reunion in New Harmony I asked Dad who were the most influential people in his life. He named his parents, quite naturally, and Marie Groth, the grocer for whom he worked. Dad said, "The moral fiber of my parents has been key: my mother for her faith and my father for his honesty. And Marie Groth for teaching me how to work." I see all three characteristics in my Dad when I think of him: faith, honesty, industry.

Dad graduated in 1933 from Bath Township High school in Osborn, Ohio. He had always hoped to go to college and dreamed of being a writer, maybe a lawyer. But the $100 he earned for college—equivalent of about $2,000 today—he gave to his older brother, Lewie, so that he could go. Lewis had always been considered the smartest of the three and funds were scarce. If Dad were disappointed in giving his college money to his brother, he never said, but I suspect it must have been difficult for him by the number of times he told us the story.

Right out of high school, in 1933, Dad was asked to set up a restaurant—actually, more like a diner—on the Base. It was a one-man operation. Every day he picked up a large vat of hot soup he ordered from a large restaurant in town and took it to the diner. He opened the diner early in the morning for breakfast and lunch. He made hamburgers, coffee, sandwiches, eggs, and more. He waited on customers and worked the cash register. He washed the dishes, cleaned up and locked up. On an average day he served 150 to 300 people single-handedly. This is hard for me to picture, for I never once knew my dad to cook a meal or clean the kitchen.

About the time he graduated, Dad's parents moved to Dayton, living in an apartment at 304 Grand Avenue nearly across the street from the Christian Science Church. Glenn could not move with them because his job was on the field, so at eighteen he lived in a small empty room at the end of the barracks which the authorities allowed him to stay in—just a place to sleep and keep his things.

At 3 PM when he closed the diner, he worked in the Post Exchange, a kind of department store for the base, until it closed, earning $96 a month (equivalent to $1,700 today). At night he took business courses—accounting, typing, and shorthand at Dickinson Business School and mechanical drawing, trigonometry, chemistry, economics, and public speaking at Miami-Whittenberg Junior College from 1935 through 1937. Though he was disappointed not to go away and attend college full time, running the diner shaped the rest of his life merely because it kept him at Fairfield Air Depot, now known as Wright Patterson Air Force Base, where the American aircraft industry was being born.

Dad was selected for a two-year apprenticeship as an aircraft mechanic—something new. Never before had there been airplane apprenticeships. "There were only four apprentices and one of them was me," Dad told me in 1999. "In those days an aircraft mechanic apprentice was responsible for understanding all aspects of aircraft. Wright Patterson was the only place set up for building, modifying, and testing planes—and the only place where the government set specific qualifications for airplane mechanic apprentice ships." Dad worked in 41 sub-departments of the Engineering Department at Wright Patterson which included the complete overhaul of airplanes, engines, and also fabrication of aircraft parts. He started there in January 1935 at an annual salary of $1080 (about $18,000 today) listed as an "unskilled laborer" according to a document I found in one of his files (Glenn Evans Files document). Standards were high; training was demanding. The nature of Dad's work was detailed, requiring accuracy. He told me, "I had to build up an engine from scratch to completion. The master that was instructing me said, 'That engine is going to be put in an airplane and *you* are going to fly in the cockpit of it!' "

For several days each week the apprentices flew in the planes that they worked on. This produced a strong sense of quality in the mechanics.

One's work had to be fail-proof, perfect. One's life—and the lives of others—depended upon it. During our time in New Harmony Dad told me once more what it was like to sit in the back of an open cockpit plane: "Lt. Sessums, the pilot, took the plane into a long power dive. Suddenly I'm hanging out in the air, loosely attached to the plane, tightly clutching onto the ring of a parachute, just in case I might need it, which it looked like I might! Some of the cockier pilots liked to scare a twenty-year old kid. After landing, Sessums offered me a candy, just to see if I was too sick to take it. I took the candy with a smile."

In a letter I found in Dad's files dated September 4, 1936, a Fairfield Air Depot foreman on Patterson field wrote of Dad "I can truthfully recommend Mr. Evans as being of unquestionable character, mechanically inclined, alert, capable, and dependable in the performance of his duties" (Glenn Evans Files, 1936 letter).

From September, 1936, through September, 1937, Dad worked the 7 PM to 7 AM shift on an assembly line at Delco Products, a branch of General Motors. He was grateful for the job, it still being the Depression. Dad had looked everywhere for a job; lines were several blocks long. He got up and went back day after day until he landed the Delco assembly line position, hoping, once again, to earn money for college. He said his position there, working in assembly and testing departments, assembling shock absorbers on an assembly line and in the rework departments where units were repaired, reminded him of Charlie Chaplin's character in the film, *Modern Times,* in which boxes continue down the revolving belt at an inhumane pace. From his Delco days Dad tells of men's inhumanity to men, of hands black with grease holding sandwiches while still working on the line, of never being allowed time to wash, of long waits to be relieved for rare restroom breaks. At the end of the shift he said he needed to use one hand to pry his fingers open on the other, they were so frozen in the position the assembly line operation required.

In 1937, at age twenty-two, Dad took Christian Science Class Instruction with Lloyd B. Coate of Dayton, Ohio. Mr. Coate's teachers were Joseph Armstrong and Laura Sargent, both of whom worked very closely with the religion's founder, Mary Baker Eddy. Mr. Coate himself had twice visited with Mrs. Eddy in her home. My father was always proud of the teaching he received from Mr. Coate and respected him enormously. I remember Mr. Coate as a soft-spoken, elderly gentleman who would bend down to talk to me at my level when I was a little girl visiting Dayton with my parents for their annual Class Instruction Association meetings.

In 1937, having saved enough money, my father finally got his wish to go to college. He told me when I asked him why he chose Indiana University, that he selected Indiana because it was the most economical and it had a football team. Dad packed a mouth guard in his suitcase in case he had the opportunity to play, but that chance never came. Work was still his main activity. Between studying and working there was no time left for football or much else.

Dad worked summers at Lau Air conditioning in 1938 and 1939 for $30 a week (almost equivalent to $500 today) operating presses and other equipment. There he learned more about tooling and began to assemble a significant tool box that later became invaluable.

Prior to attending college, Dad had always thought either journalism or law would be his field of study. But his experience in industry led him to major in business. He told me he could not forget the way he had seen people treat each other during his assembly line job. Now his goal was to study business in order to manage people more fairly, kindly. He had been fascinated with quality during his airplane mechanic apprenticeship and even earlier in his days in Marie Groth's grocery. Glenn's interest in quality, plus his growing skills in accounting, tooling, managing, and the process of production, permeated his work experience and directed his college study.

He held two jobs while taking classes: one as a librarian, the other working for the comptroller's department. The latter put him in charge of handling business for the school store, doing paper work, selling tickets, collecting money for sports events and performances held on campus, and being responsible for anything connected with cash. The head of the department frequently told Dad's cousin, who also happened to work there, that Glenn's accounting was "always correct to the penny." Marie Groth would have been proud!

Even at college Glenn's spiritual life was paramount. At Indiana University he helped start the first college organization for Christian Scientists and served as president. The organization held services on campus and provided Christian Science lecturers for the college community.

A four-year college education was not to be in Dad's future. Again, his college education was blocked after two years (1937-39) at Indiana. He was enticed to take a job for the Glenn L. Martin Company in Baltimore, Maryland, an aircraft corporation "on the cutting edge of meeting World War II's demands for bomb-carrying planes," as Dad told me in New Harmony. Martin was an outstanding company in my father's eyes, both in its standards of operations and its contributions to the nation.

By 1911, Glenn L. Martin was one of the best-known flyers in the nation. On May 10, 1912 he attracted world-wide attention by flying a seaplane of his own manufacture from Newport Bay to Catalina Island—38 miles and back. He was the first to deliver newspapers by plane, flew in a movie with Mary Pickford, *The Girls of Yesterday*, started his factory in L.A. in 1912, and invented the first automatic-opening parachute (Glenn Evans Files, clipping from *Baltimore American* newspaper article on death of Glenn L. Martin, November 25, 1951).

One of Dad's favorite stories tells of his arriving in Baltimore with little more in his pocket than enough for a room at the "Y" his first night. Dad tells of this experience in one of his addresses: "The next day was Sunday, so I found my way to the First Church. I had only five dollars, but when the collection bag came by I put in one dollar. That left me with four—which had to last till I would receive my first pay two weeks later!"

"I skipped dinner and walked to a Christian Science Reading Room to pray in the quiet study area. I knew that God would show me the way to meet my needs. He always had.

"When it was time for the Reading Room to close, I stopped by the librarian's desk to ask if she might know someone who would rent a room to me. She gave me the telephone number of a church member who recently had mentioned that she was looking for a tenant. After a brief telephone conversation I took a streetcar to the edge of the city where I found a perfect room waiting for me at 2512 Taylor Avenue. I said I couldn't pay rent for two weeks, until I got paid. The landlady said that would be all right and surprised me by saying breakfast came with the room! [We all suspect she decided that at the moment, seeing this young man's plight.] She then told me about a couple across the street who served dinner to boarders. They added me to the group, even though I said I couldn't pay for two weeks. One of the boarders I met that night was an engineer who worked at the very company where I was to start on Monday. He offered me transportation to and from the plant. When I told him I couldn't pay him for two weeks he replied, 'That's all right.' " Dad told us frequently that this experience assured him Christian Science had the ability to meet every need.

Dad worked at Martin from the fall of 1939 through 1955. When he accepted the job offer, Dad had no idea what position he would have, he just knew he would work at Martin. The position turned out to be that of tooling inspector. With his unique experience as one of the first trained aircraft mechanics at one of the largest bases at the time, Wright Patterson, Dad had much to offer the Martin Company. I have the letter Dad received from Martin's employment and personnel manager stating his position to be that of inspector—at fifty five cents an hour in 1939 (equivalent to about $9 these days) but Dad had four raises within his first year. His job was to inspect the whole airplane—every detail. He was to tag anything inoperable. Rejection tags would mean a particular part or unit had to be re-fabricated and that the plane would not pass inspection. But Dad was not satisfied inspecting and tagging. He had to know *why* the part was malfunctioning. Instead of merely tagging the faulty part, he would take it back to engineering or to whatever department the problem stemmed from and help them solve it. This was not part of the job, but his personal standards required it. He always got his tool box and checked to learn exactly where the fault lay, reporting what he discovered to the manufacturing department.

Dad observed that there was a process to manufacturing: details made up a sub-assembly unit, sub-assembly units made up larger units and so on until you ended up with the complete plane. There was a distinct procedure for the manufacturing process; but, he realized, there was no procedure for inspection. So he created one. Because of his careful inspection system, Dad was soon made foreman and shortly after that, he was promoted to general foreman. Though only a 5 foot 8 inch 170-pound twenty-four year old at the time—trivia I found in his files when he invited me to explore his life records—Dad had 325 inspectors under him.

As World War II preparations escalated, Dad's workload increased. He had hoped to be a pilot when war was declared. He figured that with his aircraft background and airbase childhood and two years of ROTC at Indiana, he had a chance. He had even contacted a long time friend—a colonel at Wright Patterson. But Dad was told he would not be accepted for flight school because so few had his special training in aircraft mechanics and that was sorely needed. Disappointed that his dream of being a pilot would not materialize, Dad put his energy into airplane manufacturing and would later say to me, as proudly as if he had been there himself: "Martin hit the beach on D-Day!"

As it turned out, Dad's process of quality control through his system for inspection was essential during the high production years of World War II—especially during the planning and production of the B-26s, Martin's own plane, and B-29s built in Omaha, Nebraska by Martin. One of Dad's responsibilities at Martin was to establish quality standards for this and other productions, meeting periodically with various B-29 prime contractors. The War Department demanded large contracts for planes, forcing the new aircraft industry to peak production. In '42 the government ordered Martin to build Boeing's B-29 bomber, and with major design changes to the bomb bay area as well. The military gave no explanation for this extraordinary command; specifications were simply to be followed.

So shortly after I was born, October 3, 1943, we moved to Omaha, living first at 5231 Military Avenue, the next year at 304 N. 31ˢᵗ Street, apartment 201. In Omaha, Dad's job title was "Assistant factory manager." He had the complete supervision of four main departments: Plant Engineering, Tool and Product Engineering, Modification and Manufacturing, and was responsible for making all necessary reports to the factory manager. Martin had 35,000 people working on the new specifications and changes. It was a grueling and exciting time for Dad.

In notes I found in Dad's old files I learned that the most difficult problems to solve on the B-29 concerned the nacelles where the engines were encased and the bom-bay. Glenn cited poor workmanship on a new project of building 5 over-run airplanes because various major assemblies used were built by "various and sundry companies." This intriguing line followed: "There is much that could be said here, but it is better that it not be written." Dad felt that the drawings furnished to the Omaha operation were not clear "probably because of the problem of so many reproductions" and his report details the problems and his advice for solving them. He wrote: "It is very important that the thickness of fittings for engine mount bolts be held to drawing tolerances….coordination of this program is a tremendous problem and is undoubtedly a unique undertaking…Martin standards in the manufacture of nacelles became procedure of manufacture and engineering and could not be changed without approval from the executive board, thus sub-contractors will have to be most careful not to deviate from the original Boeing Standards without permission, even though the deviation is an apparent improvement." (Glenn Evans Files, Nacelle B-29 report)

Dad told me many times, last in 1999 when I wrote down his exact words: "We didn't know what we were working on. We were not told, but we knew it was important to the war. All we knew was we had to meet the government's demands as fast as possible. Changing another company's plane was not easy. At first we were falling all over ourselves. Problems kept accumulating. The government was breathing down our necks."

Dad worked on this "Silverplate" project morning, noon, and night, even meeting with Colonel Paul Tibbits, the pilot who would later fly this special modified Boeing/Martin B-29 "Superfortress" aircraft. It would not be until August 6,1945, that Dad would know he had been working on the *Enola Gay*—the plane that dropped the first atomic bomb on Hiroshima.

"Seven days a week, as many hours as I could stand, I worked," Dad explained to me. "I worked with Nebraska farmers hired to help, as well as trained personnel. At 29 years of age, with no college degree, I had almost 9,000 people under me, some with doctorates. I made it my business to pick out the best people to form a task force to solve problems. People brought the problems to us and the task force had twenty-four hours to find the solution to whatever problem was presented to them. I called it *the 24-hour change request*. It later became publicized because it was a system that pinned down the problem and got it resolved quickly."

Dad explained the way the system worked: "Those on the task force had to locate the source of the problem and come back and report what it was within 24 hours. I told them, 'You don't go home until you tell us you have the answer.' I met with my men seven days a week. An 18-hour day was not at all unusual for me then. I had a cot set up in my office and sometimes I spent the night there when problems were particularly tough. Analysis would reveal which kind of problem it was—engineering, manufacturing, tooling, or procurement. Then we would take it immediately to the department that could fix it. Airplanes were built on schedule. History knows what happened. What we did helped to end the war and the Martin Company got the highest award given for the work we did."

The *Sunday World Herald Magazine*, a Nebraska newspaper, stated that Glenn L. Martin's bomber-building operation "is a story of mighty achievement—the mightiest single effort in Nebraska's history….the only major aircraft plant to meet its production schedule every month for 33 consecutive months…the Omaha-made planes were produced at the lowest cost in the medium or very heavy bomber program. No other manufacturer was able to make his costs so low while building the same number of planes. In short, the Omaha company has the best record by AAF standards—among 53 major aircraft plants in the nation. Since the start of operation, Januray 1, 1942, the plant has manufactured 531 B-29 Superforts and 1,585 B-26 Martin Maurauders. At the same time it made spare parts equal to ten percent of its production of completed bombers. Its safety record surpassed that of any other major aircraft manufacturer. At its modification Center, the company changed more than three thousand aircraft, rebuilding or refitting them for specific combat needs. Many of these were practically rebuilt. In the case of some four-motored planes, the modifications were so extensive as to require more man hours than the original manufacturer used in building the plane. Because it happened only yesterday, everyone knows that it was the B-29 plane which finally hammered Japan to her knees, and made it unnecessary to invade the home island. They know, too, that the B-29 planes which dropped the atomic bombs on Japan were Omaha-built, and were equipped here with specially designed bomb cradles." (Glenn Evans Files, *The Sunday World Herald Magazine* newspaper clipping).

In 1944 (when I was 19 months old) an article appeared in the *Martin Star* about Dad: "Plant Engineering, Tool Engineering, Factory and Modification—the details of their management all pass through his competent hands. He sees to it that all possible items are taken care of before 'the boss,' Factory Manager, Jack Bailey, takes over." This article says Dad is "emphatic in his faith in the future of aircraft. Commercial aircraft, both in the freight and passenger-carrying brackets, will come into its own in a big way in the immediate postwar period, he believes." The article also mentions

Dad's fondness for baseball and reading, and his admiration for Abe Lincoln and Charles Steinmetz. (Glenn Evans Files, Martin Star, 1944)

Joe Hartson, head of Martin's Nebraska division, later President of Martin, and my father together terminated the Omaha plant at the end of the war. As a result of his war-time work, Dad was invited to be Vice-President of Cessna Aircraft in 1945. He chose instead to return to Martin in Baltimore as Director of Manufacturing, Engineering, Tooling, and Processing because of his enormous respect for the flight pioneer and inventor, Glenn L. Martin—"right behind the Wright Brothers," Dad would say.

My father liked the sense of quality, ethics, and perfection he felt Martin represented. He was proud to work for the company that produced the Maurader, the majorly important B-26 of WWII and the Matador, produced for military security—the initial weapon supplied by the Air Force ground to ground missile staff, the first pilotless bomber. Along with Martin's production of missiles and rockets for the Air Force and Navy, P4M-1 Mercators and P5M-1 Marlin anti-submarines, Martin manufactured commercial airliners, including the 404 Skyliner for TWA and Eastern and the 404 Silver Falcon. Martin was also the primary contractor for the "Vanguard," the 3-stage missile launched from Cape Canaveral and for the Titan missile development and Martin's Denver division was the first wholly integrated ballistic missile facility in the free world. Dad was proud of what Martin produced for the nation.

He was equally proud of Martin's growth. Employment increased three-fold in less than two years from 1949 to 1951. The annual report I found in Dad's file indicated an employment figure of 22,300 for 1951. Due to the company's program of reactivating production of commercial airliners after the war and because of accelerated military demands due to the Korean War, Martin's problem became one of "finding enough people for the work to be done." The company's net income in 1950 was $3,127,774; today that would be $30,000,000 (Glenn Evans Files document).

After the war, Dad had the task of bringing together all the elements of building an aircraft: fabrication, economics, tooling, planning, research and design, etc. Dad told me "some of these take four or five years from concept. It isn't just one airplane—you can lose control of these or you can become more focused on one than the others—building all these different airplanes had to have something to unite all the parts involved in manufacturing. The term "operations management" was coined at Martin. "Zero defects" was another. We put more women than men in the production line because you had to be absolutely accurate and women were good at being exact. We decided instead of telling people what errors they did, we were going to measure their work by what they did that was correct. The quality of their work improved terrifically. The Matador was influenced by this. The Air Force saw what we were doing and they investigated zero defects as did the automotive industry." Dad is quoted in a Martin Mercury magazine October 1951: "Today, during our rapid growth and expansion, we have many problems—problems that at first thought would seem to have no immediate solution. At such time it is good to look back over our shoulder and realize that yesterday's problems—now solved—seemed just as big"(Glenn Evans Files, *Martin Mercury Magazine*, vol. 9, no. 45, October 19, 1951). Martin was a good match for my problem-solving father.

Dad was instrumental in Martin's remodeling Britain's Canberra, a low-flying bomber. The U.S. did not have an airplane that could fly low enough for the required bombing. Dad was sent to Britain to look at this from a manufacturing standpoint. Later, after the project was completed, Dad spoke to the Engineering Society in Washington DC about the Canberra. Dad said, "From what I saw, we were not going to do it the way they did—they did not have enough protection for the pilots. We had to redesign the airplane to accommodate that need. But secondly, in the manufacturing of it, they did not have flexibility. If they needed skilled people, often they were not willing to re-locate, which slowed down the process." Dad told me years later, "I did not know the key representative of Great Britain was going to be present at this talk I gave. In my talk I'd said: 'The reason the British wear monocles is that they don't want to see more at one time than they understand.' The Great Britain rep took it well and afterwards told me 'there's more truth than poetry in what you said.' "

In 1952 Secretary of the Air Force in Washington DC invited Dad to go to Wiesbaden, Germany, London, England, The Hague, Netherlands, Brussels, Belgium, Rome, Italy, Paris, France, and the USAF Headquarters, Washington, DC as part of a two month special evaluation team for NATO. The technical team was to evaluate foreign aircraft being considered for off-shore procurement by the USAF, the outcome of the trip to be reported to the Chief of Staff. Dad accepted and was cleared for access to classified material up to and including "top Secret" information during the temporary duty. I remember the two months he was gone from home—how awkward it was for my mother who didn't know how to drive and had to learn, and how empty the house felt. When he came home he had stories to tell, but most of them were over my nine-year old head. I only remember the strange tale of a foreign general with whom the team was dining, who cracked one plate after another over his head to prove his toughness. I also recall hearing of the friends he made who, by associating with Glenn, appreciated not having to imbibe extraordinary quotas of alcohol expected on this hectic-paced trip with its wining and dining. In a letter dated January 9, 1953, Chief of Staff, USAF, Hoyt S. Vandenberg, writes his appreciation for Dad's participation and in another letter, written in 1952 by a T. H. Landon, Major General, USAF, Chief of Staff, writes of Dad's NATO work, to George Bunker, President of Martin: "Mr. Evans performed his part of the overall task with a skill that is worthy of recognition. He has rendered a great service to the Air Force by his loyalty, minute attention to the job to be done, and keen analysis of the airframe production portion of this program. He has gained the respect of manufacturers throughout Europe by his straight-forward and exceptional ability to grasp the essentials of the aircraft production program. In performing his assignment Mr. Evans worked many extra hours in order to meet established deadlines. Please accept my sincere thanks for the exceptional service rendered by Mr. Evans" (Glenn Evans Files, Letters).

I believe Dad's days at Martin were as formative as his days working in Marie Groth's grocery. His initial Martin job as inspector continued throughout Dad's other positions and permeated areas of his life beyond work. Glenn inspected for faults, "tagged" the error in order to fix the problem in every department of life, even as a parent. He expected the best in any endeavor, this included in his home and family. Whether he was washing the family car or working on a production crisis as a corporation president he expected perfection.

His unrelenting search for quality, his tenacity in never giving up until the problem was solved, made him an extraordinary Christian Science practitioner. Every patient's case received his endless devotion. It was normal for him to go without sleep several nights of every week in order to handle calls and cases from around the world. Whatever it took to get the job done, to heal the situation, Dad did. Just as an inferior part on a plane was unacceptable to him, sickness was unacceptable. The tagged part of a plane must be corrected; and so must a suffering patient. In either circumstance, the only acceptable outcome was perfection. Working, whether for healing or business, was part of Dad's being and he did not separate the two.

In New Harmony, Dad explained to me how he had conceived of the 24-hour change request that enabled meeting what seemed like impossible deadlines: "One morning as I was reflecting on the situation we were in, this statement by Mrs. Eddy in *Miscellaneous Writings* came to me: 'Error found out is two-thirds destroyed.' (Eddy, *Miscellaneous Writings*, 210:6); I realized that if we could find out what the error or mistake was, we could destroy it. If we could get at the root of the problem we could correct it. And if we worked hard and fast enough, we could solve the problem almost immediately. The exact process of the 24-hour change request unfolded—came into my thought—and I implemented it."

At one point at Martin, Dad had a boss, Tom Willey, who had a reputation for being distant and difficult. Men were afraid of him. One day at the close of work, Willey called Dad into his office and told Dad to say something to the employees the next day that wasn't true. Dad told Willey he couldn't do that. Willey was angry and told him he didn't have a choice. That night, Dad told Mom he might not have a job the next day, but he had to take a stand. Dad said he prayed all night to understand justice. The next morning Willey called Glenn over and instead of firing him, said, "I thought a lot about what you said yesterday afternoon and we're going to do what you suggested." After that Willey invited Dad and Mom to his home, something he had never been known to do with anyone before. When Dad left Martin, Willey said at the farewell dinner given for Dad, "Glenn is the most Christian man I've ever known." Dad told me that *standing for honesty* with Willey caused Willey to change, transformed him in his relations with the employees, and that it also taught Dad courage. Many years later, when both men's careers advanced and their ways parted, Willey and Dad kept in touch. Willey asked Dad to speak at Cape Canaveral and Dad invited Willey to speak to Whirlpool.

Dad applied what he knew about God to solve every business problem throughout his career in many industries—at Martin, or later as Vice President at Whirlpool, or president of Warwick Electronics. Certainly by the seventies, when he left the secular business world to become one of the three trustees of The Christian Science Publishing Society, Dad had confidently demonstrated God's power to heal any business difficulty.

When Dad first came to Martin, a card was given to every new management employee listing a ten-point program—standards for managing—which began with this quotation: "Therefore all things whatsoever ye would that men should do to you, do ye even so to them." Among the ten points were these: "To make a friendly contact with all my immediate subordinates at least once a day...To learn the aims of my employees and to help them toward those aims...To win the confidence of my employees so that they will feel free to come to me with their troubles and grievances...To use common sense, fair play, and justice in the handling of all grievances... To have a humane and sympathetic understanding of my employees and their problems...All this because I, too, was once where they are now" (Glenn Evans Files, document). Reading Martin's ten points, I understand why Dad expressed pride in being a businessman. Business was conducted nobly in his day, at least in his experience. True service and ethical behavior was expected, even at the top—how far removed from the Enrons, Worldcoms, and Halliburtons of today! Years later, my father quoted these ten points in an address he gave to a large group of Christian Scientists. More than once I found he quoted Martin's standards in his talks, whether addressing business executives or Christian Scientists. His themes stress self-government, humility, honesty, pure motives, and integrity over and over again. For Dad, whether practicing business or Christian Science, it was about living a compassionate and principled life and trusting God to heal all problems.

In 1955 Bud Gray, the head of Whirlpool—a company since 1938 producing the "most practical, efficient automatic washer that advanced engineering could devise" (Glenn Evans Files, document)—offered Dad a position with Whirlpool for the second time. The first time, Dad had declined the offer due to serving a three-year term as First Reader at a large Christian Science branch church in Baltimore. "Ask me again", Dad had told Bud, whom he instantly liked. Bud said that was the best reason for refusing a job offer he had ever had. Dad suggested his older brother, and so my uncle joined Whirlpool. Dad never expected Bud to come back and ask him again. But he did. Dad had finished his stint as First Reader at Church and accepted the position of General Manager of a new division in Marion, Ohio to be started from scratch.

Dad loved Martin but the appeal of the Whirlpool offer was enticing. Thrilled by the prospect to create a new facility "from the ground up," "to put principle into practice" as Dad put it, he could set the standards of operation, hire whom he pleased, design every detail of production and management, and develop a rapport with the community. In one of my interviews with Dad in the 1990s, I tape recorded his words about this move: "I was really motivated to go to Marion because it was exciting to start the thing from nothing—I could set the *standards*, create the foundation for the entire operation. I wanted to *understand* God as Principle more deeply and this job would enable that. I gained confidence in knowing what I'd do from what I'd already seen in my life. I didn't know a confounded thing about appliances! I didn't know a confounded thing about mass production! I relied on God and on people—they [people] knew what they had to contribute was very valuable to me and that I was willing, ready, eager to listen to them. I did not know myself what the answers would be, but I trusted Principle [God], to show me the way. Here was an opportunity to have standards in everything—in hiring, ideas, management, manufacturing! At the Harding Hotel in Marion, before we moved, I made a specific study of Principle. I did not know the degree to which they [Whirlpool] had problems. Whirlpool had grown up by the seat of its pants, did not have a sophisticated plan for the future, was not organized from the top down. But Bud Gray was a moral man and I liked him, respected him. I knew this was a right move."

The first two weeks of operation, over 300 units a day were produced with 30 different dryer models. Dad wrote to his "fellow employees": "One thing we must never lose sight of is the quality of our product…we cannot lower the high standard" (Glenn Evans Files, letter to employees, November, 1955).

Every employee mattered to Dad. He considered the employees "the most important asset of our corporation." As he once said to me, "Even the janitor wasn't just the janitor—I respected him as an *individual.*" Throughout his business career Dad knew many leaders, even United States Presidents, but he never saw one human being as more important than another. Each one's individual progress mattered to him beyond their contributions to the company.

For example, he used to say of Mavis Ives, a Welsh woman who was his secretary for about a dozen years: "She could run the place!" When Mavis was promoted to Senior Technical analyst, he was sad to lose her, but thrilled for her advancement. When Dad went to Warwick, years later, he received a letter from Mavis which reads in part: "Mr. Evans, it has been a great pleasure to be closely associated with you over the past ten years. Some of those years were rocky ones for me personally and I know I tried your patience on occasion; but you were always understanding and it meant a great deal to me to know you were my friend, as well as my boss, and that I could turn to you for advice and counsel. While I was trying to be a good secretary and help you as much as possible, you were helping me far more by setting an example for good. I know I'm a much better person as a result of knowing you" (Glenn Evans Files, 1966 letter to Mavis).

Only two years after going with Whirlpool and establishing its new division in Marion, Ohio, Dad was made General Manager of the plant at company headquarters in Benton Harbor/St. Joseph, Michigan. Leaving Marion in 1957 for this new position, Dad was mentioned on a Marion radio broadcast: "We don't often specify individuals as such in our talks, but we can't forgo the opportunity to wish Glenn Evans farewell and Godspeed in his increased responsibilities with the Whirlpool-Seeger Corporation at St.Joseph, Michigan. Under the leadership of Mr. Evans, and the enlightened public and personnel relations policies of his company, Whirlpool-Seeger not only became a vital part of the industrial life of the Marion community in a short several years—but achieved recognition for contribution to the public life which has far more reaching and lasting impact than mere payroll dollars" (Glenn Evans Files, document). Within two years the Marion Division assets were $10,000,000—four times the original investment (equivalent to $82,000,000 today), (Glenn Evans Files, document).

On his first day as the new general manager at the Benton Harbor/St. Joe division, Dad went out into the plant to meet and shake hands with every employee. He saw a black man working a press whose name badge read

"Evans," so Dad said to him as he shook his hand, without skipping a beat, "I wonder if we're related." The man couldn't stop laughing for several minutes.

Dad immediately noticed problems at the Benton Harbor division. For years prior to Dad's arrival, the union was militant, strikes were frequent, supervisors and foremen were weak. Dad said to me: "People were doing their own thing—some even playing cards or eating on the job. You loose all kinds of morale with that sort of thing. I planned to change the whole wage-payment rate. There would be no more piecework. There would be a *fair* rate. Men would wear a shirt and tie. Even Bud said to Dad "You're not going to make it. They won't listen to you." But the employees did listen and morale increased significantly.

Another two years passed and Dad was made vice president for all laundry products. By this time Whirlpool had facilities throughout the world with sales totaling 538 million dollars (equivalent to $4,304,000,000 today) and climbing (Glenn Evans Files, document). In 1962, Dad was put on Whirlpool's Board of Directors and in1965 he was made Group vice-president for development, engineering, manufacturing, and profitability of all appliances.

Frequently throughout his career Dad was asked to give talks to companies on whose boards he served or for associations of which he was a member and sometimes for associations or companies with whom he had no direct link, but who had heard of him and wanted him as a speaker. These speeches Dad wrote reveal a great deal about him as well as his ideas on business and God. In the late1990s, sometime following our New Harmony weekend, Dad invited me to come to Boston to look at his files and read any of his speeches I cared to, particularly ones he pointed out as important. Being as thorough as he is, I've now read nearly all of the nearly 300 speeches in Dad's files and own copies of about twenty. I am struck that no two are the same. Each speech was crafted for a particular audience, though a few favorite stories or illustrations were sometimes repeated. I discovered several permeating themes throughout all of his writing: the importance of integrity, honesty, humility, courage, community, standards, self-government and pure motives. Whether conducting business or living life, the endeavor to him was *one*.

Dad believed that a business could not function properly without integrity in the top leadership, nor could a corporation grow by ignoring its community and or employees. Many of his speeches focused on issues concerning community, such as one given to the Marion plant in 1962 when he was no longer there but was group vice president at headquarters, entitled, *Responsibility of the Company and the Community*. In another speech before a Kiwanis Club, reported in the local newspaper, Dad is quoted as saying: *"Businesses have a prime responsibility to take part in the civic affairs of the communities in which they are located...businesses must help make the community successful and help sell it as a location for future industrial development...groups must work together for growth"* (Glenn Evans Files, document).

I found several letters to Dad sent from individuals who had heard this speech. One businessman wrote: "I do not know of any talk which we have received, which had as much discussion, and all favorable, as that which you gave." Another wrote: "Your presentation truly reflects the finest refutation of all regressive thinking and short-sighted thinking I have ever witnessed" (Glenn Evans Files, Letters).

Dad wanted quality growth in all people and all things. One time he told me that he introduced an idea at a quality assurance conference to procurement/part suppliers. He was concerned that they were not developing themselves. He told them that he was no longer asking them just to be suppliers, based on price and quality, but also by what they were contributing—not just which is cheapest. "We want suppliers that are advancing their own quality of business...stop thinking of suppliers as suppliers but think of them as *associates* in our business." They were startled to hear this, Dad told me.

In 1963 Sargent Shriver asked Dad to take "the #1 Peace Corps job in Brazil" writing, "I would personally feel that our country's best interests would be extremely well served" (Glenn Evans Files, Shriver letter, May 31, 1963). Shriver requested Whirlpool's Bud Gray allow Glenn to leave that company, writing in another letter: "we have the greatest interest in seeing him here as soon as possible (Glenn Evans Files, Shriver letters, 1963). But neither Dad nor Whirlpool decided this was for the best and Dad remained with Whirlpool. I believe that church work, once more, kept him where he was.

In 1964 Dad gave a speech, *The Right Time – The Right Man*, at Cape Canaveral in Florida where he also experienced what for him was another lifetime highlight—the launching of the space shuttle. Since the Vanguard, the Viking and Titan rockets were all made by Martin and Whirlpool was involved in preservation of space food, Dad felt he had a hand in putting men on the moon. During his last two decades, when I sometimes asked my father if there were anything he would like to do that he hasn't already done, he would answer: "I would give anything to go to the moon on a space shuttle!" I wish he could have fulfilled that dream.

In 1965, the same year that Dad became the group Vice President of Whirlpool, responsible for the development, engineering, manufacturing and profitability of all appliances, he also became the director of the American Home Laundry Manufacturers Association. He addressed a gathering of ALHMA in 1965 at The Greenbrier: "A business cannot exist in a community that is neither fit to live in—nor to work in—or that cannot provide the people it needs to operate" (Glenn Evans Files, ALHMA speech, 1965: *The Image of the Industry*). In the same speech he speaks of image not being the important thing, but "reflection" of the ideals and standards behind the business: "We live in an age when images are casually tossed about by our advertising and public relations friends as though these 'images' were the result of a copywriter's wit or a photo retoucher's skill. We think of personal images, U.S. image, Russian image, corporate image...all frequently bandied about by writers, columnists, commentators, and even golfing partners, as though nothing were real and everything depended upon 'image' alone." Dad considered image-creating a superficial, selfish, and pointless goal. Instead he said, "we are here to ask ourselves some difficult questions...to look frankly and inwardly at ourselves and help determine a course for our industry through the economic and social maze that is the twentieth century" (Glenn Evans Files, Speech).

In1966, Dad made several lengthy business trips to Japan. He developed a personal relationship with heads of companies there (I recall doing a portrait of Bill Omura when he had dinner at our home). Dad suggested a meeting between the representatives of companies from the US and Japan in the electronic industries to discuss voluntary establishment of free, fair trade. These meetings were to include key members of the US Departments of State, Commerce, and Justice, and brief meeting with chairman of the House Ways and Means Committee to compare tariffs, tax incentives, credits, allocations, interest, and consider domestic export pricing practices, and forecast on US business. In telling me about this, Dad said, "Twenty years after WWII, here I am after having helped create the plane that dropped the atomic bomb on Japan and I am going to Japan to do business. This is a very key point: If Japan had been bombed by Russia or Germany and those countries had defeated them they would have confiscated and conquered Japan—but we helped build Japan and did business with them. If people think about this, they were bombing us at Pearl Harbor and then we bombed them, and then we built them back up economically—someone we defeated. Our nation could have squelched them but we didn't."

In the late sixties, Dad served as CEO for Warwick Electronics, a Chicago-based electronics company Whirlpool had acquired. It was a company on the verge of bankruptcy, but Whirlpool auditors did not discover this until after the purchase. Only three weeks after the acquisition, Whirlpool's CEO Bud Gray came to Glenn at 2 AM. The two walked along the street and Bud said, "This is going to ruin the whole company." Dad replied, "Bud, I don't believe God brought me here to witness a failure." In four and a half years the company was made solvent and the president of Motorola told Dad that this was the most remarkable turn-around in their industry he had witnessed.

Dad writes of his time as president of Warwick Electronics in a speech, *No Half-Way Position*, he gave years later to a group of Christian Scientists:

> *One time a company I was with acquired another company which had several major problems and was almost bankrupt. The chairman of the board of our parent company asked if I would be willing to head up the new company, while admitting that he knew it would be a very difficult assignment. It seemed to me an opportunity to help heal a sick company, plus keeping 12,000 employees at work, so I accepted the challenge. After a few months, conditions proved to be much worse than anyone had anticipated. There had been deception on the part of the previous owners; serious labor difficulties erupted in several of the plants; our headquarters in Chicago went through a trying period of bomb threats believed to be instigated by a terrorist group operating in several major cities. Arriving at work early one morning, I entered my office and stared at the pile of paperwork, major decisions to be made, meetings to be held. The picture was most discouraging and seemed overwhelming. I shut the door of my office, took my Science and Health out from the desk drawer, and spent the next hour praying for God to direct*

my thought. Upon opening the textbook, these words stood out: 'Are we really grateful for the good already received? Then we shall avail ourselves of the blessings we have, and thus be fitted to receive more.' (Science and Health, p. 3: 22-24). A surge of gratitude to God and Mary Baker Eddy welled up within me. I mentally acknowledged one healing after another which I had experienced in my life. Then, leaving my office, with the desk still piled high, I walked to the entrance lobby of our main building to speak to our receptionist. I told her of my sincere gratitude for the excellent job she was doing; that visitors often remarked to me how helpful she was, always extending a warm welcome. Next, I walked across the plant to the engineering department to visit a young design engineer to thank him for his significant contribution to the development of our products. As I walked back through the plant and returned to my office, along the way, I noted the smiling faces and cordial greetings toward me from employees and supervisors. As a warm glow came over me. I thought, the responsibility for the welfare of these people and this company is not mine! It is on the shoulders of the Christ. The Christ is in every employee and manager, and they are sharing in the responsibility by their intelligent and Christlike activity. As I entered my office I felt free, though the work was still there on my desk. In a few minutes the phone rang, and one of the officers reported that a difficult problem had been solved and a two-hour meeting could be cancelled. I thought: the Christ is at work. One item after another was taken care of that day; all the way home I was rejoicing and glorifying God, not just for a clean deck, but for a clearer understanding of humility and that God governs…The company steadily improved and became well and whole" (Glenn Evans Files, *No Half Way* Speech).

While CEO of Warwick Electronics—whose many products included guitars and amplifiers—Dad met rock star Jimmy Hendrix, a spokesperson for Warwick. My guitar-playing husband, Bill, says that whenever he tries to imagine some impossibility he thinks of Glenn Evans conversing with Jimmy Hendrix—and then he knows all things are possible!

Warwick had facilities in Ft. Smith and Forrest City, Arkansas building TVs and a Whirlpool refrigeration plant with a combined sales of over a billion dollars, employing over 30,000 people. Dad flew to Arkansas to speak to the people there prior to a dinner. He noticed that the blacks and whites did not mingle. He did not want that for Warwick and addressed the problem subtly in his speech.

Glenn was asked to be the guest speaker for the 13th Annual Arkansas State dinner honoring the congregational Delegation of Arkansas on Monday April 28, 1969 at 7:30 at the Sheraton Park Hotel in Washington DC. USAF Chief of Staff, Senators and representatives, including Arkansas' McClellan, Mills, and Fullbright, were among the Washington congressmen and government officials in attendance. Dad was the first non-Arkansan ever to be asked to address this annual gathering. I had written Dad a letter in 1962 with a quotation I had encountered about "the executive man," which Dad chose to include in this talk.

In 1970, at age 55, Dad left all business affiliations, resigning to devote himself to the full-time public practice of Christian Science healing, maintaining a downtown Chicago office for that purpose. Dad's decision to leave the business world for the public practice of Christian Science was not a surprise to the family. He'd been practicing Christian Science all of his life, now it would be his primary focus. He had wanted to do so earlier but I recall discouraging him from going then—he seemed to be contributing more where he was in industry by his example. In my late twenties, I had been growing in devotion, commitment, and involvement with church and healing myself. One day as I woke and did my morning prayer, recently married, living in the Midwest, it "came to me" that the time was right for Dad to be in the full-time practice and I wrote him a letter consisting of only one large word: "NOW!" He knew what I meant and had been coming to the same conclusion and the next year started full-time practice.

Two years after establishing his full-time practice, Dad was asked by the Board of Directors of the Mother Church to come to Church headquarters in Boston and serve as one of three Trustees of The Christian Science Publishing Society, publishers of the Pulitzer-prize-winning newspaper, *The Christian Science Monitor*, as well as international periodicals. In 1973 Dad was made a Christian Science Teacher, while maintaining his work as a Christian Science practitioner and working as Trustee every day at the Publishing Society. From 1980-1985 he was appointed to the Christian Science Board of Lectureship—still maintaining his teaching and practice work while traveling throughout the United States and foreign countries. Dad continued his active practice and teaching until his death in January 2002.

Dad told me before he went to Boston that he saw this call as an opportunity to combine his business skill and love of church. To serve his church was his fondest wish. Challenges increased with this appointment and Dad found new applications for the truth he loved. He saw his church organization from the inside now and courageously went about "tagging" what needed fixing as he had always done. His public practice increased enormously and became his most important work, keeping him busier than he had ever been in industry.

I remember what a Christian Science practitioner said to me when I was struggling with more than seemed surmountable: "The mountain tops get all the wind". My Dad was a mountaintop and his days in Boston with the inner workings of the church blew plenty of wind his way for the next thirty years.

The fascinating and intricate complexity of his work and what he faced in Boston, are not the subject of this book. Indeed, that topic by itself would fill volumes. I leave its telling to one of his brave students. Nor is there better reading than healing after healing; but in this vast category of his life, my father's story intertwines with the private stories of so many it may not be anyone's place to tell it. Dad's viewpoint on church headquarters is equally difficult to expose. It is enough to say that thousands experienced healing through his faithful, loving help.

Dad taught twenty-seven annual classes—people of all ages, occupations, and backgrounds, from around the world—for whom he was often practitioner as well as teacher. He was devoted to his students. They *were* his family. Their concerns and problems were his. No teacher could have given more. Every student knew that when they called Dad for help he would be right there with them working, never giving up until the healing was accomplished. Reading the hundreds of letters that his students, patients, and friends wrote to my brother and me following Dad's passing in 2002, revealed how revered he was by so many. Every letter contained stories of healing and growth Glenn had helped them attain; their gratitude was tremendous.

People have often asked me how Dad was able to do so much. I would answer: early in life he learned the importance of trusting God and overcoming fatigue. Healing work had always been a priority, no matter how many other responsibilities he had. I recall him saying many times that one should learn to overcome the need for sleep. He spoke of this is an address:

When I was serving on the board of trustees of the Publishing Society, I was also working as a Christian Science Teacher, and including as many patients in the practice as I could get my arms around. One night I had just gotten into bed about 1:30 A.M. when the phone rang again. The one on the other end of the phone call seemed desperate and thought he was going to pass on. I worked throughout the night. There were numerous phone calls. Morning came and it was time for me to go to my office in the publishing house. The patient called again—this time to report a healing and his gratitude. Without having had a moment's sleep, I left for work with the gratitude of spiritual refreshment. That joy sustained me throughout the day, and upon returning home late that evening I felt no fatigue, only a quiet sense of rest and peace, in the comfort of God's outstretched arm…Fatigue comes upon us because of the accumulation of a number of little lies throughout the day, or some enlarged burden of dissatisfaction, constantly hovering over us like a cloud, trying to darken our day. Enlightenment will come through prayer. We should learn to pray unceasingly…Prayer is a consistent attitude of affection for all that is good. One cannot say, I love my job, but I don't love my home, or vice versa. When we have so loved that true affection becomes a part of our real character, it is then with us wherever we go, twenty-four hours a day. As we adopt into consciousness spiritual qualities of love, wisdom, intelligence, health—and express these in our work, in our home, at the supermarket, through living the moral qualities of honesty, affection, patience and humility, we shall be praying more consistently (Glenn Evans Files).

From Martin to Whirlpool to Warwick, to Church Headquarters whether General Manager starting up a brand new plant or CEO in the electronics industry, or handling an issue facing the Publishing Society Trustees— Glenn Evans incorporated his highest spiritual understanding into his daily work. To him, work and church were inseparable. He once used the Bible parable of the talents in a speech to the Chamber of Commerce in Marion, Ohio, asking his audience, *Are you and I using our talents to the fullest?* He often quoted a Christian Science teacher who once told him "You don't take your business into your church, but you do take your church into your business."

For Dad, taking his church into his work meant taking honesty and truth and compassion for fellow workers into the workplace—seeing them all as God's children. He once said in a speech entitled, *Management Today: A time for Trust,* that *"honesty isn't the best policy. It's the only policy."* The presence of

God, or Truth, in his day-to-day business enabled Dad to resolve a million dollar crisis that occurred when a TV plant burned in Mexico. That's how for months when the "Weathermen" (an underground radical '60s group) sought to bomb businesses and CEOs and my father was among their targets, he kept calm in spite of threats against his life and daily police-led circuitous routes to work. That's how he turned around Warwick, a business that had been in the red by millions at time of acquisition and that four and half years later was sound and profitable.

Dad believed integrity could grow from business to business if business leaders and top management stood for honesty in all operations. He said in one speech to laundry executives, "There are enough business leaders in this room to start lifting the standard of ethics, and by performance this could become contagious and spread to other industries until we would enjoy an epidemic of integrity in the business world" (Glenn Evans Files, Speech). I would add, that this was my father's lifetime goal: to see integrity and compassion filter throughout all of business, society, and government.

Dad instituted practical methods for achieving these goals. Always they started with the individual. On numerous occasions, he dared stand before many hundred business executives and give an address that went to the core of his spiritual understanding. For example, in the same speech just quoted, he concludes: "To get things moving, each individual could begin by some soul-searching of motives when making decisions. I think it will require goal-setting—goals that have a moral or spiritual purpose but a practical application. Each individual will have to set his own priorities by determining what is really important and gives life meaning. In my own case, I found more consistency in setting standards for myself by measuring my performance against the ten commandments by Moses, and the two great commandments by the master, Christ Jesus, i.e., to love God and my neighbor as myself. These have always benefited me in the long run—and I must say business has been good to me" (Glenn Evans Files, Speech).

Dad once told me that he was privileged to have been in the aircraft business in its heyday, the home appliance business in its heyday, and the electronics business in its heyday. I would add, that he was privileged to be in the Christian Science movement in its heyday as well.

When Dad resigned from Warwick and Whirlpool to devote himself full time to the public healing practice, he received hundreds of letters. A few especially caught my attention:

From a Bank Vice-President:

"Dear Glenn:

Your phone call on Wednesday came as quite a surprise as I had not seen the announcement in last Friday's Wall Street Journal [announcing Glenn's resignation from business to devote his life to the public practice of Christian Science]. It is too bad your decision could not be postponed a year or two in order that you might reap some of the benefits of the hard work you have put in at Warwick these past few years. Just this morning I received the October statements, and it does indeed look like there has been a turn around, especially with the Sears agreement. Those of us who have worked with you during this time know the key role you held in bringing Warwick to the point where it can compete with the other television manufacturers... Your decision to move from the business world and its remuneration and security into your new field was indeed a courageous one..." (Glenn Evans Files, Letters).

And from Sid Boyar, a Sears Vice-President: "I have been trying to put into words my feelings of appreciation and thanks to you for your cooperation, dedication and friendship. It has been most difficult because words alone cannot express the inner confidence and respect that I have for you as a businessman, as an individual, and as a friend...because of your sincerity, integrity, tolerance, and exceptional ability and willingness to understand people... Your achievements and accomplishments will long be remembered— your friendship will always be cherished... (Glenn Evans Files, letters).

From Dick Stull, VP of management Research Group in California: "I regret reading of your move from Warwick. Although our contacts over the past five years have only been a breakfast, one lunch, and an interrupted day, I must say to you that I know of no one in my 25 years in business with more integrity or common respect. I cannot, of course, base this on my own limited relationship, but am reflecting the feeling I have heard all through the Whirlpool complex these past five years. That you will devote your full time now to the public practice of Christian Science is real religious statesmanship."(Glenn Evans Files, Letters).

From Bud Gray, CEO and president of Whirlpool: "…as far as I'm concerned they're lucky to get a fellow like you to do it" (Glenn Evans Files, letters).

Victor L. Short, president of the Institute of Human Science wrote to Dad: "I urge you not to forsake completely your executive talent. In my opinion it ranks among the best…and America needs it" (Glenn Evans Files, letters).

President of Sylvania Electric Products wrote: "This troubled world needs more people such as you" (Glenn Evans, letters).

And a lady church member wrote: "I think you are one of the finest, biggest, strongest, and most loving persons that I have ever met" (Glenn Evans Files, letters).

Dad's management style and his practitioner style were a merging of his religious principles and life lessons. What he learned in business he applied to practice and what he learned in practice he applied to business. His unique style included his strong belief that the world should be producing "legions of good managers". I found an undated speech of his that appeared to be associated with Warwick days, in which Dad says the true manager welcomes responsibility—transforming it into a *personal asset*—and aims to do an outstanding job beyond the given assignment. Dad explains that *trust* is the key. Employees trust in him and he trusts in them and himself—a trust grounded in God, Truth and Love.

Dad writes:

> *where there is authority without responsibility the danger of business disaster is very real…The one element that holds back a manager, that chains him in the middle is fear….a willingness to duel with adversity is a typical characteristic of the good manager….The most successful bosses know that their main task is to build a business environment that makes it easy and natural for his people to do their best. Some bosses, of course, do a good job of teaching large groups of people how not to be a good boss. The good boss, the good manager of men, makes greater demands upon himself than he does on his subordinates. He does not shirk the necessarily difficult decisions and actions that belong to the boss alone. He reprimands, he disciplines, and when no other course is open, he alone does the firing. The good manager does his job in his own way. He doesn't attempt to mimic his boss. No two people are alike—a fact for which we should be eternally grateful—and no two managers will do the same job in the same manner. Frequently, a variety of styles will bring greater accomplishment.*

The greatest delight for the good manager is when his operation thrives after he leaves, with different people at the helm. There is no more positive indication of a job well done" (Glenn Evans Files, Speech).

In a speech Dad gave to Principia College business students in the late 1960s, *The Importance of Integrity*, he ends with this quotation from *Miscellaneous Writings* by Mary Baker Eddy, which I believe many of my father's students would say expresses his character:

The man of integrity is one who makes it his constant rule to follow the road of duty, according as truth and the voice of his conscience point out to him. He is not guided merely by affections which may sometimes give the color of virtue to a loose and unstable character. The upright man is guided by a fixed Principle, which destines him to do nothing but what is honorable, and to abhor whatever is base or unworthy; hence we find him ever the same, at all times the trusty friend, the affectionate relative, the conscientious man of business, the pious worker, the public-spirited citizen. (Glenn Evans Files, *The Importance of integrity* speech).

While I am slow to accept the concept "hero," so often over used in our society, I do know that to many my father was a hero. There is an ancient Celtic concept about the hero, found also in other cultures, that seems relevant here. It is that *resistance* often accompanies a hero's birth. The hero represents the universal, so his coming into the particular, the human world, is frequently met with resistance. "The advent of the hero is almost invariably an embarrassment…and attempts are made to get rid of him. The birth of the hero is an incongruity which challenges all self-sufficient reality, so the hero, intruder, is repelled as a potential danger." (source lost). My father experienced resistance, often for a principled stand he fearlessly chose to take. He came into this world fighting for his life and he was not about to let *any* resistance stand in his way after that. He *lived* his Welsh name, Evans, which means "the fighting man," by daily taking up his mental sword against dishonesty, injustice, adversity, sin, disease, and death. Like King Arthur, Glenn Arthur was guided by a holy purpose and his remarkable story has inspired many in their own quests, including his daughter.

five

My Mother's House

A frightened little girl runs down dark corridors in every direction. "Where are you?" she shouts, "Where are you? Please, come out! Find me! Hold me!" Like trees in a forest, columns and pedestals dwarf her, she runs between them, calling out, looking behind every pedestal, toward the top of every tower, but she cannot find the woman she is looking for. The little girl knows her mother is there, hiding, but where? It is a cruel game of hide and seek they play.

My mother would have appreciated New Harmony's gardens, for she liked beautiful things. She would not have chosen to walk the paths as frequently or as far as I do, but she would have taken her knitting—probably a sweater for one of my father's students' babies—to the coziest, most comfortable bench, to stitch contentedly while admiring the garden view. She would have been especially delighted if her grandchildren were riding their tricycles up and down the walkways. But those grandsons ride Harleys and Nissans now, and my mother is dead.

The mother robin I watch reminds me of my mother. Attentively she tilts her head to the ground hunting for worms, feeding her offspring one after another. She is diligent in her duty. As long as I have sat here the mother robin has been at it. She doesn't tire or give up. She simply continues to go about her business. Now and then her silly offspring swoops over her back as if to rouse her to hurry, but she is unmoved and steady at her task. She meets his need for food at her own pace.

I have hunted for my mother, but this robin is as close as I get: the untiring provider for her young. I see Mom at an ironing board or the kitchen sink. I see her hands kneading bread dough or cutting a perfect piecrust. I see those rough cracked fingers hulling berries and stitching buttons. I watch her make a dozen original crepe paper antebellum dresses, Scarlet O'Hara hats, and pantaloons for dime-store plastic dolls—favors for my 10th birthday party guests; other mothers would have been exhausted merely contemplating such an undertaking.

My mother made things. That's what she did. From a handkerchief in her purse, she could make a toy for a cranky baby—a mouse complete with tail—that she scooted up the baby's arm to make him laugh. She created a hand-embroidered medieval costume for my sixth grade play that surpassed even the lead actress's dress in its craftsmanship. She produced luscious chocolate tortes, topped with whipped cream, sprinkled lightly with red and green sugar, placed gently in our red wagon for my brother and me to deliver to neighbors as Christmas gifts. She made loaves of home-baked bread for the hairdresser, butcher, and anybody else she felt needed to be appreciated—bread was more than a tasty commodity, it was a gift of oneself, a true labor of love, and much easier than the intimacy of words. She stitched faultless buttonholes and pressed laundry until not a wrinkle remained. Her dinners were unforgettable, causing most family gatherings to be at our house. When she wasn't making things, she volunteered for church committees, Community Concerts, PTA, and the Republican Party. Once a week she bowled on a woman's league and every Tuesday she played duplicate bridge, frequently winning prizes. She excelled at everything she put her hand to.

Only on Sunday afternoons did she rest, putting her feet up, shoes off—but always keeping her stockings on—to read the Sunday paper from front to back. Then she would mark the lesson books for the upcoming week's Christian Science Bible Lesson—forty to fifty citations marked with blue chalk, located with numbered metal markers. Every Sunday was the same. Her allegiance to duty and perfection bound my mother in a silent "busyness". If she desired more we never knew. What did she feel, long for, care about, search for? What was her personal quest? I will never know.

On October 20, 1940, three years before I was born, my mother, Ruth Agnes Hunt, age 24, married my father, age 25, in the palm-decorated parlor of Grace Methodist Episcopal Church in Dayton, Ohio. She wore a street-length sable brown crepe dress, which she probably made herself, and a stunning hunter green beret-like hat I recall from the early home movies someone took. She carried a bouquet of bronze chrysanthemums surrounding yellow orchids. Her only attendant, her younger sister, Mary Lou, wore a hunter green dress and carried yellow and bronze mums. My father's best man was his older brother, Lewis, whom I knew later as "Unkie". Dad's younger brother, Bill, and three other friends were ushers. The simple wedding ceremony was followed by a reception at Mother's parents' home, after which the couple drove to their new home in Baltimore, Maryland, a small apartment at 1721 East Thirty-first Street.

Beyond basic facts, my mother remains largely an enigma. I know very little of her early childhood, but I find her first-day-of-school curious. She walked several miles to school, but finding the door closed, walked back home! Apparently little Ruth was not one to venture behind closed doors. The only other fact I know about her elementary years is that she was a marble champion. Many years later I recall her delight in buying marbles for her grandsons to show them how to play.

Ruth (August 10, 1916-May 6, 1991) was one of six children born to a Canadian mother of Irish and English decent, Lila Nellie Bennett, and George Hunt, of Scottish and English decent. Lila, my grandmother, was born September 27, 1888, perhaps in Chatham, Ontario, for that is where her parents, Orlando Bennett (a cousin of Robert Fulton, the steam boat inventor) and Mary Gilhooley were married April 30, 1879, according to marriage record 004796, Raleigh Township, Kent County. This fact I came upon following a serendipitous trip to Wolfe Island in 2007 in search of my roots.

Wolfe Island, full of quaint farms, wind turbines, and grassy beaches is full of Bennetts! I learned this wandering into a tourist welcome cottage inquiring about the name Bennett. Before I knew it, a phone was put in my hand and I was encouraged to speak with John O'Shea, local historian-farmer-genealogist who immediately invited my husband and me to his home for tea. This delightful happenstance meeting revealed my great-great grandfather may once have lived on the O'Shea farm. I took photos of the farm and later executed a small watercolor of it, which I sent to the O'Sheas in appreciation for their hospitality. Later Mr. O'Shea sent me genealogy papers linking our family trees. As his enclosed card stated: "I think you will find that you have many relatives on Wolfe Island," signed, "Your Almost Kin, John and Joan O'Shea."

I recall my grandmother, Lila Bennett Hunt, from infrequent visits until her death in 1970 in Detroit, Michigan. But I have no memories of her engineer and automotive-pioneer husband, George Hunt (born November 30, 1887, to Frederick Hunt and Anna MacNabb of Charleston, West Virginia—a section of the family tree not yet fully explored) who died August 1946, in Dayton, Ohio when I was only two.

George Hunt, my grandfather, drove several test cars up Pikes Peak in the twenties and thirties, at least one of which set a world's record. He was very involved in Indianapolis Speedway races, several times riding in the pace car. Perhaps his engineering skill in the early auto industry influenced my Mom's ability to take apart any broken thing and put it back together so it worked. Certainly my son Jason, got the "car gene," and has flown several times from his West Coast home to see the Indianapolis races and to find cars designed by his great-grandfather in the Indianapolis Motor Speedway Hall of Fame Museum. The picture I have in my bedroom of my grandfather standing on the Indianapolis Speedway track beside "The Hunt Special," car he designed in 1931, car 37, a Studebaker, is the only bit of him I know or have, but, from aunts I've learned he was adored by my mother. Especially close to him, when she was old enough, she manicured his nails weekly (something she did for my dad as well). Whenever I asked about him, Mom described her father as reserved, quiet, intelligent, and a very talented engineer.

Because her father designed cars, my mom grew up in the nation's automotive hubs: South Bend, Indiana; Detroit, Michigan; and Dayton, Ohio. The Hunt family lived in large middle-class houses with big porches, yards, gardens, attics, basements, and garages for their several cars. There was usually a family cat and a dog—one Airedale, a smart dog, fascinated my mother because he could unlatch the screen porch door and let himself in and out.

All the Hunts enjoyed reading, card games such as bridge and euchre, and an ongoing jigsaw puzzle. The three brothers—George, Fred, and Cecil—played every sport; the girls—Gertrude, Mary Lou, and Ruth—took up tennis, golf, swimming, and skating. Mom told me she and her brothers and sisters had parties and dances on their big front porch—there'd be games, food, singing and someone playing the piano. Their home was a center for social activity with people always dropping by. From an early age, Ruth was talented in singing and dancing and often entertained for various community functions, even sewing her own costumes.

The three Hunt girls were brought up to be ladies in all ways—tact, taste, proper behavior and dress, which often included wearing white gloves and a suitable hat. According to her sisters Ruth was meticulously well-groomed, fashionably dressed in a classical sense, and always reserved, collected, a young woman of decorum. Perhaps it started with their Grandmother Gilhooley (Gillula alternate spelling found)—a refined, elegant Irish Catholic woman, known for her impeccable English and dress. Ruth admired her maternal grandmother greatly and inherited her sense of propriety and dignity. Mary Lou, a Tomboy, the youngest of my mother's siblings, told me she admired Ruth for her cultured good manners and cool poise but sometimes resented her perfectionistic tendencies—tendencies which would later make Ruth an ideal match for Dad.

One of Ruth's most outstanding skills was tailoring, a talent she demonstrated throughout her life. As a young woman in the early thirties she entered a prominent Dayton department store's sewing competition, creating a lovely teal garment, and won first prize. In the fifties I remember watching her make her sister Mary Lou's entire wedding trousseau. I also remember her taking prizes for her sewing at state fairs and once, in the sixties, she made prom dresses for girls in the local orphanage. In high school I would design a formal dress on paper and mother would make it for me; I do not recall ever wearing a formal not made by my mother—but then going to formal dances was not something I did more than three times in my life. As in everything else, Mom was a perfectionist in sewing. More than once I watched her patiently rip out seams if they were less than ideal—even if they would never be seen—and quietly start over. She told me that she learned from her father that "a job worth doing is worth doing well." He believed that you should not waste your time doing something at which you were not willing to do your absolute best. My grandfather's high standards framed Mom's sense of precision and she lived up to his motto throughout her life. Obviously, this prepared my mom to become an ideal wife for Glenn Evans, whose own sense of standards was far above the norm.

When cleaning out a cupboard after Mom's death in 1991, my father came across her diary dated 1929-1933. He let me borrow it briefly and I read it thoroughly, even taking a few notes in the hope of knowing my mother better [By Dad's death, sadly, the diary had disappeared; though I asked about it several times, neither Jayne, my father's executive secretary who cleaned out much of our personal family stuff nor my brother had seen it. Having kept thirty-some journals thus far in my life, I can't help but wonder its unfortunate fate]. Mother would have been ages 13 through 17 when she wrote her diary. In 1929 her penmanship is careful with flourishes on tails and curls at the start of capital letters but it becomes more crowded and simpler by the fifth year.

From her journal I learned Mom went to every high school game, had roles in plays, sang in public performances, played the piano and harmonica, took elocution lessons, played football with her brothers, went to the "moving pictures" frequently, wrote lots of letters, and was meticulous about her clothes. She writes about making a hat with purple and gold feathers to match a beautifully tailored outfit she had sewn for herself. According to her diary Ruth could also be a hard-working domestic. She did the dishes most nights for the family of eight, often listening to a radio program called the "Pied Piper." She washed and ironed her own clothes as well as some for her siblings. Her January 4, 1930 entry reads: *Washed and mended my dress. Made a cake and some applesauce. Washed my stockings. Helped get supper. Went to a basketball game. Rylie* [James Whitcomb Riley, her high school] *lost 20 to 25.* Her diary typically offers fact but never opinion or emotion. Within a year several Bobs and Dicks, a Lloyd, Kenny, Tom, Joe, Jim, Bill, and dozens of other boys' and girls' names appear in the entries, but never does her diary directly reveal her feelings toward any of them. According to her sister, Mary Lou, Mom's friends were always "people of means and socially accepted." People apparently mattered to Mom for she mentions names in most entries, but not once an idea or dream.

Occasionally there was the hint of high school romance coupled with an uncommon innocence. At sixteen she writes: *Heard a light knock at the door just after I finished the dishes and was I ever surprised. It was Bob Ham and Herb. We talked and played with Mary's yo-yo and ate dates. Cards was suggested and Fred* [one of her three brothers] *played with us. Gee, am I ever dumb sometimes. Especially at Euchre. Played with both Bob and Herb. They left about 10:00 (training rules)!!!!.* The most emotion I found in her entire diary was in one short entry for 1931 when she uses the word "swell" four times about some social event and, surprisingly, writes "Ha Cha Cha!" to describe a new car some fellows drove over to show her brothers. These are expressions I never heard uttered from my mother's lips.

Mom seemed to have had a social life unlike any I knew. She would have liked me to be the social butterfly that she was. I had my share of slumber parties, games and the like, but sometimes my idea of fun was to sit home on a Friday night and draw or read a good book. I know this disappointed Mom and in reading her journal decades later I understood why.

Typical of the era, George Hunt saw that his sons went to college, but sent his daughters to secretarial school. Ruth went to Miami Jacobs in Dayton, but according to one of her sisters, Mom was intelligent, self-taught, and always wanted more education.

Aunt Mary Lou told me she thought Ruth could have become an engineer like her father. She was a skilled repairman. Whenever anything was broken around the house and her father was unavailable to repair it, Ruth fixed it. Probably this ability came from living in a household revolving around the auto industry and where father and older brothers were always tinkering. Mary Lou said that when Ruth was little she wore a pair of overalls with tools in the pockets and followed her father and brothers around, imitating them, and her Dad called her "Jim." Ruth picked up an interest in repairing things, in seeing how things were put together and what made them work. More than once in my life I'd seen her take apart a faulty toaster or radio and put it back together to work perfectly.

As well as being an excellent engineer, a prize-winning seamstress, and a precision cook, my mother held a variety of jobs at various points in her life prior to motherhood. She was a dental assistant, a magician's assistant, a Western Union PBX Operator, and one of the first women officers during World War II—a second lieutenant in the Women's Army Corps.

There's the favorite family WWII tale of the time my father drove his soon-to-be-bride out to Wright Patterson Air Force base to proudly show her where he had grown up. Because of the war, security was extremely tight. The soldier at the gate would not let my father on the base. Dad mentioned names of people he remembered who would still be at the base and attempted to explain that he merely wanted to show his future bride around what had once been his home. The soldier looked at my Mom, sitting there in her second lieutenant WAC's uniform, and said to my Dad while pointing to my mother, "Since you're with this officer, I'll let you in—*she'll* be responsible for you."

In a sense she *was* responsible for Dad all her days. She kept his ship on keel. We lived in clean and functioning homes, thanks to her. She baked his favorite cookies and served them to him warm with a glass of milk in a frosted glass—the way he liked it—while he worked in his den. She baked his bread weekly, made his suppers nightly, took charge of everything including paying the bills monthly. She invested his money wisely and kept the children cared for so he could focus on business trips and church duties. She edited his speeches, and later, attended to the human needs of his patients.

I can see her late at night standing at the kitchen sink, some radio talk show droning in the background, canning peaches—a bushel gift from the Nyes, Michigan farming students of Dad's. At midnight she would still be there. The kitchen was her realm. In this space she reigned. No one ever doubted that she was captain of that ship! The refrigerator door did not open without her okay, nor was a cookie taken without her knowledge. She seemed to enjoy the dominion, solitude, and quiet the kitchen afforded her.

In spite of the number of facts I know about Mom, I cannot recall a single time when she expressed her innermost thoughts or emotions. A woman of few words and hidden feelings, she maintained a composed veneer regardless of what happened. Precise, careful, accurate, exacting in details, she could handle a complex recipe or the complications of several tax audits smoothly (my parents gave away large amounts of their income to church and charities—red flags apparently to the IRS; I recall mom sifting through stacks of papers late at night to find what they required). Mom was scrupulously clean about everything, orderly, but the system was uniquely her own. Out of chaos she could find a missing pin or vital bit of thread. Her many gifts and abilites were obvious, but not her feelings. She did cry upon a rare occasion, but silently—removing herself before anyone noticed. She could laugh, but never with abandon. Argue, but not passionately. Love, but without touching. Hate, but hide it. Listen to my brother's songs, my father's ideas, and to Dad's students' stories.

Once when I was a busy thirty-something wife and mother admiring my mother's many fine traits, I pursued her with questions. "What was your life like when you were a girl? What was your mother like as a mother? What did you do for fun? Tell me about your grandmother. What did you do on a date? What did you want to be when you grew up? Did you ever wish your life were different than it is? How did you meet Dad? Did you ever love anyone besides my father?" She by-passed most of my questions, answered a few with a dollop of interest keeping the answers to a sentence, without embellishment. Nothing telling. Nothing to help me know my mother as a person. Until we got to the last question. Quietly, while she was peeling a carrot, and almost as nonchalantly as she threw the orange shreds down the garbage disposal, she said, "I was engaged once to a man before your father."

I don't recall now what interrupted my pursuit of that intriguing bit of information. I remember asking about him, but a pressing need of the moment kept the conversation from continuing. Probably a grandson needed attention or the oven buzzer went off. Maybe the phone rang. The topic was never mentioned again. Without a word, it was clear that that was the way she wanted it. My mother had nearly slipped and revealed a bit of her hidden inner self to me.

Mostly, I remember Mother's expectations. As her child I was to be good, obedient, kind, clean, orderly, and talk more than I did when other people were present. The table was to be set, everything on my plate eaten, dishes cleared and rinsed, food put away, chores completed, homework done, my room straightened, teeth brushed, shower taken, prayers said, and lights out punctually. This was the cloth from which my childhood was cut. Growing up in my mother's spotless house demanded perfection.

I recall one unforgettable instance. I was about 14 and had gone walking along Lake Michigan's sand dune bluffs with my best friend, Mickie, as we often did. But this time I fell some 30 feet into what I thought was sand but turned out to be a buried cement breakwater. My knee bled profusely and I could see what appeared to be bone. If I hadn't been taught to deny pain so thoroughly, I'm sure I would have felt even worse than I did. My non-Christian Science friend was alarmed and suggested she go for help. But we were in an isolated part of the beach, a long way from people, and I was a Christian Scientist, so I told her to go on home, that I could walk the three miles by myself, in the opposite direction, to my home. Somehow I did. When I got to the door, a bloody mess by now, I could no longer keep my composure and began to cry. I needed to use the toilet but discovered I could not bend to sit. I still recall my mother's angry words on the other side of the bathroom door: "What's the matter with you?! If you expect to be healed you had better straighten up right now!" I straightened up, as I always did.

We had our good times, too. Usually projects: cooking, sewing, making something. Never communicating much, but enjoying work. Making things was important to my mother, but not sharing deeply with her daughter.

When she passed on in the Spring of 1991, I had the mixed privilege and chore of going through everything in my parents' Boston high-rise, her last home. Despite twenty moves, she'd managed to discard nothing. Mom was an incredible saver. As one of six children and a survivor of the Depression, she was obsessed with frugality. We could have supplied the U.S. Army with recycled rubber bands or brown sacks if there were the need. In her kitchen there were stacks of bread pans and pie plates dating to World Wars I and II, dozens of plastic airline cups, one inside of another, ceramic casseroles I could remember from my earliest childhood, mixing bowls that had been her mother's. Her freezer and cupboard shelves were stacked with home-grown fruits and vegetables, and the jams and jellies she canned. In stuffed recipe boxes, hidden between cards and decades of crumbling newspaper and magazine recipe clippings, I found unexpected prayers scripted in her handwriting on bits of paper, randomly filed—a tiny discovery that told me more about Mom than her spoken words.

Tape was an important consumable to Mom. She would tape instructions to us on everything—such as, which re-cycled plastic airline water cup on the kitchen counter was whose. The dishwasher was labeled "Clean" or "Dirty." Cupboard doors and shelves had worn curly taped papers identifying contents or usage of items. It wasn't as if dozens of people needed directions as to where things were; no one ever used *her* kitchen. If I so much as put a glass in the dishwasher, I would probably be corrected as to its placement on the rack. Even when my boys were babies and I wanted to prepare their food, I treaded lightly in her space. Not until her death did I ever make a meal in her kitchen, and then for Dad, to whom the kitchen had been off bounds for so long, he could do little more than find the peanut butter (in his last days alone he hired a chef). Taping labels to everything was not really to tell the rest of us how to use her gadgets or where a thing was kept; it was just her way of assuring order and dominion. Over her sink were taped photos of her seven grandchildren, a great niece, the new baby of one of Dad's students, family photos from Presidents Reagan and Bush with their dogs. Her refrigerator door was a gallery of children's art, clippings, religious poetry, and favorite recipes. And among these, a bizarre little poem that my husband Bill copied and keeps on our pantry refrigerator with one of his own:

Ruth's Kitchen Poem: Original Version

Please stay out of my kitchen
From my dishwashing, cooking, and such.
You are kind to have offered to help me,
And I do want to thank you so much.
I hope you won't think me ungracious
When I ask that you leave me alone,
For my kitchen is not very spacious,
And my system is strictly my own.
So please stay out of my kitchen,
It may well prevent a few wars.
And when I'm invited to your house,
I promise to stay out of yours!

And Bill's own version:

Ruth's Kitchen Poem: Extra-Strength Version

Please stay out of my kitchen
From my dishwashing, cooking, and such.

You are kind to have offered to help me,
And I do want to thank you so much.
But I won't tolerate interference
From you or anyone here
You'd better just watch what you're doing
I'll teach you the meaning of fear
For my kitchen is not very spacious,
There's really but room for one
If I catch your ass in my kitchen
I'll return it to you well-done.

It was not just her kitchen that revealed Mom's treasures. Most home storage areas were stacked with something or other my mother was saving. She had a conglomeration of wrenches, hammers, screw drivers, pliers, electrical tape, and plastic coated wire. In a linen closet I found her many jars of assorted nails and screws, including a professional wall-size screw chart mounted on the closet door interior, illustrating types and sizes of screws. From her jumble of jars crammed with fasteners of every type, she could locate any kind of screw or nail of any size needed for any task. In another closet there were fabric remnants that must have dated back to the thirties; bubble wrap, ribbon, string—enough to tie up several dozen Christmases; dozens of soaps and unopened 5-pound bags of sugar hidden behind old bath towels and sewing paraphernalia. The next Great Depression would not catch her off guard! Parts of old toys I vaguely recalled from my or my sons' childhood were tucked in odd corners of shelved linens—all sheet sizes and dimensions labeled on little bits of paper taped to the shelves.

Her clothes closets, full of worn-out dresses along with the finest designer outfits, a mink coat, and shoes of every era of the past seven decades, revealed her need to hold on to things, to save the past. End table drawers revealed piles of photos of every relative and friend she'd ever known, most of them my father's students. Knick-knacks, tacky, but meaningful to her, sat on bookshelves containing few books, beside fine china and antiques purchased in later years.

But of all rooms, the kitchen revealed Mom most. After she died, I walked into her kitchen seeing her hand-written instructions still taped to cupboard, microwave and refrigerator—as if she had written them that morning. It was surreal. To stand in her kitchen after her death was still to be in her presence.

I did not cry when my mother died. My brother was the one to call and tell me she had passed; Dad called Rich and told him of her death and asked him to phone me. I was sorry she died but not surprised. She had been ill for months, but I was never told the full story. I believe she died from depression, not the abscessed foot I'd seen a Christian Science nurse change the dressing on when we were in Bermuda to celebrate their 50th anniversary, nor the death certificate's easy answer that her heart had stopped. I flew to Boston and spent three days helping with decisions and sorting through stuff. We took 25 large black trash bags to the Salvation Army, gave away her clothes and jewelry to relatives and those who could use them. I organized the kitchen while Rich organized mother's desk piled high with papers.

There was no funeral. My father's wish. Instead he, my brother, and I sat in Dad's Boston office and shared readings from the Bible and *Science and Health* together. Though her sisters, nieces, nephews, grandsons, even her hairdresser and butcher and many of Dad's students might have liked to honor her, no one was invited. My father said that a funeral would only draw attention to the material sense of life. So, there were just the three of us. It is not the ordinary Christian Science way but it is the "Hasidic" Christian Science way. I shed no tears, felt no emotion.

I know I loved my mother. Dad kept hordes of letters, cards, poetry, artwork I made and mailed to her throughout her life in which I freely declared my love and appreciation for all that she did. Giving, long-suffering, listening patiently to my father's students tell her their joys and troubles, she was loved by all who knew her. But she and I were not close. I can't remember her holding me as a child, though she must have. I can't remember the two of us doing any mother/daughter thing together, nor ever "hanging out" the way I sometimes did with my daughter. Cleanliness and order is what I remember. And her expectations. Always her expectations—silent (and sometimes not so silent). I tried to please her. I tried to know her. That's why I wrote so many letters; they were a way to reach for her, a way that she might accept. Being good was the surest way I knew to feel close to her. So I tried awfully hard. But rarely was I good enough. Like the time in my early twenties when I tried to surprise her by thoroughly cleaning her apartment for her, making order of her room and desk—to be a surprise for her when she returned from taking care of her sick mother for several weeks. She was horrified! And like the time I brought slides to show her of my abstract artwork that had just taken prizes in significant juried competitions. I had thought she would be proud but her reply was "It just looks like throw-up to me!"

In her last years I had disappointed her enormously. She could not forgive my leaving a 21-year marriage, nor the Church. These were not proper things to do. Tasteful ladies who wore hats and gloves in the thirties didn't produce daughters who divorced in the nineties. I was a huge embarrassment. "What are you doing to your children and what will your father's students think?!," she inquisitioned me late one night, having flown to Memphis to try to stop my divorce.

Though months after her death I sat in a tub of cold bathwater and cried for the mother I never knew, today, the strongest memory I have of her is her oft repeated phrase to me in our later years: "You have bitterly broken my heart."

six

Pillars, Pedestals, and Paper Dolls

One black stroke follows another on the white surface until a face is formed, smiling. Then another face appears and another, followed by torsos and appendages. No two figures are drawn alike. Each has a distinct height, shape, hairstyle, skin tone, personality. The young artist sparks eyes with highlights, slips necks into shadow, parts lips as if they were about to speak from the page. As she applies a final charcoal layer for definition, she gives a name to each individual. Then she draws houses for them in the background, complete with sidewalks, geraniums on widow ledges, bikes and balls in the flower-filled yard, cats and dogs on the sidewalk. She thinks up their stories, who their parents and friends are, what activities they enjoy, what they study in school, what they talk about at the family dinner table, what adventures and dilemmas they experience. Before she knows it, the young artist finds herself on the sidewalk, patting the cats and dogs, tooting the horn on one of the two-wheelers, picking a geranium blossom, and waving to one of the characters she'd just drawn. The character waves back and motions her into the brick house in the background. Inside are friends, laughter, dancing, plenty of conversation, and a delicious dinner waiting. After dinner, they read books together 'til bedtime. Some evenings, they pack suitcases and fly to Ireland, France, or Morocco—always returning to their carefully drawn home before anyone suspects they'd left the page.

In New Harmony there is a roofless church, designed by Philip Johnson, a walled sanctuary, open to sky, soy and corn fields. Its undulating altar encompasses an organic work by sculptor, Jacob Lipchitz. No pillars or pedestals are present in this incongruous structure. Only nature and space give it form. I am drawn to the free-standing arches of the north nave wide open to fields, offering an inspiring humble vista.

I am attracted to the serenity of simple things. Sky. Earth. Air. Water. Religious elements acknowledged by Native Americans, Celts, Taoists but not by Christian Scientists for whom the material world is illusory, something to be overcome. I was raised to know reality as spiritual, not material, and spent much of my youth and adulthood "unseeing" most of what my eyes were drawn to.

Having a keen imagination, however, I developed a private reality centered on drawing, paper dolls, and story. From age two to twelve, the beautifully illustrated 12-volume classic literature for children, *My Book House* (which I still have in my library) was my beloved companion. I learned that true friends are in books and art.

At eight, nine and ten, I lived in a closet. Untypical of the small late-thirties style Baltimore house my father bought for us, my closet was enormous. I never really understood why I was given the bedroom with the walk-in closet. Logically it ought to have been the master bedroom. Perhaps my parents decided that since the room was already painted a rosy shade of pink (my brother got the room with the duck wallpaper), being the girl, I should have it. Perhaps they gave me the "closet bedroom" because I was so shy, figuring if I had a big, bright room, I'd grow to match its attributes. Probably they gave me that room to keep the rest of the house neat. Art supplies and paper dolls could be stashed on the closet floor, my rain of little paper scraps hidden from view.

A big step down, the closet engulfed me in darkness until I reached high for the light cord. The light on, the door shut, under an awning of skirts and dresses, I sat alone for hours, surrounded by thousands of paper dolls sorted by families and made-up stories. This was my sanctuary. Here along with thousands of store-bought paper dolls, I drew and colored my own beautiful icons to whose lives I was devoted, away from the pillars and pedestals of family and church on the other side of my closet door.

I literally had thousands of paper dolls; it was the one gift that captivated me. Every time my grandfather visited, he had two or three books of paper dolls under his wide arm. He seemed to enjoy picking them out as much as giving them to me, as if he understood how important they were. He usually chose movie stars: Esther Williams, Debbie Reynolds, Doris Day, Loretta Young, Jane Powell, Betty Grable—I had them all, even different sets of the same actress. Whenever I would walk up to Woolworth's with my little brother, he'd spend his allowance for a small plastic car and I would spend mine for a book of paper dolls.

I had a world of characters: bride dolls, fashion dolls, miniature dolls, giant dolls 20 inches tall, Colonial dolls, Civil War dolls, families, college girls, airline stewardesses, even cowboys and old-fashioned girls with petticoats and plumed bonnets.

My favorites were my "orphanage dolls." I called them that because they were a set of nine children without a mother. I still remember the day Peggy Carter, my babysitter, gave them to me with the strong admonition: "Whatever you do you must *never ever* lose or give away these dolls!" They were loved treasures from her childhood and *I* was being entrusted with them. I fully understood and accepted this sacred responsibility. The torch had been passed and I would not drop it. These paper dolls were exquisite little works of art. Their faces were like fine portraits, each with natural, happy expressions revealing character and individuality. Perfect in every detail, even their eyelashes cast shadows across their cheekbones and curls were painted to show depth and highlight. Each doll was in a different position with accuracy of anatomy down to the bends of knuckles and knees. Their edges had been meticulously cut—neither a clothes' tab eliminated nor a toe cropped. Peggy had carefully glued their cut-out names on the back of each.

My dolls took on a reality that demanded my love and routine care. As I played with them, in my mind each began to have a distinct personality with its own idiosyncrasies. Peter and Ginny, the youngest two of the set—ruddy-cheeked, red-haired toddler twins with beautifully rendered blue eyes—were my special favorites. Ginny was a sweet, gentle, shy child who always held her head slightly down and rarely said a word. Her twin brother, Peter, in contrast, was lively, bouncy, and from time to time in delightful trouble. They were, in spite of their differences, devoted to each other. Muffin, their five-year old sister, could sometimes be very bossy, being their elder, but she was also vivacious, full of energy and ideas, a little manager who could always be counted on to help Ginny button her coat or find Peter's left sock. Muffin's companion was most frequently Beanie, blonde with brown eyes, liked by everyone. Babs, Jill, and Margaret were an inseparable trio. Occasionally, the triangle would find themselves in a tiff (which offered great story possibilities)—sometimes due to Margaret's bookwormish character contrasting with the more frivolous natures of the other two who often left her out of their fun. The oldest two, almost ten years old, were Sally and David. Sally was a tomboy with braids. She and David were usually outside playing basketball, building a fort or climbing a tree. They were often entrusted with responsibility for the others in the orphanage and could handle anything. I chose an unknown-to-me 1940's movie star doll with long beautifully painted eyelashes and gorgeous red wavy hair to be their mother (I now know she was Greer Garson). The beautiful movie star doll loved every one of her nine charges as if she were their real mother. Poised, graceful, glamorous in a subdued way, she'd given up a successful career as an actress to run the orphanage. Some male doll was never far from her side, but she was very selective and slow to be impressed.

Because I had few male dolls, I had few fathers. Fathers were not that important to my stories anyway, always boring in dull suits, off to work somewhere, never around.

My dolls were busy—experiencing every imaginable life adventure and routine—including great joys, sorrows and tragedies. They learned to struggle, endure, and survive. My imagination never lacked for a story line. Occasionally I got an idea from a book, but mostly I made up situations. I loved being the director—such power for a kid! Stories I created—and lived—with my dolls sometimes continued for seasons, each day another episode. Sometimes, I would erase their pasts and start over—like actors, they would take on new roles. These characters born on the closet floor, arranged in orderly rows and lives, were my *friends*. I knew every one of them deeply. I shared their hard times and happy occasions. I laughed and cried with them. To me, they were not mere colored images to amuse a child. They *were* my reality, often more real than the people on the other side of my closet door.

Eventually, I began to draw my own dolls and create costumes for them—including hats, gloves, parasols, and ski poles. Even when I grew older and we moved away from our house in Baltimore with my sacred closet, I still designed paper dolls. I would study my most beautiful store-bought dolls to learn how to shade or draw human proportions correctly. Once I made a doll with over seventy outfits. It took me months to design and paint the prints, plaids and satins. I spent weekends in my room creating worlds of my own.

I still have every doll. I used to get them out upon occasion to show to a lonely child I baby-sat for, or, later, to play with my own daughter. For years they lay in labeled folders inside plastic bags, turning brittle in an antique bench. But in 2009 I will get them out for Emma, my two-year-old granddaughter. She will appreciate their delicacy and details as she dances them around the living room, hiding them in sofa corners to take "walks in the woods." Playing with Emma, I will become a child again as I step back into my world of paper dolls, glad to see all my old friends once more—those friends whose lives turned out however I wished.

Outside my childhood closet, I remained shy, separate, different. Always good. Always correct. Always obedient. But never feeling fully part of the non-closet society.

Even from my earliest childhood recollection, at age three, walking hand-in-hand with my grandfather while visiting him in Dayton I was aware of my shyness. As a group of young boys came down the street in our direction, I squeezed Grandpa's hand tightly and exclaimed, "No see boys! No see boys!" It was very unlike me to speak, let alone with such force. I can still remember how frightened I was, how I hid behind his wide girth, as my grandfather tried to assure me they were nice boys. But I would not be pacified so we crossed to the other side of the street to avoid passing them. My parents found this story amusing and told it frequently to family and friends; they especially enjoyed sharing it when I was a teenager, to my dismay.

My parents chose not to send me to nursery school or kindergarten but put me in *three* different first grades due to three moves in one year. I have no memories of them beyond the cafeteria lunch which I routinely had every day: vegetable soup with homemade rolls that I can almost taste thinking of it. And a second profound recollection: children without shoes. They must have worn shoes, perhaps very shabby ones, but that's not how I remember it. I recall crying to myself, day after day, because these children had no shoes.

By the time my little brother was school age (he is three years younger than I), my parents were interested in finding a better school than Baltimore public schools seemed to be. I benefited from their choice for him: Friends School, a private Quaker institution of outstanding quality with an advanced academic program and high moral standards. Rich started at Friends in nursery school, and I started there the following year, in fourth grade.

The Friends School campus was visually beautiful: English stone architecture spread out on gentle hills where we played field hockey, with a bit of woods nestling the Quaker meeting house. We wore blue and white uniforms with saddle shoes—so as not to allow ostentation. Aside from wearing these uniforms, having tongue and beets too often and Welsh rarebit not often enough for family style lunch, I loved everything about Friends School.

A global involvement was part of the character of Friends. We learned about other countries with cultures very different from our own, sometimes collecting cans of food, books, and clothing to send to poorer nations. On Fridays, we had assemblies with international guests—once dancers from India in colorful jeweled costumes who could contort their bodies in amazing twists and turns which fascinated me.

At Friends I found friends. One of my closest classmates was Carol Grief, a bright and gentle Jewish girl who lived in an enormous mansion with a buzzer on the floor under the dining room table that her mother stepped on to call the maid to clear the dishes. Her backyard was the size of a city park with elegant old trees. We would imagine all sorts of things under the tall shady oaks while we ate a fried chicken picnic carefully prepared by her cook. Carol always told me she loved to visit my home because it was so "cozy." I believed her. I had other friends my three years at Friends School—Jackie, Faith, Lisa. Whatever we shared has faded from memory.

Though I did not know it then, Friends School was the foundation for my love of learning. It set high goals for its students and even though I was not one of the brightest or most promising, I loved its standards. I knew a certain freedom of thought there and felt encouraged, never condemned. It raised humanity to a nobility that as an elementary student I did not know how to give term or structure to. But I see now I was experiencing the beginning of the elevation of art, intellect, and ideas to the position they hold in my life today. My years at Friends are among my happiest educational memories. I can still recite poems memorized once a week for English; recall the care the stern but understanding math teacher showed me—one of her weakest students; and picture my first significant art experience—drawing from live lambs outside on the lawn. I believe that that singular art lesson, along with paper dolls and seeing the beautiful illustrations in *My Book House*, nurtured my becoming an artist.

As Friends School widened my view, I broadened at home. While drawing, paper dolls, and imaginative play with neighborhood friends occupied much of my free time, by sixth grade I discovered the love of the stage—actually, the love of writing and directing. I wrote a play based on one I found in a book and assigned roles to various kids in the neighborhood, convincing them that to put on a play would be lots of fun. I gave my brother a leading role, though he couldn't have been more than 8 years old (he reminded me of this in the late1960s when he got the lead in his college production of *Carousel*), and I got to wear lipstick playing the part of the mother. There were about seven actors in the play, and their parents and the entire neighborhood turned out to see our grand production on someone's patio. I remember being amazed that it had all come together, that people actually clapped with enthusiasm. Thus my writing career was born.

We tried a second neighborhood production—Christmas tableaux in a Catholic neighbor's basement. But it was short-lived and killed any further neighborhood thespian endeavors when Annette's father came downstairs and yelled at us for our "sacrilegious" playing of *I saw Mommy kissing Santa Claus* on the record player and for using a baby doll for Jesus in our nativity scene. I remember my stomach churning and vowing to give up directing right then and there. After that I wrote and illustrated stories just for myself.

Center stage to our lives during my elementary years was a large downtown Baltimore church. I remember a tier of white marble steps—like a pedestal for the edifice; coffered ceiling squares in the sanctuary for a child's imagination to count on a slow testimony evening; pillars in the Sunday School that separated classes like trees in a forest—was that a deer peeking from behind a pillar? I might chase him during the next hymn. Pictures, icons, statues, and decorations were taboo in any Christian Science church, so my imagination made up for what was lacking in imagery. Nor was there the inspiring minimalist quality of a Quaker meeting house that I marveled at at school. Christian Science churches come in a variety of sizes and styles, often former buildings of other denominations, or, specifically designed for the unique Christian Science service, reflecting its simplicity. But our Baltimore church was not simple, but grand, having been built in the hay-day of the movement, the early 1900s.

However, the edifice isn't what matters; what matters is the spiritual "structure of Truth and Love"—the Christian Scientist's definition of church. No physical altar, no liturgical apparatus, no baptismal font, no sacramental paraphernalia, no icons nor statuary will be found in a Christian Science church. Nor will you find a person called "preacher," for the Bible and *Science and Health* are called "the only preacher," thus, the service consists mainly of readings from these two books. Christian Scientists believe no physical symbol is capable of representing baptism (a pure heart) or worship (moral practice of God's commandments and Christ's beatitudes). To rely on God alone for one's wellbeing *is* sacrament. The Christian Scientist's communion takes place in how one lives, not in physical wine and bread. Prayer is not asking God for something, but aligning oneself with God, allowing God's presence to govern every situation. *Knowing* God, *reflecting* God *is* church. Even as a young girl I understood this.

In our family, church always came first, even before family needs. I do not recall one missed Sunday School session in my entire childhood. My brother and I were often the only children in church many Wednesday evenings. Even as a child I was conscious that nothing mattered more than God. As pillars of the church, my parents, especially Dad, confirmed by their example, my growing conviction that Christian Science was inseparable from my being. What else could I possibly think watching healing after healing take place? We were almost never sick. Christian Science seemed to keep us healthy.

My father's healing of an automobile accident that left him with a severed ear, broken ribs, and a dislocated jaw, among other injuries, occurred when I was in fifth grade. Before my father arrived home in a taxi, my mother sent my brother and me next door to the neighbors (both professional oil painters whom I enjoyed being around, who happened to be Christian Scientists) so that we would "not witness any error." Dad had refused the ambulance that the police had wanted him to take, insisting on a taxi home, fighting to keep conscious during the long ride by reciting the Lord's Prayer aloud and holding his severed ear in place. The taxi driver and my mother helped Dad to bed and Mom called a Christian Science practitioner for prayerful metaphysical support and a Christian Science nurse to cleanse the wounds. Later he would go to John Hopkins and have the ear stitched back without drugs given—with little hope from the doctors that the ear would fully mend, but it did. Dad rested in bed, praying and studying continually in spite of pain of broken ribs and dislocated jaw. One day I came in and read to him from my *Science and Health*, which he later told me uplifted him on what had been a particularly discouraging and painful day. Dad, as First Reader of a large Baltimore Church, was scheduled to introduce a visiting lecturer at a public lecture on Christian Science in two weeks. It seemed impossible that in such a short amount of time he would be ready to stand, let alone give a talk on stage before a large public audience (dressed in formal attire, as was the custom at the time, in waistcoat with tails and striped pants). But he did it. Healed, he returned to work two weeks after the accident to the amazement of his co-workers. He included his healing in his lecture introduction, for which many came up and thanked him.

Years later, several of his co-workers became Christian Scientists, largely influenced by what they had observed as my father daily practiced his faith. Businessmen gained courage in knowing him. At business conferences where alcohol flowed, my Dad ordered milk or water. Many who preferred not to drink but were afraid to go against the norm, would simply tell the waiter, "I'll have whatever Mr. Evans is having." Dad always had a throng around him wherever he went. He maintained an easy camaraderie and respect for others that drew people to him. His sense of humor combined with genuine interest in others could be compelling company. He was never afraid to ask questions, speak his mind, or share intriguing ideas, including his beliefs. Wherever we moved, people were attracted to my father, many placing him on a pedestal.

Sundays were full of pattern and predictability. My father and mother always had important church duties—First Reader or church board chairman or Committee head or Sunday School Superintendent and always Dad was a Sunday School teacher, often mine. When Sunday School and church were over, my parents stayed after for meetings or my father would visit with someone who needed his help (even when I was very young he functioned as a practitioner for others). While waiting for them, my brother and I would entertain ourselves by jumping hopscotch on the shiny decorative marble floor patterns, filling paper cups with water at the drinking fountain, playing hide and seek between the Sunday School pillars and, sometimes, someone would take us to the nearby drugstore for a package of Lifesavers—I always chose cherry, chewing every one before we got home.

After church, we often drove to a seafood restaurant for dinner—Dad's way of giving Mom a break. Mom had two main luxuries, among many, all of her married life: dinner out every Sunday and a maid once a week. Never having had either, I wonder what she did with that saved time. Bridge, bowling, a weekly trip to the hairdresser's occupied some of that freedom, along with church committees and volunteer work. But, of course, she made all our nutritious meals and even ironed our *sheets* as well as shirts.

After Sunday dinner we might drive in the country or visit Dad's brother, Unkie to us kids, and his wife, Aunt Alice, who lived on the other side of Baltimore. I remember riding in a pink and black Chrysler, and later a two-toned green Oldsmobile. My father was partial to Oldsmobiles. Somehow for Dad, the very American Olds was a moral and political decision as well as a trustworthy automobile. When I inherited his last Olds in 2002, it still seemed more his than mine. A touch of guilt accompanied me whenever I transported groceries, art materials, and my wet-pawed Bernese Mountain Dogs in his leather backseat, something Dad wouldn't have done. Now that same car, that saved my life in 2004 while losing its own, lies in a scrap yard, merely a heap of twisted metal.

As a young girl, on our Sunday drives I would become oblivious to my parents' front seat conversation with my brother's occasional interjections, because Cotty was with me. Cotty was my imaginary friend—a little boy my age. I have no recollection of how or why I gave him that name. He was kind of skinny with tousled light brown hair. Appearance did not seem to matter. It was just important that he was there. I would tell my parents: "Cotty is having supper with us tonight and needs to sit beside me" and I would pull up an extra chair; or, I'd describe for them his opinions, likes and dislikes on a variety of topics when I was afraid to voice my own. Cotty and I would have long talks together, play games, and have wonderful adventures in my mind. Every now and then he'd jump out into the real world and I'd have to tell my brother, "Watch out! You can't sit there! You'll squash Cotty! He's in that chair!" Cotty especially loved Sunday afternoon rides. Frequently we would drive by his house. Cotty moved a lot. He lived in the prettiest house I'd find on a drive. When we passed a prettier one, Cotty got a new home. Even then home mattered.

As my father's church and business demands increased, family drives no longer fit into the Sabbath. By my fourth grade at Friends, Cotty was rarely around. I do not remember exactly when Cotty left. He just faded away with the Sunday drives.

Nearly half my thirty-four moves were in childhood, due to Dad's business career. Several were prior to my starting school and three in first grade alone—none of these do I recall. There was another when I was in third grade, followed by one between sixth and seventh grades. The latter was to Marion, Ohio, a small town, home of former US President Harding, where Dad was hired by Whirlpool Corporation to set up a new division from scratch.

Because Dad was very busy as General Manager of this new division he was creating and Mom had a new home to see to, my brother and I were sent to Christian Science summer camps in Michigan to ease my parents' transition. So I did not get acquainted with our new home until fall, just as school began. I don't remember my room or any details of that house except that it was located on a large corner lot on Uhler Road next door to the home of a bunch of cheerful blonde girls and their widowed mother—the Isaly's—the same name as the Marion ice cream shop we frequented after church on Wednesday nights.

In Marion I got my period. No one had ever told me about the "birds and bees," my parents were out of town, and when I saw all the blood I was horrified, thinking I'd somehow swallowed glass. Assuring me that I had not, the baby-sitter handed me a Kotex pad, which I'd never seen before, and without explanation instructed me to put it in my underwear and ask my mother about this when she returned from their weekend away. I could tell whatever had happened to me was mysterious by her nervousness. When

Mom returned, she told me this would happen once a month, something every female experiences in preparation for becoming a mother later in life. Then she handed me a thin blue book and left the room. The book told stories about teenage girls, but if there were any facts of life in there I missed them. Such was my entire sex education.

We lived in Marion for less than two years. Most of this time Mom seemed pre-occupied with establishing home and Dad was busy hiring people and setting up every detail of his huge new operation. I do not remember seeing Dad except on Wednesday nights and Sunday mornings when we would go to church together. No matter how busy Dad was, he never missed church, usually teaching Sunday School's oldest class.

All my life I have been interested in Dad's business career and his church work because both were so much a part of our lives. And I think, too, because it was my way of having him, holding on to him. So I grew up knowing both corporate and church practices and how their problems might be solved. I never separated Dad's activities from my own. Though he was frequently away on business, whenever he was around, Dad freely shared business concerns and solutions with us. When he was home, he was the center around which we revolved. Dad communicated directly, entering a room like a bull in a china shop and a divine light combined. I was always very aware of his presence. I could tell just by the sound of his Florsheims walking from garage to house what kind of a day he had had. At dinner he would tell us about his experiences, occasionally asking our opinions. By twelve, I knew the stages of Marion's plant development nearly as well as the life stories of my paper dolls. At thirteen, I was as aware of Whirlpool's labor and management situations as if these were factors in *my* everyday life. By fourteen, I saw no separation between my father's work and our lives.

It was the same with healing, though I'd been aware of it since I took my first step. It was as if I were my father's apprentice by observation. He lived in front of us every difficulty he faced so I witnessed first-hand how he solved problems and what he relied on for his strength.

By my forties and fifties, what I had known previously made better sense. When in 1999 my father invited me to come spend a week reading his files, one of the many topics we spoke about was the Marion division—a pinnacle in Dad's accomplishments. I found his experiences compelling and his business acumen extraordinary—something I was already aware of but now understood with an adult's perspective. In reading his extensive files—somewhat like researching for a term paper—I got a fuller picture and greater appreciation for the accomplished man that happened to be my father.

Whirlpool had just purchased the Marion plant from General Motors which had had union trouble and left town. Dad told me in 1999: "GM hadn't communicated with the local people. I decided we were not going to make the same mistake; we were going to be successful—and without a union, which was a big part of GM's failure. Four different unions wanted to get hold of our new employees. They wined and dined them to gain their allegiance and vote. I knew that unions wouldn't be necessary under my policy of fairness. I held meeting after meeting to let every worker know this plant would be different; it would be rooted in fairness and teamwork."

"Immediately I set up Sunday meetings with all workers—their spouses and children included—to talk with them about how I operate and what hopes we had for the plant and for their futures. I listened to them and I took all their suggestions and questions. Some had advised me this forum wouldn't work, but it did."

"I found out long ago that *trust* is the major factor in a company, a government, or family. Trust would be the basis of my operation at Marion. The basic way to get trust is *honesty*. You have to be able to say 'I was wrong.' You've got to be straightforward with the janitor as well as top management. You have to be willing to say—and mean it—'Look, Joe, don't ever lie to me. I won't lie to you. Come to me if you have a problem and I'll work with you'. You've got to learn to trust God before you can trust anyone. Before you can trust your wife, your colleague, or boss. Life, Truth, Love—these are the only demands on man. If I violate my relationship with Truth, God, I am unable to be honest, unable to trust or elicit trust."

Dad said his management system at Marion developed "out of the woodwork". He told me in New Harmony, "I always asked myself 'What does the company *need* and what must *I* do to get it done?'"

Communication with the existing community was his first goal and what he did grew out of that. Dad was quoted in an article for the company paper during this Marion period: "In the community, as in the factory, more important than the working and living conditions, is the attitude of the people with whom they [the workers] are to be associated… all should be rightfully proud of the job being done. Everyone locally from the outset has done everything humanly possible to aid us in getting started." (Glenn Evans files, Whirlpool's *Clotheslines Are for the Birds*).

Dad wrote letters to all the city's churches and synagogues asking for their support and prayers. He wrote to the schools and organizations, inviting community participation in the success of the Marion plant. An excerpt from his letters to the ministers reads: "Since there are undoubtedly Whirlpool-Seeger folks in your congregation, you may hear, at times, of problems which concern their work. On such occasions I shall appreciate any guidance which it seems proper for you to give them "(Glenn Evans files, letter). Imagine such community communication and cooperation by corporate America today!

Establishing quality was another priority. Dad believed quality was essential and devised ways of assuring it in all operations. "You have to have engineering that is quality, a process for inspecting—a formal process," he told me decades later. "On my own I wrote down the process and designed inspection for quality into every aspect—all of this began when I was inspector at Martin. Lives depended on quality in the aircraft industry and I brought that intensity to the laundry equipment industry. These were basic principles of mine before I got to Whirlpool."

I asked him how he evaluated people's work. He said he had an evaluation system that started with managers. Periodically he called each one individually into his office for an evaluation that was based on the manager's own self-evaluation. It went something like this, as I wrote down Dad's explanation: First, each manager was to evaluate himself, then his department, then evaluate "what you think your department should have done", next "what you think you need to do to improve yourself (a course, more staff, etc). Dad would have two listening sessions like this with each manager before he would say anything. He gave each person the opportunity to learn, grow and spot needed changes on his own. He strongly honored the individual; for him, this was essential to the success of the whole operation. A "good review" was "If they gave me an *honest* report, no hedging; if they hedged, I asked them to see me again in two months."

In a 1958 speech to the American Management Association (Glenn Evans file, American Management address October 23, 1958) Dad described setting up the Marion facility. Prior to the interviewing process, Dad laid out the authority and responsibility of each position. He selected key members of his management team, interviewing persons from all across the country. Once the key group was hired, together they set objectives. Dad explained in his speech: "For each objective we set, standards of performance were established in order to measure our progress in carrying out the objectives" (Glenn Evans file, American Management address, October 23, 1958). Dad took his people through the establishment of principles and objectives for the division so each could play a part in developing the standards. He made clear to each individual his or her particular duties and freedoms. He also made clear the duties and freedoms of those reporting to each manager. Then, he selected staff for the various departments, according to functions, such as, division planning, engineering, works manager, purchasing, industrial relations, controller, quality control. His hiring criteria was based on an individual's moral integrity, management skills, an interview with the family ("If one cannot manage a family he cannot manage a company" Dad said more than once), and a discussion of what attracted them to this challenge.

Dad often changed his entire organization chart to hire a man whose particular skills or integrity he wanted. He told me, "People become slaves to organization charts when really it ought to be a flexible tool—change it for who you've got and what you've got to accomplish." Dad wanted to keep a good man when he found one. Once, a man of high standards did not know enough about accounting—an area his position was beginning to require—so he was sent for schooling rather than be fired.

Dad's way of managing was really *developing people* and in this process making success of a company. Dad cared about people second only to Principle [God] and wanted his employees to speak up and contribute. Once, he "blasted" a manager: "We are in the business of developing *people*! You haven't given me a single person out of your department!" Dad told me, "I gave him a choice: go to research where you don't have to manage people or continue here and correct the situation. He left. Two years later he came back and asked me for work, saying he'd learned what he'd not been doing."

In one of Dad's many talks to managers he stated that a good manager must work to earn authority, allowing his subordinates to be the judge of his leadership ability by their willingness to follow his direction and example. Dad points out four essential qualities of leadership: unselfishness, integrity, humility, and vision. How rare these are today, but I grew up watching these four qualities in action and know they are effective, timeless. Ever connecting spiritual ideas to business, Dad included a biblical quotation in this speech: "And if I be lifted up from the earth, will draw all men unto me." This was Dad's standard for leadership. (Glenn Evans files, February 23, 1979 speech).

The Marion division became a model for the entire company and no other plant in the country had a performance bonus plan like the one Dad established. CEO Bud Gray gave Dad great latitude. He and Dad had a very warm relationship. After Dad's first year at Whirlpool, Bud was favorably impressed with what Glenn had accomplished. Within two years the Marion Division's assets were $10,000,000—four times the original investment (Glenn Evans files).

Dad wrote to his workers in November of 1955, only eight months after he started at Whirlpool: "Only by each one of us working hard and unselfishly has it been possible to reach our present stage of production in a short time. . . it is my sincere hope that each of us will have cause, and remember, to be thankful every day for an improved way of life. May our working conditions, our home life and our friendships continue to improve each day in every way" (Glenn Evans files, November 22, 1955).

Decades later, in 1995 Whirlpool's Marion Division—still in production and still union-free—honored Dad on the occasion of Marion's 40th year. It was a wonderful event for Dad; old friends—line workers and managers alike—honored him. So many had looked up to him over the years, I think he was surprised by how highly he was esteemed. The practices he had established were still in place. It made him very happy.

By 1957 we had barely lived in Marion two years when Dad was asked to become General Manager of Whirlpool's Benton Harbor/St. Joe, Michigan Division, where the headquarters were located. So we moved again.

Our first months in St. Joe, my brother, age 10, and I, age 13, lived with Unkie and Aunt Alice in their apartment on Lake Shore Drive while my parents lived at the Whitcomb Hotel so that Dad could focus on his new role and Mom could house hunt. Aunt Alice and Unkie had no children of their own, so my brother and I were their surrogate offspring. Never having been a mother, Aunt Alice always seemed nervous with us. Playing bridge (which she taught me while there) and reading novels occupied most of her time. Though she was a member of the church, I never knew her to talk about God. Unkie was easy going, a jokester, who told us amusing tall tales I naively believed. One was about how his shock of premature white hair had been caused by a can of white paint that fell on his head. Another story pertained to figurines and a clock on their mantle. According to Unkie, whenever the clock chimed in the middle of the night, the man figurine hit the woman on the head! I remember lying in their guest bedroom, wondering every time I heard the clock chime, what awful things were going on on that mantle ledge! In the morning the figurines and clock looked innocent, but I knew that was a pretense and avoided walking too close to the mantel.

While we lived with Unkie and Aunt Alice, I walked to and from the junior high, returning to their apartment feeling a bit stifled without a home. The several mile walk was scary—I had been shown the way once, but was afraid I would make a wrong turn and get lost. Several times I did take a wrong turn, frightening myself. I knew no one and had no friends in this new town. None of my own things were with me, no art materials or paper dolls, none of my books; just clothing and new school books. My parents, living in the hotel, weren't around. I felt a bit afraid and isolated until we moved into our new home.

My parents found us a beige brick ranch house with a big picture window, located on a cove on the outskirts of St. Joseph, Michigan, Benton Harbor's twin city. There was a woodsy ravine in the backyard for privacy and established rose bushes for my mother. The large basement easily accommodated my brother's Lionel train layout and a ping-pong table. There was also a finished family room for the new color TV. The smallest bedroom was painted pink and came with matching pink twin beds—that would be mine. Rich's school was close by, and I could walk to the junior high three miles away. A new high school was being built about a mile from our house where I would start in another year. It seemed perfect. But then, at least on the surface, everything seemed perfect in the fifties.

It was a tidy time. After school, and sometimes after a cherry Coke at the drugstore near the junior high, I would walk to our new ranch house with

Mickie, my best friend, a cheerleader, to find Mom either in her pink and gray kitchen baking bread, or, in the basement mangling sheets on a monster machine that pressed out every wrinkle, with TV's "Queen for a Day" for background company. I would set the table for dinner, start my homework, then get lost in a book or sketchpad until time to help in the kitchen.

Dinnertime was very important in our home. Everyone was expected to be prompt, to participate in the conversation, and to clean his or her plate regardless of what vegetable might be on it. I recall a centerpiece of pink and aqua china pheasants, candles, cloth napkins, and occasionally re-used decorated place cards I had made for the last special holiday. Mother's meals, basic more than inventive, were delicious. No one made better roast beef with glazed carrots or more flawless mashed potatoes or smoother gravy. Every meal represented all food groups and dessert was never forgotten.

We could be a team in the kitchen, my mother and I. By her own admission, she was not an artist. But she *was* an accomplished cook. I was her obedient assistant. With her culinary skills and my aesthetic sense we were an unbeatable team for any dinner party. Sometimes I would make elaborate menus to inform guests of what was in store. Always, I could put colors and textures together: the right linens with the right china, unusual use of goblets or unexpected juxtapositions of edibles. We enjoyed working side by side with little talk.

Our family had hardly settled into our new home in St. Joe when Dad was served a supena to appear Monday, Oct. 21, 1957, at 9:30 AM. before Pierre Salinger in connection with a Senate Labor Relations Committee investigation, headed by the Kennedys. Apparently Whirlpool was accused (falsely) of hiring men to use illegal practices to keep unions out of their plants, specifically one Checov, a Communist .

Reflecting on this experience years later, Dad told me: "We'd just moved to St. Joe, I was still trying to run a division new to me while all this investigation stuff was going on. I'd already been through so much at Martin with the *Enola Gay*, etc., then, setting up a company from scratch in Marion, and now this! A great challenge might rise up once or twice in a man's career, but I was having them thrown at me, one right after another!"

Only as an adult, have I come to understand what my father faced. Communism was the most dreaded word in our nation during the '50s. Senator

Joseph McCarthy was the self-appointed leader of the Anti-Communism crusade, accusing anyone he chose to attack of being a Communist, perverting an American's right to be considered innocent until proven guilty. For Whirlpool to be accused of hiring Communists and conducting illegal practices, was devastating to Dad and everyone connected with the company.

Alexander, the man Dad replaced as General Manager at the St.Joe/ Benton Harbor Division, had hired Schefferman, a labor relations firm representing management, for the St. Joe and Clyde, Ohio divisions. Schefferman had hired Checov, a Communist, who was attempting to make illegal deals with union heads. Alexander had tried to get Dad to use Schefferman's labor relations services when Marion was forming, but Dad wanted no part of it, preferring to directly deal with his employees. Ted Huffert, a man Dad had hired to head personnel at Whirlpool's Marion plant, had appeared before the Senate Committee under oath, having been put "through the mill, coming out like pulp," as Dad put it. Dad was furious with how this good man was treated, and worried for his wellbeing. Dad flew to Washington and met with Peter Nehemkis, Whirlpool's DC lawyer, and said, "This has got to stop—get me on the stand!"

"When I appeared before the committee, Bobby Kennedy started attacking but the senator from Iowa stopped him, saying, 'I would like to hear what this witness has to say without interference from counsel.' Then I got to speak and I said "Before your committee even existed I fired Chekov." The official Congressional Committee transcript reads: "Glenn Evans, the former general manager of the Marion plant, also denied that the company knew anything about Chekov's activities. The testimony in this case was of such a contradictory nature that the chairman ordered the transcript sent to the Justice Department for study."(From p 271 of the select Committee on Improper Activities in the Labor or Management Field Report no. 1417)

Dad explained to me later that he had fired Checov when he learned Schefferman had sent Chekov to Marion without Dad's o.k. "As soon as I discovered Checov was taking managers for drinks, trying to get them on his side, I called him into my office and said 'You see that door?!, Walk out and don't come back!—tell Schefferman neither you nor he work for Whirlpool any more!' I called Bud and told him what I did after the fact. Bud said, 'Fine, Glenn, if *you* did it'."

The Senate Committee planned to bring a charge against Ted Huffert but Dad insisted on preventing that and told Nehemkis, "That man reported to me. I'm *not* going to have him go through this! It isn't right! He's a good man." Huffert was suffering emotionally from the strain of testifying and the false accusations hurled at him. Dad told Nehemkis, "I want to meet with Checov". Chekov had fled to Canada to avoid appearing before the Senate Committee. Nehemkis found Checov and Dad flew to Canada to meet with him in order to clear Huffert. Checov, a squirrely character according to many who knew him, and Dad met late one night. Dad got to the point: "A man's life is at stake—you are the one man who can clear him—write up an affidavit about what really took place—and I don't have a dime to give you!" Dad got the affidavit, flew back to Washington, gave it to counsel, and Huffert was cleared.

Early next morning back in Benton Harbor, Dad was in Alexander's office waiting for him. Dad told me: "Alexander had a higher title than I, but I didn't care. I said to him, 'This is false to discredit Huffert when *you* are the one who let in Shefferman!' Alexander looked sheepish." Dad continued, " 'Do you want to go with me to see Bud or shall I go alone?'" Dad went alone to Bud's house and within two weeks Bud fired Alexander. Scherfferman got a prison term. Whirlpool was cleared of any wrong-doing. Dad was made a Vice President of all divisions, something that had already been in the works. At age 14 I heard pieces of this drama regularly and Dad's sense of fairness and courage left a lasting impression on me.

Dad believed in men acting *honorably* and working together for honorable results. This came from his belief that *every* individual as a child of God is worthy and should be the strong pillar his Father-Mother God made him to be. In similar logic, Dad believed all conflict could be eliminated if you established a foundation of standards rooted in principle, trust and fairness. This was essential to Dad's management style. For example, when he came to the St. Joe division, Dad stopped the striking that had characterized it. He brought all workers together in the Benton Harbor High School to tell them about his plan for fairness, much the way he had brought the workers together at Marion. No one in management thought the Benton Harbor/St. Joe employees would show up for this meeting, as this plant had a long history of union difficulty and Dad was the new guy in charge. Dad's colleagues told him, "Don't expect anyone to show up to meet you, Glenn. Gathering employees together to talk with them won't work! They'll boo you off the stage! They'll not let you speak! Tomatoes will be thrown!" But Glenn did it. The employees came and listened. No tomatoes were thrown, in fact there was even mild applause following Dad's words. This began a real turn-around in Benton Harbor/St. Joe.

After telling me this story, Dad added: "People are afraid because they don't know who to trust. You go to God and you're not afraid of anybody or of any job!" And he may as well have added a line I found in one of his speeches written the next year: *"If there is one thing I learned to do a little better job of, it was to maintain one's poise through the trials"* (Glenn Evans Files, American Management Association speech, October 1958). In the margin of the speech he'd penciled: *Poise is stability, steadfastness of character or purpose.*

While all of this was going on—almost as soon as we moved to St. Joe—Dad was made chairman of the church building committee. The church members had tried for years to re-locate, to start a building program, but attempts always failed. Under Dad's direction, a lovely new edifice was built in Fairplain—the community located between the "twin cities" of Benton Harbor and St. Joe. It was paid for in full and dedicated within two years.

Prior to the church building project, at age twelve, I joined this branch church. I served on the nursery committee, the literature distribution committee, and was asked to prepare a metaphysical paper on the topic of "church building" to be delivered to the membership. This last duty was utterly daunting to me! I worked for days with a Bible concordance and my own limited sense of prayer, at the time, to complete this assignment. I was nearly petrified to think of standing up before everyone. But I did and members were kind enough to thank me afterward. This church experience encouraged my self-confidence and rooted me to my church.

One Thanksgiving when I was in high school my heart sank when Dad received a phone call that took him from the family table. A distressed church member called, asking for help. Dad had hardly taken a bite of his turkey dinner, when he left. Our time with Dad was cherished, given all his work and business trips. As I was to learn later, the elderly husband of the woman who phoned was dying and she was extremely frightened. The man's breathing gave every indication that he would not live an hour more. Dad stayed with the couple in their home, speaking the truths he relied on with a strong voice, confident in God's power to heal even this situation. Dad was gone for hours, returning late that night. The following Sunday I stood beside my father in the church foyer when this couple—the husband fully alive—came up to Dad with tears in their eyes. I will never forget the gratitude and adoration on their faces as they took my father's hands in theirs. Dad told us the whole story later. It was a memorable account that I have never forgotten, one of many remarkable healings I witnessed growing up with Glenn Evans for my father.

Sometimes I longed to talk to him—not to ask for anything—just to have contact with the man everyone put on a pedestal. But I tried not to bother him; he was busy even at home. When I was young he seemed like a giant (though he was actually a short Welshman). It was his *presence*: firm and fearless. He seemed a model for right living—still is, even after death, to many. He remains the most intriguing man I've ever known.

One day in the 1970s in Boston, walking to the Mother Church with Kay Kyser—the famous band leader of the '30s and '40s, a Christian Scientist working at Church headquarters at the time—pushing my toddler son's stroller in front of me, my father yards ahead (in any group he was the fastest walker), Mr. Kyser said to me, "You know when they made your Dad they threw the cookie cutter mold away—there's no one like him." I agreed. Definitely pedestal material—at least that's how it seemed to me growing up on into early adulthood.

Though my father made good money, we never focused on *things* in our home. My parents were fair with our needs and I don't remember ever asking for money, nor even for a new pair of shoes. We always had what we needed and I remember being well-dressed for school. My mother would drive me to South Bend—later we'd fly to Chicago on the Whirlpool jet if there were an extra seat or two—for an annual day of shopping for school clothes. I liked the design of things; Mom knew fabrics. In St. Joe, few would have the quality clothing I had, but my frugal mother always saw to it that I never had more than five or six outfits. I really didn't think much about my appearance, for my real life was the world of drawing.

For entire days I would be absorbed in the characters I drew—some from real life and some I made up. I remember inventing intricate families of eight or ten—babies crying, mothers stirring stew at the stove, teens on the phone, dogs chasing cats, eggs rolling off counters, twins running, and a father with a briefcase walking out the door. My drawn families were less neat than ours, had more siblings and pets than ours.

My brother, though three years younger, seemed older and wiser. When he was little, we played school and he likes to remind me that I was always the teacher. But as he grew, he was less at home, away with friends playing sports, involved in activities, and we did not spend much time together. Like Dad, he loved to be with people. Smart, entertaining, attractive, gregarious—even in third grade, Rich was a popular student, as genuine as his good grades. In high school, president of everything, he was sure to get an award at any assembly and could throw a football or handle a tennis racket with the same ease with which he sang the lead in the school musical or operated his ham radio. In 1962, when his cheerleader-girlfriend's grandfather died, he quietly wrote her a special poem as caring as Mom's ironing of Dad's cotton shirts. Today he lives in the Southwest and I in the Northeast; we communicate infrequently by email or phone, but he is my ever-likeable and loved brother. Our bond is strong.

Completing my childhood home of mother, father, brother, was the occasional pet: for a short time a pair of kittens, once when we were little in Baltimore, a Dachshund puppy Unkie and Aunt Alice bought for us (that a strange neighbor poisoned), and shortly thereafter, a parakeet.

Mother adored Candy, the aqua parakeet who sang at the breakfast table: "Hurry up and drink your milk, you'll miss the bus!" Amazingly, my mother would allow Candy to fly free occasionally, even to peck at the china birds on the living room mantle. Once he actually knocked one to the floor where it smashed into bits, but Mom just quietly cleaned up after him—had I caused the accident, I'm not sure Mom's response would have been as calm. He was her kitchen companion. Often I came home from school to find Candy sitting on the faucet at the kitchen sink singing sweetly to my mother as she prepared supper. But we didn't have Candy for long as parakeets were outlawed in Baltimore and he went to Detroit to live with Grandma Hunt.

When Dad was in Europe for several months for NATO in the early fifties I begged Mom for a kitten. She said if I wrote my father and he said yes we could get a cat. I did, and he answered "yes", informing me years later that he missed us all so much he would have fulfilled any request. So we got a cute kitten, but it ran away the day before my father returned. None of our animals was long-lived, nor do I recall having more than one at a time, and few were allowed inside. We had what my father called "outside animals". Outside animals never had the opportunity to wet wall-to-wall well-vacuumed carpeting nor scratch the beige silk sofa facing the picture window that looked out over our dandelion-free lawn.

I was never sure why God threw me into this perfect setting, but I harbored myself behind my sketchbook capturing it all. I drew the kids for whom I baby-sat, my brother in his Little League Baseball uniform, my mother peeling potatoes at the sink, my father marking his Bible lesson books, our occasional cat or dog, our living room, our front yard rose bushes, our back yard ravine, the neighbor's garden, even our De Soto station wagon that matched the aqua living room carpet and the feathers of the china pheasants on the dining table. I made a graphic record of everyone who entered our home from Dad's business colleagues to Mom's bridge friends. I captured every family member's facial expression while they watched the "Hit Parade," the Christmas lights defining our ranch house's perimeters in December, and the starter tomato plants on Mom's kitchen windowsill in Spring.

At school I drew the kids in my classes. This I did gladly during geometry class when the teacher—who was also the football coach—re-played last Friday night's game for the class. And once in ninth grade at a "Y" camp I sat up nights in the bathroom—the only light source—drawing portraits I'd been asked to do of girls' boyfriends from their wallet photos. They actually paid me. I left camp $60 richer. I would have drawn portraits without pay. Drawing was my way of understanding things. Still is.

I formed an early bond with paper, beginning with *My Book House* books, before I could cut out a paper doll or hold a pencil properly. I loved the illustrations—some by Racham and other noted illustrators—in those volumes of classic children's literature. I would look through the books and make up additional stories for myself when no one was around to read to me. One little girl was mean to a little boy on his way to the barber shop and another cried when a bully stole her ball and the naughty kittens who lost their mittens had my greatest sympathy, often I gave them a happier ending than the rhyme suggested. Always appreciating but never limited by the printed stories, I made up dramatic plots—with eventually happy endings. I created personalities for every character in the sepia-toned Carrivaggio-esque illustration on volume 1's cover—beyond what the simple scene suggested. I loved these books with their beautiful illustrations! A year ago I learned by researching on the internet that Olive Beaupre Miller, the originator of *My Book House,* was a Christian Scientist, a fact I am certain my parents didn't know but would have appreciated. Just a few years ago, when I had a B&B, as a guest signed in, she noted my 12-volume set of *My Book House* on our library shelves and exclaimed: "Oh, you have *My Book House*! I *loved* those books!" We clasped hands and jumped up and down as if we'd known each other for years. Recently I hunted for another set online and had it sent to my son's young daughter in Washington state. My own set I share with my local granddaughter and I sense she is coming to love it as much as I.

Paper, whether for words or illustrations, provides an amazing space of endless possibility. Unlimited freedom comes when pencil and paper get together. Everything in my 1940s-50s-60s world came under my pencil's scrutiny, whether writing or drawing, or later, serious painting. These activities have occupied most of my life. When I was a child, not understanding my fascination with creating pictures and stories, my parents tried to get me to stop. "Don't you want to put down your sketchbook and get out of that chair?—come to your brother's game with us!" . . . "Why don't you go outside for a while? It'll do you good." . . . Or, if I were outside drawing trees or the neighbors' cat: "You've been out there so long, you must be frozen. Why don't you come in?"

But I didn't stop. Instead I became prolific. Even today closets are full of my writing; my studio is filled with art and my gallery exhibits nearly 400 paintings.

Before I had the lovely studio/gallery spaces I've had these past fifteen years, when I was a busy Mom as well as an artist, I designated one 3 by 4 foot portfolio to house my best artwork. I was doing large watercolor landscapes and cityscapes then. I figured with one special place for my finest pieces, I would not need to sort through piles to find what I wanted to enter a competition or show to a client. I held high standards for what went into that black leather portfolio and kept this practice for two years in the mid-eighties. The portfolio was bulging with products of my best creative effort.

Then, one day I lost it. I could not find the portfolio anywhere. I retraced my steps of the last week and searched every conceivable location. I called the places where I'd most recently taken it. No one had seen the portfolio. My name and address were on it in big bold letters so that was not the problem. I did recall being in a hurry one day and vaguely remember taking the portfolio out of my station wagon to fit in children, cats, and dogs (as an adult I've always had many pets). Could I have left it leaning against the trash cans in the garage? Weeks went by. Still no portfolio. It simply had vanished. I was in agony.

A few days later I received a long-distance phone call from a man in St. Louis—a city my husband, kids and I had lived in years earlier—a stranger who had remembered my work from a show in the early1970s, who traced me to my current home in rural Tennessee! It seemed extraordinary that he could find me. He said he was interested in buying a piece of my work. With much sadness I told him about my loss of the prized portfolio, explaining that all my best work was gone. To this day, his response and its effect on me seem eerily profound: "Why, you can't lose what you have!" said the stranger, "it's *in* you!"

From a stranger the precise words I needed to hear! I knew he was right. I realized I did not have to suffer from this loss, or any loss; that I could go right on, as if nothing had happened, painting from new discoveries, not looking back, not hanging on to precious "pedestal" pieces. I never met that man nor heard from him again. Nor did I find the portfolio. But I've never forgotten his words.

Sometimes loss is gain.

Years ago, in preparation for moving my family out of a home I'd designed with an architect friend, I cleared the attic of what seemed like tons of my old childhood drawings. Alone, I looked at each one of them. They were wonderful—my experienced adult eyes could see that now. Studying the lines and forms on those yellowed papers, I was surprised by the detail. The drawings were a pictorial history of our family. I'd captured every significant and ordinary moment. I recognized Lisa, whom I'd baby-sat many Saturday nights during my high school days. There was my little brother curled up asleep on the couch. My Dad clipping the hedge. A portrait of Mom wearing those funny scalloped, blue-rimmed glasses she wore in the early sixties. There, too, were portraits of the international businessmen my father brought home for dinner so he could eat with us instead of out in a restaurant—several from Japan, one from Hong Kong, and a nephew of Nehru from India. There were hundreds of drawings—each accurate enough to bring back the moments in which they were drawn. I saw our screened porch in St. Joe where we played Parchessi on rainy afternoons—and nearly felt the dampness and heard the drops hitting the roof. Another drawing took me to the corner where on a hot summer's day my brother and I sold Kool-Aid—I could almost taste the syrupy sweetness. Images and memories flooded me as I waded through the drawings for hours.

Then, I threw them all away. Into big black garbage bags. Like stuffing military body bags. All those icons of the past gone. Early the next morning when I heard the trash men come, I felt a sudden ache in my stomach—so painful it awakened me and I lay there listening to every trash bag of drawings grind into the dumpster. It was a leap of faith to throw away my childhood. But for a journey to continue, sometimes throwing away the past is the *perfect* thing to do.

seven

Seeking Self

From village to village, the ugly duckling swam, searching for home. But no one welcomed her. "You are not one of us," the farmer said, slamming his door in her face. "You are not one of us," the ganders cackled, kicking gravel in her eyes. "You are not one of us," the roosters and hens crowed and clucked, together barricading the hen house. "You are not one of us," the sparrows chirped from their cozy nests, dropping seeds on the duckling's head. "You are not one of us," the loons echoed in the dark night. "Nor one of us," the Wood Ducks added from their houses along the marsh. Even several swans with their necks stretched too high, called "You are not one of us, move on, move on." Wherever she tried to land, she was sent on her way.

Day after day she wandered. Wherever she drifted or flew no one said the words she longed to hear: "You belong here; this is your home." That is, not until she became herself, until she bloomed into the beautiful swan she was meant to be. Finally, in a lake filled with other former ugly ducklings, now graceful swans themselves, she found her place.

My walk this morning in New Harmony takes me past the Orchard House— an historic home of relaxed sophistication that has been my home away from home on a number of occasions. One may rent it by the room or splurge and rent the whole house. There are four uniquely furnished large bedrooms each with private bath, and a kitchen, living room, library-sitting room, dinning room with wonderful views out glass walls to a courtyard garden and orchard. Beautifully appointed with antique furnishings and genuine art, The Orchard House has served as retreat for my family, friends, and women's studies classes I've taught. It has provided home when home was not to be found elsewhere.

In searching for *home*, my hunt has found me placing fistfuls of roadside flowers in a drinking glass to beautify a motel room for a one-night stay, planting flowers outside a rented trailer, painting interiors and exteriors wherever I've lived, creating gardens and driveways out of wilderness, laying flooring on my hands and knees, sewing curtains and pillows, refinishing furniture, decorating kitchen cabinets, faux-painting rooms with five layers of paint, hand-dabbing mortar in a stone foundation, and painting more walls than I could count. Wherever I've moved I've aimed for beauty and belonging, striving for a place that allows me to be *me*.

As soon as I was able to hold a pencil I was designing houses. From thirteen on, I drew floor plans, aiming for each rendering to solve more spatial problems than the last. Designing space on paper is satisfying in some fundamental sense and nearly addictive. I wonder now if this interest in houses had to do with looking for my right place: a way to feel at home, to fit in, to belong.

Due to Dad's work, I moved seven times before I was ten. Among these early residences were several apartments, a duplex, a row house, an apartment in Omaha, Nebraska, and a small brick house just outside Baltimore, in Towson, Maryland—the one with my big closet for my paper dolls. Ten years ago while passing through Maryland we drove by this Towson home, 703 Kingston Road, which I had not seen since sixth grade; it looked as charmingly cozy as I remembered.

At the end of my sixth grade we moved to Ohio—my eighth move; less than two years later we moved to Michigan. After two months living in my aunt and uncle's apartment, we moved to a ranch house on the opposite side of town where we managed to stay put until the end of my senior year. But the summer before I started college in Illinois, we moved to a ten-acre property along Lake Michigan where my little room had a spacious view of Lake Michigan. At college, I moved regularly, for we were required to change rooms and roommates every quarter—thus, technically I could add another dozen or so to my thirty-some moves!

When Dad became CEO of Warwick Electronics, he and Mom moved from Michigan to Chicago. At the same time, I moved into my second apartment, from St. Joseph, Michigan to Benton Harbor, where I was teaching high school, my second year out of college. After one year, I ended the Benton Harbor apartment lease in order to paint abroad five months, after which I lived in my parents' North Shore Chicago apartment's guest room for eight difficult months while searching for my next career move. A few months later Mom and Dad moved to a newly built Lakefront condo, almost next door to their previous Chicago apartment and I moved to northern Michigan for another teaching job. In the 1970s my parents moved to a penthouse in Boston, Massachusetts, then to a home on Cape Cod, then to a Boston apartment, and in 2000 my Dad, at age 85, ten years after Mom's death, moved into a brand new Art-Deco condo in Boston's upscale Copley area where he lived little more than a year until his death in January 2002. All the while, I was busy with my own moves.

Because our family lived in St. Joseph, Michigan the longest, that home is the most vivid of my childhood. The brick ranch with its large front picture window—so typical of the era—was not the most attractive house my parents looked at in their search, but it had the best location. My brother's school was in walking distance, as was mine.

St. Joseph Public High School was a new state-of-the-art school, where English and Art were my favorite subjects and I became a good student. I was inducted into the National Honor Society, became a thespian and president of the Art Club. Other than a math teacher or two, I had excellent teachers, especially in English. Once I illustrated each character from *The Canterbury Tales*, an extra credit labor of love, which my English teacher displayed on classroom walls, to my quiet pleasure. Later I created Thomas Hardy characters for her. I believe that teacher, Miss Mildred Webster, was the first person to hang and praise my art publicly. She even asked to frame one of my pastels—of Eustacia Vye—and hang it over her mantel. Years later she invited a classmate and me to her home to see it in its place of honor.

Although shy in high school, I had four close friends: Mickie, Meg, Margie, and Karen. We were each quite different, but found comradeship in our diversity. What bound us together were similar standards, shared values launched from a fifties world. We were not the popular elite, not the ones having or attending all the parties, not the drinkers, the wild set, the athletes, the beautiful people or top social leaders. We were on the fringe of all that. We could hold a class office, give parties for the most popular, and yet not be wrapped up in it all. Perhaps it was our innocence that tied the five of us together. None of us smoked or drank, unlike many of our classmates. We had creative imaginations, liked to read poetry, paint, or play the piano. We cared to question and discuss ideas, but, occasionally, still played with doll houses. Above all, we were grounded by our family structures.

We valued our families, were involved with them, not merely biding time at home until graduation. Small town middle-class values permeated our homes. Religion bound me to my family; for Meg, it was family activities; for Margie, it was a distinct cultural heritage; for Karen, it was living up to and struggling within family expectations; and for Mickie, it was taking responsibility to raise a younger sister while keeping her parents together and sober.

Mickie was the hub to our spokes. She and I would walk miles down the lakeshore, climbing dunes, picnicking, sketching, swimming, discussing our dreams for the future, while our peers were riding around in cars honking at each other. Born and raised in St. Joe, she is still there, living in Benton Harbor, walking Lake Michigan's shore, appreciating 30-inch snows and dune sunsets. We have kept in touch throughout the years, visiting one another, even more frequently since I learned just a year ago that her cottage home, filled with antiques which she sells and cats that she loves, burned in a fire.

Margie also lived in St. Joe since birth. Her Swedish/Italian Lutheran home was a bit of the Old World. To enter her house was to feel the turn of the century, to discover an unspoken "otherness," a hidden world of gray lace and brewing coffee. It enchanted me. I always felt Margie was a bit embarrassed by her home and family because she kept us from them much of the time. Margie's focus was social. She strove for recognition and boyfriends, which wasn't hard with her pretty smile and coquettish eyes. In 1961, as high school seniors, along with many others in our class, all five of us tried out for the Miss St. Joe contest (for which my mother made me a beautiful organdy dress). Margie won. Ever since then, Margie was Miss Somebody; it changed her life. She and her husband, another class member from St. Joe, now live in Indiana.

Meg's family was expressive, academic, with two teacher parents and three bright offspring who stayed in St. Joe the way geese stop at a pond on their way to some better destination. Meg's family was somewhat liberal in a conservative setting, well-read and unafraid of discussion. Her family enjoyed an intimate warmth-around-the-table that I yearned for—I, metaphorically, the waif outside in the night-snow looking in their window at the heads bent together over a book in yellow light. Last I knew Meg had married and divorced an Irishman in the IRA and was teaching piano and gardening professionally in England.

Karen, the daughter of a prominent doctor and controlling mother, lived in a big house surrounded by large trees. Perhaps the most academic of the five of us, she was an accomplished pianist and writer, but also the strangest. I never quite understood her but I was quick to be concerned about her. She did not get along with her mother and was always in some sort of emotional trauma even though she apparently had all that money could buy. She would float in and out of our group like a bobber in the tide. The thing I most remember about Karen was her letter to me in college asking me to pray for her because she wanted to commit suicide. I crafted my return letter prayerfully for hours.

My home exemplified the fifties' corporate patriarchy: thoroughly applianced, clean, comfortable, smelling of mother's home-baked bread and father's success. The keystone of our family, however, was our religion.

We five girlfriends were proudly individuals—unique in an era of conformity, when convention and belonging mattered. Matching sweater sets, little white collars, and cultured pearls prevailed. But Mickie, Margie, Meg, Karen and I were not afraid of being who we were—at least of who we thought we were at the time—nor were we desirous of pretending to be who we weren't in order to fit in.

We did not need each other, were not dependent on each other, in the way I see some young people need their friends today. Alone time was fine with any of us. We could walk to class without ever encountering each other and be perfectly happy. One of us could go to a party without the other four.

We could sit with the most popular kids and carry on mutually pleasing conversations, or, enjoy a talk with a wild "hood". Meg might miss a basketball game with us because of some family activity or I might stay home drawing, and no one was miffed. We had the usual slumber parties, dances, and games but we also honored each other's privacy. Without really being conscious of it at the time, we had the flexibility to bend to a variety of interests and tolerances, to fit in with any group or be alone.

Nor were we afraid to be honest with each other. We genuinely cared about each other and would appreciate any recognition or accomplishment one of us achieved: Mickie's cheerleading or Margie's Miss St. Joe reign, or my election into the National Honor Society. I suppose we had a certain confidence. Odd to say now in my sixties, when on down days I occasionally see my life as unused skeins of yarn that never became the intended scarf, still in an old box pushed to the back of a closet shelf.

For my sixteenth birthday, Mickie and my mother planned a surprise party. They invited handsome and popular classmates, football and basketball players, and presidents of this and that. It was held at the country club where my parents were members. There was a band and elaborate food. Everyone invited came and had a terrific time. I remember being embarrassed because my parents had told me only that we were having a family dinner there and I didn't even wash my hair for the occasion. Under Mom's and Mickie's urging, I gave a few other parties after that; or, more correctly, my mom and my friends organized parties at my house. Guys came because they liked our ping-pong table, electric train layout, and Mom's food. My mother was delighted and Mickie liked all of it. I was never comfortable with any of it. These parties were beyond my control or even my wishes. Though I usually was asked to major dances, I never dated anyone in particular but managed to be the one to patch up romances for my friends when rifts occurred. Peacemaker was frequently my role and a few times I felt like a tennis ball, not knowing whose court to land in, but wanting to make things happy for everyone. I don't think I could have supplied enough words to cultivate a male relationship of my own. My first romance and first real kiss (brief though both were) would not come until I was a college sophomore.

There was no question about where I would go to college. My parents didn't take me to visit any campus except Principia, a school for Christian

Scientists in Elsah, Illinois, atop the bluffs of the Mississippi. Art schools were never mentioned nor did I really know much about them. Had I known, I would have definitely applied to one, for art had always been my passion.

Christian Science was popular in the fifties and early sixties, and Principia, the only college for Christian Scientists, had a lengthy waiting list. In 1961, I was one of many on that list. Since my parents couldn't imagine my going anywhere else, I hadn't applied anywhere else.

After graduation from high school, a second-choice college seemed necessary, for I was still on the lengthy waiting list for Prin and it didn't look like I'd make it. My father found Rockford College in Rockford, Illinois. Years later I would learn it was one of my favorite people's alma mater, Jane Addams, but at the time I had never heard of it, nor her, nor seen the college until my parents dropped me off at the campus. Rockford's academic year began two weeks before Principia's.

Ten days after I had fully settled into Rockford, my number finally came up for Principia, which had not yet started. My mother phoned to tell me I'd be leaving Rockford that weekend, to pack all my things because she and Dad would be coming to take me to Prin. All I could say was, "I can't talk to you now, I have a paper due." I had just begun to feel a bit settled at Rockford and though the quick adjustment had not been easy, I had made a friend or two, I liked my roommate, and we had even bought some furnishings for our room together. But here I was moving again—something that seems always part of my life. Besides, Prin was where I felt I was supposed to be, where my parents wanted me to be, so I obediently packed to move out instead of finishing the paper in which I'd become invested. I sometimes wonder how staying at Rockford might have altered my life.

My memories of Prin are of beautiful English Tudor architecture by Arts and Crafts Movement architect Bernard Maybeck—including my dormitory—all in an idyllic gardened setting along Mississippi bluffs where I'd walk out to the edge to sit and think; of small classes with caring and talented professors; of metaphysical meetings prior to most activities; of wearing hats and gloves to church and heels to dinner when other college students on other campuses were in shredded jeans burning American flags (at least, at Berkley by 1964; and by 1965, my senior year, the first protests took place at U of Michigan, in my home state, where SDS was the strongest in the nation. *A Student Generation in Revolt As International Oral History by Ronald Fraser, 1968, p. 102*) I remember being forced to ask a date to our dorm's quarterly house parties which I always dreaded and avoided. I remember working on floats for football games, once in charge of one. I worked on the yearbook with the editor, a good friend, Carolyn Ruffin, (she and I would seek answers to life's biggest questions together), and my senior year I designed the yearbook cover. I remember the tiny chapel room where I hibernated many times to think when it was too cold to wander the woods or sit on the bluffs. I remember roaming the library, loving to get lost in the stacks and discovering topics previously unknown, such as Descartes' "I think therefore I am", a revelation that spurred further philosophical reading. Influenced by philosophical discoveries, I once walked out in the middle of an art history exam because it struck me that taking an exam had nothing to do with real life.

We were made to change rooms every quarter. My fall freshman room was a quint—five girls in one crowded room—initially, a terror for me. Two of those first five roommates, Jinny and Ellen, one from California, the other New York, and I kept touch, enough for them to be bridesmaids in my first wedding. But changing rooms so often, and without choice until our senior year, was always difficult for me. It seemed I was always moving. Some roommates I found to be friends, but some were crazy—like the one who enjoyed walking around nude and another who climbed out the second floor window to meet her boyfriend after curfew (hard to imagine a college girl needing to do that today!) and the neurotic one who phoned Ringo Starr in the middle of the night on the hall pay phone (before anyone heard of cell phones) and actually got through to him. There were no long-term boyfriends. One I liked—a true gentleman and the deliverer of my first kiss—asked me out several times, but I was too timid to communicate much. Making art remained my closest companion.

And I wrote letters to my parents and occasionally to Mickie at University of Michigan. My duplicity as a freshman, yet complete sincerity, shows in the following excerpts, the first from a 1962 letter I wrote to my parents; the latter, I wrote the same year to Mickie—but never mailed.:

To my parents:

I feel so very happy. Tonight I've been thinking a lot and I see ever so much more clearly how extremely glad I am to be a Christian Scientist and also what a grand opportunity I have to be going here to school [Principia].

To Mickie, unsent:

I'm not the quiet, simple girl…at night I reason and question, which winds up confusing me, depressing me, leaving me without purpose…I wish I could find someone who could answer my questions beyond the slightest doubt—then I could be satisfied, happy. Everything I've believed in has been wiped out from under me, I have nothing to stand on, so I'm falling. It began when I realized that everyone wasn't as good and perfect as I'd always thought people to be. I began to question my religion. I know that no other religion has what I'm looking for either. What am I to do? My parents, friends, teachers, are completely engulfed in Christian Science, and that's o.k., except that I can't tell them how I feel without them secretly wondering about me and trying to help me work this problem out in Christian Science…for them its right, and, I, too, believe, more sound than most religions, but what I'm looking for is Truth. I want to know what God—if there is a God—is really like. If I know God, then I will know what life is and what I am, then I can set goals, find my way. I want to know what really exists, know facts and prove them—I don't just want to be told.

The other day I was so excited; I thought I was going to find my answer in a book in the library: "Discourse On Method" by Rene Descartes, a 16ᵗʰ century French philosopher, mathematician, scientist. I couldn't believe it when I read this man's goal: "A most earnest desire to know how to distinguish the true from the false, in order that I might be able clearly to discriminate the right path in life, and proceed in it with confidence." This was exactly my desire, too! He set up a method to achieve it, so I read the entire article… I was close to the knowledge I sought, but his method didn't always take axioms I could accept, so, the results could not be right. What amazed me was that many of his ideas, I had too… tonight I read his article again… it cannot help. What can?

I can never truly be satisfied, or happy, unless I know what I am, what my purpose is, what life is, what God is, what really exists…Life is more than college, friends, things, marriage, etc.—what is the reason for all this? Why are we here? Should we live day to day and never care about anything else? I just don't believe that's all there is. And what is there after we leave earth? Surely then we'll care about more than clothes or a good education. I want to know NOW so I can lead a purposeful life.

Last quarter I began to realize that everything I believed had been told to me by a person. I began to wonder how to know that they are right; they may think they're right but may not be. They are only human, too, and may have proven their so-called facts from a false premise... And if this material world is false, anything concluded from it would have to be wrong. If all is spirit why does there seem to be matter? I began to doubt Christian Science, Mary Baker Eddy, the Bible, Jesus, and all ideas that I had grown up with. I decided I must not accept anything for fact unless I could prove it myself beyond a doubt. I cast out all my beliefs, faiths, previous understandings. I started to think what I could prove and, therefore, accept. The only fact I have been able to prove is that there is a Power, some Cause that created what is; perhaps God, perhaps not; perhaps good, perhaps not. Perhaps merely a world of ideas. Who can say for sure and prove it? If one can, there's hope. If not, I'll never be satisfied… my thoughts prevent me from studying… daily happenings are ridiculously unimportant. Sometimes I think I've gotten out of this, back to "normal." But…this problem pops back up… hard to get rid of!

Maybe 20 years from now I'll laugh about this, but somehow I don't think so. Oh, God, why can't I have the answer or at least something to satisfy and give purpose?!...If my parents really knew me they'd be disappointed; I'm unworthy of all the nice things they've done for me.

As college was a time for questioning, so, too, it was a time for discovery. I experienced the history of art first-hand via a college art abroad trip, my junior year, in 1964. The textures and angles of side streets and ancient architecture were as thrilling as seeing museum originals by favorite artists. Traveling to Greece, Italy, France, Switzerland, England and Wales gave me a wider life-view as well as subject matter for future paintings and drawings. Textures, colors, smells, the taste of new foods and cultures, and an autumn bus ride through Tuscany that "screamed beauty," (as I expressed it in my journal), opened up my world. Though it was an art history trip, not a painting trip, I drew and painted every free moment. After this trip, I entered a watercolor I'd done on location in Venice in an adult competition and to my amazement took first prize.

After graduating with a Bachelor of Fine Arts degree from Principia College in June 1965, I was hired by the Benton Harbor, Michigan School System, to teach art mornings at Benton Harbor High School and afternoons at Fairplain Junior High. I leased my first apartment—furnished with little more than a sofa bed and a desk—in a new complex along St. Joe's Lake bluff, and drove across the St. Joseph River to teach in the two Benton Harbor schools. I never really got to know my colleagues well because I was what was called "an itinerant teacher," with no set place, traveling back and forth every day between two schools (there's that *moving* thing again!). Classes were large, mixed in abilities and backgrounds, and I learned as much about life from my students that first year as they learned about art.

My first day of teaching in the high school, I talked about beauty and asked the students to write about the most beautiful thing they'd seen that day on their way to school. One boy wrote "Elonzo Parker's jacket." Elonzo, black, gregarious, was wearing a paisley tuxedo jacket with a cumberbund and ruffled shirt. Another wrote, "A ten-gallon tank of water because we don't have any water at our house." A third wrote, "the way this school functions with everything so smooth." Those responses and others moved me deeply; I still have them in a file folder.

Only 21, an inexperienced and naïve teacher, I did not know—though I learned quickly—that many of my students came from underprivileged homes and their lives were very different from mine. Many of their parents were line workers, fruit pickers, farmers, or unemployed. Two hundred thefts a semester was not unusual in the high school. I had not the least bit of street savvy. I had never had a drink, smoked a cigarette, tried a drug, experienced a French kiss, used a swear word, or heard the word "rape"—all things with which my students would have been familiar. [I remember being startled one day at Prin to hear someone call out "damn" when he dropped a heavy load of books and I didn't hear the word "shit" until twenty years later at Rhode Island School of Design.]

Sheltered, yet intellectually curious about people and ideas, I spun a life for myself out of my religion, to which I was increasingly devoted (in spite of the brief period of questioning I experienced after reading Descartes my freshman year) living out of its principles, oblivious to any particle of the world that denied its teachings. Over many years I'd learned not to see the bad or ugly; much by-passed my consciousness.

Once, without my knowledge, several boys were gambling in the back of the art room, throwing coins on a towel so I wouldn't hear the sound; I didn't catch on for days. But the hardest thing was keeping a study hall of one hundred students, some just a few years younger than I. One day a group of senior boys all dropped their books at a designated time. Another day, they put a dead frog in my desk. Once a huge black senior came up and asked me for a pass to see Mrs. Baker (hall passes were required), and I wrote him the pass. It was a large school and I did not know all the teachers' names. It turned out Mrs. Baker was his mother, and he used the pass to go home!

My teaching days were edifying, happy and full. I genuinely liked my students and teaching made me feel purposeful. I entered art shows and sold my work in local and regional galleries. I taught Sunday School and served on church committees, rarely missing a Wednesday Night Testimony Meeting. For fun I walked the dunes or played bridge with Mickie and two other female friends working in St. Joe. Weekends I would see my parents at church and occasionally have dinner with them or with Aunt Alice and Unkie. I liked my independent, grown-up life.

When I began teaching in the Fall of 1965, I also began taking evening graduate level courses towards state certification and an education degree at Western Michigan University in Kalamazoo. I received As and Bs but found the courses less than stimulating and the long drive difficult at the end of a teaching day. Nevertheless, I continued and in the summer of 1966 completed my student teaching requirement in a small town south of St. Joe.

About this time, I let my hair grow down to my waist, purchased a then-fashionable black leather mini skirt and a pair of white leather boots. I was thin and attractive. Suddenly Cinderella made it to the ball. I went out dancing almost every night. I loved rock music and dancing. Sadly, my first few years in my twenties were my only dancing days. Like many women, I was to marry non-dancers. But in '65 and '66 I danced my heart out. Saugatuck was only an hour away—a charming resort town on Lake Michigan, with night spots popular with Western Michigan University and Kalamazoo College students, as well as anyone else who wanted to dance to live music. Sipping a Coke while others had their alcohol, I met attractive and interesting people my age. I always went with girl friends and we left when we wanted, no obligation to guys that way. And I would always be home in time to prepare for teaching Sunday School the next morning. It was all very innocent, compared to today's scene.

During Spring break1966, I took a Caribbean cruise with Margie, meeting fascinating people of all ages, among them writers, artists, intellectuals, Italian musicians. Enticed by everything, I wanted to drink up all of it—even the decorative rum cocktails which seemed to be an essential flavor of the trip. Though I had never had alcohol in my life, I wanted to be part of these intriguing people—and the drinks were pretty with their colorful little umbrellas and toothpicks of fruit. I discovered I could drink a half dozen without being affected. This was totally against Christian Science. I knew that full well in some compartment of my mind. But I wanted to be part of the romance, excitement, brilliant conversation, and freedom of ship life. I wanted to explore and discover all of life! I danced with the tall handsome tour director, "dated" the Italian soloist who sang with the ship's band, laughed with a witty 70-year-old woman who had as much verve as any 18-year-old, discussed deep subjects with men my father's age. The captain and others invited Margie and me to sit at their table every night. We were as active on that ship as stow-away mice. And to my Michigan eyes after a cold winter, the sunny islands were gorgeous—ideal for trying out my new bikini and getting a tan. Descartes and God were not on board.

For two months following the cruise I continued to go out, with Margie, Meg, or Mickie, ordering a rum drink and hoping for what it had come to symbolize: an atmosphere for political and creative talk. This was during the Vietnam era and I was becoming more politically aware. I knew of no political organizations in our town of 20,000 except the Republican Party, which my parents actively supported. I knew of no art organizations. So I wrote poetry. I read. I wrote letters and packed brownies for anonymous service men in Vietnam. I was concerned about a war that I did not understand, and living in a small conservative Midwestern town did not help me find the understanding I sought.

At the same time, I continued to teach Sunday School, attending church faithfully, more than vaguely aware of the disconnect between Saturday nights in a nightclub and Sunday morning in church.

Then I had a close call.

I had a date to go out with someone I had danced with in Saugatuck—I don't even remember his name or what he looked like. When he picked me up at my apartment he said, "Go get your toothbrush, we're going to Chicago." I was too shocked and embarrassed to ask questions but I got my toothbrush and called a substitute to teach my young Sunday School class. Besides, he was a pleasant fellow who did not drink too much and he was interesting to talk to. Most important at the time, he was a good dancer.

Chicago was only two hours away on the other side of the Lake. I'd driven there many times to shop or visit museums with friends. I'd even attended The School of the Art Institute of Chicago for figure drawing one summer between my sophomore and junior years in college. Maybe his invitation wasn't that unusual. Maybe lots of people went to Chicago on dates. I didn't know; I hadn't had many dates.

In the car he told me we would be doubling with a friend of his and his date. It turned out his friend's date, an attractive blonde, was a secretary for *Playboy*'s Hugh Hefner. She lived in a fascinating exposed-brick apartment not far from Old Town. We went dancing in Old Town's night clubs, one after another. The people we were with traveled around the world and their conversation fluttered around exotic vacation places and superficial accumulation.

Somewhere in the middle of the "beautiful" people's jet-set talk, I faded to my childhood. Suddenly I was in seventh grade sitting with my family, after church on a Wednesday night, in Isaly's—Marion, Ohio's soda shop— beside church people, laughing, talking, families mixing as they sat, filling several booths. I could feel the booth's vinyl seat sticking to the backs of my legs. I licked the soft smooth cream from off the hard cold metal spoon, pushing it against my tongue. Someone was telling a joke and my father was laughing. Wedged between Mom and Dad, across from my brother and several church friends, I felt included without having to say a word. I hadn't heard the joke then nor the one my Chicago companions were telling now. All I knew was this bar in Old Town didn't feel a bit like Isaly's! *It wasn't even fun.* Conversation just breezed the surface. At Isaly's talk went somewhere. But here the music was too loud and nothing of consequence was being said. There was a Vietnam War going on but these people talked of leather handbags and who they knew. There was an emptiness. It was a startling discovery that I was not having fun here, that I had actually had more fun at

Isaly's with my family after church on a Wednesday night! Why *was* I here? What was I doing in *a bar* in the first place?!

When we finally headed back to the blonde's apartment (I don't recall her name), I began to wonder what might happen next. We were given a room with a double bed. I explained to my date that I had never slept with anyone in my life and that I did not want to change that fact now. It may have been the permissive sixties but I was still a child of the fifties. I told him I was a Christian Scientist and that the tiny bit of drinking I'd done that night was totally incompatible with my religion, which was also my way of life. He appeared to understand, for he said he would honor my wishes. We lay down side by side, fully clothed, and fell asleep—actually *he* fell asleep. Probably the two-hour drive and seven hours of dancing and drinking had done him in. I lay awake, staring at the ceiling and pondering how I had gotten here and why. And contemplating Christian Science. I was supposed to teach Sunday School in about seven hours, but had called a sub before we left St. Joe because of this date. How wrong it seemed to be in Chicago. I wanted to go home. Clearly my sleeping date was too exhausted to take me there until morning.

At dawn, he awoke, took me for a hearty breakfast in a nearby restaurant, and we headed home to Michigan. In the car I talked continuously about Christian Science—every detail. More than I'm sure he cared to know. Perhaps I was talking as much to myself as to him. I wanted him to understand why I could not go out with him again. I wanted him to know how substance-less last night had seemed to me and that that was not what I wanted. I told him I felt terrible about even lying on a bed beside him. He seemed surprised, reminding me "nothing had happened." When we said goodbye, he seemed more interested in me than ever. I told him not to phone, but he called three more times. I never saw him again.

The Sunday I returned from Chicago I called my parents immediately and asked if I could come out to their house on Lake Michigan and talk with them. Their home was about half an hour from my apartment, and I drove there that Sunday afternoon rehearsing what I needed to say. I knew they must have wondered why I had not been in church on Sunday. I also knew that they had always been honest with me and I wanted to be honest with them. I wanted to report the weekend social drinking of the past two months, which included the cruise ship experience that had started it all. I had been questioning my allegiance to Christian Science in recent hours—all night long, in fact, lying on the bed next to a snoring stranger.

It occurred to me that I could not be a Christian Scientist any longer. I was unworthy. The hypocrisy of teaching four-year-olds in Sunday School and social drinking (albeit brief) was more than I could bear. I began to condemn myself. What was the point of my life anyway? What good was I accomplishing? What did anything mean? Of course I was teaching school, doing portraits, and entering art shows, but wasn't there *more* to life?

The Lake was turbulent. Waves crashed against the shore. I sat in my parents' living room, facing the massive glass window, watching the waves as I told my story. My parents listened attentively as I told them everything. I did not leave anything out. I ended my tale with "So I do not know if I can be a Christian Scientist or not."

My mother took a Kleenex out of her sleeve, sniffled a bit, but said nothing. My father was magnificent: he listened to me without interrupting—no small feat for him. Then he said, "I can't tell you whether you should be a Christian Scientist or not; but, let me tell you why *I* am one." And then he started in with the familiar story of his birth, relaying every healing he had experienced or helped with up to the present. He spoke without interruption for over an hour. By the time he was finished there was only one thing I wanted: to be a good Christian Scientist.

But I felt unworthy. How could I be a Christian Scientist after what I'd done these past several weekends? I had broken one of the Church Manual's rules: Christian Scientists do not drink. Worse, I was a Sunday School teacher. My father directed me to an article in the current issue of *The Christian Science Journal* entitled *Self-Government.* It was just what I needed. I wanted to talk to a Christian Science practitioner but there were only two in St. Joe/Benton Harbor, and I knew them both too well. I felt I needed to go beyond my town. I wondered if the author of this article might happen to be a practitioner, as was sometimes the case. I looked up her name in the listing of practitioners—no easy task since they are listed by state, not alphabetically, and the article did not indicate where she lived. Not only did I learn that she was a practitioner but also a Christian Science teacher (a higher accomplishment) and not only that, she was located in Chicago, her office only a few blocks from the Art Institute where I had made plans to go with friends next week! I was very impressed by the synchronicity of all this.

Next week I saw the Chicago practitioner and left her office with no more desire to drink and never did again for the next thirty-five years (though very rarely a glass of Berringer's white Zifendel occasionally finds its way into my non-Christian Science life today). What is more, I found that my Sunday School teaching and church work became essential; nothing was more important to me. I was committed.

What happened in that office? What happens in any practitioner's office? Conversation. Questions. Listening. A search for answers. Much prayer on the part of the practitioner before the patient arrives. When there's the Presence of God and one is receptive, one hears what she needs. I did. I realized that understanding God was more important to me than anything else.

After my first year of teaching in Benton Harbor, I ended my apartment lease in August 1966 and moved to Benton Harbor, closer to work. My new apartment was very private, one of only four to the building. It had a good kitchen, a fireplace, an extra room, a balcony—where I frequently ate dinner—overlooking a ravine of tall trees and only a five-minute drive to the beach. My second year of teaching, 1966-67, I continued to learn as much from my students as they did from their art teacher. I also worked part-time in a women's clothing store so that I could get discounts on clothes and earn extra money for furnishing my new apartment.

In late Fall of 1966, I met Helmut Horst Heinrick Stachowske at a party at Margie's house. Helm was over six feet tall, a blonde German Lutheran whose mother could speak very little English and whose father had fought and died for the Germans in World War II. Helm had been in the Marines in Vietnam and it had influenced his life in ways I would never fully know. He fascinated me. He had been born in Germany, somewhere near the Black Forest. He knew people who were in U.S. prisons, and he smoked, drank, worked on the assembly line of the company for which my father was Vice President. And he liked to dance. I think I was taken with all the opposites he presented. I wrote in my journal at the time "opposites together are a true delight." I felt I could help Helm. He attempted to go to community college for a while and I know it was my influence. We saw each other three or four times a week for ten months.

Dating Helm, teaching full time in two schools, teaching Sunday School and attending church regularly, exhibiting my art work, still taking courses towards an education degree and certification, working part-time in a woman's clothing store, I spent what little time was leftover walking the beach with life questions.

In May of 1967, at twenty-three years of age, I walked into Benton Harbor's News-Palladium editorial office—backed only by passionate beliefs—and naively asked to have printed in their newspaper an article I'd just written called *What is the Greatest Thing in the World?*' This took guts. Overwhelmed by society's lack of goodness and impressed by a little book I had recently discovered by Henry Drummond called *The Greatest Thing in the World*, I had written an essay—for myself—that contrasted Drummond's principles with the likes of Kennedy assassin Lee Harvey Oswald, murderer Richard Speck, Hell's Angels and LSD advocates. My outrageously preachy (but I didn't know it at the time) piece began:

> *If I stood behind a minister's rostrum, or lectured in a teacher's classroom, or wrote my ideas in a lengthy novel, you would not listen, so I'll meet you where you are, Mr. Reader, on your level of what is worth respect. I will sit beside you at your local bar, or in your office lounge, or on your gorgeous golf course, and here is where you will listen. You will listen because talk is easy here. And who am I, you ask, that you should listen? I cannot be learned or a man of inherent wisdom… You would not listen then. No, I have to be just like you to have your respect, for you to be attentive…let's say that I am. Let us say, that I am an American like any other… That could mean I am a Speck, or an Oswald, or… a Hell's Angel, a Berkley demonstrator, or an LSD advocate. I might be a draftdodger, eager to avoid an ugly but real situation. I might be a politician whose own love of power blocks pure justice and whose fear of losing popularity prevents courage to stand alone, if necessary, for what is right. Or I could be a businessman whose aim for success vindicates any means…I could be a father, disgusted by my teenager's drinking, smoking, and love of sex, yet, oddly, finding these habits to be my own…Maybe I am one who claims belief in equality, yet, quickly moves when a Negro buys the home next door….I could be an idealist, frustrated by the peril of our times, concerned to the depths of despair, but not concerned enough to seek a real solution of action….But whatever kind of American I am, I am an American and that entitles me to "life, liberty, and the pursuit of happiness"… What are these possessions of mine as an American? Just*

what is life? Do I really know or do I merely exist from day to day not caring to think beyond eating, sleeping and pleasure-seeking? (News Palladium clipping of my article).

Delineating American rights, I mention Webster defines life as spirit and that liberty includes freedom to govern oneself. For the third, "pursuit of happiness," I ask the reader to consider: "When we smoke one cigarette or buy one new dress are we content? No. Very soon afterwards we want more…an endless pursuit. But we are content when we help a child ride his new two-wheeler, or when we learn one new idea, or when we watch the sun come up" *(New Palladium clipping of my article).*

I ask my reader: "What self-sought pleasure can satisfy a man with such valuable, lasting possessions as these? The problem is he does not know he has them. They are too much buried…We must dig them out…use them." I refer to Drummond's theme that the greatest thing in the world is *love* with its ingredients of patience, kindness, generosity, humility, unselfishness, and I follow with ten questions, including: "Would a truly humble person care about self-power? Would a truly unselfish person have racial prejudice?" And I end with a history lesson from Muller's *The Uses of the Past*: "that the ancient enemy to civilizations has always been 'selfishness'—the egotism of nations as of individuals. Allied with it are the ageless forces of ignorance and stupidity, greed and envy, fear and hate. Today these forces are as active as ever, and more terribly armed. As the old adage has it, most men want peace but do not know or want the things that make for peace.'" My conclusion: "We must pursue unselfishness. Idealist! You ask for a solution. Well, here it is! But will you put it into action? The answer is, simply, individual unselfishness. In a larger sense, it is love. It is not easy…demands consistency of practice… So, all my talk has been ineffectual idealism, you say? Just useless words on an old theme? Well, let me ask you one more thing, Mr. Reader, Mr. American, have you ever really tried the old theme?" *(News Palladium clipping of my article)*

It now amazes me that the newspaper published this. At first the editor questioned me as to why I wanted my article published (he'd only skimmed it at that point). But the more philosophical our discussion became, the more he seemed to see my sincerity and understand my youthful zeal. In fact, when the article was published, his prefacing notes focused on a young person's idealism in a troubled 1960s world: "If the tumultuous ways of today's world sometimes leave mature observers gasping, what must they do to conscientious young people searching for anchors in a time of changing ideologies and morals?" (*News Palladium* clipping of my article). The newspaper insisted on including my photo which I did not want, but I complied. After the piece was published I received dozens of letters praising my article—from a diversity of people, even one from a man in prison and one from a university student who hoped to meet me one day and wondered if, as an artist (a fact which the editor's notes included), I had painted pictures on the walls of my bedroom.

My days in Benton Harbor were about to come to an end. I had the unique opportunity to go on a second Prin Abroad trip—the first trip the college had ever offered specifically for art majors. I had applied to be chaperone, but being just two years out of college, I was considered too young. I could, however, the school letter stated, apply as a post-grad student. With my 2-years of teaching savings and a little help from my parents I signed up. Late August through early December, 1967, I joined art professor James Green and fourteen other art students for four months of travel to England, France, Italy and Switzerland. I had to give up my homey apartment (but moving was nothing new by this point!). I figured when I returned I would launch my painting or teaching career somewhere other than Benton Harbor.

This painting and drawing trip was more wonderful than my first abroad trip. The 1964 trip traced Western civilization from Greece to England and opened my eyes to things I never had seen before; but this second, in 1967, let me draw and paint daily. Our art professor, James Green, who led the trip, believed in art the way devoted Principians believed in Christian Science. He was a strong, if occasionally quirky, disciplinarian when it came to art production. He felt church should fit in *after* painting. Once, he asked us to shorten a Wednesday evening testimony meeting we were in the middle of because he felt it had gone on long enough. Though he may have felt an allegiance to Christian Science, I never saw an iota of religious zeal in him. He demanded our best and critiqued our artwork mercilessly—which I considered good teaching, then and now. He was much fonder of the male students than the female. We women had to prove ourselves through our wits, intellect, and artistic ability, to be worthy of his attention. Older, attractive, more expressive and relaxed on this second trip, I got along enormously with James Green and my fellow art students. Above all, I loved making art every day.

Two experiences, however, were a bit frightening—might have been more so, had I been less naive. While painting alone in a very remote section above the Roman Forum, a man popped out from behind a broken column removing his clothes in front of me, a wild look in his eyes. Some internal warning siren went off in my being, telling me to grab my paints and *run*. I obeyed, soaring down the hillside, my heart beating so loud I thought even the naked man following me could hear it. Something told me to get to crowds *quickly*, which I did. When I looked back in the direction I'd come, there he was in the distance, still staring at me, without a stitch on! Though my heart was still pounding, I felt safe in the crowds as I walked back to my hotel. At this point in my life I'd never heard of the word rape but I now think that may have been his intent.

The second scary incident occurred along the coast of Normandy. As I walked alone to the beach, carrying my paints and easel, I was feeling happy, humming aloud—the sun was shining and I was painting in *France*! I seemed to have the world to myself—not a soul did I see. I picked a couple of wild-flowers to put in my long hair and took off my shoes to feel the sand between my toes as I walked parallel to the ocean through the long tunnel-like path of tall beach grass. I noticed a man on a motorcycle some hundred yards in front of me coming my way. Some inner-warning system sounded. I felt my body build a defense as he came closer. Revving his engine—apparently for my benefit—he laughed raucously. Focused on me, he slowed his motorcycle, saying something in French and grabbing my breasts. But, maintaining my gait I frowned at him, yelling one firm "No!" He threw back his head in a loud laugh and roared down the path. My heart, a pounding drum, I took a long time to start my painting that day. Sometimes I wonder if my walk at age three with my grandfather, when I said to him, "No see boys!" was a premonition establishing this early warning system within me.

Since these incidents, I have never been completely comfortable painting alone in remote areas—this saddens me, as some of the scenes I have wanted to paint have gone unpainted due to my uneasiness. Sometimes, despite fear, I have bolstered my courage and painted alone anyway, but the work was always compromised by my preoccupation in combating fear.

After painting abroad, I returned to the States in December with a hundred pieces of art—watercolor landscapes, cityscapes, and drawings—for my first one-woman show, in July 1968, at St. Joe's Maude Preston Memorial Gallery in the public library, selling most of my work. It was a success and I was very pleased, putting more of my work in a local gallery to sell.

But in spite of the artistic energy the trip had generated, I found myself soon in a slump. I had no job and no home. While planning my July exhibition, I had rotated my time between staying with Mickie, who had kindly stored many of my things in her apartment prior to my trip, and with my parents who had recently moved to Chicago. While In Benton Harbor I also saw Helm and my cat, Sneakers—whom a Sunday School pupil of mine had kept while I was gone. But Mickie's apartment was not big enough for two, nor was it my desire to infringe on her space—especially being unemployed as I was.

I'd had two years of living on my own, but now I had nowhere to go, so I moved in with my parents, who offered me the twin bed guest room in their temporary Chicago apartment. By now, Dad was president of Warwick Electronics which had necessitated their move from Michigan to Chicago. While their exquisite North Shore condo was being built, they leased this apartment next door. Though most of my things were stored in Michigan, their guest room would be my home for the next seven months until I could figure out what I was doing with my life. I hadn't a clue how to launch a painting career—that was not something we were taught in college—and no one was hiring teachers in January. Chicago was cold, windy, and alien. I felt awful.

I took temporary positions as a Howard Johnson's waitress and subbed a little for Chicago area schools. At Hojo's, not only was I given eight tables to wait on, but we frequently did our own bussing and were expected to make the salads and sodas, make the coffee, and set the tables in a specified manner. I remember that the Howard Johnson logo on the dinnerware had to face the customer and that when we made ice cream sodas the ice cream had to perch on the *edge* of the glass, not in it, and the glass had to sit on a saucer and we were expected to serve the item holding the saucer, not the glass. One day, a nervous little man who came regularly for dinner with his elderly mother, ordered a chocolate soda. I prepared him a perfect soda with care and as I placed it down in front of him, my hand slipped and the entire soda landed in his lap! I apologized profusely, showered him with napkins, made him another "on the house". It wasn't long after that I was made hostess. When I returned to my parents' apartment after long hours at Howard Johnson's, I was often too tired from my waitress job to do anything but kick off those horrible white shoes we were required to wear and count my tips—something I didn't get as a hostess—on the narrow strip of floor between the guest room's beds.

Since there was no place to paint in the apartment, my parents and I jointly paid rent for a tiny empty room above an Evanston store for that purpose, though it was hardly what anyone would call a studio. With little light and loud neighbors, it was nothing more than an empty 9' x 10' space, where I kept Sneakers (my parents would not consider having a cat in their apartment). There I did two oils, polished several drawings and watercolors for my July show, but mostly the room was where I kept my cat and cried. Eventually, the manager of the building told me my cat would have to go; apparently, when I wasn't there Sneakers would meow like crazy. I cried profusely—as my father had as a boy when he had to give up Snubs—all the way to the ASPCA and called back several times to make sure he had been adopted, which they said he was.

Desperate times often lead to something better. I had been an ardent follower of Christian Science on the trip abroad, studying Christian Science literature and weekly Bible lessons with an independent intensity untypical of the group. In fact, for me, the trip was nearly as much about growing in healing as painting. I had had several important healings for myself and had helped others, too, during the trip.

One of the more significant healings during that trip involved my suffering from severe bowel pain for several weeks, so much so that whenever I finished a meal I had to lie down and read the Bible, often still writhing. At one point in Venice, I was in such pain I took my Bible with me into the bathroom down the hall and read while on the toilet. Nothing seemed to help. The pain was excruciating. In utter despair, I laid down my Bible and talked directly, whole-heartedly, to God: "What would you have me do, God?! Why is this not being healed? What do I need to learn? Please show me!" The answer came as strongly and quickly as I was sincere. As if spoken words, I heard: "Love God more." In tears, I answered back "But I *do* love you, God—haven't I been studying and reading regularly? Always I try to live as you would have me live!" Then the words came again. This time with pointed emphasis on the last word: "Love God MORE!" Immediately, I understood. Yes, I could always do more. I could love others more. I could go further and deeper into expressing God's qualities in my experience. I could do better at putting love into practice. I understood completely. I was changed. Completely focused on this new revelation, I rose and walked back to my room. As I did, I realized the pain was completely gone. It never came again and I maintained an increased sense of love for everyone I knew or met, finding opportunities to listen or help others continually.

When I returned to the States, before returning to Chicago, I visited Boston with the purpose of meeting a number of people at Church headquarters to ask questions of them. I wanted to know all I could about my Church and healing. And I was looking for someone to be my Christian Science Class Instruction Teacher, for I had decided to apply for Class Instruction in Christian Science, a two-week intense course that prepares already deeply practicing Christian Scientists to do public healing. My Boston experience was mixed. I met several members of the Board of Directors, one who was more interested in ordering his lunch than talking to me when I was in his office and another whose answers had less depth than my own. But one editor of the periodicals answered every question clearly, creatively, with humility and a genuineness that let me know why I had so loved his editorials during the past year. This would be the one to whom I would apply for Class Instruction several months later.

When I wasn't waiting on tables, subbing for schools, figuring out how to make a living in my field, I prayed to God to learn what He would have me do with myself. At twenty-four, I knew I belonged somewhere other than my parents' home. I longed for a place of my own. Northern California had appeal: geographic beauty, freedom, art. I wrote letters to several school districts, but no one seemed to be hiring art teachers. In the late '60s the San Francisco area was full of art-oriented young people already residing in California. My Midwestern resume did not elicit much notice. So I dealt with Mother orchestrating my life at every opportunity, more than once finding some "nice Christian Science boy" to go out with me. I tried not to be upset when she and I were at odds about my life and where it was headed. When not annoyed with me, she was preoccupied with decorating her new condo into which they would soon be moving.

I never expected my parents to leave their beloved Michigan home on the Lake to move to Chicago, let alone to move twice within their first year in Chicago. Their Lake Michigan home on ten acres, about twenty miles outside St. Joe, was superb, private, and adored by my mother. My parents had moved there from our first St. Joe residence, the ranch house with the big picture window. The beautiful architect-designed Lake home was the dream home of its previous owners who built it. Rarely have I seen a better setting. Woods and clearings balanced each other. A long curving drive through woods and dunes led from the main road to the brick house perched 125 feet above the shore. Across the entire lakeside of the house, floor to ceiling windows let in the Lake vista. In every room one lived with the omnipresent Lake, rolling with its waves, whether calm or tempestuous. Large stone terraces with outdoor benches, tables, and furnishings flanked east and west sides of the house. Hills rose protectively to the north and south, uniting structure to landscape like a Frank Lloyd Wright building. In winter, the long drive back to the house could be blocked by blizzard snows, forcing the occupants to stay cozy by the large fireplace or get out the jeep which had its own snowplow [my brother drove the jeep to high school every day, never missing because of weather]. I suggested they name their place *"Gelli Lenor"* after the Evans homestead in Wales, apropos to the high dune hills, which they did.

Later, when I started teaching in St. Joe, Mickie and I would find a dune protected by the winds and sunbathe at my parents' home in February. In summer we would take the rowboat out on Lake Michigan or walk Socks, my father's black Lab, for miles down the beach or invite my Sunday School class for a picnic. I had hours to think on this beach. This home was nothing short of splendid and we all knew it.

You do not leave Lake Michigan once you get there; love for Lake Michigan is life-long. I still have it and if I allowed myself the indulgence would think of it more often than I do. To be absent from the Lake and think about it too often can be very depressing. You cannot understand the power of the Lake unless you have lived by it; it is instant romance. It is a powerful force that changes every day, playing out emotions in wind and wave. It is a true love only other Lake Michigan lovers can understand. I suspect my mother was one.

When my Dad was asked to take the Warwick Electronics position in Chicago, my mother seemed sad. Yet it was her nature to dutifully follow her husband and do whatever he wanted. In order to make the move more palatable for her, my father went all out on their Chicago North Shore condo. No expense was spared. He even managed to give her the Lake, from the Chicago side this time. Mom seemed satisfied and genuinely pleased to work with the California interior designer my father hired. She missed *Gelli Lenor*, but in this condo she and the designer built a prize-winning kitchen with every imaginable appliance and replaced all furnishings in the entire home with rare French and oriental antiques unlike anything my mother had ever owned before. She would enjoy the quality and dignity of these fine things. Above all, she still had the Lake, if not to walk by, at least to see from the windows of her Chicago condo.

To my mind the Chicago condo always had a bit of incongruity in representing my parents. I still marvel that oriental antiques were selected by the decorator to express home for my simple Midwestern parents. My mother's kitchen was state of the art, very sophisticated and efficient, lots of oriental tiles and stainless steel—incongruous with the Depression-era bowls she used to mix dough—and not a kitchen in which one expected the woman of the house to can her own peaches.

The music room walls were striated in pale blue and the dining room had breath-taking original silver leaf wallpaper imported from a museum in France; an antique French Empire crystal and gold chandelier swung from the ceiling when there was a good wind off the Lake (later to hang in my historic colonial home's front hall and now in my Bethlehem bathroom). The main living area which had large windows looking out to the Lake, had two nine-foot sofas centered by specially designed coffee tables of glass under which slipped three-feet wide circular tufted honey-colored antique leather ottomans. Four swivel arm chairs were covered in silk. The lamps were all custom made from exquisite oriental antique vases. Special bookcases were built to house the few books and china my mother owned. There was a handsome Biedermeier bureau over which an antique Venetian mirror was hung (since my Dad's death, they grace my bedroom). The drapes were heavy raw blue silk, layered with yellow fringe, framed with matching silk-covered cornices and between them, transparent white sheers through which Lake Michigan was always visible.

Emotionally for me, things were as turbulent as a Lake storm. As exquisite as their home was, it was not *my* home, nor was the temporary apartment they rented while all the elaborate decorating was going on. In either space I felt out of place. It was a difficult time for all of us. My father was the new CEO of a company Whirlpool had bought "in the red" and he had the mighty task of putting it "into the black." Painting in Europe had been inspiring and prolific, but I was now back home and "home" was suddenly Chicago where I had never lived and where I knew no one. My friends were on the other side of the Lake including Helm.

Our relationship had already been interrupted by my four month trip to Europe, but by not returning to Benton Harbor, I was continuing that interruption. Helm was so completely beneath my parents' standards that they made no attempt to hide their disapproval. I recall locking myself in my room (their guest room) in their temporary apartment in frantic tears more than once. I yearned for privacy. I was irritated by my parents' wealthy friends, and wealth in general. An artist trying to find basics, I was aware of the war, wanting deep meaning and purpose, but here I was, all my possessions in storage back in Michigan, living in someone else's high-rise on Chicago's North Shore, traveling back and forth on winter highways to see Helm. It was not a good situation. I was blind to the problems created by the contrast in beliefs, aspirations, living styles and values of Helm and my parents. I simply felt pulled apart.

I recall my mother buying me an extremely expensive (contrary to her frugal nature) pale blue sequined designer's evening dress for a North Shore party. I knew no one in the Wilmette/Winnetka area and was forced to go. My mother had arranged a date for me through her friends. She'd made several such arrangements. As she saw it, she had to "save her daughter from destruction." She and my father were desperate to have me marry "a good Christian Scientist". I don't think they realized that some they arranged for me to go out with were not as "good" as they supposed. Besides, at the time, I was not interested in anyone but Helm.

New Year's Eve weekend 1968, I drove to Benton Harbor to stay with Helm, his mother and brothers. When I arrived at his house, New Year's Eve Day, I was met by a hysterical woman shouting in both German and English that there had been an accident. When I calmed Helm's mother, I pieced together what had happened. In early morning hours, Helm was driving back home from a night out and his car was struck and totaled. He was in intensive care and not expected to live. His mother had no car of her own and his brothers were working, unable to take her to the hospital. I drove her immediately.

I had never been in a hospital in my life. It was like entering a foreign country, only far more intimidating. As I walked the halls while his mother sat in the small waiting room of the intensive care section, all I could hear and see was fear. Everyone in the hospital seemed frightened. As a Christian Scientist I'd been taught that fear is the root of all problems. I knew I had to get close to God, Love, if I were to help Helm, his family, and myself. I had my Bible and Christian Science books in the car and ran down to the parking lot to get them.

In the waiting room, I became totally absorbed in reading and praying silently.

I also called my father to report what had happened. "I can't really work for Helm can I, Dad?" Christian Scientists are extremely ethical about not working in Science for anyone who does not request help. Dad explained, however, that in an emergency one *can* work for another and that one can always work to clear her own consciousness about the situation. I did not ask my father for help. I felt I had no right to ask a real practitioner for help since Helm detested Christian Science, made fun of it in fact. We had had many debates on the topic. I had read the Lutheran catechism hoping that he might, in turn, read *Science and Health*, but he never did.

In that sterile environment, with Helm's life in jeopardy, I dove into my books. I read randomly from Psalms, the Gospels, the mid-section of *Science and Health* where passages are especially strong, and throughout Mrs. Eddy's *Prose Works*. I ran across the familiar passage that "perfect love casteth out fear." It came to me that if love permeated the hospital, fear would disappear. I felt driven to love with all my might.

While in the hospital I worked at seeing everyone as a loved child of God. I knew I couldn't "sort of" love or be merely kind and smiley. I had to *feel* it internally, deeply, genuinely. I had to commune with God so completely right there in that hospital that anything less than love would be an impossible expression. It was as if light bulbs had come on in a dark tunnel. Love took me over. I found myself loving everyone. I struck up a conversation with a scared boy sitting nearby. We became waiting room friends and he offered me his last stick of gum. I struck up a conversation with a woman there because of her husband's heart attack who was reading a book about psychocybernetics. I watched her brow relax as we talked about the influence of thought on one's wellbeing. I spoke as if I made a habit of conversing warmly with strangers in waiting rooms, feeling no shyness, only an overpowering sense of love.

Even though I was not a member of the family and only family members were allowed in Helm's room for brief intervals, the hospital nurses let me visit him. He was unconscious, full of tubes and things, as if he were not real. I spoke aloud to him, though he was unconscious, telling him God, Love, was with him and that I was praying for him.

I felt appreciation for the doctors and nurses who were doing the best they knew. I smiled from a genuine inner radiance and felt a deep peace when I walked down that hall. I truly felt a divine presence that came from seeing God is in charge of us all, that He is Divine Love and we are held in His arms. It was as if I watched fear disappear, first from my own consciousness and then from the entire intensive care area.

That night was New Year's Eve. Helm's mother did not want to leave, so we stayed until morning. Earlier in the evening, Helm's brothers joined us. About 1:00 A.M. a black woman was brought into the intensive care section, wheeled by in a hurry, with plastic hoses and contraptions attached to her. An accident patient. Her husband paced the floor of our waiting room, distraught. I was in the middle of a conversation with one of Helm's brothers about Christian Science, our voices the only sound in the still room. As I continued, " Christian Scientists believe love ought to be the basis for all our actions, for it is the foundation of health, a preventative of disease, and a minute-by-minute demand on us, for we are all the children of a loving God." I followed with examples of healings from my own life to illustrate, and then concluded: "No problem comes to us except for the lesson of loving more." The pacing husband looked straight into my eyes. He had been listening to every word. He glanced our way frequently, slowing his pace as I continued.

A few minutes later, a doctor called the stranger out of the waiting room. And just as quickly, the stranger returned, smiling. Apparently he had learned his wife would recover. Though we had never spoken before, he walked directly to us and offered his hand, "Happy New Year to you both!" Helm's brother took the black outstretched hand and returned the greeting, as did I, and the stranger left.

What may seem a small happenstance was actually numinous. All day, members of Helm's family had been making angry racial comments because the car that struck Helm was driven by a black man. That hatred had been reversed with a handshake. In the middle of the night I had shared that God is the Father of us all and we had witnessed love replace hate through the simplest of exchanges. Love is powerful. God, Love, is the most power ever available to us. We access this power when we dwell in love and let our words and actions be genuinely loving.

Months later, when Helm was out of intensive care, I went to the hospital to visit him. As I walked towards his room, I saw a blonde girl about my age standing by his door. As I walked down the hall the first reaction that came to me was: "This is another girlfriend; I should feel jealous." And right on the tail of that came: "No! Love is needed in this hospital! Love is needed everywhere and is your reason for being. How can I feel jealous of love that heals? We need all the love in this place we can get." By the time I reached the door I honestly felt only love toward this person I'd never met. "How is he?" I asked her. "Better. I'm just leaving," she answered and left. I walked into his room with only concern that he be well. He could barely raise his eyes to say, "Thanks for coming. I knew you were praying for me. Thanks."

Months afterward, when Helm was home and I was visiting from Chicago, he said out of the blue: "You know, I didn't want to tell you this but the doctor told me he almost gave me up. He told me `something else took over'. Those were his exact words. I knew you were praying for me; I could feel it. I don't like to admit it but I know it was your prayers that saved me."

It was a few months after this that he mentioned marriage.

But I had changed. Something had happened to me, too, in that hospital. I had found a deeper confidence in myself and in my relationship to God. I had learned under dire circumstances how to heal. I'd experienced healings all my life, but this was different. This was big. I gained a new and deeper understanding. And wanted more. I desired to understand this power of Love as fully as possible. I spent hours in prayer, alone with my Bible and my thoughts. I visited Chicago Christian Science Reading Rooms studying periodicals regularly. As I learned more about *real* love, I began to see that was not what Helm and I had.

I made a continual effort to love every person I saw—first in thought, then in action. I did not let a single individual pass me without doing this. It became easier to live with my parents and they seemed to enjoy me more. I also applied what I was learning about Love to my maternal grandmother who was losing her eyesight and experiencing effects of aging. I tape-recorded readings from the Bible and *Science and Health* and other writings which I thought she would find uplifting and kept her in my thought as God's child. When her health improved, my father teased me about "hanging out my shingle" as a Christian Science public practitioner.

In early June 1968 my parents, brother and I vacationed in Kauai, Hawaii. We flew over a volcano, listened to Don Ho music while dining nightly on seafood, and enjoyed the magnificent beach. I walked the shore, reading and writing to know God even more deeply—and body surfed in my new floral bikini.

One day as I came out of the ocean, a tanned blonde young man came up to me, introduced himself, and we started talking. A Navy officer and college graduate—in school again, for something to do with submarines and nuclear weapons—he said he was from Texas, here for rest and relaxation. He asked me out for the next evening and took me to a club he had never been to. It turned out to be a stripper club and I was very embarrassed—I'd never been to such a place—which, in turn, made him uncomfortable. So we left and drove to a place where we could talk. We discussed the Navy, oceanography (his love), teaching, philosophy, politics, Christian Science, the meaning of life, art, music (he was a singer), his former brief marriage, Helm, and more. He was quick, smart, expressive, with a terrific sense of humor. As he walked me back to my hotel, I carried my sandals through a field of wet grass. When I surprised myself by stepping, barefoot, on a huge frog—the biggest I'd ever seen!—I screamed. Looking down, I discovered that the entire dark field was covered with frogs the size of small cats! I continued to squeal all the way to the hotel. My date thought this particularly amusing, but I was petrified of those amphibians!

My family and I were to leave the next day, and my friend was due to return to his Navy duty, but he phoned me late that night saying he'd write, that he couldn't stop thinking about our evening together. I was sure he was just being kind.

But he wrote me long entertaining epistles for a year—each rich in humor, wit and surprising adoration. I received a letter a day —actually, three the first day. A portion of one read:

I know you must think I am too forward for my own good. I'm not usually forward in any way. I'm a mild introvert who usually distrusts people at first meeting. This thing that has hit me has changed all that. It was hard enough to sit down beside you on the beach Friday and start talking, but to have developed the affection I have for you in two days is, by all rights, impossible and very unlike me. But, like I said, I just can't stop myself. You have had an impact on me that I have never felt before, mainly because I don't allow other people into my being. But, you came in and appear to have completely rearranged everything you found...I guess I've given you quite a shock and what I feel for myself and my actions is a sort of repugnance. I never could understand or tolerate a sentimentalist, but here it is! The monkey's on my back now. Sane people don't think the thoughts I'm having now. I've just GOT to know you better. I'm glad now that I blew my cool with you (which is what I did). I would have suffered more from not having taken a chance with you than I do now from fear of seeming to be a romantic fanatic. You have no idea of the agony I'm in now and was in yesterday. I want to let you know that I hold dear and respect everything that you are without sounding like a love-sick seventh grader. And I don't appear to be doing very well. Sorry. But how can I get you to believe me when even I can't imagine myself behaving this way. I'm dumfounded. My peace of mind is obliterated. Since I found out what a woman was I've developed an image of that perfect woman (like everybody else) and you fit that image so precisely that I'm completely stunned. There you have the entire matter. I could never hope that you see half as much in me. I know my faults. I don't fool myself. Just know that you have thrown a different light on everything I see and think. Do you see? Just a little? ...

I didn't see at all. So ignorant was I of the ways of dating, of my feelings, that I assumed his words flowed from his creative wit—not from a serious interest in me. But the letters continued:

I should interject more of my feeble explanations of what you represent to me, but I doubt that I could avoid repetition if I did. So, let it suffice to say that I'm still awed by your very existence in this maligned world. You are incredible and very, very welcome. If, twenty years from now, I could say "I have known an unadulterated, vibrant capsule of infinity named Lewis, [he even remembered my middle name] *a hater of amphibious life forms, I will have achieved at least the mezzanine on the elevator of mortal happiness. In other words, I have to acquaint myself with you as extensively as I can before life or luck takes you back to your natural habitat or me back to oblivion. See?*

I *still* didn't see. What a paragon of density I was! Surprised, overwhelmed, and happy to receive his letters, I nevertheless remained certain he couldn't be *really* interested in Gwendolyn Lewis Evans. He was a very bright, gifted and entertaining writer—and I wrote him back, though not daily. He planned to come to Illinois to see me in late October, his next leave, which I looked forward to. But life would intercept these plans.

I had accepted an art teaching position for the upcoming school year and was preparing to attend Class Instruction in Christian Science in August with Alan Aylwin, the editor and Christian Science Teacher I had enjoyed talking with in Boston, whose editorials in the Christian Science publications always hit the nail on the head for me—his words seemed to specifically address my every need to such a degree that I could almost guess his article's theme before I read it. A Canadian, Alan Aylwin held his classes in Toronto, so I flew there for the sacred, deeply serious instruction that prepares one to become a public practitioner of Christian Science healing. An intense spiritual study, Class is both like and unlike academic learning and in August 1968 it was a turning point that would take me entirely away from Helm and my Navy officer, and bring me closer to God.

In class I asked all my questions and found answers. What I did *not* expect to find in class was my future husband.

eight

A Doll's House

Long before I visited the Chicago Art Institute's Thorne Miniature rooms and admired their perfect reality, I wanted a doll's house—one my father would make for me, like other girls had. But my father didn't make things; that's not what he did. A doll's house was not just a place for a little girl's imagination to run freely, it was where small people—just like one's real family—came alive. Every little girl knows that at night when full-size people sleep, dolls wake, move from room to room, talking, laughing, dancing. When one Christmas I eventually received a simple store-bought doll house, I did all I could to make it a special home—decorating it, making pictures for its walls and finding dolls small enough to live in it. One night I made myself stay awake to peek out of my covers at my doll house. There was Joanna taking Betsy out of her crib and carrying her to her tiny high chair in the kitchen! She was telling her a story in a voice so small I could only hear whispers, but after that I always knew a doll's house was real. Years later as a young mother I built a very special doll's house complete with shingled roof, wallpaper, furniture, a brass door knocker, miniature fruit, china, books, and even a kitchen fireplace with tiny bricks on the floor that I laid in grout one at a time. I made it for my daughter who, it turned out, didn't care for doll houses at all.

New Harmony's roofless church is decked with flowers today. Along the river bank, a wedding party poses smartly for photographers. I watch a breeze blow the bride's hair out of place as she tries in vain to keep it picture-perfect. Will she keep her marriage picture-perfect? The scene reminds me of another summer wedding years ago.

I married John West on Father's Day, June, 1969. Nine years later I would write on another Father's Day to my dad: "I love the fact that John and I were married on father's day, for in a way, he is much like you—you both put God absolutely first. They say daughters pick husbands like their dads. Maybe it's true. Maybe it's a way of keeping a father's qualities with us every day." John really was nothing like my father, except for his love of Christian Science. Prior to our marriage, John wrote to me from his home in Ohio to mine in Michigan about his view of our relationship: "Our main focus in this relationship is further advancement in Christian Science and a demonstration of completeness."

John and I met in Toronto in the summer of 1968 while taking Christian Science Class Instruction, the two-week program of deep study to prepare one for the public practice of Christian Science. This gave him my parents' seal of approval. John, a moral Christian Scientist, sincerely devoted to the Cause, opened doors for all the older women, said very little in class, and smiled genuinely from under a crop of John Kennedy hair.

I had the habit of identifying classmates with passages I'd been studying, much the way one reads a novel and associates the characters' traits with their acquaintances. In his general kindness to others, John seemed to express page 312 of Mary Baker Eddy's *Miscellaneous Writings*: "Love is consistent, uniform, sympathetic, self-sacrificing, unutterably kind; even that which lays all upon the altar, and speechless and alone, bears all burdens, suffers all inflictions, endures all piercing for the sake of others, and for the kingdom of heaven's sake (Eddy, *Miscellaneous Writings*, p. 312).

At the end of class, John offered me a ride with him to Ohio where he lived and where I had planned to visit Dad's younger brother—my Uncle Bill—and his family. John lived in a suburb outside Cleveland not far from Uncle Bill's home in Hudson. During our long drive, we discussed what we had learned in class and our families' experiences in Science. John dropped me off at my uncle's home and then drove on to his family's home. After my visit with Uncle Bill, when it was time to fly to Chicago, John called and offered to take me to the airport. To my astonishment just before I got on the plane he kissed me! I was stunned. I just figured he'd given me a ride to Ohio and driven me to the airport the same way he opened doors for little old ladies. I was wrong.

That Fall I started teaching school again. Not in California as I had hoped, but in Glen Arbor, Michigan, at The Leelanau Schools, a coed private institution operated by Christian Scientists but open to students of any denomination. The schools were located in the northern part of the state along Lake Michigan in the Sleeping Bear Dunes area, some of Michigan's most beautiful terrain.

I found a small cottage to rent right on Lake Michigan in Glen Haven (population at the time: 25) just a fifteen-minute drive to school. It usually rented to short-term summer vacationers but I convinced the owner to let me rent it for the full school term. With knotty pine walls, galley kitchen, small room for art, two tiny bedrooms, a wide windowed living room viewing the Lake, and a back porch for watching sunsets, on miles of empty white sand beach—it was perfect! My only "neighbors" were an old abandoned Coast Guard house, a light house, and a couple of empty summer cottages several hundred yards away. Basically, nothing but the dunes and me. I loved the peaceful isolation, the sunsets on the Lake, the absence of civilization. It was sheer bliss for a year! I had to drive an hour to Traverse City, the closest town, to get groceries and do my laundry, but I didn't mind because of the beauty of the drive and the home I came back to where "Love," my German Shepherd-Collie mix pup waited for me, a gift from a friend of my brother's who taught Russian at the school.

I taught both humanities and studio art to high schoolers and joined the local Christian Science church, teaching Sunday School. I spent time with a seventy-year-old white-haired hermit-poet, "Uncle Whit," whose published poetry I had read for years, someone familiar to me from previous family vacations in the area. And I still received letters from Hawaii from my Navy letter-writer and corresponded with my Christian Science classmate, John West.

In two months time, after only a half-dozen times together, John and I were engaged. When he asked me to marry him I felt as if God told me to say yes. There were no bells, no mad passionate love, just a sense that this was right. I felt a Christianly Scientific love for John as he did for me.

In her book, *The Fifties: An Oral History*, Brett Harvey describes the end of that era as a time when getting married, embracing everything domestic, and elevating family life became a national obsession: "The institution of marriage had a power and inevitability in the fifties that it has never had since. You simply didn't ask yourself if you wanted marriage and children; the only relevant questions were when and how many? And the answers were, as soon as possible and as many as possible" (Harvey, *The Fifties: An Oral History*, p. 69).

In 1969, I seemed to be a decade behind. Though Harvey's book wouldn't be published, nor would I discover it, for 25 more years, I would have fit right on its pages! Fifties women "were expected to seek—and find—everything in marriage and family: love, identity, excitement, challenge, and fulfillment" (Harvey, p. 71). As one woman in Harvey's book puts it: "Marriage was going to be the beginning of my real life." (Harvey, P. 71). I assumed it would be my real beginning, too. In 1969 I could not imagine a better profession than wife and mother. Marriage to a good Christian Scientist, someone as dedicated to the movement as I, seemed paramount. Our union would follow God—a goal class instruction cemented. John and I discussed how we would live our lives serving God and church.

My parents were ecstatic about my meeting my future husband in class. They went all out for a sensational June wedding in a Unitarian Church [Christian Scientists not having ordained clergy, marry in other churches] on Father's Day with an outdoor reception in the neighboring park in Winnetka, Illinois, near their Lakeshore condo. My mother took me to Chicago's Bonwit Teller where I selected my wedding gown at a bridal fashion show. The dress had been in *Vogue* magazine that month. My parents also bought me several original Geoffrey Beene designer dresses to wear to showers and pre-wedding parties. I recall sitting in a private French rococo salon where models came in wearing gowns and dresses—like something out of a thirties movie—and I would say which ones I'd like to try on.

On the morning of the wedding, a hairdresser styled my bridesmaids' hair as well as my own (Mickie, from high school, was my matron of honor. Karen, my brother's wife, Ann, my cousin, Jinny and Ellen, from Prin days, and Bev, my new sister-in-law, were bridesmaids). To aid my mother, a woman was hired to do nothing but see that the wedding went smoothly. Mom made the bridesmaids' long pink gingham skirts with big sashes that I had designed to go with beautiful high collared, long sleeved lace and ruffled blouses from Bonwit's. She also made the dress and white pinafore for the flower girl (one of my Sunday School pupils), my going-away suit, and her own silk dress. I designed everything and Mom did the sewing. Each bridesmaid was given a basket of flowers to carry rather than a bouquet. Actor Robert Duvall's brother, a Christian Scientist in the same Ohio church with John, who had sung in the New York Metropolitan Opera, was the soloist. He and his lovely wife had given us a musical engagement party weeks earlier. My father arranged for an elaborate wedding rehearsal dinner at the Mid-America Club in downtown Chicago overlooking the Chicago skyline. After the wedding, the Berlandez Orchestra that played regularly at the Drake Hotel accompanied the guests as they danced. In the cloistered park adjacent to the church, nearly six hundred people dined on fillet mignon and sparkling Catawba juice under pink umbrellas at pink linen-clothed tables.

Our first home was a rented trailer. John had left college due to poor grades and joined the Air Force, serving as clerk to a general in Thailand. When his Air Force time was up, he returned to school, but this put him behind me by a year when we met, though he was ten months older. He was finishing college when I was teaching at Leelanau and still had a few courses to complete when we got married. He arranged for us to rent a trailer while he finished at Bowling Green State University near Toledo, Ohio.

Just married, living in a crowded trailer with few of our belongings was not easy for me. I had had, by this time, two apartments and a Lake Michigan cottage on my own, paid for by my teaching, art sales, and occasional other employment. Now I was closed in by thin metal structures so tightly packed together there wasn't room for a tree and by neighbors' loud music and yelling—people I never met (nor did I want to). Nor had I a dime of my own. While John went off to school, I stayed home, cooking and cleaning, trying to play "housewife".

Marriage to me, at that time, meant homemaking, family, responsibility, commitment, and forever. Eager to be the shining and virtuous wife, I saw my role in the "Father Knows Best" world of matrimony and domesticity to be divinely ordained, established by the will of God. Though I did not realize it at the time, it was as if I were still in my childhood closet directing paper dolls, only this time the paper doll was *me* and the doll's house was a rented trailer.

I was an ignorant virgin when I married and naively grounded in being a "good girl". To the best of my knowledge, my husband was no more experienced. That's how I figured it was supposed to be for good Christian Scientists. I'd studied neither anatomy nor biology, had been exempt from most science courses, and knew nothing about the human body. Good Scientists waited until marriage for sex which was mainly for the purpose of creating children. In Christian Science one is always overcoming the material in striving to be spiritual.

I immediately discovered marriage to be nothing I assumed it to be. Disappointed in the honeymoon—three days in Boston looking for jobs at Church headquarters—and early months of marriage in the rented trailer, I didn't feel deeply close to this person who said he loved me, except as dutiful students of Christian Science. Marriage did not match the myth. Where was the romance? Where was the intimacy? Where was the close sharing of ideas, books, dreams, plans? I had imagined long talks, cozy in bed. John was a good person, so I kept my disappointments to myself.

I took a course in creative writing at the university in order to get out a few times a week. And I began to worry. John had no prospects for what he would do at the end of the summer when he would graduate. We had to be out of the trailer by mid-August when its owner returned. *Where* would we live? *How* would we live? I spent a great deal of time thinking about these issues between planning menus and writing. John had no money. He had told me that up front. His most unusual and unforgettable proposal had been: "I have no money and baldness runs in our family but will you marry me?" (Amusingly, today at 70, he still has plenty of hair!).

A couple weeks before our lease ended, we got positions as boys' dorm house parents at Principia Upper School, a boarding and day high school for Christian Scientists in St. Louis, Missouri. Our apartment in the *basement* of the boys' dorm was two rooms connected by the tiniest galley kitchen with a small bathroom. Recently, in cleaning out a file, I found our 1969-70 contract which said our salary was $4,000 a year, plus room and board! At the time, we viewed this as a blessing and part of God's plan.

With jobs as wife and homemaker underway, I turned to my next anticipated role as mother. This, too, in the beginning was a disappointment because my first pregnancy was a miscarriage in late September of 1969. We had barely settled into our basement lodging in the boys' dorm of Principia. I knew no one at the school when the miscarriage occurred, except Lydia, the kind Christian Science nurse on campus who came and talked to me outside the bathroom door as I went through the experience.

I've had three miscarriages in my life. They have run together in my mind now, but recently I came across notes I'd made at the time of the first one. I mention being alone in the boys' dorm, singing hymns to myself and working harder than ever for a healing. John was at work, chaperoning a school dance. After the miscarriage—a term I had never heard of until I experienced it—I phoned the doctor who was to deliver the baby to let him know. He asked if I wanted to make an appointment to see him, which I declined, saying I would be fine. But my experience with the practitioner I'd called when the bleeding began was different. I wrote about it at the time in my journal:

> *The practitioner alarmed me by saying, 'Why, you don't believe that God's man can go down the toilet do you?!—that's not man!' The crudeness of it sent me into hysterical crying. I had just the night before had such progress, being alone, singing hymns in our basement apartment while John was on duty in the office that night. I had sung every hymn I knew and read references—about Elizabeth, Mary and Samuel's mother, Sara, in the Bible—women given babies when it seemed humanly impossible. It had been a glowing time. The practitioner's outright declaration that I had had a miscarriage was too much. I called her back and said I could not understand what she had said. A confusing conversation followed. She then came to see me, as she comes regularly to school to see student-patients. I felt as if she were treating me like a two-year-old as far as what she thought I knew of C.S. Her sing-song voice just didn't penetrate my thought. I told her that I didn't care if she was a practitioner I was not going to listen to anyone trying to tell me that I hadn't studied hard enough. I told her of God's presence at my father's birth, at my marriage, and in many healings I'd had. I could not understand her certainty of miscarriage. I felt strong. It came to me to love the practitioner—I had not felt it before. She apologized for her 'crude way of speaking.' The next day, however, I was very sad about the miscarriage. I fought hard to be slightly happy. Alone,*

the next afternoon and evening (John was on duty again) and knowing hymns bring joy, I went through the hymnal, singing every hymn aloud, deeply thinking about the words. Absorbed, I obeyed the words of one: "rise" And sat up in bed. Finally after a number of hymns, I was able to get out of bed, still singing, and walk into the living room. I sat there on the couch singing when John returned from the dance he had chaperoned. I was feeling truly joyful. He had brought me a helium balloon from the dance which I held—I was a picture of conquered despair. I went to church the next day.

My desire to be the perfect homemaker and mother was challenged by life in a boys' dorm. Everything I had been raised to understand about being a good wife was denied place in our two rooms below ground. Cooking was unnecessary because we got free meals in the dining hall while supervising the students. I, the eager bride, was enthusiastically clipping recipes, but there was no need. To buy extra food and eat in our apartment was not economical, but we did it now and then when the desire for a few moments to ourselves or my inclination to be domestic overrode economics. I could not clean; the woman hired to clean the boys' rooms cleaned our rooms right in line with the other dorm rooms down the hall. I could not decorate; we had no money. My other role, left to the unliberated woman I was at the time, was to please my husband and that was accomplished in spite of his long and off-beat hours on duty as houseparent.

My houseparent responsibilities were minimal. I would chaperone dances and events as I had done at Leelanau and fulfilled the unassigned role of counselor, reaching the more rebellious male students or talking to girls from the other dorm who missed what a mother might have provided. I created and taught an exercise/appearance course for girls with a housemother who became a good friend, taught private art lessons, and sometimes gave speeches for deans' meetings and student assemblies.

This was not enough. I hungered to be making art and did the next best thing I could think of: I got a job working at an art gallery part time, doing publicity for shows, taking frame orders, waiting on customers, stocking, modeling for portraiture classes, and assisting the owner in any way she wanted. I also taught Sunday School and was active on many church committees. Later, I became Sunday School Superintendent, a librarian for the

Christian Science Reading Room, and head of the church nursery for which I wrote a manual and collected creative materials and furnishings.

I longed to have a baby, especially after the miscarriage. I neither knew about nor used birth control; it wasn't necessary given our limited intimacy. I was overjoyed when on October 13, 1970, Jason, our first son, was born, naturally and without drugs—a healthy nine-pounder. We named him Jason, which means to heal or make whole.

At the time of Jason's birth I learned that I am RH negative and John is not. 85% of all people are RH positive; only 15% are like me, RH negative. RH negative blood type means that my immune system sees the baby's RH positive cells as foreign and produces anti-bodies to fight them, thus the fetus or baby may die as these anti-bodies get into the baby's bloodstream via the placenta or other means and attack the baby's red blood cells. Once these antibodies are created they remain present and the danger of death increases with the number of pregnancies. Many babies die unless Rhogam shots are given to the mother in early pregnancy or prior—shots I never had.

As soon as I got home from the hospital with my wonderful son, Mom came to help. She made brownies for the whole dorm to celebrate and I displayed Jason to the wide-eyed high school boys through the glass window in my husband's office in our apartment, which looked out into the dorm hall. The boys were fascinated by Jason; he was the pride of the boys' dorm.

I adored motherhood! I read all the child care books from Spock to the more *avant garde*, trying to be the perfect mother. I learned that my own innate sense of mothering was more reliable than the experts, and I gained confidence quickly in the ways of breast-feeding, diapering, bathing, and utterly enjoying God's gift.

Several months into mothering Jason I learned I was pregnant again. I was stunned, given the rarity of intercourse. I had just worked to get back in shape and was taking a modeling course. Professional pictures had been taken and the modeling school suggested I'd be a good Saks Fifth Avenue model.

While visiting my parents in Chicago, I made a comment one day suggesting my lack of enthusiasm about being pregnant so soon after Jason. Dad, as only he could, told me in no uncertain terms that I'd better work on my attitude. I saw instantly that he was right and went into their study where

I picked up *Prose Works* by Mary Baker Eddy and earnestly asked God why this pregnancy now, allowing the book to fall open where it would. My eyes fell on these words, a biblical quotation from John 1: 12, 13: "But as many as received him, to them gave he power to become the sons of God, even to them that believe on his name: which were born, not of blood, nor of the will of the flesh, nor of the will of man, but of God." Eddy's article that followed explained our *preexistence* as God's child: "When we understand man's true birthright, that he is 'born, not ...of the will of the flesh, nor of the will of man, but of God,' we shall understand that man is the offspring of Spirit, and not of the flesh; recognize him through spiritual, and not material laws..." Immediately blown away by this message, I realized that this upcoming birth was not of two mortals' doing or timing, but God's. Once I read this I could hardly wait for the arrival of *God's* child, for that is truly who each of us is.

Fifteen months later, our second son, Nathan (which means "God given"), was born, in February of 1972. The school gave us a larger apartment on the second floor and knocked a hole through to a dorm room to give us a room for our two sons. Sometimes my boys would wake crying in the middle of the night when a student prank occurred on the floor—a favorite was stacking a tower of empty coke cans against a student's door so that when he opened it the tin can pyramid came crashing down, sounding like World War III. Many a night I held two heavy crying babies in my arms, walking the floor, while John was in the building's first floor main office pulling late night duty. There were no neighbors to help or talk to; just me, the babies and God.

I began to wish my parents lived closer so they could see their grandsons regularly. But when my father left the business world in 1970 to become a full-time Christian Science practitioner, first in downtown Chicago, later in Boston, their lives became even more complicated, so I became a copious letter writer, telling my parents every clever thing their grandsons did—and what their daughter was learning.

Eight-months pregnant with Jason, one hot August day in 1970, with the water shut off in the dorm for several days for plumbing work prior to the start of the new school year, I found myself writing a 20-page letter to my parents, a small portion of which follows:

Thinking about past and present, I become overwhelmed by God's government of our family—three generations… from Grandma's fearless faith, taking precious grocery dollars for the purchase of her first Science and Health, through her many healings that grounded her in Science, and in turn her sons, through your never-failing trust in God, a life lived courageously, Dad, and Mom's quiet unselfishness, through Rich's inner calm, and my growth 'through deserts into paths of peace'—Look at the strength God gives us all! Do we realize the ramifications? What lives it has touched, helped, healed? Often someone says to me what a unique family background I've had. Yes, it has inspired my progress…made me strong…provides me with all I need to raise my own family. Truth lived daily. For being raised to understand God is at the core, I am grateful.

Two years later, when at the request of the Board of Directors of the Mother Church Dad moved to Boston to accept the position of Trustee of the Christian Science Publishing Society (a position he held from 1972 through 1977), I wrote to my parents:

I wonder what your life would have been like had you not had Christian Science. You are traveling that diagram you drew for us from the material to the human to the divine. How well you give up material things for spiritual! Have you any idea of the magnitude of gratitude I feel for both of you as models for right living? And don't let it go to your heads (which I can't imagine you would) or you will shatter my faith in your example!

Absorbed by church work and motherhood, I also took on the joyful task of helping students work out their problems, showing them how to trust God in their daily experience. I also found time to be a gourmet cook, give parties, decorate our dorm apartment creatively on a limited budget, and learn tailoring—making clothes for the boys and myself (complete with inner linings and buttonholes). I became active, too, in the St. Louis art community, joining the St. Louis Artists' Guild and entering monthly juried competitions. I painted regularly—usually on location for I had no studio—and put my work up for sale in local galleries and shows and took some prizes.

After three years at Prin, when John took a desk job at a trucking company and Jason was two and Nathan under a year old, we moved to a real house, 94 Thorncliff, Kirkwood, Missouri. Our new neighborhood, a suburb of St. Louis, was a wonderful mix of diverse ages and backgrounds, with charming small older homes, trees and curving streets abutting a golf course and railroad tracks. Our backyard vista of expansive, steep, green hills and trains was ideal for two little boys. We tobogganed down the golf course hill in winter and walked near the trestle to wave to the train engineers or count the box cars as they rattled by. I have happy memories of those five years playing with my sons in that caring neighborhood. In fact, all my St. Louis memories are happy ones.

In St. Louis I formed strong lasting friendships, three remain so today, for spiritually deep woman who raise their children side-by-side do not lose touch, even if one moves hundreds of miles away. What we experienced as mothers—and as woman over forty-some years—has bonded me to each one.

MaryKay, a devoted Catholic and mother of five, with a gregarious nature, love of people, and wonderful understanding of what matters most in life, and I became friends. We lived only a few houses apart and saw each other nearly every day as we watched our sons play together. Mary Kay and I have long been on the same wavelength. She once commissioned me to paint murals on her daughters' bedroom walls and today she has a number of my framed paintings in her home. She has visited me in several of my homes since I left St. Louis, and I hers, and at least twice a year we phone, finding catching up is not difficult when two are journeying spiritually, similarly.

Robin, another St. Louis friend of long duration, I first met at Prin College, but knew better once we moved to St. Louis and worked at the Upper School. A talented photographer, Robin was frequently my on-location painting buddy when our babies were young. A generous volunteer at Principia and Christian Science churches, Robin and I shared similar duties, values, and parenting experiences, and, to this day she has been a kind ally of my writing. Over the years I have loved watching her beautiful family grow through emailed pictures.

Diane, my third St. Louis friend, I knew well in college as we were both art majors. We reconnected and became very close when John and I came to Prin Upper School to houseparent, for Diane's husband worked at Prin Upper School, too. We kept in touch when I moved to Tennessee, once arranging together with another friend to put on a St. Louis portrait workshop for famous New York artist, Daniel Greene; for that week I lived in Diane's home and remember well our nightly deep discussions on spiritual matters, church, healing, parenting, art, and more—as well as rib-splitting laughter watching *Fawlty Towers* videos with her and her family. Though she recently passed away, I can only think of Diane alive, vivacious, loving her gorgeous daughters, her dogs, the deer in her backyard, and just about everything else that is good in life.

When I married Bill in the early nineties, all three of these friends loved his humor, who he is, and took him into their hearts as if they'd known him as long as they'd known me. I will always love these three women, for our journeys, though each one unique, have been similar.

Dozens of kids lived in our yard on Thorncliff. Sometimes I would invite them in for tea parties or get out paints and let them make as big a mess as they liked; other times I would make old-fashioned picnics for them in the backyard. Helping two "pirates" desperately seeking a flag for their "ship"(alias the wood pile) or hunting up poster materials for a mock national election in our front yard when Jimmy Carter and Gerald Ford were running, was all part of the fun and spontaneous creativity of motherhood.

The boys and I grew our own vegetables—spinach, lettuce, onions, peas, beans, tomatoes, cucumbers and squash; the boys sold the leftover squash, cucumbers and tomatoes in the front yard from a stand they made with my help. Paints and paper, Legos, building blocks, books, puzzles, matchbox cars and British soldiers, were in the sandbox, under the living room couch, in the bathtub, between the sheets of my bed, on the stairs and occasionally even in the refrigerator. Even my watercolor board had a layout of streets I'd drawn with black marker on the reverse side for matchbox cars—a certain remedy when painting on location with my two boys went too long and little hands needed to be occupied while I finished a painting—along with others, I still use that same plywood board today and it makes me smile to think of its history. Being the mother of two sons was the best creative experience. I drew or painted my sons in their cowboy outfits, napping with the cat, and at every possible opportunity. I also painted walls and turned the basement into a playroom for the boys and into a very small art studio where I taught a few lessons. I stitched curtains for the walkout basement windows and laid my first tile floor.

I still see those little guys in their Osh-kosh overalls and stripped engineer hats with Railroad logo patches they had selected at the train museum, which I'd sewn on their caps. Every day they chose to wear hats or some sort of costume. Later it would be cowboy hats and boots, and after a trip to Williamsburg, tri-cornerd hats and my old blouses with ties at the neck so they could be true colonials when they played Revolutionary War. Imaginative play was central to their fun. We made tents in the house with sheets and sofa cushions, and snow forts outside in winter—once a snow fort so elaborate that our yard became a labyrinth of tunnels. We built villages with Lincoln logs, wood blocks, and Legos filling several rooms. We built train layouts with detailed towns. We walked in the nearby bird sanctuary counting the different birds we saw. We painted murals on butcher paper as long as the driveway. We went to the library each week and could not be satisfied with less than six or seven bedtime stories each night.

Bath time was playtime, too. Sometimes it was difficult to find the child needing to be washed with all the toys and apparatus in the tub! Plastic tubes from the hardware store were terrific for blowing bubbles; we had several of different sizes. There were rub-a-dub-dub characters in a Fisher Price tugboat and special wooden sailboats their grandparents had sent them from Cape Cod. There were assorted sponges, kitchen utensils, plastic books, plastic men, plastic animals, plastic cars, and one weird whale that when wound up spit water and traveled in circles.

I loved all aspects of motherhood, among them the humorous things children do and say. I would gather my sons' spontaneous words into books I would illustrate and send off to grandparents. When Jason got his first pair of sunglasses he picked out red ones and after trying them on said, "They keep my eyes nice and warm!" Another time after a walk in the woods, when Nathan was not yet four, he asked me, "Mom, why did God make *ticks?*" And another time, "How do they know what size to make toilets so they fit *everybody's* bottom?" My little boys always kept me laughing.

I loved my home. It became my canvas. Lots of time to play with my sons, picking fresh flowers for vases throughout the house, baking organic whole-wheat bread, making soy pancakes and home-made peanut butter, ironing weekly and freezing vegetables seasonally were essential to the design. I "painted" every season and holiday in rich color and detail. Especially

Christmas: the truest test of quality motherhood and housewifery, (tongue in cheek). I stuck cloves in oranges, wound grape vine wreaths for the door, wrapped presents with recycled satin and lace instead of Target's best buy, put candles in every window and remembered to plug them in each night, climbed on ladders to hang fresh greenery around exterior doors, sewed original stockings for the fireplace, served 20-dish party buffets I created in my tiny kitchen single-handedly, arranged neighborhood caroling, taught my boys to make pie crust and decorate fancy cookies, strung real cranberries on thread, heated aromatic spiced cider, sprayed pine scent in every room, created handmade ornaments for the real tree which I purchased and put up myself for at least four Christmases, carved chocolate Yule log cakes made from scratch and decorated with meringue mushrooms and mint leaves, painted cookies like paintings while my sons licked beaters and bowls, kept carols on the record player and candles lit regularly. All long before I'd ever heard of Martha Stewart!

Sundays were mini-holidays. With sons sparkling in matched sailor suits (or sometimes coordinated outfits from the children's specialty shop, Chocolate Soup), we left for church by 9:00 A.M. so I could teach Sunday School or attend to my superintendent duties. John, First Reader for three years, had his own obligations on a Sunday morning as well. Being on time was crucial. The routine began at 7AM when I awoke, made German pancakes for breakfast in the kitchen and set the dining room table for Sunday dinner with the good china and crystal, napkins, and always fresh flowers. Then I prepared the roast, potatoes, and vegetables and placed them in the oven, setting the timer on Time Bake so that the meal would be ready when we returned from our two or more hours at church. I made salads on our special bird-patterned plates and put them in the refrigerator to keep cold. I fed the cats, bathed the boys, poured the juice, served breakfast, got dressed, worried about my hair, hunted for pantyhose without a run, ironed John's shirt, slung on my heels, and grabbed my Bible and *Science and Health* with the week's lesson notes for teaching my class as we sailed out the door. In the early days, a wet diaper could wreak havoc on this schedule!

Perhaps it was no surprise that I began to dream about a house in the country surrounded by nature's tranquility. While my boys slept, I designed solar houses. Some day, I thought, I'd like to have more solitude, time to paint, grow more vegetables, raise Newfoundlands and chickens on land of our own. The ideal home was formulating in my mind and it was not the one in which we lived.

My brother and his wife, Karen, started their family about the same time we did. While my brother was getting his law degree at Washington University, they lived in St. Louis. We had good times together living in the same city as new parents and members of the same branch church for a couple years. Then they moved to Kansas City, then to New Jersey, and later, Hong Kong and we rarely saw them.

I would watch my friends go shopping or have lunch with their sisters or mothers or take their children frequently to play with their grandparents—those grandparents experiencing every stage of their grandchild's development from crawling to walking, a new tooth, a first word, while knowing my children would see their Gramps and Grandma not more than twice a year. I think my mother was almost as frustrated by this as I. She used to tell Dad, "The only vacation I want is to see my grandchildren." But they rarely took time off due to Dad's Christian Science practice and church employment.

As Dad's business career dictated where we lived growing up, so, later, church work dictated how infrequently he and my mother visited their grandchildren. Dad left the business world in 1970 for full-time Christian Science practice in downtown Chicago and in 1972, at the request of the Board of Directors of the Mother Church, moved to Boston to become Trustee of the Christian Science Publishing Society, a position he held through 1977. He also was made a Christian Science Teacher in 1973, responsible for hundreds of students, in-depth classes, and annual addresses. In addition to these duties, in 1980 he became a Christian Science lecturer, touring cities all across America, Europe, and Asia. His responsibilities were massive, unfathomable to most, and his students and patients were as important as family.

In the early seventies I drove alone with my baby sons from St. Louis to Chicago to see my parents because I wanted the boys to know their grandparents. The boys were only two and three the first car trip I drove alone. I got good at it the more I did it. I would buy matchbox cars, cellophane drawing slates, and other little surprises I would wrap along with hand-made items like my "find the object" game, baggies of cookies I'd baked, and tapes of stories I'd recorded (with unexpected surprise questions for the boys inserted into the stories). Periodically I would toss one or two of these gifts into the backseat; this—along with singing—kept them busy and happy as we drove the eight hours. Another time I drove them to see my childhood home in Michigan, staying with my friend Mickie and playing on the sandy beaches; several times I took them to see my aunt and uncle and cousins on their Ohio farm. Now it seems crazy that I made these treks alone, but John, whose work sometimes included Saturdays and who read in church on Sundays could not always get away.

When my parents moved to Boston, I flew with the boys to see them for a week every summer. For several years my parents maintained both a Back Bay Boston penthouse apartment near the church headquarters and a lovely home on Cape Cod. Attending The Mother Church, visiting the museums of Boston, trips to the big library (almost next door) became part of our annual visit. Mother purchased tricycles for the boys who loved riding in the maze of landscaping and concrete paths near their Boylston Street high rise. We would make treks to the nearby fire station so the boys could see the trucks and meet the firemen or sip a perfect chocolate soda at Brigham's. My parents' penthouse was framed on two sides by a glass-enclosed patio where Mom grew tomatoes and the boys played—she even kept a tiny inflatable swimming pool out there for them. From here they could see all of Boston. When a fire engine sounded its alarm the boys would rush to follow it with binoculars. Through those lenses they discovered dogs in alleys and cats in windows, boats, motorcycles, the changing color of the sky, and found places they had walked. They never watched television in Boston; real life was much more entertaining. I, too, loved these Boston trips.

On Cape Cod, the boys loved fishing with Grandma on her dock or canoeing with Gramps on the large pond behind their home. Sunday mornings the boys would get up at dawn to ride with Dad to Sully's for fresh-made doughnuts—a ritual of every visit that the boys still recall. Every visit we would buy huge lobsters and have feasts on the deck. Mom would make clam chowder with clams the boys dug on rainy days. I would take them to Plimouth Plantation and other historic sites. Good times for all!

Often I returned home inspired. After one trip, I wrote my parents:

I never fail to learn something each trip to Boston. I can't begin to write all my observations, but when I sat in the Mother Church and heard the Bible story of the fiery furnace, I realized that their "goodness" did not keep those three men from having that horrific experience, but that their goodness and trust in God did keep them safe through it—a lesson for my own life. A church member came up to me after I'd given a testimony and said, 'When can we get you to become a lecturer?' I was shocked! To my surprise, several people were moved to tears by what I said. I told of our cat's healing after being struck by a motorcycle, of healing the flu, and of helping a neighbor with a problem. I said I asked myself if I really loved enough, and answered myself, 'I think so'…but then, I answered, 'if I really loved enough, I'd be healing like Jesus'. There is always more to do! I spoke about church work's aiding my spiritual growth and said: 'Christian Science is darn hard work but worth it, you do it because it's all that matters.' It was the best testimony I ever gave because when I stood up I felt God take over, no 'I,' words flowed.

But in another letter to my parents I wrote:

Why is lack always with us? Before I was married I never had this problem; being unlimited defined me. . . It's not that I want lots of things, it's just that when I go to the grocery I'd like to be able to buy what we need. I have had to buy two weeks supplies for $35—that demands extreme planning, home-made items, soup often, and no meat other than hamburger…kills me when Nathan says he wants orange juice and I have to tell him there won't be any for two weeks. . . .no money for eating out or movies…John spends all his time preparing to read for church and works Saturdays for the company; he doesn't seem happy with his job, nor they with him. If we hadn't received a financial gift from you and money from my art, we wouldn't be able to make this month. Our house needs painting, we need a new front door. I'm not wanting a solid gold swimming pool, just orange juice, a gallon of milk, and maybe the right to be caught up with bills!

By next month's letter I had earned money in an art show. Ever able to make something out of nothing, I tell about giving someone a house-warming party for which I made tiny chicken sandwiches, cream puffs, Peruvian cookies, and cheesecake. Mom found my letters charming, for as a child of the Depression, she appreciated my *creating* my way out of financial difficulty. She'd done the same in her youth.

One cold winter's morning when Jason was three and Nathan, two, I buckled the boys into their car seats to take Jason to Prin pre-school, pushing the lock button down on the car door prior to slamming it shut, as usual. What I did not know, as I went around to the front driver's side, was that Jason's *hand* was in the door! The wind was howling and in those few seconds, I never heard his screams until I opened my driver's door. At first he was screaming so much I did not realize what was wrong, but soon horrified by what I had inadvertently done I ran to the other side of the car, fumbled for my key in my purse to unlock the back door and release his hand. Without looking at his hand, I held him close with all the soothing words a frightened mother could find and ran with him into the house where I grabbed a kitchen towel and wrapped it around his hand so neither of us could look at it or be impressed by what had happened. I immediately called a local Christian Science practitioner and told her, as best I could with a screaming child in my arms, what had happened. She said she would begin praying for us and told us to come to her home office immediately; we did. I asked Nathan to join me in singing hymns as I drove. By the time we arrived, Jason's screams had turned to tearful whimpers. The loving practitioner said a few comforting sentences to us about God's ever-present love and control. Then, she talked directly to Jason, asking him a few simple questions, finally asking to see his hand. When she unwrapped the towel—it was the first time any of us had looked at it—she said, "Why, Jason, that is a *perfect* hand!" And it was! Not a drop of blood nor mark! The practitioner said, "Jason, you and your mother are very good Christian Science practitioners!" I drove my smiling son on to preschool.

Another time, Jason fell off a swing, fracturing his elbow (as we were told later by a doctor). He would not stop screaming in pain no matter what I did to console him. John removed himself from the situation as he usually did, insisting it was easier to heal if you didn't see the physical evidence. But the "evidence" was in *my* face as I held my anguished child, trying simultaneously to "know the truth". I thought we ought to go to the hospital, something we had never done before for ourselves or the children, to have his arm looked at since Christian Science allows setting broken bones. But John did not agree and left the room. The practitioner I called refused to help me because I was considering going to the hospital and added, unprofessionally, "What would your *father* say?!" From that day on I vowed to be my *own* practitioner and never call anyone for help again. God and I alone would do the work. I took Jason to the hospital, even got John to go with me. We had to wait two hours and when a doctor finally saw us, he x-rayed Jason's elbow, verifying a fracture, and said "There is nothing I can do, but put it in a sling—keep it in the sling for three weeks." In two weeks Jason had removed the sling himself with normal use of arm and elbow. I learned another lesson: that medical means are not particularly compassionate nor immediate.

From the moment I gave birth to Jason I realized that not a precious moment of childhood should be lost. When Jason was four and Nathan three, I pulled my boys out of Principia pre-school, where they'd had one year, in order to do "unschooling". I had become a fan of educator John Holt's "Unschooling Movement." A portion of a letter I wrote to him prior to meeting him in his Boston office is published in his book *Teach Your Own*. I wanted more time with my sons, time that I would not get again. Our "school" included trips to libraries, Shaw's Gardens, the St. Louis Art Museum, Kirkwood parks, county parks, the "Y" for swimming, and visits to the Transportation Museum.

But while I loved being with my boys, I was concerned about John who was not happy with his job. In 1974 I wrote my parents:

> *John had a talk with his boss today and was told that he wasn't putting enough into the job, wasn't working to full capacity. John says he doesn't want to stay there. He needs to make a decision…whatever he wants to do. I can't do it for him—I have all I can do with everything else! Did you know you can make three meals for four people from one fryer chicken?*

Three years later I wrote again to my parents:

> *John said he will stay in his current job, which he doesn't like, until he enters the full-time public practice of Christian Science. I told him he could start at home and heal Jason's crossed-eyes and our problem of lack before he tries public healing!*

Dad agreed with me that John ought succeed at some work prior to going into the practice. I hoped he'd find what he loved and do it.

When I wasn't occupied by money-woes, marriage concerns, church duties, domestic duties, and the joys and challenges of child-rearing, Vietnam captured my attention. I was reading *Fire in the Lake*, about Vietnam, and crying when TV news dropped battles in my kitchen as I prepped dinner. I had an idea—one I still think has merit: there should be an organization formed whose address would conclude each news broadcast, its purpose to direct viewers to a means of helping about any news item given that night—not a mere list of charities collecting money, but *action* one could take. Finding solutions to world problems became a continuing desire. I sincerely cared about every suffering individual. Was I trying to solve world problems because I couldn't always solve my own or because we are all one, and, instinctively, I *felt* for others as I had for the children without shoes back in first grade?

An extraordinary international opportunity came my way in 1974 when my parents were invited to be the guests of Karen Figueres at her home in Costa Rica—an American by birth, a Christian Scientist and student of Dad's, whose husband, Jose Figueres, had just completed his third term as President of Costa Rica. In 1942, Jose Figueres spoke on radio against the Calderon government's corruption and was arrested and exiled before the transmission was finished. Exiled to Mexico from 1942-1944, he formed his own *Partido Accion Democrata*. A year later his party joined with the intellectual *Partida Social Democrata* and in 1948 he was the leader of a revolution—a civil war of five weeks duration. He became provisional President of Costa Rica for eighteen months and was elected president from 1953-58, once again in 1970-74. Known as Pepe by his people, he was beloved for his many political and societal accomplishments. He improved banking, welfare, education and women's voting rights. He abolished the military, resolved his country's electricity crisis, and founded the Committee of the Second Republic that wrote the Costa Rican constitution. Figueres had just completed his final presidential term when my parents and I were his guests.

Karen had invited my dad several times to come for a visit—she longed to talk with him as her practitioner/teacher and she wanted to show him the San Juan Christian Science Society as well as her adopted country. In the fall of 1974 Dad found time. My parents knowing I needed a break, asked me if I wanted to go along; Dad knew I might be a companion for Mom when he was busy. For ten days I stepped out of marriage and motherhood, something I had never done. A friend kept my boys after preschool, fed them dinner, and kept them until John picked them up after work.

When I landed in Costa Rica I was welcomed by Karen Figueres who handed me a bouquet of flowers, and by my parents who'd arrived a few days before. We were hustled off to a bodyguard-driven car. En route to the Figueres' estate I stared out the windows at palm trees, vivid green hills and bright blue sky. I was reminded of Greece, Italy, and Hawaii all at once. I was glad I had brought my paints.

We arrived at the guardhouse behind an electrified gate where a guard saluted as our driver sped through as if on his way to a fire. Manicured lawns, blooming flowering plants, and a greater variety of palm trees than I knew existed greeted me. Our cottage, down from the main house, consisted of a living room, a kitchen and dining area, two bedrooms, a bathroom and a covered terrace. The wall-hanging in my room had been a gift from Anwar Sadat to the Figureses. My window let in perfume from exotic orchids Karen proudly grew, as well as the sound of boots of the machine-gun-toting guards patrolling regularly. Karen told us her husband, Jose, would not let her plant trees to conceal the ugly electric fence because someone could hide in the foliage and shoot him.

Their home nestled in lush vegetation of bougainvillea, brilliant flowers, coffee, avocado, and banana plants. Baskets of orchids hung from covered walkways around tiled terraces. Inside their home was a gracious simplicity of fine things: native wood ceilings, artifacts and rare international gifts, a museum of pre-Columbian pottery dug up during excavation for building their home, giant oriental rugs in a red-painted library.

The next day while my father met with Karen, Mom and I were driven to a fashion show put on by the Israeli ambassador. We sat with ambassadors' wives from France, Malta, and other countries which my halting Spanish kept me from knowing. What does a young housewife who speaks only English say to wives of foreign dignitaries?!

Each day was a whirlwind of extraordinary activity, far from the life of an American Midwestern mother. I painted frequently in spite of daily rain showers, the humidity protecting my watercolors from the powerful sun. One day for lunch we had baby octopus with blackish green rice. One night Karen arranged for a band to serenade Mom and me, during which Karen handed us each a beautiful orchid from her own garden. One evening we were taken to the National Library to see an exhibit of one of Costa Rica's most famous painters (though I met him, I no longer recall his name). We saw the children's library which Karen had built. She introduced us to the Minister of Culture, the Minister of Youth and Sports, and other ministers whose titles came too fast to remember. The same day we saw more art in the late afternoon, including artisans of gold, pottery, and leather. We attended the symphony at the National Theater, sitting in the government box near the Presidential box. We went to Grossi Valley where peasants dried corn, picked coffee beans, and plowed fields with oxen, while children without pants or shoes stared at us shyly. I still have a painting I did there; it nearly drips with humidity.

One dark night, about 11 P.M., Peppe, as Figures was called, took Dad to meet Dr. Louis Bouristan, a Communist whom Karen called "Rasputin." Peppe, Bouristan, and American fugitive Robert Vesco, were in the process of starting a newspaper. They wanted to talk to Dad about the newspaper business because Dad was one three trustees for the *Christian Science Monitor*. Mom and I teased Dad about his "clandestine meeting," promising to look for him if he didn't return.

One afternoon Mom and I were driven to the Russian embassy by Peppe's spooky-looking bodyguard with the strangely distorted face (he looked like he might previously have worked for Al Capone). I was surprised by the embassy. Here in the seat of Central American Communism were elegant marble halls, circular stairways, crystal chandeliers, carved balustrades, and a pool! The Russian ambassador, Vladimir Kasiminov, could not have been more gracious. We were his only guests and he offered us vodka, which much to his dismay we politely refused. After her previous engagement, Karen joined us, speaking about one of her favorite causes: freeing the Russian Jews.

To honor my father, the Figures gave a gala dinner with government ministers, ambassadors, and political officials—perhaps over a hundred in attendance. Orchids and candles decorated every table. I was seated beside the wife of the ambassador from the People's Republic of China; we discussed watercolor painting—in what little common language we could manage. Guido, the Minister of Culture, played Chopin on the piano and Peppe talked of his recent visit to Czechoslovakia, Hungary, Yugoslavia and Rumania. He said that we in the West are being propagandized negatively about these countries; that each one is an individual country and should not be seen as part of a Communist whole; that none are over-consuming as is the U.S. He said the U.S. is being fed lies by its press. He saw the U.S. as a place where faith is lost and problems of consumption, inflation, insecurity, and materialism control citizens' lives and we in turn control the lives of people in other nations. This opened my mind to a new point of view.

Karen told us about the black and the white witches that live in the mountains: primitive Indians that practice witchcraft by burying objects in the ground to harm the owner of the land. One must dig them up and get rid of them to undo the harm. Karen was popular with the people for her humanitarian work. One morning a white witch came down from the mountains and gave Karen a small gold figure that he had made to protect her from the bad witches. This same day I wrote in my travel journal: "I can not imagine how I will be able to go back to being a housewife."

Karen passionately spoke of the revolution of 1948 and how Peppe became a national hero. She told us of being in San Jose and saving her baby, hiding him in a suitcase while sending 6,000 oranges to her husbands' soldiers in the mountains—he'd hoped for hand grenades. Karen told us about *La Lucha*, the mountain hideaway where Peppe and his men retreated during the revolution, organizing to restore democracy to Costa Rica and repel Nicaraguan invaders.

One day we were driven to *La Lucha*. As we approached I saw men with machine guns on mountaintops, standing guard; an eerie feeling came over me that only increased as we drove further up the long private road. Cypress trees, banana trees, coffee plants, hemp plants, begonias, poinsettias, and a variety of tropical plants I could not identify surrounded the place, in fact, almost hid it. The lodge itself was strange and cold; Karen said it was the influence of Peppe's recent enchantment with Communist countries. Walls were bare; there were a few rough pieces of furniture; empty shelves and tables—except for one book about the Mexican Revolution. Paper and paint covered windows hiding the gorgeous mountain landscape. This saddened Karen, for following the revolution she had known *La Lucha* as a refurbished country home complete with chandeliers, curtains, and elegant furnishings. She said she had not been here for a year; both *La Lucha* and Peppe had changed since his trip to the Iron Curtain countries. Following a picnic lunch with the Vice President of the country and other government people who casually appeared, we left *La Lucha*, left Peppe and his governmental friends to their meeting.

On the long journey home, Karen told us about her young teenage daughter, walking in on her father in bed with another woman. Now I could understand why I had seen the girl crying at dinner and perhaps the reason Karen had long talks with my father. The children at times seemed preoccupied with their thoughts, sad even. Now I understood. Their twenty-year old son, articulate, gracious, and my dad's tennis partner, reminded me of a young prince as I wrote in my journal, "so princely, he has such mastery of people and circumstance." Following West Point and Harvard, he became President of Costa Rica in 1994 and from what I have read is vitally involved in the UN, in sustainable environmental issues and communication technologies. His sisters, too, apparently have and are serving the world largely, as did their mother, Karen, as ambassador and Congresswoman.

As we left Costa Rica with Karen's gifts of pre-Columbian pots, unearthed on her land when they built their home, I took more than pottery; I took a new sense of what can be accomplished by the industry of a single woman. Karen had impressed me with her intense schedule and led me to see how much more I could be doing with my life. I had also observed once again the compelling power of divine love, for my father had attracted even ambassadors to his side asking questions about Christian Science, listening to his stories of healing. My last journal entry of that trip reads: *I will be strong...do more... accomplish more good. I will grow, love. My time is God's. I will listen and obey.*

Back home to laundry and Legos, I retained insights from my visit to Costa Rica. I read more about other countries and followed politics closely. I worked harder at everything, taking on more duties at church and entering more art shows. I volunteered to paint walls at the local elementary school—hundreds of yards of nature's creatures illustrated in their environs to brighten the place. I started the habit of teatime—inviting my children's friends to join the boys and me daily in interesting conversation and delicious treats—just as Karen Figueres had done with groups of children in her nation. I listened to people, touching them on the arm as I'd observed Karen do to show care or concern. My interest in international matters grew as did my desire for the *more* of life.

Being church's First Reader took most of John's non-job time. One day I noticed he was also struggling with a physical ailment, for he would collapse, unable to walk or climb stairs and in obvious discomfort. In his mid-thirties, he seemed like an old man. He got thinner and seemed to retreat into himself, wanting to be alone with his problem and solve it, not giving in to the material evidence, not wavering from his religious beliefs. He blocked me out. Whenever I asked if I could do anything, hoping he would share with me so I could help, he refused to discuss his situation, saying he "didn't want to make a reality of it". Being a Christian Scientist, he was, of course, never diagnosed, and I could only guess that perhaps his attacks, which continued for nearly a year, were heart-related. Since he was incapable of doing much except reading and praying, I took on added duties, while raising our preschool sons, painting, and keeping our home. I wrote in a letter to my parents: *It seems as soon as I turn around, panting from rallying from the last siege of things to cope with, another fierce battle is upon us.* Some nights I'd lie awake wondering if my husband would be breathing in the morning.

As First Reader, John's duties included conducting Sunday services and preparing readings for Wednesday Testimony Meetings. During his long illness, I recall more than once doing the reference work necessary for him to create a Wednesday's readings. And many a time I put his page markers in the books on the way to church. It was not unusual to have dinner at 10:30 PM when we got home. Years later, I, too, served as First Reader. Studying, selecting themes and readings can be a gloriously uplifting and consuming work, sometimes eight hours a day, Sunday through Tuesday. If done well, the preparation generates healing for oneself and the congregation. John was eventually healed of this situation, a healing confirmed when a physical was required for a new job.

During this difficult period, one day while watching "The Wizard of Oz" on TV with my sons, I saw symbolism for my situation. When Dorothy threw water on the wicked witch, she melted. It seemed to me this was a metaphor for what happens when Truth drenches a problem. Dorothy was faithful in her pursuit of home, on her path to wisdom symbolized by OZ in the utopian Emerald City. Obediently following the Yellow Brick Road wasn't easy. The faithful path can be difficult. The "straight and narrow" path involves steadfastness, self-discipline and overcoming the temptation to fall asleep along the way—like Dorothy's poppy fields—when material thinking disrupts spiritual focus. It seemed to me that we needed the same things Dorothy needed and found in her friends: a lion's courage, the woodsman's love, the scarecrow's intelligence.

Above all, Dorothy sought HOME. She and her friends went to The Wizard as an all-knowing leader and discovered that what they needed they already had *within* them—including Dorothy's ability to find home. They had to fight the wicked witch and take away her broomstick before their freedom came, just as a Christian Scientist has to take away fear's hold to free himself. In so doing they all learned to rely on the traits they thought they lacked. The Wizard merely made them aware of who they are, aware of what they already possess. When Toto, Dorothy's faithful little dog, pulled back the curtain and revealed the Wizard for what he was—like innocence leading the way to truth—Dorothy and her friends learned that the Wizard was not in the spectacular, just as Dorothy learned that power comes from one's own inner strength—much like the discovery of God *within*. The cyclone, like any tumult in one's life, can pick us up, throw us down, push us on a journey to the God within to see who we are. Like Dorothy, we awake to see that we never really leave our true home, because it is *within*.

By the mid-seventies, as my four and five year old boys were active, growing guys, and we wanted dogs as well as cats, and my need for a studio increased, we looked for a new home to meet our changing needs. I dreamed of an intelligent, economical house with an art studio, in the country where vegetables could grow and boys could run. We considered building "an intelligent solar house." Eventually my drawings led us to an architect and then his blueprint. The house was small, simple in design, not so many square feet as one sees today. It's most interesting features were the greenhouse and bermed side designed to heat and cool the house for a pittance. There was a combination living/kitchen/dining area, a small studio, two baths and three bedrooms. We managed to purchase five acres in a remote area for a reasonable sum because there had been a murder in that area. The generosity of my parents to my brother and me at Christmas enabled us to give to church or invest in our home; thus, in spite of John's small salary, we were able to buy this inexpensive land.

We put our house up for sale by owner; it sold the first day! When I saw the young couple walking up the path to our door, her long brown hair and face reminding me of my own, I knew they would buy it. They still live there, now with three children.

We were not to get our new country home so easily, however. Since our house sold sooner than anticipated, we moved into a small four-room apartment, figuring we could live in cramped conditions for a few months during the building of our new house. But we were in that tiny apartment for *a full year*: two adults, two active little boys and all their paraphernalia, two cats, and a whole house of furnishings. I barely had room to walk between pieces of furniture let alone a place to set up a studio, so I drew images of my cluttered kitchen sink and Nathan's torn and ratty tennis shoes. I entered both drawings in shows; one, *"Old Tennies Never Die They Just fade Away"* sold, the other, *"Everything And the Kitchen Sink"* took a prize.

The house was never built. After seven months, the acreage was barely bull-dozed. The builder nearly destroyed us financially—we had paid him the first part, but he had done nothing. After months of worry, a lawyer friend from our old Thorncliff neighborhood disentangled us from this builder, we sold the land, and my dream home disappeared.

One day while in the crowded apartment, caring for Jason who was sick, and concerned about bills and a broken down car, I answered my phone to hear my husband say: "I've just been fired; but I believe it's a blessing in disguise."

Shocked, tired, I moved the cat from the chair and sat. My son, calling me from the bathroom, was throwing up again. Wooden blocks that yesterday had been a wall attacked by toy jet fighter planes were scattered everywhere around me; the two cats tussling had knocked a sofa cushion onto the floor, dumping a pile of books simultaneously; the dining room cupboard stood in the middle of the living room—there being no dinning room—a blockade to all movement and, now, a symbol for the moment. When I went to my crying son, I wanted to join him, but didn't. Instead, I prayed.

Jason was becoming ill with a fever (we never took a temperature, not owning a thermometer, but burning hot heads are a clear read). He lost weight for two days. He was passing nothing but blood clots and could not retain food. I had been up with him through the night and was frightened by the evidence every time we left the bathroom. I had no idea what was wrong. I knew that as a life-long, third generation Christian Scientist, I had my work cut out for me. I had to see through this and effect a healing—now! I also knew that to help Jason I had to first heal my own fear. I had to deal with the disarray in our lives: job loss, place, illness, lack of money (we had already sold my life insurance and heirlooms in order to make ends meet).

What could I do? I was, as I have so often been, *alone* in this dilemma. I held Jason in my arms and sang hymns to him, wiping his forehead frequently with a cold wet cloth. Soon he fell asleep in my arms. I laid him on our bed and took a few minutes to be alone with God: to be *still* and know His presence, to bring myself into His dwelling. Fear, duties, the clutter at my feet, and the problems I faced knocked at my thought like a persistent salesman. But I toughened myself against the intrusion of these mental invaders and worked for my peace. After hours of prayer, peace came with this idea: if God is all the power there really is and He is in control of His creation, I can *trust* God's ability to solve all problems lying before me now. Though not a new concept, it came with force.

I dwelt on God's nature—His love for all of His children, including Jason. His goodness. His truth. His justice. His intelligence. I began to see that I ought not be impressed by any material substance or lack of it. Neither blood clots nor money were true substance. I appeared to have too much of matter in one case, and not enough in the other. *True* substance is awareness of God. I began to ponder what constituted God's substance. I thought about God's abundance. Several Psalms came to mind. Fear left me. I was determined not to be impressed by blood clot or job loss. Nothing could touch mankind's permanent relationship with his Creator. That was my base as I walked with Jason into the bathroom when he awoke. I flushed the toilet this time with no fear, nor did Jason cry. I held my hot son with all the love I knew. He was still weak, and fell back to sleep as I carried him to his own bed. When he awoke, the fever was gone and there were no more blood clots. He was back to normal. I kept him home from first grade for another day just to be cautious and to see his energy renewed. He relished everything I gave him to eat and was back bombing Lego walls as if nothing had happened. That was the end of it.

The day after Jason's ordeal and healing, we had a snowstorm. My car was still broken and we had no money to repair it so I had to leave Jason at home alone while I trekked through the blinding snow to fetch his brother from half-day kindergarten. The hill I climbed in the bitter cold symbolized my circumstances: John's impending unemployment (he had two weeks to continue working before severance), our constant financial struggle, the car, our crowded conditions and lack of home, and my growing unhappiness with my marriage. John was a good person. We both were committed to Christian Science and loved being parents to our boys, but something was missing—an intimacy, a close communication.

As I climbed the hill to Nathan's school, my heart felt as heavy as my boots. But thoughts of calamities were tempered when I remembered Jason's healing of the previous day. My gratitude would not allow me to ruminate.

To occupy myself on the cold and windy walk, I decided to review the assignment I'd given my Sunday School pupils for the coming Sunday. I went over what I'd asked of them: to learn the Twenty-Third Psalm and ponder its meaning. "The Lord is my Shepherd, I shall not want," I began. "*I shall not want.*" *Want*! Wasn't that what I was dealing with in my own life? I repeated the Psalm with fresh interest. It was addressing my calamities. When I got to the parts "Thou preparest a table before me in the presence of mine enemies" and "surely goodness and mercy shall follow me all the days of my life; and I shall dwell in the house of the Lord forever, I was overwhelmed with enlightenment. At this moment the familiar Psalm took on new meaning. I realized that right where the enemies of lack, loss, unemployment, and disappointment seemed to be was a spiritual feast—abundance—prepared for me, of God's giving. I simply had to *see* it. I accepted the Psalm's gift of abundant goodness and mercy. Wasn't this Psalm telling me that *I dwell in the house of God*, not in a crowded apartment? *Isn't one's thinking really one's home?* We dwell in consciousness! Dwelling with God—this was my home, my abundance, my supply, my all. I need nothing more! By the time I reached the top of the hill I was nearly jubilant. Even the wind seemed to have died down. Nathan was waving to me when I got to the school. His sweet face smiling, we took hands and walked home. Like a sudden burst of sunshine on an overcast winter's day, the spiritual ideas of that uphill climb permeated the days ahead.

Six weeks later John got a new job with a dynamic corporation in Memphis, Tennessee, and we moved to a spacious home in the South.

nine

In a Foreign Land

At night when others slept, she stuffed papers into the pocket of her gown, took candle, pen and ink, and stole to the alcove where she was sure no one could find her. And wrote. She wrote as fast as her tears flowed. She wrote her story to find her voice, her place, her self. She wrote until she forgot the time and where she was. Dawn broke but still she wrote. She never heard his feet upon the stairs. Never saw him until she was caught.

"What are you doing?! Writing?! Shame! No woman may put pen to paper! Give me those papers!"

She clutched her words to her breast, but dare not utter the "No!" that was in her heart. He yanked them from her hand, read a few lines, then held her story in the candle flame until only black ash remained. "I forbid you to keep a journal—a most dangerous employment for women!" Through torrents of tears she promised never to write again, just as she had promised to never read again when caught with a book. But she went on reading and writing in secret, and one day published her private words.

New Harmony's birds swoop and chirp around the bench where I write this morning, as the sun shines bright, illuminating my words. No one else is here. A peaceful rhythm invites me just to *be*.

Like birds and sunshine, journal writing is life-supporting, self-affirming, a private place to go. A place in which to be oneself, to "speak the unthought, unsaid and undervalued" (Judy Simons, *Diaries and Journals of Literary Women from Fanney Burney to Virginia Woolf*, p. 4).

Women have always written to survive. Excluded from the public domain, women in domestic seclusion have written hidden pages to find voice, self, and meaning for centuries. While society and literature have historically perpetuated an unrealistic *male-created* female image, woman has most authentically been found in her journal.

In journals, women break the silence expected of them in a male-structured society, as evidenced in the journal writing of Fanny Burney, Sei Shonagon, Anais Nin, Virginia Woolf, Mary Shelley, Charlotte Perkins Gilman, and so many others. Eighteenth century Fanny Burney, for whom the journal was "a chronicle of personal growth," was told at age 15, as many young ladies were, that "journal keeping is the most dangerous employment young persons can have" (Simons, p.3) and so she burned all of her writing as her younger sister watched tearfully. For Mary Shelley a journal offered equilibrium in a chaotic life filled with tragedy. For Virginia Woolf the journal was a place to try out words without recrimination. For many it has been a way to say what cannot be said in any other place. A woman's journal allows her voice to be "heard" without fear of condemnation. It is where her story can be told honestly and her meaning found.

In *Diving Deep and Surfacing: Women Writers on Spiritual Quest* Carol Christ writes about the importance of story to women:

> *Without stories there is no articulation of experience. Without stories a woman is lost when she comes to make the important decisions in her life. She does not learn to value her struggles, to celebrate her strengths, to comprehend her pain. Without stories she cannot understand herself. Without stories she is alienated from the deeper experiences of self and world that have been called spiritual or religious. She is closed in silence. (Christ, p. 1)*

But I did not always know this. In the 1970s I did not yet know these women, did not know what I know now, that the repetition of daily record-keeping is good strategy for controlling life disturbances; that writing provides wholeness, preserves continuity midst brokenness, and that even reading a diary can be cathartic.

When I read my journals, I gain insight and discover patterns not available to me in any other way (except perhaps through prayer). I see where my journey has taken me day by day. Margo Culley points out that the "words for 'journal' and 'journey' like the word 'diary', have their roots in the French word for 'day.' So we might think of all diaries as travel diaries and the overriding metaphor of all journals as the journey, a journey from one 'place' in time to another"(Culley, *A Day at a Time: Women's Writing From 1764 to the Present*, p. 23).

I needed to start a journal to give me *place* when I moved to the South in 1978, for I felt out of place. Though we found a lovely new house in Germantown, a suburb of Memphis acclaimed for its good schools, this foreign land of the South was a jolt. I could not understand Southern culture. Besides the expected differences of climate, language, and slower pace, I discovered that what Yankees call the Civil War, Southerners call "The Recent Unpleasantness," or, "the War of Northern Aggression"—and that it is still a factor in daily Southern life. No Yankee, therefore, is ever entirely accepted. Certainly famed Southern hospitality showed up in courteous smiles, good manners, dinner invitations, church politeness, lace-covered conversations, and people dropping by (often when I was in the middle of washing my windows or floors—two things few white Southern women did and for which I was more than once advised to "get a black woman" to do it for me). I viewed the South as a miserably hot, humid place where superficiality hid feelings and prejudices, racism was quietly upheld, Good Ol' Boys ruled, family name and ancestry was everything, frivolous social activities mattered more than genuine accomplishment, and hypocrisy was commonplace. I found the school system to be backward and services slow. I noticed that Southern pride sometimes bred a sense of superiority and that feminine fragility sometimes hid inner strength. Southerners aversion to things Northern—especially New York City—kept a number of parents I knew from allowing their bright children to apply to colleges north of the Mason-Dixon line. Deep friendships seemed hard to come by. But I never expressed these thoughts for I observed immediately that Southerners are very sensitive to the slightest criticism— especially from Yankees. In any case, I never wanted to hurt anyone in this culture that I barely understood, so I kept my opinions to myself.

My early negative appraisal, however, would change 180 degrees over my next twenty years in Memphis. Both the South and I grew.

But for the first several years in Memphis, my journal was the place to vent. I felt like Jenny in May Sartons' *Mrs. Stevens Hears the Mermaids Singing*, who when asked why she likes to write, says "I get filled up. I feel I'm going to burst...It's something I am, not something I do" (p.192).

Whether exploding, or recording the day's events, or analyzing with introspection, a woman's journal reveals her spiritual center. In *Writing a Woman's Life*, Carolyn G. Heilbrun points out in quoting Patricia Spacks, that modern women's autobiographies are written in "the high tradition of spiritual autobiography"(Heilbrun, *Writing a Woman's Life*, p. 23). Certainly my now thirty-some journals reveal my spiritual journey. Reading them has brought me enlightenment—as if the words came from someone else—a voice supportive and spiritually sustaining. But all spiritual paths pass through darkness as well as light, as St. John of the Cross reminds us, and my journals were frequently the repository for my darkest thoughts. Yet, these same pages have carried me over rocky ground to the light, fed me when I couldn't feed myself, given me life when I thought I faced death. At times, they have been my only friend.

So in a small Germantown shop I bought a small red silk journal made in Communist China (which only added to its revolutionary symbolism) that Jason's seven-year-old eyes selected as the prettiest in the store and that night when the dishes were done, the children asleep, I wrote my first entry:

> *I had a diary once before in high school. But at nearly 36 I find the need for a diary, or journal, different—broader in scope, bolder, a haven from a housewife's routine. Housewives are intelligent. They, like most everyone, do not find a mound of ironing or a sink full of dirty dishes intellectually stimulating. Their college education prepares them little for diapers, how to care for hardwood floors, or how to maintain infinite patience with a toddler. While such abilities come quickly in the press of daily housewifery—often by trial-and-error—they rarely leave room to squeeze in intelligent responses that naturally occur in the mind of a thinking woman. Bottled up term papers on current events, philosophy and poetry flutter around my day, as I'm sure the days of many a housewife.*

So I bought a journal today. It will be my delight. My private world of views. Earthquakes, Vietnamese boat people, the Mideast, gasoline shortage, inflation, recession, depression—I'll tackle it all in my journal. Unfortunately, I cannot tackle it in life (except maybe through Christian Science). Undisturbed at 1 a.m., I write my ideas as if they mattered. With each entry I intend to tell one thing for which I am grateful. Tonight it is my baby daughter, God's gift. She rolled over to her stomach, with arched back and strong whomping legs, vigorously rolling back and forth all evening long—a smiling glorious light of strength in the world.

While John was completely consumed by his new job in Federal Express's customer service department, I was completely consumed caring for my beautiful daughter, Charissa, born just eight months after we moved to Memphis. Following one miscarriage before Jason and Nathan's births, and two miscarriages after, Charissa was born seven years after Nathan. The child of my sixth pregnancy, she ought not be here. According to medical law, if an RH negative person doesn't get the Rhogam shots, the possibility of fetal death increases with each pregnancy. Plus, I was thirty-six, then considered a bit old for giving birth.

Throughout my pregnancy I worked to understand the spiritual sense of life more fully. For nine months I studied the Bible and Mrs. Eddy's writings, prayed and practiced what I learned. I chose my father as the practitioner to work metaphysically with me during pregnancy. Charissa's birth was a miracle to many, but to me, evidence of God's presence in human lives. For this reason, her existence was uniquely important to me. And, like most mothers, I had hoped one of my children would be a girl.

In December something seemed to be wrong: I could feel another miscarriage coming. The doctor asked for a special ultra-sound on Monday. This was Friday. In tears, I phoned my father-practitioner, briefly explaining the situation and my symptoms, expressing concern about what Monday's ultra-sound might find. He replied with stern sarcasm: "Sure, Lynn Evans West, you've had it harder than Christ Jesus and Mary Baker Eddy put together!" His sentence stopped me cold. Of course I had not had it harder! I knew that! I wasn't complaining, just sad and in pain over what appeared to be happening once again. But Dad's harsh words brought me to my senses and stopped my tears. He suggested I study the Bible and textbook references he was giving me. "You have nothing more important to do than to work on this birth, put all other activity aside and focus on God without interruption!" This I did.

Study showed God to be Life. The Bible lesson that week was "God, the Only Cause and Creator". I devoured it. I also read Mary Baker Eddy's article *Is There No Death?* from *Miscellaneous Writings*, which showed me that to believe in or accept death contradicts God who is Life. What I was afraid of—my child's death—was not possible in spiritual reality. If our Father-Mother God is eternal, I reasoned as any good Christian Scientist might, then God's offspring must inherit God's *eternal* nature. I realized that to fear death gives death power and *to believe in death is to disbelieve in life*, for the two are opposites; and to disbelieve in life is *not* to believe in God who *is* Life. I concluded that to be afraid of death is not even Christian. This was astounding news. I was learning *there is no death*, that my fears for my unborn child were ungrounded, that it was not a material human baby I was awaiting, but *this very understanding of the eternal nature of being beyond matter.* I got to the point where I desired to know God as Life, whether this included another human child in my experience or not. My mind was in a new place—unlimited and deeply spiritual. I had broken through the barrier of medical claims, become calm and fearless. I *knew* all was well and that Monday's ultra-sound would prove so. I *knew* God alone would be the judge, not a medical photograph. I included gratitude for the doctor's work in my prayers. Monday's tests showed the pregnancy to be not only normal but further along than the doctor had thought.

Less than a month before my due date, the doctor presented me with another obstacle to handle. During a routine exam—but an extremely thorough internal one—he discovered that the baby, whom he had already determined was very large, was in the breech position. He said it was "too late for the baby to turn around" and explained the risks connected with a breech delivery.

I called Dad after the appointment to tell him what the doctor had said. His immediate response to me was a quotation from the Old Testament: "He shall *overturn, overturn, overturn it*, until he come whose right it is" (Ezekial 21:27). He continued prayerful work on my behalf, giving me readings to study. The final week's exam confirmed the baby had in fact turned and the head was down in the normal birth position. On February 18, 1979, Charissa Ruth West was born without drugs or complications, only two hours after I arrived at the hospital and in only a nine-minute delivery (the last fact according to the student nurse monitoring my case). We named our 9 ½ pound 20 ½ inch-long daughter, Charissa, from the Greek meaning "God's grace". She was, as the examining pediatrician told me jubilantly, "perfect." Alone in the recovery room I thanked God for the beauty of her birth. In privacy I reached for my hymnal beside my bed, letting it fall open where it would. It opened to hymn #216: "Oh, he who trusts in God's protection And hopes in Him when fears alarm, Is sheltered by His loving kindness, *Delivered* by His mighty arm." What a perfect benediction to my day!

Everything about Charissa meant bliss. She was a delight to us all. Her brothers found her to be a wonderful new toy, though occasionally too loud or too messy. They thought she was very funny and loved to entertain her, hold her, feed her, and bathe her. When I walked Charissa—dressed in smocked dresses with matching bonnets I made for her—in her carriage, I accepted the compliments in silent gratitude of passers-by who exclaimed about my beautiful baby, for I knew prior to her birth that she was really God's, not mine. She was an easy baby, never fussy nor sick, and I breast-fed her for a year. She was simply rainbows, light, and music.

Our new home was also a joy for all of us. We had been able to purchase our suburban Memphis home in Germantown rather easily because coming from a rented apartment, we had the proceeds in the bank, plus a year's interest, from the quick sale of our Thorncliff residence and land sale in St. Louis. Prices were considerably lower in the South, so we got a lot more home for our money. The recently built two-story Colonial we moved into was on a quiet cove, an easy walk from the neighborhood pool, and twice as large as our previous house—and nearly dreamy having come from the crowded four-room apartment!

Our new home had a huge front and back yard (ideal for raising Newfoundland puppies as well as creating a children's play ground), a wide Williamsburg hearth fireplace in the kitchen, another fireplace in the beamed family room, a formal dining room, living room, three bedrooms, two and a half baths, a bonus playroom over the two-car garage, a first floor laundry room, and hard wood floors throughout. John and I and our children were all very pleased. We soon added a deck for entertaining, a rock garden, and a special play area complete with wooden climbing structure, swings and an enclosed wide sand area in the treed-backyard.

Along with planting gardens and raising children and Newfoundlands, and entering Memphis area art shows, I also became involved in church duties, the boys'school, cub scouts, smocking, sewing, decorating and maintaining our lovely new home. Through it all, my dependence on God grew, as my journal entries show:

> *August 11, 1979*
>
> *The Bible lesson is about Paul at Ephesus, his trials, courage, clarity of purpose…. I see similarities between Dad and Paul. Their honesty, steadfastness, obedience to God, their trials, sacrifices, criticism, hardships, the wearing-down of daily living—these temptations never overcame Paul nor Dad. Both men endured. So must I. No matter the obstacles. Just keep on. My marriage may not be all I wish, and I do not understand why I'm in Memphis… but God brought us here. My reason for being is to love my family, community, world and God. Schedules, demands cannot beat down my joy. I can say with Paul and Dad, "no matter the trials, I carry on."*

I enrolled Nathan and Jason in the local public elementary school in walking distance from our home. I joined the PTA at the first meeting held in the cafeteria, eager to be involved in my sons' school.

In her address to parents at the first PTA meeting, the principal stated that parents were "more interested in tennis than in their children," that "parents do not pack healthy lunches and should support the school's hot lunch program," that there were "too many parental requests to visit classes," that "parents should not be in the school," and that she, the principal, was in charge, not parents. She concluded with the unforgettable words: *"Farmington School is my pail of rocks to carry in life."* I was astounded.

How could a principal do any good with such an attitude?! I was amazed that in the packed cafeteria full of businessmen as well as a double-dosage of supporting mothers, not one person rose to counter or question her statements. Never had I seen such acquiescence concerning the important matter of the education of one's children. We had only lived in Germantown for a couple of months; I had barely unpacked. Certainly there must be others here as shocked as I was by what we had just heard. Where were their voices? Why weren't long-time residents speaking out? Where was free speech? Democracy? I went home outraged.

I wrestled with my concern about my sons' school all night. I had already been dismayed when school authorities told me that because of crowded conditions, Nathan would be put in a combination kindergarten-first grade. His half-day kindergarten experience in St. Louis the year before had not been a good one: the teacher had an accident early in the school term and substitutes filled in for the remainder of the year. To follow this with a year in a classroom of half-kindergartners/half first graders seemed detrimental. And now I faced this new concern: a principal who apparently disliked her school and its parents!

The night of that first PTA meeting after my family was asleep, I began a letter to the principal. I wanted to let her know that some of us *did* pack fine lunches—on homemade whole wheat bread with organic lettuce!—and *never* played tennis! Some of us were eager to help our schools, not hinder; in fact, some of us had been schoolteachers and were sensitive to the problems with which she had to deal. She needed to know that a principal who sees her school as a burden ought not be there. A school should be a place where there are no limitations to curiosity, growth, spontaneity, and openness. Furthermore, no one individual had the right to be so dictatorial in a PTA meeting—the "P" does not stand for principal but parents!

What a far cry from the meetings and involvement I had known in St. Louis public schools. There I had painted nature murals on the dark hall walls of the elementary school to brighten and inspire—a project of many months. Students could spot a Monarch butterfly or a pelican perched on a pier as they walked down the hall. There were ladybugs on assorted wildflowers and snakes slithering under tall grasses. I had solved the problem of a noisy, manner-less, rambunctious school dining room by bringing music, fresh flowers, and tablecloths that I stitched on my sewing machine from brightly colored calico I bought—all of this had an amazing calming effect in the cafeteria. Ideas and parental service were always welcome in that public school. But things were different in Memphis.

As I sat in the armchair composing my letter to the principal, sometime after midnight, I glanced at my Bible. Its mere presence seemed to interrupt what I was doing. I picked it up and read randomly. As I read, I realized a letter was no way to go about finding a solution to this problem. Love was. I realized I was not holding good thoughts about this principal and that this was harmful to both of us. I had to *love* her, to see her as God's child—not just pretend to like her, but to *genuinely find what was God-like in her*. At first I fought this idea. I did not *want* to like this person. I wanted to write her an angry letter! But I had learned to listen to that "still small voice" long ago, so I thought about who she really was as God's child. What would cause her to feel so unhappy with her "pail of rocks"? The school was large and over-crowded, with busing problems, and a large number of disabled and low ability students shipped to the suburb. Parents—many of whom were transferred to Memphis from California, New York or the Midwest—had higher expectations than county funds would allow. Certainly these concerns weighed heavily on the principal's shoulders. The more I thought about her situation, the more compassion I felt. What did she *need* to lighten her load? What could *I* do to help? Though I was four months pregnant with my daughter at the time, I decided to go to the school office the next day to offer my services to do anything the principal needed on a regular basis.

Early next morning I went to school—passing the posted sign that disallowed anyone in the building except teachers, students and staff—and walked into the administrative office with my offer. I volunteered to run copies, sort, file, staple, aid teachers in crowded classrooms, teach art—"Whatever you want I will do," I told the secretarial staff behind the counter. They just stared at me blankly and one went to get the principal. Obviously no one had ever made such an offer before.

The principal emerged from her office, eyeing me critically, saying, "We don't let parents into the school."

"I used to teach," I replied, "I will do anything you want—if you have an office duty—stapling, filing—I could do that; I also have a degree in fine arts and teaching experience. There is nothing I won't do to help. Anything you need done. And I will do it once a week, or more often, if you like, so you can count on me."

She looked like a deer trapped by headlights. "Come into my office," she said.

We talked about the school and her challenges, about my teaching experience and what I might actually do. She told me that there were *no* art classes for grades one through four. I offered to create an art program for those grades. I told her I would try to find parents with art backgrounds and train them to help me teach some of the classes. She was delighted with my plan.

In a matter of weeks I had written a curriculum, she had gotten me some basic supplies out of her discretionary funds, and I was teaching sixteen classes of art weekly on a volunteer basis, along with a few moms I found to help.

The principal and I became friends. I discovered that she was a very religious person who really did care about the well-being of her students.

When my daughter, Charissa, was born five months later, the principal invited me to leave my baby in her office while I taught. She loved my handing her that baby! Charissa usually slept soundly in her office, but every once in a while, the principal just *had* to pick her up and cuddle her. As months went by and Charissa grew, I took her with me into the classrooms. She would sit in her infant seat watching the children, or crawl on the carpeted floor. Once I placed her in the center of the circle of students and they drew her portrait. At the end of the year, so much a part of the school were we, that the principal insisted Charissa and I have our picture taken for the yearbook.

The next year I was elected PTA cultural arts chairman and trained mothers to teach art in the school. I also wrote a handbook for teaching an art appreciation program, which was adopted by other area public schools.

In spite of my involvement, the school was not offering what the boys' needed. Nathan, who had a substitute teacher most of his kindergarten year in St. Louis, and was then put in a first grade/kindergarten combination at Farmington, deserved better. And by third grade, Jason was coming home saying he hated school, as I confided to my journal:

> *October 21, 1979*
> *Jason claims to hate school. Almost every day he comes home saying this... His third grade teachers claim he has the highest I.Q. for his age level, his reading is almost seventh grade level. I pray for answers.*

I revisited my John Holt books, thinking about the prospects of unschooling my boys.

Meanwhile, I painted, entering competitions as often as convenient. I could no more function without painting than I could leave my children. I blended the two occupations as often as possible, painting the boys in their cowboy outfits and Charissa catching her first ball. I took the latter plus a watercolor of a nude model I'd paid to pose for me and entered both in the Tennessee Watercolor Society Nashville exhibition. The two loves pulled at me along with a growing desire to help school, church, community. This passage from the Christian Science textbook became my personal motto: "*We are all capable of more than we do.*" (Eddy, *Science and Health*, 89: 22). With God "the real Doer," I felt I could take on anything, putting family, church and community first, not worrying about my own needs, like so many moms I know. I struggled to find time, considering it a decadent pleasure to sit down, viewing fatigue as error's encroachment into service to others. I mastered "evil's suggestion" that I rest, take time for myself, by working harder, remembering "God is the only I or ego; there's no Lyn to feel tired."

But in the rare free moment, I found myself reading books about living on an island off Maine's coast and planned trips north.

December 17, 1979

Depression has been trying to set in—but I do not let it—too many blessings of the past year. I read a beautiful idea today: "We fill the inn of our hearts up with guests of busy-ness and human clamor, and then there's no room left in the inn for the Christ." God must come first. I must "be up and be doing, desert not the right" as the hymn says.

Following Christmas at my parents' home on Cape Cod I wrote in my journal:

January 12, 1980

There's something about going on a journey. New reflections come. I see my life is mine to do with as seems right to me. This voice inside knows what is right. I must trust myself, my own judgment. Life is not a matter of doing what one is told to do or supposed to do; rather, it is a matter of being/doing what Father-Mother God made me for.

I have devoured ten books on the topic of education these last few weeks. It consumes me—this search for excellence in education for my boys. Unschooling is radical. But it seems right. My "friend" Buckminster Fuller says: ". . . that it takes a seventh day, hallowed for resting, and considerable preaching, praying and psalm-singing, to keep a mother housekeeper in good humor as she progressively relinquishes her own potentials to the next generation." Remember that! And take time to nourish yourself.

Charissa fell down the long flight of stairs today in her walker head-first onto the slate floor. She was crying terribly when I got to her. At first I was angry with John who was supposed to be watching her while I was cooking dinner. He had left the gate at the top of the stairs unlocked. I called Dad for practitioner help immediately. She was well instantly—as if it had not even happened. Not blaming John helped bring the healing.

By Easter, I was trying to resurrect myself, though later entries reveal it was an on-going battle not easily won:

Easter, 1980

On this resurrection day I'm inspired to rise spiritually; to make more time to study Christian Science; to be more alert to practicing what I learn; to teach my children values daily. Whirling, busy with activities and routine, I'd like more freedom for art, learning, sharing, reading, understanding God, and living closer to Nature. Oh to have land, a solar house, grow vegetables, unschool my boys!

I've always had an image of a certain kind of happy home. One where each individual helps the whole; where conversation, art, music and loyalty to family abound; where honesty, truth, and life lessons naturally happen everyday; where children are honored and listened to, feel stable, secure, intact, loved, and understood. I strive for this with little help from John. I envision a beautiful unpretentious place with gardens, vegetables, things in order, big trees, space, character, charm, solidity. A dog, cats. A house of delightful peculiarities—like Swedish artist Carl Larsen's home. Our home is not this. I am grateful for what we have, but improvement is needed intellectually and in communication. John rarely talks or shares—not even a kiss when he comes home—just off to pray or watch TV. He is a good person, plays ball with the boys, but is not always really present—void of words, input, opinions, or actions, he is content I do it all. We are not a cohesive whole. I must love more, for loving is the answer to everything.

May 13, 1980

I changed the sheets, located carpet for the stairs, ironed lots of shirts for John, folded the pile of laundry at the foot of our bed—no longer to wake up to those depressing mounds, though a healthy hill of socks awaits me! I got 3 sections of my Bible lesson done plus notes for teaching my Sunday School class. Charissa and Gentle have been a delight—she loves that Newfoundland! I love them both! Jason came home with all his homework done so we can have time together! The boys won their baseball game.

A new idea came to me—I've made invitations inviting each family member to come to a "party for solutions".

I read a few more pages in my Anne Morrow Lindbergh book, The Flower and the Nettle. She writes: "There is no time, no space, no quiet. Nothing to encourage me, and everything seems to say to me: Give it up . . . I did not feel like the `wise, gentle and firm mother' today! I was very irritable and then cross at myself for being irritable…I was trying to think out of the gloom." I know how she feels. I have had days "thinking out of the gloom," but today is not one of them.

May 22, 1980

Tonight at church I realized (one of those mini-revelations that come) how much I love listening to readings and testimonies. Christian Science and family are everything to me. I must find a way to find more time for both. My day is full of setting tables, folding laundry, ironing, driving somebody somewhere, dealing with the physical, not how I want it, out of my control. I need replenishing—I am reading A Gift From the Sea—when I get the chance. I talk to John but he doesn't hear. I feel as if my life is wasting away; that my precious years as a mother are going too fast. Something has to change. Anne Lindbergh writes, "One gets so cramped in ordinary living."

June 8, 1980

I saw an excellent film about Iran. Seems we've ruined that country over many years. For what the U.S. does to people we have no right to continue as a world power. I feel the time is coming—in my lifetime—when we will be subservient to another and know hard times. It is what we deserve. We will pay a penalty, lose what is good about the U.S., the Jefferson America (I am reading a biography of him)…We need to see that what pulls down our morals is just as destructive as any nuclear weapon. We've got to get to a simpler way of doing things. We've no right to waste, be gluttons. We've created a system we no longer can control; it controls us. I've seen this in education, government, politics, church. I think of the Bible passage: "They've hued themselves out cisterns, broken cisterns that can hold no water." It doesn't matter if Reagan or Carter is elected—a tough time is ahead. We should be saving money, growing food, limiting use of electricity, gas, water—all Americans, yes, but also, our family, now. We can do better.

June 21, 1980

I picked berries with the boys—enough for a pie. Did a painting commission. Received a letter from Isabel Bates verifying my testimony, which I'm submitting to the Christian Science Publishing Society. She wrote it has "depth and heart." Got a letter from John Holt about my unschooling questions I'd written him. Got calls to do CS practice work for others—spoke to callers with a surge of inspiration.

July 4, 1980

Charissa hated the fireworks. I think it's a silly symbol—the same battle noise that has caused countless deaths. We sat too close, the boys were afraid sparks would land on them. John would not move. John never moves.

It has been two years but still I do not feel at home in Memphis…impossible for a Yankee to be accepted!

John's new job brought us to Memphis but took him further from us. In a letter to my parents July 16, 1980 I wrote:

When John comes home all he has time for is C.S. and bed. He's gone by 6:30 AM and sometimes not home until almost 10:00. Charissa says "Daddy…Baby… hold" when he's not here. I try to keep up with the housework all by myself—do you know that I have fourteen loads of laundry a week?! Do you know how many hours of folding that is?! And how much ironing?! I need a 48-hour day! I think the American housewife-mother, without a maid, who cooks from scratch, bakes her own cookies and bread, writes the bills, and whose family never can afford to eat out, is a creature ignored, of whom most people are totally IGNORANT. Some day I'll write a book about it, when everyone's grown and gone, for certainly there's no time now! Yet, I'm not complaining. I love my kids, accept my tasks. Guess I just need a break.

For a break, I took the kids to visit their grandparents on Cape Cod. My belief that travel is often an inner journey as well as outward shows in these journal entries.

July 31, 1980

The children and I are here in my parents' lovely Cape Cod home. John, of course, didn't come. I think being on Cape Cod is the most earthly happiness attainable—the constant breeze, the ocean, ponds, marshes, cranberry bogs, gardens, woods, historic architecture, old-fashioned values, beautiful simplicity, lack of materialism, Nature's closeness. I even love the rain here! I would love to live on Cape Cod—just a small house, charming though, with magnificent views of the water and a garden. Gentle would love the water—with their webbed feet, Newfoundlands ought to live by the ocean rather than in a Memphis suburb. Charissa loves to collect rocks, play in the sand, wade in the water. She is so impressed by the ocean. Jason caught his first fish of the year yesterday. Nathan and he have fished continuously since we arrived, Mom fishing with them. The boys and I rolled in the warm waves, played on the beach. Mom—who still refuses to let me do anything in her kitchen—fixed the best flounder for lunch. Dad is the busiest I've known him to be—at least if patient phone calls are any indication—125 in three days! I hope to learn about my parents' past and write it down for my children to tell their children. I've known my mother for thirty-six years yet there is so much I do not know about her. She is so quiet about her life.

I read a few quotations last night that I want to remember. From Albert Einstein: "Only a life lived for others is a life worthwhile." From Samuel Johnson: "He that hopes to look back with satisfaction upon past years, must learn to know the present value of single minutes, and endeavor to let no particle of time fall useless to the ground." From O.A. Battista: "The best inheritance a parent can give his children is a few minutes of his time each day".

August 4, 1980

I am more me, less Glenn Evans' daughter. I see life is what I make it and I'd better pursue what matters to me. Mom expects me to function like a daughter, not a grown-up. I am not allowed to help in the kitchen except to follow orders. I am afraid to even pour a bowl of cereal for Charissa without Mom's approval. Mom works constantly. So does Dad. But I can't help them. The kids and I fit in in-between. Do they not know I am a capable person? I could be cooking meals for them! My father's practice is his real family. Keeping his home is Mom's. Their life is an established regimen. We seem to interfere. Intruders, their grandchildren and I. Sacrifices are made because we are here. I love the Cape but think we won't come again for a while.

August 10, 1980

We successfully surprised Mom with a birthday party! The boys were so excited and could hardly wait until suppertime for her presents and cake.

Today I bombarded Mom with questions about her past. She told me her mother's maiden name was Bennett and her grandmother's name, Gilhouley. Her father's side came from Scotland in the 1700's. Her father quit school at age eight to work. At seventeen he left home to become trained as an engineer and became a pioneer in the car industry. He designed cars that were tested at the Indianapolis 500 and one set a world's record climbing Pike's Peak. I am delighted to learn about my heritage.

A man visited Dad who'd worked with him at the Martin Company and told Mom and me that when Dad entered a room "it was as if Jesus entered." He said swearing, bickering, and problems ended because Dad treated people fairly.

August 17, 1980

We've come to John's parents' cottage for a week in Michigan's Upper Peninsula. Dense pine forests, mountainous hills, clear water. The houses and people seem rock solid, of the earth itself, hearty, simple, unaware of the twentieth century. We're in a cottage near John's parents' family cottage—old, worn, charming. I picked wildflowers, made bouquets for every room. The window views Lake Superior and a strong blue sky. The boys like it here, are busy playing with their cousins, fishing for hours as on Cape Cod. I've painted some. John plays tennis with his Dad every day. I observe that all three West men belittle women, "use" them, though my husband least. They seem to expect women to be docile, obedient to their every desire without accepting her rights to make choices about what is important to her. Women are expected to do laundry, watch the kids, place delectable pies on every supper table, clean and remain basically quiet and good-looking. A little ERA is needed!

Lacking a personally nurturing relationship with my husband, I continued to focus on children, school, church, community and art, which kept me busy.

September 18, 1980

   Life has been busy since school started—soccer, Suzuki piano, cub scouts, gymnastics, the whole treadmill has begun!

October 14, 1980

   I want more time to hug my boys and sing Charissa to sleep. I feel an imminent danger. Although John does not see it, our life should be <u>shared</u>. I need less hustle, more stillness. Maybe a farm? I don't know the answer, but God does….John grows more outside of us with church duties and work. He has no friends, invites no one to our home, reads no books, rarely talks, and seems content to be uninvolved—like a boarder whom I feed, whose laundry I do. I even buy his shoes. I need desperately to hug and be hugged, to laugh, paint, write more. I am alone with this. Who would I tell? Who would understand? No one can help but God. Is this selfish? It baffles me that I am writing this at 3 a.m. when I could be sleeping!

November 1, 1980

   I want days full of beauty, vitality, variety. But my days are busy with laundry, carpools, picking up after others, of remembering to cut whose nails when (dogs and kids), of budgeting, paying the house payment on time, washing floors, taking kids to soccer, piano, gymnastics. Piles of clothes grow into mountains to be ironed before a minute is found to get at it. Figuring out new menus. Kneeling on hard bathroom floors to scrub tubs and toilets, or on dirt to weed endless ivy beds, and on a hunch to find the missing bedtime toy under the couch. Running to fit housework into the baby's one-hour nap. Climbing stairs forty times up and down to put, fetch, take, carry, do. Never sitting except to pay bills, smock or sew.

   In college becoming a 24-hour a day maid was not my goal. How has this happened? Neither finances nor my principles allow for hiring help. But my standards demand home-baked bread, fresh-from-scratch brownies or cookies each week, flowers in several rooms, a sparkling home, duties as den mother, Sunday School teacher, and school volunteer. Isn't all that part of motherhood? We all wanted motherhood in our future, back in the fifties playing dolls. But did we know what it entailed? I love being the mother of my children; I'd just like to be a person, too. I would like to be me. To find a time to do my work, the way a father is a father (or at least should be) but has a career too. Why is this so hard to attain? Why do I feel guilty, ungrateful, to want an identity separate from others? I must take charge of attaining what I want. I have only one life. I ought to have some say in how it is spent. A man has this right. Why can't a woman?!

I reiterated much of the following journal entry in a letter to my parents November 18, 1980 but my obvious disillusionment is not something they ever mentioned:

Here's what I believe: to be at peace one must live his ideals, his sincere feelings and aspirations. To the degree one does not do this he experiences discord. Little of what I believe in is part of today's life. I do not believe in nuclear power plants, war for most reasons; ignoring chemical waste for industry's profit; lying politicians; the fact that our country can't get back the hostages; the feeling that our country is doomed because it has fallen from its original standards; traffic and car-pooling; bad-mouthed children that my children have to be around; materialism; yelling coaches and competitive kids' sports; injustices in the Christian Science movement; the lack of sincere practicing Scientists; unhealed situations (Jason's eyes); John's inability to give or communicate or understand me; the demands on me to solve, do, and be everything without appreciation or compensation; the fact that no time is my own; that my intelligence and creativity are relegated to trying to catch up with things like ironing, dirty dishes, weeding, bill-paying, budgeting, floor-scrubbing, tub-cleaning, and toilet bowl brushing, with my efforts destroyed 5 minutes after the many hours it takes to get it all done.

Too much of life seems insincere, hypocritical, phony, foreign to man's truest, highest nature. Why? Man should live his conscience. I attempt to, but feel frustrated. Every day seems plastic. A kind of dying. "Just keep on doing what you are doing, you're doing a good job," everyone says. "Keep up the servitude. Teach Sunday School, be scout den mother, keep on being involved for everyone's good; keep baking, cleaning, driving, child-raising. Keep giving. Don't stop to fill up, refresh, or be your own person—we need you to do all this so we can be our own persons. Stifle yourself. Your feelings don't count. For if you have any aspirations they surely must be selfish, not God-directed; your only reason for being is to pour yourself out to the rest of us." All the wrongs, inequities I've fought to stop, the stands I've taken, the giving to causes and community seem insignificant. It's as if my hopes, dreams, and very fiber are extinguished. I feel like a butterfly after little hands have brushed the dust from her and she flutters her wings for the last time.

Some twenty years later I read this and see clear signs of depression—a thoughtful, caring, energetic but over-loaded young woman calling out for help. Yet I recollect no response from my parents to this letter. It was a particularly busy time for them with Dad's lecture circuit and his demanding public practice, not to mention the growing complexities he was dealing with at the Mother Church. From about this time forward, I chose not to turn to my father or other practitioners, but to do my own work, because confidentiality was of concern to me. And my journal became the repository of my most raw feelings.

I struggled with the inequities of male and female roles, as so many women have throughout history. I had not yet read Freidan's *A Feminine Mystique* or Schaff's *Women's Reality*. I had not heard of Sylvia Plath nor Adrianne Rich. Nor even Elizabeth Cady Stanton. I knew nothing of women's studies literature which was to become so important to me later.

As den mother for 16 cub scouts, two of whom were my sons, I found myself enjoying their activities and crafts, from pinecone wreaths to merit badge projects. My favorite event was our realistic Pilgrim's First Thanksgiving, held at our house, using our Williamsburg-style kitchen hearth. I got lumber for the boys to carve their own wooden trenchers. They made their own costumes, shucked oysters like Pilgrims, played Indian games, made bread from flour and yeast, made their own butter, cooked fish and corn in the fire, and I made them a turkey in the oven. I loved this as much as they did!

But I began to see another side to holidays:

> *January 1, 1981 New Year's Day*
> *A man's holiday is his day; he's free to watch football, nap, read, etc. But the woman still changes the diapers, sets a special table, cooks elaborate festive food for the occasion and then wraps it all up and cleans it all up. Her holiday is one-tenth the size of his! Though I adore cooking, making home beautiful, I struggle to get my housework done, my mother-obligations, and still have time left for me or art. Dad says home, marriage and children should come first and no other job is more important*

than the role of wife and mother. Do I always believe that? What would it be like to be a full-time artist? Would a career take me away from mothering well? Do I have a choice?

March 2, 1981

I think marriage is a confining experience unless spouses' goals are the same. John and I are oceans apart. I do not want to raise children alone like this! I am miserable without a fully engaged partner. My art and being are drying up. I feel like all the good ideas I've ever had will never happen, as if nothing matters. I seem to be in a mire.

April 2, 1981

John's boss graded him low in all performance areas and told him he is "in way over your head . . . the only reason you've been kept around is your honesty." I feel sorry for him. He is through with his job as of April 15 and has the next five months to find another position within the company. This is the second time he has been fired. He will be in New Jersey next week. Perhaps his next job will take us North!

Dad called tonight to say Bowen died, my cousin's year old son. It is difficult to understand, given the prayer bestowed. President Reagan was shot; also his press secretary; they will make it, though. John's brother divorced his Asian wife; I liked her. We have $10 in the checking account. What is all this? Everything seems to be falling apart.

Despair, however, was *not* constant. Spirituality bounced me back. My journal was where I stored the hard times and in reading it today I must remember that fact. I tended to write during low points, when I had no one to confide in but blank pages, just as eighteenth century Fanny Burney did when she wrote in her journal to "Miss Nobody," and as so many women have down the centuries. To some extent I controlled depression by expressing my most naked feelings in writing. Enthusiasm and equilibrium usually returned with creative endeavor, community accomplishment, activity with kids, something learned, a researched spiritual idea, or a healing—any one of these lit up life.

This play of dark and light is apparent in entries in spring 1981:

April 11, 1981

The I.R.S. refund check came today—hoorah! I can pay bills! But I do not want to talk about money. I've been thinking about my recent unhappiness. Jesus (of course) had it harder. Cross-bearing is necessary for ascension.

I have just finished reading Madeliene L'Engle's A Wrinkle in Time to Jason and Nathan. Through it I've new insight about dealing with evil. We get sucked in by it—that's what happens in L'Engle's book. We fight evil with love and then good prevails. I want to be nothing but love. TV is like evil: it sucks people in, robs them of time with each other. John watches too much. I wish he liked books.

I feel like I'm in a plastic baggie and soon someone's going to twist the tie around the top—if only I can get out before they do! I find myself staring at lists—family budgets, schedules, choices, groceries, menus, things to pray about for family, world, church or community. Today I am too tired to enumerate the negative. Even the Easter rabbit cake I made cracked, drooped over, and will be a mess to serve tomorrow.

Easter, 1981

After reading, clarity is coming about what I want to do:

1. *To make a sign that says: "Flee as a bird to your mountain"*
2. *To have order in all things, from house to schedules.*
3. *To always express glorious, spontaneous love in my home.*
4. *To continue without the social but be helpful to community.*
5. *To be a very prepared and thorough Christian Scientist.*
6. *To have lots of fresh flowers every week in the house.*
7. *To heal.*
8. *To limit frivolity, socializing, TV watching to 1 hour a day for each family member.*
9. *To have tons of pencils and paper ready everywhere.*
10. *To have an orderly study place.*
11. *To always get up at 6:00; pray and study until 7:00 when I serve breakfast; lunch at noon and dinner at 6:30, regularly without interruption of the order.*
12. *To paint and read more*

April 25, 1981

I feel like I've been pushed over some kind of impasse and can't get back to sanity on the other side. I feel out of control, like something terrible is going to happen in the next few weeks. Tomorrow is my art show but I barely care. I am losing all sense of other people and things. Nothing matters. I am frightened by how I feel.

Clearly depression was an issue in this last entry, but I did not really understand the concept in the eighties. It came unexpectedly and disappeared when I turned to God or managed to immerse myself in the positive things in my life. In years ahead, I would again face depression and eventually come to understand it more fully, discovering its triggers, learning how to eliminate it, until it ceased to be an issue. But not in 1981 when I once affirmed to my uncle, who smiled a knowing smile in response: "There are no pleasures."

May 29, 1981

I have a new interest: science, especially physics and Einstein. They confirm that matter is nothing. I see more deeply that any mortal thing is valueless. Nothing in this material world gives pleasure. I also see that God alone is my guide, not parents nor a church organization. I glimpse the future fading of human church organization; but feel I will always have church inside.

I got notice from the Christian Science Publishing Society that my testimony was accepted and will be published in the July Journal.

Here's a question that comes to me: As we begin to see the unimportance of matter, the pleasure-less-ness of mortal life, how do we care about what goes on? How do we make choices when none of it really matters? When the divine becomes all, how do we keep ourselves here?

I want to be a full-time practitioner someday but not until I understand more, not until I'm driven to it by God. I want to understand God, Truth, above all, not just dance around understanding…to solidly prove what I learn.

Observation: The fewer one's responsibilities the easier it is to be calm and spiritual; the more responsibilities, the greater the challenge.

August 7, 1981

Today, my unschooling plan was approved! I'm jubilant! After months of intense research, work, and communication with the superintendent, we got it! I was told we are the first in the state of Tennessee to be granted legal permission. I called John Holt's office. Everyone is overjoyed for us. One thing I am clear on: power is with God and not men. God did this. Man couldn't. We think it is the president of this or the superintendent of that who has authority. No. The only power is with God. Life continues to teach me this over and over.

September 5, 1981

My friend, Eleanor, who teaches English at Memphis State and who I've engaged to teach the boys English, tells me I must keep a log of this unschooling experience, that I've a book here, with her editing. Right now, though, I am overwhelmed with work and lack of time; schooling my kids is my main occupation. I get less than four hours of sleep many nights due to being up with books, plans, or just thinking ahead—but I love it! The boys do not know what to expect and I am feeling my way, too, but am confident that in time it will be clear. Right now I am huffing and puffing and if it weren't for Eleanor I would not even be taking time out to write this much!

October 1, 1981

Purry died. A remarkable cat. She responded so to love. I held her in my lap most of the day. That's all she wanted in her last hours. Too weak to move, she struggled to climb into my lap when I knelt beside her on the garage floor. That's all she wanted, just to be held. She fought death, breathed hard, and then stopped. I loved her tremendously. Cancer seems an unfair end for a cat. Ten years is a long time. She was like my child. We'd been through a lot together—two moves and her motorcycle accident (she learned to trust me then and had a surprising healing). Maybe she knows how much I loved her.

Gentle has gone to be bred so we may have Newfoundland puppies by December!

Maybe this year of unschooling will be all that I hope. Maybe this year I will find more time to think, read and paint. Maybe this year I will feel at home in Memphis. Maybe this year John will communicate.

Except for one, all my hopes I wrote in this entry would come to pass.

ten

Outside Walls

In her dream she was at home, but her home was not like any she knew in the real world, for there were no walls. The ceiling was sky, her living room Nature's world. Without walls, one expanse just opened into another, endlessly. One lovely view connected to the next. Nothing locked her in or blocked her path. She held on tightly to the dream after she woke.

Here in New Harmony, there are no walls. Oh, there are garden fences and vertical stacks of brick to give form to a space. But there are no walls to limit or box one in; no blockage of ideas. Everything flows. In a single morning I can enter a dozen different spaces of solitude—a stone bench in Carol's Garden, a seat under an umbrella table beside the inn, a chair surrounded by Red Geranium's pines, an archway in the Roofless Church, a rock facing a carved message in the woods, a moss-covered brick path, the banks of the Wabash River, the top of the Antheneum, the footbridge across the water, an old park bench under a tall oak, a pew in the cozy Episcopal Church, or a kneeler in the Chapel of the Little Portion—and still have an abundance of solitary spots left for the afternoon. No limits.

"Unschooling" promised us no limits. "A school Without Walls" we called it. In August, 1981, following the boys' fourth and fifth grades, I pulled them out of the school system and began our extraordinary year of unschooling—similar to homeschooling, but more open. This was no hasty decision. I had been reading educator John Holt's books and others on the topic for years. I had even written Holt and met with him. In fact, he devoted four pages in his book, *Teach Your Own,* to quoting my letter and answering my questions.

Some states were putting parents in jail or removing their children because homeschooling was illegal. Determined not to let this happen, I wrote a 20-page proposal explaining how I could educate my sons better than the school system, and submitted my plan to the Memphis' Shelby County School Superintendent for his approval, inviting him to our home for dinner to discuss it. He declined the invitation but it helped me hurdle the blockade of bureaucracy and get his attention. I researched public school regulations and curriculum in library documents to learn their requirements and language, shaping my proposal accordingly, hoping for agreement rather than dissension. We were finally granted permission to do unschooling—the first for non-religious reasons in the state of Tennessee—for one year. A school official added: "the system could not provide a better curriculum."

I knew a great deal about Shelby County schools, having been thoroughly involved with Farmington my sons' first two years in Memphis. But my sons were not having a better education there than before my volunteerism. I saw smiley face stickers on mimeographed sheets and modest applications of academic principles where I had hoped for creative thought, innovation, and real challenge. Locally, parents who cared about education tended to choose private institutions. I was opposed to the concept of private schools, preferring the healthy mix of races, backgrounds, personalities that a public school could provide, not wanting the wealth, social aspects, homogenized sameness of a private institution. Eventually, I succumbed to private schools.

Having read Maria Montessori's educational philosophy, after two years at Farmington, I put my sons in a Montessori school. Now instead of the mimeo sheets with smiley faces coming home, nothing came home. The school seemed to be going through some sort of identity crisis, and philosophical chaos seemed to rule. John Holt's unschooling began to look like a good option. As unschooling made more and more sense to me, I studied and created my plan, and submitted it, and was jubilant when our plan was approved.

With approval of my educational plan from the County Schools Superintendant, in August 1981, the boys and I began our learning adventure beyond the walls of an institution. I took them on 147 field trips. We visited Massachusetts, New York, New Jersey, Pennsylvania, Missouri, Michigan, Alabama, Mississippi, Kentucky, Arkansas, as well as traveling throughout our new-home state of Tennessee. John's job with Federal Express included discounted airfare—provided one was willing to go stand-by—so I took advantage of this and included in my boys' curriculum, travel to England, Wales, and Canada. None of this was expensive. We drove to states when the distance wasn't over 24 hours of driving, staying with relatives or friends, and even abroad found reasonable small hotels where children stayed for free, frequently having meals of bread and cheese.

Each visit included historic sites and museums. I fashioned the trips after my own experiences in Europe, for which I had studied the culture of each country and its history. In Massachusetts, we visited Lexington and Concord and traced the beginning of the American Revolution. We visited Plimouth Plantation, Old North Church, the Natural History Museum, historic homes, Mashpee Indian area, Harvard, Cambridge, and Cape Cod. In New York, we visited the World Trade Center, the Statue of Liberty, the New York Stock Exchange, Soho, the Empire State Building, the Metropolitan Museum of Art, MOMA, Rockefeller Center, and the United Nations. The trip to England included Buckingham Palace, London Bridge, Westminster Abbey, Big Ben and Parliament, the Tower of London, Dover Castle, Stonehenge, the Roman baths of Bath, with a side trip to the Evans family homestead in Wales where they met their Welsh relatives. The boys kept journals of their travels and logged all their other learning experiences.

I arranged for them to have internships in the working world. They worked in the library stacking books, gluing or inserting cards, and whatever other tasks the librarian chose to give them. They apprenticed with an architect firm, learning how to measure and draw rooms to scale. They worked putting up fence posts with an Arkansas farmer. They worked with a printer, a businessman, a stunt-car driver, a geologist, a homemaker, and an artist.

For contact with others their age they had Cub Scouts, community league football, soccer, and baseball, swimming lessons at Memphis State University, ice skating, Suzuki piano lessons, other music lessons which included playing the flute, plus time with neighborhood friends.

I purchased academic texts and materials for both fourth and fifth grades from The Calvert School, which has served overseas diplomats and others for decades. The boys studied math, phonics, grammar, spelling, vocabulary, reading, literature, science, geography, and history. We went to the library weekly to get specific books on whatever we happened to be studying or whatever the boys were currently interested in. Robinson Crusoe, the Arabian Nights, King Arthur and His Knights, and Paul Bunyan were among the literature from Calvert which the boys particularly enjoyed. From the public library, on their own, Jason, age 11, read sixty-one books and Nathan, fifteen months younger, read thirty-three. They kept lists of their reading and occasionally I had them write casual book reports. We talked about everything they read.

To be sure they were not stuck with only their mother for a teacher, I paid a fee to our next-door neighbor, a former math teacher with a Master's Degree in that field, to tutor the boys individually once a week. They worked on a week's worth of math between sessions. We had a similar arrangement with a friend of mine who taught English at Memphis State University.

Not having set hours or rigid schedules was the best part of unschooling. For us, learning never stopped; it was throughout our waking hours. We could do math after dinner or read books until midnight if we wanted. There was always some form of schedule—but it was flexible. For instance, when we got carried away reading books about a topic and we had been at it together for several hours, we were not concerned that a spelling lesson would have to be moved to 4:00. We didn't eliminate important lessons when we ran over or got off on a tangent, we just shoved time around to serve us instead of letting it dictate. We could control time in our learning environment, something a school could not afford to do. I felt it was important for the boys to be in control of their time, and we tried different approaches, including having them design their own schedules. And they had plenty of free time to designate as they wished, whether for playing ball or imaginative games in the woods behind our house.

Another plus was constant individual attention. I was always available if they had a question. But I think what I most valued was what happened to our relationships with each other. We became closer and more independent at the same time. We got to know each other as individuals—beyond our roles as parent and child. We were *sharing learning together* and no one could take that rich experience away from us. We spent far more time together than most parents and children do. We bonded in a way that has remained with us. I never went through what some parents go through when their children leave or go on long trips or off to college. From unschooling on, we had an underpinning of trust that was deeper than physical proximity. It was easy to let my boys go, eventually, because I knew who they were and valued their right to become fully themselves.

Unschooling breaks down the artificial walls between traditional subject areas. Vocabulary and spelling could come from what they were reading in literature, which could be linked to geography and history. This allowed the boys to see things as interconnected. Often such relationships were serendipitous or spontaneous. Sometimes the boys discovered links by themselves; sometimes I pointed them out.

One of our ideas was such a success that it was published in *Growing Without Schooling*, a national publication begun by John Holt for unschoolers and homeschoolers. It all began with socks. I was so tired of seeing the boys run outside in socks without shoes when they were in a hurry or watching them let the dogs put holes in their socks in friendly play. I said to myself: "If they had to buy those socks they wouldn't treat them like that!" It occurred to me that a good way for the boys to learn about economics would be for them to learn how to budget. My parents had given the boys a little stock with quarterly dividends which helped with the boys' school supplies and clothing. One day I told the boys that instead of my buying their clothes and supplies, *they* were going to. I told them that when their dividends arrived, I would give the money directly to them. They could spend it any way they wished, but it had to pay for everything they needed, except food and shelter.

When first told about this they were elated and had visions of shiny bikes, new baseball gloves, and enormous savings accounts. We sat around the kitchen table on which I had laid the "B" encyclopedia, large note cards, a columnar tablet, an inkpad, and date stamp. They were very curious about these items and could hardly wait to use the professional stamp. I gave them each a large note card on which to write down all their needs and goals. Then we read the section in the encyclopedia about budgeting. The information included a story about a boy named Carl whose income from jobs and allowance was less than his list of needs. The encyclopedia said something to the effect: "Carl will be in trouble if he pursues this budget." It tickled the boys as they quickly looked at the figures and saw Carl's dilemma (I read it with humor which they enjoyed, something a school math lesson would not usually include). They eagerly did math in their heads to solve Carl's problem.

We talked about major budget categories. I asked them which ones would apply to them. I talked about meanings of words like "income," "expenditure," and "contribution." In order to write out their own budgets on the special lined columnar sheets, the boys first had to find out how to spell these words. They had a sacred sense about these new materials they had been given—even spontaneously running up to their rooms to find binders in which to keep their budgets. Since dividends come quarterly, we talked about what "quarterly" means. "What's a quarter of a dollar? So what's a quarter of a year? So your budget has to be for how long? How many months is that?" We talked about how needs will vary from one quarter to the next, how major categories won't change but items and quantities might.

My only stipulation was that they had to buy *everything*—even their own toothpaste (which was an excellent idea since it avoided sibling arguments about who left the cap off or squeezed it in the middle), and that they had to have five clothing outfits—one for each weekday. Old clothes would be fine for Saturdays, and for Sunday they were to determine what they would like to wear to church and plan for it in their budget.

If it had not been 10 P.M., I'd have taken them to the stores to check prices at this point. In lieu of that, I gave them an approximate figure for the cost of a pair of socks. They had to multiply that by the number of pairs they thought they needed after taking inventory of their drawers. When they had to add their clothing totals, they were astounded by the way their funds disappeared to things like socks and underwear, leaving little for things like baseball gloves. "It's not fair clothes cost so much!" I could probably have introduced another lesson here on manufacturing—how clothes are made, the people who expect to be paid for their work in the making and marketing of a mere pair of socks—but we had enough going on.

One of the boys asked what contributions were. I offered some examples, but added they probably wouldn't have any at their ages except possibly for church. To my surprise, my animal-loving son budgeted a couple of dollars a quarter to the Humane Society. On their own they put down "college fund," "savings" and Jason, my automobile-loving son, listed in his budget a "Rolls Royce fund"! When I asked about this last entry, he said he only wanted to buy a car once and he wanted it to be perfect and to last; he said if he started saving now he thought he could afford one when he was a man. [That fund didn't last long. From teenager on, he went from owning a pick-up to a jeep to a Harley to a bright red Toyota MR2, and now, at age 43, drives the same Nissan he's driven for the past seventeen years, keeping it in perfect condition. The budget lesson stuck with him apparently, for he is the most frugal of my three—though Nathan is a close second.]

I showed the boys my family budget. This was helpful when they both found themselves about $20 over for the quarter. I explained to them why sometimes we ate more peanut butter than at other times, and how the semi-monthly paycheck that has to do the house payment doesn't have room for much else that two weeks. I showed them how I had to change my ideas to fit the income—or find more income. They hated doing this part, complaining, "I can't lower my savings anymore! There's *nowhere* I can cut!" They were almost hostile!

But like all of us, they found a way. I suggested they could do jobs to earn the extra $20 for the quarter if they weren't willing to cut back. They each compromised. They calculated that $20 for 3 months was not much over $1 a week worth of work. They offered to baby-sit their sister for an hour each week.

For days, they carried their budget binders everywhere, re-thinking certain parts or just looking at it. When the dividends came, I cashed the checks and put about $250 cash in each child's hands—an extremely difficult thing for a mother to do. Then I drove them to the stores where they chose to buy their clothes. I watched Jason—who at an early age had always appreciated good design [now a graphic designer with his own firm in Portland, Oregon]—agonize over a really handsome argyle sweater, but on his own he wisely concluded he could live without it because it did not fit into his budget. Nathan proved to be especially frugal, buying just the basics, not tempted by anything. Much later, when he was college age, though he knew how to dress handsomely, for a time, I recall him wearing dilapidated Tevas held together by a string. Clothes and things were not his focus.

Lessons from unschooling have stayed with my boys. I have watched each earn much of his college tuition and go on to a successful career. Jason held down three jobs his junior year and others other years. Following his degree in graphic design from Savannah College of Art and Design, he worked for a firm in Portland, later starting his own graphic design firm, which he continues to this day.

Before Nathan was twenty, he could do anything from driving a forklift to commercial construction and was even a janitor cleaning public restrooms at his university his freshman year ("humiliating but fun," he once said). His undergrad-college major was environmental science, with a special interest in ornithology (his thesis on the Marbled Murrelet). Nathan paid for his Masters Degree in Urban and Regional Planning entirely himself with jobs as The School of Planning's IT Technician and as a U.S. Geological Survey Researcher. After his Master's, he was hired as a planner with the Cayman Island Government (a British Crown Colony), where he worked for seven years and now is the Community and Economic Development Director for the City of Port Angeles, Washington. My sons' independence started early and grew steadily, in part, because of unschooling.

During our unschooling year, it was imperative to me that Charissa, two years old then, not be secondary to my work with the boys. She went everywhere with us—just as she had gone with me when I taught art—to museums, galleries, the boys' sports events, even field trips out of town and abroad. I established a playgroup for her once a week with four other little girls, each mother having all four children once a month. I also got better at delegating independent study as time went by so that when the boys were working on their own, Charissa and I had time together. I also made her Montessori projects and self-instructive learning items kept on shelves in the large playroom over the garage where the boys and I worked, so that she could help herself to a box of sand-paper letters or arrange shells according to size-sequence or find art materials.

Charissa's birth and unschooling the boys were highlights of mother-hood that taught me to break through barricades and not be limited by obstacles that would block growth or good ideas.

Another idea outside the box of conventional thinking came when I saw the need for a Christian Science Church or Society (a Society is the same as a church but with fewer members and without a public practitioner) in our community. We were driving 40 minutes to a Memphis city church, as were more than twenty others living in our area. Thirty Christian Science families lived in the eastern suburbs and out-lying cities. Rather than the long drive to the two staid, substantial city branch churches, both of which had sufficient memberships, it seemed we ought have a church serving the growing eastern population. I prayed about how this might occur. Several others did the same. I flew to the Mother Church in Boston to meet with the Branch Churches Department to learn the practical, legal, and metaphysical ramifications of starting a new church where none had existed before. They were very encouraging of our endeavor. Eventually we called a meeting, inviting the two existing churches, and I addressed the group. I remember saying that just as a mother has a third child without forsaking her first two, so we were giving birth to a new third branch church.

Not long afterward our Christian Science Society in Germantown was formed. Our goal was to simplify and purify, to get to the essence of church. Keeping rules to the minimum, we aimed for Spirit in all we did. We decided that the business of our church would be spiritual growth and healing—not committee meetings, boring reports, literature distribution, nor striving to increase membership. We wanted to serve our community and grow through prayer, to make *the idea* of church more important than busyness. I was one of three chosen to write our by-laws—a wonderful experience, for we decided we had the opportunity to keep things simple, pure, unbureaucratic by the by-laws we established.

We began meeting in homes, which was great fun because everyone participated, even the youngest children. The membership was like a large, caring family—each dedicated to our existence and purpose. Though our congregation of about 25 to 30 members consisted largely of families, we also had several single adults, and nearly half in attendance were children.

When we actually found and began to rent a building, our enthusiasm bubbled. People who might have previously been inclined in a more traditional church setting to say no to teaching Sunday School or certain duties, rose to whatever the need was, expanding their capabilities and spiritual growth. Every member "wore six hats."

One Sunday morning, when John was serving as First Reader, and the service had already begun, I noticed that the soloist had not yet arrived, with only five minutes left before the solo. So I motioned to John from my seat that I would come forward and sing the solo. I can't sing. My offer was based on courage, rather than ability. I planned to sing the Doxology—one short verse. John, misreading my intentions, announced that I would sing a hymn appropriate to the lesson, *all three verses.* People were kind; I survived; the service continued; we all had a good laugh later. Anyone in our close-knit group would have done the same.

At first we took turns being Readers in two-month stints, but eventually we elected Readers to serve for a year—which I did. We created a children's and infants' room, started a Sunday School, purchased rush-seated chairs, had a modest podium built, painted walls, dusted and vacuumed, watered plants, ushered, and maintained a Reading Room open to the public. Older children kept smaller children in the children's room during services, ushered, handed out hymnals, took up collection, gave testimonies on Wednesday evenings by their own volition. It was a great way for kids to grow up—*involved* in church, not merely taken to it. Though there might not be more than 10 to 20 in attendance, our Wednesday evening meetings held at 7:30 were full of testimonies, including a few by children. People spoke from the heart. Church was something John and I looked forward to twice a week, a joyful place the seven years it existed.

Its slow demise began when three families—nearly simultaneously—were transferred out of state. The few remaining members worked harder, but eventually, with further membership moves, the society was no longer viable and eventually closed. A special spirit and energy permeated that Society, and while it lasted, it was at the core of my existence.

While our little Society was blossoming, national media attention was slamming Christian Scientists for raising children without medical treatment. Mostly this issue was blown out of perspective. Often those appearing on talk shows or reported by media were not daily practicing nor deeply studying. *Daily* study and practice is essential. Christian Science, or any form of spiritual healing, is not something to dabble in! It makes strong demands.

Science is largely a preventive system. It is never Christianly Scientific to neglect or allow harm to come to a child. Even in her Message for 1901 to her followers, Mary Baker Eddy says: "follow your Leader only so far as she follows Christ" (Eddy, *Message to the Mother Church for 1902*, p.4:3). One is not to be a blind follower, but a thinking individual. If a Scientist is unable to effect a healing quickly in a life-threatening or fearful situation he had better make a beeline to the best care available—including medical (not that the medical system has a 100% success rate! A recent widely publicized statistic attributes one-third of all deaths to medical means). Neglect is never correct and every Class-taught Christian Scientist knows this. Media has frequently misinformed the public on this subject. To the general public, healing seems unsafe because it is unorthodox. Because it is unconventional it isn't understood. People are afraid of what they do not understand. Many haven't a clue what is going on when a loving parent who is a committed Christian Scientist diligently *works* for a child's healing.

To effect a healing, the genuine Christian Scientist first aims to eliminate fear. She does this through deep awareness of her all-loving Creator God— Spirit, Truth, Love, Principle—who made all that is. The genuine Scientist fills her thought with love and gratitude for God and His creation until there is no room left for thoughts of pain and suffering. This is not easy in the face of sickness, disease or accident, but it is not to the five senses the healer looks. Inspiring reading helps, as this verse from Isaiah I once used in helping my son: "*Fear thou not; for I am with thee: be not dismayed; for I am thy God: I will strengthen thee; yea, I will help thee*" (Isaiah 41:10). But healing is not about reading comforting verses and doing research. It is about genuinely filling up with love until some new insight is gleaned. It is about silent *listening* and obeying. One must be devoted to the healing work above all other activities. Healing work requires an open mind, self-examination, and willingness to change. The genuine Christian Scientist seeks answers in stillness, searching for the root cause behind the problem, tries honestly to see what attitude or behavior needs correcting—and *corrects* it in real space and time.

The moment of healing is indescribable. Words fail. It is like nothing else I know. It is not something to grasp but *experience*. Healing is a moment of enormous love, learning and transformation, as only one healed can understand, and as 60-some healings in the New Testament demonstrate.

In my experience, births, sprains, breaks, earaches, falls, flu, mumps, sickness, accidents, injuries, relationships, finances, home sales, moves—were prayed about and healed without medical or conventional means. Spiritual healing was my way of life as it was my father's. I knew no other way for over 46 years. As an adult and parent I became stronger in my practice because being Glenn Evans' daughter allowed me no anonymity and often I had to heal things on my own, without the support of a practitioner. For the most part, problems that arose, whether affecting my children, myself, or concerns larger than us, I handled *alone with God*. This foundation of spiritual self-reliance would hold me steady through unexpected challenges ahead.

I am amazed to see how many people never consider a spiritual solution but depend on medication. Often medication is limited in its effectiveness, yet I have seen people give up their autonomy to become guinea pigs, trying one medication after another, boxing themselves in by advertising's insistence that we need a pill to get up or go to sleep or to feel good or not to feel anything. The slightest discomfort seems to need tranquilizing in our society. It seems easier to pop a pill than to change damaging habits. Most humans avoid self-examination and change. As a society, we seem stuck in the conventional box called the healthcare system, a nightmare for everyone, including those working in it. We have walled ourselves into this system of few healing attributes. Healing qualities of love, patience, listening, stillness, self-transformation, and devoted care seem rare in the medical way.

Yet, I have relied, though very rarely, on the medical health care system, too. I have learned to appreciate the devoted professionalism of caring dentists, doctors and health professionals who meet needs when our prayers and understanding are not fine-tuned sufficiently to solve a particular problem. Had I not had a drug to knock me out so that a steel plate and seven screws could be surgically installed in my arm following my 2004 auto accident, I would have no use of my right arm, let alone be able to paint. What if my husband Bill's melanoma had not been removed? Would he still be transforming high school students' lives today? Would my sister-in-law be here if her breast cancer had been checked sooner? What if my artistic son had not chosen to have surgery on his crossed-eyes at age twenty?

I am grateful modern medicine can cure, while I uphold the higher power of God to heal. When to rely on God alone and when to call the physician? This is not an easy question to answer. I am challenged every day to understand more deeply the relationship of these two opposite methods of care—spiritual and material means—and of our own preventative and curative role in our wellbeing. But I do know that since surgery following my auto accident, I have taken no drugs and not seen a doctor but twice in the ensuing nine years. My trust is in God, not medical means, as it has been throughout my life. My wellbeing is governed by deep prayer and practice of what I know and continue to learn about God daily.

I am glad to have been raised outside the box of conventional thinking. Many aspects of Christian Science have proven beneficial, such as a proclivity not to be fearful, but to *live* love and truth, knowing my Creator God is Love and Truth—the divine Principle governing all. Christian Science instilled in me self-reliance, self-discipline, an appreciation for good, and the ability to look deep within for answers. I also believe that much associated with Christian Science is not just specific to this denomination, but is ancient and *universal*.

When I was a Christian Scientist, I did not know that silent prayer for healing is ancient. My journey had not yet taken me to the anonymous classic, *The Cloud of Unknowing*, or to the writings of Meister Eckhart or Evelyn Underhill or Julian of Norwich or to the beliefs of Native Americans, Celtic Christians, or the Desert Fathers. Eventually I would learn that spiritual healing is timeless. Though unpopular for its necessary discipline and stillness (things little valued in society), spiritual healing has been quietly present throughout many cultures since earliest history. For me, as a young parent relying on spiritual healing in raising my sons and daughter in the seventies and eighties, I knew only the Christian Science way, and felt unfettered, unbounded, by this method. But I have come to see now that what I was relying on was not so much a denomination founded in the mid-1800s, as something quite timeless, beyond denominational limits or walls, something *universal*: my faith and trust in *Universal Love*.

eleven

"Build Ye Houses"

"Thus saith the Lord of hosts, the God of Israel, unto all that are carried away captives, whom I have caused to be carried away from Jerusalem unto Babylon; Build ye houses, and dwell in them; and plant gardens, and eat the fruit of them... And seek the peace of the city whither I have caused you to be carried away captives, and pray unto the Lord for it: for in the peace thereof shall ye have peace." (Jeremiah 29:5,7)

Intuition tells me to mix more yellow ochre into the olive. Even then I cannot quite capture the shade of New Harmony's Poet's House. Years of sun and rain have mellowed its hue in a way I cannot record. My painting lacks the power of this place. The peach tree is accurate enough. The brick walk looks like brick. The cherry tree touches the chimney just as it should. The shadows mark the edifice as happens in nature. But what about the spirit? How do I put *that* on paper? Always this is the real challenge. Students think it is all a matter of technique and skill; but a good painting is always a matter of spirit. Everything is.

One afternoon in 1983 I drove to the country to fetch Nathan who had spent the night at a friend's house in Fisherville. Winding roads took me away from Memphis. Suburbs disappeared, replaced by tall pines, fields of hay and horses. I was early, having allowed extra time to find Nathan's friend's home, and found myself departing from the directions, turning off on an intriguing side road, taking it to its dead end. Ahead were miles of pastures and on the right a forest with a "for sale" sign. I turned off the engine and felt compelled to get out of the car. Like a swimmer testing the water, I walked to the edge of the property for sale. The land called me, inviting me in.

I had stood in many forests before but none more enchanting. I looked up into tall pines and oaks against a cerulean sky just as a bluebird flew by. Boughs rustled in the breeze as I walked up the hill of towering trees. Dark dense greens and umbers engulfed me. Textures of bark and decomposing leaves crunched underfoot. The bordering wheat field blew complementary color into the mauve horizon, pleasing my painter's eye.

But more than visual pleasure, there was something about this place, an almost tangible spirit. Sounds of things unseen welcomed me. Was that a possum or fox watching me from his hiding place under the downed and rotting trunk? I came to a bit of clearing where light danced on a carpet of burnt sienna needles and I followed its glow. I was not alone. What was this presence with me? At the back of the property I found a natural spring and pond with lily pads, croaking frogs, and dragonflies. I turned and surveyed the path I'd just taken. This strange and stirring place reminded me of my childhood in Michigan, of walks along wooded dunes, of my cottage in Glen Arbor, of the autumn bus ride in Tuscany when tree leaves talked, of summer days on Cape Cod. It was North country, and I was in the presence of God.

The next day I showed the 5-acre parcel to John and our children. Of course they loved it, too. What would it take to buy it? Could we even think about it? I remembered the ill-fated building venture in St. Louis. Would this be as risky? It would also mean a commitment to the South. Did we want that? What about these years of hoping for a return North? But the land had called my name. It's spirit held me.

We phoned the realtor to make an offer on the property; he came to our home promptly to write it up. Oddly, another offer for the same property came in within minutes of ours. The realtor said this was surprising because the 5-acre parcel had had no activity for many months. He explained that he was bound to take both simultaneous offers to the landowner. We understood and he said he would let us know as soon as he knew anything.

With the weight of what we were attempting, I walked alone into our family room and, picking up my Bible, asked God: *Is this what you would have me do, God? Why did I come to this land in the first place?* I knew this purchase would have to be more than my own will.

Certainly the land was beautiful. Already I visualized a natural house there—made of wood, stained to fit in with the trees. Lots of windows to let in the out-of-doors. Economical space—nothing ostentatious. Just quality throughout. Pine floors and window benches, plenty of bookshelves, fireplaces to read beside, maybe even a Swedish bed like I'd seen in a Carl Larson painting, and an art studio with north light. Everything comfortable and cozy.

But was it what *God* would have us do? Was it right to squeeze every penny to purchase land in the South? To build here? This decision would mean roots in the South. Did I want that? Is this what God would have me do? Why had I even stumbled onto this land in the first place? I wanted this decision to be what God wanted and not merely what I wanted. What would God have me do?

I prayed with my whole heart—reaching out to the Principle that governs the universe, much as the biblical woman in the crowd reached out to touch Jesus' garment in hopes of healing. "Show me God why I came to this place. Not my will, Yours, Father." With earnest words and sincere asking—as had become, and often still is, my way of prayer—I let my Bible fall open and read where my eyes landed, deeply pondering and studying the passage.

This method of prayer brings direction. I would learn many years later in seminary that this form of prayer—of deeply meditating on a single verse or passage, often one opened to serendipitously—is ancient and has a name, *Lectio Divina.* But with me, it originated quite instinctively and without knowledge of its history. Two of my favorite Bible verses capture the essence of this type of prayer, the first from Proverbs, the second from Matthew: "*Trust in the Lord with all thine heart and lean not unto thine own understanding; in all thy ways acknowledge him and he shall direct thy paths*" and "*Ask and it shall be given you; seek, and ye shall find; knock, and it shall be opened unto you: For every one that asketh receiveth; and he that seeketh findeth; and to him that knocketh it shall be opened*" (Proverbs 3: 5, 6; Matthew 7: 7, 8). When one gets personal desires out of the way and lets God inform her path, the right course of action appears. This is prayerful meditation's gift.

This particular day, with the property decision before me and my focus on listening for God's guidance, I let the Bible fall open, and read where my eyes landed: *"Build ye houses, and dwell in them; and plant gardens, and eat the fruit of them"* (Jeremiah 29:5). Amazing! How stunningly appropriate these words! I had never read this verse from Jeremiah before. I was awe-struck. I had just asked God to show me what he would have me do about building or not, to show me why I had come to the land in the first place, and the answer came with astounding clarity and specificity.

Overwhelmed, with tears emerging, I walked to the bookshelves where we kept the 12-volume *Interpreter's Bible* to research this passage. I learned that this letter from Jeremiah to the exiles is considered by scholars to be "one of the most significant documents in the Old Testament" and "rises to the highest pitch of religious consciousness to be found in the religious history of mankind up to this time." It speaks to the children of Israel longing for a return to their homeland. Jeremiah explains they must not hope for a return to their homeland soon. Rather, he asks them to lead full, normal lives *where they find themselves*—in captivity in Babylonia. He even admonishes them to *seek the welfare of the city in which they may be living and pray to the Lord on its behalf*—a revolutionary viewpoint. To pray on behalf of their enemy! "Build . . . plant . . . pray . . ." is the essence of Jeremiah's message. "Jeremiah here shows the Jews that their religion does not depend on residence in the land of Palestine, as previously he had shown it did not depend on the existence of the temple or offering of sacrifices and his 'climax line' is You will seek me and find me; when you seek me with all your heart, I will be found by you, says the Lord. Herein is contained the paradox of all religion, learned by Jeremiah out of the toils and sufferings of his own religious quest . . . as Heidigger puts it, 'Homecoming is the return into the proximity of the Source'—not a return to Jerusalem" (The Interpreter's Bible, vol. 5 pp. 1016-1021).

Like one of Jeremiah's people, captive in a foreign place, I had longed for a return to my homeland. I'd been complaining about the South when I should have been loving it, appreciating its character, and working for its well-being. How clear the message! I could not possibly miss the point! No longer could I harbor a desire to return north. I understood instantly that I must build, plant, pray *right where I find myself*. I saw that home is not a location—North, South, East or West—but a deep dwelling in Spirit. Coming home is not about returning to some particular physical place on the planet, but about dwelling with our Source wherever we happen to be.

Desire to leave the South vanished immediately. I was awed by the revelation received and the swiftness with which I felt transformed. How could I understand so much in an instant?! It was as if a healing had taken place. No, it wasn't "as if"; a healing *had* taken place! I understood in an instant that I'd come to this parcel of land *for this very experience*: for me *to see what I had been blind to*: to make *right where I was*—in the South—*home*. The lesson was to build, plant and pray for where I found myself—in Memphis. I realized I did not need the five acres. This experience wasn't about land so much as it was a divinely given wake-up call to what I had missed seeing, missed doing, missed appreciating.

"Let the other people have the land," I said, tears still quietly flowing, as I shared with John and the kids what I had just experienced, reading the significant passages. "We don't need the land; I understand why I came to it; it was for *this lesson*. I needed to learn to build, plant, pray *right where I am*, not yearn for a return to the North. John got it—this was one of the good things about our marriage: John appreciated any spiritual insight. He was in agreement when I said, "I'll call the realtor and tell him to let the other people have the land."

But before I could pick up the phone, there was a knock at our front door. It was the realtor.

"You're not going to believe this!" he said, excitedly, walking in right past us, shaking his head. "I've never seen anything like this in all my years as a realtor! The owner did not even look at the other bid, nor counter yours! He simply accepted your bid as it was! The land is yours!"

Then I knew that the building of this home was meant to be, and said out loud, "Then, even the doorknobs will be chosen through prayer!"

By selling some stock given to us by my parents over the years plus funds from the sale of our Germantown home (whose value had increased considerably in the short time we owned it) we were able to pay for our new home, incurring a modest mortgage. Working with an architect friend who gave us a special low rate, the designing and construction of our new home took three years.

One of the first things I decided was to have a lintel for one of our two fireplaces with Jeremiah's unforgettable words carved in stone: *Build... Plant...*

Pray . . . I found a gravestone carver to do it reasonably for me. I searched for architectural antiques to bring the old into the new: an 1850 nine-foot carved wood mantel fireplace façade and stained glass windows from Michigan, beveled glass leaded windows framing the front entry, imported English chimney pots for the chimneys and French cathedral newel posts found in antique salvage shops were built into the house. I spent hours designing details and searching for special "finds", locating things myself, and doing whatever aspects of the project I could to cut costs—like polyurethaning the floors and painting some walls myself.

Unusual features of the house were wide pine floors throughout, a sun porch and entry with Mexican Saltillo tile floors, window benches, yards of floor-to-ceiling bookshelves in every room, a cupola where the boys climbed to look at the stars through their telescope, and a Swedish bed in the family room behind cabinet doors that had a stained glass window looking out to a window box of red geraniums. I put favorite quotations I wanted to live with daily in Old English-style lettering on the twenty pine ceiling beams, surrounding the words with hand-painted ivy. Seventy-three curtain-less windows brought the heavily evergreened outdoors inside.

I worked hard to establish a rose garden, azaleas, zinnias and other flowers. The gunite swimming pool was not large and I had dark paint mixed in with the cement to make it look like a natural pond, as if it had been there as long as the old oaks and tall pines. Not far from the pool, the hammock suspended between two tall pines, swung kids, cats, and Newfoundland puppies—often all at the same time. Nathan, Jason, and I worked on hands and knees to turn a piece of forest into field, planting 800 square feet of vegetables. At one point we even had chickens—but they didn't last long with the surrounding forest of wild predators. We rigged up an old-fashioned tree swing and installed a surface for a basketball court out back; later we added a skate-board ramp and a small barn.

Life was utterly blissful on our five acres in Fisherville, Tennessee! My children played with Newfoundland puppies (I birthed forty-seven), raised chicks and ducks, roamed the woods, fished, canoed in the lake, helped in the garden, picked blackberries for home-made pies, swam in the pool, climbed trees, watched a water moccasin now and then, discovered baby possum, tobogganed down the long drive in winter, and glowed in the candlelight, good food, and beauty of country life. Daily life was nearly perfect for all of us and each one of us fully appreciated what we had.

One winter weekday—when Jason was 13, Nathan 12, and Charissa nearly 5—was especially enchanting. We got a terrific snowstorm, unusual in the Memphis area. Schools were closed and our long driveway piled high with snow. We were all delighted. The minute the school closing was announced, I began frying sausages and cracking eggs for pancakes and the boys began hauling in logs and building fires in both fireplaces. Transplanted Yankees, we approached a rare Southern snow with reverence and ritual: trips to the attic for toboggan and boots; rummaging in drawers for miscellaneous mittens and gloves; laying out extraneous wool plaid scarves received over many Christmases from well-meaning Northern relatives; playing the *Dr. Zhivago* soundtrack; selecting six or seven stories from *My Book House* to read before afternoon naps in the Swedish bed; filling mugs the ones decorated with Bavarian country scenes—with steaming cocoa and an added teaspoon of my own childhood: Ovaltine.

It's still crystal clear to me: my children are young again and we are together, enchanted by the unexpected big snow. As layers of syrup-coated pancakes disappear to sounds of Russian sleigh bells and crackling fires get re-fueled under the cat's supervision, outside flakes float, swirl, beckon. Nathan is the first to bundle up, struggling with last season's boots over this year's shoes, managing with sheer eagerness to get the impossible done. With a quick "Bye, Mom!" and slam of door he fades into the white cold.

From a window bench I watch. The blurry gray amidst the white is my son. He lifts one foot, observes the imprint, fascinated by the power of pattern on a snow canvas. With careful steps, then circles, finally trails, he creates his art. Concentrating. Diligent. Absorbed in his craft. He tests and tastes his material. Lies in it. Shakes it from the trees' needles to study how it falls. Between one short red mitten and a black ski glove he crunches, licks, then molds a form and throws it, zapping a tall oak. Again and again, with increased skill each time, he lets his powerful ice missiles fly. He glistens like a cake's sugar statue, his growing arms rise to the sky in worshipful glee, his face a vessel for heaven's outpouring. He laughs as the wet hits his tongue and lashes. Laughs in the joy of the unplanned day. And runs out of my view.

Okra, the cat, jumps in my lap as my daughter brings me her boots. In kindergarten she has just learned to tie her shoes. Proudly, Charissa shows me her accomplishments: tied shoes, zipped jacket, knit hat and scarf in place. Just the boots need doing. I fasten the tricky clasp. She squirms out of my grasp, giggling. Another slam of the door. Okra and I return to our post as Jason follows his sister, carrying his toboggan.

Jason's big steps and Charissa's little ones follow a sequence of initiation similar to their brother Nathan's—tracks, circles, projectiles. Puffing, Nathan runs to them, gesturing his unmatched gloves in several directions. His ten-minute lead in this wonderland proclaims his expertise. In voices rendered to me only by vapor, my three ambassadors negotiate great plans: a snow fort for the west side of the house, a snowman for the east, then tobogganing down the drive. "Gentle", our mother Newfoundland named after a favorite hymn, "O Gentle Presence," roused from sleep in the nearby shed, buries her nose playfully in the snow and prances around the decision makers, anticipating their action. She knows, perhaps better than any, the merriment potential of a good snow. I will find my boots and join them soon. Okra, curled and asleep now in my lap, purrs.

It was the loveliest of days.

February 26, 1988, I wrote in my journal:

My home has become as full and fine as Swedish artist Carl Larson's home. It has a patina all its own of flowers, sunshine, interestingly worn furniture, and happy family times. There's character here—the beams with my favorite quotations, the built-in architectural antiques bringing the past into the present. The simplicity is conducive to Socratic thinking. I'm glad I made the closets small so as not to collect stuff. I'm glad for all of it. It is heavenly here and I am the guest of God.

Walking through our five acres of Fisherville woods every day, I always felt deeply *grateful*. It was so beautiful. The house's red shutters, the green pinewoods, gardens, and privacy, the Newfoundland puppies running at my feet—the home that Spirit led me to build.

Building this special home coincided with other building. Jeremiah's admonition was put into action effortlessly. I followed through on every creative idea that came to me.

I started my first art business: The Fisherville Studio of Fine Arts, a rented space in a charming Victorian building with large storefront windows displaying my paintings. Open to the public four days a week, the studio became my home away from home. I taught art classes to all ages, exhibiting my work and the work of other artists. I produced a small catalog of drawing and painting courses for all ages, from 4th grade through adult, and taught six classes a week. Having outgrown my home studio, I did more of my artwork in the rented studio, including portrait commissions and art competitions and remained active in Memphis and St. Louis art organizations. I sold not only my artwork but carried the paintings of several artist friends, including my dear friend Diane in St. Louis. For my after-school children's classes, I offered an additional service: I picked up kids in my station wagon at Mt. Pisgah, giving them a snack in the studio prior to class—that way parents only had to pick them up once, at the studio at 5 PM. I hired a model and offered figure and portraiture classes for adults, which, to my surprise, serious students drove from Memphis to attend. I took my adult watercolor painting students on location to paint the abandoned cotton gin down the street, the hay fields around the corner, and the historic old plantation a couple miles away where you could put your finger in the Yankee bullet holes in the mansion door and nearly hear the rustle of hooped skirts as you painted.

I was also elected First Reader, responsible for conducting Wednesday Testimony Meetings and Sunday Services at the Germantown Christian Science Society we had helped establish in a new rented space. I continued part-time public Christian Science practitice for individuals who called me for assistance in healing and one practitioner in Massachusetts referred some of her patients to me when she was out of town or unable to take more cases. This work required my mornings be still and that I take several hours for study, reference work, and prayer.

I was elected PTA president for Mt. Pisgah, the local public school a few miles from our new home that all three of my children now attended. Mt. Pisgah's enrollment of nearly 1,000 students, kindergarten through 8th grade, consisted of a wide diversity of backgrounds from hundreds of miles of communities. The great-grandchildren of black slaves, still living in shacks without electricity or running water, sat at desks next to white children whose families had owned acres of farm property in the area for generations and beside children bused in from surrounding areas—some whose families had been transferred to the Memphis area from as far as California and New York who lived in gated communities with new half a million dollar homes—and beside children from small homes erected in the 30s, 40s and 50s whose parents both worked in factories, and beside children whose parents had come to the country to follow their dream of building their first home. There were huge economic, political, social, and religious differences. As Mt. Pisgah School PTA president, I stumbled into discoveries of terrible inequities that compelled me to challenge the large bureaucratic Shelby County School System, consisting of about forty-five schools, among them ours. In the process, I became an activist for change and an advocate for children's educational needs.

My PTA Board and I established volunteer parent-tutors in reading and math, art classes where none existed, as I had done at the boys' previous school, a health clinic (created out of an old bathroom) staffed by volunteer parents, playground supervisors, a Great Books program, and purchased thousands of dollars of new playground equipment with fund-raisers. We earned over $15,000 in one year for this economically deprived school through various projects: fairs, sales, organized drives, and the production and selling of a cookbook. For the cookbook, the PTA gathered favorite recipes from parents, teachers, students; I did the artwork. My PTA board printed it cheaply, collating it on my dining table for a week.

We worked diligently to improve our children's school. Nearly everyone on the PTA Board held at least a part-time job, but our PTA work was a labor of love that we fit into our lives. And we worked *hard*. We started a newsletter on my new home computer to inform parents of County School Board decisions as well as our own school's news; later a PTA board member created the mailing from her home, freeing me for other duties. Injustices were brought out in the open and improvements made. Eventually, nine badly needed new classrooms and a cafeteria were won through an amazing rallying of Mt. Pisgah parents. We encouraged parents to attend School Board meetings regularly, to speak up, sign petitions, carry placards, campaign for changes in our school which was twenty-five percent black and had been ignored for years in favor of attention to ninety-five percent white schools in wealthier suburban areas of the County.

Spirit governed our PTA activity; many of my board members felt this, too, though only a few would know the prayer that went into *every* day of work as PTA President. It was my custom to rise early and pray daily for this school, to let God direct my actions, that each day unfold as He would have it, not as I or anyone else might wish it. This verse from Psalms centered my thought before I spoke on all PTA occasions: "Let the words of my mouth and the meditation of my heart be acceptable in thy sight, O Lord, My Strength and my Redeemer" (Psalms 19:14).

Perhaps our bravest PTA undertaking was inviting the entire Shelby County School Board to lunch—for which many took a day off work and I closed my studio. We included a few newspaper and TV reporters as well. Our invitation included parents picking up all the school board members in vans driven by parents (that in and of itself was no easy feat, as their administration building was more than an hour and a half from our area). We did not let them just ride—we had a PTA person on every van with a sheet of information we'd researched and our guests heard facts en route of Mt. Pisgah's needs. They were driven throughout the varied communities composing the school area so that the members could see the extremely diverse social and economic conditions that complicated the needs of Mt. Pisgah. We wanted them to see first-hand the huge growth of our district in recent years.

Then, they were driven to Mt. Pisgah where other parents were stationed to take them on a tour of the school—almost no board members had been to the school before; we had arranged this with the principal who was supportive, if somewhat apprehensive, of our endeavor. We showed them the roof leaks, the lack of materials in the kindergarten, the need for basic supplies and better books, the need for smaller classes and more teachers, and the tiny cafeteria trying to serve a school built for a maximum of 500 students housing more than a thousand students and teachers (lunches had to start at 10:30 in order to get everyone in and out of the cafeteria).

After touring the school, the vans brought the board members to a gourmet luncheon—complete with fresh flowers and candles—at my home, where even more parents, many having brought favorite dishes and home-baked desserts for this event, were stationed to serve and talk with the board members. After hearty conversation, on full stomachs, the Board members were driven back downtown.

For this one day we had marshaled forces in a manner I now see as quite remarkable. I had delegated each one of my PTA board members to handle one aspect of the event from a long list of what it would take to pull this off. We were creative. We researched facts and statistics in libraries and by phone, creating information sheets pertaining to the entire area. We gathered evidence indicating our area had the greatest population and residential building growth in the county, yet had one of the oldest and most poorly maintained schools. We were even in contact with Washington D.C. Both federal and local governments were interested in what we had uncovered— the former, on our side, and the latter, afraid of the Pandora's box we were opening. Months of telephoning, meeting, planning, researching and letter writing went into preparation for this one day. The School board would not soon forget Mt. Pisgah!

Another significant day, Mt. Pisgah parents showed up en mass—as we'd planned—at a public County School Board meeting. TV and press were there, aware of what might transpire: a new day in grass roots involvement in public education in this part of the South. Black and white, suburban and country, shack and mansion dweller united in one glorious whole to fight for Mt. Pisgah's children! Together we faced the autocratic and auspicious county board.

Earlier that morning, looking out my bay window into the forest of tall pines while reading my Bible lesson in preparation for being First Reader on Sunday, I read a citation in the week's Bible lesson which jumped out at me as the defense for the day before the school board: "Be still and know that I am God" (Psalms 46:10). The battle was not mine but God's. His will would be done if I would get out of the way, love those around me more, and listen quietly. I copied this Bible verse on a note card and tucked it in my purse before I drove the hour and twenty minutes to the downtown morning meeting.

We planned for fifty Mt. Pisgah parents to attend the meeting—a revolutionary number in attendance considering usually less than half a dozen parents attended from all forty-some schools. More than fifty Mt. Pisgah parents showed up. They came with homemade placards, badges, and ready voices for Mt. Pisgah. There was a palpable tension and buzz of whispers as we waited for the Superintendent and Board to appear on stage. But the parents of Mt. Pisgah were prepared. Fathers had taken off work, mothers without sitters held babies, and parents of all colors and careers had driven forty-five minutes or more from their homes and jobs to express themselves today, to save their school and children. Whatever the board intended doing, these parents did not intend to let it happen without a fight. This was the first time these parents had taken a stand against the system. For some it was a new and uncomfortable position, like a shy kid having to work a math problem at the blackboard in front of everyone. Most parents felt intimidated by the procedure of speaking before the Board, of questioning authority, of making waves.

But this community-grown current had its own energy. Parents had seen too much and been well informed by our PTA Board to sit back in silence any longer.

The School Board had ignored overcrowding at Mt. Pisgah, busing incidents (i.e. over-crowded with insufficient seats for the number of students and excessively long routes), lack of classroom materials and supplies, inequities of all sorts, and were now about to vote to redistrict our school area—chopping up its sense of community and unity—against residents' wishes. I had spoken out at other Board meetings about the neglect of Mt. Pisgah and its needs. Compared to other County schools—noting the brand new buildings built in the totally white neighborhoods—our school had been ignored because of its black enrollment. We had written County Commissioners lengthy letters, been in contact with lawyers in the Federal government responsible for assuring laws passed in the sixties to govern Memphis schools' racial equity were upheld. We were a small group of parents vitally involved in something far bigger than we knew. In innocence we had stumbled into a lion's den. But like Daniel our innocence protected us.

"You know people could throw rocks at our houses! Look how my hands are shaking! I'm so nervous!" Wanda, one of my PTA board members said to me before we went into the meeting. Knowing she was a Bible-reading Southern Baptist, I reached into my purse and took out the notecard I'd slipped in there earlier that morning. "Read this, Wanda," I said. The card's words were those I had read myself earlier that morning: "Be still and know that I am God." "That's so *good*", Wanda replied with a smile.

There seemed to be a divine stillness in that noisy room. The Superintendent and the County School Board walked on the stage. Immediately they appeared stunned by the turnout. They spotted the media, and were not about to let us have the floor. Instead of taking a vote as expected to change our school area, something about "new information having come to light" was muttered by the chairperson, and no vote was taken! It was clear they intended to shorten the meeting to avoid us. Immediately I saw we were going to lose our chance to have our say, so I passed the word we needed to get our voices heard by staying and talking to the media as well as cornering the Superintendent and other Board members. A couple of fathers who had left their jobs as mailman and small businessman stood up and gave their statements, as we had planned. Then the board adjourned its meeting suddenly and scurried like frightened mice off the stage. But the Board had heard us by our very presence. They'd seen our black and white faces, seen our signs, our badges, and heard our words.

Then we turned to the TV and press and let them interview us as long as they wanted. I was on the 6 PM and 10 PM news that night speaking for justice for our school before all of Memphis and Shelby County. TV stations continued to keep up with the story for weeks. So did the Memphis newspaper. The article in the paper that came out at the peak of our struggle read: "The county system to date has not had any community involvement . . . . the community had been dictated to . . . This is a new day. It will never be the same" (*The Commercial Appeal*, Memphis newspaper). The man quoted was Roland Woodson, an African-American and the only school Board member who listened, cared, and helped us.

We won our badly needed new classrooms—nine of them—and a brand-new larger cafeteria!

To me it was more than coincidence that the name of our school was Mt. Pisgah—named for the mountain from which Moses viewed the promised land. The freedom we sought in expressing ourselves and being heard as parents and as a community of blacks and whites together caring about our children's education had deep roots in a Biblical promise. Just as Moses looked over into the promised land, and as Martin Luther King Jr. had done prior to his death in Memphis, we, too, saw the promise delivered.

Jeremiah's message was alive in me. I was building, planting, praying every day—right where I found myself, whether for school, church, or community. I cared deeply about every cause. I was always eager to take on what the day brought whether it was a patient asking for Christian Science healing help, a Wednesday night's church readings to put together, a bunch of Newfoundland puppies to bring into the world, a garden to weed, a new brochure of studio classes to design, a watercolor demo to give for a community art organization, an art competition to enter, a portrait to do, or a PTA board meeting to conduct. I thought about my work—how creativity and tenacity are always part of hard work. To this day I cherish work.

Years later, while teaching art one summer in New Hampshire, I would meet poet Donald Hall and discover his little book, *Life Work*, in which I'd find a quotation that expresses perfectly my feeling about work. It is something Henry Moore—a sculptor I've long admired—said to Hall when the poet asked his sculptor-friend, "Now that you are eighty, you must know the secret of life. What is the secret of life?" Hall writes: "With anyone else the answer would have begun with an ironic laugh, but Henry Moore answered me straight: "The secret of life is to have a task, something you devote your entire life to, something you bring everything to, every minute of the day for your whole life. And the most important thing is—it must be something you cannot possibly do!" (Donald Hall, *Life Work*, p. 54)

Work is a privilege that means we are *alive* and have something to give to our community, our world; that we are not just passing through. Sculptor Andy Gold said in a film I once saw—and I wrote his words down in the dark theatre: "If I don't work, I don't know myself."

During my work-filled days in Fisherville I felt *abundant*, as if I were partaking in a spiritual feast. Perhaps the one promised in the 23rd Psalm? The one I became aware of seven years ago in St. Louis, trudging a snowy hill to fetch my kindergartner while repeating aloud that Psalm in preparation to teach it to my Sunday School class? The one promised even in the face of my enemies of unemployment, lack, and near homelessness?

This Psalm had led me to Southern green pastures. And, sometime, when I was too busy working for my community's well-being to notice, I'd become part of the South. In a sense, I'd become a Southerner (or as much as any Yankee can). I'd gotten to know Southerners well. I'd driven with Wanda in her van over miles of dirt roads, getting lost and stuck in the mud, looking for rural homes and shacks, as we delivered Christmas turkeys, bought by the PTA, to poor rural families (I remember the family that had no running water who stacked donated old clothes in the back room of their dark hovel when they became too dirty to wear).

PTA Board members, parents, church members, Sunday School pupils, art students, the children I tutored at Mt. Pisgah, and many others had become dear to me. My paintings hung on the walls of their homes and what they taught me remains in my heart. I'd walked beside them, felt their summer heat and rainy winters, heard their stories, and learned from them their history. And I'd done what any artist knows is the surest way to know a subject: I'd painted their culture.

How many times I drove out to the old plantation—I must have done a dozen or more large watercolors there; all sold now. I even painted its grave-yard with tombstones of Confederate officers and the many family members whose descendants I knew of the same name. How many times I stopped in front of one remote general store or another, each with a lone defunct gas pump, old signs advertising Nehi orange soda or Mail Pouch chewing tobacco, weeds growing between the cracks of front steps, often a rusted screen door I painted with a loose mix of cerulean and burnt sienna. And always, about each place, I felt the fading charm of a past era I was not privy to until I picked up my paintbrush. And once, after driving several times past an eerie funeral wreath, too long left on a shack's front door, I stopped and painted what felt like a family's eternal sorrow. Another time, in Fayette County, just a few miles across the county line, I started painting an intriguing bit of dilapidated Victorian architecture when out on the porch came one, two, three, four—finally thirteen African-American family members from inside the house—each one wanting to be in my painting! That was a chal-lenge—but how could I not?! I sold that painting to a prominent white Memphis doctor's wife for too little a price—hoping she'd understand the life of that big black family hanging on her wall.

Another time, after a year or more of driving past an elderly sharecrop-per who always seemed to be sitting on the front stoop of his small shack regardless of the season or time of day, I stopped and asked if I could pho-tograph him to do a painting of him. He didn't fully understand nor could I understand much from his toothless grin, but I got the picture of him in his 1930s leather aviator's cap that he always wore, his overalls, and grayed white shirt, his gnarled knuckles and high top toeless tennis shoes. In no obvious way, somehow he reminded me of my father. He was black as night, taller and thinner than Dad, but both pairs of hands knew hard work. Both were faithfully in their place of duty. Perhaps it was the aviator's cap. Anyway, I took his photo. I prefer to paint on location, not from photos. But I had the camera in the car and *it came to me* to stop that particular day. The next week I read in the paper, to my dismay, he had been shot to death by a couple of "joy-riding" young white men. After reading this, I immediately developed my film and sat down to paint the sharecropper's portrait—a kind of testament, I hoped, to his dignity. My time in the South, taught me continually about the dignity of every Southerner (for that matter, of *every* man, woman and child everywhere).

Sandra Sue, whom I met as a teenage student in my first Memphis Christian Science Sunday School class that I taught, saturated me with wonderful Southern culture. She lived with her family on their farm in Mississippi but came to Memphis to go to church, shop, and later, to work in an art gallery (locals consider Memphis, Tennessee the "the capital of Mississippi."). We quickly became close. At first I was her mentor, but over time, we became mutual friends during the seventies through early nineties, sharing experiences and crises in both our lives. I remember taking Sandra to Cape Cod and Boston—her first trip there—to help me with my little boys, where she encountered her first revolving door and had me take her picture going through it. Charmed by her bubbly personality, sweet Southern drawl, red hair and freckles, some might not, at first glance, catch the brilliant intelligence and sadness at her core. Sandra's depth and soul-seeking paralleled my own. Differences of age, rearing, or region never limited our friendship; we were nearly as close as sisters, though today, distance has lessoned contact but not our mutual love for each other.

During my last year in Memphis, Sandra took me several times to a Mississippi farmhouse where talented old timers gathered with mandolins, guitars and fiddles to play country music the way it used to be played. People arrived in pickups and cars from across the county, plus a few from Memphis, like me. There'd be twenty or thirty of us, barely enough seats in the basement where we gathered. People brought homemade cakes, pies, and snacks and set them out on a table in a side room, along with a big coffee urn. The main room held a close and friendly foot-stompin' crowd, surrounding five or six musicians at microphones, perched on stools or standing in front of professional sound equipment. Anyone with ability could take a turn or join in the regular musical group led by the woman of the house—her clear country sound and skill with several instruments something she'd been sharing every Saturday night for forty years. It was a rare treat to be there. The rest of the world disappeared and I felt like I was at some primal place, where life is what it is supposed to be. I felt the same way whenever Sandra and I went to hear Blues on Beale Street.

Side-by-side with Southerners I had worked and played. You don't forget people that way. You become one. The people I came to know showed me the *true* South, the universality of mankind, and I learned that living Jeremiah's words, "Build…plant…pray where you find yourself"—those words that brought me to this promised land of Mt. Pisgah—also brought me the unexpected gift of *joy in where I find myself.*

twelve

Sailing Away

She watched her husband gather the herds and pack the last trunks on top of the wagon, heard him say, "We leave home to start a new journey." She wanted to cry but her eyes were dry; they'd seen too many departures. At night, after a long day's travel and setting up camp, when everyone was asleep, she cozied herself under the quilt she'd made from scraps of clothes she'd sewn for her husband and children. Lying on no-man's-land beneath the stars, far from her last home and even farther from her new one, only then did the tears silently come.

It is time to leave New Harmony. My things are scattered all about the Poet's House because I do not want to go. I want them to root themselves in the floorboards and sofa cushions, hide from me in the hearth, or refuse to be placed in the suitcase. I always seem to be leaving somewhere.

After six years in our extraordinary Fisherville home, John and I decided, upon going over finances, that we could save money for our children's education if we moved into Memphis where both of us were now employed, for I had taken an art teaching job in 1987 at a private school in Memphis to help with kids' tuitions. By then Jason and Nathan were at Principia, the private boarding school for Christian Scientists in St. Louis where John and I first started our lives together, and Charissa was at St. Mary's, a private Episcopal day school in Memphis. An advocate of and mostly a product of public school education—other than three years at Quaker Friends School—I was slow to realize that the kind of public school standards I expected were not to be found in the Memphis area.

Jason graduated from Mt. Pisgah's eighth grade (the principal asked me to give the graduation address) and attended Memphis University School until his last semester of his junior year when he transferred to Principia in St. Louis, where Nathan had already been for two years. Christian Science was vital to John and I and we knew Principia well, approved of its values, quality, and the opportunities it afforded our sons. Initially, we investigated Prin for Jason's high school years. On our weekend visit to Prin's campus prior to Jason's freshman year, he decided he preferred to stay in Memphis and attend Memphis University School, the companion boys' school to the girls school in which I taught; however, Nathan, only in 7th grade at the time, surprised us by saying, "Send me my clothes, I'm staying!" With thoughtful prayer I was able to let him go at such a young age.

People have asked me over the years how I felt about sending my sons off to boarding school—especially Nathan who was only thirteen when he started. It was not difficult because I have always known at a deep level that these are not my children, but God's. Children are not parents' possessions. Each child has an individual personality and destiny. As I view it, my job as parent is to enable each child to find his unique path, allowing each to discover, stretch, change, explore, make his own mistakes, and grow. Since their birth, my children and I have been close, sharing creativity, principles, ideas, and interests; during homeschooling and the building of our Fisherville home, this was especially true. Loving them, how could I *not* let them go?

Nathan blossomed at Prin. His innate sense of curiosity, his love of people, sports, the out-or-doors thrived at Prin. The diverse student body—students from all over the world and nearly every state—was exactly what he wanted, something not to be found in Memphis. Through football, classes that honored thinking skills, the independence of dorm life (even doing his own laundry) and serving on the boys' governing board, he grew into a confident, capable, caring and interesting young man. Nathan graduated from Principia Upper School in 1991, and to this day maintains strong friendships established there.

Jason's Prin experience—eleventh and twelfth grades—was less positive for him, though he chose to finish his high school days there. Jason always walked to the beat of his own drum. Actually both boys do. But as an artist, Jason has that extra need to not conform or fit in a slot and Prin didn't offer him what art schools during his college years would.

After her kindergarten year at Mt. Pisgah, I enrolled Charissa in St. Mary's Episcopal School for girls, one of the best private schools in Memphis. She loved it; so did I, even though it required my making the daily hour-long trip each way from Fisherville to Memphis while running my gallery!

Prin's generous scholarships, occasional gifts from my parents, John's job with Federal Express, my art sales and teaching, along with much frugality, enabled us to manage private schools for the kids. But the greatest provision for the children's education came in 1987 when I was offered, and accepted, a teaching position for the lower and middle schools at the Custis Lee Academy for Girls in Memphis, with promise of teaching high school art when the longtime high school art teacher retired in a year. A friend who was head of the middle school had asked me to consider this opening. Busy with my gallery classes, I responded, "Why, I can't do that! I have a gallery to run." Later that evening as I prayed, it came to me that I had been too abrupt and should consider her offer. I had taught art in a variety of schools to all ages—young children, teens, and adults since 1965. For nearly four years, my Fisherville Studio of Fine Arts had given me the space, privacy, independence for my artwork and teaching. I loved owning my own business and was not eager to let it go. But I realized I needed to be open to change. I saw that a salaried job would provide more consistent income for my children's tuitions, and with my gallery closed, I would no longer have gallery rent to pay.

I inquired further about the position and learned there were twelve applicants. I filled out the application with creative teaching ideas rushing through my brain. I interviewed and, to my surprise, got the job. This one nearly missed opportunity altered the rest of my life. Within a few years, teaching at Custis Lee afforded me two blessings, one of which was the privilege of getting my Masters Degree at Rhode Island School of Design through a professional enhancement grant the school offered teachers —a vastly important experience for me.

Once I started full time teaching at Custis Lee my life took on an even busier pace. The drive to and from Custis Lee and my full school day left me little time to enjoy the woods or to take care of our Fisherville home, its gardens, acreage, and animals. Our animals spent more time enjoying our country property than we did! Around 1988, we no longer had Newfoundlands, but two cats and Surprise, a beautiful Samoyed. I felt frustrated not having time with them and our lovely home. It seemed I was always behind the wheel of my car or in the classroom. Charissa and I were in town every day and the boys only came home from boarding school for vacations and long weekends. When they were home for Thanksgiving or Christmas they sometimes brought friends with them—a happy time. But except for holidays and weekends, we rarely used the canoe, fished the lake, or swam in the pool. But I still had all of it to maintain. Obviously, moving into the city had merit— but not my enthusiasm.

I wrote in my journal, December, 1987: *I am searching for answers. I must complete my Master's degree—that's a given. I must support my children's education by working—that's a given. I must support church—that's a given. I must write because I can't not write. I must paint because I can't not paint—two more givens. How to balance it all?! I do not know yet, but if I put God first, everything will fall into place. God will guide me and I will follow.*

It was more than a house I was to leave. Building this home had been an *incarnational* activity, a manifestation of beliefs, an artistic creation full of sacred symbolism. How could I leave this unique work of art? It was one thing to sell a loved painting I had labored over, but to sell this home—every particle of which had significance—was almost more than I could bear. I remembered standing precariously on a ladder to painstakingly paint ivy on the large wood ceiling beams around favorite philosophers' and biblical quotations in Old English lettering—ideas I wanted to live with daily. I recalled polyurethaning floors until midnight with Cathy Schmid, a girl from Switzerland who needed a place to stay for a year and came to live with us. I remember sunsets reflected on the antique beveled glass doors in the front hall and my wonderful kitchen with eight windows to the woods and front lawn. I thought of the exquisite carved fireplace façade and mantel I'd found in a northern Michigan antique shop and had sent back for our living room. I recalled Christmases, snow-bound days cocoa-sipping in front of either fireplace, Jeremiah's words

"Build…Plant…Pray" on one mantle and on the beam over the other, *"Home is not a place but a power"*. I thought of my Newfoundland puppies born by my own hand, of the nights sitting up with them, finding them good homes, and burying the few that died. I thought of Jason, Nathan and me, our summer-tanned hands and feet in the knee-high weeds creating our vegetable garden, hacking at persistent tree roots that still thought the land was theirs. I remember standing by the lily pond at the back of the acreage wondering how to fence where land and water met in order to keep our dogs in. I remembered tobogganing with kids and Newfies down the long drive in moonlight; and nights in July, lying on my back in the swimming pool looking up at the same moon through pine trees, thinking no life is better than mine.

It is as real to me now as then—that feeling of knowing I had to leave but not wanting to. Could I just sail away from all this? Could I live without another sunset through those trees? Could I shed all I'd known here as easily as my carefully planted azaleas shed their blooms or the dogwoods we'd planted along the drive lose their petals?

The night of the decision to sell our home I cried myself to sleep without making a sound. With blurred eyes I looked out my bedroom window into whistling trees, listening to an owl hoot and the rustle of branches against curtain-less glass. A beautiful night; a night of agony.

Morning came quickly. Puffy lids resisted daylight, but I woke aware that last night's decision had not been a dream. John, up early as usual, had read his Bible lesson and left by 6:45 to drop off Charissa on his way to work. It was nearly 7:00 and I would need to hurry if I wanted to be on time to school. But I couldn't move.

I told myself, sternly: "You can wallow in despair over this loss or you can pull yourself up by your bootstraps and find the lesson in this experience!" From under the feather comforter I reached for my Bible on the bedside table. Before I let it fall open, I talked to God: "O.K., Father, seven years ago You brought me to this land; if You are taking us away now, show me as clearly now as You did then."

I let my Bible fall open and read: *"The burden of Tyre. Howl ye ships of Tarshish; for it is laid waste, so that **there is no house**, no entering in"* (Isaiah 23: 1).

No house! Another time in my life I had let my Bible fall open and found equally poignant teaching that brought me here. Then, as now, the message was stunning. It seemed as if I were standing on holy ground—again. Wide awake, I ran downstairs to the shelves of scholarly Biblical references to research the meaning of this passage before leaving for school.

I learned that the Dead Sea Scroll for these verses speaks to the doom of Tyre whose trading colonies were in Tarshish, a "proud maritime power". The translation for the Isaiah verses (with my emphasis): *"Your stronghold is **without house** or haven. **Sail away from your land**, O ships of Tarshish; **there is no harbor any more"** [my emphasis] (The Interpreter's Bible, vol. 5 pp.294-295).

Tyre had been grand. So had been our home and accomplishments while living here in Fisherville. I lamented our loss as Tyre did hers "like a high-land coronach celebrating the glory that is gone. Isaiah was great enough to salute the achievements and mourn the fall of a people who had accomplished so much..." *(The Interpreter's Bible*, vol. 5, pp. 294-295). Though on a much lesser scale, the comparison was obvious: good done while living in Fisherville would have long term effects for church, school and community. I wondered why Tyre had fallen from its greatness and read further: "Why was the judgment pronounced? Isaiah declares it in two lines: To abase man's pride, to humble human splendor" *(The Interpreter's Bible*, vol. 5, pp. 294-295).

This line—"to abase pride and humble human splendor"—showed me clearly why we must leave. These words silenced any doubt about moving. We said we were leaving for financial reasons; things had changed with two sons in boarding school and a daughter in private school. But financial problems are a symptom, not a cause. I had not thought of our home in a prideful way, nor was it ostentatious, but I did love it; perhaps more than one should any material thing. Perhaps shedding it was necessary for spiritual growth? God's direction was clear in Isaiah's message: pride of accomplishment needs to fall.

Our Fisherville home is not the only thing I am being asked to leave in 1988. As I research "Sail away from your land . . . there is no harbor any-more," I learn harbor means *rest* which means *fixed, settled, to remain the same.* I see there will be no rest for me, that things will not remain the same. A journey, or *sailing away* is being called for. I am not merely to sail away from home and land, but from land-locked thinking. I am being called to depart from fixed ways, settled-in ease, sameness, certitude, and to enter uncertain seas. I am to venture beyond the safe and sure, to expect the unexpected, to risk. Isaiah's wisdom makes the idea of leaving less painful while the house is on the market.

The same year, Irish musician Enya's groundbreaking *Watermark* album comes out with its top song's ubiquitous refrain *Sail away, sail away, sail away* permeating radio airwaves and shops, reminding me everywhere I go of my need to sail away. I buy Enya's CD. Seas of change are on my horizon. Bob Dylan's remark comes to mind: "He not busy being born is busy dying." I was busy dying and being re-born, but didn't fully know it. Like the ever-adapting Welsh Gwydion, I was shifting again.

While living in Rhode Island for the summer in 1988 working on my Masters Degree at Rhode Island School of Design, I glean more from Isaiah's words. I realize I'm being asked not only to sail away from house, comfort, fixity, and accomplishments, but from something I've been denying for years: discontent with my marriage. I'd expected my marriage to last. But I slowly begin to realize that leaving it is part of the journey I'm being called to take. Along with property and settled ways of thinking, I'm also to leave my husband.

From the start, some elements of marriage were disappointing, but I had denied my feelings, tried to overcome them. Christian Science, with denial at its root of practice, helped me do that. Unconsciously, I had turned to children, church, and community to give and receive the affection and involvement missing in marriage. Passionately involved with children, church and community, I became too busy to face the truth about my marriage. Creating art, babies, homes, projects to help causes and find solutions, I avoided personal desires and needs. At first, I figured this was just how marriage was—that spiritual things mattered more and I should *overcome* my wish for sharing ideas, books, intellect, decisions and responsibilities, dreams, intimacy and deeply loving companionship. Love for God, I told myself, was what mattered, not marriage-love. Furthermore, I made myself believe that whatever was missing in my relationship with John simply offered me an opportunity to rise higher spiritually. The reality was that all those years of neglect accumulated like drops of water in an ocean and the floodgates were about to open.

I looked at my beautiful Fisherville home and discovered a true marriage didn't dwell there. What I did not understand then and what I have learned since is that a couple's first real "child" is the *love* they have for each other and that if that child is not nurtured and fed daily it dies; when it dies the house is empty, no matter how many children or pets or lovely things occupy it.

Though he was a good man with high morals, John contributed little. Often I felt as if I had a fourth child. I handled so many responsibilities alone and most decisions were left to me. He went to his job, did church work, mowed the lawn, and coached our boys' teams occasionally, but our husband/wife interactions and conversations were limited to Christian Science and care of our children. Sharing books and ideas, playfulness between the two of us, cuddling, and other normal marriage acts were not really part of our relationship. I never saw John read a book other than Christian Science literature, but he did like to watch TV sports and sitcoms. He had no hobbies. The friends we invited to Christmas parties were usually people from church, neighbors, or people I knew. People liked John for his warm smile, welcoming handshake and ability to listen, but I never knew him to have a friend over. People knew, however, they could count on him at church or in the community. At work, though his efforts were sincere, his performance was sometimes less than what a boss wanted, for he was fired three times during our marriage. But John was an honest person who cared to help others and the company for which he worked. I believe much later his accomplishments and confidence improved.

I sometimes wonder if my vitality stimulated whatever life he had during our marriage—or intimidated him. I felt as if he lived through me and my doing. Other times, I thought he might make a good monk (if Christian Science had them). He appreciated me as a partner in spiritual endeavor and as something to take pride in, the way other men bought shiny new cars. As for *knowing me*—my inner thoughts and questions, who I was, what I hoped for, felt, did, and cared about, what ideas mattered to me beyond our religion, what books I read, what music, art, philosophies I studied, what I needed as a woman—he never seemed to know or care to discuss.

We were compatible in our devotion to our church, however. Our commitment to Christian Science as a way of life never waivered while we were married. It offered us a foundation on which to build our family, to give our children values and standards—honesty, decency, integrity and compassion. A certain goodness aligned us. God mattered most. These principles guided us throughout our twenty-one year marriage, and today enable John and I to remain friendly.

Though united by the same principles, our individual practice of Christian Science differed. John would spend hours in silent meditation, sometimes putting himself to sleep, and the ritual of Bible lesson reading seemed to take precedence even when a child's calamity interrupted. I felt John was in an ivory-tower isolation of his own making, blocking out human experience in order to perceive only the spiritual. He strongly believed he ought not share whatever problem he was working on, even with his wife, even when the problem affected her, too. He whisked away any enquiry as if it meant disloyalty to his healing progress.

Solving crises on the spot was not John's forte. He left the scene when Jason fractured his elbow saying he had to leave in order to see the "spiritual nature of our son," leaving me to hold my screaming child while also declaring healing truths. He had refused to be at the births of our sons because he said it would cause him to see the birth of "a mortal, not as a spiritual reflection of God." John intended not to be at our daughter's birth, too, but I insisted. It seemed to me if I could carry his sperm in my body to a full term infant, the least he could do was show up for delivery of our third child, having missed the birth of the other two. I think he was glad he was there. Of our three children he is closet to Charissa.

Unlike me, John was not a seeker. Like most Christian Scientists, he believed he already had the truth—what was there to search for?

John rarely expressed emotion—except very rarely anger when one of the boys misbehaved. I remember once he squeezed Jason's hand so tight that it frightened me. But this was unusual; ordinarily John was kind, mild-mannered, stoic, and distantly quiet.

When we tried to discuss an issue on which we had different opinions, his response was often: "I know this is not the real you" and *walk away*. Expressing something you feel deeply and having someone respond by walking away from you, is worse than if they argue. Though he claimed to love me, apathy was what I frequently felt he expressed.

Other than the first few months after our wedding or for the purpose of creating a child, affection and lovemaking weren't part of our marriage. John's kindness to strangers, could be truly that of a Good Samaritan, but I am not sure he knew how, nor even desired, to express love physically, for he once said to me: "I could never love you physically, only *spiritually*."

How did I feel about this as a woman? I was too naive in the early years to know what I was missing, though I sometimes suspected there ought to be more to marriage than I was experiencing. I know sometimes I longed to be held, or paid attention to. But filling my days with giving to others eradicated personal pain in this regard. I just figured I was supposed to grow spiritually, to *overcome* disappointments and longings. If *I* weren't happy, I figured it must be *my* fault. If I had been under the impression that marriage included conversation, cuddling, and close sharing of ideas and feelings, well then, I must have gotten it wrong, because that's not what John and I had.

What we *did* have was an ability to get along, to respect each other, and to serve our church together. Our relationship, when at its best, was a sort of brother-sister/mother-taking-care-of-son/ convenient roommates/Christian Science co-workers combination. I'm sure no one observing us thought our marriage anything other than normal. And in some areas of marriage that was true.

I entered marriage with high standards, so I took on more and more to make home and family be what I thought it should be. I spent years denying our incompatibility and held tight to what good there was. But after twenty years, hidden tears came. I would find myself unable to stop crying for no apparent reason—a sign I now recognize as depression. I got good at hiding it. Crying without a sound. Hiding in a bathroom or closet—even once at school in the art supply closet. I really did not understand why I was sad. I simply knew my sadness had to be healed and I worked at this daily.

"Divorce" was not a word spoken in my family. No one in my family had ever divorced (actually Aunt MaryLou had, but I would have been about three at the time). In fact, I did not even know anyone who had divorced. The idea was totally incompatible with everything I valued and believed. Leaving my marriage was unthinkable. Divorce was not an option. I could not even utter the word. I had been raised to be the faithful obedient child and to follow that with being the faithful obedient wife. So I denied the thought of divorce every time it came, seeing it as an "evil suggestion."

I saw no way to "sail away" from my marriage. Neither my family nor I would tolerate it. It was not something *true* Christian Scientists even contemplated—or so I thought at the time. So I denied the need and buried myself in a busy life and in my art—just as I had in childhood when there was no other place to go. Art has always offered survival.

Going to RISD the summers of 1988, 1989, and 1990 in Providence, Rhode Island became my salvation. Fellow students in the three-year program for a Master's Degree in fine arts were predominantly university and high school art teachers from all over the country and several foreign countries. We were required to take a full load of summer studio courses of our choice plus an art education seminar, and write two fifty-page thesis papers back home during the school year.

During my RISD summers, my children went to summer camp and the last two years the boys had summer jobs. My second summer away, our home in Fisherville was for sale and Surprise, our Samoyed, and a couple of cats kept John company when he came home from work at night.

In Providence, without my usual responsibilities and interruptions, I could draw and paint 'til all hours of the night. At last I could be the artist I had always been on the inside! I read voraciously as well: Plato, Hegel, Jung, Ibsen, Arnheim, Eliade, Kandinsky, Heidigger, Kierkegaard, and many others. The RISD and Brown University libraries were a smorgasbord for my intellectual starvation. There seemed to be no satiation point. Books piled beside the bed in my Providence apartment. New paintings covered my walls. I wrote every day. It wasn't that I had extra time for these activities, I *made* time for them. My energy level at RISD was astounding, even to me.

Fascinated by the intellectual discussions my first year, both in and outside class, I toyed with several possibilities for my first major thesis which I was eager to start. But nothing came together clearly until I returned home and started teaching for the new school year.

More times than I can count, precisely the right words from book or stranger—serendipitously (or spiritually directed?)—have popped into my life, powerfully transforming it. A chain of such instances occurred beginning with a 14-year old student of mine, who frequently discussed ideas and books with me after school. One day she asked if I had ever read *Walking on Water: Reflections on Faith and Art* by Madeliene L'Engle. I said no, that I had read her trilogy for children to my sons when we did unschooling but that I did not know this one. " She's written many books for adults," my student told me, "You *have* to read it, Mrs. West, I know you'll like it." I responded, from what she said about it, I would like to read it someday.

Next week in a school chapel the associate headmaster, a former Yale scholar, stated that "Incarnation is the single most significant fact about Christianity." I had never heard this before. Unfamiliar with incarnation—it was not significant in Christian Science theology—I was fascinated that I, a devoted Christian, had little awareness of it. I walked out of the chapel and into the connecting library, pondering this new discovery. Absorbed in thought, I bumped into one of many special tables set up for a book fair, knocking one book to the floor. I picked it up. It was *Walking on Water: Reflections on Faith and Art!*—the very book my student had mentioned only the week before! Shocked by such serendipity, I read the first couple pages, and was hooked. There was only one copy and I bought it immediately. I devoured it that weekend, underlining and re-reading favorite parts. It was poignant, enlightening, and precisely where my RISD thesis was headed! And *incarnation* was a consistent theme of the author's!

Illuminating incarnation as it is experienced by the artist, L'Engle's book touched my soul as it clarified my thesis:

> *...to paint a picture or to write a story or to compose a song is an incarnational activity. The artist is a servant who is willing to be a birthgiver. In a very real sense the artist (male or female) should be like Mary who, when the angel told her that she was to bear the Messiah, was obedient to the command (L'Engle, Wallking on Water: Reflections on Faith and Art, p. 18).*

That was it! I had not known the term *incarnation* until now, but what I had really been *wanting* to write about was *incarnation*! My thesis became: *The Creative Process as Incarnational Activity.*

Before I read these words I knew their meaning. L'Engle's book affirmed what had been going on in me since early childhood. Obedience had been the predominate feature of my rearing. Now that ability to obey was alive in my work as an artist. I knew how to be the faithful servant of an idea and take it where it dictates—whether for a painting, a poem, or a righteous cause. I know to nurture an idea born in me, to feed it and watch it grow on its own. I feel an obligation to enable it to live fully—no matter what it takes. L'Engle speaks of an artist's devotion to *idea* in a way that brought tears to my eyes the first time I read it. It is my favorite statement of what it means to be an artist:

> ...*the artist is someone who is full of questions, who cries them out in great angst, who discovers rainbow answers in the darkness, and then rushes to canvas or paper. An artist is someone who cannot rest, who can never rest as long as there is one suffering creature in this world. Along with Plato's divine madness there is also divine discontent, a longing to find the melody in the discords of chaos, the rhyme in the cacophony, the surprised smile in time of stress or strain.*
>
> *It is not that what* **is** *is not enough, for it is; it is that what is had been disarranged, and is crying out to be put in place. Perhaps the artist longs to sleep well every night, to eat anything without indigestion: to feel no moral qualms; to turn off the television news and make a bologna sandwich after seeing the devastation and death caused by famine and drought and earthquake and flood. But the artist cannot manage this normalcy. Vision keeps breaking through, and must find means of expression* (L'Engle, p. 143).

I am this obedient servant, this artist. It is, perhaps, the most vital fact about me. It became the *how* of my paper as well as the topic itself. Ideas catapulted into thought as I wrote, as if I had been waiting all my life to understand and share these ideas. L'Engle's quotation hung on my classroom wall and became part of my syllabus each year.

I was always eager to return to RISD. Though it was difficult to leave my children and Fisherville each summer, I was turning to a new light like winter Geraniums reaching for the sun. In exploring art and religion—partners throughout history until the twentieth century—I discovered a deeper direction for my own artwork and philosophy. I found an intellectual *home* in the ideas I was discovering that were already at my core. Enigmas I had lived with now had explanation and puzzling pieces of thought came together in a *wholeness*. Like a magnet collecting metal fibers I attracted synchronicity, serendipity, and enlightenment. And Providence, Rhode Island, became my summer home for this growth.

Providence. Could there be a more perfect name? A name signifies the nature of a thing; and, in this case, identifies the mystical quality of the place.

Some sort of strange metamorphosis took place every summer I arrived in that creative, vital and historic city. I was bombarded by images: variety of textures, shapes, architecture from the seventeenth century to the present, colleges, universities, bookstores whose windows sucked me in daily, steep cobblestone streets, highways to beaches in less than twenty minutes or to Boston in a mere forty, seafood, famed restaurants and musical night spots, alleyways with fire escapes, flower gardens tucked between Victorian houses, ethnic diversity that required grocery stores carry more than five kinds of Italian peppers, Mediterranean seasoning, Portuguese bread, and strange Chinese vegetables Memphis didn't have.

My second summer at RISD, the fashion statement appeared to be to wear plenty of black clothing, pink Mohawks or nests for hair, thick industrial boots, and purple-black lipstick—except for those of us who made our living as teachers. My Cher hair and then thin body showed no such arty signs. I was in my early forties for God's sake. Sandals and an Indian print skirt were as arty as I cared to get. But I loved observing the diversity, the craziness that often surrounds an art school. In fact, Providence provided a field day for me as imagemaker.

Images can be tricky, mysterious, and powerful. Artists come with built-in antennae for them. They are the substance of my work as a visual artist and I gather them continually. Images are ideas born visible in the imagination— that connecting link between the conscious and subconscious, where much of our brain functions occur, the place that holds our personality, intellect and spirituality together. Images bombard me at the breakfast table or at an intersection. I do not forget the pattern on the windshield made by rain nor the beauty of faded aqua and peach paint on a slum wall. Wherever I go I am under a constant barrage of images. It is as if I lead a second, secret, life in multiple layers of my mind. Images roam throughout mental strata and come together now and then to take form in my journal, sketchbooks, or a 2 AM poem. Sometimes a few burst out into daylight conversation as wild metaphor or simile, but usually I corral them into writing or a painting. When our work of seeing becomes intense, images can take over and permeate our lives.

That's what happened my second year at RISD, the summer of 1989. All the sights, sounds, colors, shapes, freedom and joy that I was experiencing, that was Providence, became symbolized in one extraordinary face.

I had just set down my suitcase to figure out the apartment lock in the charming three-story Victorian building, my home for the summer, when someone bounced down the stairs from an upper floor. His head was turned as he spoke to a friend, but he glanced my way as I looked up from the keyhole. I was stunned by his beauty. I could hardly keep from dropping the key. Never before in my life had I been so gripped by a man's image. He appeared to be about thirty. The most startlingly attractive thing about him was his expression of *joy*. I'd never seen such lively joy in a face, except in my daughter's at age two. His eyes were clear, dark and directly gazing at me. His mouth showed a kindness and an authority at the same time. He epitomized dominion, purpose, and caring all at once. His thick brown-black hair was wildly curly like my own. I knew in a glance that whatever he did it was unique and exciting.

"Have you rented the apartment?" he asked kindly as he and his friend headed toward the double glass doors of the main hall.

"Yes, only for the summer," I answered, glad that the question provided me with a longer look at him.

That night after I had unpacked and put my things in order, I lay in bed contemplating tomorrow—my first day of my second RISD summer. Anticipation was high. I would definitely go to the library and check out tons of books tomorrow after classes. And my classes: three hours each of portraiture and figure drawing, abstract painting, and illustration! For only the second time ever in my life since I'd been married—the other time being the previous RISD summer—I had relinquished my obligations as wife, mother, Sunday School teacher, church administrator, and teacher to be just me. I could rest knowing my daughter was at camp in Maine and my sons both had construction jobs for the summer at home—and one would be going to camp later. I realized how rarely I had been alone in the past nineteen years. It was a delicious feeling. No responsibilities. What a change! I snuggled under the covers with a smile.

But I couldn't sleep. I heard footsteps above. I wondered about this person who lived over me. Was it the handsome young man I'd met on the stairs when I arrived? The image of his beautiful face matched the strength in the footsteps overhead. I could hear everything he did: the closet doors closing, the dresser drawers creaking, the washer, the shower.

Each day I awoke to his sounds. I knew when he ate, washed, slept, or left. And I began to wonder about him.

Then one night while in bed with my master's paper spread around me, my doorbell rang. It was almost 1:00 A.M. Who could that be? All of my RISD friends would be as busy as I was in their dorm rooms or apartments elsewhere. Curious, I went to my door and looked out into the hall toward the double Victorian entrance doors with their long glass panels. There was that beautiful face I had met the first day, smiling at me! Apparently he had locked himself out and was trying to rouse someone from one of the five units. I went into the hall in my nightgown and let him in. More expressive close up, he warmly thanked me as his dark eyes penetrated my own from under kinks of nearly shoulder-length hair.

"Thanks," he said with a wide smile, I must have forgotten my key; I really am terribly sorry to have bothered you. I hope I didn't wake you? But (he scanned my nightgown)…I guess I did."

"It's okay, I was up."

"Thanks again! Really appreciate it!" he said with a lingering look and up the stairs he bounded.

I thought about him that night—what he did for a career, if he lived alone, if I would see him tomorrow.

A few days later, John arrived for a brief overnight visit on his way to a Fed Ex business meeting in the northeast. We talked of bills and children. While I was at class he answered the apartment doorbell. John told me when I got home that someone had come to thank me for letting him in the building last night when he had forgotten his key. John said the stranger looked surprised to see someone other than me answering the door. I was surprised, too. Plenty of thanks had been expressed last night. *Why had he come?* And why was he surprised to see my husband instead of me?

I lay awake that night beside John imagining what if I had been there alone to answer the door. Would I have let the stranger with the beautiful face in? Would we have talked? What would our conversation have been about? His work? Mine? Music, art, books? Would he have asked to see my paintings? Would we have had supper together? I was good at whipping up a gourmet meal on short notice. I listened to the footsteps overhead until I fell asleep. The next morning as I went off to class, John left to fly to his meeting and return to Memphis.

For the next several days I heard no footsteps at all. Looking up at what I presumed to be *his* windows as I walked home from class, I noticed two cats on the sill. Surely he would not leave them unattended. I carried my bulky portfolio into my studio, poured some juice, and began working on my illustrations with thoughts of those cats' owner.

I worked intently on my paintings, pleased with what I would take to class for the next day's critique. I ate a quick supper and left for the Tuesday night figure drawing session—a free offering for anyone on campus of which I took full advantage every Tuesday from 7 to 10 PM. If my class assignments were demanding, I just stayed up later. I didn't seem to need sleep at RISD.

That evening, as always, drawing and painting from the live model was a transcendent activity. I had hired models at various times over the years and loved working from the nude figure—movement and flesh colors can be an exciting challenge to capture. Even the short poses I did in water color, working in a feverish pace, pleased me. It was as if I were one with the brush and paint, as if only the creative process existed. Nothing else was real. No students. No sounds of night traffic. The watercolor brush flew over the paper, depositing the right swishes of alizarin crimson in a curve's cavity, burnt sienna brandishing the hair, Prussian blue added for just the right chemical mix. I was oblivious to all else but the absorbing process of art making.

Ten o'clock came too quickly. I packed my paints and headed up the hill to my apartment—exhausted and satisfied. Why couldn't every day be like this? Why was there housework, laundry, and carpools waiting for me back home in Memphis? The Providence night air held me in its cool breeze. Why didn't Memphis have a breeze like this? One that penetrated. One you could *feel*.

When I took my morning shower, I thought about the changes occurring in me. Ideas and art and writing and reading were now my daily life. My friends here talked about things that mattered. Occasionally Chris—my best friend at RISD—and some of the others would take me to places where we could hear blues bands. They would sip beer, and I my Coke, while we talked about religion, philosophy, deconstructionism, politics and the New York art scene. I was learning a lot and dreaded going home. I felt that for the first time in my life I was living *my* life. With the shower splashing in my face, I asked a small prayer: that whatever it takes, I be allowed to become the artist I was meant to be. My abstract painting class had opened up a new way of working with paint that excited me. Art was uppermost now. I was free to be prolific, often painting through the night without sleep. This was the life I wanted!

One morning when I stepped out of the shower onto the cold tile I met God. His words were as clear as if there were a person in the bathroom with me. I puzzled over them for days: "You will go through the desert like Abraham, through difficult times, as up and down as a roller coaster; but I will be with you and it will be *all right*. Always remember, it will be *all right*."

I did not know what this meant, but I could not forget the feeling of standing on that cold tile wrapped in my towel, hair dripping, and those lucid words. Later, they would become a staff on which to lean.

Days went by without a sound from the apartment above. Because my art was my focus, I gave the silence little thought. But I was aware that the absence of those overhead sounds created an inexplicable nervousness in me—like a kid about to be in a school play or go on her first date.

Providence had invaded my being. My summer was full of exhilarating work and consuming sensations. The beauty and grit of Providence had me in its grasp. Friendships with RISD students and professors enriched each day. I gave a few casual dinner parties—home-baked bread with Italian or Asian dishes. People would sit on the floor and talk until late. Conversations were stimulating and I craved the stories and depth of ideas. With these people, life was rich and full, and Chris, Cindy, Sylvan, Tom, Carla, Leslie and others left lasting marks on my life, like pigment on a ready canvas.

In a few days, the overhead footsteps returned. The master of the cats was back. I felt less nervous—as if this stranger's being home mattered. Curious.

My art took on an industrious fury. It was as if the energy filtered through the floorboards above and into my space. There was this feeling in my stomach that reminded me of tenth grade French class when I was secretly in love with Hunter Hughes. Ridiculous. I'm no high school kid! I'm a forty-five year old mother of three! What was happening? Midlife crisis? Or something more? It was as if I were in a Dali painting. Reality seemed to be melting.

One day at noon I happened to be home. Music above! When it stopped I heard the jingle of keys and footsteps down the stairs. I walked to my studio window and looked out at the front porch of the apartment building—I could just see a portion of the porch. I knew he would have to come out that way, past my window. I waited to see his face. As the door slammed, I was struck by a surprise: It wasn't he! All these weeks I'd been listening to someone else's footsteps and watching someone else's cats! What a fool! Why was I listening to footsteps anyway? I laughed at myself. He must live in another apartment—on the third floor, *not* the second!

In a way it was a relief. I wouldn't have to listen anymore—listening had become an obligation as well as an obsession! But it made the man with the beautiful face more remote and I wanted to have him closer. My obsession was not over. I decided to write a story about what I was experiencing. Whenever I wasn't painting, in classes, doing night model sessions, completing assignments, painting watercolors of Providence streets or out with friends, I was typing a story about a Southern housewife who comes to RISD and sees a beautiful face. My energy was extraordinarily high and solitude for painting and writing was cherished time.

With a phone call everything changed. Sally, a church friend from Memphis, needed a place to stay in Providence while job interviewing in the area. "Sure, Sally, you can stay here," I found myself saying. My other self, hearing a voice from home, had taken over. I was serving again. It came naturally. I really wanted to help her. I did not think about losing my solitude or what this would do to my work or current state of mind. She came for two weeks—the last two weeks of my precious summer. I made the most of my last days of solitude prior to her arrival, working even harder than normal, enjoying the self-imposed pace and the peace of my studio.

I also felt compelled to take a risk.

I wrote a note to the-man-with-the-beautiful-face, explaining I was an artist and his face would be an interesting study for my portraiture class. I asked if he would consider posing for me. I stuck the note conspicuously on the hall banister, labeled with the name I detected must be his by the process of elimination in consulting the doorbell labels. It was a gamble.

I went back in my apartment feeling butterflies like a kid pulling a prank. This was *really silly*! Was I losing my mind? Then, relief! At least I had *done something* about my undeclared feelings. I had to get beyond the surrealism of the summer. I would do a portrait of this beautiful head and get it out of my mind. Drawing is like that. When I draw a picture of a place, I know it intimately and never forget it. Then it is *done*. When I drive by an old barn I once painted, it's as if I'm passing an old friend. So, too, with a portrait.

Curiosity got the best of me. By eleven that night I felt compelled to go out in the hall and check if the note had been picked up. It had! The butterflies returned. Now I knew *someone* had read the note. But who? Was it the beautiful face?—or someone else? Why had no one knocked at my door to acknowledge it? Was he afraid because the last time he rang my bell my husband had answered? I worked on my illustrations until after 1 AM that night.

The moon was full and bright so I sat in my studio rocker looking out the high windows. Tears came from nowhere—as they had so frequently this past year. Had I made a complete fool of myself? Probably. It wouldn't be the first time. The situation seemed absurd. I felt terrible the entire next day, unsure of what I had done. Unsure of the whole dream-like summer.

As I walked out of the apartment the next day to meet some friends for lunch, I noticed one faded doorbell label I'd overlooked. Maybe *that* was his and not the one I left the note for! I wrote another note, sailed to the second floor and put the note on another apartment across from the one over mine, then hurried off to meet my friends. I had told them of my antics and this crazy story I was both living and writing right from the start. They found it amusing, amazing, and, smiling, encouraged me to meet this guy, for God's sake, and do his portrait. They had opinions about my "repressed life" without being judgmental and saw this little escapade as hopeful.

When I arrived back at the apartment I started an assignment, a water-color illustration for the children's tale, "The Princess on the Glass Hill." I was drawing the golden apple in the princess' hand. When I looked up, suddenly, around the corner of the building, at eye level with my windows, appeared The Face. Like the knights in the story I was illustrating, I realized I had one chance to pluck the golden apple. I had to ride up that glass hill of fear, and now was the moment! I said hello out the window and asked if we could talk for a minute. I went to my apartment door and opened it. He walked into the hall with his extraordinary smile and his arms full of groceries. I hardly knew I was talking. Words just popped out. Actually it was more like mumbling. I had given a school graduation address, dozens of chapel talks, appeared at PTA microphones before thousands of people, been interviewed by newspaper and TV, but I couldn't speak two intelligent words to him; I felt fourteen and foolish. He then surprised me by saying he'd gotten my note. Immediately I realized my first speculation was correct and that the note I had recently left on a second door was to an unknown face. He seemed very interested in sitting for the portrait but said he worked long, late hours. A musician perhaps? He would let me know.

As soon as he left, I raced upstairs and tore the note off of the wrong door and returned to my studio where I realized what circles I'd danced these past weeks because of one strong visual image. What spinning. What folly. Or was there more to this? I wanted to laugh and cry.

Time passed quickly. Sally, the friend from Memphis came and went in the two weeks as expected. I turned in my final art projects for critique. Life went on and the portrait never happened.

My last day in Providence it rained. Tomorrow I'd leave for Memphis. I packed my things and cleaned the apartment in tears.

In the late afternoon I carried the trash down the back stairs and outside. I heard footsteps behind me. Yes. They were his. I knew it before he said a thing. He opened the door for me and we stood there looking at each other. He was smiling his beautiful smile. But my smile was missing, having spent much of the day crying.

He spoke: "I'm sorry I haven't had the time yet to sit for the portrait. I really want to do it. How much longer are you here? He had his car keys in his hand and was ready to cross the parking lot to his red Porsche.

"I leave tomorrow." I answered. He seemed surprised.

"Tomorrow ?! You haven't been here that long!" Actually, the whole summer was nearly gone; it had been 8 weeks. But to one who lived here year-round, my time here must have seemed short. "Will you be coming back to Providence soon?" he asked with those penetrating dark eyes.

"Not until next summer," I answered. The reality of this sentence stuck in my throat. I could feel my emotions rising, my eyes welling up, and turned quickly and walked away toward the trashcans with my garbage bag, in the opposite direction of his car. I could feel his eyes on my back as I walked.

I knew he was not moving, just staring. Suddenly an idea came to me, and I turned around to face his gaze.

"I want to give you something." I began, "I'll leave it at your back door."

He must have thought me weird—what could I possibly have to give him?—but he gave no sign—instead, he said, "Thank you!" with one of his tremendous smiles. I turned and dumped my trash. When I turned around again, he was gone.

I had no idea what I would give him. I just had to give him something. Giving would require his receiving—some kind of wholeness binding me with Providence and him. I always had to give—it was just how I was, how I still am. I'd baked a couple of homemade loaves of bread two days earlier to use up my flour. I could give him one of those. No. That wasn't enough. This handsome face had lingered in my mind all summer as a metaphor of everything dynamic, vital, expressive, loving and beautiful. Like the pulse of Providence. No. I had to give more than a loaf of bread! Then it came to me. The painting I had done of this historic apartment building would be perfect. My art came from the core of my being. What better gift? Besides, it was a good painting. I had planned to enter it in a competition and knew it would sell for at least $500. But what was $500 compared with wholeness? I wrote a note telling him the truth: that he had the most beautiful face I'd ever seen and that I was sorry I'd not been able to do his portrait.

But that was not enough. I had to give him one more thing: the story I'd been writing. I had made a second copy. I taped my note to the plastic-wrapped loaf of bread, took it and the painting and the story and walked out my back door by my bedroom, up the back hall stairs to the third floor. Secure in knowing that he wasn't home now, I left all three gifts outside his door.

I finished packing about an hour before my husband and children arrived. Nathan had been visiting friends for several days at the camp Charissa was attending. The plan was that John would pick them up in the family station wagon and they would drive from Maine to Providence in time for dinner and I'd load the car with my art materials and we'd drive home together to Memphis the next morning. My parents would be joining us for dinner, driving from Boston.

Everyone arrived about the same time. It felt odd to be mother, daughter, and wife again. I felt as if I were a shape-shifter in a sci-fi film. Suddenly,

I had to become the several someones I used to be. And the transformation had to happen quickly. When my family arrived, I had a hard time remembering who these other me's were and I was in the middle of transition—an edgy, awkward place.

For several days, I had been apprehensive about the dinner with my parents, husband, and children. Cindy, a RISD friend, whose relationship with her female partner was as deep as any heterosexual marriage, had given me excellent advice: "Know that you can always get up and leave." Cindy, like Chris and so many other RISD friends, had been supportive of my questioning soul. Whoever I was at the time was always all right with them. I kept Cindy's piece of advice in mind throughout dinner and came close to utilizing it, but I made it through without leaving. I managed to be the expected diligent daughter and mother, listening to my father's stories and wisdom, managing brief answers to my mother's questions without revealing more than she cared to know, asking my kids about camp and friends, all while mentally still the free-spirited artist, infatuated with a handsome young stranger I didn't know, sad to leave a summer full of art, intellect, and learning.

I'd noticed Nathan had been coughing a lot during dinner and by the time he bedded down in his sleeping bag on my studio floor it was apparent he was not well. I gave him water and kissed him goodnight, settled Charissa asleep on my bedroom floor, and got into bed. John sat on the far edge of the bed, praying. I followed with my own prayers for Nathan from under the covers, then, stared at the ceiling unable to fall asleep, trying to deal with re-entry.

I had just closed my eyes and John was nearly asleep when I heard a knock at my back door, only steps from the bed. I leapt to my feet. Only one person would have access to that back door. "I'll get it" I whispered to John in case he was listening. He mumbled something like "Who in the world could that be at this hour?" My heart pounded. No more than 10 feet from where my husband lay I opened the back door to the young beautiful face staring dark eyes into mine.

His tussled hair and tight white Italian tee shirt suggested he had been sleeping or at least had come downstairs from a causal night at home. He smelled sweetly of sweat and the muscles of his bare arms shown in the dim hall light. He had never knocked at my back door before.

"Thank you for the bread…" he began sincerely, his face beaming generously. Before he could say another word I put my fingers to my lips, stepped into the hall, closing the door—my hand still on the knob—behind me. John was groggily coming this way.

"Shhh….my entire family is on the other side of this door. I can't talk now….I am SO SORRY….so very sorry about everything!"

He smiled embracingly and said softy, "It's okay. It's okay." His eyes were still staring understandingly and he did not move as I closed the door on his face and stepped back into the bedroom just as John reached my side.

"Who was that?" he asked.

"Oh, just a neighbor thanking me for some bread I'd given them."

The next morning in a stuffed station wagon with a sick son coming down with the measles—but we didn't know that yet—a customarily silent husband, and a bored ten-year old, I sat stuck in traffic on the New Jersey Garden State Parkway, absorbed in images of Providence as we drove back to Memphis. My mind was racing. The good thing about being an imagemaker is that you always carry the image with you wherever you go. It can't be lost.

Within two days of returning to Memphis, I nursed three children with measles, bought Charissa's school clothes, started teaching, confided in a colleague—the only person I knew who was divorced—that I was considering the D-word and began to look for an apartment.

Two months later I moved out.

thirteen

Frontier Journey

Pioneer Woman

Can she dig out from the day-to-day to keep pace

When 1990s pioneering weighs prairie-sod heavy?

Savage thoughts from the forsaken past attack her new fragile walls.

Rains weaken what she builds.

Mental cyclones circle.

Tornadoes give no warning.

Field fires come like breakfast, lunch and dinner.

She sought the frontier.

Left all.

Now huddled in her private wilderness, in severed-family isolation,

She scrapes together fortitude and finances, keeping children's lives and her's

Intact.

No plodding.

Plowing and planting.

"Less is more" her harvest song.

Alone, she carries.

Alone she hunts.

Are there water-witches to find love's flowing stream?

Or will dry winds blow grasshoppers where her new wheat is sown?

A dew-like melancholy hangs about NewHarmony's Poet's House. I'm sad to leave. Are they watching me go?—Frances Wright, Thomas Merton, and others haunting this numinous place? Will they come to say good-bye like the white cat at my feet? The cherry tree nods "I know you will return." I promise I will. I always have.

The white cat observes me from a garden ledge as I carry my things to the car. No doubt she has watched others come and go many times. How often I have left dwelling places! Not once was it easy. Leaving behind little pieces of me, I'm never quite sure what's left, never sure I'll have what I need when I reach my next destination, never sure that what I love about a place will still be here, unchanged, if I return.

New Harmony sends me off with gifts; I take more than I leave. Into the car trunk I pack my manuscript, my poetry and paintings, and a few pottery purchases. New wisdom rides up front with me, occupies my thought the 340 miles back to Memphis. I've had a productive two weeks in the Poet's House—has it really only been two? It seems like a lifetime. Among shadows and light I crawled and climbed to collect the pattern pieces of my life, attaching them to each other, past to present, seeking a satisfying design. These two summer weeks of 1993 have wrapped me in fresh insights and self-knowledge, like a Westward-bound pioneer comforted by her quilt.

Pioneer women of the westward movement rarely returned to their Eastern homes. Most followed their husbands without choice; others journeyed alone leaving behind all they'd known. Hoping to follow their dreams and improve their lives, these pioneer women entered unknown territory in search of a place of their own, a place to call home. Plowing and planting, battling prairie fires and disease, surviving one loss after another, they made home, as women always have. The secret of women's frontier life was the isolation it thrust upon them. Some walked miles just to watch a distant train go by. Others climbed roofs and went mad. But the strong ones survived the choice made to enter unknown territory and create home.

Frontiers are places of promise and possibility. But frontiers are also wildly unstable, unsettled, and undefined.

A frontier is first and above all the space beyond the last settlement, an unconstructed region with no organizing systems—no maps, no roads, no outposts. Frontiers are volatile environments in which men do not control the natural world and are subject to chance encounters." (Lillian Schlissel, Far From Home, p.233).

Divorce is a frontier. Suddenly single in 1989, at age forty-six, after a twenty-one year marriage having left all—home, husband, family, friends, and more—I wandered a lonely prairie, a pioneer woman on a new frontier. But I'd been led into this wilderness step-by-step.

My silly escapade in Rhode Island was a symptom of how desperately I longed to be loved. I had not known I was so desperate. The tears I'd concealed for over a year were another symptom. Once I'd mentioned the crying to a RISD friend in 1989. He asked, "Don't you recognize the clinical symptoms of depression when you see them?" "Oh, I can't be depressed," I answered, "I'm a Christian Scientist!" One well-trained in denial does not readily recognize depression, nor any other malady.

Nothing appeared wrong on the outside. Isn't an employed husband, three well-adjusted children, a beautiful house in the country, and a successful career evidence that all is well? Like a 1950s child with a *Children's Highlights* magazine looking for what's wrong with this picture, one notices nothing at first glance. With scrutiny, however, one detects an array of discrepancies. Tears have cause. Divorce is not simply waking up one day in dissatisfaction. Feeling trapped comes from an accumulation that collects like garbage. It cannot be ignored.

Boxed in, alone, and unclear of my next step, I prayed. Just as listening to God's direction had always been the prime factor in any decision I had made in the past, so it was with this one. I felt divinely led to divorce, step-by-step, and I acted only upon each idea when it became clear.

One of the first steps was to lease a small loft apartment for six months, providing me time and place to think things through on neutral ground. The moment I entered the barren white-walled unit I knew I was meant to live there—not because it was beautiful, because it wasn't, but because it told me it suited the next part of my journey. "I'll take it," I told the agent. I knew what I was doing was brave and strange and right.

At school, the Headmaster's secretary, a Catholic, supported my journey by introducing me to Thomas Merton via a quotation of his she'd copied for me:

> *My Lord God, I have no idea where I am going. I do not see the road ahead of me. I cannot know for certain where it will end. Nor do I really know myself, and the fact that I think that I am following your will does not mean that I am actually doing so. But I believe that the desire to please you does in fact please you. And I hope I have that desire in all that I am doing. I hope that I will never do anything apart from that desire. And I know that if I do this you will lead me by the right road though I may know nothing about it. Therefore will I trust you always though I may seem to be lost and in the shadow of death. I will not fear, for you are ever with me, and you will never leave me to face my perils alone.*

I loved Merton's message and pinned it where I could see it daily, beside my L'Engle quotation of what it means to be an artist. Later, I would read more by both Merton and L'Engle, who would become favorites.

John knew I planned to leave. I had told him everything shortly after I returned from Providence; I even read him the story I had written about "The Beautiful Face." He did not want us to separate, and divorce seemed preposterous to him. "Divorce is spreading across America! It's against the Bible! I won't let this happen!" He pounded his fist into the kitchen counter with more passion than I'd ever seen him express. In fact, it frightened me. The divorce lawyer I'd gone to earlier in the week had warned me to expect the opposite of whatever was John's usual behavior. I had assured him John would be different, adding, "he's a quiet, moral person."

John proposed a "contract." When the Fisherville house sold, he suggested we get a large new house in town, each living in opposite ends of it. He would do all the housework, including ironing—work he had never been responsible for before. We would live totally separate lives, but stay married "for appearances sake and for our children's sake." I was shocked by this offer. It showed me he did not understand. It wasn't a relationship of separation I wanted but one of deep sharing and loving intimacy.

The night before I left, I stood beside our feather bed in tears explaining: "I want a feather bed without two hollows on opposite sides separated by a mound of feathers in the middle! I want a feather bed with one shared hollow in the center!" I wanted to be touched, held, loved. And I wanted to give the same to someone eager to receive. I wanted to share ideas and reading, with communication at the core of our relationship. I wanted as much vitality in marriage as I gave to any cause or endeavor. I explained it wasn't housework that I wanted to leave; it was lack of appreciation. No longer could I tolerate the deadness of our relationship. It depleted my energy, wore me out, pulled me down. I was tired of doing marriage all by myself, being taken for granted. Apathy was killing me.

A few months later I read Leo Buscaglia's *Living, Loving and Learning* that perfectly expressed what I felt:

> *I have a very strong feeling that the opposite of love is not hate—it is apathy. It's not giving a damn. If somebody hates, they must feel something about me or they couldn't possibly hate. Therefore, there's some way in which I can communicate. But if they don't even see me, I'm finished—there's no way in which I can get to them. If you don't like the scene you're in, if you're unhappy, if you're lonely, if you don't feel that things are happening, change your scene* (Buscaglia, *Living, Loving and Learning*, p. 43).

My address changed October 15, 1989. On a Sunday morning while John and Charissa were at church—where I ordinarily would have been—I put a chicken casserole in the oven and laid out some buttered dinner rolls for their Sunday dinner. They knew I would be gone when they returned, though I believe John didn't think I would go through with it. I packed the barest of essentials into a colleague's pick-up and left my home in the woods for the tiny apartment I'd rented in town.

This would be the last of my days at the branch church I had helped establish, for I could not attend where John was, where friends might feel uncomfortable. Church was another place I was leaving. Now my "church" came only from within.

I had worried about telling my children that I was separating from their father. I told Jason before he went off to college in early September, a month before I moved out. He shocked me by saying, "I'm not a bit surprised. I wondered how you stayed together all these years."

I took Charissa, age 10, to see the apartment several weeks before I moved in. I told her what I was going to do and why—that this was just a separation, not a divorce, that I'd not decided what to do but needed a place to think clearly. I told her she could live in the apartment with me during the week, that I would bring her home from school (she now attended Custis Lee where I was teaching) just as I always did and cook her dinner. I explained that on weekends she could go back to Fisherville where our dog was if she liked, when her father was in town (recently, he was out of town much of the work week). I wanted her to want to be with me. I don't think she really understood, though she said she did. She never shed a tear and said to me, "If I were you I never would have married my father. He never talks."

I wasn't eager to tell Nathan, now a junior at Principia, until football season was over because I did not want to worry him and disturb his performance. Just before I planned to tell him, I had a dream in which the children and I were rushing to get on a train. The train was leaving the station and we had to run very fast to catch it. It looked like Nathan wouldn't make it. I got the others on board with me, but Nathan was further behind. I pleaded for him to hurry, to run faster, to grab hold of my outstretched hand. I woke up in a sweat. I thought this dream meant that Nathan would not accept the divorce as well as the others and would be upset.

I had been living in my apartment for several weeks when I told Nathan. I drove up to Prin to see one of his final games, then to tell him about the potential divorce. We talked in a quiet corner of the library. He could not have been kinder or more sensitive. He said that he understood, that he wondered how I could "go so long" without affection because he said he couldn't; that he and his girlfriend were closer and probably kissed more than his parents. His girlfriend was a best friend to him and someone I liked. I appreciated what he said.

All three children remained supportive—without being disingenuous with their father. They were terrific. When the actual divorce was final, I learned years later, that it had not been so easy for Jason, that he had gone wildly driving and gotten a ticket. Charissa hid her feelings and after the divorce became close to her Dad, even helping him buy his clothes, cooking his dinners, almost as if she were a substitute wife. She lived with me during the week and with John on weekends, until high school when she chose to live with me permanently. The back and forth had gotten hard for her—always a belt to an outfit or an important piece of homework was at the wrong place. Nathan never had any difficulty that I know of concerning the divorce, more focused on his own full life. All three children managed to balance their love between their parents. I am sure it must have been a shaky juggling act at times for each of them, but I have asked and we have talked about this since, and they've revealed nothing any different. I think they loved what we were to them as parents and honored the fact that we are each individuals, just as we had striven to let them be individuals, free to go to school where they chose, free to become who they innately are.

My parents, on the other hand, were anything but supportive.

Out of courtesy, the night before I planned to move out, I called to tell them about the separation. When Dad answered the phone, it came to me to start with words that must have come from God: "How much do you love me?" Dad answered with profuse accolades.

Then I said, "Well, with what I'm about to tell you I'm putting that love to a test." I told him about my apartment, about my plans to separate with the possibility of divorce.

He was taken aback and, at first, untypically, at a loss for words. Then, in his most powerful practitioner voice, after a mumbled declaration I'd heard him assert a number of times before about John not being a good provider, he thundered, "But why are you doing this?! John never beat you and he isn't an alcoholic!" To Dad, these seemed to be the only two justifications for divorce. Resonating into the phone were his final words: "Work on self-justification!" Apparently he presumed I was acting impetuously and trying to justify my actions. In an uncharacteristically nervous fashion, he began to talk about "denying the self" and suggested I work on "getting rid of self." After his brief speech, he asked, "Have you told your mother yet? You've *got* to tell your mother!"

"That's why I'm calling, Dad, to tell you *both*—you just happened to pick up. Put Mom on and I'll tell her."

"No!" he answered childishly. "You will have to call her yourself!"

This seemed ridiculous! They live together! She was in the next room! While they did have two phone lines, one was for my father's patients and family, the other reached both of them; my brother and I were encouraged to call on either.

"Call her on the *other* phone!" He was obviously angry.

"All right, Dad." Our strange conversation ended abruptly.

Given that Dad had reacted as he had, I was petrified of how Mom would handle the news. I phoned her immediately before Dad would have had time to get out of his chair in the den and find her in the kitchen. I told her why I was leaving.

She listened quietly and then said in a weak, tired voice: "I think I understand more than you know."

I was flabbergasted at how well she seemed to have taken the news! She had high ideals about marriage and family and how things looked socially. I hadn't expected her response! I thanked her for understanding and conveyed how much it meant to me.

But in less than a month, I learned by her phone calls to me that she had been utterly devastated by my news. To this day I do not know why she said what she did. I have thought about her words and tone often. All I can imagine is either she feared losing her only daughter if she showed her true disappointment, or, she knew aloneness within a marriage first-hand, and that for a brief moment she was reacting to her own longings, instead of mine. I will never know the truth.

In less than two hours after leaving my Fisherville home for my sterile apartment, I'd unpacked and placed in order what little I'd brought. I stood in the center of the one room, looking at the abstract paintings I had just hung on the cold white walls. Two summers at RISD had changed my work. It was edgier, tougher, grittier, vital. Two summers at RISD had also changed me.

I glanced around the room: one window, one small sofa, one small folding table, my books lined up along one wall on shelves I'd fashioned from cinder blocks and boards, a large easel, metal art drawers, portfolios, boxes of art materials and in the small loft above, a mattress on the floor. This would be my home for the next six months.

Why had I left? For the same reason I got rid of old shoes—I would have been crippled wearing what I'd outgrown.

Why had I left? For the same reason I transplanted a pot-bound plant into a larger container—so it could grow rather than be stunted.

Why had I left? For the same reason I work out my composition before I paint in watercolor—I can't build anything worthwhile on a false foundation.

I felt as if I were being squeezed to death by my marriage. I created a large charcoal drawing about this time that expressed my feelings and entitled it "Trapped". It was later purchased by a trauma surgeon who said the piece captured the pain of patients in the hospital's trauma unit.

I also wrote poetry:

A Dick and Jane Marriage

See Wife.
See Wife smile.
See Wife smile and dream.
See Wife run after the dream.
Run, Wife, run.
Run, run, run.
See Wife pray and plan and cook and clean and bake and sew,
and raise children
All alone
See Wife serve husband, children, parents, church,
career, school, community and more
And pour out herself.
Never filling back up.
She even buys his shoes.

Another poem I wrote at this time:
Divorce

Like ripping flesh from bone
I leave all that I have known
Ejected into cosmic space
Not aware of what I face
All alone.

With poetry, prayer, journal writing, painting, and long walks I survived. And something inexplicable happened: I found the courage to become myself. I kept a list of the most extraordinary "signs" that showed me I was on the right path—Moses-signs, like little burning bushes—that were taking place in my life. The list grew to 40 items of serendipitous synchronicity helping me "sail away".

One example: The week I moved into my apartment, I took Charissa to buy new shoes. On the store counter was a brochure advertising a brand of running shoe showing the close-up photo of a woman's face with the caption: "I don't think about what would have happened if I stayed. I think about what would have happened if I never left." I wasn't sure how this statement was supposed to sell running shoes, but I *did* know what it said to me and slipped the free brochure into my purse.

A few weeks later I learned that a colleague lived in the same apartment complex I had just moved into. She invited me over and while we were visiting, from the bookcase behind her, a title jumped out at me as if it were in neon, begging me to take it home. It was one word: *Changing*. Exactly what I was experiencing! I asked if I could borrow the book. It happened to be the autobiography of actress, Liv Ullman. As I read the book I discovered that some of her story was similar to mine. A few of her words entered my journal: "I feel that to be respected I must produce pancakes and home-baked bread and have neat, tidy rooms…my growth and my development depend on what I choose or discard in life…in me are the seeds of my future life."

In reading Ullman's autobiography, I learned she starred in *A Doll's House* and other Ibsen plays. Her comments about them spurred my interest and I went to a bookstore and purchased the playwright's complete works. Not only was *A Doll's House* apropos to my current life but so were many of Ibsen's other plays, including *When We Dead Awaken* and *The Master Builder* and *Ghosts*. I took copious notes on each play and even researched Ibsen's work in the library. I loved the psychological depth and meaning of his work; it seemed to speak directly to my journey.

I happened to mention my newfound Ibsen interest to an English teacher at school. She told me she would soon be showing the film *A Doll's House* to her class, who were reading the play, and invited me to sit in on her classes if I liked. I liked and did. During the film, pieces of my life flashed in front of me. I could hardly keep from crying.

I highlighted passages in my voluminous copy of Ibsen including this crucial conversation between Torvald Helmer, the husband, and Nora, his wife, who has just gotten the courage to tell him she is leaving him:

Helmer: *"Abandon your home, your husband, your children! And you're not even thinking what people will say!"*

Nora: *"I can't be concerned about that. I only know how essential this is."*

Helmer: *"Oh, it's outrageous! So you'll run out like this on your most sacred vows."*

Nora: *"What do you think are my most sacred vows?"*

Helmer: *"And I have to tell you that! Aren't they your duties to your husband and children?"*

Nora: *"I have other duties equally sacred."*

Helmer: *"That isn't true. What duties are they?"*

Nora: *"Duties to myself."*

Helmer: *"Before all else, you're a wife and a mother."*

Nora: *"I don't believe in that anymore. I believe that before all else, I'm a human being, no less than you—or, anyway, I ought to try to become one."* (Henrik Ibsen, A Doll's House from Ibsen: The Major Prose plays by Rolf Fjelde, p. 192-193).

At one point in the play Nora says: *"I waited patiently for eight years."* I'd waited twenty-one.

Nora was a doll her father and husband played with, as she said, "Papa used to tell me everything and I took on his opinions." I, too, had taken my father's beliefs as my own. Most of my life I had been like the paper dolls I played with as a child on the floor of my Baltimore closet—moved by others to be what they wished, to meet others' needs—just as I had cut out and orchestrated the fairytale lives of Peter, Ginny, Beanie, Muffin, Babs and my other paper friends. Now as an adult, I'd moved at the impulse of parents, husband, children, schools, employers, branch churches, and good causes. I'd been their good and faithful servant. But like Nora, I discovered I had duties to myself that I could no longer ignore. I was discovering a me *beyond* obedient daughter, housewife, mother, and activist.

I wrote in my journal: *I want to teach, write, paint, touch people's lives, love someone—a relationship rooted in creative expression, intellect, and spirituality. In my time alone I have learned: I am not my father's daughter. I am not my husband's wife. I am not my children's mother. I am God's.*

I am not defined by what I do for others nor by my relationship to them. Serving them is not my sole reason for being. Serving God by finding myself is."

I was not diminishing my roles as daughter, wife, and mother, but asserting a more basic and neglected need: to become myself.

Journal-writing saved me. In May of 1989 I wrote: *It is not possible to separate creative writing and creative thinking. . . I love words for they are the closest means we have for touching ideas, touching the spiritual.* I wrote lists of things I wanted to pray about, followed with specific healing declarations. I wrote about every thought and idea that came to me, filling journal after journal until today I have nearly as many journals as I have years.

Books became friends. I joined a Great Books group. Volumes piled up beside my bed: Plato, Socrates, Kierkegaard and others. I'd found Carl Jung at RISD and was reading him, again. I discovered C.S. Lewis and Joseph Campbell.

One evening on PBS I heard Bill Moyers' *Power of Myth* interview of Joseph Campbell. The famous philosopher-author's words made it to my notecards: "I think it is sad when people say, 'I never did a thing in my life that I wanted to do.' " Moyers asked, "What happens when you follow your bliss?" Campbell answered, "You find it" adding, "Grab every little intuition about where your bliss is and stay with it…following your bliss puts you on a track that's been waiting for you all along…follow your bliss and don't be afraid. Doors will open."

Becoming. That was the journey I'd begun. Jung calls it "individuation." It is a matter of having the courage to be who one really is and not what others dictate. For the artist, individuation is a passion. Without keen self-awareness an artist doesn't develop her unique style or particular point of view or distinctive body of work. Ibsen says that the artist is in contention with himself. Artists suffer to give birth to their creations. Normalcy must be sacrificed, as L'Engle says.

Alone in my apartment, an empty vessel of a dwelling, where Christmas turkeys were never cooked nor children put to bed with stories, I found my artist-self. Paintings erupted for days on end. I painted after school, at night, and on weekends endlessly. I wrote when not painting. My journals overflowed. I didn't seem to need sleep. Canvases came from "the stranger within." I painted Kierkegaard's "leap of faith" and Jung's "*daimon*." With Ibsen's character Rubek in *When We Dead Awaken*, I could say, "I was *born* to be an artist. And no matter what I'll never be anything else." (Fjelde, p.1074)

A strange bliss filled my solitude, an odd kind of contentment with my restlessness, a peace in being alone   similar to a Buddhist meditative *sitting with*.

Then came the abyss.

One cold January night the dark took over. It was as if all the black outside came creeping into my white apartment stealing the light. Lonely does not go far enough in describing this particular night and several others. All my support systems had disappeared. Not a best friend or family member to turn to. No one to confide in. Not even an acquaintance I dared burden. No professional to call. No church anymore. No one and nothing but myself.

I reached out—as if from some astronomical Black Hole—for *something*, *someone*, to hold onto. But there was nothing to grasp. Not even a sound, except my sobbing.

Despair hovered thick as a blanket. I curled up in it. I tried to pray at first, in my usual manner, but did not trust old ways. They had proven recently to be without mercy. I listed my losses like a defeated military general re-evaluating his battle plan:

No father

No mother

No husband

No children beside me

No family

No home

No possessions

No best friend

No church
No financial stability
No community
No support group
No professional help
No answers
No out

The tally displayed my hopelessness.

I found myself thinking about the wandering homeless of our nation's cities. Though I had a roof over my head, I felt like a wanderer in the wilderness: hopeless, homeless, rootless, without place or purpose.

Though there was not a flicker of light in this dark night, suicide was never an option. Life being eternal, I concluded suicide would solve nothing. Ending it all was not even a possibility, but simply another loss for my tally sheet. Feeling worthless, taken for granted, unloved, and abandoned, I sat on my floor without ability to move, feeling even more unappreciated than I had during some of my loneliest moments living with John.

This particular night, even God seemed gone.

God. All my days He had been with me. In every trial I'd turned to Him and found an answer. Tonight I couldn't find Him—or Her. I'd been taught that God is all good. But there was no good present—not even a hint. If God is in good and there was none, where *was* God? Had I lost God along with everything else? Had He let go of me? To lose God! The ultimate loss! I could not stop the tears.

I called out loud to the God I thought was gone: " My Father-Mother God, *what* would You have me do to *find You*? *Where* would You have me go? I have followed your signs. I have listened and obeyed. God, where *are* you? Help me now, if You hear me, if You are there. *Is there no help?* I am drowning in this darkness! Help me! If You are there, *help me!*"

Suddenly, right there in the darkest moment, I felt a slow flood of warmth—a sense of Presence, a sense of God. Right there *in the very abyss, in the darkness itself.* It was as if I were a small frightened child and He had taken my hand in His. I felt something warm. I was surrounded by love and strength. No physical being, yet this God of mine was more solid than rock, more ever-present than my own thought. I discovered my God right there *in the dark abyss*! He, my true Father who is also She, my true Mother, my Father-Mother God, was with me. I felt God's presence in a new way. "God will never leave me"—I *knew* this in an instant with complete eternal assurance. It was as if I had studied it in books for hundreds of years. Yet this was *not* an intellectual knowing, nor a worked-at healing. This was plain eternal unequivocal truth I was experiencing. God with me—*even* in the abyss! God with me, not just in "the good", but *in the very dark*. This idea was revolutionary and revelationary.

I remained on the floor facing my bookshelves. Through tears, only one title from the shelves came into focus: *What is God?* by John Haught. A RISD friend, a nun in charge of a college art department, gave me this book the previous summer, telling me she thought I was on "a significant spiritual journey for truth." I had never read the book. But this night, reading it was the only thing I wanted to do.

I read all night, finishing it, and discovered that depth is both ground *and* abyss. I read about what I'd just experienced:

> *We might gain a more concrete sense of what this abyss means if we conjure up the specter of being utterly alone without the support of other people or of status or possession. There is probably nothing we humans find more terrifying or try more ardently to avoid than the state of aloneness. . . . What would happen, though, if we allowed ourselves, or were forced by `circumstance', to plunge into the abyss? The wisdom of depth seekers throughout history has proven that "there is yet another side to the depth: ground. In the final analysis, the depth is ultimate support, absolute security, unrestricted love, eternal care. Compared to this ultimate grounding of our existence… our ordinary supports are shallow; or at least inadequate. The reason we can have the courage to open ourselves to the depth, to accept our solitude, is that there is an ultimate ground to our existence, there is an ultimate companionship in our alone-ness. . . . There is more than abyss to depth. There is also courage to accept the abyss. (Haught, What is God?, p.17-19).*

That night I found "ultimate companionship." I had found the ground of my existence *in the abyss* and *my home in God*. I knew I'd have forever a permanent closeness with God, Spirit, for God became more solid than words allow description. Immutable Emanuel. God with us. God with me. Forever.

As days passed, my religious search took me beyond denomination. While I still studied faithfully my Christian Science lesson, I also explored everything else. I came across one compelling definition for religion: *"the passionate search for depth and for an ultimately solid ground to support our existence."* A *passionate* search! Without defining my actions in those terms, I had been approaching life precisely that way. Passion for education, family, art, ideas, and God generated my actions.

It would be only several months later, during my last RISD summer, that I would walk out in the middle of a Wednesday night Christian Science church service in Providence when I heard these words from the platform: "If man is not victorious over the passions, they crush out happiness, health, and manhood" (Eddy, *Science and Health*, p. 407:10-11) and "Human belief—or knowledge gained from the so-called material senses—would, by fair logic, annihilate man….(Eddy, *Science and Health*, p. 490: 20-22). Though I'd heard these passages many times before, this time I couldn't accept them, so incongruous were they with my current experience, both as seeker and artist. Painting taught me passion causes creation, gives life. How could passion annihilate? Passion seemed to generate all great inventors and thinkers. How could it crush out manhood or womanhood? The words caused me to get up out of my seat. I left the church before the readings were over. As I hit the cool night air I started running, running as fast as I could away from the church, away from those words, as if they were choking me. The wind beat against me and the dark sky surrounded me, but I ran right through them. I ran as if all the energy of the universe were pushing me. I had listened to readings and given testimonies in the same church the two previous summers, but this time I could not sit and take it in. This time the familiar words seemed to reach out as if to strangle me. I ran six blocks home in the dark.

It had been only a few months earlier that I had experienced the night of abyss in my Memphis apartment in which I'd gained an intuitive knowing and confidence in my understanding of God. It was if the ground of my being had been solidly established then. I felt stronger and clearer in every aspect of my life. This new confidence included clarifying my next right step: divorce. At this time, I read somewhere and recorded this line: *When the decision is made in the abyss, then it is quite clear that it is not one's own decision at all. It is a decision more right than human knowing.* This is how I felt about the decision to divorce. I was being obedient to a higher power, an inner call, finding the courage and strength to face whatever followed.

John was convinced that I would not go through with my intentions and begged me to come back to the Fisherville house—which, though we'd put it on the market, had not yet sold—"just for the holidays", to give our marriage "one more chance for the sake of the children". He assured me he would change. Things would be different. I battled with guilt and lost. I decided to give our marriage one last chance. As I drove out to the house with Thanksgiving groceries, it seemed even the steering wheel wanted me to turn around and go back to my apartment; I knew in my heart that returning was wrong. I spent Thanksgiving there—even inviting my parents—as if a house full of children, their grandparents, and festivity could solve deeply rooted difficulties. So "worked on" was I by husband and parents, that I returned at Christmas to repeat the Norman Rockwell scene.

But nothing changed. John was still John. Our marriage was what it had been and why I'd left became crystal clear. With each return, I felt I was forcing something that couldn't be, and worse, I felt like a traitor to myself. I had not gone through the agony of leaving my Fisherville home the first time, the night of the abyss, the loss of friends and the disapproval of my parents merely to return and say things were fine. I had *changed* because of these events and because of RISD and my own individuation. The woman I now was could no longer reside in this marriage.

About a week before Christmas, John and I went to the closing on the sale of the Fisherville house. I had spent an agonizing week prior packing everything in cartons, crying when no one was around as I went from room to room in that extraordinary home I'd built with my soul. Stunningly, devastatingly, the day of the closing on the house, we learned the buyers' loan did not go through. I had to return to the house one more time and unpack everything. The house was back on the market. I was exhausted, bewildered, and drained from the packing and unpacking, from the holidays, as well as from my own traumatic back-and-forths between apartment and house.

While I was in this confused state, John convinced me we ought to purchase a house in town for the children's sake, rather than expect them to live in my tiny apartment and a second apartment I suggested he get. We'd planned a year earlier, when we first put the house on the market to move to town, but since separation I had been suggesting separate apartments. "What place would the children have to call home if we each got separate dwellings?" John asked. "Our children deserve a home" was the sentence that lured me into looking at houses. Home being such a vital concept to me, I did not want to deprive my kids of it!—even if my boys were a high school senior and college freshman by now. I told myself I didn't have to agree to live with John or to sign any purchase papers, but I'd take a look at houses to keep everyone happy.

By February we had another contract on the Fisherville house—oddly enough, by the same couple whose loan had failed to go through earlier—this time they had everything in order and the closing went smoothly. I packed up again—an even more arduous task the second time. The family that bought our home seemed perfect for the house that I had so lovingly designed and built. The wife reminded me of me; she and I became friends and corresponded occasionally. She and her four children and husband would have a wonderful life in the Fisherville house to the present day.

By early Spring Charissa had picked out a newly built house in a fancy subdivision she liked. Aesthetically I liked it, too. We bought it. The day I signed divorce papers, I picked out wallpaper and lighting fixtures for the new home. I remember walking into a remote corner of the lighting store and crying where no one could see me—it was all too much.

We moved in in March. I still had my apartment but let my friend Sandra use it during the week. I lived there weekends, painting some of my best art. The tiny apartment was more my home than the handsome brand new stucco house John and I had just purchased with Charissa's encouragement. The new house had a turret room for my studio, though it got little use, a giant kitchen for which I selected blue and white wallpaper, a massive entry hall for which I chose a striking dragon pendant light fixture that reminded me of Wales, and the master closet was large enough to have held a party. All this seems ridiculous to me now, but at the time, my motive was not to deprive my children of a lovely home.

I was still teaching school, painting, and exhibiting my art. That amazes me now. I have no idea how I did it all, especially with what came next.

My best friend at school, Mallory, one of several high school math teachers, provided the next extraordinary episode in my life. She and I had become close two years earlier because she was interested in Christian Science and would ask me questions. Brilliant and beautiful, she was a vivacious and popular teacher among both faculty and students. Though she grew up in rural Tennessee in a fundamentalist home she had gone on to get several degrees, and was currently completing her Ph.D. I loved her brazen vitality. We would have lunch together in the art room discussing philosophy, Christian Science, or any one of a thousand topics, sharing deeply. We could laugh or cry together and we kept no secrets—or so I thought. There was nothing I wouldn't do for her nor she for me.

When I got back from RISD my second summer, she was one of the first persons I told that I was planning to separate. To my amazement, she told me she was considering the same thing. Then she told me her incredible story, making me promise not to tell a soul. For the next four years I kept that promise.

She had fallen in love with a married man, a black man, twenty years older, a professor. Both were innovative thinkers, devoted to education and to civil rights. Their love developed out of genuine care and common interests over several years. Since both were caring and religious and married to other people, their situation was agonizing for them. Neither could break the moral code of their conservative religious backgrounds, so they lived in close affection without an affair (at least so I was told). They also lived a lie. No one knew about their relationship. My friend was certain she would lose her job at our upstanding private conservative Southern institution if anyone found out. She may have been right. I had seen people fired there for less.

She lived in great turmoil that year. Consideration of how and if to leave her husband weighed heavily on her. Her husband was a successful lawyer, a good and generous man who helped numerous charitable causes and even taught Sunday School in a large fundamentalist church. He provided them with a nice house and exotic vacations. Concern for her parents' opinions and beliefs nearly consumed Mallory; she was convinced that their relationship would be severed if she divorced to marry a black man. I am sure she was right. She was living a consuming nightmare. People's opinions mattered to her, especially those of her parents whom she dearly loved and colleagues. What if they found out? She was obsessed about anyone learning her secret. The issues of race, religion, marriage and age went against all propriety of her Southern culture, family and friends. She did not want to hurt anyone, including her husband, for whom she incongruously cared. It was a predicament of paramount proportions. And it nearly drove her insane.

One day in May she did not show up in her classroom. The students sat waiting. I covered for her, though math is *definitely* not my field. When she came to school I could see by her weary face that she was on edge. She had neither slept nor eaten properly in months. This particular day she went to the teacher's work room and lay down on the couch. A male teacher was grading papers nearby. "Take me away from all this!" she said to him with abandon. Wildly dramatic in talk and manner, I saw that she frightened those present and I was afraid where this would lead. I motioned her outside where we could talk in the spring air. Outdoors, she let down her guard and told me, her eyes welling with tears, that she could not stand it anymore. "I don't know if I can hang on!" I put my arms around her. A hymn came to mind and I sang a bit of it to her.

She had visited a Christian Science branch church several times, read the writings often, and had a couple healings, relying on my father as her practitioner for one. She kept her interest in Christian Science a secret because she knew her parents would consider her a heretic if they found out and disown her.

Mallory felt cornered. I supported her daily, as she did me while I wandered through the maze of divorce. When she was down I would leave an inspirational note taped to her desk or look in on her. No matter how busy I was, I would let her escape to the art supply closet when tears came or walk with her in the campus woods when it was just all too much for her. She was my friend and I loved her.

Eventually her situation became extreme. One day, as was our habit, I went to her classroom to meet and go to lunch together. She was in the closet at the back of the math room, crying. I hated to see her so miserable. It was then that she showed me the gun in her large shoulder bag. "Mallory, what do you need that for?!" I had never seen a gun close-up. The handgun was long and frightening. She said it was from Vietnam and that she had gotten it from her brother, and that she planned to use it on herself when things became intolerable. Though I'd never held a gun in my life, I asked her to let me keep it for her but she would have none of that. I told her it shouldn't be in school, that in fact, it was against the law to have guns in a school. She said it was for her own use and told me to go on to lunch and get two seats for us; she'd be down in a minute after she put on some make-up. She already had plenty on. I left as she headed toward the restroom.

After a quick lunch, before classes were to resume, we walked briefly in the woods beside school. She talked again about running away with her professor friend, reminding me where important documents and possessions were in her home so that I could send them to her when that time came. I had heard this before. She had written out a list, which I kept in my desk at school. Then she began to describe what to do if she killed herself, where her body would be by a big tree in her back yard. I balked. I told her she had to promise me she would *not* use the gun.

"I can't do that," she answered.

"Then," I answered. "I can't promise you what *I* will do about the gun."

Before we left school for the day, I got her to agree to call me that night. She did. She talked more positively than I had ever heard her speak in recent weeks. She said she was so grateful for our friendship, that she loved me, that she had put the gun back in the hall table and would not bring it to school tomorrow. There seemed to be a strange peace surrounding her. I was uneasy about it. Everything had improved too quickly.

The next morning she was not in school. I was petrified. What if . . . My mind could not finish the sentence. Would I need that list in my desk drawer she had given me, telling me what to do with her things in case of….? I prayed not! I covered for her first period class, told her students to do any homework they might have. My students were finishing a long-term art project and could work well unattended so I bounced between the two rooms. But I was terribly concerned. Yesterday's introduction of a gun into the picture made her absence today alarming.

After teaching my next art class, between classes, I hurried to Mallory's room. To my great relief, there she was! She was taking things down from her bulletin board, putting them into a box. She was upset, saying the headmaster had called her into his office as soon as she arrived, something about parents' phone calls he was getting regarding her classes, her behavior, and he reprimanded her for missing today's first two classes, warning her she had twenty-four hours to straighten out or her services would be terminated. But apparently she was not waiting. In bitterness and belligerence, she packed.

True, her private agony had been taking its toll in the classroom. She would sit on the floor with papers scattered around her, exercising her head in circles, or forget main points while writing at the board. I had seen this once myself and she had bluntly told me as well. She was upset with those students who wanted things easy, cared about grades more than learning, and who she said were "spoiled." Recently, both students and teachers had been casually asking me what was wrong with Mallory. I always replied, "She's just tired." She did not need their focus on her on top of everything else. A private girls' school in the South can be a terrible rumor factory.

Angry and hurt, she vented about students as she put something in her handbag. It was then that I saw the gun. I was shocked!

"Mallory! The gun! Its *still in your handbag*! You told me last night you put it back in your hall table!" I asked her about this but she brushed aside the issue; I was about to be late for my next class if I didn't hurry; I told her I'd see her for lunch in an hour. She agreed.

I knew I ought to report the gun and decided to tell the middle school head (the upper school head was out of town). She was a friend, a Christian Scientist, the one who had encouraged me to apply for the art position I had, and she knew Mallory well. I felt she would be sympathetic to the situation as well as serve my obligation to tell a school authority. I expressed to her my concern about Mallory, that I felt she needed a rest, that she was facing a very difficult situation, which she'd made me promise not to speak of to anyone. The head said I needed to get the gun and report back to her after lunchtime, which it now nearly was.

I went to meet Mallory for lunch as soon as the class period was over. She said she would be right with me, that I should go on down, that she had to put on lipstick first. She had been wearing unusually heavier and heavier make-up in recent days. She would say "I look so pale." In my opinion, she was wearing a mask, both psychologically and physically.

Ten minutes into lunch, Mallory was still not down and I was alarmed. Several teachers had been talking about her at the table because her students were spreading stories about her erratic classroom behavior—with untruthful embellishments, as school girls are capable of doing. I sat silently, hating to hear their comments and concerned about why Mallory wasn't here yet.

I couldn't concentrate on eating so I excused myself to go look for her. My face undoubtedly showed concern, but no one seemed to notice or even hear me except for a colleague who caught my look and said, "I'll go with you." A spontaneous fellow, he liked getting involved. I did not stop him. I was not sure what I might encounter upstairs. He was whistling a merry tune, unaware of how serious the situation might be. I couldn't tolerate it. I was envisioning my friend on a bloody restroom floor with a gun beside her and he was *singing*! When we were alone in the hall, I stopped dead in my tracks and faced him squarely: "She has a *gun*." He was stunned and instantly changed his tune. We agreed to split up and cover two different approaches to her area of the building so as not to miss her. My heart was pounding. I did not want to enter the girls' restroom. It was all I could do to make myself push open the door. She was not there. What relief! But she was nowhere else either. Neither of us could find her. We returned to the lunchroom and there she was, laughing too loud. Somehow she had arrived in our absence down another flight of stairs. Her eyes conveyed epistles to me. I didn't bother to eat and I knew that eating was not her priority—she'd been throwing up for months. I nodded toward the exit and she returned the nod. We picked up our trays and left.

Incongruously, it was a beautiful day, the air clear, the sun bright. I suggested we walk through the woods in the remaining lunch time. Mallory began describing what I should put on her body when it was discovered under a tree in her backyard—the same scenario I had heard before. This dead-body business was too much.

"Is there anything I can *do*, Mallory? Is there *anywhere* I can take you? Is there *anyone* who can help you? Surely there must be *someone* you feel can help you. Can't you tell your story to someone? If you just get it out it will help so much! I'll drive you anywhere!" I had said these same words throughout the last couple of months, but this time with increased passion. I, too, was coming to my wit's end.

Always, she told me the same thing. There was no one. No one must ever know.

Again, one last time I asked her with urgency: "Is there not someone on this earth who can help you?"

This time she surprised me with an answer: "Well….. maybe, your father."

My father! For a second my heart sank—but only for a second. Sure. I'd do that for her. That moment she could have asked to see God Himself and I would have found the way. In spite of all that it would mean for me, given the estranged relationship I had with my dad at this time regarding my separation, I would call him if that's what she wanted. I helped her up from the curb where we'd been sitting and walked as fast as I could with her to the nearest private phone—in the counselor's office. I asked the counselor to please let us have her office for the next hour, to which she agreed, seeing who I was with and the look in my eyes. I did not want Mallory to change her mind. As a practitioner, my father had dealt with every kind of ailment or psychological problem for many years, and I knew he could help.

When I called, Dad was out of his Boston office, so I left a message that he was to call this office number at school immediately. I suggested to Mallory that she lie down on the couch. She looked exhausted.

When I got up to leave to tell someone to cover my two afternoon classes, Mallory cried out, "Don't leave me!" Her voice was like that of a little child.

"I'm not leaving. I'm right here." I held her. She was shaking.

I tried my father again. Still no answer. It came to me as I prayed silently for guidance, to have her tell me what she wanted to say to my dad and that I'd write it all down for her as she spoke. She was very weak and did not feel capable of talking on the phone. For the next amazingly clear half hour, she told every detail of her story. Lucidly. Calmly. All of her feelings and concerns were out, now on paper. The release was revitalizing. With intelligence and coherence, she described her love for this principled, dynamic professor; she revealed fears generated by this love that had trapped her for over a year. I wrote rapidly, accurately. Then I suggested she try to sleep, which she did. I sat silently in a chair and prayed. It had been an exhausting day for me, too.

I tried Dad once more and this time I got him—he had just walked in. I asked him to get his legal tablet, which I knew he had beside his phone, and to just listen. I explained that I was calling on behalf of Mallory and that she was not able to come to the phone herself but that I had written down everything she wanted me to say. I told him about the gun first and that she was at the point of killing herself. I then relayed Mallory's words I'd written down. Towards the end, Mallory stirred and Dad asked me to put her on the phone. He spoke and she listened. All I heard from our end were Mallory's long pauses punctuated with "Yes, sir" and "No, sir." When she hung up the phone she seemed refreshed and a bit more like herself. By now the school day had ended. I offered to drive her home but she refused. She smiled and gave me a long hug, and told me that she loved me. I felt drained but calm. The change in Mallory was truly remarkable. I watched her go and told her to call me later that night. I reminded her, too, that my father had requested she call him again in one hour.

I went to tell the middle school head of the progress. She was delighted. Then she asked me where the gun was. My god, the gun! I had totally forgotten about it in all the commotion of the day's events! She asked me to get it. I ran across campus, passing students with book bags and colleagues on their way home, barely returning their greetings. As I entered the door of our building, it came to me to grab the paper basket that was propping open the door. I sailed upstairs and as I turned the corner, down the corridor, I saw Mallory cross the hall from her room toward the restroom without noticing me. Under orders, I went into her room, found her handbag on the floor beside her desk, swiftly reached in and felt the cold metal of the gun. I pulled out the only weapon I have ever held in my life and dropped it in the paper basket I was carrying. I ran back across campus to the middle school head and handed her the basket without a word. She switched the lights off in her office, as she had glass windows to the hall and wanted no one to observe us.

Minutes later, though I had no idea at the time, the middle school head took the gun to the headmaster while I ran back to tell Mallory what I had done. I felt obligated, as a friend, to let her know I had taken her gun. I did not want her to wonder why it was missing or where it was; I wanted to be honest with her. She was my *dear friend*; I could do no less. She had her back to me, finishing packing her last carton of classroom materials. She let out a tremendous sigh which surprised me—almost as if there couldn't possibly be an ounce of air left in her. Somehow it did not fit the reformation of the past half hour. I felt uneasy. She did not have the peaceful air about her that she had had when we left the counselor's office earlier.

"Mallory." I spoke gently. "I took your gun."

She whirled around with an unforgettable expression of exhaustion, evil, and hate. "What did you go and do *that* for?!" Her words—strained, attacking, devilish—sounded nothing like her own voice. I was stunned. This was *not* Mallory!

"I had to," I answered. "You know there can't be a gun in school. You know that as well as I do. In reversed roles, you'd have done the same thing."

"What did you do with it?" she questioned me with a crazed expression I had only seen in her for split seconds on rare occasions this last month. But now that expression had taken over completely. My best friend was frightening. And furious.

She picked up her box and headed to the door saying in a demonic tone, "You know I can always get another gun or do it with drugs! How could you do this to me? I thought I could trust you! We were best friends!" Her voice hit all possible pitches as she spit out sour words, ripping our friendship to shreds.

"I wanted to help you!" I responded. "I told you when you first showed me the gun that I couldn't promise you what I would do about it. You didn't give it to me when I asked. You *lied* to me when you told me you put it back in the hall table. Mallory, I don't want you to kill yourself! You can't have a gun in school! I just wanted to stop you! I had no choice! I love you!"

"Yee-ahh." She dragged out that word sarcastically, shooting hatred at me. Bitterly, she left the room, walked down the stairs and into the first floor hall where the headmaster awaited. He had received the gun from the middle school head and immediately went to find Mallory before she left the building. He fired her on the spot. A few minutes later, in his office, I pleaded he reconsider his decision. Time off, sabbatical, anything, but not this humiliation of being fired. But he would hear none of it. He told me the gun she had brought to school was loaded, and had she used it, it not only would have killed her, but was powerful enough to have "blown holes in the building". He said I had done "yeoman's work" and thanked me.

I didn't feel like a yeoman. I felt like a traitor. Yet, I knew I did the right and only thing possible.

Mallory called me a few nights later and in a slow gravelly whisper that I could hardly recognize, told me she forgave me. School officials told the switchboard to pass no calls or messages from her to me or to anyone else and if she were ever on campus I was to notify them at once.

Less than two months later I again got a phone call from her at home to say she was signed up for Christian Science Class Instruction in Boston with my father. I was shocked. I couldn't imagine the necessary transformation from thoughts of suicide to being ready for Class had taken place. Though she wasn't allowed on campus, twice notes were mysteriously taped to my school desk chair from her—one a year later at the time of my mother's death. She also phoned me out of the blue a few years later. She said she was a principal for a public school, still married to her husband—but we didn't have much to say to each other. I have never seen nor heard from her since.

One of the most difficult things about this episode was that I lost my only friend at a time when I really needed one. And I felt it was my fault.

One of the other difficulties was the reaction at school to Mallory's absence. Right after the incident, the headmaster told me, and the few people involved, to respond to all student or faculty questions as to why she was no longer at the school with the simple statement: "It's a private matter." I said those words so often I felt like a robot. And with each utterance I grew more frustrated. I wanted desperately to talk about it, to let the truth be known, but I never did until four years passed and I no longer worked at Custis Lee.

Rumors as to why Mallory left floated through the school. Some thought she had a better offer, some thought she had a nervous breakdown, some thought she quit. No one knew she was fired. No one knew about a gun, the nearly attempted suicide, or the cause of it all. No one knew the truth.

The worst rumor of all was that she had been studying "that heretical, crazy Christian Science religion" through her relationship with me and that she, therefore, was refusing to take drugs that could have helped her nervous condition. In truth, her handbag was full of pills. But I was seen by some as the bad guy, the cause, along with Christian Science, for her leaving. One of our most outstanding teachers was gone and many perceived it to be my fault. I faced hard looks for weeks. Yet I could say nothing. I clung to my promise to Mallory that I would tell no one her secret. And I stuck to the headmaster's orders that I say nothing other than "It's a private matter."

Miraculously, during this crisis and my separation from John, I kept my equilibrium. The rock-like strength that I'd found in the abyss earlier fortified me.

Late in May, I found two friends at school whom I could talk to when things got heavy. One was the drama teacher who invited me to attend his Methodist church. I felt welcome at this inner-city church of blacks and whites working together to keep their small congregation alive to what real church is about. I even did portraits for a fund-raising fair they held. The minister was down-to-earth and gave inspiring sermons.

One day in despair, I phoned this minister. After briefly telling him my story, he said, "How have you managed to *stay alive* with all you've been through?! How have you remained in one piece when none of the support systems we usually take for granted were there for you?! How have you survived so many losses in such a short time?!"

I answered with one word: "God."

He agreed with my answer, adding, "God does not want us to stay in destructive relationships." He suggested I find a book by Chiam Potok called *My Name is Asher Lev*, about an artist and his struggle to find himself in spite of his Hasidic upbringing. This book was remarkable for it seemed to describe my life as an artist living under family ties of a strict religious code.

The other acquaintance from school who became a friend was the history teacher, Bill Caldwell, the chipper colleague who had left the lunch table to help me find Mallory.

One afternoon when John was out of town and Charissa was playing at a friend's, I found myself crying, curled up on the bathroom floor in the new house we'd recently purchased in a neighborhood where I knew no one. My best friend was no longer my best friend. I phoned the Methodist minister of the church but he was not in. Then I phoned the history teacher who volunteered to come over and play his guitar. He brought some Calvin and Hobbes cartoons to cheer me up and stayed for supper with Charissa and me. I found myself drawn to his free and caring spirit.

In May, the week after the Mallory incident, less than two months before my divorce would become final, and just weeks before I was to return for my final RISD summer, my mother called from Boston at 7:00 A.M. on a school day, just as I was heading out the door, to announce she would be arriving that afternoon and to please meet her plane! To say I was surprised is an understatement. One: my mother never traveled without my father—ever.

Two: she has never been spontaneous. Three: this was the busiest time at school as it was almost over—why would she come now? Four: With all I had just been through, now this!—was there no end to crises?!

I quickly made my house as immaculate as possible before I left for school and I picked her up at the airport after school. John was still out of town. I knew why Mom had come. She hoped to save her daughter from destruction. She knew the divorce would be final in a few weeks and saw it as her duty to prevent that. Now in her seventies, she seemed more tired than usual and had difficulty walking. Until Charissa went to bed, she acted as if this were merely a pleasant visit. Then Mom turned to me and said evenly: "I understand you are about to do something totally devastating."

It was a long night. A night of inquisition. She questioned and I answered until 3:00 AM, both sleeping in my king-size bed because John was out of town and she was not able to walk up stairs to the guest room. I don't know that we had ever slept in the same bed before in our lives. I tried to answer her questions, to explain the reasons for my impending divorce. She had caught me in a state of exhaustion from the demanding end of a school year. On top of which my second RISD Master's paper would be due in June. I was also coping with divorce legalities and my best friend's near suicide and the consequent loss of my best friend.

Every sentence that was not a question my mother prefaced with: "Your father thinks…" I felt like she was his ambassador:

"Your father thinks you are being impetuous and taking this action rashly. Why are you doing this? Has everything you've lived been *a lie*?"

"Your father thinks you are no longer a Christian Scientist. Is this true? Have you changed religions? How do you rationalize divorce with what is in the Bible?"

"Your father says you are hurting many people. What about your children? Aren't you only thinking of yourself? What about people in the Christian Science movement? This will get out, you know. Some of your father's students are your friends, too, and they are disturbed by what you are doing. You are destroying them."

"Your father thinks that RISD ruined you—all that liberal thinking, all those artists and strange people! He saw peculiar signs around your school art room when we visited at Thanksgiving." The "strange signs" referred to quotations by Van Gogh, art historians Herbert Read and Kenneth Clark, Madeliene L'Engle, and one I particularly like by Neitzche: *Without risk, no creative life is possible.*

And she went on: "John tells us that you play *loud rock music* and that you *go out at night.*" I explained to her that I played rock, blues, classical and a tad of country regularly and that I did not think it unusually loud considering the size of our house. I told her I had gone out *twice* with Sandra—the friend to whom I had loaned my apartment—to Beale Street to hear the blues. Period.

When we stopped talking and my mother finally fell asleep, it was 3:30 AM. I quietly went into the bathroom and recorded the entire conversation in my journal. After no sleep and an early breakfast, I drove my mother to the airport, gave her a hug, and put her on the plane back to Boston.

A few weeks later, school was over, my second thesis paper for RISD completed, and I was in Providence for my third and final summer, renting a convenient two-bedroom apartment with Chris Lissandrello, my friend since our first days at RISD. He had called and suggested we lease a place together to save money. My parents and John thought I was crazy to say yes. They could not comprehend that Chris and I were just roommates, comrades, sharing cooking and cleaning, though I had explained several times that his wonderful wife, Gail, and their little boy would be driving down from their home in New York and staying with us on many weekends. It certainly was not unusual for male and female students to share an apartment; it was just not something John and my parents had ever heard of.

My sons were working in Bristol, Rhode Island, for the summer. Chris and I had them to dinner frequently and to an occasional gathering with our RISD friends. They liked Chris's sense of humor, his guitar playing, and his comfortable, talkative manner.

It was a full summer: painting constantly, classes, writing, reading, 6-mile walks with my RISD friend Sylvan from Palo Alto, California, and gatherings for dinner and music as in the previous two summers. Music was always part of my RISD summers: Chris's guitar or a Billy Joel concert or a trip to the Kennedy Plaza to hear John Hiatt.

Donna, another fellow RISD student, an art teacher, photographer, singer, guitar-player, who had been a dancer and done some acting in New York City, took it upon herself to "educate" me. Abused as a child, she told me she still saw a psychiatrist twice a week. She dated musicians, used marajuana upon occasion, practiced yoga, and smoked too much. She gave everyone back rubs, talked like a pogo-stick, bouncing from topic to topic, and once created a 30-foot fish sculpture she danced through. She wanted to introduce me to musicians she knew, have me try wine, and learn to play the guitar. Fortunately her follow-through was lacking and my schedule too full for any of this.

Sylvan on the other hand, like Chris, was a solid and very spiritual friend, a print-maker, whose walks and talks were vital to me that last summer. She had done lots of dream work with highly respected professionals in California where she lived. One evening in particular with Sylvan was most memorable.

I had had a dream several nights prior that woke me in a sweat and that I couldn't forget even in daylight for days later. In the dream I was in a house with many layers and levels and it was full of people, as if some sort of party were going on. I was disinterested in the party and walked through the house looking in room after room for a place that seemed comfortable, a place for me. I wanted to get away from the noise and humanity. I found myself going out a back door and into the yard where I saw two idyllic children, their backs to me, swinging on swings. As I approached them, they turned to face me and I saw the most evil I have ever seen staring back at me, laughing. So frightening were their faces that I woke up. I told Sylvan about this dream and she suggested that we have a dream session. I went to her dorm room where she dimmed the lights and asked me to lay down. She "walked me back into" the dream and when I got to the frightening part, where the children faced me, she asked me to ask them who they were. To my shock they responded, "We are you." When the session was finished I asked Sylvan what it meant that they were me. She said we all have our dark sides. That only I could work on answering that question. She explained that dreams come to get our attention, wake us up to what needs attending. Apparently some neglected part of me needed serious attention. The long-ignored shadow side stepped boldly once more into my experience.

As a Christian Scientist I had managed to avoid the negative rather successfully. It was nothing I ever let roam my consciousness. The dream seemed to be shocking me into taking a good look at my dark side, face it squarely, then let it go, in order to see clearly my wholeness. The two at first seemingly cherubic children swinging represented the male and female qualities we each have, another aspect of wholeness.

Another time, Sylvan brought me a book prior to our routine evening walk.

"What's this?" I asked, looking at the 4-inch thick book she thrust in my hand.

"Something I think you need to read," she said with a smile.

"*The Hitte Report on Sexuality?*" I was puzzled, put it down on the coffee table, and we started our 6-mile trek. When I got home from my walk with Sylvan, Chris was still away working in his studio so I picked up the book Sylvan had given me. I had never read anything like it before. I was fascinated, surprised, a little frightened, intrigued, and enormously sad. Sad because what I was reading about for the first time hadn't been part of my life and I realized I would have liked it to have been. All I could think was "I am 46 years old and I have never experienced any of this!" I didn't understand exactly why, but suddenly, I couldn't stop crying. On our next walk Sylvan and I talked about the book, about sexual behavior in a loving relationship, and I began to understand my tears: most of my life, I had longed for—without knowing it—such a relationship.

Just before I was to fly back to Memphis to appear in court for the divorce, my father paid me a visit in Providence. I was anxious about his coming. I prayed to be able to stand strong against his well-meaning manipulation, for he always had a definite and persuasive agenda. When he arrived he was serious and went straight to the topics he came to discuss (or preach). He said he wanted first to discuss Mallory and then my divorce. He spoke for a solid hour without room for my response. I timed him, because I took my heavy Swiss army watch off my wrist and laid it on the coffee table in front of me.

Dad told me Mallory had left his class after a few days, rather than staying for the required two weeks; this is never done. She told Dad that *I* was suicidal, that I had "confused her about Christian Science" and a few other preposterous lies. I have since learned about the clinical psychological term *projection*, but at the time I could *not* understand why my supposed former friend had done this. Yes, I had turned in her gun to the headmaster but that was one act over years of closeness and kindness. I had sat with her during her time of greatest need and called my father on her behalf as she asked—at a time when calling my parents was difficult for me. Furthermore, I was shocked that Dad had chosen to believe her over all he innately knew about his own daughter. His accusing me of what Mallory had told him was so fallacious and unexpected! His hammering against my divorce I had expected, but not his false accusations! It was *life* I sought, not death! Why ever else bother with divorce? I think he began to sort it out when I got a turn to respond—brief, though it was, for his tirade against divorce then became his main agenda.

He began his anti-divorce speech with specific major points: "Divorce is not in accord with the Bible nor the teachings of Christ Jesus!" He repeated things he'd said before: "John can't be that bad—he doesn't beat you and he's not an alcoholic. . . Be grateful you have a husband and just love more . . .I've put together plenty of marriages and I know it can be worked out!…Guard against self-justification, selfishness, and self-righteousness! … .You are a pillar in Christian Science and need to maintain that image . . . People look up to you, they put you on a pedestal and will be disappointed in you when you do the unexpected . . . They will wonder what you stand for if you divorce instead of work it out in Christian Science."

I was able to respond calmly, feeling a new dominion over my self and thoughts, and remained unafraid of my father. He was not able, this time, to control me.

The next morning, slipped under my door, was an eight-page legal tablet letter continuing his argument against divorce—apparently after he left, Dad sat outside my door to write what he'd left unsaid. He was never one to give up! The only sentence I recall now was his last (for I threw the letter away after reading it, and now wish I hadn't for my story's sake), something about his "praying to God to know how to be a better father" because he knew he had "failed".

While Dad was visiting me, Mom, I learned later, was on the phone with my sons in Bristol, Rhode Island where my boys were employed for the summer. Calling them from her Providence hotel room she said, "Your grandfather is trying to talk your mother out of divorce right now. She probably won't listen. It's been a waste of our time to come here and try to change her mind. Your Dad is getting the short end of the stick." Jason and Nathan told me about the call the next day. Once more I was stunned by my parents' behavior. Where was unconditional Christian love? Why bring the boys into this? Neither John nor I used our children as pawns, vowing to be decent to each other during this process.

My mother's main point seemed to center around the house. I had planned to keep the house because I had always done everything pertaining to home, and in fact, the money with which our homes had been purchased over the years was largely from my end, investments made in our homes over the years from gifts from my parents. It never occurred to me John should keep the house; I was the homemaker, not him. I was the mother, still raising my daughter and assumed Charissa and I would live in the house after the divorce.

But the very next day one of my RISD classes gave me a new perspective. I took five large watercolors (Providence houses, seascapes, landscapes) and two large oil abstracts on canvas to the critique. The teacher, Lenny Long, had each class member comment on each person's work; then, he critiqued the work fully, one artist at a time. When it was my turn I put up my seven pieces. Lenny looked at them and asked me questions before he let the class members talk. He asked me how I *felt* about doing the two very different styles and mediums. I said I liked both and found myself bouncing between the two. I added that I felt the dichotomy needed resolution. Then he asked me again: "I asked you the "F" word! How do you *feel* doing each?"

I admitted that there was more challenge, intensity, more struggle in doing the abstracts. Then he asked if I thought I could give up the watercolors. Would it bother me? I answered I thought I could, though it had never occurred to me, since most of my awards were in watercolor up to that point. Then he opened the critique to everyone. The first person said, "Abandon the watercolors, continue the abstracts!" Everyone spoke similarly, acknowledging the technical skill and accomplished level of the watercolors, but preferring the edginess and bold strength of the abstracts.

Then Lenny spoke as I took down his words. His critique of my paintings turned out to be an analysis of my life, though he did not know it. In fact he barely knew me. He began: "It's all a matter of evolution. You will never lose anything. It's *in* you. It's not a matter of giving up something. The concerns are all the same. All your technical skill, color usage, expressiveness will carry right on into your abstracts. The only thing that you will probably give up will be the American flag and the putzy azalea stuff (referring to a Providence house with flag and flowers). People will tell you 'Do not give up the flag!' It is too precious!' But you will know better. It is a scary jump from the one to the other. But you cannot walk left and right at the same time without falling down trying. There is an energy, a strength, in your abstracts. All you've accomplished previously in watercolor will come through in the abstracts. *All you've learned and demonstrated will not be lost in the change.* You have a boldness, an ability to add and subtract on the surface area. I would say, definitely go in this new direction. Go with the abstracts. Learn all you can about them. Devour books on abstract artists. Discover their vocabulary. You don't have to reinvent the wheel, just get better traction. Learn all you can, then *go on your own*. It's like this: *It's like you've gotten out of the house, you've said good-bye to everything. You've left all. Now you're out there on your own but you don't know where you're going yet. But you will. Trust yourself.* Your abstracts have a strong beginning but you are not there yet. It will be harder than the water-colors. It will be physically exhausting. I want five or six big abstracts next week, say 8x10 feet each."

I understood completely. I was stunned by the wisdom of Lenny's words. The double layers of meaning about "getting out of the house," "not losing anything," "evolution," "giving up the putzy stuff"! I sat during the next person's critique thinking about everything I had just heard, looking over the notes I'd just taken. Then, I thought of the space it takes to do 8 by 10 foot paintings. Why, I couldn't even fit an 8 by 10-foot piece up the stairs into my studio in the fancy subdivision house we'd recently purchased!

Walking up the hill to my Providence apartment after the critique class, I realized I could not do large abstracts in the house in Memphis. I thought of John not wanting to leave the house. I thought of my mother saying to Jason and Nathan that their father was "getting the short end of the stick." And I thought of a passage that came to me last winter in my apartment in prayerful solitude: *We have left all and followed thee* said Peter to Jesus who answered: *Verily I say unto you, there is no man that hath left house, or brethren, or sisters, or father, or mother, or wife [or husband], or children, or lands, for my sake and the gospel's, but he shall receive an hundredfold now in this time, houses and brethren, and sisters, and mothers, and children, and lands, with persecutions; and in the world to come eternal life.* (Mark 10: 28-30).

I thought of the The Interpreter's Bible Moffat translation I'd discovered when asking God why we must leave our Fisherville home: *To abase pride and humble human splendor.* That had been only the beginning of my sailing away.

By the time I reached my apartment it had become clear. John could have the house. I would find a small studio with 11-foot ceilings somewhere in Memphis for my 10-foot abstracts. I called John and told him he could have the house. He was very pleased not to have to move. I also decided not to ask for anything—no alimony, savings, insurance. I needed nothing but a studio. He would *not* get the short end of the stick!

The next day I made an appointment to meet Lenny Long for lunch, to pursue the wise words of his critique. As I revealed pieces of my life to him, he did the same. I learned to my total surprise that he had been raised a Christian Scientist in childhood but left it soon after as it did not accept his lifestyle nor meet his needs. I bought one of his smaller prints to remind me of him and the wisdom he taught me.

To change from award-winning watercolorist to abstractionist seemed right. But also brave. Like stepping off the planet. Like divorce. Lenny's analogy about getting out of the house but not knowing where you are going was right on target. Changing without losing. That was his point to me. He had said *you can't lose anything.* Seems I'd heard that somewhere years ago. *You can't lose what you are. It's in you.* A stranger had told me that several years earlier after I'd lost a portfolio of my best work. Now another stranger was telling me again.

On Independence Day, Wednesday, July 4, 1990, I got my independence. I flew to Memphis, just long enough to appear in the Tipton County Courthouse and stand before a judge who asked me if I wished to sever my marriage to John West. In less than five minutes a twenty-one year marriage was legally terminated. I flew back to Providence the following Sunday where RISD friends came to our apartment to celebrate with Chris' famous pasta with clam sauce.

In August, my third and final RISD summer was over, and I returned to Memphis where my realtor showed me only one place—a light-filled condo within walking distance of The Memphis Museum of Art, near galleries and the main library. It had *14-foot ceilings and 9-foot windows*—perfect for painting large abstracts! I took it.

All I lost was the putzy stuff.

fourteen

A New Path

A Poem for Easter

It's three days before Easter
and a couple thousand years after
they crucified Christ like a criminal and I
have aunts and uncles and cousins who won't speak
to me the black sheep of the family
whose return to the fold they pray for
but I have to be white if I come back
wagging my tail behind me
so I baa in my own pasture and eat the greener grass I run in
with the wind to my back now
no longer trusting their blinding whiteness I
search for the Shepherd in new fields that smell of wild onion
as well as sweet clover

In the summer of 1993 I cross the narrow toll bridge into Illinois with New Harmony in my rear-view mirror—an image I will hold long into the bleak Memphis winter of the upcoming school year. Images in the mirror are always closer than they appear. Yesterday, after packing up my paints and writing materials, I paid my last visit to the *Chapel of the Little Portion*. Today it's with me on my drive home from New Harmony. No icons in that tiny chapel, no cushioned seats, no carefully arranged floral bouquets. Only light from the clerestory windows casting a cross shape on bare plaster walls. There's room for fewer than six worshipers on several low, crude wooden benches. Remains of one votive candle suggest an earlier lone visitor. This is a chapel made for solitude. A massive millstone serves as altar in the center of the single room. Textured with chiseled lines radiating out from its hub, it is a powerful centering image that pulls one to the nucleus of her being. This altar sits in the center of the chapel in a town centered in my family's native state in the center of this nation in the center of our solar system in the center of the universe. I *feel* these concentric circles. In New Harmony's sacred vortex I have learned, once again, that I dwell not in a house, but in internal space. Here is homecoming.

In July 1990, after receiving my divorce, I took my own name, Gwendolyn Evans. There was a new gait to my step as I walked to my RISD classes, past Providence's historic homes, and the white clapboard 17th century American Baptist Church. The sign for next Sunday's sermon caught my eye: "A New Attitude." I'd never been in this beautiful historic church, but was drawn to that Sunday service because everything in my life was *new*.

The female minister, Kate Penrod, preached on never being separated from the love of our Father, God. Only the week before my human father came to talk me out of divorce, but failed; he *had*, however, succeeded in severing our relationship. He let me know I was no longer his loved child. So it was comforting to sit in that pew on July 15, 1990, and hear a sermon on the Fatherhood of God—a father I could not lose. The hymn we sang spoke to me; I copied its words on my program, transferring them later to my journal:

Fatherhood and Love
Be still, my soul: the Lord is on thy side
Bear patiently the cross of grief or pain.
Leave to thy God to order and provide;
In every change He faithful will remain
Be still, my soul: thy best, thy heavenly Friend
Through thorny ways leads a joyful land.

Be still, my soul: thy God doth undertake
To guide the future as He has the past.
The hope, thy confidence let nothing shake
All now mysteries shall be bright at last.
Be still, my soul: the waves and winds still know
His voice who ruled them while He dwelt below.

Be still, my Soul: the hour is hastening on
When we shall be forever with the Lord.
When disappointment, grief and fear are gone.
Sorrow forgot, Love's purest joys restored.
Be still, my Soul: when change and tears are past.
All safe and blessed we shall meet at last.

Comforting my grief, the sermon and hymn addressed my longing for Father, reminding me that without husband, father, or home, I still dwelt with my true Father—God. I thanked the minister in her office, shared how her sign called me in, how her sermon addressed my need. After hearing bits of my story she said: "Stay strong in the days ahead!" How often her counsel comes back to me!

I know the ever-presence of God—something every Sunday School child is told but doesn't always feel as an adult. God in the dark and light of our days and nights, speaks all the time to us; sometimes shouting. I write of God my Father knowing I mean also God my Mother (language inadequately expresses the Divine). I search for God beyond denomination, seek *universal* Truth and the presence of Love. I aim for God *in the moment*.

In 1990 books on world religions, theology, spirituality and philosophy accompany me on my new solitary path. I write my own prayers and beliefs in my journal. I test my beliefs in daily life, discard what no longer makes sense—a method not unlike my old friend Descartes'. The former theatre director at school once told me what works for him is to periodically write "Here's what I know today...." and fill in the blank. He says it keeps emotions at bay, offers him direction. I try it. I find uplifting thoughts everywhere. The school chaplain serendipitously hands me a Bible passage translation of

Isaiah 43: 18-19, which stays among those inspiring my new frontier: *The Lord says, "Do not cling to events of the past or dwell on what happened long ago. Watch for this new thing I am going to do. It is happening already—you can see it now! I will make a road through the wilderness and give you streams of water there.*

On August 11, 1990, I write out my new relationship with God:

1. God is Supreme Good, Spirit, Truth, Love, all-powerful and ever-present.

2. God is Creator of All, the principle behind what is—my only Father and Mother, who never leaves Her child comfortless. I am not alone. I trust me to Her care—just as He/She cares for all.

3. My reason for being is to serve God by being the creative person She made me to be; to do less is not to serve God or oneself.

4. I listen to Christ Jesus but also to the wisdom of the Old Testament, to Buddha, Plato, the Tao, diverse thinkers and philosophers I am discovering, and to daily experience.

5. Humility and honesty are essential characteristics for those who seek God. Dishonesty and willfulness are signs of distrusting God, forfeiting His guidance and power in one's life.

6. Love is paramount. It displaces fear, heals instantly, sometimes means getting no return but is always the best course. Giving love is the goal, not getting it.

7. God gives ideas; it is my duty to be the servant of every good idea that comes to me.

8. I must never forget that I am on a spiritual journey. Like that of the creative hero, it is not easy but it is abundant adventure and endless learning.

When my final RISD summer came to an end, I faced the challenge of driving large canvases and all my gear back to Memphis by myself. Bill Caldwell, Custis Lee's gregarious history teacher, offered to fly up and help. He'd never seen Boston or Rhode Island and it sounded like fun.

The school's confirmed bachelor, known as BC, had a way of cheering up colleagues by describing the precise *Far Side* cartoon one needed, or just by being his witty and humorous self. Knowing I was going through a divorce, Bill had been solicitous of my welfare during the school year, stopping by my classroom to ask how I was doing. I began to have feelings for him. He had been the one to join me in looking for Mallory that traumatic day in May and one time during the last weeks of school had come to my home when everything weighed heavy. He was always uplifting someone—one of his gifts, along with guitar-playing, humor, and intellect. The summer of 1990 he phoned me twice from Santa Fe, New Mexico, where he was attending St. John's College Great Books Master's degree summer program and I'd written him letters about my summer's intellectual, artistic, and spiritual discoveries. We were becoming friends.

After my divorce, his calls were more frequent. My RISD friends teased me about this potential "relationship", but I knew Bill was eight years younger and my mind was full of all the changes I had to face when I returned to Memphis. At the same time, I could not deny a growing fondness for and fascination with Mr. Caldwell. We visited Lexington and Concord—where this American history teacher had never been—as part of our trip home and found we could talk endlessly about everything. It was a good road trip, the first of many. Our creative natures and love of books blended well, and by September we were "dating" (if that's what one calls it in one's middle years).

Just before the school year started, now a single woman with a master's degree with honors, I moved into my new light-filled loft-bedroom condo with its 14-foot ceilings and 9-foot windows—a perfect home for painting.

The century-old building, built as an elementary school in 1909, contained a dozen condos. Early black-and-white photos of the children and teachers who attended here lined the entry hall. Being in the elementary years of a new life, I felt at home, though my condo's 950 square feet was a third the size of any house I'd ever owned. I loved its openness and light. From my bedroom loft, open to the studio and living space below, I looked out to treetops through tall windows that extended between both levels. The hardwood floors and tall ivory plaster walls suited making and displaying art. The galley kitchen was smaller than most closets in my previous homes, but its high ceilings and old glass-front cabinets made up for any limitations. There being no fireplace, I purchased a carved antique German mantel with money from my painting sales and put it in my living space near my old gate-leg table and new brown paisley down-stuffed sofa. I had a carpenter build a cozy bed-loft with a surround of shelves for Charissa—up the first set of stairs, prior to our shared bath and my sleeping area.

Though everything was new, I felt guided each step, really since separation before the divorce. Actually, always. Signs as clear as white blazes marking a trail led me, have always led me.

Charissa lived with me during the school week and with John on weekends in the large subdivision home we'd purchased immediately after our Fisherville home sold. A year later, John sold that house and purchased a slightly smaller less expensive subdivision home, continuing to have Charissa on weekends. I was busy painting in my turn-of-the-century condo with 14-foot ceilings and seeing Bill on weekends when I did not have Charissa. Bill and I visited bookstores and libraries, went to the repertory theater, enjoyed hiking in state parks. In school, we were determined not to even look at each other. If I saw him coming down a corridor, I went another way. It was pretty silly. But a private girls' school loves rumor, and we wanted privacy in this new and fragile relationship. By November, however, we could not hide the fact that we were in love.

I told my children about BC a month after we began dating. Bill and I even went to see a couple of Nathan's football games in St. Louis. The boys seemed to like him (everyone always does) but I am sure it was awkward for them to think of their mother dating. Charissa knew Mr. Caldwell from school and seemed to accept him readily. She was very close to her father at this time but Bill was not a father figure, as much as a popular, amusing teacher and friend of her mother's. I told my parents much later as they were not really speaking to me—at least not in a friendly way.

Christmas 1990 and New Year's were difficult. Bill had previous plans for a long canoeing trip in Big Bend National Park, in Texas, with St. John's College friends, and I would be in Bermuda for my parents' 50th anniversary, an event my brother had arranged for all Evanses to attend. Rich had even wanted to invite John (though he doesn't recall that now).

My kids and I arrived some days after the others, and pulled up to the Cambridge Beaches Hotel to find family members, including my parents, attired in tee-shirts with Glenn and Ruth's photo, a caption below reading, *Fifty Years for Ruth and Glenn*. There were no tee shirts for us (which was fine by me!). Things got odder. When I went to register there was no cottage for Ms. Gwendolyn Evans and family, only for *Mrs. John West!* I had not been Mrs. John West for six months! Someone in the family was still rubbing it in.

A divorced woman in the midst of fifteen Christian Science relatives, I was not someone anyone seemed glad to see. My aunt and uncle would barely speak to me the entire week. My mother was tired all the time and easily avoided me due to an abscess on her leg, for which a Christian Science nurse was always at her side. Mom rarely left her cottage and had next to nothing to say to me, though I tried to visit with her several times. She did not seem healthy and I was concerned about her. I'd brought photos of a recent exhibition of my artwork in a major Memphis gallery as well as a few pictures of the kids to share, but neither she (nor anyone else) seemed the least bit interested. Karen, my sister-in-law, though busy with Rich and her four kids, did go on a walk or two with me, otherwise I was pretty much alone. My kids had a good time snorkeling, scuba-diving, and sailing with their cousins. I survived the awkward event but wrote caustically in my journal December 25, 1990: *Midst all the perfection, I am a flaw on this family…It is quietly made clear that I am to feel just enough disgrace—not enough to look like anyone is doing this disgracing, for that would be imperfect of them—to know that I have upset the King and Queen and their kingdom.*

Every evening everyone made great effort to laud my parents. Once, my uncle circulated a menu on which we were asked to put our kudos and praises for Ruth and Glenn. I don't recall what appreciative message I wrote but I did find the activity strange for a family that values humility.

Then there was the video. Back in Boston, Mom had arranged for someone to make a video from old home movies—a several hour history of the Evans family from 1939 to the present. Interesting to be sure, but yawns were also present during the lengthy after-dinner premier in Bermuda. Afterward, Mom handed me the video saying she had "a copy for *each* of us". Later I learned mine was *the only* copy made—even my parents did not have one! The video began with a twenty-second hold of a still shot of our family taken one Christmas at John's and my Fisherville home about four years earlier. There I was looking at what no longer was. I guess that was the point. Aside from being an historical record, I guess the video had been made to punctuate my divorce.

The remainder of the holiday the kids flew to Florida with their Dad to his parents' home. I sat alone in my Memphis condo—except for 10 minutes early on New Years Eve at a party given by someone I didn't know on the third floor of my building and another short visit to a colleague's. That week was one of the loneliest I've known. My previous holidays bustled with activity surrounded by family—for 21 years I'd prepared Christmas dinners with all the trimmings, followed by a quiet family New Year's. Now I was alone. And *I* had caused this change. I had to sit with it. I wrote in my journal: "I feel like an empty house."

So I painted. Big abstract canvases. And I wrote: voluminous journal entries and poems late at night when I ought to have been sleeping. These acts gave me *place*. To create, I've learned, is to work one's way to God.

Where to go to church was problematic. The branch church, the Germantown Society, I'd help start in the early eighties closed after seven years, having lost a third of its members due to career moves and job transfers. But I would not have gone there anyway at this point, because I was changing. While still adhering to most of what Christian Science taught, I continued questioning its teachings and the behavior of some Christian Scientists as I explored other religious viewpoints.

Bill had been raised Presbyterian, and had a Master of Arts in Religion degree from Philadelphia's Westminster Seminary, aside from his Vanderbilt degrees in History and English. When I asked what propelled him to go to seminary he answered "to face my own personal demons." After seminary, he stopped attending Presbyterian churches and started attending a small Episcopal church where he occasionally played the guitar.

I had recently heard an inspiring talk by an Episcopal priest, a guest speaker at school, and was pleased with my private conversation with him afterward. When a colleague, who knew Bill and I wanted to find a church we could attend together, suggested we visit Calvary Episcopal Church in downtown Memphis—a lovely historic structure and the oldest church in the city—we decided to visit. Though leery of its iconic and Catholic roots, I went open-minded. I discovered a place of architectural beauty, glorious music, and an inspiring story-teller rector, Doug Bailey, whose slight East-coast accent reminded me of my Baltimore childhood.

Doug's words conveyed messages straight to my heart. I wasn't sure what to make of the procession of long-robed clergy—something I'd never experienced—nor of the icons imbedded in the pillars (which I learned later represented the four gospels writers, Matthew, Mark, Luke, and John) but I knew I was meant to continue here when in front of me in the pew rack I found a notice for *The Journey Course.*

Of late, the word *journey* had special meaning for me. I had found it in everything I was reading, from Joseph Campbell to Thomas Merton to Carl Jung. I had adopted *journey* as my own. It seemed *more* than serendipitous that this downtown church, which neither of us had ever visited before, would be offering a course on that particular subject! I knew I was meant to take the course.

Though this was a large church, with hundreds in attendance at three services each Sunday, I boldly decided to call the rector to ask him a few questions and ask about *The Journey Course.* I called Doug on Monday, on my lunch break. At the time I had no idea how busy he was (now I am nearly embarrassed that I bothered him with my questions). Then I did not know he had walked with Martin Luther King and Desmond Tutu, was highly respected nationally, that his church had nearly two thousand parishioners with more than thirty outreach activities. He had his hands full, but Doug answered my theological questions with patience, sincerity, and as if I were the only person he had to talk to that day.

Bill and I signed up for *The Journey Course.*

Doug had created the course years ago, and it had become popular within the Memphis area, attracting persons of varied denominations and backgrounds. Anywhere from 70 to 120 persons would be in attendance. Based on deep questioning and soul-searching, the course was an exploration of the human journey. Wednesdays after school, Bill and I drove an hour downtown to attend the 15-week, 5-hour a night, commitment. After the first year, Bill and I became part of the ten-member Journey team: those who worked with Doug in planning and teaching the course. This was often the best part for me, often the most inspiring time of my day. After our planning session from 5 to 6, we ate dinner in the church basement together, followed by a brief church service in the sanctuary, and then returned to the basement for the course from 7 until 9 or 9:30. At 9:30 the team went up to Doug's office for a recap of what had transpired, sometimes not leaving until after 10:00. Recap was another favorite time. The team became close in the most core way one human being can know another. I always felt God's presence in Doug's office. It was a kind of *home* to all ten of us after whatever our day's work had brought us as lawyers, artists, teachers, interior designers, writers, businessmen, housewives. In that room we were one.

"My most helpful image of the Christian faith is the journey" Doug would say in the first class. An avid hiker and outdoorsman, he likened the life/faith journey to a hike, a road trip, a quest, pilgrimage, search, odyssey. But this excursion is not about ascension or destination he would quickly add. He would say, "life is full of pit stops and mountaintops." No "victorious Christians" were in his analogies.

The variety of people in attendance was no surprise since Doug embraced everyone and viewed church not as a building or denomination so much as "the community of the changing," the place that enabled *metanoia* (Greek, meaning change, transformation) to happen. Certainly with all the changes I had gone through in the past year, this made me feel right at home!

Doug took the stories of the Bible as well as real life experiences, along with the best of literature, film, and philosophy to convey his teaching. He was a gifted story-teller and his stories and examples were true, touching one at a primal level. Believing the unexamined life is not worth living, Doug invited us all to explore the depths of our lives, both positive and painful. What we experienced in those sessions was profound. Doug called it: "*doing theology.*"

More than anyone I have ever met, Doug Bailey understood humanity. He genuinely *loved*—the way the sun just shines. His compassion was the most Christ-like I have encountered. He knew deeply those in the 12-step alcoholics' program, the woman in the hospital dying of cancer, the child in Sunday School. And he knew each by name in his large congregation. When you spoke, he listened, giving you his time even if he had an agenda backlogged into tomorrow (which he usually had).

Doug began each Journey session with opening prayer and welcoming comments that introduced the theme for the evening. He followed with an intro question that everyone answered, around the room, one by one. He would begin: "My name is Doug Bailey and …." filling in the designated intro question. We would all follow suite. For example, once the question was "If you were going on a trip and you knew that the essentials—food, shelter, etc. were provided—what would you take?" One man said his laptop.

A woman said photos of her grandchildren. Bill said his guitar. I said my journals. Answers revealed what mattered to each person. Another time the question was "My name is…and my religious or spiritual background is…." Another was "My name is… and a moment when God was very present for me was when…" One of my favorites was "My name is… and one of the moments in my life when I had to own up to my own brokenness was…" The question was always an opportunity for revealing, sometimes deeply personal sharing, but a question that could be answered in a sentence if one preferred, and one was always free to pass.

With a theme developed, we broke into small discussion groups. Some nights we got so "into it" in our whole group that we ran out of time to break into small groups, our whole gathering becoming an intimate sharing. Never before had I experienced such deep group intimacy, such discussions of honesty and spiritual depth in a large gathering. Many of the most inspiring times of my life happened in *The Journey Course*. We were human beings working out together our deepest selfhood. Each session was a transforming experience. There was nothing that couldn't be discussed. Every topic and every point of view was heard and valued. Perhaps that in itself was what I marveled at most.

One night as everyone answered the intro question: " My name is… and…" as we came to the final row a young blonde woman stood up, began her intro response and then said " I am *angry* with God! My father died tonight in the hospital!" The room became perfectly still. We listened as through her tears, a torrent of angry words rushed from her lips. She was mad at God and didn't hesitate to tell us. We could feel her pain as if it were ours. Some of us wondered how Doug was going to handle this. I no longer recall exactly what he said (and he told us later he felt his words very inadequate; but Doug often felt that way even when he was marvelous; he didn't seem to know how good he was at what he did), but what I *do* remember is the compassion that flowed to that woman both during her emotional dialogue and after—from Doug, from all of us. Doug made us see that this was life, too. That, as Doug put it, "shit happens" (as the bumper sticker says) but right in the middle of it is God *walking with us* through our fears, anger and even death. Doug would remind us of Jesus' compassion for humanity, by pointing out the shortest sentence in the Bible: "Jesus wept." Jesus suffered on our behalf *because* of his extraordinary love. His Father, also our Father, is Love itself and never far from our agonies. Doug taught that dark places are part of the journey; in the dark, the journey feeds us in unexpected ways. I don't know that it was that particular night, but I recall Doug saying "the God who acts in our darkness shows us the fierce face of love". Frequently he quoted Buechner: *The place where God calls you to is the place where your deep gladness meets the world's deep hunger."*

Doug's eclectic references included saints and sinners from Abraham and Moses to Peter and Paul, the prodigal son, Dr. Zeuss's *"Oh, the Places You'll Go"*, *"La Dolce Vita,"* *"Fried Green Tomatoes"*, the candlestick scene from *Les Miserables* (already a personal favorite), Robin Williams' *carpe deim* message in "The Dead Poets' Society" (also a personal favorite, I showed the film each year to my students as ground for the year's art-making), *An Interrupted Life* by Etty Hilleson, *The Hound of Heaven* by Frances Thompson, a poem by Robert Frost, St. John's *Dark Night of the Soul*, Kushner's *When Bad Things Happen to Good People*, Tolstoy's *Brothers Karamazov*, Carl Jung's statement, *"Called or not called, God is here"*, Henri Nouwen's *"YOU are the glory of God!."* Doug also gave us a wide spectrum of human stories to show us that God is everywhere, that church is not about going somewhere to sit and listen but that "faith is meant to be lived on pavement," and inseparable from our journey.

I learned new concepts along with new theology at Calvary. Words like *metanoia, redemption, ritual, mercy, mystery, woundedness, trinity, theology, liturgy, sinner, saint, sacrament*—words which sounded complicated, but which I learned were not the untouchables my background had led me to believe. Redemption, for example, is about transformation—something I'd just lived. Mystery is not a frightening lack of knowing, but a means to explain the inexplicable for humans who haven't God's omniscience [I would soon discover even more about mystery and mysticism through the writings of Evelyn Underhill and many early desert fathers and mothers].

Woundedness, another new concept I valued, was something I'd experienced, too. Now I viewed it *not* as something to overcome but as something to examine for its spiritual significance. When Doug told us about the apple trees in North Carolina (his home state) being wounded on purpose to grow better fruit, I understood. When Doug said one evening that "Faith is most formed in weakness, need, and inadequacy" I understood that, too. When he said "Many times we see more through tears than through dry eyes" I knew he spoke the truth because I'd *lived* that in the past few years.

My life had *experienced* his words. I saw that wrestling with questions without answers is okay and very human. Certitude and control often miss a struggle's blessing. As Doug would say, "We are all amateurs, all beginners, there are *no Christian professionals*, no *life* professionals." The journey does not exist to make us Christians or Episcopalians. Evangelism to Doug was, as he put it, "One beggar telling another beggar where food can be found."

Having come from a place where ritual and sacraments did not exist, I was now surrounded by them at Calvary. At first this was a bit of a leap for me. But learning that "sacrament is an outward and visible sign of an inward and spiritual grace" helped me bridge this chasm. I realized that when I am making art I'm in a ritualistic act. I am making a kind of sacrament in a sense, for the outward painting conveys my inward meaning. I grew to appreciate the order of the liturgy (though I could never "bewail my most horrible sins" or whatever those words are in one liturgical version). I loved the flowers, music and beauty of the service. Some people came just to hear the magnificent choir and orchestra; at Christmas time it was practically impossible to find a seat for Calvary's performance of Handel's "Messiah." Calvary was always an artistic and spiritually moving experience.

What I was learning in—and out—of Calvary at this time influenced my concept of prayer. When Teresa of Avila was mentioned in one Journey session, I was eager to read all I could about her and got every book on her in the wonderful church library, Memphis' main library, and in a nearby women's bookstore. Moving quickly over parts too Catholic, I stayed with her spiritual core. I loved her tenacity, her honesty, her feistiness, her courage, her life story, and her understanding of prayer's power. I related to Teresa's comment that "Mental prayer is, as I see it, simply a friendly intercourse and frequent solitary conversation with Him who, as we know, loves us." (Teresa of Avila, *The Life of Saint Teresa of Avila By Herself*, p. 63). Conversation with God! That's what I'd been doing all my life! Here was someone from the sixteenth century who understood and experienced prayer as I did!

Julian of Norwich, a thirteenth century anchoress, also dropped into my life because Doug mentioned her in the *Journey* course. She and Catherine of Siena, Hildegarde of Bingen, and so many women I came to "know," dynamically lived their relationships to God daily in ways similar to my own experience. They had healings, overcame difficulties, devoted themselves to God and helping others, but not one of them had ever read the Christian Science textbook! The deeper I read and the more life I lived, the more the Christian Science Church seemed narrow; I grew away from it.

Doug would say "The Church should not lie to people; we must tell as best we can the naked, liberating truth." I did not feel the Christian Science Church always told the naked truth.

I was privy to facts and details concerning wrongs and divisions growing in the Christian Science Church from the mid-seventies until I left the church in 1992. I witnessed or knew things taking place at the highest levels that were not, at least from my perspective and that of others I respected, in accord with its teachings. Fear, arrogant power, love of money, and pride seemed to try to dominate over the simple directive its founder had given when she wrote in her textbook: "The vital part, the heart and soul of Christian Science, is Love" (Eddy, *Science and Health*, p. 113:5-6). I'd been part of the remnant carrying on pure Science in spite of dismaying Church changes and praying daily for truth to be revealed. Sometimes it nearly wore me out. To learn of one injustice after another was overwhelming. This church stuff required deep prayer, along with whatever else needed prayerful healing in oneself, family, branch church, community and world—on top of church meetings, church duties, church committee work, and more. Eventually, life experience caused me to seek less church and a more *universal* view. If asked why I left Christian Science, though the reasons are complex and varied, my simplest answer to that complicated question would be Church hierarchy's hypocrisy.

As I devoured books by a variety of theologians and scholars and began to attend Calvary regularly, I noticed the differences between what Christian Science taught and what traditional mainstream Christians believe. I struggled many a late night with concepts from both Christian Science and traditional Christianity! I came to see the human and divine differently than I had previously. I realized that certitude and the righteous-judgment of "victorious Christians" is *not* Christianity. I appreciated that Episcopal history, service, and liturgy stem from the earliest Christians. Calvary not only met my need for knowledge, but filled up the empty holes left inside me after what I'd been through in the last few years. At Calvary I found outstretched arms literally and figuratively and received the unconditional love from strangers I'd hoped for but not found in some of my Christian Science family and friends. Calvary Church manifested the *mercy* Doug's homilies illustrated— one of the primary principles of Christianity.

With Calvary, Bill, classes, my children, and art filling my life, 1991-1994 was a productive and mostly positive period. I entered artwork in the largest competitive exhibition in Memphis, and *four* of my pieces took prizes, including "Best of Show" for a piece I titled "Individuation," a Jungian term that had come to mean much to me. My large abstract oil, "Gestation for a New Life," took second prize in the oil category and another abstract, "Little Blue," took second in mixed media. I got the Grumbacher Gold Medal for "Trapped," a piece I'd done just before my divorce, purchased by the trauma surgeon. All these pieces were born out of recent life experience. Intensely honest, these prize-winning pieces confirmed my new direction.

One day in early 1991, while I was recording grades in the library, Bill walked over to my table and plopped a newspaper on top of my grade book, tapping an airline advertisement for low airfares to Boston. Bill felt it was time we made a visit to my parents so they could meet him. I was not sure my parents were ready, but something told me to honor his suggestion.

When I phoned my parents later that day, they seemed willing to have us visit, though not eager.

"What does he look like?" my mother asked coldly. When I answered that he had a beard and slightly long hair, my mother snipped, "What's the matter? Can't he afford a haircut?!" adding, "I'm not going to any special trouble, you know—no fancy dinners!" I assured her that was not what we were coming for and that no meals were expected.

We arrived at my parents' Boston apartment about 6 PM, April 12, 1991. I had told Bill that if they were argumentative we would leave and stay in a hotel. I wasn't sure how this would go. Dad opened the door and gave his usual lecture-circuit smile. I gave him a hug and introduced Bill. Mom was in the kitchen. To my amazement, the dining room table was set with good china, silver, and flowers. What happened to "no fancy dinners!"?! Mother had prepared a Southern meal, complete with ham in red-eye gravy, biscuits and grits! I had *never* known her to make grits before in my life, nor anything Southern—and I'd never known my Southern Bill to eat them before!

She and Bill found a common interest in history—conversations about the Depression era and World War II. Though a bit awkward at first, the weekend went better than expected. On Sunday we attended the Mother Church with my parents, and then my frugal Mom suggested we go to The Budapest, an expensive Boston restaurant, one of my favorites. Mom had never suggested going out to eat before; usually that was Dad's delight. Before we left for the airport, my mother gave me the first embrace I'd had from her in several years.

The weekend had been quite a surprise. Three weeks later I would receive another. On May 6, 1991, at age 74, my mother died.

How providential that Bill suggested our Boston trip when he did! Had we not gone, I'd never have seen my mother alive again, never have had that final hug, nor would she and Bill have met.

In her last days, Dad, who seldom cooked, fixed Mom's meals and took them to her in bed. Since Christmas, she'd had a bandage that needed changing on her leg, but the real cause of her death I'll never know—all the death certificate said was that her heart stopped.

Dad had called my brother Rich to tell him of Mom's passing, and Rich called me at 7:30 AM. I got on the first plane for Boston. There was no funeral. Mother was cremated and Dad asked that the funeral home dispose of her ashes. He and my brother picked out the coffin, several models up in price from the plain pine box that most were cremated in. "We don't want people to think Christian Scientists don't care," Dad said when I questioned why not a pine box since it was going straight to fire. Back in his office, Dad had my brother and I read some passages he selected from the Bible and *Science and Health*. Rich and I spent the rest of our visit packing and sorting Mom's things, making order in the apartment so Dad could function efficiently without his partner of 51 years. Dad wrote a letter to mail to relatives:

To Our Beloved Relatives,

Your phone calls and notes of loving support at this time embraces all of us, and assures me that no power of separation can withstand the power of divine love.

Lynn and Rich and I appreciated the thoughts of you who joined us in spirit in our special service of prayer for our beloved Ruth.

The following pages of tribute hopefully provide a means of sharing our love with each other. I pray these few examples, representing the many received, bear witness to the fact that the good expressed in one's life is everlastingly effective from heart to heart.

On behalf of our immediate family, and all of you, I thank God for his lovingkindness and everpresence.

Gratefully yours,

Glenn

Aside from several grammatical and punctuation errors and the misspelling of my name (but so it always was), the letter was a Christian Science statement that reached Presbyterian and Catholic relatives on Mom's side of the family with a coldness that several remarked about to me later. Aunt Marylou, Mom's younger sister, told me that she had wanted to be included in a funeral for her sister. It was hard for those who were not Christian Scientists to understand Dad's point of view. A booklet was enclosed with Dad's letter: written tributes from Dad's students and other Christian Scientists, with photos of Mom—created by one of Dad's students—a kind gesture but only one-way communication and more of a production piece than the sensitive exchange non-Science family members sought who wanted to say what *they* felt about the sister, aunt, or grandmother they'd lost. Recently in cleaning out files, I came across my copy of this booklet and re-read it. The tributes show how much she meant to Dad's students and other Christian Scientists, as these few examples reveal: "Ruth is the very essence of love!"; "...one so tender and true, whose expression of motherhood and genuine unselfishness continues to be an inspiration to me."; "Her gracious and loving manner was so precious. She was just that kind of person that opened her heart to you;" "Ruth is such a powerful example of true womanhood and motherhood." "Ruth's sense of family was so strong..."

I wrote a poem about my mother, which I entitled, *My Mother Died Today*—six stanzas that later became ten. It ends in part:

Her memory bakes and cleans in silence still
Her touch, as modest as in life, unfelt,
Her service, unforgotten,
Her struggle, finally at rest....

While in Boston helping Dad and Rich, I wrote in my journal:

There is no room for me in my family. That I am to blame for my mother's death hangs over Dad's apartment like a blanket. I caused her disappointment, her depression, which led to her death—this is the rumor among relatives, the whispers among some of Dad's friends and students. My father is noticeably uneasy with me. He could not call me to tell me of Mom's death himself but left that deed to my brother. I am not trusted nor relied on nor shared with anymore. Rich is essential but I am forced out—perhaps by God for my journey? My first mistake was to be a daughter and not a son. Divorced, I will always be "outsider" to Dad. I have not done the big things he and Rich share as businessmen; I only draw pictures…I have sorted, thrown out, organized Mom's clothes; cleaned refrigerator and freezer, labeled foods; ordered the living room; made trip after trip to the incinerator with trash; been to the funeral home to help with arrangements; cleaned the kitchen and prepared meals for the three of us; selected jewelry of Mom's to give to relatives or special friends as Dad requested; filled dozens of garbage bags with clothes for the Good Will. I am here only for "women's work," wallpaper to my father and brother's conversations.

Dad denied having contact with John once we separated but I learned through the children and others this was not true. In fact, I was their frequent topic of discussion. Yesterday I told Dad I phoned John to notify him of Mom's death. Today while Dad was out, John called returning Dad's call to him. When Dad came back I gave him the message but he denied ever calling John! Truth seems more talked than lived here.

The next morning about 6:30 I wake before Rich and enter the dining room to see an envelope at my place and one at my brother's. Inside mine is a note in Dad's handwriting thanking me for the work and cleanup I've done with an enclosed check. I am being paid, apparently, for coming to help Dad following my mother's death. Dad, of course, has already eaten and is in his office doing his morning prayer and study. I knock on his office door to tell him he needn't do this, that if family means anything it means coming when your mother dies to be with your father—without pay! He insists I keep the check (money has often been his way of showing gratitude). He begins to randomly speak of the wife he just lost, then suddenly begins to cry. I have never seen Dad cry before. I cross the room, put my arms around him, hold him, and tell him it is okay to cry. But with my words, I feel his back stiffen as he moves away from me, immediately gain composure, once more in control, firmly saying, "We will get the *victory* over this!" He walks me to the door and I leave as he wishes and return to the dining room to my cold cereal.

I decide to write Dad a letter. Writing has always been something I do when I cannot speak or when no one wants to hear me. When I finish, I copy the letter into my journal and slip the original under Dad's door. This is a portion:

May 9, 1991

Dear Dad,

We are sculptors. Our human life is our clay. Human isn't a bad word. Don't be afraid to be human. Jesus was human. That's good company! To me, Christ Jesus, the transition between the divine and human (incarnation) is the most significant point of Christianity —the divine meeting the human need. But only God is the Original. We are imperfect, changing, because we are learning. We are not God. It is o.k. to express our feelings, not a sign of weakness or failure. In fact, it is honest.

Someone recently talked to me about "Abba-love" which translates "father-love", more accurately: "Daddy-love". The connotation is of a small child sitting on a father's knee enveloped in his arms, or, at a mother's breast—a very intimate, warm, close inseparable parental love—this is abba love. This is God's love for you! Especially now. And for me, for everyone. This is the love that has guided you always and that is still guiding you. Even in the abyss God is there holding you. I heard someone say recently "God is not found at a safe distance from grief and hurt but smack through the middle of it." Smack through the middle God is holding our hands.

I relate to your current challenge, for divorce is like death. Both force one to seek God's direction more than ever. I am continually amazed by His signs, provision, guidance... God is abundantly in us—in every man, woman, child, in every race, creed, background. You have dedicated your life to God. So have I, though differently.

Jesus went specifically to the fallen. He chose them. They were teachable, ready to listen for they had nothing to lose. They could take the risk of Christianity...

God does not love us or reward us because we are perfect, nor love us more when we are successful, good, or strong. He loves us right through our mistakes, with all our "warts". We are perfect in His eyes only because He is our Father/Mother...this is what God's mercy is about. God forgives, looks through our human frailties to our hearts, to his precious children and says to us: "I love you no matter what." Mercy was Jesus' life work for humanity. His work wouldn't have been necessary if we were already perfect. Conquering, victory, victorious, fight, battle, defend—we hear these war words a lot in Christian Science. Perhaps we need less war and more grace...

My father never mentioned this letter.

A few days later I drove with two friends, Ann and Eleanor, to a conference in North Carolina. Ann, an architect, a Christian Scientist, she and I had raised our children together back in Christian Science Society days; her husband, Harry, also an architect was architect for our Fisherville home and he I had been First and Second Readers together in the Germantown Society. Eleanor, a Quaker and college English professor, had taught my boys English during their homeschooling year. She and Ann had been Memphis friends since childhood. Years before, Ann and Eleanor had come with me to Cape Cod and Nantucket one summer when my boys were young. While my parents were away lecturing, we young women, my little boys, and Sandra as babysitter, had their Cape Cod home to ourselves for a week. The seven of us rode bikes, ate lobster, enjoyed the beach, canoed, and after the kids were in bed we sat around talking late into the night. Albeit infrequently, Ann, Eleanor and I were grounded in sharing ideas.

I no longer recall how we decided to take off on this trip to Epworth-by-the-Sea for a conference called *Journey into Wholeness*. Perhaps it was because we had read books by a number of the conference speakers and spirituality mattered to all three of us and the word journey drew me. We rarely got together because our work and personal lives went in three different directions; this conference in May of 1991 offered us time together as well as time alone. Each of us was questioning her career, life direction, and marriage (two of us were divorced then; now all three are). Attended largely by psychologists, Jungian analysts, and philosophers, the *Journey into Wholeness* conference gave us time to sort out our changes.

While there, I wrote in my journal: *This conference cannot take me into wholeness. Nothing can but me. I am discovering how very strong I am. Not my divorce, my mother's death, my leaving Christian Science, the loss of friends or home—none of it can separate me from my Rock, God. Whatever comes, I can deal with it through God. The chapel chimes are playing. I think of the Christian Science Church. The Episcopal. The*

American Baptist. My Buddhist readings. My Quaker childhood school. I think of all the ways men and women have to come to God. And I realize He is right here beside us in the midst of these differing ways…

In early summer of 1991 Bill hiked the Colorado Trail and met up with my kids and me in Keystone, Colorado, where I'd rented a friend's condo for a short vacation to paint and enjoy my children. We all hiked together and this gave my children a chance to know this man who was becoming more than my best friend.

Bill and I were slow to commit. However, by the end of summer, a year after our first road trip, Bill and I decided to marry.

Since I'd had an "over-the-top" wedding first time, I was happy to let this ceremony be in Bill's mother's Presbyterian church to honor her. On teachers' pay, we were not planning anything fancy. Bill arranged our honeymoon: three days in South Carolina to visit Fort Sumter staying at a nearby B&B. But we did go all out on a unique wedding invitation we made ourselves. Believing too much is made of wedding ceremonies and not enough thought is given to the marriage itself, we created an invitation lightly spoofing the ceremony. We had so much fun creating it! Anyone who knew Bill or me would understand, and everyone invited would be in that category.

We called it the Caldwell-Evans Wedding Kit and sent it in a plain brown envelope. Inside were many pieces to entice the recipient to laugh—as we had continually throughout its creation! In a tiny zip-locked plastic bag were crumbs of chocolate cake (home-baked) suggesting it be taste-tested by the recipient, results to be reported to the Caldwell-Evans Wedding Committee as to its fitness to be the wedding cake recipe. I'd drawn the main wedding players in their underwear (including the minister) as paper dolls with wedding clothes to cut out, so that if some folks could not make the wedding they could at least "play wedding at home." There were samples of three suggested invitations from ultra-flowery prose to our favorite: "Bill and Lyn get hitched , October 19, 1991, 11 AM, Be there." There was a chain letter of alliterative names of famous people (…Harry Krishna, Hardly Kosher, Leona Helmsley, Buddy Holly, Holly Golightly, Peter Pan, Peter Principle, Princess Leia, Pasta E. Pepperoni, Patty Hearst, Donald Trump, Donald Duck, Ronald Reagan….) protesting our invitation to which the recipient could add his name. There was an order form for a black velvet portrait of the bride and groom with Elvis and for an interpretive dance video of the wedding. Included was a warm fuzzy 2-inch square of baby blanket for those afraid of weddings.

Every Sunday we went to mid-day dinner at BC's parents' home. His grandmother was always there. Known as Miss Francis or Fanny and Tat to family, Bill's 95-year old deeply Southern grandmother, asked us for weeks, if we had invited her dearest friend to our wedding. We hadn't. But every Sunday dinner, Tat would ask, "Bill, you *have* invited my best friend Charlotte to the wedding, haven't you?" Bill would say something like, "Grandmother, you know we are trying to keep it small" and then change the subject. Finally BC got a call from his grandmother: "Bill, you WILL be inviting Charlotte, won't you?" It really wasn't a question as much as an edict. Finally, he gave in, "Yes, grandmother, we will send an invitation to Charlotte." Within minutes of the invitation kits hitting the mail boxes, Bill got another call from his grandmother: "Bill, You DIDN'T send one of those invitations to my friend, Charlotte did you?!! WHAT IN THE WORLD WERE YOU THINKING?!" "But, grandmother," Bill replied, "you insisted!" The family still laughs over this.

On October 19, 1991, fifteen months after our relationship began, we stood before Bill's sister, Lib (a woman who lives up to her name), an ordained Presbyterian minister, and said our marriage vows in his mother's church, following a buffet breakfast which I prepared all by myself for our guests. Bill's siblings, my children and brother were in the wedding party. My father came and read a Psalm, though it was obviously difficult for him. No other relatives of mine and few of my friends attended. Colleagues from school and all of Bill's family were there. I wanted (searched for and found) a black blues singer to belt out "Amazing Grace"—and she did, the most soulful rendition I have ever heard. This 1700s hymn had taken on special meaning for me after I read all the verses and learned of the circumstances under which it had been written, the *divine change* in the human heart that leads one home, which it represented. It seemed pertinent to my life: *Amazing grace (how sweet the sound) That saved a wretch like me! I once was lost, but now am found, Was blind, but now I see. 'Twas grace that taught my heart to fear, and grace my fears relieved. How precious did that grace appear The hour I first believed. Through many dangers, toils and snare, I have already come; 'Tis grace hath brought me safe thus far, And grace will lead me home*".

The school music director, a friend of ours, created an original piece of music to accompany my walking down the aisle. I walked alone. No one was "giving me away" like some object. Barely a size 4 then, I purchased a simple antique turn-of-the-century high collared fragile cotton lace dress that came just to my ankles and I made a wreath, adding fresh flowers, to wear around my curly shoulder length hair.

The most important thing I made that day (and a few days beforehand) was the breakfast we served to everyone *before* the wedding. The church had notified us after our invitations had gone out that they had mistakenly scheduled two weddings and receptions that would interfere with each other—and the other party had priority, being a member of the church—did we want to cancel they asked? It was too late for that! I decided we would do things a bit differently than the conventional way. Instead of having our reception as planned for the church basement following our wedding, we would have a breakfast *before* the wedding, enabling our wedding to be over with before noon, freeing the entire rest of the day for the other wedding and reception.

I decided to do the reception myself to save money. I rolled out croissants in my condo's small kitchen for days, cut fruit, baked quiches, cooked sausages and more. And twenty minutes before everyone was to arrive, there I was on my wedding day in my jeans—but with the wreath already in my hair—setting out the buffet with two high school students of mine I'd hired to help. I had ordered a superb 3-tiered chocolate cake, which I decorated with flowers, scattering petals on the cake table. After an hour of breakfast and socializing in our wedding garb (Bill and I are not superstitious), BC's younger brother, Andy, rallied everyone upstairs to find a seat in the sanctuary. The ceremony went rather like most weddings—other than the spectacular Bluesy solo. After the ceremony, family came to our now shared condo for lunch I'd prepared ahead.

Our early years of marriage were full of hikes and road trips—the first summer we visited dozens of states to see everyone either of us knew—about 50 stops across the nation. We slept in sleeping bags under the stars (we never use a tent), stayed with friends, or in B&Bs. It was great! On the road I read aloud Pete Seeger's autobiography or we listened to Dylan, Clapton, the Beatles, Robert Johnson, or Guthries, Woody and Arlo. We especially loved the Southwest and even drove to New Mexico from Memphis twice in one summer (we drove back to Memphis mid-summer so I could be with Jason for his eye operation which was successful; and then BC and I drove back to the land of enchantment we so loved).

Both bookaholics, reading was our shared passion. Lucky for us, the huge main library was in walking distance of our condo.

A year prior, I'd begun a study of the history of Mary Baker Eddy and Christian Science in Memphis' main library. Mrs. Eddy is a complex character, sometimes to be admired but sometimes remarkably strange. Her textbook, *Science and Health*, also contains what appear to some to be tautologies, discrepancies in logic, and even a few plagiarisms—along with inspired wisdom. The religion departs from traditional Christianity, though its healing principle comes awfully close to the teachings and practice of Christ Jesus. I researched Quimby and other peculiar issues connected with Christian Science—a complicated labyrinth, for a good bit of Mrs. Eddy's history is difficult. There are episodes of bizarre behavior, selfishness, pursuit of wealth, egotism, and love of fame, none of which I could understand in a religious figure and I began to suspect that my father's "dearly beloved leader" was not mine.

More recently, however, I have read Stephen Gottschalk's *Rolling Away The Stone: Mary Baker Eddy's Challenge to Materialism* and found it a well-researched and insightful explanation of Christian Science and its founder. That and Robert Peel's trilogy on Mrs. Eddy, which I read years ago, present a balanced, accurate and thorough depiction of this phenomenal woman and her unique religion. For the average person, neither the founder nor the religion is easy to comprehend. Language often dis-serves spiritual matters, but these two authors have managed to tangle with this problem admirably where others have failed. So many books on Christian Science and Mrs. Eddy have an axe to grind, a mean angle, a bitter personal story, a misinterpretation of major points, a lack of understanding that stems from not having whole-heartedly *practiced* the religion's principles. I believe Christian Science can never be understood to the slightest degree unless it is whole-heartedly *practiced*.

Another enigma was the superstitious attitude regarding Animal Magnetism that many Christian Scientists held. This puzzled me. Animal Magnetism—like a viscous troll under a train track—was lying in wait to derail any good Scientist from his or her path—unless he or she were quick enough to dispel A.M. through consistent prayerful study. Some Scientists seemed nearly obsessed by the concept. I recall a Prin housemother requiring each of us girls in her dorm to study the lesson one-on-one with her once each quarter, at which time animal magnetism's threat seemed her main point. Though Christian Scientists do not believe in a personal devil, A.M. always seemed to me to fill that role. If one were not alert, one might come under attack of "malicious A.M." The preventative was consistent specific prayer and devotion to the Cause. Though as a practicing Scientist I "handled" A.M. as we were taught, deep down it never actually made sense to me. With a good God being *all* the power, where did this other power come from? If it were mere illusion or mental suggestion as was explained, then why did it have potential power? This foe Scientists fought seemed unworthy of focus if one accepted the omnipotence of God.

Denial would be the third conundrum. Christian Science denied everything unlike God. If I were afraid, I had to immediately refute my fear. If I were in pain, I had to immediately know it was a lie. If my feelings were deeply hurt by unjust treatment, I had to instantly dismiss such selfishness on my part as unacceptable. Whatever darkness came, *it did not really exist and was to be denied.* I got good at not seeing or accepting pain or hurt at an early age. Eventually, I no longer recognized it. Through denial, I became incapable of knowing what I really felt or who I really was.

In my study of many religions, theologies, philosophies and psychology in the early nineties, I began to see what I now see even more clearly: the detrimental effect denial can have on one's life, the build up of repression that can result and later erupt in dire ways. This sentence stood out to me in my reading of Alan Watts book *Myth and Ritual in Christianity*: "A truly problematic evil arises in human life when the necessary dark side of existence is not accepted and 'loved' along with the light" (Watts, Myth and Ritual, p. 83). Quite stunning at the time, this passage touched me in the way truth does. It was the start of recognizing that a lifetime of denying dark and emphasizing light had left me with serious shadows.

Certainly I had tried to sort this out from an early age—I had plagued every Sunday School teacher with this question: "If God is only good, the only reality, how can evil even *seem* to be?" Their answers ranged from useless to intriguing, but I always managed enough contentment to get past this philosophical problem and remain devoted to Christian Science—until now. Now my *own* relationship with God was getting me through; my *own* life had become my very best teacher.

Today I find myself appreciating and benefiting from many religions and philosophies, including Christian Science. When I read the Christian Science Bible Lesson, which I do regularly midst my eclectic practice, I find inspiration, but I do not read slavishly, rather I glean out the kernels that strike me as wisdom. I do the same when I read any religious, spiritual, or philosophical text. I have learned that it is my life that I must listen to, first and foremost. If I remain open and listen to that voice within, the wisdom I need at the time is there to teach me, heal me, enable me to grow spiritually. When a principle resonates, I pick it—as if a spectacular bouquet is being gathered. A variety of magnificent "flowers" inspire my life. Discernment leads the gathering.

In late1991, about the time I was carefully composing my letter of resignation from the Christian Science Church, someone identifying herself as a representative of the Christian Science Mother Church Board of Directors called to say that they wanted to print one of the articles I'd written for the *Christian Science Journal* entitled *This Is Why I Am A Christian Scientist* in a book. It had previously been printed in several languages and in another book. The woman who phoned said it was one of their "most well received articles." "I am no longer practicing Christian Science" I replied, "but the words I wrote were true when I wrote them. God remains my center, and I see no discrepancy in my *direction* only a change in my *denomination*. Please feel free to do whatever you think is best."

For Christmas 1991, seven months after Mom's passing, my brother suggested we gather the whole Evans clan in Bermuda once more so Dad could have Christmas with family. I remained the black sheep in the eyes of uncle and aunt (confirmed in words spoken to me by a third relative) and my mother's absence was quietly considered my fault (confirmed by the untypical silence and stares I received). But this time my husband, Bill, was with me as well as my children. I was too busy to worry about what a few people might think.

When we arrived, my brother caught my attention immediately. He seemed subdued, preoccupied, unwell. Rich, his wife Karen, some of their kids and mine, Bill and I went together to a Christmas Eve Anglican service on the island (Rich for the music). I noticed that my brother, whose talent is singing, did not have the strength to stand and sing, but sat silently in the pew, his head bowed. Clearly something was wrong. Christmas Eve I wrote in my journal: *"Rich, I noticed... is not himself. I told Bill, he is either at a near-death experience or is facing divorce—but of course it can't be divorce because his marriage is such a good one. Rich said he had something to talk to me about but that it would be very difficult.*

Karen asked me to go for a walk with her the next morning. I also had the promised talk with my brother. I wrote in my journal: *"Both have told me that their marriage is in jeopardy. Karen wants to leave."*

In more walks with Karen, she poured out to me her whole story. She was very much in love with someone else, a seriously ill neighbor and family man whom Rich knew as well. Rich's career took him to Asia for his work much of the time and Karen was able to spend many hours with this man. When she described him, she spoke with such love and longing, the way a girl might speak of her first boyfriend. Karen told me they had plans to "sail around the world together." She seemed to yearn for the free life he pictured. As we walked along well-landscaped paths between pleasant pink stucco cottages, Karen spoke of "wanting out of this marriage" and of her growing objections to Christian Science. She was confused and upset about what to do next and cried a lot. My heart went out to her, for I knew the lonely path she was on. Though it was my dear brother she wanted to leave, I somehow understood her.

But I understood my brother's side, too. Karen had told Rich of her relationship over the phone while he was on business in Asia, far from home. He told me he walked the streets alone until late that night in despair. He had no one to turn to, but God. He told me how much he wanted to fix his marriage, whatever it might take. He was devastated by Karen's decision to go. I yearned to help him. With compassion for both, I felt their pain deeply. I was also concerned for their four kids. Most of my vacation was spent talking separately with Karen, Rich, and their children.

That vacation was equally busy for Bill who had never met my aunt, uncles, cousins, nieces and nephews—most of whom did not really want to know him, nor get his humor. With conversations with Rich and Karen taking me away from Bill much of the time, he was left largely to his own devices, entertaining my kids, snorkeling, and reading. One night when I told him I would again be off talking privately, Bill nestled himself in bed with an Agatha Christy novel he'd found on one of the cottage's library shelves—until Rich's youngest son, Owen, about 9 at the time, came in to bounce on the bed telling his new Uncle Bill the plots of all his favorite movies.

I recall putting on wet suits and snorkeling in the ocean with Owen, Bill, and Charissa—all of us holding hands under water as we swam gently through reefs of brightly colored shimmering fish, as if life were suspended in ethereal aqua-blue breath for a blissful moment, away from the trials we faced on land.

Back in Memphis, I completed my letter of resignation to the Christian Science Church and mailed it February 4, 1992, drafts of which I found on my computer recently:

Dear Mother Church:

This is perhaps the most difficult letter I will ever write. It is a culmination of hours and days of prayer and careful thought.

Throughout my life, Christian Science has been the basis for my spirituality, defining my identity as a child of God, enabling me to experience many wonderful healings and rooting my living and activity in God. For this spiritual foundation I will always be grateful. For twenty years of teaching Sunday School, serving as Sunday School Superintendent, First Reader, chairman of the board, part-time practitioner, one of several to establish a new branch church, etc. I will always be grateful. Each job was a valuable learning experience. For every hardship or dissension in branch church or the Christian Science movement, I have learned patience and to go directly to God. For every slow or difficult healing with one of my children, with friend or stranger, or self, I have learned to rely on God alone. Listening to God has become my way of functioning. Obeying Him has directed my every move from one city to another, one career to another, one home to another. And from marriage to divorce.

Divorce was unheard of in my family. My devoted Christian Science parents were shocked. They could not accept divorce nor the imperfect image they saw it putting before the community…In my darkness I found God alone to be the solid ground of my being …I realized that in the very dark itself God was there, that I had nothing to fear, no opinions or judgments to consider but God's. I let Him direct my every step. I began to realize I am not my father's daughter, I am not my husband's wife, I am not my children's mother (which is not to say I do not deeply care for, tend to and love them!), I AM GOD'S. It was a sacred experience, this learning. Beyond denomination.

My journey with God is sacred to me, the most valuable thing I have…It has led me to appreciate His universal presence–in every one, in every church, in every place.

When my Christian Science family could only condemn, I found the Methodists, American Baptists, Presbyterians and Episcopalians ready with mercy. I discovered an amazing grace. I found that God's love is truly non-denominational. In fact, I found that mercy is an essential element of Christianity. My spiritual study has been continuous. Understanding my true Father is my most important goal; it is the basis for my life, my art, and the reason for my being.

For the past sixteen months, Calvary Episcopal Church in downtown Memphis has been my church home. The "Journey Course" and other classes and community services of this church have taught me much. The membership is composed of all walks of life, great diversity yet unity. The symbolism I find here has profound meaning, not rigidity. The ritual is the outward expression of a great inward spiritual substance stemming from approximately 2,000 years of Christianity.

In one brief letter I cannot do justice to all the growth, lessons, changes of my journey; nor is it necessary. I simply need to tell you that the universal concept of God's love and church has led me to wish to join Calvary; therefore, it seems right I inform you of this and end my membership in the Christian Science Church.

In the early eighties I wrote an inspired article for the Christian Science Journal called "This is Why I Am a Christian Scientist". Everything in that article is as true today as then—the healings, the ideas. The only difference is that in response to the last line "Why isn't everyone?", I now know the answer. Perhaps it is because God is bigger than any one denomination. Perhaps it is because there are many valid ways to know Christ. Perhaps it is because concepts of mercy, incarnation, grace, mystery (not having all the answers) and scholarship are essential parts of Christianity to some as they have become to me.

A word about my father. No finer Christian Scientist lives. His example has been enormously important to my life. I know of no one more devoted to the Christian Science Church than Glenn Evans. He has sacrificed everything for it. Few will know all he has given and continues to give to the Christian Science movement and mankind. He has faced adversity fearlessly time after time for healing after healing. I will be ever grateful for the privilege of growing up in proximity to such spiritual leadership, devotion, strength, honesty, integrity, moral courage and love.

I do not know where my journey will lead. I cannot say where my religious base will be in another ten years. I only know I am with God each step of the way. He alone holds my hand and He alone is my reliance.

As Doug Bailey, rector of Calvary, has rightly said to me, "we need to cherish the fabric of our religious past as well as our present", so I take with me many principles of Christian Science. Drinking, smoking, drugs and doctor-dependence are not part of my experience nor have I any faith in them. Moral integrity and daily striving to learn more about God are still my roots. If healing is of Christ, then it is universal, non-denominational, open to everyone.

I would hope that not a single precious Christian Science friend or family member need be lost to me because of this move I make. Yet, I am aware of the righteousness often bound in the Christian Scientist, aware that talk may unfairly flow and criticize, and I realize that friendship and family ties may be severed by my action. But one of the lessons of the past four years of my journey has been that risk-taking, when God-impelled, is necessary. A certain courage is required of Christians. I have faced loss, death, isolation, condemnation, and survived what I call the abyss with my hand still tightly in God's. I know I can do it again—and again and again – if need be. I only wish to follow my highest sense of spiritual right.

Thank you, Christian Science Church for your essential part in molding my beliefs. May we all, as true Christians, love each other always.

Most Sincerely,

Gwendolyn Evans Caldwell

The following day, February 5, 1992, I became baptized in the Episcopal Church, which I followed with weeks of confirmation classes to join the Episcopal Church. I wrote of this event in my journal:

This is the most risk-taking thing I have ever done. My father, relatives, and friends of my past will likely be lost to me. No one here can understand that. Not even Bill. They cannot comprehend what I have left and how extreme my action will seem to all those Scientists I have known since my birth, in college, in churches where I have worked. My past is bound up in Science. I have no jubilation for what I have done; it is too serious for that. It simply was the next right step on my path. I love what I am seeing in this church I have become part of tonight; it fits me, my art, my values, and my desire to be in a community rooted in history and meaning...I know it is where God wants me now. But I have left something that was once just as meaningful and full of healing. I cannot forget my C.S. life. It will always be part of me. Doug has said as much.

My new path led me to Julian of Norwich and Teresa of Avila, who in turn, led me to women's studies where I would learn what I was already discovering on my own, well stated by Alice Koller in her book, *An Unknown Woman*: "*you can't be a woman until you're first **a person*** (my bold), and that *my life will have to be all mine, not anyone else's . . . no one else can take its measure*" (Koller, *An Unknown Woman*, P. 255).

fifteen

A Room of Her Own

Dark turns to light as she climbs the stairs to the cupola and opens wide windows to let in the rising sun. Sitting in the faded yellow chair, a stack of books at her feet, pen and journal in her lap, she faces the mountain view, breathing in the cool morning air. She watches a bird fly to a tall pine, fold her feathers beneath her breast, and settle into a newly made nest. She flies off again and again, but always returns to her safe roost. The woman observes her own reflection in the glass, then, looks outward to the glowing horizon, as she picks up her pen.

Arriving back in Memphis after my reconciliation with Dad and two-week stay in New Harmony's Poet's House, I have few days left before the 1993-94 school year starts. I help Charissa get ready for her first year of high school, finish unpacking boxes from our recent move to our Davidson Cove house, welcome home my son, Nathan, from Alaska and Bill from his 75-mile Appalachian Trail hike, and keep my appointment I'd arranged with the surgeon prior to my trip, whose words "Nothing's certain" traveled with me to New Harmony. The surgeon, tells me upon examining another set of mammograms: "It appears you have nothing to worry about, but we'll take another look in December. The unchanged shadow just appears to be part of you."

Shadow will always be part of me.

Shadow is part of woman's universal story. I discover this in 1991-92 when I dive into women's studies, reading more than 100 books in a year on the subject, each, to my surprise, telling pieces of my *own* story. Every woman's voice is also *my* voice! What a discovery! A whole *family* of women traveling my journey with me!

"Listen to this!" I say to Bill as we lie in bed reading books, then I tell him some fascinating tidbit I'd just read (as he, too, shares bits from his reading—often history, but sometimes an inane Dave Barry column or some obscure fact about the Beatles). I might read him Anne Sexton's poem *Rowing Toward God* or the powerful short story, *The Yellow Wallpaper* by Charlotte Perkins Gilman, or details of Mary Shelley's tragic life or Alice Walker's *In Search of Our Mother's Flower Gardens,* or Leslie Marmon Silko's *Lullaby,* or chunks of Jane Addams' *Twenty Years at Hull House* or paragraphs about Anne Hutchinson's unjust ordeal with Winthrop in colonial America, or about 19th century Dorothy Wordsworth's self-effacement in deference to her brother's fame—she, equally the poet, but relegated to merely picking up his apple cores.

Sharing discoveries is foundational to our marriage. So is creativity: Bill with his humor, and I with art. We both are writers, too. Wonder, learning, and intellect typify our togetherness as well as a love that, in the beginning, seemed to surprise us both. A consummate teacher, fellow bibliophile and questioner, Bill craves learning as much as I. How many wives, lying awake pondering a theological question or ambiguous reference, can roll over in bed and ask their husbands why things are as they are—and get a precise answer—or, at least, a tangent of related facts, or, humor to cause jousting laughter? Sometimes I'd ask him questions to place what I was reading in a larger historical context and off we'd go from one subject to another. When he was reading *The Man Who Saw Infinity* Bill fed me fascinating mathematical morsels until I wondered how I could have disliked math in high school and omitted it from my college study. Sometimes he liked what he learned from my reading enough to include it in his history teaching, such as assigning his students Jane Addams' *Twenty Years at Hull House.*

Two favorite women's books of mine, however, never made it into his history classroom: Virginia Woolf's seminal feminist marvel, *A Room of One's*

Own, and Mary Collson's lesser known story in Cynthia Tucker's *A Woman's Ministry*.

Perhaps the single most personally significant women's studies book I encounter in 1991-92 is *A Woman's Ministry* by Cynthia Grant Tucker, about Mary Collson, a 19th century Hull House worker with Jane Addams, who for thirty years was also a Christian Science practitioner.

Most conveniently (and providentially) there is a scholarly women's bookstore within walking distance of Bill's and my condo—not far from an old-fashioned drugstore known for its delicious ice cream sodas where we stop for lunch after each bookstore excursion.

One Saturday morning—about the time I am writing my letter of resignation to the Mother Church—this book about Mary Collson, with the words "Christian Science Practitioner" on the cover, nearly jump off the shelf and into my hands. I sit on the bookstore floor reading as if there is only this book and me in the universe. Bill, the only male in this woman's bookstore—but who never met a bookstore he didn't like—patiently sits in a rocker skimming several historical books he finds. After an hour of entranced reading, I buy Tucker's book, finish it that weekend at home, highlighting in tears. What Mary Collson learns and leaves touches my own story.

A reformer and feminist of the nineteenth and early twentieth century whose goal is the betterment of society, Collson is a successful Christian Science practitioner with a bevy of patients. For thirty years she practices, with numerous healings to her credit, including healings during the deadly influenza pandemic following World War I when 20 to 40 million lives worldwide are lost—but from this disease every one of her patients recovers and she remains untouched.

Collson experiences disappointment with Christian Science, too. She discovers it is not the reform she had hoped it to be and eventually believes it is unscientific. While visiting slums and settlement houses in London she studies Kant at Oxford. His concept that "the only good in the world is the will to follow moral law...regardless of profit or loss for oneself" (Tucker, *A Woman's Ministry*, p. 122) leads her to re-evaluate Christian Science in this light. She concludes that Christian Science is "a philosophy of getting" where the motive is "always the desire for gain, whether the object be perfecting health, worldly prosperity, or some other commodity of the good life." (Tucker, p.122) And *this,* she decides is perhaps behind the joyfulness, assumed to be spiritual, displayed by many Scientists. Though I know first-hand the real joy a genuine healing brings following great suffering and despair, I find myself in agreement with some of her findings; her analysis fits simplistic Pollyanna Scientists I have occasionally encountered.

Along with Alice Hamilton, her former Hull House colleague, who teaches at Harvard Medical School, Collson tries to ease post-war hatred of Germans by speaking publicly and privately. She helps Russian famine victims, even becomes a shareholder of the *Communist Daily Worker,* but is disappointed in the liberals' lack of interest in religion's healing power as a viable answer for humanity's plight. She protests mass arrests of Communists, raises funds for Quaker feeding centers, works for women's suffrage, helps disease victims, and follows Jane Addams' pacifism lead and Charlotte Perkins Gilman's admonition that women keep their solidarity in the anti-war cause and "march by the thousands." In 1914 Collson marches with 1,500 women in black mourning dress, down Manhattan's Forty-Second Street (Tucker, p. 141, 143).

Disillusioned by Christian Science and those who practice it—a disillusionment I understand—Collson experiences enormous dread one day as she leaves for her Christian Science practice office. Unable to breathe, she gets off the subway and takes the bus, but cannot move when she gets to her stop. Collson writes of this experience:

> *Since I seemed unable to make the effort to get off the bus at this point, I decided that if I rode around the loop, perhaps I could make it on my return. The result was that I spent hours repeating this trip, for every time I caught sight of my office building I felt glued to my seat. I said the Lord's Prayer and 'the scientific statement of being' over and over. I repeated the 'definition of God' and everything else that I could think of as statements of Truth with power to exorcise animal magnetism. I declared that this experience was unreal, that it was a dream, and I repeated these declarations until, as in a dream, the bus began to appear to be floating along, rather than rolling over the pavement. It was almost like a phantom bus, and with the Ancient Mariner I could easily have said that Death and Life-in-Death were casting dice for my soul*

(Tucker, p. 127).

Tucker explains Collson's bizarre episode:

> *Then in recoil from the horror of this travesty, Collson grasped the railing on the bus. It was real, and as she held it she proclaimed that the whole material world in which she lived was a real world. "In detail I declared the buildings were real—made of real brick and real stones—and the people about me were real human beings, right-minded, sensible people going about reasonable tasks in a sane and normal manner." She pulled the buzzer, got off the bus, and took the subway back home. Exhausted, she threw herself on her bed and slept...* (Tucker, p. 127-128).

Reading this passage I cried, for I, too, had discovered *real* railings! I knew the weight of her decision to leave what she'd been devoted to for thirty years. I understood the upheaval and bereft state such a decision leads to. The aloneness. Collson took charge of herself the next day as Tucker describes:

> *Awakening to the aftermath of the previous day's grotesque episode, Collson set to work readjusting her thinking...accepted responsibility for her near nervous breakdown, acknowledged that she had allowed herself to be controlled by the very sort of dogmatism she had deplored... She had sought an escape from her problems by accepting as absolute the authority of Mary Baker Eddy—'a human being no different than myself,' she realized—and in so doing, she had let herself be reduced to a state of humiliating submission to a man [Farlow, her CS teacher, who falsely accused her of being in love with him] for whom she had no respect. She also decided that her hysteria had been induced less by her relation to Farlow than by her gradual acceptance of the doctrine of animal magnetism. The preoccupation with M.A.M. had alienated her from the rational world of empirical experience, with the result, not uncommon among Eddyites, that she addressed her problems through 'unreasoning superstition instead of with practical understanding of natural causation.' On the Fifth Avenue bus, some instinct toward survival had changed the direction of her thinking, and that, she believed, 'had saved the day.' Without further postponement, she sat down and wrote to The Mother Church asking to have her name dropped from the membership roll... February 12, 1914* (Tucker, p. 127-128).

One of Collson's Christian Science friends, a newspaper editor who had joined the Eddy-ranks through knowing Collson, and left it shortly after she did, told her upon leaving the church that he had come to view Christian Science as "one of the worst of human systems" (Tucker, p. 155), finding it an enormous strain for "'a fluid imaginative person'" (Tucker, p. 155) for he found the doctrine's attempt to divide the whole of life into truth and error cruelly artificial and 'really an awful blasphemy'" (Tucker, p. 155). Collson herself eventually came to believe that the Christian Science movement was "founded on deceit" (Tucker, p. 165). Once she saw this, Collson was through with organized religion.

When she left the church to which she had given her life for three decades, Collson found herself friendless—much the way I found myself after five devoted decades. Tucker writes, "As Eddy metaphysicians, whose standing depended on the denial of all unpleasantness and the depreciation of human personality, she and her colleagues had 'never honestly' talked about their problems with each other or formed the close friendships that grow from such exchanges" (Tucker, p.160).

Today I count half a dozen Scientists as true friends; but I'd known hundreds. Dissent can bring loneliness. Tucker writes about Collson's loneliness:

> *There was no social life connected with the Christian Science church,' she [Collson] testified, 'and I personally found my relation with other practitioners to be more competitive than cooperative.' 'We all [thought] alike and talked alike and only [vied] with one another in the precision of our yea, yea, and nay, nay, and our accuracy in repeating what the Monitor had to say about anything and everything.' Indeed, the lack of solidarity among the organization's women had so disappointed her feminist expectations of Science, that when she finally left the movement, she found she had no friend 'to whom to say goodbye' outside of her own clientele. 'The years I should have been gaining real strength by living a normal life in wholesome contact with the affairs of the world, she lamented, 'I was indulging in pipe dreams of metaphysical intoxication. (Tucker, p.160).*

What if all those years putting Church first—meetings, committee work, practice, study—I'd been painting and writing? Would my career have blossomed sooner or fuller? What if I'd played as often as I wanted with my children instead of balancing their needs with dozens of duties as a Christian Scientist with numerous church obligations? Would my constant desire for more time have been eased by eliminating church commitments? No is my final thoughtful answer. I would not be who I am without that phase of my journey. Work as a dedicated Christian Scientist built my organizational skills and mental capacity, enlarged my knowledge of the Bible, enabled healings for family, others, and myself without reliance on medical means, enriched my spiritual depth, rooted me in good, made God my focus, gave me a moral foundation, and launched my search for Truth, though that journey eventually led me away from church. Nothing has been lost, for Christian Science established my solid faith in God.

I do not hold the animosity Collson seems to cling to toward the Christian Science Church. Indeed, I am grateful to have been raised in such a spiritual context, to have grown up valuing honesty and a moral approach to life, to have watched my father's stalwart healing example, to have raised my children largely free of common sicknesses and fears, to have had Christian Science's comforting principle to lean upon during hard times, and to have had the privilege of class instruction from an excellent Christian Science Teacher. Above all, I treasure the definition of an omnipresent impersonal good God—Spirit, Life, Truth, Love, Principle, Mind, Soul—which Christian Science taught me and which I still cherish. To grow up knowing we are all God's beloved offspring is liberating in more ways than I can count. I value that Christian Science taught me to work diligently for all things reflective of God's *goodness*.

But in questioning mode at age 48, I found Mary Collson's powerful story awakening. I'd lived the dichotomy of significant healing while experiencing the peculiar idiosyncrasies of the Christian Science movement. I'd seen its self-important personal and political tempests-in-teapots that wanted to loom more important than a world-view. Denying unpleasantness and the metaphysical bogey-man—Malicious Animal Magnetism—no longer made sense to me (if, in fact, it ever truly did). In grasping *real* railings neither Mary Collson nor I could continue to accept fully that to which we had devoted our lives. Collson's intelligence, feminism, pacifism, and deep longing to improve humanity led her away from Christian Science, just as similar passions led me to where I am today. Though I have greater respect and appreciation for Christian Science than Collson had in the end, many of her points are well taken and Tucker's book became helpful, among so many other life-impacting books during this period of my life.

I am surprised to learn that the author of *A Woman's Ministry*, Cynthia Tucker, is a *Memphis* State University professor—living not far from my own Mid-town home. Yet, why should this surprise me? This sort of thing seems to occur rather frequently in my life. Without hesitation, I find Cynthia Tucker in the phonebook and call her Sunday evening following my marathon reading of her enlightening book. She is happy to speak with me and at the end of our lengthy phone call, we continue our conversation the following weekend at the women's bookstore. I learn of her childhood experience with Christian Science and we exchange our personal stories. She shows me many letters she's received from former Christian Scientists during and after the writing of her book and gives me the stack to take home and read. We visit again when I go to her home to return the letters. I realize I am finding ground on which to stand. I am not alone—neither as a woman figuring out her place in this world, nor as one who has chosen to leave the Christian Science Church.

I am in the profound process of *awakening*.

But *in* this process, I don't realize that's what I'm doing—until I encounter Maria Harris's book, *Dance of the Spirit: The Seven Steps of Women's Spirituality*. In her feast of a book, Harris explains that *awakening* is the first step in removing *masks*—not just the masks of make-up, high heeled shoes, and dissatisfaction with our bodies, but more important, the compulsive pleasing of others, the keeping of expected roles, the "peaceful agreement when we are actually raging in disagreement, and the masks that keep us not only from seeing ourselves but being ourselves" (Harris, *Dance of the Spirit*, p.16). In unmasking, we "face—and stare down—all the lies about ourselves we as women have been taught, and to which we have agreed" (Harris, p. 17). I discover I have been agreeing with more lies than I knew. Only recently have I begun to hear my own voice within and claim my identity.

Harris teaches me about disbelief:

if we want to take part in the full Awakening of the Spirituality to which we are called, if we want to take on our vocation to be bearers and birthers of the real

God—the God who is God—then we must learn to practice disbelief. We can say it quietly or we can shout it. But when told we are inferior or unworthy because we are women, then we must say something. And in the face of the lies about our spiritual incapacities, there is only one thing to say. And it is "No, I don't believe that. Not any more." In such words reside the power of Awakening. (Harris, p. 18).

Harris' words remind me of Nora's in Ibsen's play, *A Doll's House.* I am learning the *universal* similarities of women's journeys and find comfort in knowing I am not alone. I see, too, that before I ever laid eyes on Harris's book—I was *awakening and unmasking on my own.* But what I learn and practice of Harris' seven steps telescopes my progress. She teaches me about life's shadows and woundedness (as some of my earlier Episcopal reading had done) and bolsters my growth. Throughout 1992 my path to self-knowledge is guided in the most serendipitous manner, confirmed by every book that falls into my path, as if by magic.

This mystical process continues when I "run into" Alice Koller's book, *An Unknown Woman,* on another visit to the women's bookstore. In just the first few pages I realize her story is also mine. I take her home with me and underline intensely as I discover we unmask similarly.

One winter in the 1970s, Alice Koller, a college professor and writer, leaves all for an isolated cottage on the shores of Nantucket to live deliberately alone, with only her dog, Logos, for company and her journal to "talk" to: "I'm here to understand myself, deliberately to turn myself open to my own view...I'll write down everything I can remember, so that I can see the full extent of it, pick out some patterns in what I've been denying for so long... to get it all written, no matter how ugly." (Koller, p. 40).

Minus Thoreau's convenient return from his self-imposed Walden "isolation" several times a week for conversation and a good dinner prepared by others, Alice Koller remains utterly alone for four months. At the "outermost edge" of her life, she asks herself the hardest questions in order to strip away habits of living for others, in order to *know* herself: "I'm going now to a place where no one knows me. In this place I'll tear away all the sham and all the acting. If anything at all is left, it will at least be mine. No one else's standards will guide me. No one else's reasons" (Koller, p.15).

The process of learning about herself is a unique kind of edification. Koller writes:

What sort of knowledge is this, that it can't be taught either by specific example or by abstract precepts? I think it's that knowledge Socrates meant when he said that virtue is knowledge but that it can't be taught. It can't be taught, but it can be learned. You have only to set yourself to be both teacher and learner at the same time. What you learn is something true of yourself alone. (Koller, p. 260).

I, too, have been both teacher and learner. Like Koller, I question and write to find my authentic self—I just don't get to do it in a Nantucket beach cottage.

I write to survive. Even as a child in imaginative play, somehow I knew my stories enabled me to be me. I jump into women's studies and learn that writing *her story* has often been woman's *only* way to know she matters.

Deena Metzger writes in her excellent book, *Writing For Your Life*:

Sometimes the simple willingness to explore one's life story asserts the reality of the individual, which is otherwise so often undermined. And as it is almost impossible to disentangle or distinguish the process of writing from one's development as a person, this, in itself, is the beginning of healing. The writer has an urgent desire to tell the truth and a sensitivity to the necessity of story (Metzger, Writing for Your Life, p. 45).

About this time I submit a detailed proposal to write a women's studies course for juniors and seniors—a course, I realize, that might appear controversial and particularly awakening for Southern young women in an elite private girls' school. To my surprise, without a history degree, I win the grant over all the other history proposals submitted.

Eagerly I begin the arduous, yet joyous, course creation. I write as if I've no other occupation (yet, I have all the same demands). As books pile up on my desk, bedside table, and sofa, I go through reams of paper in planning this course which becomes more than an academic project; it is a vast undertaking, a *cause* that has my complete devotion (not unlike Christian Science was?). I love what I am learning, and can hardly wait to share with these girls my exciting discoveries. My earnest desire is that they grow up with a clearer understanding and appreciation of themselves and their potential than I did. I hope they might sort out what it is to grow up female in a patriarchal world, uncovering women's hidden story to inspire their living. Likely they do not know "there is a masculine bias at the heart of most academic disciplines, methodologies, and theories" ((Belenky, Clinchy, Goldberger, and Tarule, *Women's Ways of Knowing: The Development of Self, Voice, and Mind*, p.6) and "when women's mode is treated as deficit, women come to believe that they cannot think and learn as well as men" (Belenky, p. 16). I want these students to know the best of women's thought, the finest of women's literature, women's history, and women's ways of knowing—ways often "neglected and denigrated by the dominant ethos of our time" (Belenky, Clinchy, Goldberger, and Tarule, *Women's Ways of Knowing: The Development of Self, Voice, and Mind*, preface).

In the process of writing this course, I consciously incorporate *women's* ways of knowing into my methodology. I come across an obscure but interesting fact which inspires the course's framework. The first piece of quilting an Amish mother teaches her daughter is called a *9-piece*—nine fabric squares stitched together into a pattern. Using the quilt metaphor, I design my course in nine parts that together make a whole, calling my course *Herstory 9-Piece,* implying the passing on from one generation to another, mother to daughter, of woman's *story.* I decide my students will stitch a small pillow of meaningful scraps—bits of their life—whether a remnant from a girl scout uniform or a favorite pair of jeans, a slice of lace that reminds them of a special event in their lives or perhaps merely a color or design personally metaphoric—simultaneously learning woman's ancient skill of sewing (I will learn that most have never sewn on a button and can't thread a needle!). They will also keep journals, as women have down through the centuries. Along with copious reading and research papers of their choice—for this will be an academically rigorous course—they will interview three women of different ages whom they admire or find interesting with a base set of questions. They will also call their busy fathers and make an appointment to interview them—this turns out to be the most difficult assignment: in one class, only *one* girl was able to get face time with her father—but that, in and of itself, teaches much to these young women.

On one of the first days of class I read aloud to my students this brief but electric passage from *Women's Ways of Knowing:*

We do not think of the ordinary person as preoccupied with such difficult and profound questions as: What is truth? What is authority? To whom do I listen? What counts for me as evidence? How do I know what I know? Yet to ask ourselves these questions and to reflect on our answers is more than an intellectual exercise, for our basic assumptions about the nature of truth and reality and the origins of knowledge shape the way we see the world and ourselves as participants in it. They affect our definitions of ourselves, the way we interact with others, our public and private personae, our sense of control over life events, our views of teaching and learning, and our conceptions of morality (Belenky, p. 3).

Class discussion follows on the main point: women often do not feel heard even when they have something important to say because society's concepts of truth and how one learns have been articulated and formulated throughout history by men, while attributes associated with the feminine—such as "interdependence, intimacy, nurturance, and contextual thought" (Belenky, p. 5-7)—have been ignored. The baseline, against which *both* men's and women's intellectual development is judged, has been, and remains, masculine. It is time to hear *her* story.

Part of my *Herstory 9-Piece* course includes a New Harmony weekend retreat for students. The girls and I make and sell home-made bread (imitating a colonial woman's skill) to earn money for our trip. I rent the entire Orchard house so that every two girls share *a room of their own*. The workshop retreat turns out to be transforming for the girls.

So successful is *Herstory 9-Piece* that several adult women ask to audit it and I re-write the course for women of all ages— first teaching this adult version around my dining table, then at Calvary Church, and later in my public art gallery. The original course includes a retreat to New Harmony. Eventually, *Herstory 9-Piece* becomes a 100-page syllabus with a seven-page bibliography (I still teach it occasionally).

I want to share women's studies with my daughter, too, that she might grow into her fullest self. An idea comes to me to do a New Harmony Orchard House retreat for Charissa, now in 8th grade, with two other mothers and their daughters. Each mother shares a room with her own daughter but we break up into pairs, mixing mothers and daughters, for various projects and gather as a group for discussion. We talk about what it means to be female, what women have contributed to society, read stories of and by women of all ages, create personal works of art, write, walk, talk, swim in the Inn's indoor pool, learn how to like being alone, try meditation, cook meals with everyone participating, connect with each other and our deepest selves.

One of our last gatherings in the Orchard House living room, I take the "first woman's symbol," an apple, and cut it in half horizontally, revealing the seed star inside, as I have done for every *Herstory 9-Piece* class on retreat since. This idea came as a *gift*—intuition is one of women's most reliable *ways of knowing*. I show the seed star to the girls and their mothers and say, "Just like this apple, at the center inside each of you is a star waiting to radiate outward. The apple grows beyond its seed and core; so do we. Without a core the apple could not have grown, could not have served its purpose. We need to find our centers. Without a center a woman is like a lop-sided wheel that can't function. Our roundedness requires a center that balances our lives. Time for centering is not selfish; it enables outreach—like a star that can't keep its light to itself but must shine on all." I pass around seed-star slices of apple for each to eat in an unspoken *communion* (a ritual I would not have known prior to finding the Episcopal Church—how all things fit together!). We discuss how to find one's center, how it clarifies who we are and helps us become the givers women innately are. I tell the girls and their mothers that we reach beyond ourselves in spite of any personal emptiness, woundedness, or inadequacies we may feel, because women seek *connection with all things* and know relationship matters.

Women are spherical for a reason—our roundedness connects us with earth itself. Instinctively we understand earth's seasons, planting fall bulbs to become spring flowers, just as we understand our body's cycles. We know our girlhood spring leads to a menopausal winter, that raising a child well at five will help him function at fifteen, that our daughters will one day be mothers like ourselves—though different, wiser, stronger, we hope. We know circles and cycles tie life's pieces into a meaningful whole. As women, we feel entrusted to protect the circular continuity of all life.

As a woman ever in the awakening process, I've learned to honor time. Not mere instructions have taught me how long to bake a cake or steam broccoli, or when to rock a baby back to sleep or when to let him cry. Intuition tells me. Intuition tells me when to ask a patriarch a question, how long to soak baseball uniforms to get out grass stains, how to make a fabulous dinner out of nearly nothing, how long to hold off house cleaning when pressed by a hectic week at work, how long to put off resting or shaving legs because others need me.

Women understand we don't have enough time for ourselves. We understand priorities. We stir the family supper while on the phone with a friend whose marriage is falling apart. We read waiting in carpool lines because ideas matter even midst routine. We recycle, fight for causes, teach Sunday School, join organizations we believe in, and magically tuck PTA meetings and orthodontist appointments into imaginary cracks in our 9:00 to 5:00 jobs. Between breakfast, lunch, and dinner, women slip not just what matters in a day, but all that will matter in a hundred years or more. Perhaps because we give birth, we know how precious life is. A woman cherishes each day not just for herself and her family, but because she loves the light radiating from her center that enables her industry, caring, connecting and vision.

Bettina Aptheker, an author and professor whose work I find especially helpful in teaching my course (I wrote her as I did Madeliene L'Engle and Deena Metzger, each one taking time to write me back, encouraging my journey) writes in *Tapestries of Life: Women's Work, Women's Consciousness, and the Meaning of Daily Experience* a powerful paragraph including a quotation from Deena Metzger:

> *Each day is a tapestry, threads of broccoli, promotion, couches, children, politics, shopping, building, planting, thinking interweave in intimate connection with insistent cycles of birth, existence, and death." Some of these things also happen to men, but not all of them, and they don't happen in the same ways because most men in the United States are not ultimately responsible for maintaining personal relationships and networks. They are not primarily responsible for emotional work. They are not primarily responsible for the children, the elders, the relatives, the holidays, the cooking, the cleaning, the shopping, the mending, the laundry. Their position as men, even as working-class men and men of color, gives them access to more resources and status relative to the women and families of their communities because the society institutionalizes a system of male dominations* (Aptheker, Tapestries of Life, p. 39).

Women, at least women in the awakening process, look for meaning in the ordinary. The numinous must be present in daily routine. Like living quilts, women link segments of time, persons, places, and events into a pattern, stitching yesterday's patches to today's and tomorrow's. The design becomes a warm, functioning *whole*. On some primal level, even before I stitched my first quilts (brightly colored bunk bed quilts for my young sons), I knew women are quilt-like. No one told me; I just *knew*.

My maternal grandmother's quilt on my bed is made from pieces of clothing that clad everyone of her six children. I pull her quilt up around my neck and feel somehow I know my grandmother better for it. What were her thoughts the day she put in the bit of red gingham? What about the day she cut a piece from Aunt Gertrude's old print dress and Aunt Mary Lou's checked blouse and Mom's party dress? What emotions and events are represented here? What stories of past lives? I can only guess. But I am closer to these women because of my grandmother's quilt.

Quilts offer an essential resource in reconstructing women's history because frequently women left no written evidence of their lives. Quilts have provided a record of women's lives, their community, their politics, their children, their cultural heritage, their causes and concerns. Women's history is stitched up in quilts. As one quiltmaker said: "My whole life is in that quilt… All my joys and all my sorrows are stitched into those little pieces…I tremble sometimes when I remember what that quilt knows about me." (Aptheker, p.38)

Embodying woman's *dailiness* in an art form, the quilt has been the subject of artists and authors such as Judy Chicago, Sue Bender, Alice Walker, and so many others. Elaine Hedges explains that the quilt throughout history has been "a vehicle through which women could express themselves; utilitarian objects elevated through enterprise, imagination, and love to the status of an original art form. . . . In 1845, a Lowell, Massachusetts woman described quilts, as 'the hieroglyphics of women's lives', and so they were." (Aptheker, p. 68)

Sue Bender, author of *Plain and Simple: A Woman's Journey to the Amish*, one of many whose words inspired my course, describes her first encounter with Amish quilts in a New York City department store exhibition: "those stoic Amish quilts, with their Spartan shapes, sent shock waves through me—a grown woman mesmerized. These are dramatic words, but that's what it felt like. The connection was immediate and electric…My busyness stopped. The fragments of my life became still. I was coming home, connecting to a part of me that I had ignored, even depreciated. I felt calm." (Bender, *Plain and Simple*, p. 11).

Quilts tell women's stories. Without *story* a woman is lost. I open my *Herstory 9-Piece* course with Judith Christ's marvelous words:

> *Without stories there is no articulation of experience. Without stories a woman is lost when she comes to make the important decisions of her life. She does not learn to value her struggles, to celebrate her strengths, to comprehend her pain. Without stories she cannot understand herself. Without stories she is alienated from those deeper experiences of self and world that have been called spiritual or religious. She is closed in silence. The expression of women's spiritual quest is integrally related to the telling of women's stories. If women's stories are not told, the depth of women's souls will not be known"* (Christ, *Diving Deep and Surfacing*, p. 1).

Listening to students' stories, I cherish each one, for story is the way women give meaning to what they know, believe, and do. Dailiness creates her story and story tells her journey.

In childhood I was *"doing* story" but I did not realize this fully, nor articulate it specifically, until in adulthood I wrote in my journal September 27, 1992:

> *I realize I am a storyteller. I have always been a storyteller. When I was a child I perpetually made up stories with my dolls and paper dolls. My earliest drawings were narratives; I drew stories. I wrote plays on paper, acted them out with neighbor friends, and in my head on a hot summer's night when I couldn't sleep—or any night in order to drift off to a place I'd rather be... Why is it, then, a surprise to discover I want to write? At some hidden level I've always known it. I think my life work is to tell stories in pictures and words. But how can I take care of my family, and do this work? I need to sell 20 paintings a year—if I could do that I could contribute enough to buy me freedom to do my work.*

This sounds like Virginia Woolf's declaration: *"A woman must have money and a room of her own if she is to write"* (Woolf, p.4). My copy of this address by Woolf delivered to female college students, published in 1929, is well worn and marked, for I *love* its truth. Each time I watch British actress Aileen Atkins' rendition—a video I share with my women studies classes—tears come to my eyes, but I notice no one else's eyes are dry either.

Ms. Woolf exquisitely exposes the challenge women face as writers, but her point is applicable to every woman. My favorite section begins: "Let me imagine...what would have happened had Shakespeare had a wonderfully gifted sister, called Judith, let us say" (Woolf, p.46). Ms. Woolf goes on to describe the robust and scholarly life of Shakespeare, his ensuing success, and then contrasts it with the outcome for the equally talented "Judith". She would *not* have gone to school nor even been allowed to read or write, might even have had her writing burned when found out as happened to 18th century Fanny Burney. By her teens, Shakespeare's Sister would have been betrothed, no matter how hateful the marriage, and would have been beaten by her father had she dared complain.

But knowing the poet's soul lying within Judith, Ms. Woolf imagines Shakespeare's sister would have gathered up "a small parcel of her belongings, let herself down by a rope one summer's night" (Woolf, p.47) and taken the road to London.

Like her brother she hopes to act, but the theatre manager merely laughs at her. "Yet her genius was for fiction and lusted to feed abundantly upon the lives of men and women and the study of their ways" (Woolf, p. 48).

The actor-manager takes pity on this penniless maiden, takes her home, and soon she finds herself pregnant with his child. Woolf writes: "...who shall measure the heat and violence of the poet's heart when caught and tangled in a woman's body?—[She] killed herself one winter's night and lies buried at some cross-roads where the omnibuses now stop outside the Elephant and Castle" (Woolf, p. 48). Woolf explains that "the mind of an artist, in order to achieve the prodigious effort of freeing whole and entire the work that is in him, must be incandescent, like Shakespeare's mind...There must be no obstacle in it, no foreign matter, unconsumed....That one would find any woman in that state of mind in the sixteenth century was obviously impossible" (Woolf, p. 56).

Woolf's moving ending *lives* in me, comes to me each time I pick up a brush or compose at the computer. It is especially with me when I long to stay in the moment of my writing or painting, but am interrupted by a child's phone call, or the necessity of another dinner to prepare:

I told you in the course of this paper that Shakespeare had a sister but do not look for her in Sir Sidney Lee's life of the poet. She died young—alas, she never wrote a word. She lies buried where the omnibuses now stop, opposite the Elephant and Castle. Now my belief is that this poet who never wrote a word and was buried at the crossroads still lives. She lives in you and in me, and in many other women who are not here tonight, for they are washing up the dishes and putting the children to bed. But she lives; for great poets do not die; they are continuing presences; they need only the opportunity to walk among us in the flesh. This opportunity, as I think, it is now coming within your power to give her. For my belief is that if we live another century or so—I am talking of the common life which is the real life and not of the little separate lives which we live as individuals—and have five hundred a year each of us and rooms of our own; if we have the habit of freedom and the courage to write exactly what we think; if we escape a little from the common sitting-room and see human beings not always in their relations to each other but in relations to reality; and the sky, too, and the trees or whatever it may be in themselves; if we look past Milton's bogey, for no human being should shut out the view; if we face the fact, for it is a fact, that there is no arm to cling to, but that we go alone and that our relation is to the world of reality and not only to the world of men and women, then opportunity will come and the dead poet who was Shakespeare's sister will put on the body which she has so often laid down. Drawing her life from the lives of the unknown who were her forerunners, as her brother did before her, she will be born. As for her coming without that preparation, without that effort on our part, without that determination that when she is born again she shall find it possible to live and write her poetry, that we cannot expect, for that would be impossible. But I maintain that she would come if we worked for her, and that so to work, even in poverty and obscurity, is worth while (Woolf, p.113-114).

This passage, this utterly sublime and eloquent piece of writing, tells truth so powerfully! It never fails to put a lump in my throat and, then, a pen in my hand. Women writers *will* be born! And I intend to be among them.

Charlotte Perkins Gilman was yet another woman writer in which I saw myself. Reformer, pacifist, author of many treatises on women's issues and of *The Yellow Wallpaper*, Charlotte read and wrote voraciously, attended RISD as did I, desired self-improvement, and worked to better the lives of women everywhere.

In her autobiography she writes of her mother's disappointment in love, which led her mother to deny Charlotte "all expression of affection as far as possible, so that she should not be used to it or long for it" (Gilman, *The Living of Charlotte Perkins Gilman*, p. 10-11). Charlotte quotes her mother: "I used to put away your little hand from my cheek when you were a nursing baby…I did not want you to suffer as I had suffered" (Gilman, p.10). Charlotte feigned sleep because when she was sleeping was the only time her mother caressed her. She writes, "how rapturously I enjoyed being gathered into her arms, held close and kissed" (Gilman,p. 11). But her balanced appreciation of her mother is evident: "If love, devotion to duty, sublime self-sacrifice, were enough in child-culture, mothers would achieve better results; but there is another requisite too often lacking—knowledge. Yet all the best she had, the best she knew, my mother gave, at any cost to herself" (Gilman, p. 11). I could say the same of my own mother.

Perhaps because of her mother's high expectations for her daughter, coupled with lack of expressed affection, Charlotte developed a keen inner life, much as I did. She developed a love of books and beauty, much as I did. Charlotte writes, "My passion for beauty dates far back; in picture books… the colors of the worsted mother used, loving some and hating others; in bits of silk and ribbon, buttons,…a little cloak of purple velvet, deep pansy-purple, made over from something of mother's that enraptured my soul" (Gilman, p. 18). I relate to this—even to the purple coat, for one Easter, I wore one of the same color my mother made for me complete with carefully embroidered pansies on the lapel.

Intelligent and curious, Charlotte once proved a math problem that did not match the "correct" answer in the text. Charlotte took her slate to the teacher for checking. "This one is wrong," the teacher said. "But I have proved it," Charlotte said. After the teacher did the problem herself, she confirmed that Charlotte had been right and the book wrong! Charlotte writes of this experience. "This was a great lesson; science, law, was more to be trusted than authority" (Gilman, p. 19). Once in 6ᵗʰ grade I purposely spelled "gray" the English way, "grey," because it was printed on my British-made crayon and I wanted my teacher to know I knew the less common spelling; unlike Charlotte, my answer was marked wrong and when I spoke to the teacher about it she said, "We're *not* in England and that's not how it is in *our* spelling book."

Another time Charlotte's curiosity got the better of her. In the customarily hushed classroom, she wondered why they had to sit so quietly. What would happen if someone called out? She selected a tiny word to experiment with, "it", and called it out loud. "Who said that?' the teacher promptly asked. Up went Charlotte's hand. "Why did you do that?" the teacher asked, knowing Charlotte to be a scholarly child of decorum. "I wanted to see what would happen." Charlotte answered. Another lesson: *"things debarred may sometimes be done—in safety"* (Gilman, p. 19). Unlike Charlotte, I would reach adulthood before trying a bold act.

Perhaps the most important lesson of both Charlotte's childhood and mine was learning "the use of a constructive imagination" (Gilman, p. 19). After an early supper followed by much reading, came an early bedtime imposed by her mother. Though she was rarely sleepy, Charlotte discovered, as had I, the possibilities afforded by imagination. "I could make a world to suit me," she writes (Gilman, p. 20). I did the same.

Charlotte is described in Ann J. Lane's *To Herland and Beyond: The Life and Work of Charlotte Perkins Gilman* as having *"electric energy and vitality"* (Ann J. Lane, *To Her Land and Beyond*, p. 106) as well as periods of immobilizing depression which left her unable to care for her home, husband, and child. She sought out Dr. Weir S. Mitchell, a popular physician addressing the many illnesses plaguing "ambitious and imaginative" Victorian women. Mitchell's "moral medication" treatment was a travesty that included bed rest, avoidance of writing, reading and intellectual pursuits, isolation from family and familiar surroundings, being over-fed by a nurse, and culminated in orders to return to women's work: care of home, husband, and child. Lane writes: "That a woman's life might have a 'distinct purpose' like that which informed 'the lives of men' was apparently beyond him" (Lane, p. 118). Charlotte writes that after precisely following his directions for many months, she "came perilously near to losing my mind" (Lane, p. 121).

But Charlotte used this low point to shift her life into a different direction. She left her husband, took her child (whom she later gave up), and moved to Pasadena, California to begin doing "exactly what I pleased" (Lane, p. 123). As Lane writes, Charlotte "expended enormous amounts of energy trying to do what was expected of her, first by her mother, then by her husband, and finally by her doctor. For the first time, she was truly declaring her independence" (Lane, p. 123). She began writing novels and short stories; among them, one particularly brilliant short story, and now famous psychological work, *The Yellow Wallpaper*, first published in 1892.

Gilman's powerful Poe-like story gripped me. Equally wrenching and perfect as *Thelma and Louise*—the academy award-winning film which came out the summer of 1991 when I was first discovering Women's Studies—*The Yellow Wallpaper*'s dark truth is timelessly woman's tale. I began to memorize it in hopes of doing a dramatization of it one day. And I created a painting with bulging eyes behind torn collaged yellow wallpaper. Somehow, parts of my life with Dad, John, Christian Science, as wife, mother, and community servant, glittered in the shadows of this horror story. Similarly, after seeing *Thelma and Louise* I created a painting of the same title, which still hangs in my gallery today. Though I was neither Thelma nor Louise, nor the docile Victorian doll who goes mad in the *Wallpaper* story, I understood them. I've learned that most married women do.

In marrying Bill Caldwell in October 1991 I resurrect myself as wife, homemaker, and mother. I tell his Mom: "It is a good thing I raised two sons before I married Bill!" She laughs, knowing my meaning. For forty years Bill has never had any responsibilities to anyone other than himself. His family, like so many in Memphis, has always had a black maid and cook—Blanche, who came to our wedding as well as Tat's funeral—and none of the domestic chores expected of children in a Midwestern family had been part of this Southern boy's experience. Nor as an adult had he pets, houses, or significant others to care for. Taking on a wife and her existing family was quite a change (though my sons were on their own by that time). Bill had never thought about a mortgage, nor did he want to. He would have been perfectly satisfied with a tent—what was this house stuff for anyway?! Savings accounts, insurance—who needs them?! Certainly not a bachelor! And in many ways Bill remained a bachelor into our marriage.

Aside from our age difference, Bill's attachment to his mom was my greatest concern in considering marriage. Frequently, a Southerner considers his childhood home *still his home*, even though in adulthood he's created a new home of his own, with his own family and responsibilities. When in his parents' home, Bill reverts to the child he was, drifting off to book or magazine, not responsible for adult participation. We discussed this. I also told him I'd not likely be giving him children, which he claimed he didn't want, though his sisters suggested I do so if possible.

Just before our wedding, Bill and I purchased together the condo beneath mine, which had come on the market. We connected the two units with an impressive 24-step internal stairway that we had the building's architectural firm design and a contractor build. The lower condo had been the original boiler room of the old school and included a finely functioning brick fireplace as well as a sunken living area with exposed brick walls, a tiny kitchen, a bedroom (which became Charissa's) and an exterior door to a patio. The original unit that had been mine since my divorce remained intact: studio, living and dining area, galley kitchen and sleeping lofts. We enjoyed our dramatic 1,800 square foot new home with its seven levels of living space. Evenings we would read together—happy soul mates by fireside, as our favorite Blues music filled the air, or snuggle in bed, watching the moon out of our 9-foot windows.

In June 1992, the first summer following our marriage, Bill and I set out to visit everyone either of us had ever known: sisters, brothers, cousins, aunts, uncles, school and college friends, staying in each home for a day or two—quite a road trip and great fun! Bill and I discussed ideas, philosophy, history, read books aloud to each other, playing tapes of our favorite music. To save money, I prepared meals ahead that we kept in a cooler and we slept in sleeping bags, hiking and visiting national parks and historic sites between stops at friends' homes.

Our first stop was Nashville, staying with Bill's sister, Cathy, her husband and three active sons. While the guys went fishing, Cathy and I went out to lunch. Cathy, a full-time mom, petite, with sandy short hair and a wide smile, talked about her mom and dad. She surprised me by revealing her father's alcoholism and their mom's frequent phone calls for solace to her and Lib (Bill's other sister, the Presbyterian minister who married us). She said her mom was often in tears or anger and at a loss as to what to do about her husband's drinking.

Bill never mentioned his dad's drinking until the day before our wedding. I'd wondered why most Sunday dinners at Bill's parents' home—Bill's weekly custom, now ours—his Mom would say Bill Sr. was "napping and won't be joining us." When he did join us, I'd been puzzled how harsh he could be with Bill. Now I began to understand. Cathy and Lib were the first to face the alcoholism problem and wanted to get help for their dad at a rehab center, but Bill wouldn't confront him, Cathy told me, adding "I wonder how much longer Dad can go on."

Always a keen observer, I wrote in my journal June 17, 1992 that I wished Bill's family were able to face this issue but feared they did not have the courage. Bill's mom seemed to me to be a classic enabler, manipulatively seeking sympathy from her grown children. I hoped we'd manage to keep our independence and not become part of the engulfing web that intertwined members of his family. I suspected Bill's dad's alcoholism played a role in the co-dependency I'd observed.

Bill's sense of humor, quick wit and intellect suited him for the jester role to brighten his family, just as for colleagues at school. Though he never joked about his family, he did throw out a few zingers about mine: "I met my mother-in-law and two weeks later she was dead"… "Lyn's sons—one's a horse thief and the other a motorcycle biker!" Even Charissa was the brunt: "Who wants to live with a *13* year old?!" Hard for me to hear, but I knew, of course, he meant no harm and genuinely loved my kids. I have learned a quick-witted humorist can't keep himself from constantly cracking original lines.

One Sunday at their house, Bill's dad—bright and interesting when sober—pulls me aside and whispers that he had to go to his mother-in-law's every Sunday and he doesn't want us to have to do the same. How kind of Bill Senior to suggest this! I decide one Sunday a month I will prepare dinner for our friends and my children [at this time, Charissa lives with us but is sometimes at her Dad's on weekends and Jason lives in his own apartment but is always glad for a good home-cooked meal]. Two Sundays I won't do dinner but will paint, for which there's never enough time. The fourth Sunday we will go to Bill's mom's.

Surprises show up in any marriage. In ours, some of Bill's cultivated habits—especially anger over things that don't go his way—are difficult for me. I'd not noticed these traits prior to marriage, though he had told me, "I don't do emotions." Actually, he is the most emotional person I know—he tears up playing "Deportee" on his guitar, cries at movies, cringes at the sight of blood or needle and feels things more deeply than he acknowledges. Sometimes he rages if a screw doesn't turn properly when fixing his computer or if traffic moves too slowly, or if a student's parent gives unjustified criticism, or if his eyeglasses are dirty, or if he can't find a book he's looking for. Our first few years of marriage I confided my frustration with his anger to my journal.

Also in the early years, money is an issue. In my marriage to John I'd kept the budget, paid the bills, made most financial decisions. Bill wants to handle everything, while blaming me for expenses—everything from the unexpected bathroom plaster repair that cost $700 to his car repair of $1,000 —which I had nothing to do with. Such costs are normal in adult life, but Bill has had few adult problems to deal with and avoids money discussions as he does talking about emotions.

I knew from the start not to expect gifts. Valentine's day, anniversary, Christmas, birthdays did not matter to Bill. "One day is like another," he explained before we married. He detested buying gifts for anyone, didn't do it, in fact. He saw no need to single out a particular day or event for recognition. Hearing this, I told him he needn't get me a ring when we married; so he didn't, neither engagement nor wedding. Long ago I'd purchased a plain gold band (with painting money) to wear in the art room instead of the lovely diamond and platinum family heirloom John had given me (when I divorced, I gave the heirloom to our oldest son to keep for his future bride) so I used my gold band when I married Bill.

Over the years, however, Bill changed. He began to remember special occasions with flowers and dinner out. I feel appreciated and there is no subject we cannot fully discuss, emotions and finances included. We evolved a pragmatic system of shared financial responsibilities, each handling particular categories; it works beautifully. In any marriage, people grow, change, adapt, and meld harmoniously to each other—provided they communicate, are compatible, have similar goals and interests, like as well as love each other. Eventually, as couples learn to resolve issues and to compromise, they instinctively think as *one*, with respect for each other's individual viewpoint. Today we are at the point where we know what the other thinks or means without using nouns or finishing sentences!

Writing helped me find my way in this new relationship—as it always has in all of life. Writing is one of the places where God speaks to us, where we come face to face with who we are. I've learned it doesn't matter if we write about lettuce leaves or metaphysics, we'll find ourselves in what we write. Writing and art-making show me who I am, where I'm going. I wrote in my journal in 1992: *What do I want? Just to write an honest account of my life and leave it behind. Nothing more.* Guess I'm doing that.

By my 49th birthday, I realized the time had come to "sew the quilt." You can't fuss with pieces forever! You've arranged them over and over, now *sew*! Connect the fragments! Scattered pieces can't comfort—they have to be made into a *whole quilt.* When you are half a century old, you want to be in life's dance—not on the sidelines waiting. You realize how little time is left. You want to paint and write all those ideas that have been interrupted by duties, the bits and fragments just waiting to come together. You want to do it *today* not tomorrow!

One night reading Annie Dillard, appreciating her luscious and exact use of words, I crave to be a writer, if not on Cape Cod as she does, at least in Memphis. I sign up for a writers' night course at Rhodes College in the fall of 1992—as if I'd time for such a thing! I slip writing in between all I'm doing, frustrated by the lack of *time to create* after teaching school all day and care-giving all evening.

I go to my second Rhodes class a bit nervous, sitting to the side. In the first class I'd learned, as we introduced ourselves around the room, that many people taking this course make their living writing. Will I measure up, be good enough to even be here? Who am I to think I can write?! Other pieces read before mine seem so polished; perhaps mine will be inadequate. I tell myself what I know is true: I want criticism—that's why I'm here—I need to discover whether or not what I write in my room is a voice worth hearing in the world. I liked RISD critiques, so I can deal with whatever is dished out here. I'll be strong. It's my turn; I read my piece and am relieved and surprised by the favorable comments afterward from teacher and students. It is the *first* time I feel validated as a writer (other than when my articles were published in the *Christian Science Journal*). I had no idea how my writing would be received; I had written to *survive*, not to get published. But in recent years having my voice *heard* has seemed important. Women throughout history have shown me the importance of *finding my voice* and using it. I am stunned when a classmate says "You have a lack-of-self-esteem; you preface your reading with insecurity but what you read intimidates us all". Did she really mean this? I don't think I have a problem with self-esteem, nor do I believe my work could intimidate anyone in this room! Though validated, I am confused when I leave that night. I go home energized and write until after midnight.

Only a month into our marriage Bill takes a group of students to Washington DC for a week. Night is hard but day is not easier. I cry but do not know why I am sad. There are more important things to do! I need to stop this muck! But I feel powerless. Clearly another onset of depression comes, which I did not recognize then.

I love Bill with a love so immense it almost alarms me. In our first months together, I sometimes imagine I am a replacement for someone younger, prettier, he might have had. This feeling comes when occasionally letters and phone calls come from former students and people in his past. At such times, I wonder if my role is just harbinger for someone else to enter his life. Perhaps that Rhodes College classmate was right: I have self-worth issues?

But I can't face that tonight. Nor can I sleep. I write a poem and call it "Sometimes I Have To hold My Own Hand." Somewhere in the creative dark, the wisdom of a thirteenth century anchoress helps me sleep, Julian of Norwich's words: "*...and all shall be well.*"

Depression continues the next day and night. I teach well, like an experienced stage actress whose inner turmoil never shows, as she flawlessly performs her role. Then I go home from work and write so as not to melt, polishing last night's poem, but getting little sleep.

When Bill is gone, I feel as if half my body and half my soul is missing. Yet he seems to carry on without me. In my depression, I imagine him charming everyone and somehow feel unloved because of it. Does some former love linger in his heart? My imagination runs on. The new drama teacher told me today: "Your husband is the *weirdest* man—you are the *only* one I know who could possibly live with him!" We do seem well-matched except for times of my depression and his anger. He also has dark recesses I'll never be allowed to enter. But tonight I feel my own dark. It is very cold at 2 AM…my body shakes in spite of the extra blanket on my bed. It is so dark. I need *light*. I always need light. Finally I drift off to sleep asking myself, "Why can't I just be happy like everyone else?"

The next morning is no better. I want to be sweetness and light, to deny the error and go on, to be a delightful person, caring, moving forward, unafraid—the person I often am—but today I can't. Today I feel worthless, exhausted, depressed.

When Bill returns from his trip the depression vanishes as suddenly as it came. All is well. That weekend we go to the library and Wiles-Smith drugstore for chocolate sodas, hike in a nearby park and take long naps together.

In December, less than two months into our marriage, Bill falls in school while in the library. He is taken to the hospital without the upper school head or anyone bothering to tell me. When I am eventually told, I rush to the hospital and learn he has a herniated disc and will require immediate back surgery. I stay in the hospital with him four days and nights and keep the medical personnel from killing him. Not aware he just had back surgery, nurses nearly fling him off the gurney to his bed—but I halt them just in time. I catch the wrong meal being delivered to him—the name on it is the patient in the next room! I prevent the wrong late night pills from being given to him. I hold his plastic urinal for him, keep him calm when he gets frustrated, and read to him from a few good books. The next two weeks back home—our Christmas break—I nurse him, read to him, help him walk to the bathroom and back to bed, and cook his favorite foods. We spend Christmas alone in our condo playing music, reading, and watching lights on our tall tree reflect in the 9-foot windows—a close and gentle time.

I finish my second May Sarton book over the holiday, *Journal of a Solitude*, and am reminded of Jung's message that we must embrace the shadow in order to grow. Four years ago at RISD I encountered Jung. He influenced my art and thinking then and still does. I marvel that always just the right author or thinker appears when I need him or her. Each prepares me for my next experience. Had I not read Jung prior to my significant abyss before divorce, for example, I would not have understood that darkness as well as I did. Each step of the past four years seems to have been orchestrated by a Grand Conductor.

By January, Bill is mended and back at school and I am filling winter nights with painting and writing.

I write these odd words on January 9, 1993: *If my father dies, I will become an artist.* What does this mean? I think it means that when the daughter in me dies, I will be free to be fully an artist. When I am no longer a man's daughter or wife, but completely my *own* person, with my *own* voice—which I *am* finding—*then* I will be fully an artist. The time is coming. I hear a tiny voice inside ask: "But are you *good enough?*" I answer: "I must be or every part of me is pointless." I am a birth-giver, a servant, of whatever ideas hum in my ear until I make them incarnate. Perhaps my job is incarnation?

February, dark and cold, has always been a dreaded month. February 1993 is no exception. Everything wrong seems magnified in February: the broken microwave, the smoke alarms needing replacement (Bill collects them on his desk), the closet door off its hinges, the front door entry flooding when it rains, not enough room for my new paintings, the botched bathroom repair job, a year with only three functioning stove burners, Charissa's need for privacy and her unhappiness at school, a school to which I was giving enormous energy, my studio's reams of unfiled papers, and running into Bill's former students wherever we go. I feel both sad and hectic and frustrated there's *never enough time.* I write a poem about not being able to catch my breath. How petty this list sounds now, but in February, as I say, everything is magnified.

After a trip to take art students to see an exhibition in Holly Springs, Mississippi when we return, Bill and I go to the theatre where he runs into an old female friend. Though I am standing beside him, he does not introduce me. They have a long conversation as if I'm not there. It stings. Early in our marriage, Bill never thinks in terms of "us"—he always says "*I* went… or *I* did… even when we both did. Later I mention this bothered me, but he says nothing. This has happened before. What am I to him? A cook, maid, and occasional intellectual companion? I imagine one day someone will sweep him off his feet and her youthful radiance will capture his heart when he's not looking, and in spite of his honorable intentions toward me, he will fall in love with her and I will have no place—just as I feel I have no place when he meets people from his past. Better I leave before this happens, I tell myself. My mind swirls, little pieces of thought trip over each other. Nothing makes sense. It is, after all, FEBRUARY!

The same month, my frustration with school issues grows. Never have I given so much for so little. My professionalism is exemplary, even I know that. I love my students. But I long to go beyond this private school's box where too many games are played, injustices and antagonisms churn, and where creativity is not honored. Most administrators and teachers can't even *find* the art room on campus, let alone *understand* or *respect* the subject I teach. Art is the stepchild of the school. Ideas I want to try often get rejected by administration. Especially frustrating when my largest oil painting, a triptych, hangs in Memphis' Brooks Museum of Art in February and April. I begin to read professional want ads, redesign my resume, and apply for college teaching positions in Colorado and Oregon. Bill, who has been at Custis Lee for twenty years, but who has always loved the West, says if I get a job out West he would eagerly move.

It is no longer February! Spring Break has sprung! Bill, Charissa, and I hike in Amacaloola Falls State Park in Georgia, having a perfectly glorious time. We visit Jason in Savannah where he has recently moved to become a graphics design major at Savannah College of Art and Design. He has a charming old carriage house apartment—ideal for him.

Later the same month, I take a group of women studies students to New Harmony and write in my journal our last night there: "It is too glorious to put down in words what we women have shared here!" I'm loving teaching and all's right with the world! Did I mention it is no longer February?

This has been a particularly difficult year. I've struggled to find my God as I stand somewhere between Christian Science principles and new Episcopalian ones. I've struggled with new freedom from my first marriage and the restrictions of my second. I've organized an elaborate school art show (something I established when I came to Custis Lee), which takes enormous effort. I've completed my own paintings for a large gallery show of my newest work. Too busy, I've felt like loose swatches, not a *whole* quilt.

May 13, 1993, I ask God what He'd have me do. Answers lie where they often have for me: in books. I read Bernie Segal's *How to Live Between Office Visits* and Brenda Ueland's, *If You Want to Write.* The former keeps me loving life and the latter advises me to "keep a slovenly journal." I follow Ueland's advice and write everything I know to be true, warts and all, as I've always done.

With Charissa having a bedroom and bathroom all to herself downstairs, the loft I'd built for her when I first got my condo has become my "room of one's own." A mattress on a platform, surrounded by books with a light above, it is a place where I retreat to read and write.

Charissa, now a modest eighth grader not wanting to find Bill in his boxer shorts sitting at his computer when she walks out of her room, wants "a real house," rather than the openness of our condo, which offers little privacy. "I want a door I can close," she says. I understand this. She wants *a room of her own*. We consider moving out of Midtown to the suburbs, closer to school. I love our quirky seven-leveled condo with its high windows, studio light, and overall drama. I like its proximity to bookstores, museums, and Memphis' big main public library. But my daughter needs to be near friends and school for the next four years of her life. We put our combined condos up for sale.

I find an ordinary Memphis story-and-half brick house, practically characterless, in a cul de sac of elderly residents. We can afford it and it is within easy walking distance of school. I intuit as I walk to its front door with the realtor that we are *meant* to live here. The location is perfect and there is sufficient space for the three of us—even a room for the boys when they visit. There is a bright eat-in kitchen, which I will paint white and paper with a blue and white pattern. The main living room's beige '60s grass-cloth walls I'll paint red, its built-in bookshelves, white. The glassed-in porch serves as a small art studio, which I eventually paint white to enhance the light. There is a dining room, a private bedroom with its own large bath for Charissa, a master bedroom with smaller bath for Bill and me. The second floor has a guest room for the boys, a third bath, and a huge carpeted den for Bill, which we line with Home Depot bookshelves we paint brown. The house works out fine. There are a few interesting trees and shrubs in the small backyard and eventually I plant an English garden out front. We take in "Surprise,"my Samoyed whom I've missed dearly, and our cats, Oreo and Butterscotch, the pets having been at John's house since the divorce, for they could not be in the condo. Charissa has her "real home" by summer—the same summer I meet Dad in New Harmony and then have my painting/writing retreat in the Poet's House. We manage not to move from this house throughout Charissa's high school years.

Occupied with *new* home, *new* marriage, *new* family (Bill's), *new* church, the *new* challenge of mothering a teenage daughter through her high school years, a *new* gallery exhibition of my art, and teaching not only art but also my *new* Herstory 9-Piece women's studies course, I sometimes long for serenity.

Books on Buddhism and Taoism offer respite. I try to practice the Buddha's 4 Noble Truths and 8-fold path. In September 1993 I am inspired to go to a bookstore to buy *The book of I Ching*. There are several versions; I am not sure which to purchase as I thumb through each carefully. This Asian fortune telling is new to me—and I only have money for one book.

A broad, bearded, towering man about my age, dressed all in white—yes, from head to toe in white tee shirt, white pants, and white Birkenstock sandals—points to the copy currently in my hand and says, "This is the one you want. It's better than the others."

Startled—who is this person I don't even know giving me advice on buying books anyway?!—I look up at him and reply, "I do?" How could this stranger know which one I wanted? Why was he talking to me in the first place?

"You haven't done the I Ching before have you?"

"No," I respond. How could he tell—does it show on your face or something? Did I *look* like a philosophical novice?

He tells me he has been doing the I Ching for decades, says it is remarkable in its accuracy. "I'm an engineer by profession but I believe in magic."

"I'm an artist," I disclose. We begin, there between the stacks, to talk about ideas—philosophy, literature, science, world issues, and what matters. I cannot believe it! Five minutes ago I had never seen this stranger—now there isn't a thing I can't ask him. He tells me he spends his life searching and reading in bookstores and libraries. He says he never met anyone who talks as fast, and with so many questions, as I do, except his great aunt. He tells me I have a very high I.Q. and that I am more *mathematical* than an artist—now there's a surprise!

"Now I will show you how to throw the I Ching," he says taking three pennies out of his pocket. We straddle a bench, as if riding a horse, facing each other. I throw the pennies (heads=yang; tails=yin) and he tells me it is a "very strong reading." Something about thunder, but I didn't get it all, too amazed by this serendipitous meeting to focus on details.

"You won't even need the pennies after a while", he says.

"What do you mean?" I ask.

"You'll find your message *everywhere*," he smiles as I thank him and move in line to purchase the copy of the I Ching he'd suggested.

That night at home, I throw the I Ching, and look up its meaning in my new book. This particular hexagram invites me to proceed on my current path, practicing introspection as I go. To practice introspection requires finding that quiet place, Virginia Woolf's room of one's own—even if it is only a chair—and sitting still. Busy-ness would prevent my sitting still.

The next evening I ask the I Ching if Custis Lee is my right place and my throw reveals I am to place my talents at the service of the ruler and public. I take it to mean I am to stay at Custis Lee, at least for now.

I am reading Plato, again, who tells me similarly: *If one cannot find happiness in the celestial order, it is because of not being about to obey heaven...Human life in the world has a mission...with this direction there is life, without it there is death. If one cannot find happiness in this mission, this direction, this order, everything else is empty and false. That to which heaven directs humanity is only good; if one can find happiness in that command, then this is obeying heaven.*

At the beginning of the school year when I show my students *The Dead Poet's Society* to set the foundation for art-making, Robin Williams' character's familiar line about *sucking the marrow out of life* speaks to me passionately once more. We read and write poetry—and make art—because these means express the *passion* of human life! I am *here*! My students are *here*! All of us are *here*! Life *exists*! Our unique identities bring a verse to life's drama! As Williams' character says, "The powerful play goes on that you may each contribute a verse." My hands are over my heart. I've seen this film a dozen times, but am affected by certain scenes over and over again. Most of my students, unlike myself, have *not* seen the film before, and will try to go on to math or French class, dry-eyed, unmoved, but will be unable.

I assign my Advanced Placement students Ranier Maria Rilke's classic, *To A Young Poet*—a hugely inspiring little book for any artist or writer. My copy is heavily underlined; I re-read its wisdom as often as possible. A young poet asks Rilke for advice on becoming a writer. Rilke responds honestly, passionately, with words that go straight to my heart:

Nobody can counsel and help you, nobody. There is only one single way. Go into yourself. Search for the reason that bids you write; find out whether it is spreading out its roots in the deepest places of your heart, acknowledge to yourself whether you would have to die if it were denied you to write. This above all—ask yourself in the stillest hour of your night: must I write? Delve into yourself for a deep answer. And if this should be affirmative, if you may meet this earnest question with a strong and simple 'I must,' then build your life according to this necessity; your life even into its most indifferent and slightest hour must be a sign of this urge and a testimony to it. Then draw near to Nature. Then try, like some first human being, to say what you see and experience and love and lose (Rilke, To A Young Poet, p. 19).

Like the male counterpart of Virginia Woolf, it seems to me, Rilke calls us to find our inner sanctuary where we are alone with our art. He writes what I have been learning, that *in the deepest and most important things, we are unutterably alone* (Rilke, p.23). Rilke reinforces what I already know: an artist craves solitude because it is the birthplace of creativity.

Works of art are of an infinite loneliness…Everything is gestation and then bringing forth. To let each impression and each germ of a feeling come to completion wholly in itself, in the dark, in the inexpressible, the unconscious, beyond the reach of one's own intelligence, and await with deep humility and patience the birth-hour of a new clarity: that alone is living the artist's life: in understanding as in creating (Rilke, p.29-30).

As I assign his words to my students I am reminded I must be ever vigilant in listening to my inner voice, must "be attentive to that which rises up in you and set it above everything that you observe about you. What goes on in your innermost being is worthy of your whole love" (Rilke, 46-47). I honor Rilke's admonitions and feel what he describes.

But I struggle with the responsibilities of *ordinary* life—my children's needs, home duties, meals, bills, constant cleaning and all the etcetera any Shakespeare's sister knows—and how to still have time leftover for art-making or writing. Would a *female* Rilke have written the same advice? Would she have had *time* to even *write down* her advice to a young poetess?!

382 | Gwendolyn Evans Caldwell

I read Thomas Moore's *Care of the Soul* and learn what everything else I'm reading teaches: that self-knowledge is the soul's foundation. Moore says what I already know, that if we are not caring for our soul daily through spiritual practice, such as sitting still, prayer, or meditation, we may grow empty, feel meaningless or depressed.

Sitting still is not easily attained, but I do my best. Most unlikely, four days in a row I throw the same *I Ching* message: *revolution, change*. I turn 50 in a couple weeks. Half a century! There's a change! My periods have stopped—almost like clockwork—the beginning of menopause. Perhaps because of prayer and meditation, this change comes to me symptomless. Change, ever with me, always has something to teach me.

I read *Creative Visualization*, which I have read before, and other books which inspire my meditation. I apply affirmations to my family, Custis Lee, world peace, my next mammogram which I will learn remains unchanged from August's, my paintings selling, our condo selling, my writing, and my Achilles tendon; I have been wearing supportive hiking boots daily, regardless of my outfit, for several months. The Achilles situation is strikingly healed— as if it never had been and in spite of a doctor's dire predictions. Though no longer a Christian Scientist, I maintain my health the way I always have, by prayer, having no faith in *materia medica*. My paintings sell, so do the condos. I even find time to write more. The power of prayer is constant.

Advice of writer Judy Blume makes my journal: "…until you pull it out of your own heart it really doesn't work." And Erma Bombeck: "That's the way to write—being absolutely straightforward and saying exactly what you mean without trying to impress anyone." Honest words. I write my poems or prose over and over until I get the clearest meaning. But writing is not easy after a full day of teaching—for besides my regular classes, I teach *after* school adult art classes which prevent my coming home to husband, daughter, dog, cats and duties as quickly as I'd like. Laundry and dinner prep await. Shakespeare's sister may live in us but it is tough work letting her out!

In the evening, Charissa interrupts my poem-writing to read her 5-paragraph essay to me, due tomorrow. My husband swears at Bill Gates once more from his computer upstairs and my hand shakes until he stops. It is quiet for a few seconds and I get back into that writing zone where poetic images run, play, and hide. But then Bill comes downstairs to tell me about his computer glitch that nearly ruined his hand-outs for tomorrow. I listen; and the poetry disappears. He runs back up to work. Now I am alone except for Oreo and Butterscotch, our two cats cruising the back ridge of the sofa. My daughter now in bed, missing her cats, calls them in their native tongue: "Meow…Meow…Meow…" Guitar chords waft down from above (Bill has distracted himself from technical difficulties). Cat calls continue. My poem has given up for the night. I listen patiently for the quiet to come again. Suddenly the music stops—my husband has probably found a book to read. The cats have answered Charissa's call and are gone to her bed. I am alone. Precious silence. My pencil puts down a few rhyming verbs. Then the phone rings and I am the logical one to answer it. It is Nathan in Oregon needing some advice and money. When the call is over, I look down at my slippers and think about laundry. I realize that the teacher's meeting that ran so late today took away my early evening laundry time and I have no clean underwear for tomorrow. I look at my watch: 10:45. Might as well do a full load. Before I sort clothes, I look in on my daughter now asleep, two cats curled up cozily by her neck. It is a picture I might paint if I had the time. My husband, too, is now in bed, snoring, an open book on his chest, his glasses and light still on. I remove his glasses and turn off the light before starting the washer. I walk back to my legal pad with its bits of poem scattered outside the lines. I sit still for a minute, but the muse is gone. I listen to the breathing of my sleeping family, as I had listened earlier to their noise and needs. I hold them in thought now, loving them all, and put myself to bed.

Dark shadows gather in days ahead, but I row toward God (as poet Anne Sexton might say). Through each black storm, I cling to what I trust—the God-Rock found in the abyss one night but also known to me since my first breath—as I hum the words of an old hymn I've posted above my kitchen sink: *No storm can shake my inmost calm while to that rock I'm clinging, Since Love is lord of heaven and earth how can I keep from singing?*

sixteen

In the Valley of Darkness and Dreams

Dark snakes hide in tall grasses but I fend my way through dense foliage to pick Delphiniums. When the snakes stir, I take my bouquet inside. I return with my daughter who wants to pick her own Delphiniums. I lead her to gardens far from snakes. Nevertheless, one slithers toward us, and coils to strike. I quickly grab its rattling tail and squeeze tightly to protect my daughter; oddly, its tail becomes its head. I am bitten and feel the poison's hot liquid flow into my body. "I knew this would happen," I tell myself. When I wake I still feel the heat.

Summer 1994 I am not in New Harmony. The previous summer I'd reunited there with Dad, then wrote and painted in the Poet's House for two blissful weeks. But this summer I teach outdoor watercolor classes in Memphis, finish painting my studio, make bookshelves for Charissa's room—white with hunter green walls, her choices. In July, Bill and I take Charissa to Boston to visit colleges and her grandfather. In August, Bill and I drive to Tacoma, Washington, to see Nathan, working construction there for the summer. En route, Bill and I hike in the Badlands and Glacier National Park and follow the Oregon Trail.

When we moved into our house in June 1993, Charissa and I began after-school walks together, sharing our thoughts and dreams. We continue the practice throughout 1994. One day she tells me she dreamed her dad drives up in front of her friend's house where she's playing. His eyes are swollen and red from crying as he tells her his mother died (though in reality at this time his mom is alive). We conclude I may have been the mother he lost.

In a dream I share with Charissa, I am roaming institutional buildings, crawling in blocked off corridors because a terrorist group has taken over (this is six years before Columbine, eight years before 9/11, and nineteen years before Newtown!). When I get outside, I see people creep in the grass, so as not to be targets. But I don't understand the danger and proceed across an open field eager to reach home. I am shot by a masked gunman who kicks me to make sure I am dead. After he leaves, Tom, one of Calvary Church's Journey team leaders, appears and I get up and walk home. The dream teaches me I need less institutional chaos and more spiritual peace in my life.

In another dream, I own a condo—old world, quaint, textured, a garden only I can enter. But I cannot locate it or my key. I roam common areas cluttered with people, looking everywhere, searching up and down stairs, under archways, behind bougainvillea on Tuscan balconies, to no avail. An Asian man who speaks no English shouts to me from the street that he knows where my condo is, acting out his message as if doing charades. Without locating my home, I wake up just in time to get ready for school.

In another dream, I own an overgrown property—house, art studio, barn, even a pig shack! Bill, Charissa and I had just moved in; boxes and piles surround us. Charissa is about 5 and dozens of her friends are here for some creative project, giggling, running in all directions. A reporter comes to shoot photos of my studio but it's locked; he never speaks to me. He publishes an article stating my gallery is a travesty, nor am I included in his map of galleries. Tom and Sandra (real life art friends) appear in the dream to say this will end my art career.

In another dream, I'm in my house (not any I've actually owned) preparing for my mother's arrival (though in real life my mother is dead) when a stranger, comes asking for work. Out of compassion I hire her, give her a room, feed her, but she doesn't work. I ask her to make a cake I will ice with caramel frosting, my mother's favorite, but she doesn't. Meanwhile, a gang of teenage boys with machine guns and knives takes over the woods where my three dogs play (dogs I once had in real life). Worried for my dogs, I call them inside and comfort them, while readying for Mom's arrival. The stranger I'd hired asks me to wrap and mail a package for her. I take it to the post office, frustrated she ordered me when *I* employed *her*. Busy caring for everyone in this dream, I wake exhausted.

Jason phones to tell me *his* dream. "You died." he says. "I run frantically through your house looking for you—there's no furniture, just abstract paintings on every wall, with poisonous snakes and cats wandering. I can't find you. Finally, I find your nightgown, but not you, and screaming, I run outside, down a hillside to a river, beside which are grave markers. Gramps' and Grandma's names are on headstones; an empty plot is next to them, where you'd been, but aren't. Someone says you've been moved to a new plot, away from your parents because you shouldn't be buried beside them."

Amy Tan, in *The Hundred Secret Senses* says "We dream to give ourselves hope." From August 1993 through 1997 my quantity of dreams suggests I need hope. Certainly the hope that dreams provide enables us to survive. Without dreams we are at a loss. It is as Rabbi Wolpe says, "Failure is a loss of dreams" (David Wolpe, *Making Loss Matter*, p. 71).

In January 1994, juxtaposing dreams and reality, I merge poetry and paintings, into a box series based on women's studies themes. I create these artists' books from found object containers—biscuit tins, wooden cigar boxes, recipe boxes, bullet boxes, old typewriter ribbon cases, even metal mail boxes—which I distress, paint, and transform. Inside each I place a poem written for each themed container. These art objects become communal when the purchaser stores her own poetry along side mine. Rooted in a book-making course I took my last year at RISD, my series deals with opposite aspects of box: being boxed in and keeping precious treasures safe. I am devoted to this body of work.

The regimented, narcissistic, bureaucratic world of academia can be a kind of box. But I step outside of it and teach the way I make art—passionately, creatively, enthusiastically, with my whole being. Even so, my desire to leave Custis Lee grows, as my journal reveals: *Some teachers live through their students' lives because they don't have any of their own, but the teacher who is also an artist is burdened by lack of creative solitude—how to give one's all to inspire others, yet, keep ones' own creativity?!*

Solitude arrives with February, during an unusually cold week-long ice storm that hits Memphis. I lie awake in the pitch-black listening to the eerie sound of old trees cracking and limbs falling, praying none strike our roof. By morning we've lost two birches and a neighbor's tree has fallen in the cul de sac. School is cancelled for a week. I love the free time the electric outage affords, preventing chores—but, happily, I can read and write by flashlight. I cook over Bill's tiny camp stove and we eat by candlelight. The dark stillness feels like homecoming. But after days of doing nothing hi-tech and reading and sleeping his fill, Bill comes down with a case of cabin fever—a clangor in the darkness.

The following week I write about another kind of dark: my inability to provide financially as much as I'd like for my children—especially the boys at college (I did not ask for alimony). Free writing becomes a kind of talking to God to help me delineate issues rather than ruminate. Prayer by pen I call it.

I've journeyed a wilderness path but manna isn't coming... God, I have lost friends, family, things, and survived, but tonight I need solutions. I want this house to be a true home for Charissa, where she can bring friends. She needs a dresser, a chair and a functioning computer. The dining room needs carpet, the hall needs painting, our bedroom needs curtains, and Bill's office, a phone. I want the squirrels out of the attic, the toilet fixed, and to pay more toward the boys' college. God, show me my path.

My path becomes clearer when February passes and March arrives. I discover Natalie Goldberg's book, *Long Quiet Highway*, having loved her *Writing Down the Bones* years ago. I write in my journal: *"I know every bit of her highway! I yearn to find my place, too... Leaving teaching seems imminent. I'd like to walk into the school office, as Goldberg did, and eloquently quit!"* The bug is in my ear for future action.

Yet, I love teaching. It's the bureaucracy and administration that frustrates and tires teachers. Weeks later when I take another group of students to New Harmony, so glorious is our time, I know I must teach. I love my students. I write in my journal: *Teaching involves full spiritual listening as much as Christian Science healing work or making art.*

One night after washing dinner dishes, I rag the dining room walls a blend of three colors of paint to suggest old-world plaster, and concoct a textured mixture to apply over hall walls, transforming peeling wallpaper. When I'm done, I decide hall and dining room look spectacular. Since its only midnight, I move to the kitchen to blend ingredients for hand-made paper to take to school tomorrow for my eighth grade class. I step in my studio to grab an assignment for my AP seniors and to glance at my artwork I'll display this weekend when my studio will be part of a public tour of a dozen Memphis artists' studios. Not until my head hits my pillow an hour later do I realize I'm exhausted.

April 5, 1994, I write in my journal:

> *Writing and painting can no longer come at the <u>end</u> of the day when I'm tired. I long to let a poem get past incubation...TIME! I'm a teacher—but also an artist. If I cannot pursue spiritual interests I will remain exhausted, for we are exhausted by what we don't do— not by what we do. I've not been fully following my bliss, captive in a box I somehow allow. Box is the perfect image for my art. Is there no outside the box? This box, this coffin, shuts out the light. I close my eyes and through the wooden lid I see above me people throwing down dirt; I watch it fly in my face. Buried, I rest in peace.*

Four days later, bounding energy eradicates all darkness. Bill and I wake early for an array of activities—odd since we tarred the roof leak until 1 AM. We visit Brooks Art Museum to see the *Nabis* exhibition, among my favorite painters, then, stop at the main library which we miss since our move to the suburbs, on to Wiles-Smith drugstore for chocolate shakes (like old times), then to a plant sale at Dixon Gardens. At Home Depot we purchase two new unfinished rockers for the front porch—something without which no Memphis home is complete. I paint them a thirties color—between aqua and olive. I run to Seesels for the week's marketing while Bill starts his routine nap. While he sleeps, I put away groceries, make a cake, and plant all the plants we just bought—I will have a wonderful English garden in a month or so! I paint flowerpots to coordinate with the rockers and when they dry I put geraniums, marigolds and begonias in them, placing the potted plants strategically on the front porch and around the back stoop. I try out one of the freshly painted rockers listening to the neighbor's wind chimes after swinging on the front yard tree swing that Jason made for me. Bill wakes, comes out with his banjo and sits in the other rocker, and begins pickin' and frailin,' Scruggs style, "Cripple Creek" and "This Little Light of Mine." He switches to guitar to play my favorite, "Statesborough Blues." Surprise, our Samoyed, sits at our feet while Oreo investigates the new garden and Butterscotch cleans herself in the sun on my lap. Bill and I rest in the quiet joy we share.

I go in and chop green and white onions, garlic, peppers, carrots, celery, lettuce, cheese, and spinach for a Southwestern dinner, Bill's favorite. After dinner and walk, we read. Bill falls asleep before10:00, but I am awake, saturated by the beauty of today, and engrossed in reading.

One of several philosophical books I found in the library today, is *Man's Search for Meaning* by Viktor Frankl, psychiatrist and Auschwitz survivor. Frankl teaches that suffering is essential to a meaningful life, that there is meaning in darkness, and transforming darkness into beauty redeems it. I believe his words, try to do this in my ordinary living, and I add Frankl to my favorites:

> *If there is a meaning in life at all, then there must be a meaning in suffering. Suffering is an ineradicable part of life… Without suffering and death human life cannot be complete… The way in which a man accepts his fate and all the suffering it entails, the way in which he takes up his cross, gives him ample opportunity— even under the most difficult circumstances—to add a deeper meaning to his life … The greatest courage is the courage to suffer* (Viktor Frankl, Man's Search for Meaning, p. 86).

Frankl describes how the beautiful thought of his wife (whose death he is unaware of) *transfixes* him, lifts him out of the horrible conditions in which he finds himself, something I, too, have found love and beauty can do. He sees that "love is the ultimate and the highest goal to which man can aspire:"

> *The salvation of man is through love…a man who has nothing left in this world still may know bliss, be it only for a brief moment, in the contemplation of his beloved. In a position of utter desolation, when man cannot express himself in positive action, when his only achievement may consist in enduring his sufferings in the right way—an honorable way—in such a position man can, through loving contemplation of the image he carries of his beloved, achieve fulfillment* (Frankl, p.49).

My second book of the night is *The Hungering Dark* by Frederick Buechner, a Pulitzer-finalist theologian Doug Bailey frequently quotes. Along with Buechner's *The Sacred Journey*, *The Hungering Dark* uplifts me, for this writer knowns first hand dark despair and the way out of it. A third Buechner book, *Listening to your Life* touches even my understanding of *hiraeth* and home:

the Kingdom of God is what we...hunger for... even when we don't know its name or realize that it's what we're starving to death for. The kingdom of God is where our best dreams come from and our truest prayers...The Kingdom of God is where we belong. It is home, and whether we realize it or not...we are all of us homesick for it (Frederick Buechner, *Listening to Your Life*, p. 305-306).

Later I will discover his book *The Longing for Home* and once again see our connection as seekers of true home.

In May I re-read Joseph Campbell's *Hero with a Thousand Faces* that I'd used in preparing my Master's thesis. This leads me to shamanism. I find Morton Kelsey's *Transcend: A Guide to the Spiritual Quest* in Calvary's library and learn that shamans, a unique society of spiritual men and women thought to have originated in Siberia, exist in various forms in most cultures. They know the secret of breaking through one plane to another. Intense in religious devotion, the shaman is a guide and guardian of the soul who combines masculine and feminine qualities and functions as intermediary between the people of his culture and the spiritual world. Wounded through spiritual crisis himself, he is willing to suffer and return as a healer for other wounded beings. On his journey he crosses a symbolic bridge, experiences rites and trials leading to mystical realities. "Bridge," a frequent shamanistic motif, represents a dangerous passage or tense situation about the reconciliation of opposites—day and night, light and dark, heaven and earth. The shaman learns that *out of brokenness comes wholeness*. My "personal shamans", Buechner, Frankl and Campbell, teach me how to live in the dark. I write in my journal: *"I want to be a shaman when I grow up!"*

April 25, 1994, Nathan calls to say he's writing poetry—my football-playing, soccer-playing, skate-boarding, snow-boarding son! He reads me *There's No More Dog on the Porch*, a poem generated by his dreams. His poem tells of walking by a neon-green house every day where a yellow dog is always on the porch. Just seeing the dog each day means Nathan will have a great day. One morning it is raining and the dog is gone and Nathan has a bad day. The poem speaks of loss and change—losing friends, fun, youth's adventure. Nathan tells me about his nightmares, in each one he dies in a different horrible way. We talk about finding meaning in dreams. I read Nathan a few lines from Frankl, adding, I will pray for him. I may be dealing with my own dark, but the mother bear in me still fights for her cubs—even if this one's 6-feet tall! By his next phone call, Nathan's nightmares have ended.

On rare nights, I have nightmares of my own. In one, I cross a bridge, that popular shamanistic symbol, as a headless horseman in flowing black cape and gloves wildly gallops by, nearly scooping me up. His head—only a skull—pops up, staring fiercely at me. I back away and wake. Intuition tells me the rider symbolizes death. I decide to see a counselor to learn about this dream. I do not watch horror films, never have, so if these dark dreams have a source, I want to know it.

My first encounter with counseling was in 1989 prior to separating from John. Learning of my potential divorce, parents of a friend of Charissa's encouraged me to see a counselor they knew. Then, I felt myself an errant Christian Scientist in visiting a counselor, but he informed me in our only session that I was "many women" and the "Amazon" and "Aphrodite" parts of me needed to be let out. He explained I'd been the "Nurturer" to the neglect of other aspects of womanhood.

This experience, plus Sylvan's dream work with me at RISD, prepared me to say yes in 1994 to an artist-friend's suggestion I visit her Jungian analyst regarding my headless horseman dream. Having read Carl Jung, important to me since RISD, and several books by Jungian analysts, such as John Sanford's *Healing for Wholeness,* I felt comfortable enough.

As I relay my dream, the analyst suggests the rider crossing the bridge may reflect an unconscious concern about cancer or death. The bridge may represent a life transition, given the many changes I have undergone. He amazes me with further insights. I make another appointment for myself, a colleague and two friends to go together, sharing the doctor's exorbitant fee. My friends' dreams are fascinatingly complex and I let them use the hour rather than ask about my own. But through these two sessions, I learn dreams come to bring to light what we are ignoring. Dreams have purpose. Only the dreamer can decipher the exact meaning, for their symbols are one's own particular iconography.

Sometimes we don't need dreams; ordinary life teaches us—similar to what the white-clad man in the bookstore told me about the I Ching: *eventually one doesn't need to throw sticks or pennies to know the future; it's obvious in the ordinary.* A highway sign can be a message. Often, a book opens to the exact words needed. Or a stranger says precisely what one needs to hear. And on May 10, 1994, while dining in a Chinese restaurant, a mere fortune in my cookie—*"Joys are often the shadows cast by sorrows"*—sums up my life at the time.

School clamors with intense end-of-the-year demands, grading, reports, inventory, extra responsibilities and meetings, meetings, meetings. I feel confined, stored, lidded, contained—and angry—a roar against years of duties and quiet obedience, of living up to high expectations, both those placed upon me and my own. And I wonder, rather randomly, why I've always lived in cities chosen by men, always served men, always done what they expected. Am I thinking of my father? John? Bill? I loved all three. No it isn't the men personally in my life I am feeling anger toward. It is anger toward the patriarchy. For men who make a dollar for every 75 cents women earn. For men who run our government, monopolize power, determine how things will be, take us for granted, assume we will cook and clean while they have leisure. I am all women everywhere as I jot down these words for a future poem: *Maybe the nervous breakdown doesn't come to 'the mad woman in the attic' at 3 AM, but at 10 AM when the sun is shining and her lipstick's on straight.* I never finish the poem. Being a woman I haven't the time.

In July 1994, Bill, Charissa, a friend of hers, and I visit Dad in Boston over the fourth, watching the city's spectacular fireworks from his high-rise windows, while the Boston Pops plays on his TV. We also spend a few days with Dad on Cape Cod at a cottage belonging to one of his students. Bill and I have the *perfect* bedroom: three sides open to the sea. While here, beaches of my past roll into every soothing shoreline walk.

Jayne, Dad's executive secretary and friend, joins us. Jayne, a couple years older than I, is my father's best friend since Mom's death. Slim, petite, dark-eyed, with shoulder length salt and pepper hair that swings when she walks, Jayne is always fashionable, often in Saks suits—or on the Cape, in white slacks and crisp striped shirt, a fuchsia cardigan wrapped about her shoulders. Dad's *confidante*, companion, and assistant in his Christian Science practice, Jayne brightens Dad's days in new ways with her appreciation of beauty. She sees that his apartment has fresh flowers and is well decorated, encourages him to attend a concert or eat out more than he might, and helps him with his wardrobe as well as his filing, phone calls, and students.

At 7 AM, Dad and Jayne sit on a bench facing the bay, reading their Bible Lesson together, then walk the shore engrossed in Christian Science talk. After lunch, they disappear—off to buy Dad some shirts. At dinner, we watch Jayne share bites with Glenn, as if the rest of us are not here. Bill and I sneak smiles at each other. It is apparent to everyone on this trip that Dad loves Jayne. Later, Dad tells me he thinks my brother—in the midst of divorce—should marry Jayne. She is not Rich's type—older, too stylish, high maintenance—besides, Rich has another agenda, as Jayne may herself. Eventually, Dad admits his love for Jayne to me, but worries how it would look to his students if he asked her to marry him, she 30 years his junior. He asks me to be his John Alden (as in the Pilgrim legend where John Alden speaks to Priscilla Mullens on behalf of Miles Standish, when John himself loves her) and fish out any interest Jayne may have. I learn she loves who Dad is and his work, but marriage is not her desire. For the rest of his life, Jayne and Dad remain a good working team.

When we return to Memphis, Charissa stays with her dad, while Bill and I drive 7,000 miles out West and back. Bill and I excel at road trips!—playing music—Woody Guthrie, the Beetles etc., laughing, reading out loud, discussing every topic from philosophy to US tariff policy. We visit national parks and museums, hike, discover new things together, sleep under the stars, and adore each other. He even lets me stop and paint *en route*, while he cozies up with a good book or pillow or keeps crowds at bay that form to watch me paint. Once as I was painting in a Colorado Ghost Town, he turned to spectators to remark, patting his chest, "It does a teacher proud to see his student do so well!" Bill kids, too, suggesting we call Bill Gates to volunteer to travel for him, since he's too busy; we'll send him postcards of our adventures—this, of course, would be a full time occupation and we'd have to quit our school jobs. Such are our fantasies on the road!

We stop first in Chicago to see Bill's sister, Lib, and the dream-like Redon exhibit at the Chicago Art Institute, which my brother had phoned to tell me I *must* see. He was right. Then we drive through Iowa corn fields, the Dakotas, and Glacier National Park.

We drive through a Western dreamscape unlike anything I'd ever seen before: rippling rock formations and changing colors of South Dakota's Badlands and Wild Sage Wilderness. I'm convinced wilderness is my place. In spite of this state's extreme winters, I could live here. We drive for hours on rough back roads, passing a huge slithering rattle snake, a multitude of popping prairie dogs, swift cottontail rabbits, deer, bison, and antelope, to reach a remote rim of a grassy prairie, some 40 miles from the visitor's center, where we hike to a camping spot almost too spiritual to speak of. But I do speak of it in my journal and art, for the place touches my soul. We pitch no tent, as is our habit, so we can see the sky and feel the air. Other campers' sites are tiny dots of green, red and blue, far away midst the swaying grasses. From my sleeping bag in the early morning, I watch the sun rise before anyone else is awake. Not a camper stirs nor lights a lantern. The prairie, beyond, the sky above, seem endless. The full moon over my shoulder greets the sun peaking out pink in front of me. I sit in buffalo grass and survey the circular vista in perfect silence. I have never been happier. Sounds travel far—the occasional call of crow or coyote. Otherwise, the quiet is heavy with the past. I imagine an Indian hunting buffalo under the same moon and sun—before the white man came and took away his life. I think I hear his song. Bill emerges from his sleeping bag beside mine and we begin our oatmeal ritual.

We have been living out of our cooler—Swiss cheese, tabouli, broccoli, shrimp, tuna, and chicken salads, blue corn tortilla chips, tomatoes, bananas, grapes, cereal, yogurt, whole grain bread, and peanut butter—planned and prepared before I left home.

We decide to splurge and spend a night at a B&B in La Grande, Oregon, and visit the nearby Oregon Trail museum. I purchase books about women who traversed the Oregon Trail and read aloud their stories as Bill drives. We are both blissfully happy.

Watching the Western landscape as we drive, I imagine what it was like in 1850 to cross this rugged land: She is out there still— that lonely woman, whose husband leaves her for business hundreds of miles from their isolated "soddy" homestead, leaves her alone for months with all survival chores on her shoulders. Their journey out to Oregon had been cruel enough, but the isolation made women go mad. I thought I saw her one day—the woman who chased after far-away trains, just to hear their whistle and be reminded she was not alone. Another day, I thought I saw the one whose children died in her arms as she waited, still holding their dead bodies for days, until her husband returned. And the independent one who bought her own land and made it work—she is there too. They are all out there still. I hear their voices when the wind howls.

In Tacoma, we stay briefly in the house Nathan and his friends are renting for the summer. He and Mariner, his buddy since Prin days, take us to Defiance Park for a glorious day hike through tall pines. I make homemade bread and pizza, enchiladas, and salad for the guys. Bill plays guitar with them. Nathan, Bill and I hike and spend the night at Cape Lookout Campground on the beautiful Oregon Coast. August 2, 1994 we hike and camp on Mt. Rainier, our tarp fastened between two huge trees, underneath our sleeping bags lie on a ground cloth over soft pine needles. I collect wood for a small fire on the grill. Where trees and sky are all you have—that's the best! I give Bill a hat I bought for him at REI, for tomorrow he turns 42.

School, and the hectic pace of another year, begins when we return to Memphis.

A former student visits campus and greets Bill with a showy public display of affection, an-over-the-top hug and kiss. She'd phoned him at home to tell him she was coming to see him and another long time teacher told him, in front of me, "she can't wait to see you!" A colleague who has been at Custis Lee longer than I, whispers in my ear: "Bill has always been a big flirt!" This does not comfort me. I did not know this when we met—was his attentiveness to me merely flirtatious? Bill needs fans. A teacher once told me, "Bill craves attention." In a weak moment, I confide to my journal: *Bill believes he can have it all—capture young maidens and have a wife cooking and cleaning at home.* Even then, I knew better, but I wasn't listening to me, didn't tap into that divine voice within. No, I was letting self-doubt rule, as women often do. In time I would learn depression's triggers and see how ludicrous it was to doubt my husband's love. But not right away.

Bill and this former student take a long lunch together—for the rest of the afternoon, in fact, beyond the school day. I am not invited, nor am I even introduced. After school I drop Charissa at her Dad's and return home and enter a severe depression.

I write, but stop for tears. Neither Buechner nor Frankl help. Nor Teresa nor Julian. My mind becomes dark. I enter my bedroom closet—a place of joyful childhood play, comforting in some odd way, like entering a womb. I close the door and curl up on the floor, keeping the light off. I have never done this before. I am still there when Bill arrives, when dinnertime comes and goes.

Bill calls me. But it is as if I cannot hear him, as if I am in a cement tunnel far away. Finally he finds me in the closet, but I do not want to be found. He wonders about dinner and why I am in the closet. I say nothing. I have no voice. I am in some dark place that is not where reality is. I stay in the closet listening to him walk to the kitchen and fix the only meal he ever prepares: popcorn and a peanut butter and jelly sandwich. I almost do not exist. I half-heartedly look for a glimmer of light but there is only a bit of God the size of a sequin shining. A heavy lid is on top of me, closed tight. I do not care if I get out. The darkness is deeper, different than the abyss five years ago in my white apartment when God's warmth came. This darkness is sinister. It wants to keep me with it forever.

Bill finishes his sandwich. I hear him put his plate in the sink and walk to our bedroom and open the closet door; but I am not there anymore. I crept out to a corner of the dining room where he'd never think to look. Still mentally curled up, I sob silently so he won't notice. I am good at quiet. No one can see or hear me. If I am very, very quiet maybe I can disappear and he won't find me at all. Ten minutes pass. Then a strange thing happens. From around the dining room entrance, a plastic baggie filled with Nestle's chocolate Crunch, bounces on the end of a stick, like a cat toy! This dancing incongruity flits back and forth across the dining room entry as if a puppet performing some hilarious ballet by some unseen hand for some unseen cat audience! I find myself suddenly laughing. How can I not?! This is too *funny*! Two hands, as if disembodied, clutch the side wall. Then my husband's smiling face pops sideways beside them, just before he jumps out in front of me and drops the bag of chocolate in my lap. I am still laughing. Instantly this humorous gimmick pulls me from the depths! I marvel to this day at the power of humor, for where I had gone was very far away indeed.

Bill has little to say about his lunch date; it was nothing to him. I tell him it triggered my depressive state, but he says I worry too much and dismisses my fears.

October 2, 1994, the day before my birthday, I vent in my journal: *Tomorrow I will be 51 years old and no one will care. What's one birthday more or less, anyway? Everything is process; destination is nothing. But sometimes, life seems a disappointing dream. The trouble with having high standards is that life is always a disappointment.* I copy this last sentence on a note card, pin it to my bulletin board—next to another line I wrote the week before: *TRUTH: Half of it is none of it.*

Journal-venting continues: *I need nature, but I'm surrounded by ticky-tacky houses repeated on every cove without creativity—each more aesthetically tasteless than the last. My house doesn't reflect me—in spite of Herculean efforts. Teaching takes all, art loses... I meet everyone's needs but my own. Sometimes I think I want the life of a hermit or sage—would there be days when I'd be sorry? If I chose to live on nothing, some days would I want something? If I found solitude would I be lonely? Tomorrow will not be a happy birthday.*

Too busy with teaching to ruminate for long, I eagerly create a National Gallery project for the middle school, plan and take a trip to DC to complete it, enthusiastically work on my adult women studies course, a constant joy, and continue on Calvary's Journey team. Life is full and happy. Whatever got me down disappears. Is it because I am reading *Womanspirit Rising, War Against Women,* and *Women and Self-Esteem?*

January 13, 1995—it *would* be the 13th!—while walking with Bill, discussing our shared anger over various school situations and policies, I fall on wet pavement. In the flash of falling, I think, "No longer a Christian Scientist, I can't ethically rely on a system I left! This is *real* pavement and it's going to hurt like hell!" It does. My arm blows up the size of an elephant's leg. Bill insists on taking me to the hospital, though I want to wait to see if the inflammation will go down. I look up inflammation in the dictionary and discover one definition is anger. Precisely what I was engaged in when I fell.

At the hospital's emergency room, I am told I have broken a bone in my right hand. I cannot write, type, cook, teach, paint, dress myself, nor lift my arm higher than my hip for the next four months, even though I see a doctor and a specialist. Everyone has a different theory. My whole arm is put in a cast for six weeks (which later I am told is the wrong thing, causing a frozen shoulder and Reflex Sympathetic Dystrophy). I am given a cortisone shot I do not want; it does nothing. A handless artist, for along with my injured right hand, my over-worked left hand has been put in a splint, I take 2 weeks off school. When I return, I try to teach, paint and draw handless.

After the cast is off, I have physical therapy for several months. Though I have a high tolerance for pain, I find the therapy excruciating. I take my Bible with me but cry, not so much from pain—which I am never able to rate when asked—but for the spiritual desert in which I find myself. This is the first time I have relied on the medical profession and I find it unsympathetic, inaccurate, and confusing. And, worse, I feel I have forsaken God. Once more, my journal becomes the repository for frustration, though I can barely scribble with my left hand. I note that healing has existed in all cultures and times, is universal and available to all—not the domain of one denomination. I take "Christ Jesus healed" as my mantra and expect healing.

I find *The Healing Path: A Soul Approach to Illness* by Marc Ian Barasch which makes the startlingly relevant point:

> *In shamanic initiations, a symbolic dismemberment of the body*—[like the loss of hands?!]— *is a necessary prelude to spiritual reconstitution….The underlying agenda of the healing sacrifice is the surrender of whatever impedes the greater stream of our life: We must relinquish a part of ourselves, perhaps an entire pattern of identity, which we have cherished and clung to even after it has become an obstacle to our growth. We may be asked to face a painful truth, heal an ancient wound, realize an unexpressed potential, or change a relationship… Sacrifice is a word that comes from the Latin meaning sacred and to make. That which must be given up, far from being discarded, is the very thing in need of transformation and renewal. Heralds of illness may, if we pay them sufficient heed, announce the nature, origins, treatment and psychological significance of illness all at once.*

Wow! How perfectly this fits my situation! I am reminded of Frankl's statement that there is *purpose* to suffering, for what I am going through is teaching me that that which I must relinquish is what needs transformation.

I set out to find the purpose of my handless situation. One of my adult women's studies students suggests I re-read the *Handless Maiden's Tale* in

Women Who Run with the Wolves by Clarissa Pinkola Estes, Ph.D., one of the books in my *Herstory 9-Piece* bibliography. Literally a *handless* maiden, I obey.

The tale is about a young girl whose father is tricked by the devil into chopping off her hands. She *cries* and *wanders*—two acts which Estes explains *protect* her. Immediately I realize I have been doing both all my life, that somehow these two acts have protected me. I also see the significance of the father/daughter relationship. I understand my tears better when I read that they are made by the *soul*, that "tears are part of the mending of rips in the psyche where energy has leaked and leaked away" (Clarissa Pink Estes, *Women Who Run With the Wolves*, 404). Wandering is "a resurrection into a new life and a death in the old" (Estes, p. 411). My wandering has involved many moves and changes. Estes explains endurance leads to strength. I understand this even better today, for approaching 70 I now know what a strong woman life has made me.

Estes says it sometimes takes her seven months to teach this tale because it "pulls us into a world that lies far below the roots of trees" and contains "material for a woman's entire life process," giving us "the key journeys of a woman's psyche" (Estes, p. 388).

I easily relate to the maiden in the tale who becomes handless in surrendering to her father:

> *In cutting off her hands, the father deepens the descent, hastens the* dissolution, *the difficult loss of all one's dearest values, which means everything, the loss of vantage point, the loss of horizon lines, the loss of one's bearings about what one believes and for what reason…The old self is gone, and the deep self, the naked self, is the powerful wanderer* (Estes, p. 413).

Like the maiden, I've been this naked wanderer in order to become my self, and, as do hers, eventually, my hands return to me.

How do the hands return? "As we practice the deep instinctive knowing about all manner of things we are learning over a lifetime, our hands return to us, the hands of our womanhood" (Estes, p. 449). It is *using* the deep *knowing within* that will give me back my hands.

From Estes and other reading, ideas flood my mind. Eventually, I have eleven boxes of note cards on this and related topics. Wounds of accident, disease, and psychological trauma are teaching tools, windows to the soul. As I wrote in my notes, Campbell says:

If a life is going outwardly contrary to its inward need, nature will not permit this disaster without making some effort to correct the situation" for *"the familiar life horizon has been outgrown; the old concepts, ideals and emotional patterns no longer fit... the passing of a threshold is at hand...marking a new period, a new stage, in the biography...Our wound is the place where the Self finds entry into us. The wound is also the treasure...Body symptoms are not just to be healed, repressed or cured. They are potentially meaningful and purposeful conditions. They could be the beginning of fantastic phases of life, or they could bring one amazingly close to the center of existence...the symptom may be the part of you that is trying to grow....*

My reading encourages letting go of disturbing school issues. While many teachers complain, some leave, others are fired, I focus on what I love doing with my students. Buechner reminds me to heal and I apply this to school as well as myself: *we are to be above all else healers, and that means...we are also to be healed because God knows you and I are in as much need of healing as anybody else, and being healed and healing go hand in hand.*

Healing is rooted in love. In May, I receive an invitation to demonstrate this once more. My cousin Ann calls to invite us to a luncheon celebration of her parents' 50th wedding anniversary, June 3, 1995, at her home in Ohio. Her parents, Uncle Bill and Aunt Ruthie, are among those who opposed my leaving the church and who perceived my mother's death to be my fault. Neither had come to Bill's and my wedding (Uncle Bill's gift to us was a note saying he was donating to my mother's Christian Science association). Though I love my cousin Ann, I can't imagine attending this event.

"Ann, do you *really* want me there? Your parents don't like me and haven't spoken to me in over 4 years."

"I know, Lynnie, but *I* want you there! This has gone on long enough, and they can be damned if they don't like your being there! This situation needs to be *healed!*" I've never known Ann to swear and she adores her parents. I see she really wants me there and I need to go—to support Ann's healing attempt, if for no other reason.

It may be awkward for my relatives and not easy for me. But I hope for healing. As I think deeply about my aunt and uncle, the love I've had for them all my life comes back in full. I recall the many happy times on their farm swimming or gathering around Aunt Ruthie's farm table, eating fresh green beans from her garden and Uncle Bill's joking with my toddler sons as well as his in-depth talks with me. I remember when I was living in Chicago with my parents in my early 20s when he flew in to take me out on my birthday—dinner and a comedy club—almost like a date. Once he gave me a book on Impressionism inscribed: *"To my favorite niece, my favorite artist Monet, my favorite painting, page 37."*

As I ponder these things, it *comes* to me to bring a gift: an oil portrait of Ann's only child, her teenage daughter, Julianne, Uncle Bill and Aunt Ruthie's only grandchild. Ann mails me photos of Julianne and I begin work—my *first* artwork since my fall on the pavement which took away use of my hands. I work on a 24" x 30" canvas. I still cannot raise my arm above my waist, certainly not high enough to paint, let alone to do a life-size oil portrait! Nor can my stick-like fingers move a brush sensitively. Yet, it is clear to me I am to do this portrait.

I hold my arm up with my left hand supporting my right elbow and make beginning charcoal marks. Every few minutes I rest my arm from the discomfort (which some might call pain). My stoic Christian Science background keeps me from taking painkillers and from paying attention to the pain. This portrait is painted by an inner fortitude I can't explain. My desire to see healing in a relationship is behind every stroke. I keep loving images of my aunt and uncle in my mind as I work, forgetting their disapproval of me. I think about my cousin Ann, her husband, Gary, and their daughter, Julianne, and the purity I hope to portray. Eventually, when painting, I feel no pain. After days, when I am finished, I know it is one of the best things I have ever done.

On June 2, 1995, Bill and I leave for Ohio, the custom framed painting, carefully wrapped, lying in the back of our station wagon, and arrive at Ann and Gary's farmhouse where I help prepare for the big event. Bill, Charissa, Julianne and I go into town for last minute party groceries. I flute a watermelon, mix punch, cut up fruit, decorate and set the tables with Charissa, while Bill kindly strings Ann's guitar (she's a music teacher). Nathan and his girl friend arrive. Dad and Rich, too. Rich, in the process of divorce, has everyone's full support—but that is another story. Aunt Ruthie's sisters and their families arrive. And many more. Some from as far as Florida. It will be quite a surprise for Uncle Bill and Aunt Ruthie! Everything goes well in spite of a little drizzle, for the big rented tent keeps us dry. When they arrive, Aunt Ruthie and Uncle Bill are overwhelmed to see a hundred familiar faces. I make a point of keeping out of sight. After a grand lunch, gifts are opened. Because of its size, my gift is the last to be opened, actually, unveiled. As Uncle Bill takes off the wrapping, a hush fills the tent and then a gasp from Ann as she sees my rendition of her daughter for the first time.

"Oh, *Lynnie*! She exclaims, "That's not a portrait of Julianne, that **IS** Julianne!!" She is touched to tears.

So are Uncle Bill and Aunt Ruthie. Uncertain how my gift would be received—they could have hated it!—I'd positioned myself behind a pole at the back of the tent. Everyone claps and heads turn my way as Uncle Bill spots me, opens his arms wide, motions me to come forward. It seems a long walk to the front of that tent, my heart pounding. My uncle and I look at each other as if no one else is present. I see only the man who loves Monet and me. I see the man in plaid shirt, cowboy hat and boots, his tractor behind him, ready to pull a load of hay and cousins. I see the man who could pick up Julianne, when she was four, under one arm, and Charissa, when she was three, under the other—like a pair of giggling baby calves. I see the business-man turned Christian Science practitioner and Committee on Publication, respected representative of Christian Science in the Ohio legislature, whose ways are gentle and strong. I see the man watching Letterman or Carson, shooting the breeze with my high school sons. I see the man who is my Dad's best friend. And he is smiling at me. I love him; I always have.

He wraps me in his arms, gives me a kiss, whispers in my ear, "There's a lot of *love* in that painting, Lynnie". Everyone continues to clap as if they knew—as if they knew they'd witnessed a healing. Aunt Ruthie, like a little bird chirping at my side much of the rest of the day, tells me how much she loves the portrait, even the custom frame, and asks what's new in my life and when can I come for a visit?

I am reminded of *Les Miserables'* candlesticks scene—when the priest gives to Jean Valjean, the one who robbed him, the heart of true Christianity. Technically, Julianne's portrait is one of the best I've done, but spiritually, its significance is without measure.

If you've gone through divorce, a wedding anniversary celebration may not be your favorite place. There will always be memory triggers, the outsider-feeling, and Pollyanna platitudes in after dinner toasts. Aunt Ruthie and Uncle Bill's celebration was no exception. A toast was given praising the exemplary marriage we'd come to celebrate, emphasizing a perfect marriage is assured if you work at it. For my brother and I who had worked ourselves nearly to death, twenty years each, on our marriages, both ending in divorce, this statement prickled, at least my ears, if not my sibling's.

Marriage is like shoes. You want certain things in a pair of shoes. You try on several until you find the right ones. Sometimes you go to several stores. Sometimes you never find the shoe you want; it's just an image in your mind. If you finally find the beautiful pair that seems to fit just right, you walk in them pleased with your comfortable choice. Some are such a good fit and so well made, they last forever, remaining old friends in spite of wear. Others fall apart way too soon. Some never fit, maybe because you were too busy looking at style, not focusing on fit. Others lose their shape, or walk through too many storms and just aren't the same shoe you took home. They have changed. Maybe they squeak too much. Maybe they don't hold your foot close enough or maybe your foot has gotten bigger so they pinch. Some shoes you just outgrow. They don't meet your needs anymore. They don't support you. They just take up space in your closet. Maybe their style is stuck in the past and you want to move forward. Maybe they hurt you, cause pain, and you are not going to take the torture anymore. They might even cripple you if bad enough, preventing you from walking at all. So for any of these reasons you decide to discard the shoes. Maybe you give them to someone who doesn't have any shoes. Maybe you throw them out. The main thing is you can't keep shoes that *won't let you walk your journey.*

In July, Bill and I visit Rich at Tenacre, in Princeton, New Jersey, where he has taken an apartment until his divorce is final. I read, write, and work on my courses for the coming year, full of new ideas. Inspired by a recent writers' workshop I attended, I apply to Warren Wilson College's MFA Writers' Program. I may not get in this competitive program. A month later I learn I don't. Another passing dream. I write for solace: *Writing redeems. To use words is to partake in incarnation because God is the Word, and the Word and words are linked... Perhaps God puts us where we are uncomfortable, where we would never choose, because that is where we grow. Sometimes busy being the warp thread I miss my pattern.*

Writing continues to be my solace when in Mid-August the school year begins with all its craziness. By September I write I'd like *to live on an island off Maine's coast and write children's stories or illustrate myths in an Oregon studio or write poems in Wales or live in a New Mexican adobe and paint landscapes.* I just can't figure out how to pay for any of these exotic roofs over my head. So I don't pack my bags. I keep my day job, remind myself a woman earns only 75% of what a man earns, that writing and painting can be done anywhere. I might like to paint French haystacks and Rouen Cathedral over and over in different light like Monet, to fragment color in loose strokes and capture the moment. But my days fill with duties Monet left to his wife and housekeeper.

Duties prevent focus on writing and painting in October. Upon turning 52, I find myself in wilderness again. Perhaps I never leave it? Perhaps it is the human condition? Jesus was driven to wilderness and John the Baptist was of it. What does this say about wilderness? It must be God's country, the place where man encounters Him/Her close-up. In Mark, after God tells Jesus he is well pleased with him, the next verse is, "*And immediately the spirit driveth him into the wilderness*" (Mark1:12). So, I guess, as soon as one pleases God he is driven into wilderness? I think wilderness is wherever we find ourselves that is difficult, but where we gain strength and direction *because* it isn't easy—like woundedness and suffering. I am oddly at home in this hardness. Just as I felt at home in South Dakota's Wild Sage Wilderness. Perhaps wilderness is my turf.

My journal helps me deal with wilderness. After another birthday, I write: *Autumn: the season of aging. When the body stops, the mind ought to be allowed to roll ahead with all those dreams that couldn't squeeze in between carpool, dinner and the 8 to 4 job, couldn't squeeze in because needy arms took all you had. Loving them into bloom, you gave and gave—and loved doing it—but now it's your time. But is it? Ideas I once wanted to follow sit like sludge in some recess of my mind and I see the doors and windows of my life shutting.*

When you wake before dawn, answers stand out like dripping-clean wet windows after a thunderstorm, all the grime and fog washed away. My journals holler with ideas wanting to become paintings and poems, begging to be knocked into being. When school and home demands won't let me give them birth, I write: *A human needs 9 months to be formed, an Asiatic elephant 608 days; all my poems get is 4 to 6 AM on an occasional sleepless night-morning.*

Calvary's Journey course starts again and I'm inspired to read *The Way of Perfection* by Teresa of Avila. Her writing affects my life, as it still does. Under her influence, I frame self-goals of humility, compassion, and detachment of things. I decide for birthdays and holidays, we should not give gifts but shed one thing. I would enter a convent at this point, if I could still come home and see my family, walk my dog, and have Friday night pizza with Bill.

Spurred by Teresa and the Journey Course, I begin an independent study of prayer. I know prayer requires humility, stillness, trusting, living under God's awning. It has long been my routine. But I want to see *all* perspectives. I manage to make diverse theologies come together in my mind—like some silver-glowing spiritual quilt wrapping me up. God, for me, the universal governing principle of Love and Truth, includes some traditional Catholic and Episcopal definitions but also Buddhist, Taoist, Hindu, Hebrew, Quaker, Christian Science and more. I love Celtic Christianity and Native American beliefs because they stay close to Nature and find prayer in the ordinary. When I pray, I want all the above, this holy conglomerate, to commune with my Mother-Father God.

I've long known prayer isn't telling God what to do or what we want. *Listening* to Him (I also mean *Her* and Principle and Truth) is what prayer is, for me: first getting on God's frequency, then turning up the volume. Being in a quiet place helps, so there is no interference. Jesus' phrase "Enter into thy closet" comes to mind. But prayer also means action; it isn't about sitting in a cozy chair and thinking pleasant thoughts. Without action, prayer is like trying to paint without paints. Action never happens in an ivory tower, but takes us down to earth. Sometimes I don't want to go there. But if I avoid the muddy places, they just follow me until I face them. Prayer is finding God in unexpected spots and moments each day. He is in every face, beneath every mask. Prayer is listening how to love more. Ego likes to bombard humans with self-important things to do, so they won't sit still and listen, but the discipline of prayer stops the bombardment.

I don't think it is possible to separate prayer from ordinary living: how we greet, think, work, care. Prayer also requires emptying garbage. I have to take out the trash I find when I go deep into myself—or at least transform it like a found-object artist. Prayer is simple, but not often easy. Many times I wrestle—like Jacob until he got the blessing. Prayer blesses, teaches, redeems, heals and reminds me I am always in relationship with God. Throughout 1995-1996, prayer is my path out of darkness.

I sign up for a silent retreat for women at St. Columba, a woodsy Episcopal retreat center outside Memphis. Never having done anything like this, I do not know what to expect when I drive there on October 27, 1995.

I arrive a bit early this glorious fall day, check in, unpack my things in a tiny cell-like room, and go for a walk, gathering leaves. A Golden Lab (with something else in his mix) follows me on my walk—a lovely companion; the world is full of spiritual beings and many of them are *not* homo sapiens!

5:00 PM thirty-some women gather in the dining room. Talking is permitted only at the reception and dinner; the rest of the weekend is for silence. I know no one but am less fearful of this gathering than most. I spot one of Calvary's assistant rectors, and enter the group of women talking with her. I discover not all here are Episcopalian—some are Catholic, Presbyterian, Lutheran. Two are talking about their *spiritual directors*. Whatever those are, they seem to be very important to these women.

"What's a Spiritual Director?" I ask

Someone explains, "They've been around for centuries; its an ancient term—a spiritual director is a companion or counselor, a spiritual friend, except they make a point of not advising, but of listening with you for God's voice."

"Are they Episcopal clergy?" I ask.

"Can be, but also Catholic—I had a wonderful monk for one once. You'll find spiritual directors in most religions," another answers.

"But what do they *do?*" I ask.

"Well, it's not easy to explain. Perhaps the best way to learn about spiritual direction is to read about it. There's a great little book by Alan Jones on the subject—but I don't know where you'd find a copy. Maybe back in Memphis you can order it. There is a small library here and a few books for sale for the retreat, but I doubt there's anything on spiritual direction; its not common reading. You might check, though."

I listen a bit and then wander out into the hall where not more than a dozen books are lined-up for sale. I run down the titles—many familiar books I have seen at Calvary, some I have not. I suppose I will have to wait until I get back to Memphis to learn more about Spiritual Direction. But then, near the end, I spot a thin, unassuming blue paperback with the words: *Exploring Spiritual Direction* by Alan Jones! Of course—why should it *not* be here?! I need it now! If L'Engle's *Walking On Water* could fall off a library table at my feet and set the course for the rest of my life, why should I be amazed that Alan Jones' book would turn up at my first retreat?!

Though I read many things on this retreat, I *devour* Alan Jones little book. The Preface introduces spiritual direction as *The Art of Arts*; I am impressed already. The second paragraph says *spiritual growth is concerned with companionship: first, companionship with God, and second companionship with our fellow human beings* (Alan Jones, *Exploring Spiritual Direction: An Essay on Christian Friendship*, p.1) I keep reading. I come to the line: *A human being is a longing for God and nothing less than God will satisfy us*" (Jones, p.18). Yes! I am at home in spiritual direction.

After dinner we gather in the chapel to hear readings. Two specifically stick: *Beware the barrenness of a busy life* by Socrates and Mark 6:31, *Come away to a lonely place and rest awhile*. Quiet has always been my place. The chapel is cozy, simple in design with large windows to the woods. A crude driftwood cross hangs above the altar. I want to make one like it when I get home. As communion takes place I am reminded I need sacred ritual—that is why I brought the vase of dried flowers, why I collected leaves, and why I take the bread and wine now. My spirituality is connected to nature, art and beauty.

I find myself wishing Dad could know Teresa and Julian and Doug Bailey and this chapel with its simple driftwood cross. Episcopal means more than Journey and Doug. It includes these women here who seem the epitome of grace and generosity. Episcopal means openness, acceptance of who we are just as we are, embracing arms that leave no one out and a rich heritage of tradition, history, and saints—real people like Teresa, Julian, Hildegarde, Catherine and others who have been so much a part of my journey.

I used to have trouble with the word "saint"—just as I had trouble with the word "sin"—when I first transitioned from Christian Science toward traditional Christianity. But I learned it wasn't that complicated. Saints are human beings devoted to God whose life stories of healing, transformation, and wisdom teach us. Sin was a bit trickier.

I look out into the woods from my pew and reflect on how easy it is to be here. What a treat, this retreat! I look forward to meditating uninter-rupted and purchase two more books—one by Buechner and one by Henri

Nouwen, before retiring to my room. I skim Buechner and discover Nouwen for the first time. Nouwen, spiritual writer, professor at Harvard, Yale, and Notre Dame, is an author who will remain essential to my journey. He is a man "deeply conscious of his longing for home" as (Henri Nouwen, *Finding My Way Home*, preface by Sue Mosteller Literary Executrix, Henri Nouwen Centre, L'Arche Daybeak, p.15)

Nouwen's *The Path of Waiting* addresses my waiting for place, job, and purpose:

> *Waiting is a place between where one is and where one wants to go. People don't usually like a place like that… To wait open-endedly is an enormously radical attitude toward life. It is trusting that something will happen to us that is far beyond our own imaginings. It is giving up control over our future and letting God design our life… The spiritual life is a life in which we wait, actively present to the moment, expecting that new things will happen to us… beyond our own imagination or prediction. That, indeed, is a very radical stance toward life in a world preoccupied with control* (Nouwen, *The Path of Waiting;* now reprinted in Nouwen's *Finding My Way Home, p.97*)

Nouwen's words remind me of French philosopher and Christian mystic Simone Weil's words which she'd written in her journal and I'd copied into my own the previous month: *Waiting patiently in expectation is the foundation of the spiritual life.*

Waiting is all I could do after my fall. Everything had to be done for me. I was in the uncomfortable place of *not* doing, of relying on other people's hands because mine couldn't function. I was in the position of *waiting* on God's action, not my own. "My soul is waiting for the Lord"—I read once that this is the theme of the Hebrew Scriptures.

During the retreat I research "falling" in a theological text about the doctrine of the Fall—a completely different fall than mine, but I find connection for it suggests falling pertains to "falling away from the divine purpose" *(Essays Catholic and Critical, p. 243)*. Certainly my anger at the time of my fall was far from divine purpose!

One of the puzzlements of my Episcopalian life has been the concept of sin. It was not major in my Christian Science background, nor is it something I am inclined to dwell on. As Julian of Norwich writes, so it seems to me, all is well done by God and "sin is nothing" (The Classics of Western Spirituality: *Julian of Norwich: Showings* The Paulist Press, p.137)… "I did not see sin, for I believe that it has no substance, no share in being…" (*Julian of Norwich Showings*, p.225). Crucial, too, is Saiving's essay in *Womanspirit Rising* which contends that doctrines of sin do not provide an adequate interpretation of the human situation because masculine experience, which has been the basis for establishing most theology and doctrine, is not the same as woman's. The will-to-power, pride and self-assertion may be man's temptations, but woman's temptations are more likely to be dependence on others for one's self-definition, her powerlessness and negation of self. Selfless in service to others, she may feel she has no right to her own life. Saiving calls for a redefining of theology regarding sin to include the feminine situation because *a theology based solely on masculine experience may well be irrelevant* (Carol P. Christ and Judith Plaskow, *Womanspirit Rising*, p. 41). I agree.

When I return from the retreat, I phone a local spiritual director, a female Episcopal priest that another Episcopal priest at the retreat referred me to. I drive to her office in a Mid-town Memphis Episcopal Church, take a seat on a small settee across from her desk in her soothingly dark Tuscan-red office. She takes a side armchair near me. Virginia, as I am asked to call her, is such a thin wisp of a woman a light breeze might blow her away. About my age, in white clerical collar and gray blouse, she exudes genuine humility. She sits quietly and waits for me to speak first. We talk about *being and not doing* and about sitting in silence to hear God. She hears bits of my story and asks a little about my work as an artist and teacher. But mostly she waits for me to speak. Spiritual directors do not direct. Nor do they charge, yet she gives me nearly two hours of her time. I feel this is the beginning of what I've been searching for. There's depth and peace in her office and both stay with me when I leave. I write in my journal: *I must keep all this in my heart for there are more truths and revelations that have come that I cannot write about for they slip from words.*

November 1995 Bill takes a group of juniors to Washington DC as he has many times. It does not help when one of my students confides to me while he is away, "Mr. Caldwell always sucks up to girls." Is this true? When the phone rings one night while he is gone I don't answer. Why do I not pick up? Why do I let the phone ring and ring? I feel a hard knot inside me that understands why. I do not want to be patronized, asked token questions about my day, don't want to be crossed off his to-do list, don't want to ask him the expected questions and hear the expected answers about museums, Congress, and the like, while *not* hearing about his charming the dinner table of eight which he won't mention. I don't want the absence of words to force me to fill in blanks. I don't want to hear silences of words unspoken—the words he edits out, the experiences he overlooks or erases from memory, replacing them with "I can't remember" and "I don't know." So how can I pick up the phone? It isn't February but it is beginning to feel like it! When Bill returns he tells me how much he missed me and I tell him the same. February disappears.

On Oct. 31, 1996, Halloween—a holiday I particularly dislike—witches and goblins ring our doorbell and I stuff Nestle's Crunch bars into their plastic pumpkins, then clean the kitchen, work on tomorrow's lesson plans, vacuum the living room, fold Charissa's laundry, put away Bill's shoes, and, before I go to bed, write in my journal: *I am sick of self-reliance. I scream a silent wide-mouthed scream spitting soundless sound that is only heard in my head.* In contrast to mine, Bill's routine means coming home after school to retreat to his den to play banjo, guitar, or harmonica, to enjoy his computer, read books, plan hikes, grade papers—free of house work, laundry, meal preparation or clean-up, shopping or responsibilities outside his career. Women's work, it seems, is never done. Sometimes the unfairness frustrates.

Other times, if I get my duties done, we sit side by-side, cozily reading and talking together, as content as if we are an old couple living in a Welsh cottage by the sea. Bueckner says: *The life you clutch, hoard, guard, and play safe with is in the end a life worth little…only a life given away for love's sake is a life worth living.* When I read this I am once again reminded that giving does not impoverish, that loving even *through* the housework, inequities, and disappointments is what a woman does. I close my journal, turn out my light, and give my dear snoring husband a kiss.

One day Bill has a *terrible* day at school—his students are extremely upset about their grades and he walks out enraged. Though he has been there twenty years, Custis Lee is not always the best place for Bill. We commiserate on our individual school experiences while walking Surprise, our Samoyed, often driving to Shelby Farms' hiking trails and lake. Surprise scares up birds from the weeds and chases squirrels he never catches, his thick long white hair blowing in the wind. We love him dearly, this shaman of a dog—as most good dogs are.

Bill and I release our school tensions chopping garlic, peppers, and mushrooms Friday evenings after the long school week. While I knead the dough, blend the pesto (fresh basil, pine nuts, parsley, garlic, and olive oil), and assemble the pizza (my secret ingredient: a trail of honey across the tomato sauce), Bill catches the Lehrer News Hour. By the time the pizza is in the oven and the aroma in our kitchen suggests a village in Sienna—a smell even Surprise appreciates—our stress has disappeared. Friday nights Bill and I are like a comfy pair of old slippers.

Thanksgiving 1995 Charissa, Bill and I fly to Boston to be with Dad. We dine at the Algonquin Club on Commonwealth Avenue, a staid and elegant men's club, with its black leather hooded chairs with tiny side windows, oriental rugs, grand imposing staircase, huge pewter chandeliers and superbly served cuisine where for three decades Mom and Dad, or Dad and Jayne, and any of us children and grandchildren when in town, have been privileged to be Dad's guests. Jason, his girl friend, and Nathan fly in from Oregon—the boys have not been here for years. My brother is here, too, with Blythe, a student of Dad's, divorced mother of six, whom Rich will marry when his divorce is final. The next night we dine in a Japanese Restaurant on Newberry Street, sitting on the floor, our shoes off, with bamboo boats of shrimp, skewered fruit and wrapped delicacies spread before us. I realize that none of us are with the one we started with. Dad is with Jayne, not Mom; Rich with Blythe, not Karen; I am with Bill, not John. What does this say about family, society, the times, the complex nature of relationship?

For Christmas 1995 we fly to Oregon where Jason now lives, drive to a cabin we rent for a week near Trillium Lake in the Mt. Hood area, park our car and hike our stuff into a remote log cabin in the mountainous woods with Jason, his girlfriend, Nathan, and Charissa. I cook holiday meals in the log cabin kitchen, the boys find a Christmas tree and decorate it with pine cones and handmade ornaments, build fires we read by, snowboard, ski, and hike in the snow, play games, and watch the star-filled sky without another soul around but our family. We haul some of our gifts and suitcases out to the car the night before we leave only to discover the next morning that our car window's been smashed and our car broken into, our Christmas gifts and suitcases'contents stolen. But the good and relaxing week together lasts longer in memory than things lost.

In the new year, two women who took my *Herstory 9-Piece* course invite me to lunch at Memphis' Peabody Hotel. Somewhere between salad and dessert they propose marketing my course across the nation! They have apparently discussed this between them for some time, thought it out in detail, and decided I must travel, teaching my course in workshops throughout the United States!

"Your course has gotten *under my skin*" one says, pinching her forearm. "I think every woman in America should know about it!"

"Are you open to this?" asks the other.

Stunned, I answer, "Well, I don't know, I never thought about it—but it sounds great! You're talking about something year round? I would stop teaching?"

"Of course; we intend to make this your career. We'll need photos, your resume, a bio. You'll have to create a speech—that's how we would begin. Maybe a video, too."

"Won't this require money?" I ask

"We have it all figured out. We'll take proceeds from producing and selling baseball caps with women's logos and give it all to you—that's how strongly we feel about this!"

Both are successful women. One in marketing and business, the other a successful commercial artist. They bubble with ideas. I am as delighted and excited as they are. It seems too perfect.

It turns out to be just that. In March, I give them my bio, photos and resume and I resign from Custis Lee, effective for the upcoming1996-97 school year. I write speeches. Weeks pass, but I hear nothing. Finally, I call and learn that *both* women have taken jobs in different states, one on the West coast and one on the East! I am no longer a priority.

Left high and dry, having resigned from Custis Lee, with no other prospect for employment, I file with Carney Sandoe & Associates, a private school placement agency. I ask the Assistant Head of Custis Lee, for a recommendation and ask my request be kept confidential, which he promises to do. But within two days he tells the Headmistress, who stops me in the hall and says,

414 | Gwendolyn Evans Caldwell

"I hear you've applied to Carney Sandoe. I know Carney." I was shocked my confidence had been breached. Lately, prospects and disappointments have been striking me like missiles in a mid-East war!

Facing unemployment, an idea comes to create a home art business which I will call *Seeds: Growing Creative Ideas.* I create a unique, artistic brochure of many pages, offering private classes, portraits, art for interior design and corporate art placement. This gorgeously creative piece of graphics gets many compliments but few takers when I mail it out in May, as my final days at Custis Lee wind down. But I look forward to what art positions Carney Sandoe may have to offer.

About this time, a former student phones. A friend of hers is in a coma and she asks me to pray for her and him. I agree to and tell her to love more than she already is, that perfect love casts out fear, and that Love, God, is the only Healer. I remind her she is not alone. I add it is not her job nor mine to heal; it is God's. Ours is to love. When we hang up, I prayerfully work and write until after midnight. Some weeks later this student calls and asks if we can go for a walk. I listen to her life challenges and choices, as I have for so many young women and girls over the years.

"If I could just be you!," she says to me as we walk past incongruous English country homes in East Memphis, "If I could put myself in your body, I would."

She stuns me. First of all, this slim and attractive twenty year-old *really* doesn't want my body! And, second, she doesn't know all there is to know about me. She is a Bible-reading Christian who wants to find God in her choices. She appreciates that I want Him in mine, and knows much of my story, shared on other afternoons.

She is not the first young woman to seek me out. Several dozen young women come to mind—girls I met teaching Sunday School or at Custis Lee, girls who ask many questions and seek answers, just as I did and do. They would find me after class, phone or drop by, we'd share our stories and, together, try to make sense of the world. Sometimes, one would call in desperate tears. I always took the call or offered a room or fetched them if need be. I cared about every one as if she were my own soul. When one girl wrote a college paper on my life, I remember asking her why me. She replied, "Because you live courageously trusting God and I want to do the same." I don't tell all of them—just ones ready—about my darkest days and unlived dreams. At 16, 20, or 30—they need light, not dark. But I do wonder why God has had young woman seek me out. Even now.

In May, I receive an interview offer to teach at a very prestigious private school in Washington DC. There are over 100 applicants for the position and it comes down to me and another. The Chairman of their art department, knew me and my work from a two-week workshop both of us attended years earlier. When she sees my name as one of the applicants she is immediately interested, reads my attached resume thoroughly, and phones me. She tells me she is looking for someone with "rigor" and that my application stands out to her not merely from knowing me previously but because of what it contains. She asks me to come for an interview. In order to do this I ask permission from my Upper School head for a friday off. I ask her to keep this confidential. However, before I leave to fly to DC, she tells the headmistress, who stops me in the hall to say she knows where I am going, in fact, she says she knows the head of that school and will tell her all about me! She knows nothing about me, my art or teaching, for she hasn't visited my classes nor have we discussed my work. I tell her calling is unnecessary because I have already given references, the process is past that point, now down to two candidates.

Bill and I very much like the DC area and the school (over 50 nationalities are represented, many diplomats' daughters, it even has a women's rights organization). We look forward to the potential move. Everyone involved seems to like my teaching methods and philosophy, and the slides I've brought of both my work and my students' work. I teach a couple of classes and receive praise from both art teachers. At lunch I nearly choke on my soup when the art teacher I'd be replacing says to me "I think you've got the job—the other person doesn't have your abilities."

Sunday we have dinner at the home of the department head, my friend who initially invited me to interview. She discusses real estate with us, what possibilities we might find for a home in the area. She offers to call private schools on Bill's behalf, even gets up from the table to phone a colleague at a prestigious boys' school about history openings. She is as excited as I am about our working together.

Bill and I are thrilled with the DC prospect. Monday morning, the headmistress makes a point of finding me to ask how my interview went, adding, with a strange smile, that she phoned her contact there about me. Instinct tells me to say little, besides, I have a class.

Two weeks pass. I hear nothing from DC. Finally I receive a call from my friend there with whom I interviewed, the head of the art department, saying it has been decided the position will go to the other person, a man. I can't believe it! Surely a man is less appropriate for this girls' school—they'd been so impressed with my women's studies experience besides my qualifications as an experienced artist and art teacher! I am incredulous! I'd been given such enthusiastic praise! Why, she had practically had me moving in! I can *not* understand.

"*Why*, I have to ask *why*?"

"Well…he…ah… he seemed more laid-back".

More "*laid-back*"?! I can't believe my ears! Nor be more puzzled. Where's the desired "*rigor*" she was looking for in "*laid-back*'?! Then it comes to me: my school's headmistress had phoned. Why hadn't I thought of that immediately?

"By any chance," I ask, "Do you know if the head of *my* school spoke with the head of *your* school?"

There was a heavy sigh on the other end of the phone. "Yes," my friend answers.

So *that* was it. She was under orders *not* to tell me, but she could respond with a simple "yes" if I happened to ask the right question. Clearly the Headmistress of our school prevented my getting this position.

When I leave Custis Lee, I am given a leather briefcase which I return with a note. I don't want gifts for my dozen years—as if they could buy me off, as if what was done to me was just fine. It wasn't. I write letters and make small watercolors to give to the teachers I've worked with and cared about over many years, which is most of them.

The Headmistress, has been there only two years but has managed to make mincemeat of the place, alienating and firing teachers at will, lowering the academic emphasis, controlling with an iron hand, instituting pep rallies and mindless activities for both students and faculty. She did, however, redecorate the house provided for her.

About this time, following a routine physical required for teaching, since I am no longer a Christian Scientist and no longer exempt, I'm told by the female physician that she recommends I see a psychologist, that I may be depressed. Hmmm. Let's see, lost my new career to travel around giving women studies' workshops, for which I resigned my teaching job, and lost my best offer for an ideal new job in DC, thanks to the headmistress of the school from which I resigned. Depressed? Do you think?!

I see the psychologist three times. I take her lengthy tests and ask if I may take notes when she talks, which is fine. She tells me I have anaclitic depression, which she says is usually seen in institutions or orphanages where children have abandonment issues. She says I have "issues with emotional abandonment," that my depression is not age-related nor menopausal but stems from childhood, a lack of nurturing, not being held nor stimulated enough. To my surprise she adds, "some have died of this." She says "Custis Lee is like the Christian Science religion for you. Who to *trust* is your concern. Working with girls may trigger issues from your past. If you work in an institution you must have a *voice*, some empowerment; otherwise, you are better off working for yourself."

She tells me I identify more with my dad than my mom—no news there. She tells me I crave knowledge "and a compatibility of ideas". She says "the support and closeness of your husband is absolutely essential for your survival—even any unintentional hurt he causes is similar, for you, to your parents' treatment of you and will have a negative impact. You two should talk every day. It is important your husband not keep things from you, nor lie even in the smallest category. You do not need criticism. Your partner must give *trust*—important because of transference with your father. Your dad and Bill are very similar—bright, talented, charming, appealing, and have influence with others. You respect and admire this, but it frightens you, too, just as your father misled you in religion—though aspects of your religion have been good. Anyone held in awe is a risk for you. Thank goodness you had personal strength!—which you, also, probably got from your father."

"You and Bill are bright, competent people; you will not end up homeless [I had told her this is my greatest fear]. Bill did not get adequate parental attention, which explains in part his need for attention now from so many.

You both need to understand transference. Neither of you should ever work for an institution that denies the individual's best interest. It is your nature to be anxious and blame yourself for every mistake, but you will be successful. Work to keep your anxiety level low. You don't seek control but you need it to overcome anxiety. Especially in social situations. Push yourself to socialize so panic attacks do not come of this. Carve out time for yourself creatively—not creating only with the need to sell. You have the same humanity as everyone, yet you are particularly unique: your self-esteem is at the same time both very high and very low."

I never really thought about myself in these terms, but I feel much of what she says makes sense and am glad I took notes during our meetings.

Unemployment hangs over me. June is too late for worthy teaching positions to come. We drive to Colorado for an interview we'd lined up where an art teacher and history teacher are needed, a charter school, that we learn may not exist longer than a year—bad choice. We look for teaching positions in other Western states, but find nothing. Private schools usually line up their teachers by early summer and neither of us wants to teach in public where discipline is more one's task than ideas. If we taught math and science we'd have found something, but the best of art and history teachers are a dime a dozen.

I decide to meditate on the Sermon on the Mount and Proverbs 31— my self-proclaimed summer 1996 project, taking notes on all that comes to me on how to do/be better: Do good to your husband; work hard, prepare well, be strong, never be idle; give to the poor; take excellent care of your household, children, animals, and all within your charge; dress attractively but also "dress" in honor and strength; be joyful; speak wisely, kindly; paint or make what you can so your works praise you as God's child. Affirming my purpose and place, I make lists of successes in my life. I make lists of what I am grateful for. I make a list of what angers me to get it out, and then affirm I have better things to do than be angry. I record all of this in my journals, filtered with to-do lists, Martha Stewart recipes, notes on how to refinish furniture, grocery lists, venting, goals for when the summer is over, painting ideas, pieces of poems I hope to write, and quotations from books I am reading. Inspired as we drive West, I design garments to sew, handmade books to sell, and more—for my new business, *Seeds: Growing Creative Ideas.*

While out West, between hikes and interviews, I paint a series of large watercolors in New Mexico, finishing them over the next four months back in my Memphis home studio.

In late July when we return home, a Calvary friend invites me to go to a CASA program, an organization of court-appointed child advocates for child abuse cases. I'd always felt I'd like to help in that arena some day. Though I've had no personal experience with abuse, it strikes me as one of the greatest evils in society. I find myself impressed with the lawyer's presentation and embark on the 6-week training program to become a certified CASA volunteer. I receive my badge and papers, following thorough checks, and am given my first case, all cases being confidential.

By the time I get my second CASA case I am discovering cases have similar elements—usually drugs, alcohol, poverty, and dishonesty. Driving on the highway one day I see a billboard: "Poverty is violence." My CASA work shows me this daily. I enter slums and dark corridors with strange smells. This is not my world. I do my CASA interviews with a bit of trepidation. Usually I find two warring factions pulling on the child because whoever gets custody doesn't pay child support. It's a matter of finances—not love of offspring! I am shocked. The cycle repeats. How do we get rid of abuse? Do we first tackle poverty? Or alcoholism? Or remove drugs? What's the answer?

As a creative problem-solver, I think I ought to be able to solve at least the cases brought to me. As a CASA volunteer I am expected to interview the children involved, their parents, step-parents, extended family, the hospital or doctors involved, the schools and teachers, friends and neighbors. Usually this means twenty or more in-person interviews and twice as many phone calls per case. I am legally privy to children's private records and must monitor the situation constantly. Then I write a report—usually about 20 pages, kind of a term paper, which goes to the judge. Finally, I appear in court, stand before the judge and recommend permanent removal of these children from their parents, or not. In my two cases, based on the facts, permanent removal is the recommendation.

After just two cases, this seems an overwhelming responsibility. Who am I to play God and permanently remove children from their parents? What if somewhere down the road (though highly unlikely) the parents got sober or changed? What if the kids were lying, as I found can be the case? One young girl who appeared to be innocent on first interview, I later discovered had 35 school offenses for aggressive behavior inflicted on others. Finding the truth is difficult. When I spoke with a mother, her infant crawling on a dirty floor, I could feel her pain and problems as a single mother of three—not so on another case when I sat with a mother in front of her 4-foot TV screen, her professionally manicured nails gesticulating, while her daughters, now living with their grandmother (often the case), did not have more than a change of underwear. Sometimes fathers lied persuasively, denying they'd abused their daughters. As I pieced together the varying stories I saw that nearly everyone was lying—even grandmothers would tell me whatever best served their interests. I wanted to send all the adults back to childhood and re-raise them! The maize of deceit—a place I've never been comfortable—got to me, and after six months, I quit.

I never was able to turn off the cases. As long as I was working on a case it was in my living room and bedroom, even in my dreams. I called and asked the lawyer who was in charge if there was anything else I could do, directly hands-on with the kids. He suggested I work with abused kids placed in immediate temporary care when first removed from their homes. They might be there a day or several weeks. I was assigned 10 teenage girls to work with for several hours each visit, teaching them art. I had them do self-portraits. At first most were unsure of making any mark on paper, but with encouragement and demonstrations, every girl eventually had a fine life-size head and, to some degree, a likeness. By the time our projects were finished, I'd gotten through the tough crust of life that hid their true selves. I took photos of them with their portraits and hung them in the cafeteria. They were so proud. They hated to see me go, touching my hand or arm every chance they got, as if I were a rare bird. Perhaps in their eyes I was.

Volunteer work is good, but I need a paying job. A number of Custis Lee AP Art students take private tutoring from me. I've sold a painting or two and created hundreds of hand-painted wooden ornaments, "Gwen's Girls", each unique, marketing them locally and in other states. I sell some—but the time I spend on each 8-inch figure is barely covered by the income they produce.

Mainly, I work on completing the dozen large landscapes I started in Taos, New Mexico. Upscale Taos B&B owners who had watched me paint on location had said they would like to have my work in their lovely old adobe establishment. I'd promised to send them photos when all paintings were complete. I devote myself to this huge work for four months—and mail photos of each 32" x 40", matted and framed piece to the B&B owners. I feel these pieces are my best work to date. The B&B owners say my work is wonderful, but that they've decided they don't want to take on the responsibility after all of selling expensive art work on top of their business. I am crushed.

About the same time, I receive a call from an art agent who travels to galleries throughout the US representing artists and selling their work. He has just seen some of my work at a Memphis gallery and wants to see more. I invite him to my home studio and he takes about $4,000 worth of my work—not the framed Taos pieces, however, for he only deals in unframed work. I sign an agreement, happy my work is about to take off, as he assures me it will.

I never hear from him again. Months, and years later, even after doing everything in my power to locate him, I am left hopeless of ever retrieving my work. I feel raped, a pile of bones heaped on the floor. Never again can I trust anyone.

One thing after another has been thrown at me. Had I not been reading about *abandonment—surrendering* material goods, associations, and possessions, I might have taken these disasters harder. But I had recently started a course called *Practical Wisdom*, held at my spiritual director's church and moderated by her. Based on a course of questions, the class gathers under Virginia's gentle leadership 7:30 AM Thursdays—an early half hour drive for me—to discuss such ponderings as *Have you ever really paid attention to what keeps coming up in life even though you may try to prevent it or escape it?* And hundreds of other self-reflective questions. Our group includes men and women on their way to work, housewives, university students. In this class I explore St. John of the Cross's *Dark Night of the Soul* which speaks to my recent darkness and inspires my art.

On my way home from my first Practical Wisdom class, my car turns in and parks in front of Memphis' Civic Gardens' Japanese Garden. I'd been here once before when home-schooling my boys long ago. This morning, the garden is not yet open, but I find myself walking through the entrance, and buying an inexpensive membership because only members are allowed to enter early. For the next year, I come every Thursday after class to walk the paths, sit by a pond, or under the red-roofed pavilion when it rains. I meditate, think, and write. God brought me to this peaceful sanctuary. It is my *manna* in the wilderness.

Lack of regular employment over the past six months, is difficult; teaching privately doesn't remotely compare to a salary. I substitute in local public schools, though it is more like baby-sitting than teaching, more frustrating than academic. The Upper School Head, perhaps feeling guilty about having told the Headmistress about my DC interview, wants me to sub—not something I would have liked, given the circumstance, but which I would have done for income—but this is nixed by the Headmistress.

When not working on my new business, I study the Native American Ghost Dance Religion at the main library. Enchanted with all things Native American since our summer out West, I read everything on the topic I can get my hands on, much of it primary source material. I am pulled to the world of Native Americans. I want to capture their hope against all hopelessness—perhaps, as I want to capture my own hope against my hopelessness. They faced annihilation of their beliefs, sustenance, culture, and their very existence, yet remained hopeful. Perhaps in them I see myself.

Spirit meant *everything* to Native American life. Similar to Campbell's idea that dreams are the mode for spirit to enter one's being, dreams support Native Americans' reality. Their source for imagery and ritual, dreams jump right into their daily life. For them, *religion is not isolated from other cultural manifestations. For them, the supernatural breaks into the every day* (The Religions of The American Indians by Ake Hultkrantz). Religion and dreams do the same for me.

In the summer of 1889, word circulated among tribes of a Messianic prophet who had come to earth to rescue the Indians from their misery and restore their ancient ways. They clutched at this possibility. Representatives were sent to find out if the story were true. Medicine men and mighty warriors, Short Bull and Kicking Bear, who were among the leaders to spread the new religion, found the prophet at the Paiute Reservation at Walker Lake, Nevada. His name was Wovoka, a sheepherder and shaman. Healed of a feverous illness, Wovoka "returned to life" to tell his people:

"I have talked with God [Wakan Tanka]. Soon now, the earth shall die. But the Indians need not be afraid. It is the white men, not the Indians, who should be afraid for they will be wiped from the face of the earth by a mighty flood of mud and water. When the flood comes, the Indians will be saved. The earth will shake like a dancer's rattle. There will be thunder and smoke and great lightening…Then, when the flood has passed, the earth will come alive again… The land will be new and green with young grass. Elk and deer and antelope and even the vanished buffalo will return…And all the Indians will be young again and free of the white man's sickness—even those of our people who have gone to the grave. It will be a paradise on earth!"

Wovoka told the tribes that Wakan Tanka wanted them to prepare for this paradise with honesty, goodness, hard work and no war. They were to perform a specific dance and sing songs that Wakan Tanka had taught Wovoka. This paradise was expected to arrive in 1891 with earth's trembling as signal for all Indians to tie sacred eagle feathers in their hair which would transport them to the sky while the new land covered the old. The ghosts of all dead Indians would come alive. Until then, Indians could "die" by glimpsing moments of this paradise in dancing the Ghost Dance and singing the Ghost Dance songs, which would relieve them of their despair.

The dancers, eyes closed, wearing "bullet-proof" (which they weren't) holy shirts decorated with crows, eagles, crosses, and other symbols, held hands in a circle, crying, wailing, staggering or swooning as the dance went on for hours, even days. During the trance like state they saw visions of the return of the buffalo, their beautiful land and people. As one source said: *They desperately danced the Ghost Dance in a final attempt to survive, for Buffalo, land, spirit, prayer, all the basic fundamentals of life were lost—taken by the wa'sicu—white man. What was left, not even human dignity.*

But the U.S. military forbade the Ghost Dance Religion, viewing it as a dangerous resistance movement to unify tribes. This led to the *massacre of sick, starving and unarmed Indian women, babies, and elderly men at Wounded Knee, South Dakota on December 29, 1890.*

Mooney's *Ghost Dance Religion and Wounded Knee* contained primary source material by a U.S. soldier who visited every tribe to write a detailed report about the Ghost Dance Religion. This passage from his book struck me deeply and encapsulated my next body of artwork:

The lost paradise is the world's dreamland of youth. What tribe or people has not had its golden age, before Pandora's box was loosed, when women were nymphs and dryads and men were gods and heroes? And when the race lies crushed and groaning beneath an alien yoke, how natural is the dream of a redeemer, an Arthur, who shall return from exile or awake from some long sleep to drive out the usurper and win back for his people what they have lost. The hope becomes a faith and the faith becomes the creed of priests and prophets, until the hero is a god and the dream a religion, looking to some great miracle of nature for its culmination and accomplishment. The doctrines of the Hindu avatar, the Hebrew Messiah, the Christian Millennium, and the Hesunanin of the Indian Ghost dance are essentially the same, and have their origin in a hope and longing common to all humanity (James Mooney, The Ghost Dance Religion and Wounded Knee, p. 657).

I *love* this! *All* religions and belief-systems are born in *hope and longing common to all humanity!* Just when my own life needs hope, I am compelled to express mankind's shared longing for hope. I paint intensely. An artist's job is to protect humanity's dreams and myths. Campbell says somewhere that "The artist is the only one who can keep vision alive." Painting, the artist participates in myth. I make myth for months in 1996-97.

While devouring Native American material, I also study Celtic Christianity and the influence of ancient Celtic pagan beliefs and myths on Christianity. Celtic concepts resonate with me: healing, Nature, animals, transformation, rebirth, spiritual individualism, the importance of women, the significance of water (whether springs, rivers or wells), gardens and groves, the rejection of the doctrine of sin, the value of small things and small joys, duality of darkness and light, finding God not in afterlife but *now*, in ordinary routine and *"the very thin 'divide' between past, present, and future times; places where a person is somehow able, possibly only for a moment, to encounter a more ancient reality within present time; as places where perhaps only in a glance we are somehow transported into the future"* (Edward C. Sellner, Wisdom of the Celtic Saints, Revised and Expanded, p.34).

The first presence of Christianity in Britain dates to about 200 AD—at Gwent, in Southwest Wales. Christian saints and monks who left the deserts of the Middle East sailed to the coasts of Britain, Ireland, and Wales, desiring a simple life of solitude and work. Often a hermit who cleared land and built himself a hut, the early Christian was joined by others until a community of 10 or a 100 formed—but without monastic regulations and authority. In Britain and Ireland monks and nuns led a simple life with much flexibility and freedom to pray and meditate as each one chose, meeting together only once a day for worship. These earliest Christians were not farmers, but collected berries, nuts and roots. Because the pagans before them believed women equal to men, the Celtic Church in the British Isles adopted this stance, even establishing "double monasteries" where men and women lived and worked together, women holding powerful positions as frequently as men (Davies and Bowie, *Celtic Christianity*, p. 8,9).

Just as I become more Catholic and Episcopalian in outlook than I was raised, I discover in November of 1996, Ellie Wiesel's *Four Hasidic Masters*, a book of inspiring Jewish wisdom. I read of rebbes (a rebbe is a sort of rabbi of rabbis or spiritual teacher) who move others to joy but struggle with melancholy themselves. They combat sorrow with exuberance, dancing and prayer. "Absence of passion leads to indifference" says the Holy Seer of Lublin (Wiesel, Four Hasidic Masters). He *expects* ecstasy and imagination. Not to express oneself freely is a resignation worse than despair. Rebbe Barukh speaks of faith as part anguish: "Faith and the abyss are next to one another, even one within the other." How well I know this! I am reminded of my night of abyss prior to divorce in my sterile apartment. These ancient Jewish masters are saying things I've experienced! They, like the dessert fathers and mothers, Celtic Christians, saints and Ghost Dancers are also my shamans.

All ideas inter-relate. Mythology and belief systems unite in my mind. I see this unity as the *hope* of humanity. The circle dance of Jewish Masters is the circle of the Ghost Dance is the circle of Druids, of Stonehenge. The crow of the Native American Ghost Dance Religion is the raven of Celtic spirituality and the black birds flying over corn fields at New Harmony.

I am shown this oneness in a most extraordinary way one day, alone in my studio. I work on studies for my Ghost Dance paintings, listening to Native American flute music, when on my paper appears a pattern exquisite in its simplicity and meaning. My hand draws curved V-shape lines across the top of the paper—like kindergarten birds. Under them appear stone-like/Indian-like shapes in a circle—the shapes might be stones of Stonehenge or blanket-wrapped Native Americans shuffling slow steps in a circle dance. I am in awe! I have created my first piece about the unity of human hope. It is as if I were in a trance like the dancers. I do more pieces capturing that last sentence in Mooney's paragraph. Transfixed, I am the servant of a work that has its own energy. Never before have I experienced such a complete dispensation of time and space. I work on this project as if on hallowed ground. Sadly, I complete only four paintings, never finishing the entire body of work, as events in my life change.

In October 1996 to get away from their work in Boston, Jayne and Dad come for a visit. After several days in Memphis the three of us drive to New Harmony for a short stay in one of Mrs. Owen's rentable houses, the 1825 Duclos House. Jayne will have the lovely bedroom with private bath and I will sleep in the twin under the alcove between kitchen and library. Dad likes privacy for his practice and will take a room in the inn close by. I prepare meals for us in the Duclos kitchen. Dad and Jayne walk New Harmony's many paths or work in his room on his lecture and practice, while I write on the porch swing.

One night, Jayne and I stay up late talking, the way females do. We share thoughts about the complicated man we mutually love. I learn it has not been easy for her to work with Dad; something I might have guessed.

During one of his monologues—I cannot call it a dialogue—Dad brings up Doug Bailey, whom he'd met in Memphis just prior to our trip when I invited Dad to come to the Journey Course with me. "Doug Bailey is a good man—you haven't overstated him." But then Dad begins to tear down the tiny bit he knows about Episcopal theology that Doug represents. He refutes several traditional doctrines about Christianity and adds, "Jesus did not mean for us to go out and sell all that we have." Not a surprising statement from a capitalist businessman (albeit one who gave away much of his earnings to help others). But I think that is *exactly* what Jesus meant! I say nothing. Dad is on to "sin" now, a topic he neither accepts nor understands. He says religions other than Christian Science emphasize it but that "no where in the Bible is it emphasized." That might be news to most Christians! He worries I'm following the *person* Doug Bailey rather than God. Nothing could be further from the truth and I try to say so in the few seconds before his next discourse: on standards and self-government.

Dad cannot discuss my religion with me. He can't even let me mention my views. He is not interested in Julian, Teresa or any other historic Christian. He is very uncomfortable discussing any religion other than his own.

St. Francis of Assisi day is the day after my birthday and Mrs. Owen invites Dad, Jayne and me to attend the blessing-of-the-animals-service in the Roofless Church that evening, followed by a candlelit dinner as her guests. Dad does not want to go. In fact, he is not eager to meet Jane Owen. He likes to control his time—and ours—completely.

So I go alone. It is a lovely event, European in feel, including children, dogs, cats, birds, goats, and choir processing with candles from the church to the lawn beside the *Chapel of the Little Portion* where picnic tables topped with white cloths and more lit candles offer us an evening supper of spare ribs, vegetables, and rolls. I happen to sit beside a Catholic priest, Father Earl, who is also a metals artist. We begin a theological discussion that continues when I meet him the next day at his Church of the Holy Angels. Somewhere in our discussion he tells me "it is more important to *believe* than to *know*," reminding me of the Einstein poster I hung in my classroom: "Imagination is more important than knowledge." My father thinks it is more important to know.

I paint the fresh roses in our living room and give the watercolor to Dad before he and Jayne leave Sunday morning. Mrs. Owen invited Dad, Jayne and me to join her for Sunday breakfast but he'd refused; so Mrs. Owen drops by on Sunday morning just before he leaves—it is one of *her* houses we are staying in, after all! Dad is on the phone; she waits patiently for him to finish. She says to Dad, "Your daughter has waited a long time to get you here." She has forgotten our New Harmony visit in '1993, but her point is well-taken. She expected Dad to take part in New Harmony. She is saying more than her words. She is really asking, *"why can you not participate in your daughter's journey? Why do you resist her so?"* I walk her out to her golf cart (which she rides all over the village) and thank her for last evening. She says to me, "Your father is shriveling up!" She has read *In My Father's House*, the brief story I wrote about my father's life and mine; she sees him narrowing from the man she'd read about. She may not know, as do I, his focus has always, and only, been Christian Science.

For the next five months I continue teaching private art classes, paint, participate on the Journey team, attend the Practical Wisdom course, and try to establish my new home business, Seeds. But I also add working as a paste-up artist at Cleo Wrap, a wrapping paper design company, in November and December—nothing creative, but I am grateful for the work. I'm encouraged by the department head, who knows I am an artist, to do Santa illustrations on speculation. I spend hours of my own time on several; nothing comes of this except praise and rejection letters for the waste basket—same fate as the poetry I sent off for possible paid publication. My next work opportunity is a temp job surveying customers about Proctor and Gamble products—UGH!

Bill's time with colleagues and students keeps him in a world I am no longer privy to. He gives his sense of humor and intellect to others all day long, bringing little home but a tired body. Some days I feel I am merely the cook in his kitchen, the body in his bed and less important than his computer.

In January 1997 I have a one-woman show at the Memphis State University Fogelman Gallery of my 12 large Taos watercolors, some done in the pueblo just before a storm, all revealing the amazing Southwest light. The gallery does not advertise the show, however, as I'd been told, and few see the exhibit. Not one painting sells. I spent $2,400 in framing. Gratefully, a couple months later I conduct a several-days watercolor workshop in Arkansas for which I am well paid, almost enough to pay the framer.

Colleen, an artist-friend for 15 years, a beautiful woman and successful watercolorist, asks me if I'd like to teach the Arkansas workshop for her. I run into her in the Memphis gallery where we both have paintings. Raised in a Christian Science home, though not a follower, Colleen used to occasionally attend our Germantown Christian Science Society where I'd been her daughter's Sunday School teacher. She tells me she's just had two breasts removed and cancer is now in her liver. I am stunned. Leaving the gallery, I step on the escalator thinking: *What right has cancer to travel through her beautiful body?!* I repeat a resounding "No!" as I ride the moving stairs." No! No! No! No!" I shout all the way to my car. A man unlocking his Ford stares at me, but I don't care. "No! no! no!" I repeat all the way home. I throw my keys on the sofa, get out my Bible and other books, a legal pad and pen, and pray for Colleen. For many hours straight I write a dozen pages as thoughts come. I mail them to her. She calls to thank me for my words and I promise to continue to pray for her. She improves to everyone's joyful amazement—due to her own fortitude and good medical care as well as prayer—and paints her best work in the next five years before she dies.

When I can't sleep, I read or write. One evening in January 1997, I read Hildegarde of Bingen—and write in my journal: *I worry about not having done anything useful before I die. Seems whatever I do, a door slams in my face—this whole year! I can hear them—bang, bang, bang! There's nothing left to enter.*

As I ponder this, I find myself in a strange daydream—like a night dream but I am awake. I've never experienced this. I close my eyes and stare at closed doors. I push one open, but discover behind it universal space, a starry void. I would step into outer space if I entered so I don't. I try another door. It is the *same* door. All the doors are the same door! Why is the door knob shiny brass but the door plain? The void is like the sky seen through a telescope. I turn the doorknob and quick jolts of filmy-clad females with lovely faces, flash by—blonde: a little child and the other, ageless. The older female smiles knowingly. The child beckons me. Frowning, agitated, she points to the space, wanting me to hurry, to leap beyond the door into the void.

Suddenly a dragonish thing appears—dark green and black, flashing on the other side of the door. The women are gone and I have gone through the door. I am falling and worry my filmy dress will float above my head. It feels restful—the most rest I have had in days. Gentle. The dragonish thing watches me, takes my hand. He is playful, smiling, not a bad fellow, really. He licks my forehead like a dog might. Then shapeless things like bears or rocks—I can't tell which—attack me. The dragon hurries off afraid, he is not the friend to save me. My attackers eat at me like lions at prey. But when they've had their fill and are gone, I put my hand to my head, and though it is pounding, it is intact. Only my womb is gone! Where it used to be there is a huge hole through which I see the dark sky. My hair is blond like the little child's now. I get up and look for my womb. I find shapes to try to fit in the hole—like a child's toy sorting box—but they are too small and fall out.

A giant womb appears, like a planet whooshing toward me, filling up my hole, knocking me over. The planet-like womb is so huge, it amazes me it fits. I put my arms around it like I am pregnant and smile. I laugh. I die. The dragon tip-toes back and looks at me sadly and moves out of the picture. The child and adult female peer down, smiling at each other and me. Surprisingly, I wink at them but remain dead. They turn and wave good bye to the viewer (odd there is one, I think later). I believe I've had my first vision. This is weird. I am not asleep. I think of the Ghost Dance trances. I know sleep deprivation is one way to experience a trance. Did I set myself up for this with little sleep and two days of Hildegarde? I drift off in real sleep.

Next time I meet with Virginia she asks me what I *want*. I answer that I want Bill and me to remain soulmates, to be close to my daughter and sons, to have a purposeful job, and to find success as an artist, but uppermost, I want God—I want His undeniable Presence to come *through* me. Virginia asks if I am ready to "go up the mountain of fire." I say yes, though I'm not exactly sure what that means. She begins an explanation of the Daily Office in the Episcopal prayer book. Office means work, she explains. Every morning I am to spend 15 or more minutes with this reading, con-sisting of a Psalm, another biblical reading, silence, a hymn, prayers for myself and others, the Lord's Prayer and a Collect (biblical passage used in liturgy). In the following months the Daily Office ties in perfectly with my life and art—themes of renewal, purpose, hope, patient waiting, and "the treasures of darkness".

I write in my journal: "everything is happening, yet nothing is." In seven months I have had 42 different jobs or job-related attempts, completed 16 new paintings and who knows how many Gwen's Girls ornaments. I have edited and re-edited my resume, sending it off numerous times. Nothing has changed. I do not have a job. Yet I am at peace. My focus on "the dying" or abandonment of self —detachment from things and associations—brings this peace. Pierre de Caussade says "The soul that truly abandons itself to God has nothing to fear from the most violent storms..." for it has its " being in God only, in possessing nothing more than God alone, no other sup-port, no other help, no other hope!" My hope has always come through God. Virginia and Doug speak of my "fire," something each has told me has to do with my "fierce passion" for life and God. Every Celtic church in Britain and Ireland kept a fire burning as a sign of God's presence. I feel this fire, God's Presence, in 1997 in spite of hard times.

Bill's increasing dissatisfaction with Custis Lee, leads us to a Boston teacher-placement conference—kind of a meat-market format—February 19, 1997—where, among others, a New Hampshire private boarding school expresses interest in us.

Back home, I see a want ad in the Memphis paper for an immediate art teaching position in a local public middle school. I apply, interview, and get the job. I sign a contract to teach March through June, finishing out the year for a pregnant teacher. They will pay me wages far better than Custis Lee. But I will have enough students to populate a small village—1,100!

Before I start this job, Charissa, Bill and I go to New Harmony during the first couple days of their Spring Break to get away from what has been a challenging school year for Bill and a battle for me in finding work. We stay in the Duclos House—where Dad, Jayne, and I stayed in October. We write, read, walk, talk. I make French toast and cocoa. Bill devours books he has brought, while Charissa and I visit the inn's exercise room and swimming pool. Mrs. Owen's secretary drops by and invites us to do yoga with her and to have lunch with Mrs.Owen. Bill visits with Mr. Owen who is very ill. After our 3-day respite, Charissa visits her father for the rest of break while Bill and I fly to Boston to see Dad for a night, then drive through a blizzard to Vermont for job interviews. We sign on to teach at a New Hampshire boarding school for the summer, hoping it will lead to something permanent.

After Spring Break, I begin at Collierville Middle School. Though I admire the principal and assistant principal, I soon discover my assignment is horrific. As if teaching 1,100 students every week weren't bad enough, I even have two classes simultaneously in two *different* rooms—60 middle school students!—every conceivable kind of humanity. As I suspected, my job is more about keeping order than teaching art.

But I enter the scene expecting transformation. Where no art existed on white walls we soon have sheets of work. Where crayons—the only art material in evidence—were used primarily by students as projectiles before, now they create art, along with paint, pastel and charcoal. I dare to take my classes outside to draw from nature. Students take turns posing in sports positions while classmates draw them. Sweet girls stay after class, so jubilant I have come, bringing me gifts and appreciative notes. Boys who beat each other up don't know what to make of me, but settle down after the first two weeks because they are having fun making real art. One boy wheeled in by an Aid, whose name is Mark, with disfigured limbs and helmet, unable to speak, barely able to raise his head or hold a pencil, lights up when I proudly show his contour drawing to the class—how difficult it had been for him to manipulate the pencil!—but there it is—a drawing of real movement and design!—as interesting as any museum drawing by Ellsworth Kelley. Thrilled for him, I walk over to his chair, and staring into his eyes—our faces six inches apart—I tell him, "This is a *beautiful* drawing! Exactly what a contour drawing is all about! You have done a superb job! I love it! I am so proud of you! Will it be o.k. with you if I show it to the class and hang it on the wall for everyone to see?" He smiles, makes an affirmative sound, glows in a way that makes *all* my struggles disappear. I write him a note, praising his drawing, to take home to his parents. Later, I ask the aide about his condition and am told he hasn't long to live.

On March 25, 1997, Bill receives a 2-page typed memorandum from the Headmistress, accusing him of negativity, of not using enough facts in his history classes—after saying he is a good teacher in the first sentence!—absurd criticism since she barely once set foot in one of his classes! None of it makes sense! It is a horrid letter and the antithesis of truth. Bill will never get another teaching job if she has her way. So unfair! Her evaluation will be part of Bill's permanent file. In her office, she tells him he is "a negative influence on the faculty." This would shock every colleague, parent and student if they heard it, for what he really is, is their *hope*! The truth is, his scholarship, creativity and humor make their days bearable. His care and concern for the intellectual development of his students is extraordinary. He is one of few to have brought genuine intellectual depth to that institution! I have never witnessed a finer or more professional teacher—and would say the same were he not my husband. But the Headmistress, who has been there but two years to Bill's twenty, calls in the Associate Head, and they denigrate this accomplished professional. Bill is accused of not teaching "dates"—an unsupported, ridiculous accusation based on two girls not knowing the dates of the Civil War when asked by the Assistant Head. Ludicrous! Bill takes his students way beyond dates, into critical and analytical thinking (as well as dates). He is an expert at teaching kids to *think*. Then the Headmistress tells Bill she knows he has applied with a teachers' placement service, for she is on its board. Ah, so this is the root of it all! She does not want him—among the cream of the faculty—to leave unless *she* instigates it. How would it make her look? A number of teachers besides Bill and I are displeased with her running of the school. Since this headmistress's arrival in1995-96, it has seemed honesty, openness, ethics, and confidentiality have disappeared. Two years she will be gone and a new head hired.

Though Bill has not resigned yet in the Spring of 1997, we list our house with the realtor used in my past four moves. Like Ghost Dancers dancing their last hope, we pray our interviews, or perhaps our contracted summer positions, will lead to permanent new positions.

Easter, 1997, I am at Virginia's church, sharing a simple ceremony of feet washing, something I've never done. As Jesus did to the disciples, Virginia washes my feet, saying, "This beautiful woman would drink the ocean of God if she could, for she reminds me of Peter who said 'Lord, not my feet only but also my hands and my head!" I am surprised by her words, yet, sometimes I *do* feel as if I *am* trying to drink the ocean.

Privately, she tells me not to worry about getting answers; they will come. "You try hard to grasp things; simply rest. *Let* God grasp you. *Trust* even when you don't see. *Hope* even when things seem hopeless. You tend to see the world in brilliant white and darkest black. Julian's *All shall be well* means to accept the awful darkness, too. Living *through* brings answers. There will be an Easter for you. Whatever happens, its all God-stuff." I feel like a child in the wilderness, feeding on Old Testament manna that becomes New Testament bread of life, and that each Sunday is represented in the sacrament.

April 16, I come home late after keeping after-school detention for two naughty boys, frustrated by the evils children inflict on each other, only to watch Zaire's tragedy on TV as I fix dinner. I do laundry, scrub toilets, playing Paula Cole's *Where Have all the Cowboys Gone*, read before bed an Eskimo shaman's words that true wisdom "lives far from mankind, out in the great loneliness…reached only through suffering." Before I turn out my light, I write in my journal: *An artist needs a nest, a loose bit of sticks, prickly full— a base to support her flight; but she can't fly from a cage.*

In May we take a long weekend to fly to Los Angeles where Bill has an interview, but we learn quickly the school is not a good match for him. In L.A., I write: *We are both worried—no lined up employment, our home is for sale but we've nowhere to move, our daughter starts college this Fall, and we have less than 3 months to find jobs for the upcoming school year. Bill has one more interview—in Pennsylvania.*

Via the placement service, Moravian Academy in Bethlehem, Pennsylvania contacts Bill. This outstanding school is a perfect fit for my husband and he accepts their offer of the position of History Department Chair. Founded in 1742, the school has a bright, diverse student body representing every religious and ethnic background. We plan to stop there en route to our summer positions in New Hampshire.

I barely have time to get our house in order for the real estate agent and pack for our summer teaching in New Hampshire. Charissa, who has just graduated, looks forward to staying home, having independence and a summer job. Calvary Church friends who have just sold their home and are about to move and need a place to live for a few months, will live in our home with her.

My last visit with Virginia, I ask what she perceives to be my particular reason for being. She answers, "Your purpose is *redemption*; you are capable of being a redeemer for others." That word came up in connection with my Native American Ghost Dance religion and Celtic art series, too! The redeemer is like Campbell's "hero" who enters the depths of darkness to return and help his people. Virginia says redemption means " to find light *in* the darkness, to transform, heal, uplift bad to good, take what is hurting others and ameliorate it." Like a shaman, perhaps? I hug Virginia good-bye. I will miss our visits. But I am used to leaving people, places and things.

Bill and I look for a house in Pennsylvania en route to our summer teaching stint in New Hampshire but find nothing. From our Easton, Pennsylvania motel room window, I watch Hell's Angels in black leather come out of Mac Donald's and get on bikes. Will we find a home here? Will this place change us? Memphis seems soft-edged by comparison. Bill's school will be good for him, but what will be here for me? Will I find a job and purpose? Why has God brought us here? Why has everything about this move seemed difficult? Even when we went to get in our car to start this twenty-hour trip, we found two cedar trees had fallen across our driveway, blocking our path! Rather symbolic. I tell myself, if we find a home, get Charissa to Boston University where she's been accepted, and I find a job, then there is hope.

Our summer jobs house us in a pair of student rooms with twin beds, a couple of dressers, and little else. We have many duties besides teaching, for we are responsible for 5th and 6th grade boys. We supervise nightly study hall and dorm time, chaperone after school sports, social events and weekend activities, while divvying out discipline in this rule-obsessed institution. We eat meals family style with the students in the cafeteria. We are on duty 24 hours, 7 days a week, with a rare day off to do laundry.

As the summer unfolds, Bill and I decide these are feral children. Boys with hi-tech computers stuff themselves with dress-boxes of candy sent from home but cannot tie their shoes or bother to use their toothbrushes without my reminding them. Our work is mammoth. Our jobs would rob us of whatever sanity we have left after an already unbelievably difficult year. But, as always, I like my students—especially a talented Ukrainian boy and two Korean girls who attach themselves to me like barnacles. Bill, however, not used to disciplining anyone and unfamiliar with middle school, has many frustrating days. With countless duties and no privacy it is a hard summer for both of us.

While in New Hampshire, our Memphis house sells. We've only *one weekend* to find a new home in Pennsylvania—on our drive back to Memphis. We sign papers for a duplex in Easton, ten minutes from Bill's new school, then drive on to Memphis with only a week in which to pack all our belongings and move.

seventeen

Back Roads to Brigadoon

People parade through my house, not realizing this is my home. Nearly naked, I run up back stairs to dress, to my high-ceilinged bedroom with tall windows where I find a woman in a red-feathered hat walking her Newfoundland puppy. I don't seem surprised by her being in my bedroom. I tell her I raised 42 Newfies and does she know they save lives? But she doesn't hear or see me and walks out the second floor window and disappears. I put on a thirties gown and return downstairs where hundreds of people mingle, conversing, dining, ignoring me in my own house. I puzzle over this dream.

New Harmony is no Brigadoon—for along with its mysticism, it has *real* farmers, grocers and innkeepers—but as if it disappears in some hundred-year mist, I visit there no more.

After teaching the summer of 1997 in New Hampshire, purchasing a home in Easton, Pennsylvania (by phone calls and a brief on-site look en route back to Memphis), we pack up everything in Memphis in less than a week and drive back to our new home in Pennsylvania. Nathan, who has come along to help, drives the Mitsubishi packed with Charissa, our old dog, Surprise, and cats, Oreo and Butterscotch—each cat constantly meowing in his/her own kennel—suitcases, boxes, brooms, vacuum cleaner, hangers of clothes, and miscellaneous stuff. Bill and I drive the Honda wagon, wedged in by plants, computer, treasured paintings, and Grandma Hunt's silver.

Once more I leave one place for another, the known for the unknown. For twenty years Memphis has been my home, the only home Charissa has known. Bill, too. This is a substantial change for all three of us.

Before leaving our New Hampshire teaching stint, I received a note from the man who hired us for our summer positions. One sentence stands out: "All great adventures begin with unequivocal risk and undaunting faith." I take this wisdom with me to Pennsylvania.

The journey proves to be rugged—not just because we have only seven days in which to pack and leave, following a grueling summer, but because the thousand-mile trip from Memphis to Easton incurs two unforeseen calamities.

North of Knoxville, Bill hits an 18-wheeler. He is alone in the car. I am driving the Mitsubishi with Charissa and Nathan so we can visit for a couple hours. I watch the accident happen in front of me. Bill steers too far to the right and collides into the left side of the truck. The right front end of our car is damaged but neither Bill nor the truck driver is hurt; the truck incurs minimal damage. Amazingly, the Honda still runs, so after waiting for the police and exchanging information, a bit shaken, we continue on our way.

The more agonizing tragedy happens in Virginia. I drive the Honda, while Bill takes a break following his accident, and Nathan drives Charissa and the animals in the Mitsubishi. Suddenly both kids make hand-signals indicating we should pull off at the next exit. They seem agitated. We exit into a gas station. Nathan pops out and comes to my window and says, "Mom, Surprise just died."

Surprise, my Samoyed, was an unexpected Christmas present that Charissa had urged her father to give me (and her) one of our last years in Fisherville. A ball of white fluff with a red collar, he was an adorable pup. Over his thirteen years, I adored him. My silent companion and confident, in whose deep ruff I could bury my tears or laughter, was missed terribly during the divorce and after when I couldn't have him at my Lennox School condo. As soon as Bill and I moved into our Davidson Cove house, we took Surprise along with the cats (John moved out of his suburban home he'd purchased after the divorce to an apartment). Surprise liked living on Davidson Cove and had charmed a neighbor or two into bringing him treats. A watch dog when necessary, he was, above all, a soul-friend.

Nothing prepares you for death. I had seen some signs of aging in Surprise, but never expected to lose him—especially without me by his side. When I look in the kids' car, I'm shocked to see him lying so still. I wish he were only sleeping, that I could wake him with a call and look into his loving eyes once more. It's even worse, he died in the *kids'* car. We all stand in tears alongside the highway. I suggest we find the closest veterinarian and ask him to bury Surprise. Amazingly, in a few minutes, we find a country vet who handles everything compassionately for a reasonable fee, even allowing us time alone with our beloved pet before we leave him forever in northwestern Virginia. Exhausted, the four of us travel in silence the remainder of the trip, except for an occasional sigh or tear. Sometimes I still cry for that dog.

We experience no other disasters—other than getting lost in Allentown after dark.

Very early the next morning, Nathan and I pry up all the old mauve carpet in our new home, in a whirlwind attempt to tung oil the revealed hardwood floors beneath (which I had checked prior to purchase) before the moving van's arrival. Bill and Charissa clean the upstairs and vacuum. By the time the van arrives all is ready. Nathan flies back to grad school at University of Tennessee the next day. The very next weekend, Bill and I load Charissa's stuff for her first year at college into our Honda for another road trip—this time to Boston University—and Bill starts work at Moravian. I do most of the unpacking alone.

Our new home at 355 Shawnee Drive, Easton, Pennsylvania is located in an area known as College Hill, perched on a high hill, near Lafayette College, with tall old trees, in a neighborhood of charming turn-of-the century houses, many larger than ours (I will paint them when all the boxes are unpacked). We are within an hour of New York City and a couple hours to the ocean, and only thirty minutes to the Appalachian Trail. Boston is only six hours away. I decide I will like living here.

Our 1913 white stucco Arts and Crafts Movement "twin," as duplexes are called here, is half of a large home. There are nine-foot ceilings on the first floor with wonderful old chestnut woodwork—beams, moldings and a coiffered ceiling—one of the attractions to the place. I call our home

"Cymru Cottage" for there is a very Welsh feeling about this area (in fact, I will discover a group of Welsh-descendents, a St. David's organization, which I join; Bill and I attend three programs which conclude with Welsh food and singing old Welsh hymns). To the side of our front door I hang a small slate I paint with flowers and the words, "Cymru Cottage." I have a contractor install my German antique mantel around the fireplace (which I had originally purchased for my Lenox School condo); it looks as if it were made for this home (in every home I have installed something that I couldn't remove—a subconscious insurance against moving again? Or, a desire to connect to the home's future by leaving behind a bit of me?). In the dining room, against a series of existing windows to a sunroom, I lean three antique stained glass windows from my Fisherville home—the new owner replaced them with storms and kindly gave me the originals. We put new Berber carpet in the sunroom which overlooks the hillside where I plant a perennial flower garden the following spring. The very tiny kitchen faces the front of the house with windows looking into large oaks and up a hill toward lovely old houses. There are four bedrooms: one for Charissa, one for Bill and me, a guest room for the boys when they come, and a den for Bill (which we fit with built-ins eventually). There is a walk-out basement where I do laundry and keep my garden tools. The one-car garage is across the little drive that leads to our house and three other homes. The unheated attic is 17' by 27' and I designate it my art studio.

The couple who live in the other half of this house are older, their grown children frequently visit with grandchildren. They are both heavy smokers, and I smell smoke in our home, increasingly unpleasant. But when I sit on our small front porch, evenings, watching the fall colors, not found in a Memphis autumn, I am grateful for this house and Bill's new job which brought us here. I feel peaceful for the first time in many months.

My first two months in Pennsylvania are filled with unpacking, organizing, sanding floors, re-finishing antiques, painting walls, executing large watercolors of the College Hill area for my future attic studio/gallery/classroom—and keeping Charlie, the neighborhood bully cat, from attacking Oreo, who will not leave our doormat, and Butterscotch, who refuses to go outside at all.

I decide *Seeds Studio at Cymru Cottage* is what I will call my art business here. I send out a flyer to advertise private art classes for adults and children, but no one calls. Nevertheless, I plan to use the attic as a studio—a place to teach, once I am known, and display my work. I paint the attic walls white and stain the beams dark chestnut. I set up my art tables and easel and create a small corner with a mattress by the window for my "room of one's own," adding a shelf for writing materials and journals. There's no heat up here, so I bring up a down comforter to wrap around me when I write. I paint in two sweaters or a jacket. Eventually I hope to add heat and skylights. I sub a little at Bill's school, Moravian Academy, and learn how wonderful and exceptional the students are. I continue to look everywhere for a permanent art teaching or art-related position, but find nothing.

We frequent the small public library and I check out another insightful book by Thomas Merton, in which he says God speaks to us in three places: in Scripture, in our deepest selves, and in the voice of the stranger. Here in Pennsylvania, I hear God in all three.

We attend a lovely historic Episcopal church at the base of College Hill in Easton. The rector is nothing at all like Doug Bailey—more coolly academic than out-reaching—but I am drawn to the quiet female assistant rector. Our first Sunday we are given a loaf of home-baked bread—a custom of this church to welcome newcomers. The note accompanying the loaf invites us to make Trinity Church a place "where you can be fed with the Bread of Life," which reminds me of my days in Memphis' Japanese Garden when I prayed for manna and learned that the manna of the Old Testament becomes the Bread of Life in the New Testament and the sacrament on Sunday. God has fed us manna every step of the way in bringing us out of wilderness to this place of employment, home, and new possibilities.

One morning in prayer I read in Exodus: "I am the Lord thy God, which hath brought thee out of the land of Egypt, out of the house of bondage" (Exodus 20:2). I study the commandments that follow this verse, accept them as my occupation, for I have no other.

Studying healing, I realize how little it is understood or appreciated in standard Christianity, though more than a third of the gospels deal with little else. I have noticed that healing seems to make ordinary Christians uncomfortable. Medical means seems the only trusted method. The assistant rector asks me to speak to her Sunday School class about healing. I enjoy the preparation and opportunity.

My three-word mantra in my transition from Christian Science to Episcopalianism—*Christ Jesus healed*—continues to be my rock. I love its simplicity. Jesus did not know denomination; he simply healed every sincere seeker.

Bill comes down with a severe case of sinusitis. After three weeks with medicine and no relief, I ask him if I can pray for him. He agrees. The first day my Bible falls open to Psalm 140 where I read about "the violent man" and it comes to me Bill's anger must stop. Where does this otherwise delightful and humorous man's rage come from? I write: *"When the violence goes so will BC's sinusitius."* I tell him this and in a day his sinusitus is gone. Even he acknowledges this healing.

I show the paintings I've done of College Hill homes to the two galleries in Easton, along with my box series; both owners like my work but have full exhibitions scheduled a year in advance and can't accommodate me; they encourage me to come back in Spring.

I write to the Allentown Art Museum for work but there are no openings. I take my resume to several local colleges and have two interviews—again no positions are available. I place an ad for my classes in the local newspaper, to no avail. I discover a poetry reading group which meets across the river in New Jersey and attend a few times, reading several of my poems which are well received, and ask if anyone knows of writing jobs; no one has any suggestions. I remain unemployed until the middle of November.

One day we go to the Allentown Market and buy groceries—one chicken breast, an onion, a handful of fresh spinach, some good rye bread for the bean soup I plan to make. We are having a good time because we have no grocery list, no agenda, and are free to look at all the amazing stalls and their wares, savoring each one's unique offerings, choosing carefully, carrying little. Somewhere in the Allentown Market I turn to Bill and say: "You know, I would rather be poor with *you* more than with anyone else I know!" Bill smiles and squeezes my hand.

Meanwhile, I am put in contact with a new gallery in Sun Valley, Idaho. I send them slides of my New Mexican watercolors that I had shown at

Memphis State University's Fogelman Gallery. They very much like my work and want it for their opening. I pay over $800 to have my work shipped out to Sun Valley where I've been told wealthy clientele will appreciate my style. What I am not told is that the new gallery does no real publicity and because the gallery is brand new, few see my pieces. Not a single painting sells. Once more, I am completely frustrated.

I paint a charming historic house en route to New Hope, New Jersey, (a popular tourist art town about 45 minutes from Easton), have post cards made of it and mail them at considerable expense to B&B's throughout the nation offering to do watercolor portraits of their B&Bs from their photo. No takers, in spite of everyone telling me "what a great idea!"

Our first Thanksgiving in Easton, Dad, Jayne, Charissa, Nathan, and Jason come, for which I cook up a storm, write individual poems for each, arrange dried grasses in vases, finish painting the guest room walls, buy new towels and make a sign up sheet for our one full bath. Bill takes the boys and Dad on a hike. We take Dad and Jayne to the Christian Science church in Bethlehem Thanksgiving morning.

About two weeks prior, I find a newspaper ad for a deli position at the Moravian Bookstore, an upscale shop that fills three charming buildings on Main Street in the historic section of downtown Bethlehem. The book store/ gourmet deli/restaurant/gift store sells high-end Christmas ornaments, books, gourmet food, kitchen and home accessories, and serves breakfast, lunch and dinner. I get the job. They give me a white apron and I wait on customers, make sandwiches to customer's specifications, dish up and prepare deli food, stock beverage refrigerators, package scones, supply shelves, wash pots and pans, write the menu on the menu board, load cases with bowls and platters of food, work the cash register, microwave, coffeemaker, and change the drip pans—all for $7.25 an hour. I drive 30 minutes from home for this, including many weekends. At age 54 with a master's degree with honors from one of the top three art institutions in the United States, I find myself on my hands and knees cleaning an industrial refrigerator's drip pan. Over time, I grow to appreciate learning recipes for Moravian's stuffed portabella mushrooms and popular scones; but after four months, I quit.

It depresses me not to have a real career. Some days it's difficult to put on my shoes. I keep my shoes at the foot of the bed where I can see them when I wake so it will be easier to climb out of the covers. I pray and walk every day to control depression. I write in my journal: *Stillness is the first necessity for manifesting your desire.* It is easy to practice stillness here, where after 7 months I still have met no one and see no one every day—aside from a rare visit with Nanette, who lives in the other half of our house but who is usually gone because her job is cleaning houses.

When I am not refinishing furniture, planning my new business, or painting local scenes, I work—again–at figuring out what my purpose is. Bill says, "psychologically it is honesty; socially it is justice" and adds, "You could fly a balloon around the world if you knew it was your purpose."

Depressed on February 10, 1998, I write in my journal: *I have nothing. No job. No career. No art sales. I have no real studio for the first time in my adult life... At 54 I make minimum wage. At my age my father was a CEO! What's wrong with me that I can't be successful?!... we create our own reality, but I don't feel like I'm creating this darkness... Bill does not understand—he is busy with his wonderful new job—I am like a story he is reading in detachment. I wish Surprise were here. I hate when good dies.* It is February once again.

One day it seems impossible to get out of bed. My tennis shoes at the end of the bed seem too far away. Bill is gone to Moravian and I am alone. I could stay under the covers today and it wouldn't matter. But, I am Glenn Evans' daughter, and somehow I reach for the shoes. I find myself walking up the hill, to the top, through a passage of woods to the edge where the vista overlooks New Jersey. It is hundreds of feet down and I do not like heights. But this day, I go to the edge. I wonder what it would be like to fall. To just sail through the air and land on those rocks far below. How would it feel? That would be one way to not have to worry about my lack of employment or purpose! I stand there for a few seconds thinking about that option. But then I back up, having scared myself sufficiently, and walk home quickly, enter my kitchen door, find the phone book, and look up "psychologist" in the Yellow Pages. I find one that mentions women specifically and make an appointment—a huge step for this former Christian Scientist!

The calm young blonde psychologist is easy to talk to. I visit her for many months and learn about myself: that I have to work through my Christian Science past, that I am too cerebral for my own good, that I need to do what I love—mostly stuff I already know.

I do better when the sun is shining. On Valentine's Day I wake saying, *This is the day the Lord hath made, be glad, give thanks, rejoice,* then go over the Lord's Prayer. When I get to the debts and debtors part, I realize if we are to get out of debt—the $15,000 the move cost us!—I must *forgive my debtors,* those who I feel harmed me in any way: the art agent who disappeared with my work, the Headmistress and Upper School Head and others. Forgiveness doesn't happen overnight—nor just because I want it. I must work for it. I must truly see each individual as a beloved child of God—this Valentine's Day and every day. Our Valentine's Day celebration is simple: I make Bill a card and he plays me tunes. We have only $16 in the bank but we have each other.

Before I leave the deli job, I apply for and get a job working at the Crayola Museum, a hands-on children's museum which promotes Crayola products and attracts thousands of tourists. Though the pay is only a dollar more an hour than the deli job, I think it may lead to something bigger—like writing art curriculum for the museum.

But I learn quickly my job in the Crayola Museum is no more rewarding than the deli position. My main duty is to demonstrate materials and supervise children at various art-making stations. It turns out to be more about disciplining children, setting up, cleaning up, stocking supplies and selling Crayola products. At one station it's my duty to say over and over to each group coming through: "This is Model Magic! Model Magic is a Crayola product that can be molded into any shape and dries hard in just minutes…" as I manipulate the nontoxic Play-Dough-like substance into tiny animals or figures. Sadly, making sculpture samples is the best part of the job. I am required to attend meetings—but not paid for my time—to plan the periodic, thematic changes for station activities. Here my 24 year-old boss, who holds only an associate art degree from a local college, institutes concepts like copying rather than promoting originality. I am deeply frustrated by the clamps put on my ideas at these sessions. Though she knows I have a RISD masters degree, she seems to shoot down or ignore whatever I suggest. Dealing with her, the vacationing public, busloads of wild, unsupervised children, and constant physical clean-up finally gets to me.

One day a museum co-worker who knows of my art degree and experience, says to me: "maybe you can work your way up". She means well, but at 54, with only a few good years left, I am not looking forward to "working my way up" at the Crayola Museum! I think of Diane, Robin, Karen, Debbie, and other friends I've known most of my life who do not have jobs—nor is their working requisite for family income as mine is. I feel frustrated, frozen in a foreign role, down-sized and downwardly mobile, as if I will never be able to realize my dreams. I begin reading self-help books: *The Zen of Making a Living* again, several of those parachute books, *Finding Your Perfect Work*, Deepak Chopra's *Seven Spiritual Laws of Success*, and *Do What You Love the Money Will Follow*. I'm not sure I agree with the last one, but I do the work sheets in each with nearly as much diligence as I worked to save Mt. Pisgah School. I endeavor to find what I am meant to do in this world. I discover I have too many interests to fit in a slot. Starting my own business interests me, but the lack of start-up money and living in a new city where I know no one, prohibits this. I want a career that utilizes *all* that I am and love. I conclude that the more I express my true self the more success will follow. Chopra offers a quote from the *Upanishads* IV.4.5.: "You are what your deep, driving desire is. As your desire is, so is your will. As your will is, so is your deed. As your deed is, so is your destiny."

About this time, a course at the Bethlehem library is offered in the Hindu Uphanishads by a swami. I enroll in my first serious study of Hinduism. I find some of it reminiscent of Christian Science. Later, in the spring, I will go hear the Dali Llama speak when he visits a Hindu Center in New Jersey.

One day I apply for a higher paying curriculum-related position that I see on the bulletin board in the Crayola Factory workroom, feeling I have an excellent chance because I am already an employee and because I am over-qualified for it. Though the several required interviews seem to go well, I do not get the position. In fact, to my surprise I am phoned and let go from my regular job! They are cutting back on their hourly employees and I, being the last one hired, am the first one to be let go. I am stunned! Things couldn't get any worse!

I sit on my sunroom floor and weep. I have no one to talk to—I still haven't met anyone in Easton—and Bill is teaching. Who to call? My life has hit bottom.

I decide to call Dad. Helping people is what he does for a living. Surely as his daughter I can talk to him and he will listen. I phone him and explain my situation through a few leftover tears. He begins: "You know when *I* was between jobs as a young man….and he continues with all the familiar stories of his life. I cannot get a word in edgewise. My heart is sinking. I hold the phone away from my ear for a few seconds—he is still telling me *his* story and not listening to mine. When he changes the subject to some new project of his, I listen, offer a comment, thank him for his time, and hang up. Except to catch up on his life, I will not call him again.

I sob, rock, pull my long hair. Butterscotch stares at me from the window ledge. Then, tired, I stop. When I get still, I hear a voice as clear as if someone were in the room with me: *Do nothing, just BE.* Where did this come from?! It has the sound of God. I hear it again. *Do nothing, just BE.* I am silent before this unexpected wisdom. Suddenly I am undisturbed, enlightened. I get it! I am to *just be me*—and not do what is not me—in that will come my rightful work. I decide to paint, write, and not worry about employment.

I miss not having a spiritual director and ask the associate rector at the Easton Episcopal Church if she would consider being my spiritual director. Turns out she has a degree in spiritual direction and is delighted. We meet monthly. One day when I go early to her church office, I look at books on her shelves. I pick up one entitled *Mysticism* by Evelyn Underhill, a 500-page book about the development of spiritual consciousness. My quick skim tells me it is wonderful. Beth tells me to keep it.

Underhill is a huge influence on me. Her writing explains all I have experienced. I learn this is a classic work for those in the field of spirituality. Underhill speaks of awakening as a "a disturbance of the equilibrium of the self, which results in the shifting of the field of consciousness from lower to higher levels."(Evelyn Underhill, *Mysticism*, p. 176) Like L'Engle, she reminds me that "travail is the normal accompaniment of birth" (Underhill, p.177). My recent travail advances my purpose. Underhill widely opens the doors of contemplation and spiritual consciousness for me, affirming my finding the inward in the outward. Through Underhill I find Ruysbroeck, Augustine, Dionysius, *The Cloud of Unknowing*, and again, St. John of the Cross and Teresa of Avila. Underhill tells me all mystics "speak the same language and come from the same country" (Underhill, p. xiii). Their country is mine. I check out of the library every book Underhill has written and devour them.

I pray daily about lack and the need to earn a living. Within three days, three amazing things happen: 1)I receive a long-distance phone call telling me that a very large oil abstract painting I had in a Memphis gallery has just sold and I will be receiving a check for several thousand dollars 2) I am asked by the Easton Episcopal Church to do a pen and ink of their historic façade that they could use for their stationery; 3) Virginia, my former spiritual director in Memphis commissions me to paint an oil of my concept of Teresa of Avila for hanging in a new woman's center she is creating. So much manna all at once! I am in awe and grateful. I learn that just *being* leads to right work.

I reread Teresa of Avila's autobiography and other works to inspire the painting I am to do. Her water analogy for prayer interested me then and I reread it to inspire my painting. Teresa likens prayer to watering a garden, explaining there are four kinds of watering. *"A beginner* [in prayer] *must look on himself as one setting out to make a garden for his Lord's pleasure, on most unfruitful soil which abounds in weeds"* Teresa of Avila, The Life of Saint Teresa By Herself, p. 78). She explains that, first, we could draw water by from the well, which involves a lot of effort and work. Second, we could turn the crank of a water wheel and use aqueducts to obtain water with less labor, which Teresa says is the method of the prayer of quiet, without striving. The third way to water a garden is by employing irrigation by river or spring: when God helps us so completely he is nearly the gardener himself and we are not, a very deep and soul-sustaining form of prayer. And the fourth method of prayer comes like heavenly rain, when least expected, saturating the entire garden so that it is never dry; this form of prayer comes through great detachment from self-interest and requires enormous gratitude and humility. Teresa advises the gardener not to grow discouraged, nor to be concerned when tears come— *"tears gain everything; for one kind of water attracts another"* (Teresa of Avila, *The Life of Teresa of Avila By Herself,* p. 129). God will help in all trials. Union with God, means nothing parched; all is water.

I decide to do three things to bring me to level four of "watering": First, I will list what I am grateful for. Second, I am going to live with one goal: to please God by doing that which best stirs me to love. Third, I am going to make quiet time every morning. I don't let my geraniums go without watering each morning and I won't let myself go without it either! I drink six glasses of water each day, but I don't always take care of my spiritual thirst as I should.

In April 1998 I take on a strange piece of research. It comes to me to read all of my journals and look for a pattern of depression—when and how it began. I discover that between 1979 and 1998 I mention depression 81 times. I go back through the same nineteen years and tally how many times I am exuberant. The tally for exuberance during the same period is 50. I note that periods of heavy depression are usually in winter, usually February, often followed by spiritual peaks. When spirituality is strong, depression is rare to non-existent. I also note depression doesn't affect me when I am deeply engrossed in art-making, writing, or causes. And I note that I am down when I feel unloved, as I'm sure most human beings are. I also remind myself that my journals are *not* a balanced reflection of me, for they became the repository on my darkest days; on happy days I usually didn't take time to write.

Karen Evans, my brother's first wife, lives only ninety minutes away from me in New Jersey. She and I were in college together and later shared raising our children. Our friendship included deep conversations, love of art, and a Christian Science background (though Quaker and Asian influences eventually became more her focus). Now that I am in Pennsylvania, she pops back into my life. Both questioning, creative, and avid readers, Karen and I have much in common. She has not found her way since she got the divorce she wanted. When we get together for lunch she cries over the loss of her marriage. We share feelings, ideas, visit an organic farm and several bookstores, sit in front of a fire in my living room with cups of tea and talk about our journeys. On her birthday, we have a lobster picnic at her charming place in Oldwick, New Jersey. She and her new love interest, also a bibliophile, visit Bill and me for several dinners in our home. Unlike me, Karen doesn't have financial concerns—in fact, she has not had to work in 30 years; my brother has generously seen to that. She makes trips to Europe and attends workshops across the US. Our situations are not the same but our questions are.

One day in the dentist's office, waiting to get my teeth cleaned, I read a line in a gardening magazine: *"When we needed money, I knew that the answer was in the garden."* This stops me short—the way the Nike ad had in the shoe store years before, only this time the message is about my career. I've been designing my future art business, *Seeds Studio at Cymru Cottage*, because I see creativity as a seed that germinates and grows to full bloom in paintings, poetry, and more—as back in Memphis I had attempted to launch *Seeds: Growing Creative Ideas*. I think about my days meditating in Memphis' Japanese *Garden*, how answers came when I was still. I think about Jesus in the *Garden* of Gethsemane—a trial in the garden that leads to his resurrection, of Adam and Eve in the *garden*, and of Teresa of Avila's *garden* analogy. *Garden*, I decide, is a word I value. *Garden* is a place in consciousness where seeds—ideas— grow. I look up *garden* in the Bible concordance and read many references, among them Numbers 24:6: "How goodly are thy tents, O Jacob, and thy tabernacles, O Israel! As the valleys are they spread forth, as *gardens* by the river's side…which the Lord hath planted….He shall pour the water out of his buckets, and his seed shall be in many waters…." And 51: "he will comfort all her waste places; and he will make her wilderness like Eden, and her desert like the *garden* of the Lord; joy and gladness shall be found therein, thanksgiving, and the voice of melody." It seems to me my desert time is about to become a watered garden! I write February 25: "I am a well-watered garden full of seeds yearning to grow and bloom for others to enjoy."

I study Scriptures and spiritual writing because that is one of the places God speaks. Actually, He speaks to us continually in the serendipitous, in the sign along the highway, in a stranger's words, the shoe store, or the magazine we read in a dentist's office. The problem is *not* with God's neglecting to send us messages. The problem is with us *hearing* the many he has already sent.

One night I fall asleep asking God: What is my garden to be? What would you have me do? If art is my being, but so is spirituality, what work combines the two? In the morning, God answers. It can't be 6 AM yet, I can tell by the sun. But I am awakened with "instructions" to go find a book I haven't seen since we moved here over a year ago. It is Alan Jones' *Exploring Spiritual Direction* that I'd purchased and read on retreat over a year ago and had not read since. I have no idea which of many sets of shelves to find it on, but I put on my slippers and wander the house until I find it. I open to the preface. Its heading is *"The Art of Arts."* If I read not another word I have my answer. I am an artist seeking the spiritual and here is a work—spiritual direction—that is called *the art of arts*! I reread Jones' book to learn how one becomes a spiritual director. I discover that Jones is a spiritual direction professor at General Theological Seminary in New York City. Before the day is out I am on my computer searching for an application to that seminary.

I learn from my spiritual director, that she attended the same seminary! After months of writing complex application responses, that in a sense are spiritual autobiography, I mail my application. I will be able to pay for this as well, for coincidentally and unexpectedly, my father bestows a monetary gift to his two children that eases my state of unemployment and will cover the first year of this Spiritual Direction master's degree for which I am applying.

Meanwhile, wanting to reach out and connect to my community, I volunteer to work for one of the Easton Episcopal Church's charities, Third St. Alliance, a large Victorian home that shelters abused women and their children. The church has taken on the task of repairing, cleaning, painting and making lovely rooms from ones badly in need of renovation.

In the Spring of 1998, I take on this volunteer work with great zeal, selecting paint colors and designing interiors other church members and I will paint. My goal is to make the rooms as inviting as the finest B&B. I faux paint walls myself to create a Tuscan ambience in one room—complete with framed watercolor paintings on the wall (my own—ones I decide I can live without) and hand-painted ivy vines. I create a special grape vine wreath for each room and sew decorative pillows. I shop at discount stores to find attractive new linens to create comfy beds. I paint butterflies on a periwinkle wall in another room, adding a hand mirror and fresh plants on top of newly refinished dressers. I buy lavender soaps, pretty combs, and place a book beside the bed, a seat cushion in the window. I passionately want these women to have a lovely home. To be homeless is the worse thing I can imagine. I do this volunteer work for months.

But this is not enough. The more I see what the lives of these women are like, the more I want to do. I tell the director of the home about my CASA experience and offer to help more directly. She says she would be thrilled if I could take a young mother and mentor her. I said I would love that—this would *not* be the first time I mentored young women!

I am assigned Darcy, a 23-year old who just gave birth two months ago, but also has a four-year-old and a 6-year-old. Her husband, like her father and uncle before him, had abused Darcy and her children. Her husband sexually attacked her 6-year-old daughter and gave their 4-year-old son a concussion.

The courts ordered him to keep away from Darcy and her children after he poured gasoline all over himself and set their home on fire—a fire in which she lost everything. With her husband in jail, she moved into Third Street Alliance while her older children went into foster care.

My assignment is to help Darcy get organized. With my own money I buy her a day-planner, file container, files, markers, pack her a picnic basket lunch of homemade bread sandwiches, fresh fruit and homemade cookies, and make her a grape vine wreath with flowers, acorns, and pine cones I find walking up the hill behind our house (wreaths unnecessary, beautiful, nature-born, handmade, show someone cares and say *home*).

Darcy's 8 by 10-foot room overwhelms me, piled knee-high with every sort of commodity: mounds of clothes, baby equipment, canned goods, food packages, toys for her older children who come to see her twice a week (though they've been in foster care for three years; Darcy tells me she won't give them up because her mother abandoned her when she was eight and she was forced to live with her abusive uncle). I have seen messes before, but nothing like this! Even her large walk-in closet contains huge garbage bags full of clothing and more toys and long shelves loaded with free community-given pantry food, enabling anyone to eat well. Yet, junk food packages are open everywhere in the room. She has more food in her space than I have ever stored in my pantry!—even when feeding a family of five! And the large trash bags of clothes—given to her by various agencies—are like black mountains midst the clutter of dirty clothing.

I begin to show her how to make order while hearing her tale. Twenty minutes into our appointment, she tells me she has to catch a bus in the next 30 minutes—though we'd arranged to have the whole day. She tells me I can stay in the room and clean it myself while she's gone, but I know that's not part of the deal. She then "borrows" 35 cents from me to make a phone call to Child Aid because her 2-month old son has to start day-care tomorrow (which Child Aid pays for) because she returns to work tomorrow, taking a 6 AM bus, traveling over an hour each way. She is breast-feeding her baby so I can imagine what "fun" this will be! I'm disappointed because I know it will take the whole day to get her room in order, but I say nothing other than that I will have to make a second trip for us to finish. As it turns out she is on the phone so long, down on another floor, that she misses her bus. The reason she had to catch the bus, she tells me, is to pay on a storage unit she owns; if she does not pay on it today, her belongings will be confiscated (basically a kitchen table and, unbelievably, more children's clothing and equipment). The storage unit is an hour's drive away. I drive her, saying "Just this once, but never again." We make what seems like a major moving expedition, up and down old Victorian floors, to load my station wagon with her stuff to take to the storage unit; it seems intelligent to take as many unnecessary items clogging her room as we can since she owns this storage unit.

When we get to the storage place, she goes into the office while I stay in the car with her baby. She's gone so long I begin talking out loud to the baby, telling him he might not have a chance to hear it again, but I want him to know and never forget that he is God's beloved child. A strange moment, the 2-month old looks at me as if he understands.

About 15 minutes later Darcy appears and says "we'll have to go back". "Heck no"! I think to myself, and say, "What seems to be the difficulty?" Turns out she lost the key to the unit a month ago (I had asked her before we left if she had the key); now she'll have to pay $60 to get a locksmith to break it open! No way am I going to pay $60 at this point! I ask her: "Where's the office?—there's *got* to be a solution to this problem and I am *not* leaving until we find it!" I hand her her baby, pray solidly, already feeling prayer's effects as I enter the office. I select a Mid-Eastern gentleman to tell my story to (my other options being an 18-year old kid who looks like he just woke up and a young girl shuffling her shoes).

Turns out this is only the second day on the job for the Mid-Easterner (whom I will refer to as Mohamed). I say to Mohamed: "I volunteered to bring this young woman here today to store all that she owns in her life in her unit; it has taken us over an hour to load the car and another hour to drive here and I am NOT leaving until we get her stuff put away; there MUST be a solution to this problem; I believe that human beings should help each other, that is what we are here for, and I will not leave until this problem is solved; I am SURE that if we all think creatively together there must be a solution." Then I look deep into his eyes—past his eyes really, into his heart and pull it out and hold it between my eyes—and speak heart-to-heart. "This young woman has experienced a very hard life and NEEDS A BREAK!" Our eyes communicate. I know he understands and feel he will do whatever he can (of course it does not hurt our cause that the baby cries and Darcy whips out a breast to feed him, holding him awkwardly in her arms). I pray, think creatively, and ask questions all at once.

By now we have the attention of all three employees, mostly spurred by Mohamed being new, questioning them for answers, and the endless wailing of the baby. I ask: "Is there a place where we could just keep the stuff for a few days until the social worker can get her the money to get the locksmith and then transfer it all into the one unit?...Can I talk to the manager?...Is there a small space and what does it cost to rent for a day? The manager is not in, the three behind the counter are the only ones around. There is no small unit to be had for a day. Then as I pause for thought, I hear Darcy say, what I take to be a tiny bit of Christ-presence because of its lightness in a dark moment—the kind of thing Bill might do to ease tension. With somewhat of a smile she says to Mohamed: "Gee, have you ever known anyone to have a problem like this before?—I mean have you ever known of *worse* problems?" I smile. Mohamed answers: "Yes, I have known of worse problems." But Mohamed is not thinking on a small scale. He replies, "Once, I was told the wrong date and time for a final exam when I was in college far away, not in this country, and so I went on the wrong day and found that the final had been the day before and I had to go to college for another whole year." "That's awful!" I respond, trying to imagine his full story. And I add, "Yes, there are worse problems than the one we face (and I thought of a friend I have with cancer) but I do believe we are put here to help each other even in the small things if we can; if we all help each other there are always solutions." "Yes," answers Mohamed, "I, too, believe that; we must all help each other". Then it hits me: "What does it cost to rent the smallest space for the least amount of time?" The young computer guy, finally awake, punches in a few buttons and answers, " 5 feet by 5 feet for $29.95—it doesn't matter if you have it for two days or a month; it's still $29.95". I look in my wallet and start to count what I have without saying a thing. I have $25 and do not want this on a credit card. Mohamed leaves saying something I did not catch and returns, *emptying his wallet on the counter*, saying "We must all help each other. You pay half and I pay half." Tears, that no one sees, I hope, fill my eyes. Deeply moved by the "face" of God I see in this man, in this moment, in this crazy day, I hand him back his ten and twenty and say "What you are doing is *wonderful*; the $5 will be enough—thank you! Thank you so very much!" I am not sure Darcy fully appreciates what has just happened. "Did you see what he did for you?" I whisper. She thanks him. I get his name and write a letter the next day to his boss and one to Mohamed, too, praising his actions, leadership, and adding in his boss's letter that my Dad as CEO believed hiring someone of true moral character is the most important thing, adding that my Dad would have hired Mohamed in a minute for *any* position!

It is late in the afternoon by the time Darcy and I return to her room. She mentions she plans to walk eight blocks to the Laundromat to do her laundry. I know the time that will take from her organizing—my goal for her before she has to start back at work tomorrow—so I offer to do her laundry for her—"just this once". How much laundry can just one young woman and a tiny infant have anyway? Two or three loads tops, I figure. Wrong! She is thrilled with my offer and to my utter amazement—kind of like '50s circus clowns getting out of a car one after another—she begins to pull one huge garbage bag of laundry after another out of her closet, from under her bed, and from stashes unimaginable! Trip after trip, I schlep bags down six flights of Victorian stairs to my car around the corner in the parking lot. She yells after me, "I won't have to fold it when it comes back will I?" Astounded, I call back, "No Darcy, *I* will fold every item carefully myself." Driving up to College Hill I mumble whatever have I gotten myself into. I sort the clothes on my basement floor, start the first of what will become *10 loads* of laundry. Stunned by all of this, I begin to count how many items her two-month old baby has been given by the five social agencies that are in charge of Darcy's case. This little baby has a wardrobe *double* what *all three* of my children (put together) had in *all of their childhood*! I fold each bootie and garment as if it were for my own. I get Bill to help me carry the many clean stacks to the car. I have spent *nine hours* doing her laundry! By 10 PM the folded laundry is back in her room—which I realize will never be organized, for their isn't a dresser large enough to hold her material possessions. Never again do I do anyone's laundry but my own family's.

In March 1998 I am reading Peter Marshall's sermons in *Mr. Jones, Meet the Masters*. Peter Marshall says our problem is not so much that we don't know what we should do as it is that we know perfectly well and don't want to do it. What is it I *don't* want to do? I *don't want* to be homeless or without purposeful work. Am I dreaming to think I might be an artist, a writer, or a spiritual director? How will we eat or pay the bills? Is it wise or foolish to follow my bliss? God doesn't answer loud enough for me to hear yet.

Easter is coming. Why do I not like Easter? Some flaw in my character? It's the hoopla. Easter's fuss, like Christmas's, is not humble enough. Every year there's this Pilot story, the cross, the thorny crown, the stone rolled away, doubting Thomas (though, actually, I relate to him), the seaside breakfast, donkeys, palm leaves, and celebrating trumpets. I like the workday Jesus better: the one who heals and teaches saying "go and tell no man". I don't need a stone to roll away to tell me life is eternal, to confirm God's in charge, or to tell me Jesus died for our sins when I can't accept that an *all-Good* and *all-powerful* God created sinners. I have experienced God's presence in my ordinariness and know God as an ever-available Friend. Some degree of crucifixion comes to those who follow God; I've not been afraid of that. I've entered black holes and waded, waited, and wailed through to the other side.

In May 1998 Charissa and I drive to Knoxville for Nathan's graduation from the University of Tennessee: his master's degree in Planning. His thesis book is impressive. I make lunch to celebrate his graduation, including a chocolate cake I decorate with tree and blue bird for his love of the environment (his undergrad degree). After a party with his friends, he and I stay up all night talking until 5 AM the morning of his graduation. My son is strong, independent, hard-working, humble, and generous. I'm impressed by this person that my child has become. His expertise with GIS, computers, the environment, and planning is in demand. I see in Nathan someone who has overcome many challenges, who understands himself, who loves people, never judges, accepts and enjoys each person for who he or she is. He tells me he believes in God but not denominations. And when I ask him how he has overcome so many challenges, this environmentalist answers: by learning *not* to choose *un*sustainable actions, to select "*sustainable*" behavior. It is a privilege to know Nathan—as it is to know my other two children. They are individuals I respect for what they have made of themselves.

In August both boys visit and hike prior to Nathan's starting his new job with the planning department on Grand Cayman Island. Bill's Mom and sister visit, too. We finish up the summer with a drive to Boston to visit Dad. About this time, I turn down two jobs—a part-time art teaching job that would pay under $7,000 annually (which I realize I would take on as if it were full time) and a job to assist an entrepreneur market a new art product—not a good fit.

I am reading *The Third Spiritual Alphabet* by Francesca de Osuna—a book Teresa of Avila says directed her life, her concept of mental prayer, and influenced her becoming a nun. In reading this 600-page book I feel a bridge has been crossed from my past as a Christian Scientist to my present as an Episcopalian—or more accurately, as one who doesn't believe in denominations at all. I write in my journal that this may be the "most important book I've ever read." Osuna was ordained a Franciscan monk in 1519-20. His monastery near Guadalajara was a retreat house of 5 isolated hermitages. Those in residence were strictly dedicated to meditative prayer. Osuna created maxims to guide meditation which he arranged alphabetically. He reduces everything to the law of love. Like Augustine's philosophy, Franciscan spirituality was nourished by Platonic tradition. I like Augustine's story—his life of lived lessons—and both he and Osuna become companions for my journey, along with Teresa and Julian. Interestingly, I find more garden imagery in Osuna:

> *If you desire your prayer to be heard by God…you must first be baptized in the fountain of tears; thus you will be able to beg God confidently to direct your interior road straight to him, and if you wish your conscience…to be the Lord's garden, be careful that it is not dry and, as safeguard, set in it an abundant fountain of tears so that it will be fresher and blossom more profusely. Remember that if you are to be the little paradise of the Lord, you need a river of tears flowing from the place of your delights, which is God, and you must desire him alone whom you can purchase with the tears you shed for love of him alone…* (The Classics of Western Spirituality, The Paulist Press, Osuna, *The Third Spiritual Alphabet*, p. 283).

Of tears, a subject I know well, Osuna writes they are *as efficacious in the devotion of recollection as the most learned teacher, and many people, just by weeping for the treasure hidden in recollection, discover great riches and with no one else to guide them through the sea of tears realize that it is the Holy Spirit piloting them through a strait more narrow than they could imagine. When the soul rests from weeping, it sees itself in the company of that which it sought through tears and is content in the unmistakable certainty that its tears are no longer present because the One who caused them is no longer absent. They know from experience the meaning of the Lord's words: 'Blessed are you who weep now for you shall laugh.' ....And so it happens that those who weep...wash their eyes in order to see God spiritually; after the tears well up and pour down from the clouds of their eyes that were opened, the sky of their souls is cleared of all darkness and cloud of sadness, leaving such an interior clarity that their souls seem crystalline and perfectly clear, penetrated by divine clarity and filled with the joy Tobias describes in communion with God: 'after the storm, Lord, you bring tranquility, and after the tears and weeping you infuse joy'* (The Classics of Western Spirituality, Paulist Press, Osuna, *The Third Spiritual Alphabet,* p. 275).

My highlighted copy of Osuna's book offers wisdom on everything from contemplative prayer to pragmatic application. His chapter on meekness is the finest interpretation of the subject I have ever encountered. His large embrace of humanity filters throughout every page, and his understanding of love inspires. He gives me enough to contemplate for a lifetime.

Along with Osuna, I probe the earliest Christians and desert fathers and mothers. Their stories fascinate me. I am drawn to Origen and his concept of the "third eye:" Beyond the eye of the body and the eye of reason there is a third eye—corresponding to the 'spiritual sense,' which sees God, and this is the 'eye of contemplation.' Study of contemplatives continues throughout my ordinary days. I "grab life like a drowning man"—words that come to me one morning when I wake.

September 20, 1998, I leave for Grand Cayman Island. Nathan sends me a ticket to visit him, to help establish, decorate, and create his first real home in his first career position as planner for the British Government. In less than seven days I sew pillows from fabric the color of Caribbean waters, paint five paintings of a conch shell from five different directions, framing each watercolor to hang down an entry hall, stretch some of my old oil canvases to mount for Nathan's living room, paint a lamp base, create a coffee table out of glass blocks and plexiglass, arrange sofas and tables, place a bowl of fresh island limes on his dining table, beside his own handmade pottery.

Georg, a level 4, and possibly 5, hurricane is potentially going to hit while I am here. Every store is boarded up and free hurricane-tracking maps are available in every store. But by my stay's end, the storm has not yet hit. As I fly over Cuba's green mountains and empty roads on my return flight, the pilot tells us to look out at the clouds on the left side of the plane—there is Georg!

An island is a strange place to live. Surrounded by water in the middle of the ocean, my son's new home could be covered with water, wiped out by the slightest ferocity of wind and rain. This fragile, pure beauty of color, sand, waves, and Palm trees could disappear. We should all go up in a plane and look out the window more often and think about what we see, our insignificance in the universe. Instead we put headphones on and rivet our eyes to TV screens or pages of print.

September 28,1998: I dream I am in a new house with a bunch of beautiful powerful tigers coming through all the doors and windows. The home is *full* of windows and doors. I am busy locking out the tigers. United Van Lines pulls up to take my things; I'm moving again. I keep sealing up boxes and keeping out tigers. The same night, I dream that Jayne and I are organizing and cleaning up Dad's home while he is away. We decide to flip his mattress and when we strip his bed, we notice it is full of wet blood. Two years later a version of this premonition will come to pass.

October 3, 1998: I am 55 today. Bill is away for my birthday canoeing with students. Charissa is traveling and working in Wales, Jason lives in Oregon, and Nathan on Grand Cayman, my father in Boston, and my mother is dead. Bill put a card under my pillow before he left, but no one else remembered my birthday. It's what becomes of housewives and mothers. Years of caring for others breeds neglect of the caregiver. Others have always come first so why should that change? What could a caregiver possibly need? She's self-sufficient. Able to solve all problems. Like the earth, she's always there. No one seems to know that like a faithful houseplant she requires watering.

We neglect mothers: Mother Earth as well as mothers in general. A mother never quite achieves personhood; she's more an institution—like church, school and the post office. She's never seen as an individual with wants, needs, desires—just functions. The assumption seems to be that she doesn't require care because she gives it. One day, when no one's looking, institutions and mothers fall apart.

I make myself a chocolate birthday cake and call Karen, my friend and former sister-in-law, to share it with me; she brings lasagna—one mother/housewife/giver to another.

That night I dream I'm addressing an audience of thousands. I talk about God and spirituality, and ask who is certain and who has questions? I expect no hands up for certainty, but all of them go up. I tell them I do not have all the answers and am stunned they believe they do. Thousands think they know everything, so why are they listening to *me*, their speaker? I wake up feeling this vivid dream is important but have no idea how.

I am reading lots of Meister Eckhart, another favorite mystic, and also Gill Gillian's biography of Mary Baker Eddy. I seek to know every spiritual person's path.

In March,1999, I compose a letter to my father asking to interview him, as I have before, but with greater thoroughness so that I might someday write his story. I explain in the letter that I believe his perspective is valuable because of the changes he has witnessed in the world and because of his solving business problems as he heals and healing as he solves business problems. I include fifty-five questions I wish to explore with him. He is delighted with my five-page letter and we plan a future visit.

For Spring Break, Bill and I fly to Grand Cayman to visit Nathan. While snorkeling with my son, I see a shark not more than five feet away. Nathan calmly points it out and, unafraid, we slowly swim in the opposite direction. Always at one with nature, Nathan loves diving. He and Bill deep sea dive while I paint watercolors of palm trees, pink stucco buildings and colorful boats, while thinking of current wars and news of suffering in other nations. I am reminded of my first grade and the children without shoes. Injustice intrudes on paradise.

I lie in the sun reading Annie Dillard's *The Writing Life*, hoping to unlock the secret of writing through her wisdom and brilliant use of words: *"One of the few things I know about writing is this: spend it all, shoot it, play it, lose it all, right away, every time. Do not hoard what seems good for a later place in the book, or for another book; give it, give it all, give it now. The impulse to save something good for a better place later is the signal to spend it now. Something more will arise for later something better…Anything you do not give freely and abundantly becomes lost to you. You open your safe and find ashes"* (Dillard, p. 78)I walk Seven-Mile Beach, thinking about good writing, listening to the island music, watching waves for sea turtles, finding bits of beach glass, collecting tiny shells and broken pieces of white washed coral.

I ponder Dillard's quotation of Michelangelo' advice to his young apprentice: *"Draw Antonio, draw, dare and do not waste time."* And Dillard's own advice: *"Push it. Examine all things intensely and relentlessly...Giacometti's drawings and paintings show his bewilderment and persistence. If he had not acknowledged his bewilderment, he would not have persisted...Rico Lebrun, taught that 'the draughtsman must aggress; only by persistent assault will the line image capitulate and give up its secret to an unrelenting line.' Who but an artist fierce to know—not fierce to seem to know —would suppose that a live image possessed a secret? The artist is willing to give all his or her strength and life to probing with blunt instruments those same secrets no one can describe in any way but with these instruments' faint tracks... Appealing workplaces are to be avoided. One wants a room with no view, so imagination can meet memory in the dark"* (Dillard, p.78). I pick up my drawing and painting tools to convey more than pink and palm, for I realize paradise is not what I want to paint.

A few weeks after we return home, on April 12, 1999, I receive notice I am accepted into General Theological Seminary in New York City! This summer will be the first of three towards my Master's degree in Spiritual Direction. I am happy, with a sense of wonder and a quiet unknowing about what it will entail. My spiritual journey has included the dark night of the soul that St. John writes about, but it has also included self-control, self-discipline, and a clear-headed innovative prayer.

I go to Boston to visit Charissa at BU and to interiew Dad. While there, I call Jenny, a former student of mine who is attending Boston University, who plans to be a doctor. She has double degrees in Western philosophy and Asian medicine and has even completed a practicum in a mental ward. Next fall she starts medical school. I taught Jenny 4th through 12th grades, including AP art, at Custis Lee. Artistic, creative, insightful, funny, spiritual, and extremely intelligent (whether the subject is physics, English, chemistry, calculus, the environment or animal care) Jenny is unique among those I have taught. She and I often shared long talks over the years, but now that we are no longer student and teacher, our friendship is freer, deeper. We meet for lunch on Saturday, May 8, 1999, at Legal Seafood over stuffed lobster.

We talk as if long lost friends, yet, as if we had just seen each other yesterday, rather than three years ago. After we conclude our non-stop catching up, she glances at my hand and offers to read my palm. Surprised, I give her my hand. She gives a light laugh at what she sees.

"What ?" I ask, curiously. No one has ever read my palm before.

"Very interesting! You have such *defined* lines. Very strong on the creative, as I'd expect, but also on the rational. See this line? You will have a *very* long life. You are a very old soul (I'd mentioned previously I thought I had eight good years left). You've lived many lives."

Surprised, I ask Jenny about this and other spiritual work she's been doing.

She starts to explain, but interrupts herself. "Excuse me, but they are here."

"*Who's* here?" I scan the restaurant for a familiar face.

"Your three spirits." Jenny answers. "They are telling me things…I am sorry but I need to interrupt…I know this seems crazy but…they are telling me to interrupt…"

"No, go ahead" I assure her, for I trust this girl. She is, above all things, honest, level-headed as much as she is creative. Instinct tells me to take out notepaper and write down every word she says. I write as fast as she talks.

"The spirits are telling me to tell you that you will live a long life and that your 60th year—or your 61st or 62nd year—will be very important …I see an image…I see you digging holes on a beach, running up and down and digging hundreds of holes as if in search of buried treasure. You have a shovel and you keep digging and digging and digging. You dig until a ship or boat with white sails—for purity, I think—comes in. You get your closure, your clarity, with the ship. You stop digging. It is as if everything you've searched for is suddenly clear, answered. Its *not* that there is something on the boat that you are looking for, its just that you no longer *need* to dig—everything makes sense, as if you understand TRUTH."

She tells me that the spirits are telling her I must meditate no matter what, that *that* will help focus my intensity. "In stillness is Truth. Right now in your life you are being given *time*. More free time than ever before or than you will have. Yet you are like a flitting bird—anxious—the spirits want you to be still, to just sit down, just sit down in the bottom of the cage and then the door of the cage will open and you will hear the sound of your own voice and it will be Truth. Your mind will be open when you meditate—that's when it's healing. It's like you are throwing out a net—out too far. You can't do it that way. Focus *in*. Re-emerge like a phoenix. Use the net on yourself. I see you blooming like a flower—I see a daisy, white, purity—I don't know why. You cannot cast your net so far—it gives your power away. You need to pull it back in. Then you will be stronger. I see that your head and bones won't hurt anymore—I don't know what that means. [I wonder years later in re-reading this if it references my future auto accident]. Soon you won't need to pass out the love you have to others, it will just come out. Find Love, the Atman. The Seen Self. Right now you do not have an anchor—you are at sea, rolling over and over. You are in huge waves right now, overturning, but you will be beached on the shore. Your anchor will come with the boat. You will stand in the center. People will be around you. Use the time you are given now to regain your power. Sit down, experience a sense of calm and healing. You have to heal yourself before you can help others."

Whew! My hand and mind are exhausted from following all of this as fast as it came. Never before have I experienced anything like this! Every word Jenny spoke came as if it were pure truth. Though I can be a cynic about such things, I felt no doubt from the time she began telling me what the spirits were saying. I *knew* this was truth.

Jenny tells me they are gone now. I ask her what my spirits are like. Can I see them? Jenny repeats that I have three—two masculine and one feminine, but not in the human gender sense. I ask her if it is more like two yangs and a yin and she says yes.

"They have always been with you, in your other lives, too." I ask her how I can hear them more often, more directly. She says there are *signs*.

"The signs are telling you things all the time, nearly *bashing you over the head* with what you need to know! Do not worry, they are always with you. We need to *ask* the spirits. Also, we must be *grateful* to them—they like gratitude—I learned this from a woman I visit."

"Jenny, how does this spirit world fit with you as a scientist, with your love of organic chemistry?"

She tells me there is no separation or conflict, that the 117 elements are laws of energy and they are completely compatible. "It's all one."

Suddenly she says, "I see a house, there are gutters that need cleaning out, leaves clogging them. The spirits tell me to tell you: you must clean out the leaves. Like Feng sui. You must check your pipes, have them cleaned out; it may be expensive, but it will be more expensive later if you don't do this now." [In my next home, gutters are always an issue].

Jenny continues: "We have to forget in order to be able to learn."

This made good sense at the time.

Then she spoke of my father, whom she does not know, though she did meet him once long ago when he visited my classroom. "I see an image—he is dead...he has lost his life because of his stubbornness. I see that at his death he may not be able to speak, something about his not being able to speak and a problem with breathing. He is surrounded by people, so many people, but they are all blind. I see blindness. He will come to understand you at his passing. Your father is afraid of his own mortality because he never can strip away his own ego from his accomplishments. He will not listen. The spirits are dismayed by this. They see it as a loss. They feel they haven't gotten through. I see a bull—a red bull—the ego...his ego. He dies with regret. He looks back. His marriage was a TV program, wasn't solid, she was like a feather to him, floating around, she always had to do the right thing—a mirror for him, but she had no substance of her own."

I do not understand what this means but I believe it on some primal level. I ask her about Bill. She says she could not work with him, could not do this spirit work for him because they are not compatible (they did once have a bit of a clash as teacher and high school student). She says, however, that "he expresses concern for you... You are so BIG to him, so much, with so many moving parts—its as if he wants to fix things for you, but there are so many parts he doesn't know where to begin, or how to help; he is overwhelmed."

Jenny says to me very pointedly: "You do not see what you do. You do not give yourself enough credit. You do not acknowledge what you have done. You do so much but, for you it never is enough. Recognize that you cannot feed the world; you can't give everybody shoes. You want to be a bird, to have wings. You get tired but do not acknowledge it. Don't grind down the stone. *Meditate*, the spirits are imploring you—that's how they speak to you."

It is as if a big coastal wind has come and gone. We talk now of her boyfriend, her college experience, and my going to seminary in June. We walk out into the crowded mall after a spiritually significant meeting that I will not fully understand for some time—if ever. I treasure what passed between us and hold it close.

Back in Pennsylvania, I take my morning walk up the hill, praying silently the Hindu Uphanishads prayer I learned in class with Swami: *Hara hara maha deva*…. A prayer about emptying oneself. I am already empty. If I empty more I might disappear. And as I reach the vista, I look for the unseen me who writes and paints herself on the page. I wanted my mother to hold me like she did other people's babies, and listen to me more than she did talk-radio. I wanted my father to invite me more often into the room he called others into. I wanted John to SEE *me*, not just as someone to go to church with and save the world with. I wanted Bill to give me all the wonder I saw in him, to love me in ways that John never could. I wanted love from each of these people.

But only God's love is lasting. This God that is Life, Truth, Love, Principle, Mind, Soul, Spirit of Christian Science. This God I also met at a Memphis Methodist inner-city church. God I knew through Doug Bailey and the Episcopal Church. This American Baptist Church God I found in Rhode Island. This Quaker God from my school days. This God of Buddhists and of the Hindu Uphanashads. And of the dessert fathers and mothers I've come to know as friends. This God of light and dark—of St. John's dark night and of Christ healing. This God of incarnation and mercy who calls sinners and saints. This God who must know Kosovo as well as the Third Street Alliance. A God of *unknowing*. God in every day people and places.

Then it hits me. God is like the mother in *The Run-Away Bunny* I read to my children when they were small. She does not leave me no matter where I go or what I do. I cannot hide from Her or run from Her. She, my Mother-God, is always there loving me and all Her children. This complex yet simple knowing of God takes me to seminary next month.

Journal entry, June 6, 1999: "I am at seminary. *Seminary!* Nearly staggering to think about! Ten years ago this was not even imagined, known, nor wanted. Yet, here I am! This adventure is unlike anything I have ever done."

I read today in *The Cloud of Unknowing*, that amazing fourteenth century anonymous classic, as fresh today as the day it was written: "*Do not pray with words unless you are really drawn to this….by the work of contemplative love man will be healed*" (The Cloud of Unknowing, p. 149).

At seminary I SEE what I already knew. I write in my journal which we are required to keep: *I am a mystic, always have been. I haven't done anything ever without God.*

Classes are academically intense. My favorite is *Introduction to Christian Spirituality* with Dr. Koenig. The mystical tradition was something I had begun to discover on my own prior to arrival at seminary, but this course offers me scope, depth, discipline, terms, and historic perspective on the subject, enabling pieces to fit together in some vast whole. Never before have I known such intense and significant academic study. I love the reading and assignments. Even the final exam, which many fear, is exciting to me. We had to create our own essay question and answer it. The question I wrote was: " '*Studying the human experience of God is not viewing through a telescope a bush burning in a distant desert. It is taking a chance on hearing our name called at close range.' Sandra Schneider's vivid metaphor suggests that Christian spirituality cannot be merely intellectual but must be a 'project of life-integration' rooted in a yearning for God that leads to life transformation. How is this yearning and path to transformation interpreted by the authors we have read and by my own life?*"

I get an "A" but the best is Dr. Koenig's written comments: "*This essay is remarkable for its thoughtfulness, accuracy, completeness, and inclusion of personal experience.*" I'd done what I'd hoped: knit together my life with what I was learning.

All the early Christian writers that we read and studied from 4th century Gregory of Nyssa through 16th century Teresa of Avila yearned for God, were *called* by God and interpreted their lives as well as the Scriptures existentially, experientially, ontologically with the intent to unite with God through Christ. Each offered his or her particular spiritual journey to the whole community. I loved their journeys, never tired of hearing about their struggles and successes, much as I had loved hearing my Dad's healings.

This course taught me most profoundly, that Christian interpretation is not just intellectual but *requires* transformation. The early Christian writers cannot be appreciated from a cold detached distance. One must be fully engaged, prepared to *experience* what she reads about, ready to hear her name called by God.

In seminary I learn one cannot come to God without first knowing oneself. According to every author we read, self-knowledge is essential to the spiritual journey. Augustine says that the search for God is also the search for self. Teresa says "we shall never succeed in knowing ourselves unless we seek to know God" (Teresa of Avila, *Interior Castle*, p. 38). Through the names of God which Pseudo-Dionysious, the inventor of mystical theology, gives, I learn about *kataphatic* and *apophatic* interpretation and discover the term "brilliant darkness" which I feel I've already experienced to some degree. And in the stories of the early Christians I find pieces of my own story—just as I had in women's studies. Their yearning is also my yearning. They sought to love as they were drawn to God's love. For them perfection was loving God and mankind. Today some Christians talk about being perfect in the sense of following rules, expected behavior, adherence to dogma, but perfection's original meaning in the time of the early Christians meant loving God and loving others. Bondi writes "To be a perfect human being, a human being the way God intends human beings to be, is to be a fully loving person, loving God, and every bit as important loving God's image, the other people who share the world with us" (Bondi, *To Love as God Loves*, p. 17). I write in my exam that "To live out of this love for God is not only the purpose of the early Christians, but mine."

Gregory of Nyssa in his *Life of Moses* calls the early Christians "beacons" and so they are for me. He sees the spiritual journey as one of continual progress in which we penetrate, without sense and intellect, into a higher type of knowing founded in *yearning* and thereby gain access to what is invisibile, incomprehensible in other ways, and there we find God. This transcendence is the *via negativea*. It is also the place where healing occurs according to *The Cloud of Unknowing*.

Assigned to do a class presentation on *The Cloud of Unknowing*, I find myself drawing. I create a detailed illustration of *The Cloud of Unknowing* to explain its meaning. The professor asks for a copy and permission to use it in her other classes.

My seminary experience shows me I have given birth to myself by the yearning for God that has led me to launch into historical traditional Christianity. I've lived Gregory's depiction in his *Life of Moses*, which says Moses' birth on the river symbolizes birth into spirit, "naked before God" in the turbulent stream of life. In Gregory's writing, I hear my story, just as when I read Augustine's *Confessions*. Both lived in the fourth century, but I find in them a deeply spiritual validity for today that draws me, as when

Gregory writes, "...none of those things which are apprehended by sense perception and contemplated by the understanding really subsists, but that the transcendent essence and cause of the universe, on which everything depends, alone subsists" (Gregory of Nyssa, *The Life of Moses*, p.60). How similar Gregory's words are to Christian Science! How comfortable, too, am I with the words of the anonymous author of the *Cloud* when he (or she) writes: "if you are seeking God alone, you will never rest contented with anything less than God" (*The Cloud of Unknowing*, p. 61). This line becomes all the truer the longer I live. I will re-read all these fine spiritual thinkers not just at seminary, but throughout my life.

My brain expands at seminary. I love the intensity. But I am glad, too, for our weekend retreat to a monastery along the Hudson. When I am not reading or praying, I sit in the garden and paint and write a little poem:

Work of Art

A little painting of a peony
Is not who I am nor what I want to be.

The silent *Cloud* is more my place
Than color, from, line, and space.

I put away my brush and paint
In perfect stillness sit and wait.

God's love comes, flowing into me
Without image, more perfectly I see

In unknowing, I am known
In unknowing, the seed is sown

Creating is only done by Thee
And the work of art is really me.

One Sunday late in the seminary experience I write in my journal: *So, God, where do we go from here, You and I? I see who you would have me be as if 'in a glass darkly.* I am a foreigner here. Am I an Episcopalian? A Christian? Or still a Christian Scientist? Or something else? I have come to seminary to learn the contemplative life, to develop my spirituality. But here, surrounded by traditional Christians, I realize I am not and cannot be a traditional Christian.

In the strange forest that is Christian Science there grows a tree in the midst of it that is truth. There is such a tree growing in every deeply spiritual religion. This truth is *universal.* It declares that we are all God's children, loved, able to know healing, held forever in God's likeness, *not* helpless sinners. This truth tells us that we are beloved, though we sometimes miss the mark, lie, lust, harm, puff ourselves up. Our mistakes are the school for learning our path. By our struggles we find God's mercy, forgiveness and love. In this universal truth is our home. It has nothing to do with dogma, the complexities of theology, the politics of organizations, nor the peculiarities of denomination. Love doesn't need a trinity, a baptism, a Eucharist, a ceremony. What Jesus came to do as way-shower, teacher, healer—wasn't it all about love?

One of the brightest parts of seminary for me is the poetry course. I need this outlet from the very cerebral state that is seminary. I have missed creative opportunity. Poetry spills out of me when I am in this class as if it has been strangled, gasping for breath, and is at last set free. The poetry class uses the title of one of my poems for the cover of our class collection: *Sparrows in the Weeds.* My poem came after observation in a Chelsea park, where it seemed to me all mankind, in its amazing variety, is like sparrows pecking at weeds popping out of cement, wishing for grass that isn't there. My poem is also about a homeless woman I saw enter the park, dressed, oddly for July, in winter clothing, needing a cup of cold water in both the physical and biblical sense.

Though I love it, poetry is not my purpose. Is art? Spiritual direction? It comes to me that my purpose is whatever comes down the pike and steps in front of me. It isn't "out there", but *right in front of me.* It doesn't come with thunder claps, but in small raindrops.

When I return home from seminary I sleep straight for 15 hours.

In late July Bill and I visit Dad in Boston. I am reading Dad's files and interviewing him again—this time with tape recorder as well as legal tablet. Our time together is productive. This Herculean task to know my father and write his biography takes me through all of his many file drawers. He is eager for me to do this and brings out many particular files he wants me to see. I read and take copious notes dawn to midnight. I ask him the 55 questions I'd sent him months ago. New questions come from what I discover in his files and from my instant curiosity. As I've found before, Dad loves this process of articulating what matters to him.

He repeats for the hundredth time the story of his birth, of working in Marie Groth's grocery, of playing football and his first healing. We are interrupted by the ringing of Dad's phone—as we so often are during any visit—I start to get up, but he puts his hand up indicating it will be o.k. for me to remain in the room while he talks with this patient. I hear him tell the patient to STAND, meaning to take a stand for his health and wellbeing as a child of God. When he finishes, we resume our interview. He remembers exactly where we were and states: "This century is the most significant in the history of mankind." He demonstrates his point with inventions and changes he has witnessed over his lifetime. He speaks about the importance of contributing to our century—he quotes Paul in the Bible: "*Now* is the expected time" and adds, "the lost opportunity is the greatest of losses! We can't just wait and wait and wait—we must *do*!" He loops his commentary into the importance of *sequence*—how one thing leads one's life into its next phase, concluding: "every trial contributes." I watch him gesture with his hands, his knuckles the size of large walnuts.

Dad says the main theme in his life has been "putting Principle into practice." Certainly that is what I witnessed growing up in his house.

I ask him who his closest friends have been over his lifetime. He says His brother Bill always. He adds from 1955 to 1972, Sid Boyar, a top executive with Sears, was a good friend; Sid was Jewish and the two respected each other's beliefs.

One evening in particular, as we sit in his office and I watch the sun's setting glow out his window, I ask a series of questions to which I invite his first quick response.

Me: "What would you like most to say to mankind if given the chance?"

Dad: "Love one another."

Me: "What do you consider the most important impetus in your life?"

Dad: "Principle in action."

Me: "Do you have any pleasures?—what gives you joy?"

Dad: "When someone I have worked to help says 'I am healed.'"

Me: "Does anything make you angry?"

Dad: "No. Sometimes something tries but it doesn't get that far."

Me: "What change would you like to see most in the world or society?"

Dad: "Selfishness changed into unselfed love."

Me: "How do you now view marriage?"

Dad: "It is an opportunity to demonstrate our relationship to God."

Me: "Tell me about Mom."

Dad: "Before I got married, we had rough times courting because it was done when I was in Baltimore, by writing. We had a couple of brief visits. There was warmth and real caring. I asked Ruth to play tennis. I wanted companionship, rather than being alone. She was a good cook. She took responsibility for the home. She worked charitably—with the Air Raid warning center and at Western Union. They asked her to join the WACs. She was gone three months for the training and we'd only been married for 1 1/2 months. She didn't express her feelings much but her sincerity was deep and dependable. She was shy and never said 'I love you.' I gave her all my money I earned and she spent it wiser than I could have. She was never jealous. We had a wonderful time on the lecture circuit together later in marriage. She talked about herself then—things I never knew. There was always a trust between the two of us. Ruth never lied to me once in her life."

Me: "What has disappointed you in life?"

Dad: "When people aren't obedient to God."

Me: "What do you consider your biggest accomplishments or successes in life?"

Dad: "Overcoming fear. Especially in my earlier experiences."

Me: "Do you see a thread running throughout your life?"

Dad: "Consecration, commitment, dedication which grew out of honesty and caring."

Me: "What is one moment you particularly treasure and why?"

Dad: "It would involve my mother—her example—I see her reading the textbook with the dictionary beside her."

Me: "What do you think has been your greatest accomplishment and why?"

Dad: "When I was a young man telling my boss, Tom Willey, I would not tell the people a lie. It changed that man and it freed me, taught me honesty and courage."

Me: "What are your particular views on death?"

Dad: "Death is darkness. We should always keep the light within us. People who pass on have a foundation in light."

Me: "What do you think are the common misconceptions about Christian Science and what would you do if you could to correct them?"

Dad: "The only way to correct the misconception is by steadfast healing."

Me: "If there were no Mary Baker Eddy and no *Science and Health* what would you see yourself doing today?"

Dad: "I can't imagine. Science is Christianity. I can't think of being anything other than a Christian Scientist."

Me: "Tell me about your class—your association of Christian Science students for whom you are Teacher."

Dad: "My students are African, Parisian, farmers from the Midwest, eastern Phds—every walk of life—18 year olds and 100 year olds. It is the most important work I do, to teach and to heal—for the two are inseparable. I interview each student at the end of each class to see what they got out of it, to not let them leave with a question or concern."

Me: "Tell me what is most essential in the healing work."

Dad: "You have to be Christ-like in thought and action. Be willing to put aside your most cherished beliefs, interests, whatever you most love to do with your time. Lay it all down. And get freedom from fear."

Me: "What do you do in healing?"

Dad: "Someone calls—don't see them as a patient, but as God's idea—before you pick up the phone. Whatever you hear on the other end of the phone—stomach problem, accident, etc.—*deny* that any child of God can have it. Stay with this person until he or she is free. I have to maintain a perfect view of the individual when they come to see me. I listen with compassion but not sympathy. I work with them until they reclaim their qualities of God. I work until they get the spiritual view. And don't leave them until *they* know they are God's loved child. When a person calls you, see what is going on in their life, business, marriage, family. Find the problem. "

Me: "How do you think your brand of Christian Science differs from that practiced by most church members?"

Dad: "You have to lay *all* on the altar. We teach by what we are. What I love is Paul. He lost his sight to *see*. When people come to Boston, or any place where they've not yet demonstrated humility over power, have not fully seen that power is only God's, and are unable to say 'I can of my own self do nothing,' then that's when trouble comes. One has to be honest."

Me: "Tell me about a couple of recent healings."

He relays many, closing with: "You have to decide if you are going to accept the 5 physical senses as law or God's law of freedom. God's law is all the law there is. Knowing this is essential in healing."

Dad says when he has a day of 40 calls, plus appointments, one case helps him with another, though there's never a common solution, for each need is *individual*. When he has an extreme case, or a child's case, he stops everything and does nothing but work for that situation without sleep or interruption. He works with the concept of "NOW" in emergencies and that there can be no separation of the individual from God.

"You have to be willing to *take a stand* to be healed." Dad explains. "Don't worry about being the only one. *One* is enough. Sacrifice is necessary. Lay *all* on the altar. The only power the problem has is the power you give it. Laws are thrown at us continually: eat this, don't eat that, run, exercise, etc. etc. etc. I don't care how many people believe these laws! The only law is the law of God—God's law of harmony and love! Love washes away fear. Love is *crucial*. I find myself loving more with every call. My love gets greater because if they call, then, dear God, that means they want what *You do*, what *You are*, what I love."

"God's whole plan is complete. I have wanted to be obedient to that plan. I have set everything aside for what He directed. If I can do it, anybody can do it. I didn't have a lot of money, not much education or intellectual prowess. Early on I devoted my life to understanding God through Christ Jesus' example. My concern is on the street—the unnecessary suffering going on in the world. How is God as the answer to be portrayed? One way: by example. *There is no other way.* Look to Spirit, not matter—matter only gives pain. I am getting an intensity of calls now—more than ever before. People *must* claim their divine inheritance! "

"I had a conversation with myself about death: 'Glenn, do you really believe there is no death?' I answered, 'I do. I'm not afraid of death.' Then I asked myself, 'Glenn, do you believe *anyone* out there believes in death?' 'Yes,' I answered. 'then, Glenn, you have more work to do!'"

At the end of one of our intense conversations, Dad says, "What I am seeing in this world is so stupidly unnecessary—people floundering without standards, without a system. Jesus relied on God. So did one lone woman without degrees: Mary Baker Eddy. This is the need of our movement: reliance solely on God. We need to forget about sleep. I could be president of this country tomorrow—it would be a snap—let me answer any question! If you have one thing—honesty—you don't have to worry about anything else."

Several of my questions pertain to the Christian Science movement—a topic on which Dad has always had many opinions. Dad opposed the selling of Bliss Knapp's book ("like Judas selling Jesus for silver" he said), church video conferences, church TV, the trade edition of *Science and Health*, the watering down of content in the periodicals, and the control by the Board of Directors, rather than the Manual-based balance of power with the branches and Publishing Society. He felt branch churches were following *persons* in Boston too often instead of turning directly to God in prayer to heal church-related difficulties. We talk during this visit, as we have before, about Dad's being asked to be on the Board of Directors, of the cover-up of his "firing" from the Board of Trustees and the directors falsely reporting in the Christian Science Monitor his wish to return to Chicago which was untrue. We talk about injustices and events as complicated as Watergate.

On one of my last days in Boston, Dad speaks again of the importance of *sequence*—that everything contributes to one's path—every trial and every person one meets, one step in life leading to another. He told me: "As I think back on my earliest days, I never expected to be anything great. I wanted to be useful, to help mankind. I couldn't depend on academics for my confidence—I didn't have much. I put my trust in God. Whatever I've done, I owe to God. My Church has taught me that; I want to strengthen my

Church, do whatever I can to set right the fallacy that's governing it today—I would do *anything*."

How he managed to stay in Boston and be the stalwart beacon during the church's dark days and decline I don't know—actually, I do know: by staying close to the Principle that governed every day of his life, by remaining fearless in his stand, and by loving his enemies. Many Christian Science practitioners and teachers, as well as those working at headquarters, sought his help as the movement dwindled in the seventies, eighties, and nineties. One day someone may write a book about this much larger story.

Back home, I attempt to write my Dad's biography, which I call *In My Father's House*, which I never finish. And I try to figure out how to utilize my seminary experience and find permanent work. On July 22, 1999, I write in my journal: "I love mornings because they mean fresh starts, new beginnings, chances to start over, to reach goals, like a white canvas before a painting happens."

Fresh ideas come unexpectedly following a trip to the library to get books on starting a business. One book calls me, but I brush past it because it is a large contemporary novel, something I rarely read. Next visit, the same book calls me again. Without even taking it off the shelf, I glance at its title and author: *Gardens in the Dunes* by Leslie Marmon Silko. *Gardens* attract me. Silko is already a favorite author—her story, *Lullaby*, I read out loud to my women's studies classes with Native American flute-music playing in the background. "Well, not now," I tell myself, "I'm here to find books about business for starting *Seeds At Cymru Cottage*." The third time I visit the library there it is again, calling. "O.k., o.k. I hear you!" This time I take it down from the shelf and look at the first page—a Native American story, not something I have to read just now, so I leave it. But the fourth time I'm at the library, it nearly grabs my arm and wrestles me to the ground. I read the jacket flap, turn a few pages, and decide, at least, to check it out. At home I read 50 pages and understand why it worked so hard to get my attention. It's about the Ghost Dance Religion, Wovoka, and the Messiah! The topic of my paintings a year ago! And about Celtic Christianity in the British Isles! And Silko *connects the two* just as my art had! How continually books affirm my life and show me the interrelatedness of all things!

In July, the Bible is the book that guides. I renew study of the ten commandments. Moses says the commandments *are* our life and thus I feel compelled to reread them frequently, examining my life in their light. I sit on my garden bench and meditate. Our region is having a dry spell—watering is forbidden (though my neighbor is out with her hose any way)—an arid time to match my own dryness in finding permanent employment and purpose. I go into my computer and work on my business plan with ideas inspired by Silkos' *Gardens in the Dunes*, St. Teresa's garden analogy, and the Ten Commandments.   After a visit to Bill's brother and family in DC, we drive to Ohio to visit my cousin Ann and her family in Ohio—she and I can beans and peaches from her farm. While there, Ann asks me to help her de-clutter and decorate her home. We stay up all hours of the night and rise early to accomplish amazing changes that please her. I realize I love this home work and add helping people organize their homes as a possible component of my new business.

On the way to Ann's, Bill and I stop at a B&B where our overly-air-conditioned room is so freezing cold it is hard to believe it's August. Some might complain to the management, but Bill and I chose to lie in bed shivering and laughing. His humor brimming with comments like, "*If it weren't for my wife's hot flashes we'd freeze to death!*" ... "*I want to go to the bathroom but I'm scared I'll slip and fall on the ice.*" ... "*Now we know why the toilet seat is fur-lined!*" ..."*I guess we're practicing to be Canadians!*"...And my personal favorite which he shared with the hostess next morning at breakfast: "*I wondered every time I opened the door if the light would come on*" [think refrigerator]. His quick and very funny sense of humor is one of the reasons I married this man!

In September I take care of seven of my brother's ten kids while he and his wife, Blythe, go to Europe for two weeks. School is starting and I drive them to their schools, enforce study halls each evening—no easy task—check their homework, attend various parent/teacher meetings, keep house, cook meals and teach the kids how to take care of their things and appreciate order. I discover more socks in their laundry room than I'd imagined existed in any one place. I wash them all and begin the daunting task of sorting. I end up with 67 matched pairs and 54 unmatched loners (their partners no doubt gone to the sock heaven that every dryer in the universe seems to funnel them to). It comes to me to call a family meeting that night—after laying out the matched pairs on the lovely Tudor living room sofas. The kids, who were supposed to do their own laundry but rarely did—each claiming his or her labeled laundry basket had been stolen by another—were so impressed by the sorted pairs of socks, their admiration nearly left their eyeballs and saluted me: "You did *all this*, Aunt Lyn?!" Then with humor and order I continued the meeting, going over behavior expectations—like not sneaking down the back kitchen stairs for ice cream after 1 AM—and rules for study hall and bedtimes. I made the kids wholesome meals to replace their love of candy and quick frozen meals. I stayed up late in the kitchen to play friendly cop reminding a pair of ice cream seekers that a hearty breakfast would be their next meal. On Saturday morning I posted a sign-up list to work with each one for an hour, teaching them how to scrub their bathrooms with ammonia and how to organize their mounds of CDs, videos, and tapes. Though of course it wasn't the season, one day I made them a complete Christmas dinner with all the trimmings, inclusive of small gifts at their places. I had a couple of drawing lessons with the youngest son—at the time a budding artist. Cleaning, I noticed there were Bibles and *Science and Healths* everywhere. One day I made a count: 56! More than unmatched socks!

In October, I return to Boston to work on Dad's files, taking notes, observing once again that his speeches are the core of who he is. One day Dad walks into the room after finishing with a patient and says, "No one can be helped if they don't seek the spiritual. No one can seek the spiritual cluttered by the material." This fit with my experience at Rich's and Ann's. I realize that de-cluttering is something I have a knack for and I soon find my business plan encompassing this concept. My business will have three parts: (1) Art Works—my painting, (2) Word Works—my teaching and writing, and (3) Home Works—helping people make order and beauty in their homes where chaos and clutter had been. Though a bit unsure of how to start this venture, I write my plan for months, filling the rest of my time with prayer. As my plan begins to gel, I learn that it is *illegal* to have a home business in College Hill where we live! All my work to turn the attic into a studio seems sadly halted. But germinating ideas grow in spite of having no place to bloom. Drawings and plans fill my sketchbook, journal, and computer files. So that I might live where I could start my business, we gingerly consider moving from our duplex. It would be nice to have a whole house.

One day in December I see a newspaper ad for a house in the Poconos. The Poconos never occurred to us; we'd never been there. I call the listing agent, Marianne Higgins. We meet at her office and she drives us to the property. Immediately I do not like it. The phony door knobs, the pervasive royal blue carpeting, and the steep cliff are all wrong. But as Marianne takes us back to her office, she drives through a mountain vista above the Delaware River, down a hill and into a misty hollow where a small 18ᵗʰ century village lies beside a stream. Immediately I think of Brigadoon, a favorite fifties film, in which a beautiful, colorful Scottish village appears only once every hundred years, disappearing in the mist until its next revival.

"What *is* this place? " I ask as we pass over a little stone bridge beside a quaint general store. Out of the valley haze, what an enchanting place has risen into view! I feel as if we *are* in Brigadoon!

"This is Shawnee-on-Delaware and I live here," Marianne Higgins answers.

"I'm meant to live here, too," I answer almost unconsciously, aware as I speak of how odd my words must sound—but it is as if they come from some place other than myself. Bill and the realtor give me a strange look. I have no idea why I said those words.

"Are there any houses for sale here?" I ask.

"No, most have been in families for generations or are summer homes or time shares. It's a small village. I don't know of one for sale."

But as we come around a curve, there it is: a small crudely-made "for sale" sign by a driveway in front of a eighteenth century Federal stone and clapboard farmhouse, overgrown with ivy and weeds, beside a cascading waterfall. "What about *that* one? I ask.

"Oh, that one" she seems surprised it is for sale, "I will have to check—but you don't want that mess—the floor plan is all broken up inside."

"Will you find out how much they want and if we can see it?"

A few weeks later we have an appointment to see the house. The listing agent tells us it dates to 1736. The vernacular Federal clapboard and stone home sits on nearly an acre of land, its backyard dominated by towering trees, a dramatic 60-foot wide waterfall, and flowing stream. We enter the original paneled front door and step into the house's run-down neglected spaces. But I see past the trouble. I see the wide original hearth, once an eighteenth century kitchen now part of the dining room, and imagine my family gathering for Thanksgiving. I see the original plaster walls and amazing wide-plank floors, the pie stairs, the wavy glass windowpanes, and the separate entrance to the perfect place for my potential art studio business. I don't even mind the small poorly applianced kitchen with its dingy linoleum, for it looks out over the boulder-ensconced waterfall. There are five or six bedrooms depending on how you count them, 4.5 baths, a deck off the kitchen that gets good sun, facing the falls and tree-sheltered yard. The house is close to the road but I'm told the row of trees across the front just inside the long picket fence bloom purple and white lilacs in spring and there are no neighbors on either side. I imagine seeing a play in the Shawnee Playhouse, diagonally across the street, and enjoying a deli lunch in the Shawnee General Store, across the little bridge. Tourists, traffic, soot, mouse-droppings and cobwebs aren't in my vision. We make an offer. Two counter offers later, the house is ours.

At our Legal Seafood lunch W months ago, Jenny Wilson told me, "I see you meeting a woman with a name something like Heather, with an 'H', to sign papers—but I don't know what it means." Her name is *Higgins*— and February 4, 2000, we sign papers with her to purchase our home in the Poconos. Something I never dreamed of over a lobster lunch in Boston. Sometimes when we aren't looking, dreams drop at our feet.

eighteen

Deaths

Sometimes I wonder if they are standing around watching—my mother, father, grandparents, their grandparents before them, aunts, uncles, my sister-in-law, friends and colleagues, special dogs and cats I have known—standing in that space we occupy after death, checking on those of us still here. When it is our turn to die will they greet us or chastise us for not being better than we were? I hope we don't meet, that we just move on—except for the dogs and cats whom I'd like to see again.

New Harmony Rappite cemeteries are grassy areas without headstones, no material markers of who lies beneath, but they are remembered for their architecture, inventions, agricultural and industrial accomplishments.

Shawnee's past I will come to know through the historic house that becomes our home when we move in in March 2000. That day, I come across this: "The house, perhaps more than any other symbol of American life, fulfills the ideals of life, liberty and the pursuit of happiness" (Merrit Ierly, *Open House: A Guided Tour of The American Home, 1637-Present*). Pursuit of happiness doesn't come easily in our village home: no kitchen and no bathroom for two months, and mice in our bedroom the first night—in spite of paying for pest service prior to moving in. We discover traffic in front of the house is four times what it was on the lazy Sunday afternoon when we first saw the property, and soot from the busy corner collects on everything. We knew the exterior would need painting but are surprised to learn all five fireplaces need repair. Later we learn several huge trees must come down at a $1,000 a pop, plaster and plumbing work is needed and the house's foundation needs securing.

My favorite response comes from the historical architect I pay to walk through the house and make recommendations when he advises us to "re-do the foundation."

"*The foundation*?! Well then, what's holding up the house?" I ask, puzzled. His reply: "Imagination?"

As if this weren't enough, we inadvertently become park rangers for tourists who, ignoring the private property signs, litter and wander our yard, photographing and climbing our waterfall—as if we are part of the Delaware Gap National Recreation Park only a mile down the road! Booming Latino and Rapper music from New York cars, speeding by without stopping for the stop sign, vibrates the house. Motorcyclists pass in roaring clusters. Sirens from frequent fire engines and rescue trucks pierce our dinner conversations. Over the next ten years, twenty cars will take Hollow Road's curve too fast and crash into our yard—some young drivers will wait in our living room until their parents fetch them. Night buses take skiers to the mountaintop, their glaring headlights and gear-shifting keep me awake.

But structure problems give me the most sleepless nights. I dream about leaky pipes, arcing wires, mildewed walls, cracking plaster, peeling paint, and the five faulty fireplaces. Besides historians, I hire electricians, plumbers, contractors and painters as we can afford them. Some things improve with money. Other things I learn to fix myself. I scrape, prime, and paint the lengthy old picket fence surrounding our property and eventually pay to add another stretch of picket and gates to go across the drive with two entries. I lay a flagstone walk and gravel the driveway. I give more than three coats of white paint to the third floor suite—previously "decorated," I'm told by a neighbor, in a psychedelic mural in the1960s by a high-schooler who's goal seemed to be to use the darkest blues and brightest greens he could find.

I plant, rake, weed, scrub, dust our two-centuries old money-pit relentlessly, confident I can transform it into the lovely vision I imagined when first I laid eyes on it. I will resurrect it from the dead! If only I work *harder*! Sleep is a thing of the past—I may as well be the Mother of a newborn—in a way I am! I wake at 5:30 with creative ideas for transformation. I draw out plans for the master bathroom and a small gourmet kitchen and find Mr. Wright (a contractor who is truly Mr. *Right*) who likes and understands my drawings and is as honest as they come—a rarity in the Poconos I discover. Hiring ethical workers is the most difficult part of renovation.

As months progress and my new art business begins to flourish, the house and I develop a love/hate relationship. Three months after moving in, exhausted by a full day of renovation, I write in my journal: "This house is the opposite of what I wanted—a sanctuary it is not!"

My art business—*Shawnee Falls Studio: Art Works, Word Works, Home Works*—however, takes off, with gallery space for my paintings, a tiny retail section for selling materials to my students, a class space large enough for three six-foot tables and a model stand, and a small painting area for me. I hang dried bouquets (made by a Michigan friend I've known since high school, Connie, a professional dried flower grower/arranger) upside down from the ceiling beams for a touch of charm, place iron and copper ladles that a neighbor crafts on the mantel, fill shelves with some of the books I love for sale—themes of spirituality, decorating, home-making, women studies, bound volumes of my poetry, and my Herstory 9-Piece syllabus, along with a Nova Scotian artist's beautiful hand-made journals decorated with flora she collects along Canadian shores. In creating this studio/gallery, I hold to a line from the *Field of Dreams* film: "If I build it, they will come." And so it proves to be.

I offer six different classes. Enough to make a small livelihood. I genuinely enjoy the adults who take drawing, watercolor, figure, portraiture or my Herstory 9-Piece course and I love working with high school juniors and seniors eager to get into Pratt, Parsons or RISD. A few of the wealthier villagers and a few tourists buy my paintings. First Fridays of every month I open the gallery in the evening with a show of my newest work, a delicious reception, and I do a demonstration of a particular medium. BC entertains with guitar, connecting music to the art show theme. While the gallery/studio space is not large, it is more than I've had in recent years and being open to the public Wednesday through Saturday gives me exposure. I love my new business.

Bill is happy with our new home, too. Our backyard waterfall views and our proximity to the Appalachian Trail, where he hikes most afternoons, make up for his long commute.

I take on the difficulties of our historic house, solving every problem, transforming our village home into an historic beauty with character and modern convenience.

I soon learn, however, that rednecks are more prevalent than art purchasers. While I sell art to the occasional Manhattanite or local lawyer or the few who understand art is as important as bread, I have had to cut my painting prices for this small village. My work is not being seen the way it was in metropolitan areas like Memphis or St. Louis. While I have created all the charm an historic village studio implies and love living in history—adding, by my own labor, perennial gardens, stone pathways, plants, artistic garden ironwork and handmade wreaths—I do not have the quantity of business, nor the serenity, I'd hoped for.

From the day we move in I work diligently nonstop to bring this dead house back to life. I saw the potential life in it from the first and do not give up in restoring it. I learn how capable I am and how endless my energy is for unlikely chores. Day after day, month after month, year after year, I learn to plaster ceilings, stain floors, and how to use milk paint. I scrub, wax and polish, appreciating the centuries-old wide-plank floors, pie stairs, and moldings. I polish iron hardware, door latches, and the iron fireplace tools and the primitive chandelier I commission local artisans to craft for the house. Exhausted after laying the gravel driveway, I write in my journal: "I am a strong woman and tomorrow I'm gonna go sit in the sun!" But rarely do I actually sit. Work dominates.

The good parts are: the feeling of putting *life* into a thing thought by many to be dead, the sense of accomplishment, the continual learning of new skills, and the beauty of nature surrounding us.

From my new kitchen, I view the roaring waterfall in spring, its magical ice formations in winter. When I take my students outside to paint in summer, hummingbirds appear in the trumpet vine and the perennial gardens I planted add gorgeous color. When the huge yellow maple by the driveway brilliantly announces autumn, my favorite season, I gather grape vine to make wreaths to decorate my home and sell in the studio. On a cold October morning when the light is bright and tree colors vivid, nothing seems more spectacular than my home. It feels the same in January when the sun shines on three feet of snow and the dogs and I toboggan together in the back yard. In summer I love picking Delphinium, daisies, roses, coneflowers and zinnias for my students' still-lifes. I decorate deck, walkways, doors, and gardens with favorite quotations I paint on wooden signs ("One cannot possess more than peace in a garden of her own"—Alice Walker), and with buckets, terra cotta pots, a Cayman conch shell, a buoy from Nova Scotia, baskets, a '50s tray from my childhood, a yellow and blue picnic table cloth from Provence, and wreaths of my own making. I can't decide which is lovelier, my home at Christmastime—little candles in each window, snow and twinkling lights creating an enchanting wonderland—or, in Spring when eight lilac trees are in full purple bloom in front and hundreds of yellow daffodils fill the back yard. At these times, I am immensely satisfied and cannot imagine calling anywhere else home.

In autumn 2000, Bill and I drive to Princeton for a weekend at Tenacre—favorite getaway of my Dad's, a quiet place for Christian Scientists to rest and study, but now open, also, to others seeking spiritual solitude. Diane, my new spiritual director, an Episcopal priest whose husband was my poetry teacher at seminary, lives in Princeton, and I visit her for the first time. We become spiritual friends. I once read that "Anyone without a soulfriend is like a body without a head."

While at Tenacre, I read Buechner's *Sacred Journey* in which he refers to lectures he gave at Harvard, " I made the observation that all theology, like all fiction, is at its heart autobiography, and, that what a theologian is doing essentially is examining as honestly as he can the rough-and-tumble of his own experience with all its ups and downs, its mysteries and loose ends, and expressing in logical abstract, the truths about human life and about God that he believes he has found implicit there" (Buechner, The Sacred Journey, p.1). I want solitude in which to do Buechner-work, for I am eager to learn from my own autobiography.

About this time, I encounter Rabbi David Wolpe's *Making Loss Matter.* I connect immediately to his thinking for all the losses many moves have made in my life. The premise of his book is that "all of life is a series of losses, which, if woven correctly from the sadness, can stitch a richer emotional fabric of our days" (David Wolpe, *Making Loss Matter*, p. xi). The rabbi's words speak to my core—as significantly as L'Engle's quotation about artists and Mooney's quotation about the Ghost Dance. He says "The only whole heart is a broken one" (Wolpe, p. 7) and that we all experience brokenness and the transformative power of loss because "Losses are the stuff of life" (Wolpe, p. 9). With my many moves and losses I relate.

What I find most interesting, as an artist, is the relationship Wolpe makes between loss and creation. Loss drives us to create and gives meaning to our lives; without it we can't grow. I know that I paint, in part, because of this fact.

Wolpe writes extensively about the loss of home and the exile that causes. He quotes a Holocaust survivor: "A home is something you lose" (Wolpe, p. 23). After 33 moves I understand this well—but, gratefully, without the devastating suffering a Hollocaust surviver knew. Throughout his book Wolpe explains what my life has taught me: "We spend our entire lives in search of home, for we must be exiled to live. . .We will lose a succession of homes in a lifetime. With each leaving, a piece of ourselves stays behind. Home is not only the walls and fields but the bit of our soul that rests, that finds peace in that place" (Wolpe, p.25). I have experienced this in every move I've made! "Losing our homes in the world is creative and making them inside ourselves is healing" (Wolpe, p. 47). With each home, I've been constructing home *within*, too. As industriously as I've been renovating my Shawnee house, so I have been renovating my interior spiritual dwelling, often without realizing it.

This interior home deep within matters most, for it is the lasting home that cannot be destroyed. When Wolpe says "No human being on earth is at home" (Wolpe, p. 46), I know he speaks truth, for I continue to learn more fully that home is not the material house I seek, desire, or create, but is where I spiritually dwell.

Not only does Wolpe unite home and exile as a process, but, to them, adds another of my favorite themes: redemption. "The opposite of exile is redemption. Exile is the loss of home, and redemption is the finding of a home, a real home. Redemption is a product of the love of others, of our strength, of memory, and of faith. Together these factors combine to make real the prayer of the exile, that he might one day be truly at peace, really at home" (Wolpe, p. 44-45). This reminds me of what Virginia, my first spiritual director back in Memphis, said to me just before I moved when she told me that she felt *redemption* was my purpose, that I was meant to be a *redeemer* in this life. Now Wolpe is telling me redemption means finding home! Finding home = redemption. Redemption = finding home. I am uplifted by this exciting discovery that seems a new important thread to weave over the warp strands of my life.

Reading Wolpe shows me that what I am doing with my Shawnee home is reflecting my faith in God. "The faith that creates a home is the faith we have in our ability to generate a worthy place" (Wolpe, p. 45). When I select a paint color, move a chair to the right spot, refinish a lost antique, repair a crumbling stone wall, plant a garden, or create a fine meal to share in front of the historic hearth I just scrubbed, I am—by these faithful acts—praising God, thanking God, just as He/She is caring for me and all His/Her creation. By not neglecting what needs doing, by not letting dirt deteriorate nor anger ruin, by cleaning, watering, fixing, changing, improving, working, I am faithfully generating a worthy place. The daily chores that can sometimes seem so boringly routine, so undesired, so mundane and trivial, need to be approached joyfully, with the consciousness that the tiniest chore reveals our love of God and others. I take *care* of my home because to do so is a reflection of God's care for me and all creation. It is my opportunity to thank God. When we manage this mindset and these acts, we are paying attention to what really matters.

Wolpe says "As the seed contains the fruit....so exile contains the essence of redemption within itself. If we can love, if we can believe in the possibility of figuring out a place for ourselves in this world, we can endure losing home. For we will create a new one"(Wolpe, p. 45). As I work to create a home of God-like qualities—beauty, peace, harmony, honesty, joy, love, generosity, originality, inspiration—expressed in every choice or task I undertake, I am letting the seed of exile bloom into the redeeming fruit of true home. I know I could even endure losing my home and once again find myself wandering in exile to an unknown place where I would then create a new home. It is the creating and dwelling that matters, not the house itself.

The spiritual mark each home leaves on us contributes to our inner building. "Each place we leave is a room in the home we build inside. The mortar is the belief that each home was necessary to make us who we are. We should not dread leaving or tremble at the unknown places where we have to go. We are wanderers all, children of the wilderness" (Wolpe, p. 44). Those words again! Wandering and wilderness! Like Old Testament Jews, the Navajo, the Native Americans seeking Wovoka, the women of the Westward Movement, the dessert fathers and mothers, and the Celtic saints! Like me. We have all wandered, hopefully seeking our dreams. Such good teachers are wandering and wilderness. Wolpe says wandering in wilderness, being in exile, 'is the prerequisite for growth." (Wolpe, p.36). He shows, as life has shown me, that "an idyllic home is a dream" (Wolpe, p. 38). Dreams help us through the wilderness; certainly they have me. And when Wolpe says that redemption is "the most basic dream" (Wolpe, p. 79), I am with him.

This wise rabbi has connected all the themes of my life: dreams, home, hope, wandering, wilderness, and redemption! Like Mooney's Ghost Dance comment that speaks of mankind's universal dream, the dream of redemption is something from which we cannot separate. Home is where we start, always are, whether we see it or not, and where we end. Our need is simply to see this and live out of this knowledge.

I redeem our 1700s house, a project that continues as long as I call it home. In 2000 I also prepare it to beautifully receive Dad and Jayne for Thanksgiving and my kids coming for Christmas. Redemption filters into how I teach my art classes, which are growing. I give more than how to mix paints and wash color across a sheet of Arches paper. I pull out the individuality in each student, go to any length to reach them, to meet their particular needs. Even my *Herstory 9-Piece* class has a waiting list, and I am selling some paintings. We have a new puppy—Zermatt, a Bernese Mountain Dog—a breed Charissa and I researched and loved instantly (Charissa, finishing up her degree as a French major at nearby East Stroudsburg University, is living on the third floor in what we call her "French garret"). Life is full. Home is inspiring, challenging, satisfying.

The following March Bill and I go to Grand Cayman again to visit Nathan and enjoy the island. The guys dive while I paint and we hear of Nathan's success at work.

Two months later I get a call to help Mary Kay, my long-time friend in St. Louis, create a new home for herself, as an empty-nester. I fly to St. Louis to help her decorate her new home in a gated community. I draw her rooms on graph paper, place furniture and possibilities, help her shed what is no longer needed, visit fabric stores, advise her about kitchen cabinet choices and paint colors, plan the design and arrangement of art and meaningful objects.

One night at MaryKay's, before I fall asleep, I think about what Diane, my spiritual director, said on my last visit: "Listen to yourself, especially to that which you might not want to hear." I lie awake listening. I think about the leaky pipe in our basement we just had repaired—and the work we had done when an exposed chord of live electrical wires was found—and the repairman who recently came because we had no hot water. As soon as I return home next week, the chimney men come, then the tree trimmers, and the restorers to cut out and "explore" the foundation. Listening to this list I hear, and subdue, a dizzying cacophony of calamity. Before retiring, I write in my journal—always a sure way to *listen* to myself : *Home is not about wires and pipes and brick and mortar as much as it is about building relationship with God. Home is about where we dwell mentally and spiritually.*

In MaryKay's guest room it comes to me that perhaps my focus on home could be more spiritual. The material work weighs me down. I should be healing every situation that arises. I elect to take each problem on as if it were a case to be healed. What do I know about healing? A lot and nothing. I did it, lived it, witnessed it all my life. The way of healing is love—to just *be* it! But always easier said than done. And always so much to learn.

Outside Marykay's kitchen window lies a lesson. On the wall above the window my Catholic friend has painted in 6-inch letters a wonderful reminder: "Rejoice in the Lord always." Outside, is a birdhouse with three healthy babies, cared for by devoted parents. My second and third day, however, though the parent birds appear faithful in their parental duty, suddenly I no longer see babies. It appears to be an empty nest. A nasty grackle circles and I wonder if he has killed the baby birds. Are they dead? But on Sunday morning, my last day, I again see the babies! They were merely hidden down in the straw—the grackle hadn't gotten them after all! There was only the *appearance* of calamity, the *appearance* of death. The truth is, all was well. It strikes me that this is similar to the healing process. We simply need to see beyond the negative, even something as startling as death, to what God sees, to the spiritual sense of things.

The same Sunday morning, I find a book on MaryKay's shelves containing the writing of Sirach whom I'd never heard of (I later learn this is a second century BCE text, originally written in Hebrew, included in the Septuagint and part of the Catholic biblical canon) and I copy into my journal the line that my eyes fall upon: *Hold fast to your duty, busy yourself with it, grow old while doing your task…wait for the light* (Sirach 11:20-21). I realize that like the parent birds with their task uninterrupted, even when danger or trouble circles, I must continue with my tasks as a good steward of my home. I pray about this, then pick up my Bible and let it fall open for further reading; it opens to Job and this amazing serendipitous match: "In my own nest I shall grow old; I shall multiply years like the phoenix" (Job 29:18). My remarkable lesson of the weekend in helping Mary Kay seems to be: Be constant, diligent, and faithful in caring for and praying for your home and community. I'd been glad to get away for this long weekend, leaving behind renovation, housework, the pace of scheduled classes and being open to the public. I'd hoped for a rest in St. Louis, but with all MaryKay and I had to get done that hadn't happened. But my true rest came this last day, this brilliant Sunday morning, when the lesson gained from observing the birds and reading *was* a spiritual *rest*. I am reminded once again to fit more of this kind of rest into my life back home.

In spite of the problems surmounted and the beauty I have created in my Shawnee home, in two years, moving comes to mind. With our front door and second floor bedroom just ten feet from heavy traffic, our home is not a place of peace. More and more I want *peace*! Working in my front garden, I can expect to be asked directions four or five times in an hour by tourists who think nothing of yelling at me from their car windows, just as they think nothing of flinging cigarette butts and Styrofoam coffee cups over my freshly painted picket fence into our lovely yard—and I will be the one to pick up their trash. Their music and angry slurs towards those daring to stop at the stop sign at our corner would interrupt my serenity except that I've learned to put on *mental* amour when I garden and tune them out.

The house continues to present difficulties. The chimney guy who came to fix the fireplaces—to whom I paid $5,000—did not really fix the fireplaces. I'm advised to take him to court—but there goes my precious peace and time if I do, so I don't. The exterior painter, who I learn later hires prisoners for his crews, whom I paid a quarter of our annual income to, overlooks his young prisoner's painting door edges shut; otherwise the painting job looks good. I clean up after them and in a year, re-paint a peeling section myself. We re-do a bathroom, necessitated by a leak, and another bathroom just to improve it. I discover the tile man doesn't lay the tile properly—the same one I had to call daily to get him to show up—and I have to have it corrected. In every case I got at least three bids, but this was still no assurance of quality. The roofer took a year to show up and a half year more to belabor the job of replacing a few worn slates. The floors collect pet hair, which mingle with pollution and traffic soot, clogging the spaces between floor boards, so I vacuum and scrub the floors on hands and knees to make them shine—a 36-hour operation. It's an endless full-time job to be a good steward of this home; no wonder moving comes to mind.

The place has an edge. It is not sweetness and light, though the beautiful waterfall and stream in our backyard might suggest otherwise. Instead it seems to be eternal challenge—the opposite of the haven sought. But I tell myself, if I just work harder, save more money to spend on this place, I can fully transform it into quality, beauty and serenity. As its owner it is my job to *redeem* it, to bring it back to life. I sense I have been placed in Shawnee, just as in Memphis and previous locations, to build, plant, pray for the community in which I find myelf.

June 17, 2001, I calculate in my journal: *I've moved an average of once every 1.4 years, living in 8 different states just in these past 13 years! Between '89 and '92 I moved 7 times in 4 years—that's an average of a move every 6 months! In my life, I have had 33 moves. In her 22 years, my daughter has had 15 different homes, though in only three states—an average of 1.4 moves in her young life. What does this mean? Each move seems a kind of death of an old life, leading to rebirth.*

Bill's Dad is suffering from cancer, complicated by his alcoholism. Bill goes to Memphis to be with his family for a few days. I call Dad on the phone to tell him my father-in-law is dying of cancer and maybe he'd like to write him a note. A long silence. This man who heals by profession, who has all the answers, hasn't a word to say. "I could do that," he finally decides. I give him the hospital address. He repeats it and hangs up. No message of hope, just awkward silence and abrupt end. All phone calls with Dad end similarly.

Bill returns to Memphis ten days later for his dad's death and to spend Easter with his mom. "I haven't called home in a week," Bill sometimes says. Home to him will always be Memphis, his mom, and the house he grew up in—not the home he and I share. For all his intellect and liberal politics, Bill is a Southern boy at heart.

I paint new works on location for my gallery and prepare for a special one-woman show I am to have in Moravian's gallery at the end of September. Most artists settle on one style in one medium. But I cannot—any more than I might settle on one place to live. I need the journey of diversity. Each style serves me in a different way. Variety reflects a woman's life—fragmented, interrupted, full of diverse duties, needs, and abilities. I love the diversity of mediums and subjects: portraiture, landscape, abstraction, the spontaneity of watercolor, the richness of oil, the purity of pastel—just as I love each of my three children and could never single out one as favorite. Painting is a struggle as well as a love. Gauguin said "painting is like man—mortal, but living in a constant struggle against matter." I know this struggle when I try to put spirit into the matter of canvas and paint.

Painting, teaching classes, cleaning house, I worry that it is already September and I have nothing purchased to wear to my son Jason's October wedding. He has chosen a wonderful woman to wed. I loved Victoria the minute I met her. We relate instantly. She is deep, humorous, creative, ever evolving and full of questions, with strong artistic ability in music and art. When I first met her I felt I'd met a rare old-soul who I would love forever even if she weren't marrying my son. A talented artist, illustrator, bag-pipist, Victoria plays the guitar, banjo, and more instruments than I can recall. Her closeness to nature, especially birds, is nearly magical.

The story I most like about her is when she and Jason came to our home for a visit. It was one of those cold wet mornings and eight of us were in various stages of prepping outside to start a walk—tying shoes, adding jackets, hats and gloves. Suddenly, a little bird flew into a front window and fell to the ground, to all appearances dead. Just as quickly, like a bird herself, and without most of us even noticing, Victoria knelt down and gently scooped the poor fellow into her hands, quietly moving away from everyone. With her head very close to the little bird's, she whispered to him. I could see no one else was paying attention, but I watched Victoria with her feathered friend. In a few minutes she gently raised her hands up to the sky and away the little bird flew.

She and Jason plan an outside wedding in the Portland, Oregon's Hoyt Arboretum, where they met when he did the park's graphic design signage and she its illustrations. In honor of their mutual Scottish heritage (Jason's Scottish lineage comes via my father's mother, a Kelso, as well as my mother's McNabb line), Jason will wear a McKabb tartan kilt, the wedding party will be led to an old oak by a bagpiper, and the ceremony will be conducted by a Celtic minister. Because I am to have a small part in the wedding ceremony I decide to go to Boston in late September to look for a dress for this special occasion.

A week before I fly to Boston, the second week in September, 2001, while cleaning the kitchen, I glance up at the TV's morning news program to see a plane hit one of New York city's Twin Towers. I wonder how anyone could be so stupid to get that far off course. How do you run your airplane into a multi-story building in New York City?! In moments, I realize this is about much more than bad piloting. I phone Bill, Dad, John, and kids before the second plane hits the Twin Towers, telling them to turn on their TVs; none of them were watching until I phoned. Then comes the second plane. Riveted to the TV screen, I put down my cleaning rag. Will more attacks occur? Nothing like this has happened before. It seems as unreal as one of those disaster films the airlines always seem to be showing on long-distance flights. But this is happening only 70 miles from my home! Like everyone else in America, I sit transfixed. Immobilized by disbelief for the rest of the day and night, I can do only one thing: make art.

When terrible things happen against humanity, artists have to *do* something or they will explode like Madeleine L'Engle says, we can't make a bologna sandwich when vision breaks through, craving expression. I rummage around for a large blank canvas, grab my oil paints and brushes. It is about 11 AM. I paint what I feel and what I have seen only an hour earlier, adding to the painting as the days go by.

But before I paint, I make a sign and post it on top of the stop sign in front of our house: *TODAY: A time for EVERYONE to pray and love more!* Since moving to Shawnee, I have endured the road rage, swearing, rude behavior that occurs outside my front door. It occurred to me that such behavior has the same root as that of terrorists: hatred. All the daily anger in front of my house is a kind of terrorism, a hatred we cannot afford if we would stop others from hating us. I realize that not just in NYC but right in my village exists a tiny bit of terrorism. It occurs to me that if we expect to get rid of the larger kind, we have to get rid of even the tiniest bit of terrorism—even the little hatreds we occasionally express. We must *love more*. So I put up my sign, realizing, of course, few will understand, in fact, few will bother to stop for the stop sign on which it perches. Even fewer will see the connection between their anger and that of those who would plow into the towers on 9/11.

Zermatt is confused. He does not receive his normal walk. But the cats curl up on the radiator as if nothing's changed. For several days, like most Americans in the aftermath of 9/11, I seem incapable of moving more than a few feet from my TV, as if it is some oracle about to tell the future. I seem to need to watch to make what happened sink in. One son calls, then another, then Bill. Dad calls when, across from his condo, a SWAT team enters the Westin Hotel on Huntington Avenue in search of a suspected terrorist. We talk on the phone as Dad watches the real scene outside his window that I am watching on my TV. Weird. Everything seems uncertain, unstable. The lives lost are beyond my comprehension. Smoke, dirt, papers, pieces of people fall. A reporter mentions the Stock Market lost over 800 points and is still falling, another one says the airlines are nearly bankrupt—including the one I am supposed to fly on in a few days when I go to Boston to see Dad and find a mother-of-the-groom dress.

But before I fly, I finish my 9/11 painting. I ask God what else I might do to help; I have a hunger to help. It comes to me to do portraits of 9/11 victims for their families. "It's what artists *do*," I tell the local newspaper reporter who comes to do a story on me and my oil painting a couple days after 9/11. The painting is full of shreds of gray canvas—like the fluttering papers and debris we watched tumble down. There is a suggestion of a fireman and a rescue truck, but mostly abstract layers of jagged diagonal lines and shapes that cannot begin to do justice to the agony of the reality. A woman walks into the gallery a few days later to see the painting and says, "Oh, this painting is not hopeful!" "No" I reply, "9/11 *wasn't* hopeful!" But I think about her words and the importance of hope and redemption in this world. Another painting comes to me, which I title "Hope," showing humanity crossing the Brooklyn Bridge, going from the black ugliness of destruction to the light and color on the other side.

The several-page newspaper article with a photo of me and my 9/11 painting also conveys my desire to do victims' portraits for their families.

Over the next six months as my offer spreads, via a grief counselor in NYC (who is one of my painting students) and several more newspapers—including an article in the international *Christian Science Monitor*—I complete nearly thirty victims' portraits from photos sent. I call my endeavor *The Portrait Project: Remembering Their Spirit.* I draw each in full color, life-size, in the medium of soft pastel, trying to infuse the spirit of each individual into the portrait, based on information sent to me. I am impressed by how much joy is expressed in their faces—these were good, contributing, caring people of all ages who didn't deserve this sort of death. But then does anyone *deserve* death? I cry through the first portrait, which I work on past midnight—the young blonde woman was the same age as my first-born son who will be marrying next month; her casket contained only one arm.

I fly to Boston just nine days after 9/11, wondering if my plane could also become a target. I wear a red, white, and blue ribbon—which I don't wear on the way back, for my understanding changes—nor do I hang a flag in front of my house like so many—instead I paint a cloth red, white, and blue, with the word peace in the center, encircled by an olive branch and the words: "Let it start with me." I cannot understand the eye-for-an-eye mentality that seems to obsess many of my countrymen after 9/11—how can anyone want to do to another the same horror inflicted on them?! How can war help? This tragedy makes me want to love more, not fight.

I visit Dad in his new condo—an amazingly gorgeous and sophisticated piece of art deco architecture newly built, across the street from Neiman Marcus, Tiffany's, and other upscale shopping and fine restaurants and next to Boston's Public Library. I could barely imagine my plain Mid-western father choosing, especially at age 86, this residence.

"I would never have this place except that it serves God," Dad tells me. Later that night in bed I think about this sentence. It seems to me that this condo serves God the way Back Bay slums served their residents when they were torn out to make room for church employee's town homes; the same way the Church's I.M. Pei architecture provides its recycled air conditioning water for inner city children to run through on a hot August afternoon, since they no longer have the cool green park to play in that used to surround the Mother Church. But Dad has an innocence when it comes to areas not his expertise, material possessions being one. He usually relied on Mom, then

Jayne, to help him choose his clothes and the things that surrounded him, for they were never his focus.

The robin's egg blue carpet and walls—selected by Jayne in conjunction with a Christian Science interior designer (a friend Dad and I knew long ago, whom I suggested for her decorating talent)—are peaceful, attractive, and not obviously ostentatious. New custom built-ins beautifully and efficiently house Dads' many files. New silk upholstered chairs will serve his visiting students. Everything is ordered, lovely.

Though, if one were to look at the decorating receipts (as I had occasion to do later) the understated beauty reveals itself to be extremely expensive. The prices of the silk drapes, silk covered chairs, leather designer chairs, leather ottomans, and a few choice oriental antiques, do not suggest frugality. One might feed a thousand orphans in a third world nation for years with the total amount. I was uneasy with this, but kept my mouth shut. Dad had the right to do *whatever* he chose with his hard-earned money. How unselfishly he had worked since boyhood!—and was still working in his eighties! I only hoped it was *his* choice, not anyone else's. In any case, the new décor expressed harmony, peace and beauty—the first two qualities essential for Dad's work, and the last, the concept Jayne introduced into his life, which both she, as a lover of beauty, and I, as an artist, valued.

Along with beauty, Jayne loves quality. She expects and demands the best of everything—in ideas and things—beautiful and sometimes expensive things. Her small studio apartment in walking distance to the Mother Church and Dad's location, houses few but quality material possessions, and a wardrobe of designer clothes. Dad loves quality, too—in people and ideas. And he loves Jayne. Dad is generous. Dad no longer wants to rent but *own* his Boston home. Somewhere in these facts lies the genesis of the condo purchase. Actually, Dad also purchases a second smaller condo unit on another floor for guests, where I stay when I visit.

The day I arrive is also the day a terrorist threat is made against the city of Boston. A scare regarding water contamination. Almost no one is on the streets. When I go shopping for my dress for Jason's upcoming wedding, I am nearly the only one out. Eerie. Three clerks in a boutique on Newberry Street assist me in finding my dress—an expensive long, slender, black dress with bead work at the top of a thirties style net overlay which I plan to wear to every wedding and special occasion for the rest of my life. And seven clerks in Saks help me find shoes. They have no other customers.

After dinner, Dad discusses his perspective on life—one flowing, non-stop sentence. About 10:30 he begins to ask me a question—a question that continues until after 11:00! The gist of it is, "why aren't you a Christian Scientist, you have so much you could give to the movement?!"—though he never actually gets it out that simply. The next day I hear old story after old story—over and over—about Pearl Harbor, the building of the Enola Gay, God's law, self-government, warehouse windows and the bee-bee gun, his experiences in industry, his Christian Science demonstrations, his example for others, etc., etc., etc. I listen once more. It has always been my primary role in his home.

At times it is painful to sit in his office and listen –like lashes to the heart. He struggles so with what I am and what he would have me be. I hear it in his voice. He can barely hide his disappointment. My father genuinely believes he understands the mysteries of life, but I am an enigma to him. His concrete certitude fills cracks where others have reasonable doubt. In 86 years no storm has shaken his Christian Science foundation. Every day I know more why I have left denominations. Love is *universal*, without particularity or partiality. I know this from the top of my head to my toes.

I think about Dad and realize he is really lonely but acts happy. He has his students but if he lost Jayne I think it would kill him. Their interdependence is convenient for both, but not necessarily the best for either. Even self-reliant Glenn Evans needs human relationship.

When I return home I offer a gathering once a week at 7:30 AM for anyone who cares to come to my home to share, from *any* point of view, our best thoughts and prayers about peace, terrorism, the war, etc. I open these meetings with a brief apropos Bible reading followed by silent prayer, then everyone's sharings, and we end with a light breakfast I serve. I call it "Morning Meal." It turns out to be a big success. Sometimes as many as a dozen or more people come and share their thoughts. I do this for several months.

I hang 23 pieces of my work at Moravian the following week, including the oils "9/11" and "Hope", and sell a few pieces and prints.

Now that things are quieter, I take time to write my thoughts about 9/11 in my journal:

What is this tightness in my stomach each morning lately when I wake?—Is it fear? Am I the one to fear now, the way Afghan women have feared behind their veils for centuries? Or the way children in Northern Ireland have feared or in Israel or Palestine? How much worse their fear must be than mine for all these years! My fear is but a recent thing. Is God telling us we cannot continue to let suffering happen anywhere in this world? That we are not safe, will never be safe, until no suffering person remains? That our brothers and sisters cannot be allowed to suffer while we have wealth and abundance in our nation? Or will we continue to be afraid of those not like us? Will we waken from the lull of materialism and self-satisfaction, merely throwing money at the problem of terrorism? Or might we educate ourselves and others out of complacency? Might we do the hard work of transformation, see deeply into our enemy's face and find there the face of God?—the one universal God in whose image and likeness all the world was made? Evil is that which we do not know about God. We must get busy knowing God.

I wake at 4:00 AM, again at 5:00, and finally rise at 6:00 to write more:

This nation cannot go back to normal, cannot continue to shop until it drops, cannot wallow in its materialism any longer. No. There has been a change. Now let there be a transformation! A death of the old narrow US and an awakening by our nation to a new, more universal outlook that includes and embraces others. And may each one know it starts with himself. It starts with me. Everyone everywhere must say in his or her heart that 'it starts with me.' Each one must allow himself to be transformed by this 9/11 experience and not just return to 'normal'. Each one has the possibility of creating a new, more globally-caring normal. We cannot take liberty, justice, equality for granted. Had the Talaban or the terrorists grown up in safety, plenty, peace, would they now rage? I read that many of them grew up orphans in a dusty land where want is all that's plentiful and war their play. How could they be other than they are? They may never have known a safe and loving home.

And I keep writing:

If one—just one terrorist were in your home right now, seated comfortably on your sofa in your living room, in conversation, could you love him? Christians are called to do this, as are followers of most religions. Could you hold the child within him, letting him cry on your shoulder for all his many years of suffering and deprivation? [For certainly all terrorists have been driven by despair]. *Would it not be possible to prepare him a fine meal and give him a warm bed after hearing the horrors of his life? Could your expression of love transform him? If you answer no to this, then indeed we have a long road ahead. For it will not be by bombs and technology that we win! It never has been so. It will come only by our extraordinary and courageous brotherly love—the lovingkindness of Jesus and Buddha. The kind of love an ordinary (but exceptional) priest in Les Mis had in giving a poor robber a pair of golden candlesticks, changing his life forever. The kind of love that has to be worked at daily. The kind of love that does not come easy. Far more difficult than saying "have a good day" to a stranger or giving Christmas gifts to one's family. This love requires contemplation, prayer, forgiveness, and it demands we* change. *Every day. The kind of love that lets us find a way other than anger even when anger may seem justified. The kind of love that does not believe a person is evil, because God made all His children in His image and likeness. What we do about evil has been the problem of centuries and will never be easily solved. But we can always re-define ourselves, conform our ways, habits, and actions to greater love.*

In October Bill, Charissa, and I fly to Portland, Oregon for Jason and Victoria's wedding. Many family and friends, fearful to fly so soon after 9/11, do not come. But my Dad and Jayne fly from Boston. Victoria wears a lovely white satin princess dress with a dark green velvet cape she made herself. She also made shawls for each of her bridesmaids to wear. She is a creative woman who makes furniture, quilted art, illustrations, and unique carved bird-doll images I carry in my gallery. She designs a drawing of the two of them to use as table décor—each as a bird, she a crow and Jason a white bird. Bagpipes begin the ceremony as the bride and groom walk in through the woods. We gather by a tree where I've hung a wreath they asked me to make; beneath it the couple say their vows before the Celtic female minister whose service is a delight. But only a year later, this wedding's reason for being will die in divorce and Jason's heart will be broken. He will recover and become stronger, and in 2009 marry again—to a lovely red head with the same sensibilities as his own and together they will make a wonderful home surrounded by amazing organic gardens.

In November 2001, Bill's entire family of siblings and their offspring come for several days at Thanksgiving—seven little children among them, a total of 15. I bake and make all sorts of specialties, arrange rooms, line up sleeping bags in the second floor's long hall when I run out of rooms. We play monopoly, checkers, chess, do art projects, take walks, chase the cats, play with the dogs—we've just added Geneva, a second Bernese Mountain Dog to our pack—and when it is over, having had a good visit with all, Bill and I are nevertheless exhausted and vow never to do this again.

In December, Jayne calls and asks if we would invite Dad to come for Christmas. I am surprised as I have asked Dad throughout his life, numerable times, to come for Christmas, and while there were a few such visits when my children were young and Mother was alive, his usual answer has always been, "that is my busiest time of the year and I cannot leave Boston." Thanksgiving was our usual get-together time. Jayne explained that she had plans this year of her own for Christmas and I was aware of a new romantic relationship in her life. We arranged for Dad to spend a week with us, arriving mid-day December 17 and staying through the morning of the 22nd, when we would drive him to Tenacre in Princeton, New Jersey, his favorite place. Since Mom's passing, Dad usually went there at least once a year for rest and study and to write his association address. He told us he wanted to be there for Christmas, plus a few more days, so he could write. My father, along with Mrs. Eddy, believed that Christmas is not about Santa Claus, gift-giving and merry-making, but a time for intimate closeness with God, for gratitude, stillness, and spiritual study. To spend Christmas in a well-appointed, quiet and private wooded Tenacre cottage, with meals delivered to your door, was the best Christmas Dad could imagine.

When Dad arrived he visited Bill's classroom at Moravian, walked the village with us, enjoyed my home-cooked meals, and we shared the opportunity to catch up. We took him to visit Chadds Ford, visiting the Wyeth Museum, decorated for the season, and to the sing-along Messiah presentation at the Shawnee Playhouse across from our home. We took him to a neighbor's Christmas dinner party we were invited to where he seemed to enjoy singing carols and visiting with folks he didn't know. Bill and I listened to his stories of the past and his view on current politics. We went for walks together with the dogs and appreciated the beautiful snow that fell. I prepared all his favorite meals and did an early Christmas turkey dinner on the 21ˢᵗ ,which he seemed to relish. We gave him a couple of gifts to open—Dad has always liked receiving gifts, I think because he received few in childhood.

The last morning of his stay, I woke about 5 AM to the sound of running water and got up to investigate what new problem might be occurring in this old house. Water was gushing from the guest bath faucet and could not be turned off. I ran downstairs to the living room where Dad had ensconced himself on a sofa with his books. He had risen early, showered, shaved, dressed, packed, taken his bags downstairs, and was reading on the sofa with a magnifying glass (he refused to get glasses). He explained he could not turn off the guest bath faucet, that it had broken when he tried, and so he decided to just let it run because he did not want to wake us. Apparently it had been running for about an hour—probably our oil tank, which heated both radiators and water, would be empty in short order and our next bill would be astronomical! I said I would take care of it and then prepared his breakfast right away. I awakened Bill, called the plumber who couldn't come, and then called Jim, our neighbor who can do anything. For the next 4 hours Jim and Bill worked on the shower and eventually fixed it while I dished up Dad's pancakes, bacon, and eggs and then the two of us talked in the living room.

Dad shared ideas he had gleaned as a life-long Christian Scientist, many stories I'd heard countless times. But I listened patiently. Somehow I had the feeling this was the greatest gift I could give him—to listen. As I listened, I noticed Dad seemed older, less sure in his step, less powerful in his tone, and in general, less in control. At one point he took a speech out of his briefcase he had given to some group long ago and asked me to read it aloud. It was the familiar telling of his life as a young Scientist and the healings he had experienced. When I was finished I told him how good I thought it was.

"You can keep it. I have another copy in my files" he said. He added that he felt that this speech was an important message for today's Scientists on how to live daily life *practicing true church*. I agreed that's what his manuscript conveyed. He said he thought it might make a good article for publication in the Christian Science periodicals. The periodicals had changed in recent years in Dad's eyes—he felt they were watered down, more secular. I told him I thought it would make an excellent article, particularly for the *Christian Science Journal*—a publication I was familiar with, having had several of my own articles published in it years ago. I offered a few suggestions and changes which he liked immensely.

"I could do a little editing for you, Dad, later, on my computer and email it to you."

"That would be great." His face lit up like the Christmas tree in front of him.

I suggested he might also try working on it at Tenacre. He said, smiling, he wished he could take me with him to Tenacre to work on it for him, adding "and you could help me on my association address, too!" It was nearly like old times—my Dad and I, squirreled away together, working on ideas in Christian Science. He said he really needed someone to write with him, to put down the ideas as they came to him, to order it on the page, to make sure important facts weren't omitted—facts so familiar to him that he sometimes forgot to include them.

As I looked over the speech, I realized it wouldn't be too difficult to turn it into a solid article. The thought came to me, "Why, I could do it right now at my computer while we are waiting for the plumbing to be resolved!" But I did not say this to him, in case I couldn't complete the editing before we left to take him to Tenacre.

He was a bit nervous about the time it was taking Bill and Jim to solve the shower problem; this was delaying his plans to be at Tenacre. All his life Dad needed to be extra early to everything. It was not as if anyone were waiting for him at Tenacre; he did not have a set agenda. I assured him we could make up some time driving, that on any account we had not planned to leave Shawnee until 10:00 AM. It was important to him to get there by lunchtime. I assured him we could still do that and left to clean the kitchen, leaving him to make a couple of phone calls to his patients.

Meanwhile, I did a fast job of the kitchen and took Dad's speech to the computer and scanned it in. I moved paragraphs, filled in missing parts of ideas he meant but had left out, added story bits he had not written but I knew were important to the whole, changed tenses and grammar, clarified pieces for the reader, made it less of a speech and more an article, etc. The work flowed. It was as if the writing were happening all by itself—such a time for a writer is always a gift. In little more than an hour it was done—by 9:30!

I ran downstairs, "Dad, I have something to read to you". I read the article in its entirety, stopping only when he made a remark. When I had finished, he asked to read it aloud for himself pausing at every addition or word change, as if tasting each morsel of it, discussing the improved version with such excitement. He loved it. He seemed amazed by the appropriateness of the additions—"My lands, how could you remember *that* story?!—its perfect there." He could see the increased clarity. He read it again aloud by himself. When he was done he got up out of his cushy sofa seat, stumbling over the Berner asleep at his feet, to get to my chair as I, in turn, stood to come to him. He told me "You are a remarkable woman!" and gave me a kiss and the kind of hug that squeezes the breath out of you. I saw a tiny tear slide down his face. He was truly moved that I had re-worked his writing into an article that expressed everything he'd tried to say. I promised to email a copy to him and Jayne and gave him another copy to take with him. As if on cue, Bill and Jim came down the stairs, triumphal in their plumbing war, and we got Dad to Tenacre in time for lunch. Not for a year would I know the outcome of the editing I had done for Dad's article.

Christmas is a restful day, as it should be. I read with a cat on my stomach, Geneva, our Berner puppy, at my feet, Zermatt, our older Berner, to my side, a husband on the facing sofa. All seems right with the world. We had a large Christmas eve dinner with friends Walter and Pam who live on the mountain above us and today I have no work. I finish Camus' *The Stranger* and continue David McCullough's *John Adams*—a great book about a great man, perhaps my favorite man in all of history. Adams, a staunch journal-keeper, with whom I agree when he writes, "The only way to compose myself and collect my thoughts is to set down at my table, place my diary before me and take my pen into my hand. This apparatus takes off my attention from other objects. Pen, ink, and paper and a sitting posture are great helps to attention and thinking." (McCullough, p.66).

In the evening, my big *gal lute* of a puppy, all 90 pounds of her, leans across my legs on the bed as I write. Her wavy hair soft against my body, her huge dark brown eyes set in piercing whites follow my every move and thought. She knows me as if we've had a past as old as this house. I tell her she will be a best friend forever and bury my face in her fur, lost in black fluff, while she pants a comforting steady rhythm, always watching me. I am as important to her as she is to me, and as is her larger brother-Berner on the floor beside me, whose body once fit in the palm of my hand. My love for my dogs is a piercing love beyond the normal human kind of love; it goes to some other dimension.

New Year's Day I am sick in bed with a102 temperature. I have only recently begun to take temperatures, usually dogs'. I don't like it and rarely do it, unless Charissa or Bill insists. This time, Little Miss Efficient Nurse Charissa lectures me about Tylenol. "If you don't take two Tylenol right this minute I am going to call a doctor and make an appointment for you right now! I will drive you to the hospital myself!" I have never taken Tylenol or any pill before. I break my pact with God and take the capsules—so difficult to swallow both physically and mentally! My spiritual director tells me "God can be in the Tylenol," but all my life I have *not* relied on medicine but have been trusting God, not leaning on anyone or anything else. Now I have broken that trust. This fact is worse than how awfully sick I feel. Our pact was: I would rely on God in everything and He, in turn, would take care of me. I intended to have the courage to stick with God. But I did not do this. Our bond is broken. I failed God. My agreement with God is gone because of two Tylenols that did nothing to relieve my illness and I never take them again.

During this illness, I feel depressed, old, and very, very sick. I wonder how to pull myself together, back to that initial vision I had that my life is mine to create—lovely and full. I am not dead I tell myself. I live in a free country. I can handle this. I just need to live *gratefully* every day—to love *more* and do better.

But I feel, too, my slavery to the needs of this vastly demanding house. Neither Charissa nor Bill seem to understand that I *work*; because my studio business is at home, it seems to them I haven't pressing work. But my gallery is open to the public 4 days a week, my 6 or 7 classes are each two or three hours long, and my painting, ordering, writing, and running of this business is fully time-consuming—especially on top of historic house demands. I am fully employed but because it is under the home roof, it is assumed I am there to do laundry, dust, scrub, cook, grocery shop—and apparently eat bon bons in my free time! I resent this. They tell me to slow down but do nothing to take up the slack, to takeover any duties. It is difficult to run a profitable one-person business. I am interrupted in everything I do. And I am exhausted.

It is not just my immune system that is being tested with this sickness, it is my convictions, my strength of belief, my faith. I trusted that *Christ Jesus healed*—my mantra—that is where I've rested since leaving Christian Science a decade ago. But now I am in some malaise of belief. That which I *believe* has always been my foundation, my strength. Now it seems weakened—like this house's foundation before we had it restored. Not weakened for good, but *re-arranged*. I feel shattered. Some wonderful mosaic has to be made of my brokenness.

Once more I must re-create myself. What really matters? What do I love? These are the questions that count. Answers will re-create me in my next metamorphosis. So I write out once more at this place and time what really matters to me. The list has not changed: God, beauty, Truth, honesty, my children, my dogs, space, solitude, goodness, Nature, the good in anything anywhere, making art, writing, teaching, my family, ideas, learning, books, creating, improving anything, helping anyone who hurts, healing, being appreciated, being heard, hard work.

The sickness continues for weeks. I cancel classes, close the studio. My face is deformed with blisters. My form has been taken from me. What will my new form be? I glean I am being called to *re*-form. Ahh! To *trans*form!

Uplifting by flowers, a note, a kind word or a phone call do not come. I am alone. I review my spiritual self and physical self, habits good and bad, my need to meditate more, to express more love, to slow down are issues the illness brings to the fore. Gratefully, I begin to see myself more clearly, who I really am becomes more fine-tuned. The me I am *not* dies; a welcome death.

Just as I begin to recuperate, Jayne calls to say Dad fell on the streets of Boston, was bleeding, but walked home alone to continue his calls while a Christian Science nurse bandaged him up. Dad fell several times and is dealing with "a blockage problem" she says. Jayne said Dad's problem "has existed for awhile" on and off for over a month. He kept his problem to himself at first, then Jayne became his nurse and practitioner. I look up blockage in the dictionary: "internal resistance of an individual to understanding a communicated idea, to learning new material, or to adopting a new mode of response because of existing habitual ways of thinking, perceiving and acting." The dictionary's wisdom seems remarkable. Prayerfully, I allow my Bible to open. It falls open to King David's charge to his son before his death—like a premonition speaking to my own relationship with my father: "Now the days of David drew nigh that he should die and he charged Solomon his son, saying, I go the way of all the earth; be thou strong therefore, and shew thyself a man; And keep the charge of the Lord thy God, to walk in his ways to keep his statutes, and his commandments, and his judgments, and his testimonies, as it is written in the law of Moses, that thou mayest prosper in all that thou doest..." (1 Kings 2:1). Perfect immediate teaching! I look up the same verse about King David's death, that my King James Bible had opened to, in the Harper's Collins Revised Standard Study Bible and read: "Be strong, be courageous, and keep the charge of God, walking in his ways and keeping his commandments, laws, testimonies, as written in the law of Moses, so that you may prosper in all that you do and wherever you turn." This compels me to study the law of Moses, the 10 Commandments, once again, and I write out what I learn.

About a week later, Jayne calls Rich on a Wednesday night. Rich calls me Thursday morning after again speaking with Jayne. He tells me Dad sounds "sleepy, weak." Rich has decided to fly to Boston; he wants me to consider coming. According to Jayne, since the first week of December Dad had had some difficulty involving food and elimination. That would mean he was dealing with this situation to some degree when he visited Bill and me before Christmas, though we saw no evidence of it, and neither Jayne nor Dad mentioned a thing at that time. I'd thought he looked a little fuller in the midriff than usual in photos taken while he was here, but this was more a vague observation than anything noteworthy. I recall him thoroughly enjoying all the home-cooked meals I made for him—especially the chocolate torte with whipped cream, home-made vegetable soup, and complete turkey dinner. I figured that explained the tummy increase noticed in the photo. But apparently he had been working on this problem for some time, while continuing his work as a practitioner, still taking cases and preparing his association address.

On Thursday, January 24, 2002, my brother flies to Boston. He calls me late that night from Dad's condo, suggesting I come up tomorrow. He suggests I might help with nursing care, meals, clean-up in order to free Jayne to focus on taking Dad's calls and association business. Rich says Dad was in some discomfort, apparently caused by no bowel movement for some time, but adding, he seems alert, on top of things, and in expectation of healing. Rich says he'll call me tomorrow after he has a better chance to evaluate the situation. I ask why no one had called me until now. He said Dad and Jayne had only phoned him the day before. I wonder why I had not *also* been phoned the day before. I could have cancelled my classes and driven there immediately had I known. I decide to leave for Boston the next afternoon.

Early Friday morning I cancel my classes and call my brother, now in Boston, to let him know Bill and I will arrive in Boston between 10 and 10:30 PM that night. Rich is glad, thinks it the right thing, says he'll leave Dad's condo door unlocked so we can slip in quietly in case Dad's sleeping.

About an hour or so later, to my surprise, I get a call from Dad. In a weak voice barely recognizable, he tells me it isn't necessary for me to come to Boston.

"Dad, it's no problem, I have already cancelled my classes." I assure him that my coming is no trouble. "I called all my students first thing this morning and I have a sign out that the gallery will be closed tomorrow. As soon as Bill gets home from school we're on our way!"

"You did?" He sighs. It seems as if he is dismayed that I am free to come. "Right now I just have so much on my plate," he continues. "So many calls coming in, uh…" He has difficulty breathing and needs to pause often between phrases. "So many patients' cases I'm handling, uh…*this is not a good time for a visit.*" It is an apparent struggle for him to speak. That he musters force for these last words is significant and I pick up on that instantly. I have been his daughter too long. When Dad does not want to do something or does not want something to happen, he can be adamant. He is adamant now.

"Dad, I'm not coming for a *visit*—I'm coming to *help*. I can do things!"

"There's really no need…uh… we're really making progress here and I..uh…should be back to where I uh…need to be in no time…uh…we have everything covered…uh…there's a lot of progress."

"But I could at least…"

He interrupts quickly and firmly, "Laurie [his cook] has the meals taken care of…we don't need you to cook. Jayne and Rich are here to take care of everything …uh…there isn't anything for you to do. [I think: How about sit beside my father while he's terribly ill?] And, we really don't have room for you and Bill with Rich here right now."

"We can sleep in sleeping bags on the floor, Dad, or get a hotel room".

"No…uh… you don't need to do that. We *really don't need you*." he speaks more quickly and firmly.

I can be a slow learner sometimes. Finally I get it. *He doesn't want me there.* I'm stunned. Just to see if I'm maybe misreading this, I ask, "Dad, are you saying you *prefer* I not come?"

"Yes, I think it's for the best…uh… there's no need for you…uh… to be here."

"I don't want to do what you don't want me to do. If you don't want me there, then I …" Suddenly an idea strikes me. Maybe Dad can't rationally decide this; I should talk to Rich, so I ask Dad to call him to the phone. Dad doesn't really answer me; I hear him mutter and fumble with the phone buttons, then disconnect. We never say good-bye.

Five minutes later Rich phones. He is surprised Dad called me and says he had no idea that Dad had done so. I tell him about our conversation. Rich says, "Let me talk to him and call you right back."

Rich calls me after talking to Dad and says, "There seems to be an issue of separation with Dad, but I still want you here."

"An issue of separation". Only a Christian Scientist, or former Christian Scientist, would know what this means. My father, knowing me to be a non-Scientist, feels a separation between us that conflicts with his work as a Scientist; in his view, my presence would be an *intrusion* to the healing process. And I had thought we had been making progress! Are we still so far apart? Has the improved relationship been a facade these past several years?! What was our Christmas visit only a few weeks ago about if not a shared spiritual closeness? Does he not know my love for God is as strong as his? That I, too, believe in healing? Suddenly I realize that because I chose to leave his church I will *never* be worthy in his eyes. Rich, Jayne, and Dad's students receive his love, a love to which I will never be entitled. I am only his first-born child, but they are followers of the Truth he holds dear.

It is an appalling realization. My father doesn't want me.

I tell my brother: "I awoke this morning knowing it was my right place to be in Boston with Dad and you. But after his phone call…I don't want to upset him, or intrude, or be perceived as impeding his healing. I was blamed for Mom's death; I don't want to be perceived as interfering with Dad's healing. If he really doesn't want me…"

Rich, a much broader thinker than our father, replies, "I still think you should come. This isn't just his decision; *it isn't just about Glenn.* Glenn has things to learn in this experience. Truth is what this healing requires. I'll call you again at noon."

Rich doesn't wait until noon; he calls me back about an hour later and says: "My dear sister, of course you should be here. *I want you here even if Dad doesn't.* I love you and I want you here for *me.* Come!"

We leave as soon as Bill arrives home from school, shortly after 4:00. The traffic is thick; we do not make good time. We reach Boston, travel down Boylston Street, pass the Mother Church, up Exeter, around the Westin, to One Huntington Avenue: Trinity Place Condominiums—my father's home. We give the doorman our car keys and ask the concierge not to ring the apartment—my brother said he would leave the door unlocked so we could enter quietly should Dad be sleeping. We take our bags and walk through the marble and gold rotunda to the elevators. The twelfth floor seems farther than it is. My thoughts are mixed as they were in the car coming. Because I've come here will my help be rejected? Did he *really* not want me here? Could my coming upset him enough to cause his death? No, I know better than that.

On our drive, somewhere near Waterbury, Connecticut, a passing thought had come to me that it would be good for all concerned if Dad passed on in his sleep before I arrived. That way he couldn't be upset by Bill's and my presence; but, if that happened, I would not be able to talk to him in any meaningful way *one last time.* I always felt we had one more corner to turn, one more understanding to achieve between us. We could not be deprived of that! Besides, no one said he was *dying,* only that he was very ill and working alertly on the problem. I was coming to help any way I could. So why this premonition of death? I attacked the negative suggestion—how preposterous to think he was dying! He was alive and fighting for healing—just as he'd done thousands of times for others. "One ought never give up! Never give into a problem! Never accept death!" His own words. He always lived up admirably to his Welsh name, Evans: "the fighting man". How could he now do otherwise?

There was purpose to my visit. I was coming to read to him, sit with him, clean, fix and do for him—as I always had. If he liked, I would even read to him from the Christian Science textbook, *Science and Health,* as I had as a little girl, a big girl, and even in New Harmony when that textbook was no longer a major part of my life. I would tell him once more how much I loved him and how many peoples' lives he had affected for good. I'd ask him questions, listen to his stories. Read his speeches to him. If he were in pain I would help him through with strong declarations, the Lord's Prayer, a Psalm, my own faith in God. I would *not* leave his side. My father never intended to die; he told everyone he planned to live forever. He, and those he told, more than half-believed it. Why, he had barely moved into his new condo less than a year ago! He had things to *do* with his life! Healing. Teaching. Growing. And he and I had come so far in re-establishing our deep closeness—couldn't we go all the way? We had to finish that!

As Bill and I got off the elevator, an odd sensation came over me—a kind of *knowing* that this was the end; yet I turned the handle of the door to his apartment with hope. I saw my brother, his back to me, his hand holding his forehead, standing in the dim crystal light of the sky-blue hall. As we entered, he turned and I knew his words before I heard them: "We've lost him! Our father just passed moments ago."

"We haven't lost him", I answered quickly, responding instantly like any good Christian Scientist might, one who knows there is much more to life than the physical body. I felt a release as the three of us—Rich, Bill and I—embraced in a kind of football huddle. We took a moment to honor this extraordinary man who happened to be our father. Thirteen minutes earlier I would have stood beside his bed and held his hand along with my brother; thirty minutes earlier I could have said good-bye.

Rich took us into Dad's bedroom, past the wall of gold-framed family photos, into the crisp royal blue and white bedroom, so fresh from a decorator's eye. There in the vastness of his king-size bed lay a little Welshman, his eyes closed, his mouth wide open as if about to receive a cup of cold water. But no cold water came. He was dead. His skin was gray-white against the dark browns and burgundy of his paisley robe that Rich had, in propriety, thrown across his legs. Immediately I was aware that this was not my father. My father was so much more! This was but the shell he'd left, like some hermit crab moving on.

Rich had had a hard day. Earlier that morning he had bathed and shaved Dad in Dad's never-before-used marble Jacuzzi. No easy task, but much easier, under the circumstances, than Dad's customary walk-in shower, impractical under the circumstances. Rich helped Dad into his Indiana U sweatshirt and the paper diapers Jayne had bought for him several weeks ago. His abdomen was greatly swollen out of proportion so that he could not fit into any pants. What a sight he must have been! According to Rich, he and Dad had a good laugh over this get-up—so incongruous for my take-charge dapper Dad! Good they could find humor. His extended abdomen was most likely causing him more pain than he had ever known or would ever give in to. Dad could only sleep in short spurts. He had difficulty breathing and talking. Rich said his voice did not sound like him, weak, strained, gasping sometimes. I had noted this in his phone call—in fact, after hearing the details, I marveled that he phoned me at all. How desperately he must not have wanted me to come that he would go through the pain of phoning! How extremely uncomfortable he must have been with our relationship! How deeply painful my not being part of his church must have been for him these past twelve years!

Earlier, searching for ways to be helpful, my brother said to Dad: "I need to ask you a hypothetical question, Dad. If someone came in to your bedside right now, say a neighbor, and said to you, 'Glenn, I know this Doctor So-and-So at Mass General, a fine fellow, and I could take you down to see him and he could fix your "plumbing" and get you back to your old self and you could continue your work'—how would you answer him?"

Dad said very clearly, "I know exactly how I'd answer him because I've already asked myself that question. I've thought about it carefully. *It would completely undermine my entire life.* I cannot go that route."

Rich understood. He read Dad the current weekly Bible Lesson on Truth, followed by reading, at Dad's request, *all* of the weekly Bible lessons for the next two months!—over 90 citations! A call came in from a patient—Dad took it as if he were undisturbed in his routine of healing. He had been taking fewer calls in recent weeks, but now Rich got him to let someone else handle his cases. Just this once, his only focus should be healing himself, not others.

Between naps, Dad worked prayerfully. He wrote out the synonyms for God—Life, Truth, Love, Principle, Mind, Soul, Spirit—in shaky handwriting, one to a sheet of paper, and spread them all over his bed so that he could focus clearly on each one, striving to be fully present in the meaning of each. Rich said Dad was lucid most of the day and only occasionally seemed to be "somewhere else".

Dad talked with Rich about his spiritual discoveries and about his brothers, parents, grandparents, aunts, and uncles. Dad said he wished he had known his father better. Rich and Dad discussed Truth and the need for honesty. They focused on ascendancy, getting thought higher than the problem.

In the evening Dad asked to get out of bed and have dinner in the dining room, something he had not done for a week or more. Neither Jayne nor Laurie, the cook, were there—*contrary to what Dad had told me on the phone*. It was Jayne's day off and Laurie came only once a week. Rich prepared dinner—a cup of re-heated potato-leek soup Laurie had prepared several days ago. He set the table in the dining room, put a pad on the silk chair seat, and helped Dad walk slowly from the bedroom he had not left in days. Dad asked to watch Lehrer's TV newscast, part of his normal routine, though Rich observed he wasn't always following it. Doing his normal routine seemed very important to Dad. Rich smiled when Dad asked for a juice glass of Coke with ice and peanuts. All our lives Coca-Cola was a rarity, a party-item, usually served in juice glasses, reserved for birthdays, celebrations and special occasions. It seemed appropriate I thought, smiling, as I heard of his simple last request. He was going to have some small good human things before he left this world. He deserved them. Not much to ask. Just a juice glass of coke and a handful of peanuts.

Dad and Rich sat in the living room following dinner and talked briefly—but Dad would sometimes drift. Rich saw him getting sleepy, "Dad, why don't we go back to the bedroom—wouldn't you like that?" "That dear bed" Dad responded. It *was* dear to him. Dad worked on so many healings from that bed, especially when late-night calls came. After a long day it was like dropping into open arms he once told me. Across his bed was draped a navy fleece blanket that the kids and I had given him many Christmases ago on which I had had embroidered "God is Love"; he loved that blanket and more than once remarked what a reminder it was during a hard case. This bed had supported him especially well these last weeks when he could go nowhere else. It had become a kind of precious home. Yes, it was a "dear bed". Rich helped him walk back to the bedroom, slowly, straddling to support him, and then returned to the kitchen to do dishes as soon as Dad fell asleep.

About 10:00, Rich saw the row of Belgian crystal hall lights come on and thought it was me arriving. But suddenly there was Dad standing in the kitchen! Rich was startled. He was amazed that Dad could have made it to the kitchen by himself. Dad started to try to open the Sub-Zero himself, saying he wanted a pitcher of ice water and another glass of Coke. Rich got them for him and Dad insisted on carrying them by himself back to his bedroom. Rich again straddled him, helping to support his walk, but allowing Dad to carry his beverages. At bedside, Rich leaned down taking the water and glass from Dad, setting them on the table, as Dad sat on the edge of the bed. As Rich stood up, Dad fell backward, gasped, starring past Rich, through Rich, through the hall light, through everything. Rich said it was as if he were suddenly somewhere else, as if he were "busy doing something else." What he was busy doing was dying.

There were no last words. So much happened in a split second. Rich took his hand, phoned the practitioner, saw the body convulse before stillness set in—an awful experience for him. Rich said aloud "God is All", still holding Dad's hand. He swung Dad's legs up onto the bed before the body became stiff and closed Dad's eyelids, but could not close his mouth. How quickly it all happened! He wondered if he should call 911 or try to resuscitate the body. But the immediate answer that came was No. He threw the paisley robe across Dad's legs and knelt beside the bed for a moment. Then, he walked out of the room to the front hall, with its sky-colored walls and crystal ceiling lights casting rays across the soft carpet. He rested his forehead in his hand and realized he was utterly alone. His wife was hundreds of miles away with their children, his father lay dead on the bed in the next room, neither Jayne nor a single student was here, nor his sister. *Where's my sister?! She should be here by now! I want my sister!* he thought to himself, he told me later. Just then, I opened the door and walked in. Rich turned, sighed in relief, and told me the news.

Dad passed away in his Boston condo Friday, January 25, 2002 at 10:40 PM—just thirteen minutes before I arrived.

Then began the surrealistic all-night parade of 911 guys in helmets and boots fresh from a fire, EMS workers, police who had to keep everyone out until each faction of government did their job in proper order, and finally at 3 AM, the funeral parlor men in black arrived who were "sorry for our loss" as they zipped up my father in a plastic bag and took him away. I never saw him again.

The next day was awkward and busy. My brother, as executor of the will, called a 9:30 meeting for Bill, Jayne and me at which he read the will and delegated duties. He and I would meet with the funeral home in the afternoon and he would stay over Monday to contact lawyers and banks. There would be no funeral nor memorial service, just as there had been none for Mom. Dad would be cremated, like Mom, and the ashes disposed of by the crematorium. My father believed in the unreality of the body and wouldn't have wanted it any other way. The greatest urgency was composing and getting out a letter for Dad's Christian Science Class Association members and another to the Association board. He and Jayne spent most of the day working on those projects and related tasks. They conferred about Dad's confidential files, sorting and throwing out papers. All of Dad's patients had to be notified. Jayne and Rich made hundreds of phone calls. I was asked not to answer the phone when calls came in, since most were Christian Science-related. My only assigned task was to make three phone calls to selected relatives and write "the family and friends letter." No longer a member of the church, I couldn't help with anything else. Dad's life had been Christian Science. Tidying up after that life was reserved for Christian Scientists. I was shut out in his death as I had been shut out of his life these past dozen years. Hurt and anger welled up inside me, but I did not know that's what it was—I had no label for what I was feeling and assumed it was just a natural reaction to death. Over the next month my feelings would become clearer.

Sunday morning Rich suggests the three of us read the Christian Science Bible lesson out loud together, pausing periodically to reflect on its meaning in relation to Dad. I read the Bible portion, my brother reads the *Science and Health* citations and Bill reads a Psalm as benediction. We share a few memories about Dad and laugh over new puppy stories (we each have new puppies at home). Rich and I peruse the household as to what we should do with Dad's stuff. Rich wants Dad's black leather office chair and the antique oriental lamps and I can use the tufted leather footstools. Dad's framed portrait will go to one of his students, a few things are set aside for family members, and the remainder will be boxed and shipped to various grandchildren starting their first homes. Our minimal work finished, Bill and I leave for home Sunday afternoon. It had *not* been the weekend I'd expected.

Two weeks later we drive back to Boston to meet with Rich, his wife Blythe, Jayne, and lawyers and divide property. I notice an odd smell about the car. Maybe it's from taking the dogs hiking yesterday? But no, this is not their smell. It must be my coat—I hadn't worn it since I laid it down beside the body when I entered my father's room the night he died. Or maybe it is because this morning I put on the same wool sweater I wore that weekend when I washed his stained bed linens?

No, the strange smell is still with me when I slip between the dry-cleaned sheets of Dad's third floor guest suite where Bill and I stay while Rich and Blythe sleep in Dad's condo's sofa-bed. I sniff one sleeve of my clean pajamas, but it smells only of Bounce. No, the death smell is not in my clothes, but in my nose. I cannot breathe without that smell. I cannot sleep. This smell is as piercing as the sirens outside.

Besides the smell, there is this heavy weight I feel on my abdomen—as if there is a boulder on my belly. At the end, Dad's belly was heavy—is this the weight I feel? It seems as if Jayne, Blythe, my brother, my dad and mother are crushing and burying me 'til I cannot find myself. They would replace me with some cartoon of who I really am, manipulating, placating, patronizing me. They dance on my abdomen, chanting their beliefs, but I manage to jump up and run into a closet. It is the closet of my childhood! I am six years old playing on the floor with paper dolls and drawing pictures; no longer do I hear their words. I hear my own voice in this safe place—round and full and brave. It is not the meek voice of the ever-obedient daughter, nor the rallying sound of the devoted Scientist. It is my own true self speaking. Let it be heard! Let it not be hid! I will not submit to their superiority and silent criticism but stand up for my true self!

I wake as the sun rises—the glow peaks behind the brick wall that is the view from the guest condo window. Today we sort through and make decisions regarding the stuff of my father's life here on earth. Blythe, Jayne, and Rich take over Dad's office, Jayne's office, and the hall files. They talk in quiet tones I cannot hear. They sit on silk chairs somberly reflecting and sharing who my father was, what he did, and what should now be done with his writings, his files, his things. I pass by them on my way to the kitchen to clean out the refrigerator—a task they allow me to do, for which I am well-qualified. The phone rings again and again, but I do not answer it, as instructed—who knows what I might say to the Christian Science caller on the other end? Why, I, a non-Scientist, might even have the audacity to offer a comforting sentence not found in *Science and Health*—or even one that is.

As I take a basket of old jars to the incinerator/trash room, I realize that I am angry. Why should I be angry? Grief is what I am supposed to feel, isn't it? Why anger? I realize that I cannot get over the fact that Jayne called Rich three days before my father died, but never called me. Not to call Glenn's firstborn child was not Jayne's decision to make. She said she tried, but I have an answering machine, and with my business open to the public I am most always home, always reachable. I do not even have a car, because I've given mine to my daughter who's working two jobs and going to college.

I feel very detached from Jayne, Rich, Blythe, my father and mother. It feels like a divorce—messy and full of hurtful shards. It seems I keep shedding people, places, and things. What is family anyway? In that moment, I decide it is the place that wounds more deeply than any other.

Mid-day my brother tells a story, after I finish the kitchen work—a story that has popped up whenever someone realizes "Lynn" is going unnoticed. The story is one of those false legends that occasionally crops up in a family history, something that didn't actually happen but that is told so many times it feels like it did. Dad told the story over and over, principally because it was the only story he knew relevant to his daughter's love of art. As the legend goes, at age thirteen, I got the family to sit in the living room every Friday night for months and read together *The Metropolitan Seminars in Art*, a series of art books with plates of famous paintings. The truth is we did this *once* and not at my suggestion, but *Mom's*. She had purchased the art volumes as a way to connect me to the family. We went to Rich's Little League games, football games, wrestling matches, his band concerts, and his plays. "This is what we can do for Lynn." But the book series was over our heads and everyone was miserably bored. Yet, time and again throughout my life Dad told of how he and the rest of the family came together "so Lynn could teach us all about art." Dad usually brought up this story in defense of never taking me once to an art museum or gallery, or whenever it was embarrassingly obvious that too much of a conversation focused on my more accomplished brother. "Remember the time we read those art books together with Lynn?" he would say. I'd smile a little and let it go. Now it was different. I was a grown woman, and as I listened to my brother tell a brief version of this tale, I rebelled.

"That never happened!" I said. Rich looked startled. "We did it *once*. Everyone found the series exceedingly boring and we stopped. The only use *The Metropolitan Seminars in Art* got was when I took them to school once I started teaching."

I might have dared to add, but did not: "The truth is you were all too busy to notice me. You did not share my childhood, nor now my adulthood. You do not know me. None of you ever knew me! Not one of you can love me enough now for the pain of 58 years! For that's what's behind a shy child's quiet: pain. The pain of not mattering, not belonging, not measuring up, not fitting in. Don't tell me how I felt! You were not *me*!" Certainly my having just recovered from illness and Dad's death contributed to this selfish venomous thinking, but, in it, too, lies a kernel of truth.

Back in Shawnee, the smell of death surrounded me for months.

Ever since I first met her, I knew that Jayne likes to make things smell good—part of her beauty ethos, an ethos I appreciate as an artist. Under her management of my Dad's condos, room sprays, soaps, cologne, creams of every sort and size filled drawers and cupboards in every bathroom, bedroom, guest room and even the kitchen. Dad—a man who never wore a fragrance in his life—had six Crabtree and Evelyn hand lotions unopened under his bathroom sink when he died—all purchased with his money by Jayne. Was this about covering up ugly real odors with good scents? Was this about covering up unpleasant truths? About good conquering evil? Sometimes it seemed to me that issues involving purchasing the right commodities or dry-cleaning sheets (amazing in itself), plumping pillows perfectly on sofas, matching Dad's ties correctly to his shirts were considerations nearly as important to Jayne as Dad's practice work was to him. But I have observed that women sometimes make household order when order can't be made on a higher level.

Not just this weekend in Boston, but for several months after Dad's death I feel anger toward the religion that I served passionately for 46 years— a religion that is no longer mine, that detoured me from myself, told me, in fact, I had no self, that robbed me of years I might have spent becoming a better artist or writer. Instead I tabled my own desires, put priority on establishing churches, reading lesson sermons, teaching Sunday School, serving on countless committees, studying, praying, healing, speaking and writing for the church that formed me and filled me with its certitude. Though this anger will abate over the next decade, in 2001, dealing with my father's passing, I address, in my mind, my father, my mother, Jayne, my brother and all the rest, by paraphrasing Virginia Woolf's words: *"Beadle though you are, you can never remove me from my turf! Never keep me from the largess of my mind!"* (Woolf, *A Room of One's Own*).

After a few morning details, Jayne, Rich, Bill and I are driven in Dad's car by a condo employee (Jayne's thoughtful idea so we don't need to park) to a law firm Jayne arranged for Dad to use in writing his will. We sit in big black leather armchairs across a table larger than my living room as we meet for the first time with lawyers whose hourly fee matches my weekly income. They dip us through their sticky glaze of information as reams of paper and details pass over my head. But my brother is quite brilliant with these lawyers. He, himself a lawyer, asks all the right questions. I am grateful he is here to make sense of things. He executes well. Jayne, Bill and I are in his good hands.

The lawyers explain the codicil—Jayne gets 20 % of the interest from my Dad's trust; my brother and I each 40%. My share of the principal will go to my children when I die. Jayne will also get her entire office of furniture: sofa, desk, computer, tables, chairs, lamps, etc. This was not in the will but my idea since she had selected the furnishings and decorated the room and loved those pieces. Rich agreed. Later I would find the receipts for the condo and realize how much had been spent of my father's money to give him a beautiful condo Jayne had decorated with the interior designer. Dad would have done anything for Jayne.

About four months after Dad's death, with my anger dissipated and smells gone, I wake one morning thinking about the potential *Journal* article I edited for Dad when he visited at Christmastime. It comes to me to send his article to the Christian Science Publishing Society with a letter of explanation. I take another hour to polish it and mail it off. Months pass. I receive a letter back stating that it will not be used. I think to myself, well at least I tried. I had attempted to take his life story as a Christian Scientist full circle for him—my last act of devotion, a final gift for him. I knew he would have appreciated it.

A few days later, the Nyes, a couple who I knew since my Michigan childhood, long-time students of my Dad's Association, call to express their condolences about Dad. As part of the conversation, I happen to mention this last piece of his writing I'd help edit for Dad. They ask if they can read it and I email it to them, glad someone will read it, even if the church publications don't want it.

More months pass. A distant relative, a Christian Scientist, calls in regards to my inquiry about family history I am investigating. In the process she says to me, "That is *so* fine that last article of Glenn's! Everyone is talking about it!"

"What last article?" Had Dad had something published just before his death and no one told me?

"The one you sent to the Christian Science Publishing Society."

"How did you know about *that*?! How did you *see* it? It was rejected!"

"Our church got a copy. In fact, *every* church got a copy—it circulated with the John Nye letter."

"*What* letter?" None of this makes sense to me.

Finally I get the full story. John Nye, Dad's student whom I had emailed the article to, had been praying and composing a letter to the Board of Directors and *all Christian Science churches and practitioners everywhere throughout the world* regarding the declining state of the church, in hope of awakening members to facts. As an addendum, he had printed out and included the emailed article I'd helped Dad write! He never told me and I had no idea!

I phone John Nye and learn about his gentle fight to ameliorate critical church matters—some elements decades-old. He apologizes for not telling me about including the article in his mailing, never realizing he ought to have asked permission. He'd been so taken with the content of Dad's article which detailed the true meaning of church expressed in one man's life, and so stunned that it was rejected by the Church publication editors. He had circulated it at his own expense along with his letter exposing church problems. He tells me he has heard from so many people all around the world—all positive and so grateful for Dad's article as well as supportive of John's brave efforts to straighten out the church. I realize how pleased my father would have been. How long he had been in this same fight! Standing for principle, uncovering the evils in hierarchy, praying with all his might for a return to the purity that Dad knew to be underlying his beloved church! My little part in editing that manuscript one wintry morning and then following through to try to have it published, emailing it to the Nyes—it all was a series of God-directed acts that would have thrilled Dad, perhaps *did* thrill Dad even after death. I felt a rush of warmth fill me, a deep completion to our relationship that I had not felt in years. I knew my love for my father had motivated my role in this and its gift was world-wide—far beyond anything I might have expected!

In the summer of 2003, Karen, my friend, my brother's former wife, is dying of cancer and comes for a brief visit at my home as she and Chrissy, her sister from California, cross the country moving Karen to Chicago where she used to live. Karen steps out of the car, frail and thin, but with the same natural smile she has always had, and says to me, "I was so afraid I wouldn't see you ever again!"

"Of course you will! Many times!" I answer back, hugging her, feeling her bones. But I am wrong and she is right.

We sit in the sunshine on my deck overlooking the waterfall, as we talk about death. I make a special grilled chicken salad for dinner and give them the third floor suite of white rooms. The bed linens, walls, tables, built-ins under the eaves, lamps—everything is painted white—I love white for its purity, possibility, and refreshing openness. When decorators or magazine editors attribute qualities to color, I always think they ought to bestow upon white the characteristic of *imagination,* of possibility—like a clean white sheet of drawing paper before the design begins. White says we can do anything! White says we have its comforting support for whatever we need or want. It gives us permission to fill it with what we love and who we are—and no questions will be asked nor anything demanded. White doesn't try to dominate like red or yellow, which really knock us into paying attention to every detail of the space they occupy. Nor is white like blue—a team player needing others. White can stand alone in confidence, but welcomes others. I love white. I purposefully put Karen in the white room.

Karen shows me her outstanding paintings before she leaves the next morning. They are the best she has ever done—her usual expert color choices—periwinkle, chartreuse, corals, rust-reds, pale blues and aquas—but new and innovative shapes. Sometimes subtle, always imaginary, whimsical and playful, her work is somewhat reminiscent of Paul Klee's, but uniquely her own, so expressive of Karen. I tell her she must have a show—these are too good to sit in her home unseen. She is not sure she can manage a show and I fear it will never happen. Perhaps she knew then, that she would be dead within 5 months.

There are all kinds of deaths. Some are actually good, like the death of even the tiniest injustice.

A pair of 1930s Bessie Gutmann prints that hung in my previous home's laundry room, and now hang in my bedroom, once hung over my childhood bed. As a little girl, I contemplated their meaning in great consternation. One depicts a little girl, about three, with bouncy brown curls (like my own at that age) in a pale dress and blue Mary Janes (a little girl I somehow felt was me) feeding an ice cream cone to an adorable puppy. Clearly the little girl and her puppy love each other—a precious scene, entitled, "The Reward". The second of the pair shows the same little girl standing in the corner in punishment—the implication being she is in trouble for sharing her ice cream with her beloved puppy; the title of the second piece: "In Disgrace." As a child, I suffered with that little girl nightly, puzzling over why her generosity toward her canine friend was judged to be so wrong. It occurs to me in adulthood, when I stand ironing beside this pair of prints, that they represent good and bad, or, *justice and injustice*. Metaphorically, like this little girl, I stood in the corner much of my life "giving away my ice cream"—not doing the right thing in my parents' eyes, not measuring up to their expectations.

One day in 2003, I defended the little girl in those prints. It took me to age 60 to do it, but I vindicated her! One hot summer's evening, I took my panting Bernese Mountain Dogs in the car and drove down to the ice cream stand. I bought two baby-size cones of luscious vanilla ice cream for them. It gave me such pleasure to watch Zermatt gulp big bites and Geneva close her eyes licking as if nursing, or experiencing Nirvana, from the cone I held for her. In fact, Bill and I have bought ice cream cones for our dogs on more than one occasion since. And never do I go home and stand shamefully in the corner; we go home in glee!

Another good death is the death of being owned by a man. No man owns me. I used to think my father did. Later, it was husbands, or the patriarchy in general. But today, no one does. My confidence took a long time coming, through growing and figuring out again and again who I am, reinventing myself like a Welsh Shapeshifter. But always the death of one me brought birth of a new me.

Good, too, is the death of things. Shedding things. Like my lost art portfolio years ago. Like homes I've loved and left. People, too. Loss keeps the journey going. I can say goodbye to almost anything now. It isn't always easy, but I can do it.

When musician George Harrison died, his friends and family gave him a concert, "The Concert for George," and made a CD recording of it to celebrate his life. Often I paint in my studio, grateful for the music his death brought together. I listen to Eric Clapton play "While My Guitar Gently Weeps" and think I might just now die in utter satisfaction. His music is a religious experience. How can sounds be so perfect?! How can music take me, affect me, like this?! No other consciousness matters but this music this minute! This song gets blood out of a turnip, fills my house with bouquets, births Newfoundland puppies, paints abstracts as fine as Rothko and Rauschenberg, meditates like Merton or Main, rings true like Rilke's writing, sends soldiers home from Iraq, lets the Democrats win for a change, gives me Christmas with my far-away children, heals the suffering, feeds the poor, and holds me as no human ever could. It goes all places at once and nowhere. It is dancing and love-making, peaceful solitude and joyful chaos. It is collapsing in sweet exhaustion after climbing to the top of Mt. Hood. It is sailing on Lake Michigan when the waves are high. It is feeling a babe in my womb and mountain dogs in my winter bed. It is rising out of the abyss as Jesus showed or *sitting with* as Buddha teaches. It is opposites together, dark and light, life and death!

Next to honor George comes "My Sweet Lord" and I know its o.k. to die now. Yes, as the song suggests, I really want to see you, God—my God that has been with me in every particle of life, God that can create, through mere men, music. "All things must pass away" —except music, words, and art—these three carry me transcendent beyond myself, yet, to myself.

So when I face a death in this life, I take a bath by candlelight with George's CD or Johnny Cash's "Hurt," or Leonard Cohen's "Hallelujah," and let music wash my brain clean—just lie there soaking, listening. Music. Words. Art. That's all I need, alive or dead.

nineteen

Village People

"What in the world were you moving boxes in the middle of the night for?!"

"I wasn't moving boxes. I was in bed all night—exhausted."

"But I heard you! You were shuffling boxes!"

"Maybe you were dreaming."

"No! I was awake and I heard you."

"Well, it wasn't me. Maybe a village ghost?"

I never had a ghost experience my many visits to historic New Harmony. But I have three ghost stories to tell from living in my eighteenth century Shawnee home. The first experience occurred our first night after moving in. Bill was certain I was up all night moving boxes, though I was actually sound asleep. I denied his emphatic accusation next morning and was sure he had dreamed it until he kept at it. My husband deals in facts. He is not one to believe in the un-provable. Only at 7 AM when I put on my slippers and went to the bathroom and he heard my steps did he realize it *wasn't* the same footsteps he had heard during the night. "It wasn't you." He offered quietly when I came back into the bedroom. "What I heard was shuffling—like someone sliding boxes down the hall."

"That's what I tried to tell you. I never got out of bed last night; perhaps we've a ghost?"

The second occurred a couple months later when Nathan came to visit with his girlfriend, staying in the room down the hall in the oldest part of the house. At breakfast, his friend, a bit shaken, told us she woke in the middle of the night to go to the bathroom and when she returned to bed, the door slammed shut and she saw a transparent woman in a white gown with long gray hair at the foot of the bed. The slamming door was impossible because there is no window nor draft in that part of the house. The woman, however, I was pretty sure was the same one Bill had heard the night we moved in.

"Charlotte!" I said. "It must be Charlotte who lived here for more than five decades and died in this house a couple years before we bought it. She was loved by everyone in this village. I'm sure she's a good spirit—I've been aware of her presence since we moved in. I keep finding her gray hair pins everywhere. I saw a photo of her once: She wore her long gray hair piled up on top of her head, held in place with pins."

The third ghostly experience happened to me when I was alone in the art studio, about a month after Nathan's visit. I would turn on lights and they would suddenly go off. Or I would turn off the lights when I left the room and when I came back they would be on. This happened several times. It was pretty strange, because this was new track lighting that had been installed by a reputable electrician when we moved in. I felt someone from the past was trying them out—previously, there had not been ceiling lights in this part of the house—just as they had wanted to check us out when we moved in.

I'm not really sure what I think about this ghost stuff, but I do know that after a few years of intense labor and dollars galore spent on our Shawnee home, I do believe we belong here. We fit into this quirky village (population about 300) where our property with waterfall and stream sits in the heart of the Village, at the busy corner of River and Hollow, across from the Shawnee Playhouse, Stony Brook Inn, and the Shawnee General Store, and a mile from the 70,000 acres of Delaware Water Gap National Recreational Park. Some disgruntled old-timers remember when tourists had not yet taken over and a dog could lie in the middle of the crossroads. We live among families whose kids catch the school bus in front of our house, B&B owners, yoga instructors, banjo players, writers, actors, musicians, fellow artists, school teachers, carpenters, laborers, volunteer firemen, farmers, retired grandmothers, permanent tourists, real estate dealers, a college dean, a computer expert, and an international mogul whose resort and dynasty may overtake the village one day. Peculiar natures seem to be the norm here. None of us walk to the beat of the same drummer nor visit over backyard fences. Yet, somehow I am at home in this village without a stoplight (though we do have our ignored stop sign).

New Jersey-ites, New Yorkers, and others from some place else come to our village along the Delaware River to recreate, picnic, boat, hike, hunt, play golf, ski, shoot paintballs or deal drugs. They are the topic of many letters to the editor in the local paper (or at least a close second to the letters written by fundamentalist Christians advocating liberals leave their country). These "guests" of Monroe County litter, swear, and honk when a driver in front of them looks both ways before turning from Hollow to River, or if the school bus takes longer than ten seconds to let out its passengers—the same tourists and new transplants from the city whose booming music shakes my house walls as they pass by. The Park Ranger told me 5,000 cars travel these two roads in front of our house daily—but I didn't need him to tell me—I *hear* them!

If I am in my front garden—on hands and knees weeding the bevy of perennials I have spent 8 years encouraging—tourists perceive me as their tour guide, not a deeply absorbed gardener whose to-do list makes time in the garden precious. "Which way to 209?" is my favorite question. In truth, one can get to 209 going left, right, or retracing the path from which he came! So I put down my trowel and crank up the old knees and reply, "Turn right, here, go down to Buttermilk Falls and make a right—you can't miss it. My husband, on the other hand, if home from school for the summer with less of an agenda, happens to be asked the same question, he invites the tourist to pull into our driveway for detailed directions—off the dangerous road where stopping to ask a question is sure to elicit honking, yelling, swearing and a few fingers in the air, or, worse, an accident. But the motorcycle gangs don't ask questions. They fly through the village, their engines hitting the highest decibels possible.

But when the summer sun is bright mid-week and the waterfall glistening, I feel as if we live in Provence. I carry a salad with broiled chicken breasts—prepared with herbs from my garden, garlic and lemon juice—to the umbrella table on our deck where I keep a huge bouquet of picked annuals in a white pot. I light a candle in an old canning jar, and plug in my CD player with Nana Mouskouri's *Vielles Chansons de France* or, sometimes, Mississippi Delta Blues or, occasionally, when it is a very hot day that feels like I'm with my son on Grand Cayman, Bob Marley. We sit down to this joyous meal, only to have it interrupted by the roar of revving motorcycles—not two or three, not even a gang, but *herds* of them! Provence disappears. I get a rude reality check. This is *not* the south of France, but Monroe County, PA!—home to bikers, deer-slayers, Nascar devotees, and more Red Necks than Memphis ever had.

In winter, we don't get bikers. We get skiers. Bus loads of them. In the middle of the night (cheaper ski rates then). I lie in bed and watch headlights cross my ceiling while bus brakes screech to a halt less than a dozen feet from my window—at least the buses obey the stop sign. Some of these snow bunnies and snow boarders don't come by bus; they have their own SUVs or sports cars—whose radios are as capable of rocking our walls as those belonging to the summer folks. After imbibing a bit too much, some get in their vehicles and drive from Shawnee Mountain down Hollow, take its severe curve at 40 instead of the posted 10 MPH, skid, and end up in our yard, about twenty feet from the waterfall—dozens of tourists have done so in the ten years we've lived here. Sometimes we trek out in the snow to see if we can help, but more often volunteer firemen arrive within minutes and pull them out. Sometimes we invite them in—like the young high school girls from New Jersey who were too distraught to wait outside for their parents.

Our backyard waterfall attracts tourists like visitors to Grand Coolee Dam. People climb over our picket gate when it's closed to get a photo or knock at my back door to ask if they can wander the creek's island of boulders, our private property—each one certain he or she should be the exception to our "private property no trespassing sign". Once, I walked outside to call the dogs and spotted two men *peeing* in my backyard stream!—they didn't stop even as I approached to ask them to leave.

What fun Village life!

As the historical marker on our property indicates, Shawnee-on-Delaware, located in the Delaware Valley, Monroe County, Pennsylvania, was founded by its first settler, Nicholas Du Puy (spelled numerous way in various documents), who purchased 3,000 acres, including the island of

Shawano and Manwalamink, from the Minsi Indians in 1727. He was the grandson of French Hugenot refugees from Artois, France who came to New Amsterdam in 1662. Du Puy was among those to establish the Dutch Reformed Church in 1750, where the Shawnee Presbyterian Church, re-built in 1853, now stands, its graveyard full of the earliest Shawnee settlers. From my kitchen window I look out at what remains of the 17th century stone grist mill. After cascading over boulders at the top of our property, Shawnee Creek runs through our land, past the mill, on its way through the village to the Delaware River. But before there was a grist mill or church, Shawnee was Indian territory. The Moyer's property, across Hollow Road from us, was thought to have been an Indian fort. When the building's stone walls were partially torn down, a double wall with port holes and nearly 75 arrowheads were discovered. In the early 1800s our home was the home of Mrs. Sarah Wilson and her relatives—"ardent church workers and kind to the sick and needy" (Frank LeBar, *When the Days Were Not Long Enough*, p. 23), and in the adjacent small stone house (joined to our house at some point) lived a young couple, Bill Nye and his wife. I was told that in the 1920s our home was an ice cream parlor and that during the Depression it was abandoned and an impoverished black man took up residence. The Sittig family purchased the home in the thirties where they raised six children, and their grown children sold it to us in 2000. I've read a good bit at the historical society about Charlotte Sittig but I'd like to know about Sarah and the other women who lived here before them. I'd like to know what they cared about and what spirit they contributed to this home. I always intended one day when I got the time, I'd do the research.

In the fifties and sixties there was a plan to flood this region, known as the Tocks Island Dam project. It would have created nuclear hydro-electric power plants to service the surrounding megalopolis from Philly to New York City. After displacing thousands of people, taking homes that had been in families for generations, the federal government discovered the rock was too unstable for a dam—in fact any dam here would be outright foolishness. So the government, in its wisdom, got the bright idea of renting the houses it took—mostly to hippies, known as squatters, because after a while no one was collecting money for the homes as they fell into poor condition, many without utilities. It wasn't long before everyone was bulldozed out. Today the area is part of the national recreation area, but one doesn't have to be here long to hear the story of Tocks Island and feel the strong undercurrent of hate generated by that entire debacle.

But one of the best parts of being here is the nature trails. Almost every afternoon, Bill, the dogs and I hike part of the six-mile McDade Trail (to be twenty miles when completed) that parallels the River, or, the Appalachian Trail, just a five-minute drive from our house. Mornings, until the resort owners put up a gate to keep folks out, I used to walk from our house with Geneva and Zermatt along the shore of the Delaware River to watch the sun and clouds play with the mountains on the Jersey side. Genny would chase geese and Zermatt hope for a human to greet. In July, we walked the dogs to the free concerts on the Resort's lawn where folks gathered with folding chairs and blankets to listen to live music: John Phillip Sousa, barbershop quartets, Broadway show tunes, country, rock or Blue Grass. Zermatt especially loved this, for he knew half a dozen children would sit down and climb on him, adoring him. In winter, we dragged our toboggan behind the Village's Fort Depue—once the defense against Indian attacks, and now the Manwalamink Water Company. If there were no school, the dogs would be deliriously happy, chasing children's sleds.

God has given me just the right amount of community a writer and artist can handle. Just enough neighbors to make life interesting, and none too close.

When I'm out of milk, or when I think our house guests "need" a Ruben sandwich, I walk across the little bridge over River Road to the Shawnee General Store, decorated with hanging flower pots and country antiques, where young proprietors (and proud parents of two young girls) Teresa, in bandana to keep her hair back while she's at the griddle, and Bill, in backwards cap at the cash register, wait on me. Bill is a musician whose band does local gigs and Teresa has a degree in psychology—a good thing if you run a General Store, where you can learn anything about anybody. They've worked hard to make a go of their business. I've painted several watercolors of the General Store as have my students.

Teresa's Mom, Maggie, about my age, whose family is one of the old-timers in the village, and her husband, Vince—one of our *good* supervisors that many of us in the village helped get elected to prevent further greedy development in our township—live at the top of a big hill (or small mountain, depending on where you are from) in an architecturally interesting Victorian that rambles with beams and vistas, and occasional Christmas parties. They, like many in the village, are related to other villagers. I am continually learning that someone I have known here for ten years is related to someone else I've known (I recently learned that Reggie, my electrician, is related to band leader Fred Waring's daughter-in-law, Bev Waring). I'm still figuring it out. Someone needs to draw a Village family tree!

Catty-corner from our front door is the Shawnee Playhouse located in the historic Shawnee Community Center, from which famed bandleader Fred Waring's radio programs once emanated and now where young actors from New York City and talented locals put on favorite summer musicals or occasional winter dramas by emerging writers. Every December, a symphony and professional singers delight area residents with the Messiah sing-along.

Up Hollow Road, friends Jill and Jim by their own talented hands have created the most intriguing home and gardens in the area. Supportive of my gallery openings my first year in business, they've shared humor and a beer with Bill around our kitchen table, or rescued me from some house calamity. Jill, with a ton of red hair, is in her garden working every day, when she's not at her hospital job in New Jersey where she is a psychologist or when her lupus isn't too bad. She recently got her landscaping degree and started a garden mentoring business, Hollyhock Dreams. She helped mentor my own gardens into being when I first moved here and she's taught landscape design classes in my studio. Jim, as big and strong as Paul Bunyan, a sergeant at the local jail, is actually an artist with rock and iron. Recently, his work has gotten notice and I can't afford him anymore. Now he creates designs for unique ironwork or elaborate outdoor stone fireplaces for wealthy home-owners in New Jersey and even as far as Montana. But a few years ago, Jim forged beautiful andirons and iron tools for our wide-open hearth fireplace. I did an oil painting of him in trade for part of the cost—seated in his armchair with his favorite goblet, handmade bolo, boots, and cigar. Jim hand-hewed a copper ladle for me, for serving punch at my gallery openings, and delivered me quantities of rocks for my paths and gardens (which I laid myself). We used to venture to antique shops and salvage yards together for great finds. Jim has been there for us when our shower wouldn't turn off, the Christmas tree fell over, and the original hardware on our doors needed re-bolting, as well as executing half a dozen iron projects for our home.

High atop the hill overlooking the village, in a large Victorian house (once owned by actor Don Amiche), live Pam and Walter Wyckoff, with whom we've shared occasional walks, dinners, and gardening tips. Walter, probably nearing eighty [deceased in 2013], grew up here in Shawnee, a history buff and sometime oil painter, he knows more about this village than anyone living. Twenty-some years younger, Walter's wife, Pam, a physical therapist, knows as much about people and gives intuitive massages. I faux painted their kitchen a Tuscan yellow for them in trade for a couple massages.

Rose Ann, a gregarious former elementary school teacher who now sells Longaberger baskets and is an avid Red Hat Society lady, runs The Stony Brook Inn across River Road from us, with her husband, Pete, a former New Jersey businessman who is found poolside in summer flipping burgers with a beer in his hand. About my age, they've been together for more than two decades, *sans* marriage vows—until a few years ago when one July they invited their friends and neighbors to a pool party at which they surprised us all by whipping out Karl, the local Presbyterian minister, and getting married in front of us! That was icing on the cake. They'd just survived devastating damage from their *third* flood in 22 months which had eradicated their pool into a sea of mud—just shortly after invitations had gone out for their party. I couldn't imagine they would still be able to have their gathering, given all the belongings out on their driveway following the flood and seeing the muddy water that had eliminated their pool. But with unbelievable hard work by them, Rose Ann's son, Rich, and some good neighbors, the pool was in full operation by party-time—complete with surrounding deck, decorative pots of red geraniums and outdoor furniture.

The other Village bed and breakfast owners, Cindy and Gordon, parents of lovely blonde daughters and now proud grandparents, moved here to buy and operate the Gate House Inn, the rambling turreted B&B down River Road that used to be Fred Waring's home. Cindy, a good friend of Rose Ann's, is also a member of the Red Hat Society, and in-laws with the Kirkwoods who own nearly everything in Shawnee.

Janet, editor for the "Dignity" section of the local newspaper written for retirees, and her husband, Peter Taney, music teacher for Shawnee Institute, a boarding school serving challenging and challenged children just beyond the Village center, and their daughter, Joy, to whom I've taught art since I arrived, have had a professional folk band, the Juggenaught String Band, playing regular gigs of what they call "Appalachian Juju music"—that is until Janet's death from a brain tumor a few years ago. Bill, my husband, used to take his guitar down to Peter's and they'd fiddle around; in winter, they occasionally cross-country skied the golf course together.

Across from Peter and Janet's, reside the thirty-something Siptroths. Michele, a lovely mom and elementary school teacher, her husband and daughter have faced floods three times—I saw them canoeing in their driveway during the last one. Their daughter has posed for my portraiture class and she and her Mom have taken care of our pets when we've been out of town.

Barbara and John Ligouri, once professional rock musicians, offer our dogs backyard play dates with their black lab, Emily, who is smitten with Zermatt as much as he is with her. While our dogs run around her yard, giving play signals to each other, Barbara, busy raising two kids and caring for her mother with Alzheimer's (until her recent passing) brings me a mug of Chai tea while we visit. Barbara has a heart of gold, and works unselfishly to support every good thing in this village. She gets petitions signed to stop bus pollution, attends township meetings faithfully, helps with school book sales and girl scouts, is a deacon in the local church, makes jewelry in her cozy Victorian kitchen to aid the Shawnee Preservation Society, and is one of those generous women every community needs. Barbara, and her village-friend Chris, who works in a mental ward and whose outspokenness I've sometimes admired, would gather their kids (and I my dogs) and we'd meet behind Ft. De Puy to sled. In warmer weather Barbara and I would walk, she venting her parenting challenges for my two cents of wisdom. Barbara will remain a good friend wherever life takes me.

Two of the six Sittig siblings brought up in what is now our home by their classical musician father and Village-Matriarch mother, Charlotte (whose hairpins I mentioned earlier), had a presence in the village when we moved in. Like their marks from childhood sword fights, dart games, psychedelic art experiences, and phone numbers penciled on our 260-year-old walls, their stories of earlier Village life were legend. Charlotte, who died in this house, owned an antique shop where I have my art studio. Once someone who had known the Sittigs, came into my gallery and told me it was stunning to see the place so "empty," as she said Charlotte had antiques "stuffed floor to ceiling." Jim Sittig and his brother down the road have tried to watch out for the political maneuvers and development ideas some powerful men would enact to overtake this charming village, but Jim moved away, selling his historic home to the resort owner who owns most of the village. Jim remembered quieter times in Shawnee, and told Bill and me when he was a kid he climbed the waterfall's island of boulders to fish in the stream. We've spied a few sunfish and trout—also, a river otter once, a bear, and every year a pair of Mallard ducks, deer, and the blue heron who comes in spring and summer. The heron, graceful and elegant, prunes himself until spotted by a Berner; then, he takes off like a Para dactyl and flies through treetops downstream, his wing span phenomenal to stand under! He and the waterfall remove traffic from my mind; only then can I imagine the Shawnee Jim Sittig knew as a child.

Another old-time Village resident is Colleen, in her late seventies, who lives in the cutest sky-blue cottage, makes the best baked beans (so good I commissioned her to make a big batch for Charissa's wedding) and throws a 4th of July party every year. She has come to a number of my gallery openings and usually brings friends. Her son, John, and his wife, Norma, own a large and lovely historic home about the vintage of mine, but spend some time during summer months in the adorable little white cottage behind Colleen's house, and have been true patrons of my art with more than four of my best paintings of Shawnee hanging on their home's walls.

Dr. Holly, a children's psychologist and very bright young woman with a storied past, became a good friend when she and her husband, Al, also a doctor, moved here recently. She took over where I left off in the fight to save Shawnee from greedy development, and started the Shawnee Preservation Society to protect the history and environment of our village. About twenty years younger than I, Holly has the intensity, intellect, humor, spirituality, and breadth I like in a friend. We met at soul level, often viewing the world similarly. She was the only Villager there for me after my devastating car accident, even accompanied me in April 2006 to Philadelphia Federal court for my accident case. Her husband Al did yeoman's work in helping us re-do our endless picket fence—a noble task for which he merely accepted meals in exchange for labor plus one of my best oil paintings of France. Holly moved away when she and Al divorced and I haven't seen her since, though Bill still walks our dogs with Al Sunday mornings.

The Barretts, owners of mountain top property, with their long-time roots to Shawnee, and their relative Charlie Garris, a former local mayor, with his idyllic *Country Living* setting up the road from us, remain powerful political township protectors—especially of their own particular portions.

Michele, the beautiful yoga teacher who gave Bill and me yoga lessons and used to live in a white cottage down the lane, got married in Scotland and moved out of the village. One Christmas, I paid for my entire family of visiting kids, spouses, boyfriends and girlfriends, to have a private family yoga session with her. Her skillful healing manner was especially helpful after my auto accident.

Roy, the young, local resort-employed computer expert, whose village apartment hosts a rare harpsichord and framed Gregorian chants, has on two occasions rescued Bill and me from a computer emergency at no charge.

Charlie and Ginny Kirkwood who own the Shawnee Inn and Golf Resort gave a party for us when we first moved to Shawnee. Charlie, a Harvard graduate, and Ginny, a Peace Corps worker in Thailand in the sixties, about my age, are also producers and owners of Shawnee Playhouse and many other Shawnee enterprises. They are on a variety of Boards, own several businesses in Asia (I've never been clear exactly what) and about half the Village. The Kirkwoods started the Shawnee Institute and Shawnee Development Inc., which had or has connections to the controversial PRD (planned residential development), and opened the Village's new restaurant, Sam Snead's Tavern, in walking distance to our home (recently changed to the more complicated name. The Gem and Keystone) and there have been Kirkwood connections to the Village timeshares, the miniature golf course up on Buttermilk Falls Road—the latter made out of fake stone which my Southern mother-in-law when visiting called "double ugly." Though frequently out of town, owning a flat in London, a home in Michigan, something in Thailand, and I am not sure what else, the Kirkwoods bring an international flavor to the village by employing international workers to work for their businesses. We have fed home-made pizza on a number of occasions to young Russian, Polish, and other East-Europeans employed at the Inn, several of whom remain good friends of our daughter; one friend from Poland was in Charissa's wedding party. In our early years here, Ginny and I "did lunch" a few times, shared movies out, and with our husbands enjoyed Asian meals prepared by her Thai cook. Ginny might describe herself as Village Mother, inviting all the children of the village to dye eggs at Easter and decorate cookies at Christmas. But her favorite sponsorship is the annual sing-along Messiah.

Marianne Higgins, who sold us this house, and her lawyer husband, Dan, who did our closing, live further up Hollow in a lovely historic home. I don't see her often except at the annual women's Christmas party where gifts, cookies and gossip are exchanged (though after the first couple years, I chose not to attend). They commissioned several paintings from me: one of their historic home to include their grandchildren, and another of a local woodsy scene where fine summer homes used to exist before the Tocks Island fiasco, near McDade Trail. Their daughter, Mary Ellen, is the librarian and comes to many of my gallery openings. The Higgins family members are advocates of keeping what's best about the Village.

But frustration with local power and politics has curbed my own activism.

About the time I was recovering from my auto accident, preparing for Charissa's wedding in May 2005, and surviving flood #2, I learned that 1,571 town homes, timeshares, and homes had been approved by our township to be built on top of the mountain above our village, without any real concern for the environment, water-runoff, flooding, sewers, wells, infrastructure, city services or roadways. It seemed unbelieveable that anyone would allow this! I gave up sleep and devoted myself to studying this matter, reading the township codebook and relevant documents that I procured from the township and county planning commission.

The week before Charissa's wedding, I work at this as if it is my only endeavor. It is my village home and its people I'm fighting for, afterall!

It is just eight months since my car accident, and I am in the midst of preparing for Charissa's wedding, for which I will feed nearly 200 people, making the food and decorations myself (other than the Memphis Bar-BQ she wants flown in). The wedding will be outdoors in New Jersey at her husband-to-be's family farm overlooking the Delaware Valley, and she will wear the same Italian wedding designer dress I wore when I married her father. With John and Bill—one Dad on either arm—she will walk down the aisle. The day before the wedding I will give a luncheon for the bridesmaids and the morning after the wedding a brunch for 40 out-of-town guests. For weeks my kitchen table is covered with tiny terra cotta pots I stuff with plant foam, moss and a single twig on which I hot-glue name cards for each wedding guest. Fifty yards of tulle, silver trays, plastic champagne goblets, flatware, folded linen napkins and hundreds of tiny tin pails and baskets in labeled boxes line the upper hall of my home awaiting the day when they will decorate the red gingham clothed tables—a Provence, France garden theme (Charissa was a French major and three times in France), with large pots of fresh blooming red geraniums everywhere. My energy, surprises even me, given my condition just six months ago, but I have learned there is not much a mother won't do for her child. Or her village.

So it really is not that difficult to stand up at the township meeting April 25, 2005 before the three supervisors, their lawyers and the PRD developers, to ask 18 carefully thought-out questions. I have done my homework. I have studied and researched documents untiringly, and spoken with my planner son on Grand Cayman. I have learned much about planning, developers, politics, and related terms and topics in the past 48 hours! The supervisors and their lawyers, who appear to enjoy intimidating citizens, are unprepared for my questions and professionalism. I stand firm when the solicitor tries to intimidate me. Many residents like what I say and we begin to organize ourselves.

Four days before my daughter's wedding I call a meeting of concerned villagers in the community center—the same location as the Shawnee Playhouse. A group of us Villagers have engaged a land-use lawyer to attend. This grass roots movement grows, developing a strong life of its own. This is perhaps the first time villagers have had a voice in their own community. Though I have said I will not lead anything beyond this first meeting due to my daughter's wedding, I encourage villagers to organize. They hold another meeting a few days later and before the week is out hire the lawyer to write an appeal to stop the PRD. They also make plans to incorporate, establishing Shawnee Preservation Society. Everyone who can throws in a $100 or more to help the cause, and we join them. In another month or two my friend Holly is elected president of the newly formed Shawnee Preservation Society and by the following fall, we have campaigned for and elected two competent and caring Villagers—Vince and Brian—to fill two of the three supervisor township government positions and hopefully to eradicate the powerful greed and corruption of many decades.

One day it strikes me that this entire experience—far more complex than the few words I write here—validates my having moved to the Poconos. I never thought about it when it was happening, but in hindsight I see perhaps I was brought here not just for redeeming an eighteenth century house but to play a small role in a greater redemption.

This being said, I also realize that even the Shawnee Preservation Society and the election win of two new supervisors won't keep traffic from my door or invaders from my back yard. The more I read and think, I realize my home's location will always be a problem if peace is my goal—and it is. One day a traffic light could go in at our busy corner when the road in front of my house becomes the collector road for the new 1,571 PRD units. I read in a document that the previous township board granted this PRD the right to condemn and "confiscate" homes along Hollow Road in order to widen the road. My home might be a likely candidate, unless its history prevents its confiscation. I also learn that Hollow and River are projected to receive 6,000 vehicles daily once the PRD is complete.

Though I've just decorated a guest bedroom—for which I designed, plastered, and painted, hiring a wonderful seamstress, Olga, to make curtains, pillows, duvet, bench and arm chair slipcovers and for which I built, stained, and hand-decorated a lovely French armoire—I begin to realize that leaving my Shawnee home is inevitable.

What's happening in Shawnee is not an isolated situation. Developers everywhere milk the earth to death, take their cash and retire far from the mess they created. Schools are forced to add temporary classrooms to accommodate increased enrollment. Police stretch themselves to handle new streets and more crime. Services are strained, from sewer systems to water. Construction causes water run-off, erosion, flooding, and other environmental problems. Though there are fewer services and more problems, taxes are higher. Those of us who've thrown money into historic homes for years will watch our investments dwindle while new traffic lights blink in our bedroom windows. With no impact fees required of developers, as in this state, things will only get worse.

In spite of the Village's passionate new unity, I nail up a "for sale" sign in front of our house right after Memorial Day, 2005. I take it down by Thanksgiving when I have second thoughts. In Spring 2006 the sign goes up again for several months.

While the house is on the market in the summer of 2006, Bill and I travel to New Mexico, the "land of enchantment" that we've loved and hiked several times before. This spell-binding state's brilliant light, crisp air, mountain vistas, beautiful architecture, rich history and diverse culture, enchanted us once again. I lap up Canyon Road art galleries, paint adobe and desert landscapes, and feel as if I belong. We marvel at sunsets and the perfect climate and enjoy everyone we meet—people who've moved from many states to call New Mexico home. We even look at a few houses for sale. Wouldn't it be nice….

About twelve miles outside Santa Fe, the realtor drives down a dusty road and then another and another, makes a steep, narrow, winding climb and then I see the house in the spectacular New Mexican light: a 20-foot tall one-story rosy adobe sitting up boldly away from everything and anyone, its back-side bermed a bit into the mountain, between "Lone Ranger" rocks, overlooking a breathtaking 350-degree desert and mountain panorama, nearly *in* the sky, its 14-foot high windows shining in the brilliant morning sun. This wonder-of-a-home is *it?*—the house she's taking us to see?! No, it couldn't be… surely its too much. "This is it" the Realtor affirms parking beside what *feels* like my future home. Unusual angles with barely a walled room inside—just open spaces soaring to thick viga beams, this house is extraordinary, unlike anything I've seen. The outside is inside here. The sky comes right in and takes over. There's even lawn, fruit trees, and raised garden beds. Expansive, yet, not large in square footage, there is no superfluity—just a kitchen, 2 bedrooms—one with a loft, 2 baths, an open living and dining area off of which is a small greenhouse. There are two fireplaces, one a kiva, tile floors that remind me of Provence, huge vast walls for paintings, tall windows facing the sun and the most magnificent view. But above all, there is a *spirit* about the place—there's even a meditation room—enveloping me in infinite light, sky, and rocks. A true sanctuary! I cannot let this beautiful property go, even when we fly home to Pennsylvania. We email the realtor we'll make an offer on the "Lone Ranger" property when our house sells.

But the housing market is saturated. Months go by. Our Shawnee home does not sell and the New Mexican magical sky house is sold to someone else. It would have taken a miracle for things to fall into place, but then, it wouldn't be the first time my journey took a miraculous turn. As much as I wanted this sanctuary, I know it is not my will that works things out.

We visit Bill's sister in Chicago and while there browse the University of Chicago's bookstore where a book *calls* me to take it home. Not merely in the stacks, but boldly front and center this book I could not miss; its title suggests my life story: *Searching for Home: Spirituality for Restless Souls* by M. Craig Barnes. Barnes writes, "the right place isn't something you choose, but a place that chooses you, molds you, and tells you who you are" (M. Craig Barnes, *Searching for Home: Spirituality for Restless Souls*, p.17).

The "for sale" sign goes down again when a bright new idea based on a long-held dream develops one afternoon when Bill comes home from school and says, "Listen to this…" and reads me a paragraph from one of his students' papers. It's wonderful. I ask him to read me the entire paper. And then another and another—all 15 papers! The course, World Religions, is a semester elective Bill teaches. The first day assignment had been to put the word "Religion" at the top of the paper and freely write for the remainder of the class period. The results were exquisite revealings. Each one poignantly representing religious views as diverse as Seik, Hindu, Buddhist, Catholic, Unitarian, Baptist, Jewish, agnostic. I love their obvious *yearning*, their questioning, openness, intelligence, and brilliant articulation of difficult ideas. Above all, I love the honesty shining in their words, the rare humility not often seen in high-school students.

Somewhere in the middle of Bill's reading, it hit me: Bill is one of few who could so perfectly teach a class of such diverse beliefs, so extraordinary is he at honoring all perspectives. While Bill reads the last paper, I silently marvel at the opportunity he and those students have together—a classroom so diverse in ethnicities and religious backgrounds it is like a mini-United Nations village! I am thrilled he is their teacher and that these diverse students' journeys might one day lead them to solve a few of the world's problems. I see clearly, as if a tiny epiphany, what a *gift* my husband is to his school and to these bright students. I'd already known he was a gift of a teacher, but this time the thought comes that we ought not move to New Mexico or anywhere that would take Bill away from his students. He is making such a difference in these students' lives. It comes to me that it is my small contribution to the world to stay and find satisfaction here, so that my husband can continue to do what he is doing right where he is. He once told me that he knew his job as head of Moravian's history department was "the job of a lifetime, so perfect a match."

Part of my epiphany suggests I make lemonade out of the traffic lemon of the 5,000 cars passing our home daily. What if I were to open our home as a B&B? Ever since Bill and I first stayed in a B&B I'd been intrigued about running one. This B&B dream seems the logical extension of my gallery and studio. I want to create a place where artists and students might stay for my week-long painting workshops, being catered to with elegant, beautifully served breakfasts in a serene setting. So in the Fall of 2006 we took our house off the market and applied to the township for B&B approval.

After months of meetings with township supervisors, complying with their many requests, we received permission and prepared for this new venture. I carefully planned every bit of this undertaking and used the money I got from my auto accident to fund it all. We hired reputable contractors to build the perfect new gourmet kitchen I designed, complete with thick granite countertops, stainless steel appliances including a SubZero refrigerator and Wolf gas range, bay window with yellow and blue Pierre Dieux print-covered down cushioned seat, and French doors opening to a new 500 square foot deck overlooking the falls, and new vestibule (tiled in Saltillo tile I ordered from New Mexico—my token reminder of a favorite place). I even incorporated the antique beveled glass windows from my Fisherville, Tennessee home into the new B&B entry (generously sent to me years ago by that home's new owner who preferred plain glass).

As many trials as we had when we first purchased this house popped up during this 2007-08 renovation, but of a different sort. I had more to do as the designer, procuring as well as planning the granite, the cabinetry, the flooring, hand-wrought iron fixtures from Connecticut, wood flooring from Maine, and, we had the challenge of no kitchen for either Thanksgiving or

Christmas. Somehow we survived, washing dishes in the half bath sink. With all the challenges and work, sometimes our decision seemed less than ideal. Often blissful, beautiful, sunny, art-friendly places I'd researched to move to would dance through my thought.

One night, unable to sleep thinking about all the things needing doing and tired from all I'd done that day, it came to me: *You* have work to do here, too—its *not* just for Bill's job you stay. You want to paint, then keep painting—here! You want to write, then keep writing—here! You want to do a B&B to allow this house to be a beautiful gift for others and pay its way, then go forward with your B&B—here! Make *here* the place that matters. Heal what you don't like—sleaze, drug dealing, the new neighbor's pit bull, the ever-increasing traffic, community conflict, and environmental issues—take them on in your prayers and actions. Grow every glimmer of good you find. No, it won't be easy. Here, I will never have a Ponderosa pine or a solitary beach, but I will have *work in the present moment* which can be life at its best.

In June 2008 I become a fully operating bed and breakfast! I call my extended business: *Shawnee Falls Studio, Gallery & Guesthouse* and pay my talented graphic designer son to create a beautiful new website for me; it is even more impressive than previous ones he'd done for me.

The results of all my hard work as a B&B hostess are rewarding. Guests come from all over the US and many foreign countries—China, India, Estonia, Russia, Denmark, Ireland, England, France, and more. How many fascinating and surprisingly deep conversations happen! It is a delight to meet so many interesting people. At the request of many of them, after nearly two years in business, I write a cookbook, *Bodacious Breakfasts and More*, published in 2010. Making sumptuous breakfasts, creating art and home, teaching students and meeting people from around the world are the best parts of doing business.

I remember when a member of the Canadian Parliament dropped in the gallery with his wife and we got to talking about Nova Scotia, then politics and history, so we finally all had to go out to dinner to continue our conversation! There was the Israeli gentleman who asked to take pictures throughout our home, inside and out, who gave me his address, inviting me to come to Israel anytime as his guest. There were the two women tourists who came, shaken, following an auto accident that delayed their trip, staying at the inn while their car was being fixed. We had a long talk, mainly spiritual, and they asked if they could visit my waterfall. I told them "It's yours while you're here—anytime night or day." I saw them out at my meditation bench facing the falls several mornings and evenings. Bill pushed many children on our tall tree swing that soared out over the stream while their parents shopped in my gallery. And over the past ten years, hundreds of my students have painted this house and its property from every angle in every season. Several New York artists have come in to chat, telling me my work belongs in a bigger city, something I've known since the day I moved here, but dismissed holding to my conviction: "If I build it, they will come."

But by late 2010, I begin to yearn for peace. At 67, it is no longer easy to lift mattresses and clean toilets. Though my daughter has been a good help, coming once a week to help me clean bathrooms and vacuum, I maintain the place mostly myself—dusting, vacuuming, laundering, ironing, baking, menu-planning and printing, grocery-shopping, record-keeping, gardening, creating nine fresh flower arrangements weekly, while my gallery is daily open to the public and my art classes continue. I love the respite of playing with my precious granddaughter, Emma, when her mom is here to help with computer issues or to vacumn, but the B&B gallery and guesthouse is a demanding operation. Though I love creating quiches, coffee cakes, scones, croissants, and home-made bread, and don't mind waxing antiques or polishing silver, I seek a more serene life for my last decade (give or take) on earth. As wonderful as this B&B business is, I see its end in sight.

I once thought this village might replace New Harmony. Similar in age and size, though the two villages seem worlds apart spiritually. New Harmony provided instant peace; Shawnee, constant challenge. But both have been good teachers.

Can a *village or house* be a shaman? Can a house be a *theophany*? I am sure of it—at least my Shawnee home has seemed so, especially at Christmastime.

When it is Christmas Eve and snow is lightly falling, candles wink in windows, gathered greens and pine cones decorate every mantle, the now-sparkling tree, that we chopped at Beck's Tree Farm only a few miles from here, fills the living room with shining light and fresh pine smell, cats curl on chair cushions and Berners sleep on sofas—one shared with Bill—Christmas carols play, and dinner is ready just as Charissa and her husband and daughter jingle in at the kitchen door, I see no house problems. I forget I spent hours on hands and knees, scrubbing and waxing floors to a luster that will fade with wet paws and people.

My home-made hors d'oeuvres, cookies, brownies, tortes, and crudités in French iron tiers on china plates I've collected and inherited over the years, the platter of stuffed turkey surrounded by twice-baked potatoes, a casserole of sweet potatoes with a pinch of cinnamon and garlic, an array of vegetables—arranged like an artist's still life—are a visual feast that all will enjoy. On one wall, the antique Irish hutch filled with blue and white china—much like my ancestors' Welsh cupboard—sports a seasonal headdress of ivy and holly boughs with bright red berries. The primitive black iron chandelier is dimmed, and my family and dogs are beside me in this nearly magical setting. I am blessed to be here.

For certain, this house has had plenty of non-magical moments, too. The ivy growing *inside* one deep window sill when we moved in made me wonder if several centuries of entangled ivy ran throughout the innards of this home we'd just purchased, just as I wondered if mold and mildew were hiding behind every wall until we installed air conditioning and the mold inspector found nothing and the ivy never grew back. When a leak showed up in the first floor guest bathroom, looking like an offshoot of the sixty-foot long waterfall in the back yard, I watched the authentic Moses Eaton stenciling I'd finished in that room drip into oblivion. But then I liked the washed out effect and the ripped out sheet rock revealing the original stonework which we left exposed. Before we made electrical improvements, lights on the second floor occasionally flickered when I ran the washer and drier while simultaneously ironing and playing music. In the early days, before we had the floors professionally skimmed and polyed, splinters from floor boards lodged in my feet and hands. In those days, holes invited mice and voles inside and ladybugs appeared out of nowhere when the weather was warm. But re-pointing the entire basement foundation (which Bill and I did with John Liguori's help and Rich Whitesell's powerwashing) and instigating regular pest service has kept us rodent-free.

Why did we choose to live here? Maybe we didn't. Maybe it chose us. Certainly most of our time these ten years thus far were spent being good stewards of this place! Perhaps we came because of the waterfall in our own backyard cascading over boulders, beside a yard outlined with daffodils. Perhaps we came for the village's initial charm and its people. Perhaps because when you *work* at something and put your heart and soul into it, you end up loving it.

As a rigorous teacher, my house has never let up! She taught me patience, kept me humble and healthily exercised, showed me that I can't fix all things. As in my home, so in life, I cannot do it all. Perhaps the work of this house exists to keep me seeking answers. It tells me I will never find perfection anymore than I will ever have working batteries in all the smoke detectors at once.

Every time another crop of problems rose, I would stand at my kitchen window and watch brilliant sunshine flicker through the trees and onto boulders around the waterfall. No one has a finer kitchen view in all the world! Just as another repair bid would seem intolerable and moving to a new house seemed a far wiser choice, afternoon shadows would play on centuries-old floors and textured white walls trimmed with gray-teal molding—no cinematography was ever lovelier.

In this house I've lived with the past daily, something few get to do. Through solid original paneled doors, showing wear of times I never knew, I enter my apricot hue-ed dining room (painted by my hand, inspired by Provence, France), once kitchen to this home, to dust the spokes of spinning wheel and wide hearth mantle. The huge stone fireplace shows off Jim's hand-forged iron andirons, his hand-made tools, equally massive in scale, hang to the right. Bittersweet tangles with dried gourds, collected last fall, across the mantle. One of few paintings from my childhood —a favorite oil by an artist neighbor from my childhood, who may have inspired my own artistic career—hangs above, depicting a blizzard with isolated farm house, glowing lights in its windows. My almost-eleven-foot antique table, that once graced an English Manor house kitchen, reigns beneath the flowing lines of the black iron primitive-style chandelier I commissioned to be made to bring the waterfall, glimpsed from the window, inside. In the center of my dining table sits a 24-inch round pottery platter from New Harmony, its swirling pattern a vortex reminding me daily of that centering place that runs through my life like the stream in my yard.

Who would not wish to paint and read and write where hawks and eagles soar?! I climb the craggy boulders of our island to get closer to the waterfall.

I hear my ancestors' voices. They are in this place. All of them: the Welsh, Irish, Scotch, English, French and Scandinavian. They knew a bit of rocky land, laboring and loving it, accomplishing home. Nature's beauty has urged my untiring efforts as it must have theirs. I have always known we aim for beauty in our lives in order to reach the numinous.

Though I have had larger studios and audiences than my studio here affords, I have been as prolific here as anywhere, and my students seem to have appreciated what I afforded them. They convince me that even if there is no place for them to hang their coats or spread out materials, they are happy in this quirky historical space, loaded, inside and out, with subject matter. They do not mind when their pencils fall and roll between floorboards, or the radiators hiss on a cold morning. They come here for the same reason I stay. This house is *alive*, spitting out character in every direction!

This house is unique, full of individuality, like this village, like me. None of the houses I looked at when we thought we were moving had the quirky originality and authenticity of this one—the textures, woodwork, iron hardware, plaster walls, unusual curved ceiling over the pie stairs, wide floorboards, the odd-ball arrangement of rooms. Even my bed-linens are happily mis-matched: a dust ruffle I made, along with curtains, from expensive twin bed spread fabric once in my mother's Chicago guest room (that Jayne was throwing out) and an old faded floral duvet—well-worn by the presence of a now full-grown 125-pound Bernese Mountain Dog who is afraid of thunderstorms. But the Oriental rug connects well enough to the Beidermier chest of drawers I inherited. The twin lamps I purchased to sit on top of the chest, in front of the also-inherited antique Venetian mirror, have the right look, though less connected to other lamps in the room. Beneath a window sits Bill's grandfather's desk, opposite the bed, by the wall that used to peel paint until I solved that problem recently by painting all the walls in that room Celtic gray—a kind of muted aqua I chose as much for its name as its hue.

I enjoy finding interrelatedness in diverse furnishings. The green leaves in curtains and dust ruffle *do* match the blue-green crown molding my model's carpenter-husband installed to match the room's historic chair-rail, mantel, and doors. There *is* actually a hint of peach, same as the sheets hue, in the red and yellow flowers of my mother's old fabric. On closer scrutiny, I detect that shapes in the twin lamp bases repeat in the floral pattern and the tone of the wood chest harmonizes with the Oriental rug.

Some days I dream of a well-planned minimalist décor, where everything is streamlined, tied together. But when I've had a day of working on house projects, serving several pairs of guests a fine four-course breakfast, taught a couple of three-hour classes, put together a good supper, played my favorite music, and retreated to our bedroom with books and journal, a cat or dog or two, and Bill beside me, I realize what I've always known, that beauty is more than furnishings deep. My artist's eye rests with a work that likely will always be in progress.

After recently painting the bedroom and hall, I painted baseboards black and the wall beneath the living room chair rail chartreuse apple green—novel, yet, stimulating with the old teal gray trim and coral sofas. I did this decorating, in part, to prove to myself that I had not lost use of my arm, that I could mount ladders and problems, swishing paintbrushes in spite of my slightly stiffer wrist caused by the auto accident.

Proudly I survey these changes and realize that perhaps most things are finished here (though I knock on wood). I am feeling good about my home, at peace with it, satisfied with all I've done, comfortable with what little, if anything, is left undone. Like the ivy once imbedded in its 1700's stone, my Shawnee village house has grown around me—as if entangled in my bowels, heart and lungs. I have invented a way to breathe within its difficult binding. It has become part of me; and in this becoming, the question of my leaving it sometimes disappears. Perhaps a new need may pop up and take a lifetime to fix—just as it may take a lifetime to become fully me. Neither house nor I are perfect. And I'm o.k. with that.

The house's imperfections ground me as much as its beauty, reminding me that perfection is not the thing to seek. Imperfections are only opportunities for new possibilities. This house has taught me to embrace imperfections, so I try to embrace my own. Imperfect humanity thrives and clings to me like ivy on stone. I cannot yank it off, I can only prune a bit. My house and I share the ravages of time and the need for regular maintenance. Never again will I possess the innocence of that three-year old whose photo hangs on my bedroom wall, her upward face trusting and eager; no longer am I that child.

Nor am I the size four I see in my wedding photo, the one with Bill tickling and me laughing. We've experienced much change, this village house and I.

My village house has taught me to laugh rather than cry over things beyond my control. It has shown me again and again that I cannot execute every plan I devise, and that what will come is far more amazing than anything I might imagine.

I walk from room to room, appreciating the blend of history and fresh refurbishing. Its unique story gives a house a *living* personality. Idiosyncrasies of house, like those of a human being, create personality. Certainly this village and its people have shown me this. Both house and human edify, amuse, irritate, frustrate, and please. And both humans and houses are altered by everyone they come to know.

What I do to this house and what has been done down decades by others before me mingle. I love the fact that in 1740, someone dressed like Martha Washington ascended these stairs I mount now, cooked meals in my fireplace to feed her family of probably seven or eight, baked bread that wafted its yeasty aroma throughout these rooms—but not likely better perhaps than my own bread baked in new ovens. The woman who walked across these creaking, sagging floorboards of my bedroom then—did she feel the joy, despair, loneliness, and questing spirit that I have felt here in my time? I see her gather baskets of laundry and take them to the creek behind the house while her children play nearby. I see her brush away loose hair from her brow along with the annoying gnats that I, too, deal with on a summer's day. She labors with emotions carefully folded up inside—like the stacks of dry linens she puts into the same hall cupboards where I store mine.

She reminds me as she passes through the same textures and shadows I move through, why I am in this 260-year-old place with all of its foibles. I am here for the five fireplaces that tell me of hearth and home, though none of them work as well as I'd like. I am here for the knocks and pops of radiators that speak and keep me company late at night when I write. Never alone in this house, I have had more than occasional mice and friendly ghosts to keeps me company. Every particle of the house *talks* to me.

This village house, like the women who have lived in her, has her own personality. She has not been an easy shelter—the most difficult of all the homes I've lived in. When first we saw her she never promised to be trouble-free, never claimed she could easily be resolved. But we took her anyway. She has a strong character, more complex than most humans. The web of her history, simple beauty and charm caught me, pulled me in like the spider webs catching prey in her nooks and crannies. I am her prisoner as well as caretaker, as perhaps, women here before me have been. Like a nursing child, she feeds on me, occupying time and energy I would give to writing and art. She hasn't let me leave, holds me tight, because she knows I belong to her. Trapped though we women have been here through the centuries by her, we've each managed to retain our separate individualities and to appreciate hers.

The house is, I come to realize, perhaps my best friend. Like the rarest of true friends, she argues with me, doesn't always tell me what I want to hear. I respect her. She has an I-told-you-so attitude now and then, but I have learned to live with that. She can be pushy, nearly arrogant at times, but she never allows me to become self-righteous about my home. I can take very little pride here. She can infuriate me—rather, she causes me to see why being infuriated is pointless. She makes me sad sometimes, for she can be dark in winter when I am tempted to think of my losses. But then, she puts her arms around me and tells me of her own; we cry together and smile when she reminds me *she* still stands after all these decades and so can I. She puts me in my place. I am but one passing through.

She causes me to live with the unsettled, even on the edge of disaster. She proves a truth to me: there is no safe harbor in this world. Certainly not in material places and things I cannot rest satisfied in this life, for there will always be the unpredictable, unfixable, and unsolvable. The unknown sealed spaces above the third floor attic rooms symbolize that I cannot see and know everything I wish to know. Up there do squirrels gambol about and chew hidden wires causing unseen damage, keeping downy nests of Berner hair? Are leaks waiting to erupt under my newly repaired slate roof? What's behind the dining room ceiling crack—will it open wide and rain down plaster one Thanksgiving? I do my best, but am sometimes an uneasy steward of this lovely historical conglomeration. We dance an uncoordinated dance, my house and me; but we *are* in this dance together!

twenty

Lost and Found

And when she saw the white ship come in, she stopped madly digging on the shore. For there it was, laid out before her: her treasure found.

The nineteenth century Harmonists' first and last settlements were in Pennsylvania, their New Harmony, Indiana, location sandwiched in-between. Pennsylvania may likely be my last state, too, but I would not have thought so a few years back.

Prior to death by traffic, our dear cat, Oreo, used to bask in the morning sun, sitting on Doonesbury—the comic section of the newspaper Bill left spread out on the kitchen table each morning. Though I'm not an advocate of cats on kitchen tables, I occasionally let Oreo sit where he wanted, scrubbing carefully after, for, converting cat years to human, he was 97 years old. His littermate, Butterscotch, the runt of the litter, remained with us into 2010 at 101! She slept on the radiator by day and walked our anatomical landscape—ribs, stomachs and bladders—by night. Her loud yowls if we were not up when she wanted or not feeding her promptly at 6, might irritate, but I have also known these two cats to be the source of unexpected insight.

The vet told me most pet owners would elect the hard convenience of euthanasia at this point, but we didn't consider that action. At Butterscotch's last vet visit we were told, "She's as healthy as an ox!" and I joked to Bill on the way home: "Must be a Christian Science cat." Over twenty-some years these Arkansas barn cats made four moves with us, accepting as home wherever we've settled—including the tortuous trip from Memphis to Pennsylvania thirteen years ago, when Surprise, our thirteen-year-old Samoyed, their possum-catching partner, died en route. These Southern felines adjusted to the northern climate, survived College Hill's devil-cat, figured out how to manage Shawnee's deep snows, and watched Charissa, their primary owner, grow from child to married lady and then to Emma's mother—Butterscotch even tolerating Emma's toddler tugs.

Butterscotch, especially fond of my allergy-prone students—and they, oddly, equally fond of her—became the art class mascot. In his last months, Oreo, made Geneva, our Bernese Mountain Dog, his mother and she gladly took on that role, licking his fur and grooming the old cat nightly. Though Oreo sometimes missed when he jumped to a window ledge, he, amazingly, jumped (to my horror) from deck to a ledge a story above ground level to get my attention at the kitchen sink. If it weren't for Shawnee traffic, he'd still be here, purring in my lap evenings. Before her demise, Butterscotch slept in the curve of my body or on Bill's stomach and looked into my eyes as if she knew her time here was slipping away. But, as long as there was a spark, a spring, a purr, and no pain, she remained with us, fully loved and cared for. When her time was up, Emma, our three-year-old granddaughter, asked to help bury her in our back yard, tiny spade in hand, offering the only eulogy necessary: "We'll be seeing you Butterscotchy!"

As I see my own days slipping away, I realize my cats have taught me how to grow old gracefully. I hope when I become elderly there is someone to feed and hold me, as I have them.

One is essentially alone in death or any tragedy. When you are in the place of loss, calamity, or disaster, you are *alone* with it. Along the way you may have a supportive friend or two, but you enter this world alone, fumble through, survive, and ultimately meet death alone. You have but one place to turn—yourself. The *deep inside* that each of us has, if it has been developed in ordinary times, rises to the calamitous occasion, as it did for my son Nathan and his bride in September 2004.

Nathan's wedding to Alison, for which I was little more than a guest, was in Thunder Bay, Ontario, Canada, the bride's hometown. They met and worked on Grand Cayman, loving all the island life offered. But when category 5 hurricane Ivan hit in 2004 it wiped Grand Cayman off the radar screen. The island was devastated. Communications were impossible. I did not know for several days if they were dead or alive. For months they had no phone, water, electricity, or normal food, sleeping in 100 degree heat with a machete beside their heads for protection from looters, collecting coconuts from fallen trees to eat, and walking four miles to fill a several gallon plastic container with water to drink and bathe in—their cars destroyed. Not until Thanksgiving would Island services return. Once the island airport was semi-functioning, I sent boxes to my children and for general island relief. I had phoned hundreds of acquaintances, congressmen, diplomats, businessmen, priests, the Red Cross, and everyone I could think of trying to get help for the island, because it appeared to be ignored. I read whatever blogs and emails I could find about Island conditions nightly. There may be governments, churches, organizations and agencies whose task it is to help in time of crisis, but I learned bureaucracy keeps them from immediate response when needed. I discovered that even a mom's efforts have limitations. Eventually we would pay for a week's rest and relaxation for them in Boston (city of their choice). We drove up to visit them one day and learned the details of their horrific experience.

Hurricane Ivan, when it came to the US, brought lesser devastation to Shawnee via a Fall flood. Another flood followed in Spring 2005. Two 100-year floods in just seven months! The village suffered with large trees down, roads out, electric impaired, houses and inns flooded. Our neighbor and fellow-Innkeeper, Rose Ann, found her basement in five feet of water, her freezer chest overturned by the water's force, dumped food as it rolled over and over. Nearly every neighborhood porch was crowded with basement furnishings and the road where I walk my dogs eroded away. The Shawnee Inn property looked like a sea of mud instead of a stately golf course resort. In the first flood our basement got merely damp in one small section; but we rounded up $1,000 to have the carpet and floor cleaned, throwing out the extra-thick padding I had recently installed. The second flood was just as harmful, though we were spared again.

No one dreamt that a *third* flood would follow in July 2006. *Three* 100-year floods in 22 months!

I have no tidy answers for calamity. I do not presume to understand natural or human disasters. I realize floods, fires, and hurricanes are nature's pattern, but when a disaster like Katrina or Ivan affects *your own* child or *your* neighbor, such acts seem sinister.

I never seem to give up trying to figure out the old problem of evil—why it is and how to get rid of it. Though I might like to, I cannot change others or the world. I can only improve myself and in the process, hopefully, add to other humans doing their best, all of us together enlarging goodness in this world. I always come back to the fact that the only thing each of us really has to work with is his or her own life. *All I have to work with is my own life.* What I choose to do with it, make of it, for self or others, is my only means to help the world. In this process, I turn to God, that "voice" that across ages and religions, is described *within*, known intimately through meditation, prayer, and listening. The God within our own life is behind every genuinely good or truthful thing we experience. I am only one small speck in the universe, but it matters what I do because if *each* little speck acts from the God within, then, with everyone trying, the world just might be one big compassionate village! Too naive? Perhaps. But again *the only thing I have to work with is myself.*

I have wondered why I didn't die that day on my way to the Bucks County realtor's office, wondered why that car that rammed into me didn't do me in. My car was totaled. Numerous experts said I should have died. The EMS worker said it was a miracle. What is a miracle but the hand of God? I've been asking God to show me for what purpose I'm still around. Sometimes I fancy my dad prevented my death, that it wasn't just his big Olds '98 that protected me—that God assigned him to take care of me that day. But this really isn't my view of God at all, more the one hinted at in Christmas films like *It's A Wonderful Life*.

I believe I didn't die that day because I had more lessons to learn in this particular station. Like a train, I couldn't pull out for a new destination until I took on what I needed here. I had to be stopped before I became a runaway locomotive. There I was in my free will fixing to move again, away from my House-of-Many-Problems, but God knew it wasn't my address that needed changing; it was *me*. God guides us to places that promote our learning; moving is not a matter of willful decision-making. It sounds so simple when the words come: I had to learn to be *more grateful for what I already have, who I already am, and where I already dwell.* How many times I have had *that* one to learn! How many times I have taught it to my children and others! So why am I having to learn it *again?* Because until I *thoroughly get it* I can't go home.

Until I find my place *right where I am,* midst problems and imperfections, I'll never be home. Until I find in my home's brokenness lessons for my *own* brokenness, I am not ready to move. Until I find genuine glee instead of annoying traits in both those close to me and the community in which I find myself, I may not move. Until I *sit* with hardship and depression, sickness and suffering—something my yoga instructor, spiritual director, and three serendipitously purchased books *all* told me one February, I can't move. Until I find light in darkness and grasp hope in despair, I have no place to go. Until I make the art of a lifetime that is in me, I am not finished. Until I follow my children's suggestion and slow down—a rest I know includes longer walks in nature, meditation, prayer, time for candle-lit baths listening to K.D. Lang's mellow "49th Parallel" with an Amy Tan novel—I must not move. Until I enter that cave of the heart and listen *consistently* to the voice inside that links me to a power bigger than myself, I won't find home, for it isn't a house I need to find to feel at home; it is *home within* I need to find to be at home.

Like women of America's 19th century Westward movement, I have accepted change while holding close *hiraeth*—my longing for home in its deepest meaning. For me, as for them, "The vision of home was a longing for life as it could never be, a vision of time without change. Formed for the road, men and women on wild and lonely American frontiers dreamed of home as the still point of all their departures" (Schlissel, *Far From Home,* p. 243).

I have wanted to call a beach *home* ever since my years on Lake Michigan and my many visits to Cape Cod. Though I am able on a windy day to almost hear the waves in land-locked Pennsylvania—as if I am tucked away in some quiet white dune beside tall rustling grasses with an endless shoreline before me—I know—and not just because of the motorcycles racing by—that dreams of perfect locations, empty beaches, and tranquil mountaintops are fleeting. It is as Wolpe says, "an idyllic home is a dream" (Wolpe, p. 38). Who knows?—global warming may, sadly, eradicate beaches one day. My "beach" has become the vista of infinity, the eternal walk, the coming home to Spirit.

Years ago I read in Maria Harris' *Dance of the Spirit* that the "truest meaning of 'coming home' is not a coming home to a mother or child, a lover or spouse; it is coming home to ourselves. Being at Home means...simply Dwelling in a place where we can be who we are. We are Home; we are always at Home." (Harris, *Dance of the Spirit: The Seven Stages of Women's Spirituality*, p.102).

Nor need I dig for answers, for inexplicable *whys* and *what comes next*. Where I am now is focus enough. The animals and many homes I have loved have taught me this by their impermanence and demands. They tell me it is not a future destination I should focus on, but *this very moment*. What matters is asking questions of and saying yes to the present. Saying yes to the place I'm in. I know this best sitting on my deck chaise, writing, my dogs beside me, where Butterscotch and Oreo would have joined them only a few years ago.

Home has always been my internal *still point* from which I have journeyed out. But home has also been the external walls and doors that have locked me in, harboring, shaping, inspiring, blocking, and building me. Home's center and boundary is God—how many spiritual writers throughout the centuries to the present have told me that! God's mansions compose life's labyrinth. Roaming these "rooms," I've found new viewpoints at every turn. Some corridors have been dark. Others bright and too brief. But guided on, I've not lingered in ease, nor accepted a fixed view. Instead, my path has led to new risks, questions, and lessons.

The *asking* of questions matters more than the answers. As Henri Nouwen says, "Painful questions must be raised, faced, and then lived... avoid the temptation of offering or accepting simple answers...Beware of easy answers or guarantees." (Henri Nouwen, *Spiritual Direction: Wisdom for the Long Walk of Faith*, 2006, p.7). One who claims he—or she—has all the answers is not the one I trust. The answer man's self-righteousness glares too boldly; he is not Joseph Campbell's hero, the nomadic Buddha, nor the Christly savior. He knows no imperfection, sees no error in his ways, nor does he know mankind's plight. All is well with him even when it isn't. Self-appointed benefactor to his fellow-beings, he can right their wrongs if only they will listen to *him*, for he has answers for everyone.

But the questioning man or woman is unfixed in opinion or place, lives with life's complexity and embraces mystery. She is a sojourner, wanderer, a creator of her own path. Wounded, she has felt life's pain and her brother's hurt. She loves because she's been unloved and heals because she's known suffering. Imperfect, but held in *chesed*—expansive lovingkindness—she knows God's mercy, and aims to be merciful. Answers lie in her questions.

I no longer need to know everything. I used to think I did. My longing and digging for truth made me think it was attainable. I know better now. A *flowing mystery* resides in all things. Mystery, not the bad word I grew up thinking it to be, is not about what we don't know; it is about what we know by *un*knowing, as the thirteenth century anonymous *Cloud of Unknowing* author elucidates. This profound knowing, what we know beyond ourselves, what we know by intuition—rather than by reasoning, thinking hard, or being told—is unattainable intellectually and is the *Sommum Bonum*.

I look back and find my search for home has caught up with me, come after me when I wasn't looking. I discover I am at home in my *own* "skin, "knowing and *un*knowing. Like the Celtic Christians, I am at home in the *ordinariness* of life, where prayer and daily work are not separate. I find the "face" of God in cats and dogs, in children, husband, neighbors, guests, students and strangers, and, even in the young woman who slammed her car into mine nearly ending my life.

I am at home when I dig in my garden or cook in my kitchen. I am at home writing at my computer or painting in my studio. I am at home when I hike to the top of a mountain to watch the sun set or clean up the yard after spring rains. I am at home when I work diligently to make my house sparkle or at the end of a long teaching day when I still have housework. I am at home when I listen to a neighbor's woes or receive a call from one of my children asking advice. I am at home when I discover an inspiring new book or reread an old one. I am at home when I pick the first summer tomato from my garden or make an autumn wreath from grape vine growing outside my door. I am at home when I listen to Grieg or Sibelius, Rory Block's Blues or anything by Leonard Cohen. I am even at home when I'm sore from hauling wood or hearing disturbing news—for I've learned to *sit through*, in a Buddhist sense, the unpleasant—and to focus on love when the less-than-loving rears up.

I will never feel at home with the world's dishonesty, cruelty, injustice, arrogance, violence, greed, and warring. I do not *sit through* these "darks" easily for their evil would trash all I hold dear: truth, beauty, love. These shadows move across my mind like an evening storm, teaching me to cherish light all the more.

The relationship of shadow to light is vital to me—both as an artist drawing and as a human being seeking home. I can never lose shadow any more than I can lose light; one requires the other. In their pattern—their *interrelatedness*—I find myself, and God, and home. Celtic theologian Esther de Waal echoes this truth I am learning when she writes: "we cannot hope to stay in the Garden of Eden where all is well...None of us can evade the darkness" (Esther de Waal, *The Celtic Way of Prayer*, p. 115). Humans can't create safe lives locked away from suffering, for suffering pushes us to evolve—like pushing to give birth. I will continue to ask how to end humans' inhumanity and will forever hope every man, woman, and child may find peace and home. Asking hard questions seems, eventually, to lead to balance, wholeness and action.

I wrote in my journal in 1965 that opposites together are a true delight for the wholeness they bring. In 1989 I wrote in my RISD master's paper about the wholeness the journey home brings, quoting Madeleine L'Engle's *Walking on Water*, that book that serendipitously fell at my feet (literally) as I searched for my master's thesis:

> *Coming home. That's what it's all about. The journey to the coming of the kingdom...the purpose of the work, be it story or music or painting, is to further the coming of the kingdom, to make us aware of our status as children of God, and to turn our feet toward home* (L'Engle, *Walking on Water*, p. 163).

My *hiraeth* core has sought home passionately—from New Mexico to Nova Scotia, and once sent us driving 2,000 miles in a weekend to see 60 acres in Wisconsin. Realtors have probably shown me a hundred houses. I've drawn floor plans of the houses I looked at, planning how each would function if we were to live there. Searching Realtor.com and city-data.com became tasks as regular as checking email. Books ranking cities on various attributes, from climate to crime, on where to retire or how to find one's perfect spot, on what the best art towns in America are, stacked up on my library desk and bedside table—all heavily highlighted, their data turned into graphs and charts. Yet, none of this energetic single-mindedness brought me home.

Barnes book, *Searching for Home,* spoke to me of things I know and need to know: "The real home for which we yearn isn't the place where we grew up or the new place we're hoping to build, but the place where we were created to live. Paradise." This Presbyterian minister author says we weren't created "to roam the earth lost and confused but, rather, to live at home with God, which is what defines Paradise." He explains that we are nomads moving toward home, for "there is no way to find home without leaving home. It is a grace to be told to go." (Barnes, *Searching for Home,* p.13 and p. 30). I realize that like the hymn I hired the Blues singer to belt out at my wedding, my journey has been an *amazing grace.*

As a nomad, I've discovered God jumps unexpectedly into our ordinariness to light the way. Then, hope blooms as bright as my flower garden in August sunshine. I live for such moments! God's presence in ordinary life is the most precious thing I know. It gives me my greatest joy.

Wandering, moving, has seemed my destiny, framing my life pattern. No place is perfect, though I'd thought one might call me, take me in and hold me for my last decades. But now I see life is an *infinite* journey—a going, doing, changing that never ends, never set or safe. Desiring a human home to be an ever-satisfying still-point of tranquility and belonging is an illusive dream. Yet, at the same time, without dreams and hope we could not sustain ourselves.

The universal dream of mankind is the lost paradise imbedded in all cultures, yearned for by many peoples throughout history, uniting us all in a common hope. Without hope there is failure the Dalai Lama says, reminding us, "Under no circumstances should you lose hope" (The Dalai Lama, translated and edited by Jeffrey Hopkins, PhD., *How To Practice The Way to a Meaningful Life,* p. 39). Hope guided the Native American Ghost Dancers—as it does all of us—beyond struggle and loss. My favorite quotation bears repeating:

And when the race lies crushed and groaning beneath an alien yoke, how natural is the dream of a redeemer, an Arthur, who shall return from exile or awake from some long sleep to drive out the usurper and win back for his people what they have lost. The hope becomes a faith and the faith becomes the creed of priests and prophets, until the hero is a god and the dream a religion, looking to some great miracle of nature for its culmination and accomplishment (Mooney, p. 657).

This hope for a paradise or saving place of peace and belonging—this *hiraeth*—that takes us on a nomadic journey, leads, finally, within. Home, as I have learned over and over, is not a place but *a spiritual power within*, a coming home to our Divine Source, as Rilke puts it, "Your solitude will be a hold and home for you even amid very unfamiliar conditions and there you will find all your ways" (Rilke, Letters to a Young Poet, p.) I no longer need *hiraeth* to manifest itself in mountaintop or beachfront property.

When the time comes to leave this house for another, God will show the way and I will follow.

One day in the Spring of 2010, Zermatt and Harley (our new 5-year-old rescue Berner we got after Genny died of cancer) run across the chartreuse lawn to drink in the cold stream, their coats glistening in the early sun. Curling ferns perk up along the bank and a roof-top-tall dogwood spreads white blooms against spring's budding woods, a vivid contrast to our newly painted pumpkin-colored house (a much happier and equally historically correct choice than its original maroon). Bright pink tulips and yellow daffodils nod next to old stone walls and little green shoots in my gardens promise perennials by summer. I imagine Oreo (no longer with us) lying on the deck, sunning himself, his tail twitching as he watches a dove pick seed from the feeder.

Spring rains suddenly arrive mid-morning swelling Shawnee Creek and our waterfall, as I call my dogs in and watch the water rise. Will this village experience another flood? The stream touches the daffodil border of our yard and encompasses the dogwood tree Bill used to mow around that we fear may disappear into the creek. From the top of the waterfall, roaring waters bombard the boulder island of our property; they've been cutting a deeper and wider channel, slightly changing course a bit these last three years, slicing into the bank where our 175-foot Hackberry tree—our rope swing tree—no longer stands, wiped out several years ago by a heavy storm.

I take a canvas and try to capture the raging creek the only way possible: in paint. My brush rushes the oil paint across the surface, mimicking the fury of the storm outside my window.

What if the several 200-year floods should become an *annual* event? What if water rises to the short stone wall in line with our house? What if it roars into our basement and weakens our very foundation? What if everything we've done to rehabilitate this centuries-old structure in the past ten years washes away? The insurance wouldn't be enough to start over. We don't even have flood insurance (our home not in the FEMA map's flood plain). But floods have ravaged much of the village south of us. What if our home were hit next time?

My hundreds of paintings and reams of words on paper might sail like flotillas down to the Delaware, never to be seen again. My books—friends that charted my life course—and my note cards of ideas and dozens of journals would become soggy, illegible and lost. My blue and white china and hand-thrown pottery, with which I enjoy setting an inspiring table, would shatter under the water's force. The English manor house table might float like a raft down the current, along with the Irish hutch and other antiques collected slowly over a lifetime. Children's photos and things hand-made would be gone forever. I would be like a homeless Hurricane Katrina victim. No longer a nomad or wanderer figuratively, I would know the experience first hand.

I might have to mourn what had been, but, then, I would look for a new home and start all over—the *hiraeth* in me would have it no other way.

As much me as my skin or breath or thought, *hiraeth is me.* Yes, sometimes I've wanted *hiraeth* to incarnate into a perfect *actual* place, but *hiraeth* is not physical. It is *much more* than a longing for home in any ordinary sense. It is the place within that validates one's best dreams and aspirations, a nurturing present hope and future pasture. All my life I have sought this deep dwelling, this right to be, this "room" of my own, this belonging spot where I am called, welcomed, part of, where all my puzzle pieces fit and I can truly be me, where my purpose happens. *Hiraeth* affirms my identity beyond anyone else's determination of what I am. Neither my father's house, nor my mother's, nor any other, can claim me. I dwell on my own—in the place my own journey has taken me to, where my yearning meets my God, and I am embraced by Love. *Hiraeth* led me. Without it, I would still be in my father's house.

Because of *hiraeth*, I could survive even floodwaters. Nothing can wash away *hiraeth*. If destructive storms ever ravaged our property, I would stand on the awkward shore our land would have become, cuddling my dogs, and look into Bill's moist eyes. We would huddle together, making a house of ourselves. We'd take a moment to mourn our lost home: Bill would speak of cross-country skiing in the village and guitar-picking on the deck and I would recall art classes, Christmases, B&B guests, and family gatherings. Our animals would look bewildered—but they would be less upset, not needing things we humans think we need. They'd have what mattered most to them: their humans. And, in truth, so would we. Though we might pick through remnants when the sun would finally shine, we'd say goodbye to what had been our home. Then, we'd start walking—not on an endless beach—but *right where we are*, like the Navajo, who call themselves "a wandering people," imagining their journey to be a unifying universal circle bringing order to the world. Like Navajo and nomad, we'd set out once more to leave and find home.

The rains have stopped. My oil painting has a good beginning. I lay down my brush and go outside with the dogs. A bit of sunshine peaks from behind fading clouds. Harley gallops down to the creek for a drink. Zermatt brings a squeaky toy to me, his big brown eyes holding me in endless affection. The sun is beaming now, filtered through wet trees, hidden somewhat, as always, by the mountain crest. The three of us tumble to the ground and lie on the damp grass as I stroke their black hair. If she were still alive, Butterscotch would be climbing my belly for her share of attention. Oreo and Genny would be here, too, if they could; are here, really. I look up through dripping treetops toward the bright sky this hollow we live in too often hides, listening to the waterfall and wind chimes, ignoring the traffic, watching sunlight and shadow dance across my home's old stone walls, illuminating their beauty and imperfections. Today I am not in a hurry to bake, make beds, do laundry, accomplish to-do lists, nor will the studio open or the phone be answered. Today we will just lie in sunshine. And when Bill comes home, we will hike a trail together at twilight.

twenty one

The Thirty-Fourth

Hundreds of vivid paintings splash across my dream with myriad hues of aqua, green, turquoise, fuschia, orange, rust, peach, ivory, and warm grays like driftwood. People dance among them, singing, happy. I am singing too. We are in one grand celebration together.

I haven't been to New Harmony for 17 years. For three decades its peace and simple beauty offered me respite and home when I needed it, taught me to be centered like a good potter's pot. Now I find no particular place necessary to centering. Like the many apples I sliced open to expose the seed-star within for the women and daughters I taught on retreat in New Harmony, so within each of us, at our core, lies the seed-star of our hopes and dreams. In our radiant center, lies our home. It's just a matter of looking deep within.

By 2010, no longer driven to hunt for place or purpose, I was content. All the work for my Shawnee home, gallery and B&B business, convinced me I'd reinvented myself for the last time. My Shawnee nest seemed complete.

But I should have known better. Contentment is simply the harbinger of change. We are not meant to get too cozy. We are on journey, always changing, evolving, altering our circumstances. There is no end. No arrival. No final found place or situation. As soon as you think you've found something final, it won't be, for change is always just around the corner. How can we be settled, satisfied, when we exist for *the new thing, the fresh idea, the risk, the learning experience?* How can we ever be settled when life is an *infinite* process?

One day driving out of Moravian Academy, I notice a "for sale" sign in front of a house across the street from the school, on Pond View Court. The ivy-covered stucco English Tudor, surrounded by dogwoods and evergreens on a quiet cove acre, with a tiny glimpse of Green Pond waters, *calls* me, much as the Fisherville land had three decades earlier. I am not looking for a house, but I check out the listing on the internet when I get home. The interior photos suggest tasteful warmth, a bit of history reflected in stone and beam, though it was built in 1997. In spite of its high price tag, it entices me to phone a realtor to show it to us. The architecture intrigues and the location is ideal. After nearly a dozen years of 40-minute one-way commutes, wouldn't it be grand for Bill to *walk* across the street to work! How much more time we would have together! A few days later we look at the house with a realtor.

Walking up the flagstone path to the old Castle-like door with its iron hardware, I note the neglected window boxes, the invasive ivy, the missing chunks of mortar between the bluestone slabs. But I am not deterred by these negatives. Certainly we've handled over-grown ivy before. Certainly I've handled *anything* and *everything* before! A strong awareness that I am meant to see this place, guides me inside.

Once inside, I know I'm *home.* Thick as layered quilts on a cold night, I'm wrapped up by this house. Everything about it speaks my name, from the voluminous space—ideal for paintings—that greet me, some thirty feet high over the dining and living areas with exposed beams and wide wooden circular stair to a loft library—perfect for our thousands of books and BC's office. But what clinches the fit is the phrase hand-painted in old English lettering in the front entry hall, above the front door: *Touched by the hand of God*—words I might have chosen myself; and above the door from the family room to the garage: *Love one another*—just the right reminder by which to exit.

On the second floor I discover a 26-foot long photography studio with huge sink and enormous storage areas—a potential painting studio!—and a billiards room with sky lights and its own separate stair down to the garage and outside—an ideal future art gallery! And beside the prospective gallery, a third room suitable for small art classes.   Conveniently on the first floor are the two bedrooms, each with its own bath and large walk-in closet with floor to ceiling shelving, each large enough for several Berner and Newfoundland nests as well as human beds—rooms so large that Bill decides we could put basketball hoops at either end! The immense butler's pantry where I quickly envision my many sets of china, pottery collections, and chef's gear, beautifully and conveniently displayed, makes up for the long galley kitchen with its outdated appliances. Two thirty-foot-long steps open the dining room to the handsome beamed and book-cased living room with massive real stone fireplace and heavy wood mantel. Here I imagine wonderful conversation with family and friends, following beautifully prepared gourmet dinners. Two flagstone patios, one through French doors from the living room and one from the family room, lead to two separately fenced yards—one for dogs, the other for quiet contemplation. There is even a small south-facing picketed garden area for herbs, vegetables and flowers, though now overgrown with ivy and tall prickly weeds.

The designer-owner, who built the home in 1997, moved to California shortly after we'd viewed the house, leaving the selling of her property to the local realtor. Though I knew it was out of our price range—and above the price of any house in the area—I watched the listing for many months. Then one day I noticed it had *sold*. With a history of home experiences behind me, I pondered why I'd been led to see it, why it had seemed so right for us; pragmatically, I put the house out of my head, but not out of my heart.

Two years pass. Then in the Autumn of 2011, I happen to notice that the house is back on the market! How strange! Did the new owner not like living there? And it is listed with a lower price! As ensuing months roll by, I watch the price decline further (and the ivy grow). It seems that the house had sold to a wealthy elderly woman who lived in the house only a few months before entering a care facility and dying. Her distant relatives were ready to rent the property by the time we saw it again. One thing led to another, and in March 2012, the house became ours! Certainly I had not anticipated a thirty-fourth move in my sixty-ninth year!

I will not spoil the joy of being in our new home with tales of the agony of negotiating the sale, selling our Shawnee home, ending my B&B and gallery business, packing, moving 400 paintings, thousands of books, all our furnishings and antiques, then unpacking, remediating ivy, remodeling the outdated kitchen, and improving this house. Suffice it to say, *we are here*!

Every morning Harley and Heidi (our Landseer Newfoundland puppy whom we got shortly after our beloved Zermatt passed), and I walk with Bill across the street to Moravian Academy where Bill teaches and students greet us. Instead of a 40-minute commute, Bill now has a 5-minute walk with wife and dogs through Moravian's beautiful campus to get to his classroom—and the only walkers' gate for the fenced campus just happens to be directly across from our yard!

How did this happen?

I think our dearest dreams and wishes—even deeply buried ones we do not know we have—come true when we keep faith and don't get discouraged—or if we get down, pick ourselves back up in the attempt to *learn* what needs to be learned. Depression and adversity are actually great teachers. In my case, every move has involved learning something. Every move has come of evolving and reinventing myself—seeing things from a new perspective that comes through *listening within*, then acting on what is revealed. Never has a move or change been merely about moving to a new location or getting something bigger or better. No. Always it has centered on *lessons* that I needed to learn, insights that have enriched my life and led me to a new work or new-found understanding. Often the unfolding of these lessons happens in amazing, spectacular ways that we could never orchestrate ourselves.

This time, learning came as a *gift*, a directive to long-sought harmony and contemplation. This move offered Bill and me more time together, without wasted highway hours. We find ourselves in a community that offers more than we knew when we bought our home. We are surrounded by historic farms as well as conveniences like an extraordinary supermarket, ethnic restaurants, movie theaters, stores, parks perfect for painting or walking, hiking trails, community center with pool and fitness facilities, the oldest organic farmer's market in the nation, the historic canal tow path trails along the Lehigh River, and downtown Bethlehem, "The Christmas City," with its rich past and historical architecture. Opportunities abound here that we had not had in Shawnee. Moreover, in our new Pond View home there is a spirituality reflected not merely in the biblical quotations the original owner had lettered above the exit doors, but in the quiet solemnity of the home itself, a feeling that God is present and Love's work will happen here, radiating out beyond this inspiring space. Pond View calmly invites my prayerful contemplation. Every day overflows with reasons for gratitude.

Now I am not foolish enough to believe that life is one rosy resolution after another! Challenges are ever present. That's part of this mortal experience. I would have it no other way. How else would I *learn* anything? I believe we live solely to *learn*. And in the process of learning, healing is often the magnificent side effect.

I couldn't die on my drive to Bucks County in 2004, searching for a perfect house to move into, because I hadn't yet learned all that my Shawnee house had to teach me; but by 2010 I had. And when a place has taught us all it has to teach, it isn't our right place anymore. We are guided on.

The day of my auto accident when Charissa brought me home from the emergency room, I sat up in bed to try to read my mail—the one thing I thought I might be able to do. She helped me open a large manila envelope. Inside was a three-ring notebook apparently mailed by my alma mater to the class of '65—sort of a where-are-they-now collection by fellow classmates. I thumbed through it, mildly interested, glad to have something I could do with one hand, something to distract me from the pain and mental images of the accident, something to help me avoid taking the pain-killers my daughter was eager to have me try.

Towards the end of the notebook, I came to a name I remembered; reading his update I learned he works in editing/publishing. I've been *writing* all my life! Granted, mostly in a hole, too busy figuring out my voice to actually have the guts to venture into the labyrinth of publication—but wanting it, once I realize you don't have a voice unless it is *heard*. So I dared to write this near-stranger-once-friend and he emailed me back and we wrote and read and learned who each other had become in four decades. And he heard my voice, read my story—amazingly, *all* of it—tells me I am a writer—and if you are reading this, his encouragement spurred my voice out of silence.

Fiction can't compete with truth's surprises.

So as I roam through my saga this February 2013—a month I have come to love for its quiet winter solace—I see patterns. Patterns that have a central theme of *hiraeth*, that longing for home in its deepest of meanings. I have learned that the home we yearn for comes to us when we faithfully love and care and work for the home we have, including the people and pets within it and the community surrounding it.

My dogs lie beside me as I check my email this Valentine's Day. I see Bill has sent me a message in answer to my question to him at breakfast this morning before he left for school: "What would you like for Valentine's Day?" His email reply to me is almost poetry:

(Since you asked) What I Want for Valentine's Day:

When I wake up in the middle of the night and get back in bed and I can hear your breathing—that's what I want for Valentine's Day.

When I wake up in the morning and reach over and feel you there beside me—that's what I want for Valentine's Day. If you're not there, I'll assume you got up early to read or write. That's fine too.

We could have breakfast together. I'd like to eat whatever you cook, or else we can have cold cereal together. We can turn on the news or the weather. That's what I want for Valentine's Day.

If you have time, we could walk the dogs to school. If not, I may see you three go by out the window while I'm teaching. That's what I want for Valentine's Day.

When I get home, we could go and walk the dogs together, or else I'll go walk them and come back to you. That's what I want for Valentine's Day.

We can have dinner out, or not, and watch the evening news, or not.

We could watch a TV show or movie together, or we could read books. That's what I want for Valentine's Day.

We could go to bed and you could promise me we'll do it all again tomorrow. That's what I want for Valentine's Day.

Beautiful. What do *I* want for Valentine's Day? To get an email like this from my husband.

What do I want today or any day? My nearly seventy years have taught me it is to dwell in Love, to love and be loved. For I have learned that what we really yearn for, whether we know it or not, is *a dwelling made of God, Love*; a home *with* God, Love. My *hiraeth* journey has taught me that we want divine Presence with us—to experience God in our *ordinary* daily living. We want God's compassion, justice, beauty, and principle guiding our journeys. Coming home is never about coming to a particular place or person, though persons and places matter, but coming home is, finally, *coming to God, Love*, where we always have been and always will be. To learn this fully takes a never-ending lifetime.

I sense yet another shift coming, and wait patiently to discover what the next chapter in my life will teach.

Bibliography

Abingdon. *The Interpreter's Bible in Twelve Volumes.* Abingdon Press, 1952.

Anonymous. *The Cloud of Unknowing.* Edited by William Johnston. Image Books by Doublday, 1973.

Aptheker, Bettina. *Tapestries of Life: Women's Work, Women's Consciousness, and The Meaning of Daily Experience.* The University of Massachusetts Press, 1989.

Barnes, Craig M. *Searching for Home: Spirituality for Restless Souls.* Brazos Press, 2003.

Bender, Sue. *Plain and Simple: A Woman's Journey to the Amish.* HarperSanFrancisco, 1989.

Belenky, Mary Field, Blythe McVicker Clinchy, Nancy Rule Goldberger, Jill Mattuck Tarule. *Women's Ways of Knowing: The development of Self, Voice, and Mind.* Basic Books, Inc. Publishers, 1986.

Bondi, Roberta C. *To Love As God Loves: Conversations with the Early Church.* Fortress Press, 1987.

Buechner, Frederick. *Listening to your Life: Daily Meditations with Frederick Buechner.* Complied by George Connor. Harper San Francisco, 1992.

Buechner, Frederick. *The Hungering Dark.* Harper San Francisco, 1971.

Buechner, Frederick. *The Longing for Home: Recollections and Reflections.* Harper Collins Publishers Inc., 1996.

Buechner, Frederick. *The Sacred Journey.* Harper Collins, 1991.

Buscaglia, Leo. *Living, Loving and Learning.* Ballantine, 1985.

Buscaglia, Leo. *Love: A Warm and Wonderful Book About The Largest Experience in Life.* Fawcett Crest by Ballantine, 1972.

Campbell, Joseph. *The Hero with a Thousand Faces.* Princeton University Press, 1968.

Christ, Carol P. *Diving Deep and Surfacing: Women Writers on Spiritual Quest.* Second edition. Beacon Press, 1986.

Christ, Carol P. and Judith Plascow. *Woman's Spirit Rising.* HarperSan Francisco, 1992.

Culley, Margo. *A Day at a Time: The Diary Literature of American Women from 1764 to the Present.* The Feminist Press, 1985.

Davies, Oliver and Fiona Bowie. *Celtic Christian Spirituality: An Anthology of Medieval and Modern Sources.* The Coninuum Publishing Company, 1997.

De Waal, Esther. *The Celtic Way of Prayer.* Doubleday, 1994.

Dillard, Annie. *The Writing Life.* Harper Perennial, 1989.

Dreamer, Oriah Mountain. *The Call: Discovering Why You Are Here.* Harper San Francisco, 2003.

Earle, Mary C. *The Desert Mothers: Spiritual Practices from the Women of the Wilderness.* Morehouse Publishing, 2007.

Eddy, Mary Baker. *Science and Health with Key to the Scriptures.* Christian Science Publishing Society, 1971.

Eddy, Mary Baker. *Prose Works.* Christian Science Publishing Society, 1925.

Estes, Clarissa Pink. *Women Who Run With the Wolves.* Ballantine Books, 1992.

Evans, Glenn. Speeches and Files.

Flinders, Carol Lee. *At the Root of this Longing: Reconciling a Spiritual Hunger and a Feminist Thirst.* Harper San Francisco, 1998.

Flinders, Carol Lee. *Enduring Graace: Living Portraits of Seven Women Mystics.* Harper San Francisco, 1993.

Frankl, Viktor E. *Man's Search for Meaning: An Introduction to Logotherapy.* Touchstone Books by Simon and Schuster, 1984.

Gilbert, Sandra M. and Susan Gubar. *The Norton Anthology of Literature By Women: The Tradition in English.* W.W. Norton & Company, 1985.

Gilligan, Carol. *In a Different Voice: Psychological Theory and Women's Development.* Harvard University Press, 1982.

Gilman, Charlotte Perkins. *The Living of Charlotte Perkins Gilman: An Autobiography.* The University of Wisconsin Press, 1990.

Goldberg, Natalie. *Long Quiet Highway: Waking Up in America.* Bantam, 1994.

Goldberg, Natalie. *Writing Down the Bones: Feeling the Writer Within.* Shambala, 1986.

Grant, Cynthia Tucker. *A Woman's Ministry: Mary Collson's Search for Reform as a Unitarian Minister, a Hull House Social Worker, and a Christian Science Practitioner.* Temple University Press, 1984.

Gregory of Nyssa. *The Life of Moses.* Translation and introduction and Notes by Abraham J. Malherbe and Everett Ferguson. The Classics of Western Spirituality. Paulist Press, 1978.

Hall, Donald. *Life Work.* Beacon Press, 1993.

Harris, Maria. *Dance of the Spirit: The Seven Steps of Women's Spirituality.* Bantam Books, 1989.

Harvey, Brett. *The Fifties: A Women's Oral History.* Harper Perennial, 1993.

Haught, John F. *What is God? : How to Think about the Divine.* Paulist Press, 1986.

Heilbrun, Carolyn G. *Writing a Woman's Life.* Ballantine Books, 1988.

His Holiness The Dalai Lama. *How to Practice: The Way to a Meaningful Life.* Translated and edited by Jeffrey Hopkins, Ph.D, Pocket Books, division of Simon and Schuster, 2002.

Hultkrantz, Ake. *The Religions of the American Indians.* University of California Press, 1981.

Ibsen, Henrik. *Henrik Ibsen: The compete Prose Plays.* Translated by Rolf Fjelde. NAL Penguin Inc., 1978.

Jones, Alan. *Exploring Spiritual Direction: An Essay on Christian Fellowship.* Harper San Francisco, 1982.

Julian of Norwich. *Showings*. Translated from the Critical Text with introduction by Edmund Colledge, O.S.A. and James Walsh, S.J. The Classics of Western Spirituality, Paulist Press, Inc., 1978.

Koller, Alice. *An Unknown Woman*. Bantam, 1981.

Lane, Ann J. *To Herland and Beyond: The Life and Work of Charlotte Perkins Gilman*. Meridian, 1991.

Le Bar, Frank. *When the Days Were Not Long Enough*. Traford Publishing, 2006.

L'Engle, Madeleine. *The Rock that is Higher: Story as Truth*. Harold Shaw Publishers, 1993.

L'Engle, Madeleine. *Walking on Water: Reflections on Faith and Art*. Harold Shaw Publishers, 1980.

Metzger, Deena. *Writing for Your Life: A Guide and Companion to the Inner Worlds*. HarperSanFrancisco, 1992.

McCullough, David. *John Adams*. Simon and Schuster, 2001.

Mooney, James. *The Ghost Dance Religion and Wounded Knee*. Dover Press, 1973.

Murdock, Maureen. *Father's Daughters: Transforming the Father-Daughter Relationship*. Ballantine Books, 1994.

Nouwen, Henri J. M. *Finding My Way Home: Pathways to Life and the Spirit*. The Crossroad Publishing Company, 2001.

Nouwen, Henri J. M. with Michael Christensen and Rebecca Laird. *Spiritual Direction: Wisdom for the Long Walk of Faith*. HarperSanFrancisco, 2006.

Osuna, Francisco de. *The Third Spiritual Alphabet*. Translation and introduction by Mary E. Giles, The Classics of Western Spirituality, Paulist Press, 1981.

Potok, Hiam. *My Name is Asher Lev*. Fawcett Crest by Ballentine Books, 1972.

Richards, Brinley. *History of the Llynfi Valley*. D. Brown & Sons, Ltd., 1982.

Rilke, Ranier Maria Rilke. *Letters To a Young Poet*. Translated by M.D. Herter Norton, W.W. Norton & Company, renewed, 1962.

Saint Teresa of Avila. *Interior Castle*. Translated and edited by E. Allison Peers. Image Books by Doubleday, 1989.

Saint Teresa of Avila. *The Life of Saint Teresa of Avila by Herself*. Translated with an introduction by J.M.Cohen. Penguin Books, 1957.

Saint Teresa of Avila. *The Way of Perfection*. Translated and edited by E. Allison Peers. Image Books by Doubleday, 1991.

Sarton, May. *Journal of a Solitude*. W.W. Norton & Company, 1973.

Schlissel, Lillian, Byrd Gibbens, and Elizabeth Hampsten. *Far From Home: Families of the Westward Journey*. Schoken Books Inc.,1989.

Sellner, Edward C. *Wisdom of the Celtic Saints*. Bog Walk Press, 2006.

Simons, Judy. *Diaries and Journals of Literary Women from Fanny Burney to Virginia Woolf*. University of Iowa Press, 1990.

Tan, Amy. *The Hundred Secret Senses*. Ballantine, 1995.

Tan, Amy. *The Joy Luck Club*. Ballantine, 1989.

Ueland, Brenda. *If You Want to Write: A book About Art, Independence and Spirit.* Gray Wolf Press, second edition, 1987.

Underhill, Evelyn. *Mysticism: A Study in the Nature and Development of Man's Spiritual Consciousness.* Meridian, 1974.

Weisel, Elie. *Four Hasidic Masters and their Struggle Against Melancholy.* University of Notre Dame, 1987.

Williams, Gwyn A. *When Was Wales?* Black Raven Press, 1985.

Wolpe, David. *Making Loss Matter: Creating Meaning in Difficult Times.* Riverhead Books by Penguin Putnam Inc., 1999.

Woolf, Virginia. *A Room of One's Own.* Harvest Book by Harcourt Brace & Company, 1989.

Acknowledgments

I am indebted to Neil Soderstrom, Charissa Grandin, Jason West, and Bill Caldwell, without whom this work might never have become a book. I am grateful also to Sandra Harris, Mary Kay Boland, Robin Towle, Hilary Barner, Jinny Ewald, Blythe Evans, Jane Gaeta, Tara Sutherland, and to Spirit, God, without whom I would have no story to tell.

Made in the USA
San Bernardino, CA
20 April 2014